# THE REDEMPTORIST
## ON THE
# AMERICAN MISSIONS

# THE AMERICAN
# CATHOLIC TRADITION

*Advisory Editor*
Jay P. Dolan

*Editorial Board*
Paul Messbarger
Michael Novak

*See last pages of this volume
for a complete list of titles.*

# THE REDEMPTORIST

ON THE

# AMERICAN MISSIONS

Joseph Wissel

Volumes I and II

## ARNO PRESS
A New York Times Company
New York ● 1978

Editorial Supervision: JOSEPH CELLINI

———◆———

Reprint Edition 1978 by Arno Press Inc.

Reprinted from copies in the
    Redemptorist Provincial Archives

THE AMERICAN CATHOLIC TRADITION
ISBN for complete set:  0-405-10810-9
See last pages of this volume for titles.

Manufactured in the United States of America

———◆———

Library of Congress Cataloging in Publication Data

Wissel, Joseph, 1830-1912.
    The Redemptorist on the American missions.

    (The American Catholic tradition)
    Reprint of the 1920 ed. privately printed and
issued in 3 v.
    1.  Redemptorists in the United States.
2.  Spiritual exercises.  3.  Sermons--Outlines.
I.  Title.  II.  Series.
BX4020.Z5U548    1978        252'.02        77-11322
ISBN 0-405-10867-2

# THE REDEMPTORIST ON THE AMERICAN MISSIONS

VOL. I

# THE REDEMPTORIST

ON THE

# AMERICAN MISSIONS

## VOL. I

CONTAINING THE DIRECTIONS AND SKETCHES FOR
THE VARIOUS EXERCISES GIVEN BY THE
REDEMPTORIST FATHERS IN
THIS COUNTRY ON

## MISSIONS

BY

JOSEPH WISSEL, C.SS.R.

THIRD REVISED EDITION

PRIVATELY PRINTED

1920

THE PLIMPTON PRESS
NORWOOD·MASS·U·S·A

# Approbation

𝔚𝔦𝔱𝔥 𝔱𝔥𝔢 𝔖𝔞𝔫𝔠𝔱𝔦𝔬𝔫 of the MOST REV. PATRICK MURRAY, our Father General, I hereby give to the Fathers of the Congregation of the Most Holy Redeemer in this country, and especially in our own Province, for their exclusive use, the third edition of "THE REDEMPTORIST ON THE AMERICAN MISSIONS," by the Rev. JOS. WISSEL, C.SS.R. It is based on our holy Rules and Constitutions as well as on our authorized customs, and has been examined with great care by myself and two of our missionaries. It is to serve as the authorized guide and handbook for Missions, Renewals and Retreats.

E. M. WEIGEL, C.SS.R.,

*Sup. Prov. Balt.*

BROOKLYN, N. Y.
FEAST OF ST. MATTHEW
Sept. 21, 1920.

This work, whether in whole or in part, is absolutely and exclusively for the use of the Fathers of the Congregation of the Most Holy Redeemer.

E. M. WEIGEL, C.SS.R.,

*Sup. Prov. Balt.*

# PREFACE

The Redemptorist on the American Missions
is herewith presented in its third edition.  Nearly half
a century has elapsed since it first appeared, a modest
volume, in which an attempt was made to embody and
hand down to posterity the wisdom and experience of
our first missionaries in this new field of their apostolic
labors.  So well did the undertaking succeed that it
was hailed with delight by the Brethren, and proclaimed by the Very Rev. Father Provincial, Joseph
Helmpraecht, as the norm according to which our
Missions in this country were to be conducted.

Ten years later the venerable author, who in publishing the first edition had concealed his identity
under a quotation from the Imitation of Christ — *"Ne
quæras, quis hoc dixerit, sed quid dicatur attende"*
(Imit., lib. 1. cap. 1) — was commissioned by his
superiors to prepare the second edition.  This was
published in 1885.  But it was in reality a new work
in size and content, covering in three volumes every
department of missionary activity: Missions, Renewals,
Retreats to the Clergy, Seminarians, Religious Communities and Educational Institutions.  The Sketches
were complete and comprehensive; yet they left to the
individual freedom of arrangement and choice of composition and expression.

At home and abroad, among our English-speaking
Brethren, this work has proved an inestimable treasure,

a veritable *vade-mecum* on the Missions. With the growth of our own Province and the spread of the Congregation among English-speaking peoples, the edition has long since become exhausted; and for some time the demand for a new edition has been persistent from all sides. It is to meet this demand that the present edition is published.

With the exception of a few alterations necessitated by the promulgation of the New Code of Canon Law and the publication of the Provincial Statutes, the text of the previous edition has been preserved. The matter contained in the seventh and eighth chapters of the First Volume has been distributed, as belonging more properly there, to the respective Sketches; yet in such wise as to preserve the text. By this arrangement the young missionary in his use of the Sketches has before him in his work the object of each Sketch and the manner in which each Sermon should be delivered.

To diminish the bulk of Volumes One and Two, the appendix containing the German texts employed in the Sermons and Instructions has been eliminated from these Volumes and published in a separate pamphlet.

All the quotations from Holy Scripture have been carefully verified. The citations from St. Alphonsus have been traced and registered according to the Centenary Edition of the Saint's works; and the references to the Rules and Constitutions are made in accordance with the numbering of the latest edition of the Rule (1895). The former are indicated in the foot-notes by "C. E."; the latter by "R." The other abbreviations will be readily recognized.

No effort has been spared to make this new edition worthy in every respect of the great work that it is intended to assist in carrying on in the footsteps of those who have gone before us. May our Blessed Redeemer and Mary Immaculate, the Patroness of our missionaries and of our beloved United States, bless the work undertaken for their honor and glory.

Thomas W. Mullaney, C.SS.R.

# CONTENTS

# Contents

## SECOND PART

### SKETCHES FOR MISSION SERMONS

#### (First Series)

## THIRD PART

### SKETCHES FOR MISSION SERMONS

#### (Second Series)

## FOURTH PART

### INSTRUCTIONS FOR MISSIONS

## PARTICULAR INSTRUCTIONS

## FIFTH PART

### MINOR EXERCISES

ROSARY:

MISSIONS FOR CHILDREN:

# FIRST PART
## DIRECTIONS FOR GIVING MISSIONS

# THE REDEMPTORIST

## ON THE

# AMERICAN MISSIONS

## CHAPTER I

### IDEA AND NECESSITY OF MISSIONS — OBJECTIONS AGAINST MISSIONS

#### 1. IDEA OF MISSIONS

CATHOLIC MISSIONS are of two kinds: the Foreign and the Home Missions.  The object of the Foreign Mission is to carry the glad tidings of salvation to the nations that sit in the shadow of death, to plant the Cross of Christ in heathen lands.  The Home Mission finds its field of activity among those who already possess the faith.  Hence a Home Mission, or simply a Mission, consists of a series of Sermons and Instructions preached, in connection with the administration of the Sacraments, to an organized congregation, for the purpose of making them better Catholics.  The discourses of a Mission form a compendium of the entire Christian doctrine.  They comprise the Word of God, brought from heaven by Jesus Christ and taught to the nations by the Church, through the operation of the Holy Ghost.  The object of the Missions is to preach *"Christ crucified"*; [1] for, as the Council of Trent says, [2] all the mysteries contained in the life and doctrine of Jesus Christ are united in, and

---

[1] R., n. 54          [2] Cat. C. Tr. I. 5.  ¶ 5.

3

emanate from the one mystery of the death of Christ
for the salvation of mankind; and when preached to
the people, they derive their salutary effect from the
merits of Jesus Christ.   The missionary of to-day continues the work of the Apostle, who says: *"Nos autem
prædicamus Christum crucifixum."*   A true Mission,
therefore, is that which, after restoring the grace of
God to those who have fallen, renews the people in
their belief in Christ and the Church, teaches sound
principles of morality, and re-establishes the pious frequentation of the Sacraments.

Hence it follows that a course of Sermons well-
adapted to move the people to compunction and to
induce them to receive the Sacraments, may be called
a Jubilee, a Retreat; but it is by no means a Mission.
An illustration will bring out the distinction that we are
emphasizing.   The owner of a house engages a workman to paint his house, to repair the roof, and the like.
But may not other repairs be greatly needed at the
same time?   And would not the renovation be more
thorough and the work more complete, if a contract
were drawn up to overhaul the entire edifice, and the
workman bound himself to repair whatever he found
defective anywhere?   It is this thorough renovation
that is the work of a Mission which is given in a
parish.

The Mission, it is true, cannot treat in a special and
detailed manner every article of Faith, every Commandment or every Sacrament, since the Mission does
not bring the Christian religion to the people for the
first time, as the Foreign Mission does; it merely repairs whatever has become defective.   Now, the
*Eternal Truths* form the foundation of a true Christian
life.   The first and principal object of every Mission
is to imbue the hearts of the people with the knowl-

edge of these *Eternal Truths*. These, therefore, are
to be preached in detail. Having enlightened the
people on these points, the Mission must instruct them,
both in general and in particular, in their Christian
duties. As for the other truths of our holy Faith, one
or the other doctrinal discourse may be delivered, in
order to renew or confirm the people in their faith,
according as they are found deficient in any one point.
Finally, upon the minds of the people must be strongly
impressed the means of perseverance, in regard to
which the greater part of them may have become
neglectful.

It is because this fundamental idea of the nature
of a Mission is lost sight of, that missionaries, to the
great detriment of souls, are apt to make serious
mistakes in the giving of Missions. The following are
some of these mistakes:

*a*. To preach a few good, soul-stirring sermons until
all the confessions have been heard, and then to close
the Mission.

*b*. To shorten the sermons on the *Eternal Truths*, or
to combine two of them.

*c*. To preach mostly controversial or doctrinal sermons for the benefit of a few Protestants who may
happen to attend the Mission. The conversion of non-
Catholics is more easily effected by considerations on
the *Eternal Truths*. These considerations make the
same impression upon them that they do upon careless
or ignorant Catholics.

*d*. To preach the same sermons and instructions to
every congregation to which a Mission is given, without a change in the use of the arguments, the style, or
the applications, as would be required by the character
and the needs of different classes of people.

*e*. In giving Missions in this country, to follow the

same plan that is followed in Catholic countries, by copying the sermons preached there by eminent missionaries and reproducing them here without the necessary changes.

*f*. To reproduce on Missions an ordinary sermon that was preached on a different occasion outside of the time of a Mission, if such a sermon does not contain all that should be contained in a Mission-sermon treating of the same subject.

*g*. To be astonished at the abuses, the ignorance, the stupidity, and the sins, found among the people to whom a Mission is given, and consequently to grow disheartened. As well might a watch-maker be astonished at finding defects in a watch that has been sent to him to be repaired.

*h*. To fancy that the entire work of the Mission rests upon the missionary. The missionary must direct the people to the road that leads to heaven; the pastor must conduct them onward; and, what is the most important thing of all, God must bestow His blessing on the efforts of both. *Missionarius plantat, parochus rigat, Deus autem incrementum dat.*[3]

## 2. NECESSITY OF MISSIONS

Here is meant only a *relative* necessity. Strictly speaking, there is no sinner who *cannot* be saved, but most sinners *will not* be saved, without a Mission. The necessity of Missions may easily be understood, even when there is question of well-regulated parishes, presided over by good and zealous pastors.

This visible world makes a deep impression upon the heart of man; the allurements around him exert a most powerful attraction; the bad example of the

---

[3] Cfr. I Cor. iii. 6.

wicked exercises a pernicious influence over the human passions: so that the supernatural is soon lost sight of; the fear of sin and of its consequences disappears; man falls, and speedily contracts a sinful habit, which he finds it impossible either to check or to overcome.

What is worse, sin is excused, the evil of mortal sin is no longer understood, its fearful consequences are scarcely ever thought of, and the most sacred laws of God are violated without a pang of remorse. Faith begins to grow weak, the Sacraments are neglected, and total blindness of spirit and obduracy of heart take possession of man. Many of those who have thus fallen still frequent the Sacraments; but they are constantly rising from sin and falling back into it; in fact, they live most of the time in sin.

Again, many persons do not approach the sacred tribunal with the proper dispositions; hence they never receive the benefits of absolution, even when it is not refused. Others never confess their sins as they should confess them, and many conceal them altogether. All these add sacrilege upon sacrilege, and continue doing so for years, even until they have reached old age. We have reason to believe that not a few are so overcome by shame that they would rather die in despair than confess their sins.

Besides, there is in this country a large number of Catholics who entirely neglect their religious duties. There are others who have become apostates; and many are no longer known to be Catholics.

How are these wayward souls to be reclaimed? The *ordinary ministry* can no longer reach them. The influence brought to bear upon them by the very best pastor produces no effect. These sinful members of his flock either have become accustomed to hear his voice, or they never hear it. How many Catholics go regularly to Mass, but never hear a sermon! Some hear a sermon occasionally, and even occupy the first pews in the church, but they never approach the Sacraments.

The Church has a regularly established *extraordinary ministry,* and in the exercise of this extraordinary ministry the Mission consists. She has Religious Communities of men whose sole duty it is to train missionaries for this extraordinary work. Having received extraordinary graces from God, and being furnished with extraordinary faculties, which they have received from the Ordinary of the diocese, these missionaries come as extraordinary messengers from heaven, and in a short time effect a reformation of the parish by bringing back to God souls that otherwise would never have thought of amending their lives.

St. Alphonsus writes: "When we begin a mission, the greater number of the people of the place are at enmity with God, and deprived of His love; but five or six days have scarcely elapsed, when, behold, numbers, as if roused from deep sleep . . . begin to weep over their sins, and conceive the desire of being reconciled with God." [4]

The Church has always understood the necessity of "Home Missions." She has for this reason approved and established certain Religious Orders, whose vocation it is to give Missions. Such Orders are the Franciscans, the Dominicans, the Jesuits, the Passionists, the Lazarists, the Redemptorists, etc. Benedict XIV, speaking of the Missions, says: *Quocirca neque novum, neque incertum, neque a nobis excogitatum dici potest hoc remedium, quod populi corruptelis corrigendis proponitur. Antiquum illud est, malis curandis aptissimum et fortasse* UNICUM, *quod tot episcopi*

[4] Circular, July 29, 1774.

. . . *magna cum utilitate suis in diocesibus adhibue-runt.*" [5] He compares the missionaries with the companions of Peter and Andrew, whom these two Apostles requested to come and help them to drag their nets out of the water, because *"they enclosed a great multitude of fishes."* [6] — Another proof that the Church ardently desires the work of the Missions, we see in the indulgences that she grants to those who attend a Mission. — Father Segneri asserts, what every missionary knows, namely, that the necessity of Missions has become general, even in those cities in which a course of Lenten sermons — one of which is preached every day in Lent — is regularly delivered; and he adds: "A Mission of ten days is of greater benefit than all the Lenten sermons of ten years."

### 3. OBJECTIONS RAISED BY SOME PASTORS AGAINST MISSIONS

Many are the objections raised by pastors against having Missions. The following are a few of them:

"In my parish everything is in good order." But can you look into the hearts of the people? perhaps things are not in good order there. Many have spoken thus, and have afterward found that they were in error.

"My people have great confidence in me." Perhaps this is so; but for that very reason the people may find it too difficult to manifest to their regular pastor the secrets of their hearts.

"Missions cause a momentary excitement; beyond that they do no good." Hear the words of Pius VI: *"Propositio enuntians, irregularem strepitum novarum institutionum, quæ dicta sunt exercitia vel missiones*

---

[5] Gravissimum, Sept. 8, 1745. §10.          [6] Luke v. 6.

*. . . forte nunquam aut saltem perraro eo pertingere, ut absolutam conversionem operentur, et exteriores illos commotionis actus, qui apparuere, nil aliud fuisse quam transeuntia naturalis concussionis fulgura; — temeraria, male sonans, perniciosa, mori pie, salutariter per Ecclesiam frequentato, et in verbo Dei fundato injuriosa.*" [7]

"Missions lessen the authority of the pastor; the fact that he calls for outside help, shows up his weakness." Listen to the words of the prophet: *"Behold, I will send many fishers, saith the Lord, and they shall fish them; and after this I will send them many hunters, and they shall hunt them from every mountain and from every hill, and out of the holes of the rocks."* [8] Cornelius à Lapide says that these fishers are the local pastors, and the hunters are the missionaries. The work of the hunters does not lessen the work of the fishers.

"The missionaries gain the entire confidence of the people; the pastor is nothing after the Mission." This is not true. On the contrary, the people will be thankful to the pastor for the Mission that he has secured for them, and love him the more for his kindness to them. It lies in the designs of Divine Providence that during the Mission the people should repose entire confidence in the missionaries; for on this confidence shown by the people depends the success of the Mission.

"I have had Missions, yet afterward the people were as careless as ever." This is not altogether true; yet let us suppose that it is true; can it be expected that by the Mission human nature must necessarily be transformed, and become, as it were, as hard as iron and steel; that the devil will be for-

---

[7] Auctorem fidei, prop. 65.          [8] Jer. xvi. 16.

ever banished from this earth and confined in hell; that the face of the earth will be changed; that there will no longer exist any liquor-saloons; that all houses of infamy will be burnt to the ground? "Would to God," says St. Alphonsus, "that every converted sinner persevered till death." Then the crowds around the confessional would gradually diminish and the precept of annual confession might be abolished, since venial sins need not be confessed. The sins that are committed after the Mission do not prove that the conversion of the sinner was not sincere; they prove the weakness of human nature. The Galatians received St. Paul as an angel of God. They would have plucked out their very eyes and given them to him, if this had been possible. Yet the Apostle had occasion to be astonished at their perversion.[9]

It would be well if those who find fault with the Missions would inquire into their own lives. Have they kept the resolutions that they made during their annual retreat? Have such pastors of souls kept alive in the hearts of their people the principles of Moral Theology which were laid down by the missionaries? Have they exerted themselves to urge the people to put into practice the means of perseverance so highly recommended during the Mission?

"The Mission entails a heavy expense upon the pastor." As a rule, we have found that the contrary is the case: pastors make money by the Mission. Some priests have even said: "I am in great straits; I must have either a Mission or a fair." It is true, missionaries should receive some remuneration for their own support. No matter what others may do, the Redemptorist Fathers are satisfied with whatever donation the pastor can afford to give them from

[9] Gal. iv. 14, 15, and i. 6.

the income of the Mission, and they will gratefully accept it so long as the houses of the Congregation have not sufficient revenues.[10]

Let us, in conclusion, quote the words of the immortal Pius IX: *"Sacræ missiones, ubi operariis idoneis commissæ fuerint, valde utiles benedicente Domino esse constat, tum fovendæ bonorum pietati, tum peccatoribus et longo etiam vitiorum habitu depravatis hominibus ad salutarem pœnitentiam excitandis."*[11]

[10] R., n. 45, 69, 70.          [11] Enc. 8. Dec. 1849.

# CHAPTER II

THE DISPOSITIONS OF THE MISSIONARY —
HOW HE SHOULD PREPARE HIMSELF
FOR THE MISSIONS

## 1. Missions, Our Special Vocation

Every Redemptorist should be a missionary. Other priests, whether secular or Religious, who have not the vocation to be missionaries, must, before undertaking the work of the Missions, ask themselves whether or not God has called them to it; for on having or not having this special vocation will depend their success or failure in giving Missions. It may happen that men of great talent, seeing the extraordinary success of the Missions, will say: *"Let us also get us a name,"* [1] and will also enter upon this spiritual battle-field; yet not being *"of the seed of those men by whom salvation was brought to Israel,"* [2] they will themselves fall and cause *"a great overthrow of the people."* [3] The Missions that they give will do more harm than good, owing, on the one hand, to the want of experience, and on the other, to the absence of God's special blessing.

For the Redemptorist this vocation was decided when God called him to the Congregation, the special end of which is, "the preaching of the Word of God to the poor . . . by means of Missions, catechetical instructions and spiritual exercises." [4] What a powerful motive for thankfulness to God, Who has mani-

---

[1] Mach. v. 57.  [2] Ibid. 62.  [3] Ibid. 60.  [4] R., n. 1.

fested His goodness and mercy to us by selecting us, though most unworthy, to discharge the duties of so sublime a vocation! [5] It is, therefore, the duty of every one to prepare himself as well as possible for the great work that God has destined him to do. No true Redemptorist will neglect to make himself a useful and efficient worker on the Missions; but he will employ for this purpose his time and talent, his physical and mental powers. Like a soldier of the regular army, he must be well drilled in the various tactics of the spiritual warfare. In a word, he must be ever ready for war, though he may not be called to the fight. *"Huic operi omnes potissimum incumbent."* [6] If, therefore, a Father be employed in performing the duties of Pastor, or of Lector, or of any other office, he is not on that account exempted from keeping the primary and the principal rule of the Institute, namely, that of becoming an efficient missionary. Let him, therefore, hold himself in readiness to do every kind of work that is within the limits of our special vocation, and be at the disposal of his Superiors, who will avail themselves of his services, when, where, and as they may judge best. Ordinarily, the Fathers of the Congregation should not go forth to labor until they have reached the age of thirty. *"Ordinarie exire non poterunt ante trigesimum ætatis annum."* [7] St. Alphonsus was very strict in regard to this point.[8]

## 2. Our Missions should be Given in Accordance with the Spirit of our Holy Rule

There are different missionary Orders and Congregations in the Church, and all are working in the

[5] R., n. 49.

[6] R., n. 49.

[7] R., n. 1281.

[8] Circ., June 27, 1773.

same spirit and for the same end. Yet each one has its own peculiar spirit, and one differs from the other in the manner in which the work is accomplished. God will bless the work of a Religious only when he performs it according to the spirit of his Order and of its Founder. We, the Members of the Congregation of the Most Holy Redeemer and the Sons of St. Alphonsus, will find the spirit that should be the soul of our Missions well expressed and clearly explained in our Rule (n. 47–53). Every word therein gives evidence of this spirit. *"Look, and make it according to the pattern that is shown thee there."* [9] It is strongly recommended that our missionaries should frequently read and ponder those words of the Rule. If they prepare themselves for this work and execute it in accordance with those directions, they will surely draw down upon themselves God's special blessing.

### 3. Preparation for the Missions

The chief and *general preparation* for the Missions, the preparation that is absolutely necessary for a Redemptorist, consists in his constant efforts to be a good Religious. The missionary Order, with its educational establishments, is the military school in which valiant officers are formed for the carrying on of the spiritual warfare. The missionary is to go forth to engage in battle with the powers of darkness. Before he sets out for the Missions he should act like a king: *"Qui, iturus committere bellum adversus alium regem, sedens prius cogitat, si possit cum decem millibus occurrere ei, qui cum viginti millibus venit ad se."* [10] Let there be nothing left in him of the spirit of pride, worldliness,

---

[9] Exod. xxv. 40.  [10] Luke xiv. 31.

vanity, self-indulgence, self-will, which favors rather than destroys the cause of Satan. Otherwise he will never effectually drive away the powers of hell from the place where he is giving a Mission. How can an officer of the army successfully fight against the enemy in battle, if he, at the same time, espouses his cause in his sentiments and general conduct? The powers of darkness do not fear those missionaries who are practically in sympathy with them. The primary and essential quality of a missionary, therefore, is that he should be a saint.

Sanctity in a Redemptorist necessarily includes a great desire on his part to promote God's glory *by saving souls*. The Redemptorist desires to *redeem* souls by applying to them the price of the redemption wherever he can do so, at whatever cost of labor, hardship, or sacrifice. He that is not penetrated with this spirit, says Father Smetana, should blush with shame whenever he signs himself a Member of the Congregation of the Most Holy Redeemer. [11]

The *particular preparation* for the Missions comprises the following points, taken from the Constitution entitled: *Qua mente ad missiones accedendum est*. [12]

1. He must profess, and constantly practise, especially on Missions, all the virtues of which our Lord and Redeemer, Jesus Christ, gave us the example when on earth, and endeavor to resemble Him as much as possible *in re et in modo*. — 2. He should particularly possess a very high degree of humility, so as to be able to undergo every kind of humiliation, the inseparable companion of every missionary. He should never, therefore, seek his own glory, but should labor simply for the glory of God. — 3. He must also be firmly established in the practice of mortification, in

---

[11] *Spiritual Exercises, Med. xxii.*    [12] R., n. 47–53.

order that he may courageously face sufferings and privations, such as, *"hunger, thirst, cold, pain, labor, and inconveniences of every kind, even death itself, if by suffering them he can save only one soul and rescue it from the fetters of sin. . . . Whosoever proposes to himself a different end, becomes a robber of God's honor and an enemy of souls."* Let him say with St. Paul: *"Nec facio animam meam pretiosiorem quam me, dummodo consummem cursum meum et ministerium verbi quod accepi a Domino Jesu."* [13] —
4. To all this the missionary must unite great confidence in God, which consists in being fully convinced that God will assist him, both in the work of his own sanctification and in the work of saving souls. The degree of his success in apostolic work will be in proportion to the degree of his confidence in God. This necessarily implies the spirit of *prayer,* which must precede, accompany, and follow every exercise of his ministry. — 5. Finally, *"he must have all his discourses, sermons, and instructions well prepared, carefully written, and committed to memory."* This does not imply that in delivering his discourses he must absolutely follow his manuscript, as if he were not free to deviate from it whenever the inspiration of the moment, or other reasons, requires him to do so. The discourse delivered by the missionary must necessarily be free and enjoy a certain latitude of thought, otherwise it will lose what we might call that "paternal familiarity" which is one of its essential qualities. Nor is it always possible for him, when we consider his limited time and opportunities, to have his discourses thoroughly well prepared, though he should always have at least a full sketch of them, which at his leisure he should carefully write out. He may not

[13] Acts, xx. 24.

even have sufficient time to prepare full sketches of his sermons and instructions. Notwithstanding all these drawbacks, he should always be ready to obey whenever a command is given to preach a sermon for which he is not sufficiently prepared. He should make no excuse, but merely state his deficiency in the present case. He should remember that, provided he does what he can do, God will do the rest. To keep him humble and to prevent him from yielding to sloth in the future, God will rarely permit him to find out the good results of his discourses. There have always been great missionaries in the Church who have thus wisely acted under the difficult circumstances just described.

The fact that one is a Redemptorist does not make one a missionary. The dispositions that a missionary must have and the preparation for the Missions that is required of him by his Rule, constitute the prerequisites for becoming a Redemptorist missionary. Such a true missionary will not only be able to sanctify himself, but he will also be the means of converting thousands of souls. *"Attende tibi et doctrinæ; insta in illis. Hoc enim faciens, et teipsum salvum facies et eos qui te audiunt."* [14]

God, Who sacrificed His only-begotten Son for the salvation of mankind, uses all the means in His power to save the souls of men, especially of those who are members of His Church. Hence by a special Providence of God the extraordinary ministry of the Missions has been established in the Church in order that by it those souls may be saved that are beyond the reach of the ordinary ministry. The missionary comes for an extraordinary purpose; he desires to produce an extraordinary effect. The missionary is, therefore, an

[14] I Tim. iy. 16.

extraordinary messenger from God. *"Angelus Domini exercituum est."* [15] Our missionaries should be imbued with this thought while they are engaged in preparing themselves at home. Let this thought accompany them to the places where they are to give Missions; let it govern their conduct during the Missions; and let it animate them both in the pulpit and in the con-fessional. Thus will they be what they are expected to be, true *angels of mercy.* The remembrance of this thought will also fill them with the needed encouragement when they are cast down by their own numerous shortcomings and miseries. *"Noli dicere, Puer sum, quoniam ad omnia, quæ mittam te, ibis: et universa, quæcumque mandavero tibi loqueris . . . Ecce dedi verba mea in ore tuo . . . ut evellas, et destruas, et disperdas, et dissipes, et ædifices, et plantes."* [16] The same thought will confirm them in the spirit of holy obedience when they are called upon to do what in their opinion they have not sufficient strength and ability to do. It will, above all, prevent them from being elated by the success which they meet with in their Missions, as they are convinced that success is the work of God, to Whom all honor and glory must be given.

What a sublime vocation! Yet how great are the difficulties that must be overcome, and that are likely to discourage even the bravest! To seek to be relieved from going on Missions is not a rare temptation. The missionaries experience the hardships, the privations, the humiliations necessarily connected with their apostolic work. Nature shrinks from such things. They are also the witnesses of the many relapses of those who attend the Missions. Upon their mind is left the impression that the Missions do not, after all,

---

[15] Mal. ii. 7.    [16] Jer. i. 7–10.

effect so much good.    Besides, they meet with so many
other difficulties occasioned by their brethren, Superiors.    It is, therefore, quite natural that they should
wish to be free from the work of the Missions and to
be employed in some other work.    Others have not
even the courage to assume the responsibility of laboring on Missions.    They say with our Lord: *"Si pos-
sibile est, transeat a me calix iste."*    Let them take
comfort from our Lord in the garden of sorrows.    He,
too, saw before Him the tortures, the humiliations, even
the death, which He was to undergo for the salvation
of mankind.    He foresaw, at the same time, that,
after all that He had to suffer, only a small minority
would be saved.    However, when His heavenly Father
signified to Him His will He submitted, offering Himself as a sacrifice:    *"Verumtamen non sicut ego volo,
sed sicut tu."*    Let Jesus be your model.    *"Vade et fac
similiter."*

# CHAPTER III

## 1. How Missions are to be Accepted

Our missionaries should never intrude themselves upon pastors or their congregations. To do so would be an act of great imprudence. Let them simply hold themselves in readiness, preparing themselves in the manner described in the preceding chapter, and waiting till God calls them. God knows best when, where and how to use their services. We should, therefore, never ask directly for Missions, nor praise our work above that of other missionaries, for the purpose of displacing them. As far as our missionaries are concerned, there is always enough work for them to do.

The motives for which Missions are asked are various, and more or less praiseworthy. All Missions should, however, be accepted as far as time and opportunity will permit, since thereby the main object — the salvation of souls — is generally gained. When, however, pastors ask for Missions shortly after they have had a Mission or a Renewal, they should be informed that only after four years [1] can a Mission be again given to their parishes. At least, in this country, an interval of five years should elapse between the last Mission or Renewal and the next Mission. Too many Missions are injurious to the people; for many

[1] Cap. Gen. 1746, stat. 19. (Codex C.SS.R., p. iii, p. 488, n. 1383, stat. 19).

of them yield to their sinful habits more easily, neglect even their Easter duties with less scruple, hoping that soon there will be another Mission, during
which they expect to settle their consciences without
difficulty.   No parish, however, should be longer than
seven years without a Mission.   During such a length
of time things change considerably.   Children grow
up and become men and women.   For them the world
wears a different appearance.   Young men and young
women marry, and have consequently new duties to
perform.   These and other things having changed, another Mission becomes necessary.

### 2.   Previous Instructions to be Given
### to the Pastors

After a Mission has been accepted and the time
for it has been fixed, the pastor should be kindly informed to attend to the following points: 1. To ac-
quaint the bishop of the diocese of his intention to
have a Mission; to ask his permission to have it, and
to obtain from him the ordinary jurisdiction for the
missionaries.   2. To announce the Mission to his congregation about a month previous to the time fixed
and every Sunday thereafter.[2]   3. To prepare his
people for the Mission by speaking of it in his sermons and instructions, and to have public prayers
recited every day after Mass, or at least on the in-
tervening Sundays, for the success of the Mission.   4.
To have a penitential cross made according to a plan
that should be sent to him.   5. To have a sufficient
number of temporary confessionals made; the loca-

[2] Some missionaries are not in favor of this, as it gives time to the
ill-disposed to create opposition.   Announcements of the Mission,
four weeks in advance, have, however, been found necessary in
this country.

tion of which should, however, be left to the choice of the missionaries. 6. To make arrangements for the sale of such articles of devotion as are usually purchased by the people during the Missions.

Pastors should also be requested not to join to the Mission any other religious exercise that might interfere with the exercises of the Mission. It is best to separate the Mission from every other devotion, even from that of the Forty Hours. Pastors should be warned against announcing how long the Mission is to last. Nor should the missionaries on their arrival inform the people of this, as it is then difficult to know what the spiritual needs of the parish are, and the people, knowing how long the Mission is to last, are apt to neglect the first exercises, which form the essential and most important part of the Mission. It is also very necessary to inform the pastors that according to our Rule and custom the confessions should be heard exclusively by the missionaries. Hence it should be previously ascertained how many confessions may probably be expected, so that a sufficient number of missionaries may be sent to give the Mission.

### 3. Behavior of the Missionaries Toward the Pastors

Some pastors show an eagerness to interfere with the missionaries in their arrangement of the exercises and in other matters connected with the Mission. Such a disposition, if allowed to have full sway, will prove injurious to the sacred cause and be a source of great annoyance to the missionaries. It is, above all, most necessary that harmony and good feeling should exist between the pastor and the missionaries; yet, at times, it may prove extremely difficult to preserve this happy accord.[3]   It may be, perhaps, possible, by gentle means, to convince the pastor that, owing to their traditions and extensive practice, the missionaries are proficient in the work of the Missions.   Should he, however, not be open to conviction, let the missionaries patiently bear with him, let them treat him respectfully, and act toward him as if they were well satisfied. Through their Superior they should confer with him as to the spiritual wants of the parish, the common abuses existing among the people, the occasions of sin, the principal vices, etc.; and consult him about the time most suitable for the exercises.   They should be careful not to criticise his management of the affairs of the parish, even though his shortcomings may be very grievous, and about these they should never speak to other priests, either during or after the Mission.   Imprudent zeal not only does no good, but does a great deal of harm and brings upon the Missions the odium of the pastors.   Generally the pastors and their assistants are willing to take upon themselves the burden of singing High Mass on Sundays, of saying the last Mass on week-days, of giving Benediction of the Most Blessed Sacrament in the evening, of distributing Holy Communion during and outside of the time of Mass, and even of instructing the ignorant and converts.   They thereby make themselves generally useful, to the great relief of the missionaries.   Should they, however, be unwilling to perform these duties, let the missionaries perform them themselves, without showing any displeasure. God will give the needed strength.   Let them say with St. Paul: *"Omnibus omnia factus sum, ut omnes facerem salvos."* [4]

---

[3] Cfr. R., n. 60, 61.          [4] I Cor. ix. 22.

## 4. The Favor of the Bishop of the Diocese should be Secured, and from Him should also be Obtained Extraordinary Faculties

Missions should not be undertaken without the knowledge and permission of the Ordinary of the diocese. Not only should the pastors arrange with their bishops everything that concerns the Missions and the missionaries, but the missionaries themselves should try to secure the favor of the bishop of the diocese and ask his blessing for the Mission that is to be given. They may visit him, or if this is impossible on account of the distance, they may communicate with him by letter. Moreover, in order that their apostolic labors may be as fruitful as possible, they should through their Superior ask the bishop [5] for extraordinary faculties in addition to the ordinary faculties.

Very few bishops will be unwilling to grant these faculties, especially if they are acquainted with the needs of the Missions.[6] The missionaries should have a knowledge of all the extraordinary faculties that the bishops, by concession of the Holy See, can give in particular cases. They should study Father Putzer's little work, entitled *Commentarium in facultates apostolicas*. They should also be well informed in regard to the special faculties granted by our privileges.

## 5. A Mission should be Given Only to that Parish, Exclusively of Every Other

There is another important matter that should be attended to before or immediately after the arrival of

[5] Cfr. R., n. 132.
[6] Codex Juris Canon, canon 899, 900.

the missionaries. In his *Exercises of the Missions,*[7] St. Alphonsus says that the Mission must be given exclusively for the congregation that belongs to the parish. A Mission in which the people of different congregations participate is no Mission, because the people from various other parishes will hear only a small number of sermons and instructions, and thereby not fulfil a most essential condition of the Mission. Again, if the church is crowded with strangers, the people of the parish will find it very unpleasant to go to church, and this circumstance may be alleged as an excuse for not attending the Mission by those who scarcely go to church on ordinary occasions, and who are the very persons that need the extraordinary graces now offered to them. The pastors of the neighboring parishes will also more easily dispense themselves from the obligation of having Missions in their own parishes. They are apt to think that their congregations have had the benefit of a Mission, while, in fact, only a small number of pious souls attended it. All this fully applies to the present times. Add to this, that the people of a parish dislike to be deprived of the right of occupying their pews during the Mission, when it is of the highest importance to them to be present in the church. The missionaries should, therefore, discourage, by all means in their power, the attendance of strangers at their Missions.

## 6. No Penitents from Other Congregations should be Admitted

If strangers should not be allowed to come to the Mission, it also follows that their confessions should not be heard, because: (1) they are not prepared for

7 C. E., Vol. XV. p. 284.

making a mission-confession, which differs from the ordinary confession; (2) their presence near the confessional will keep away the people of the parish, especially great sinners, for whom the Mission is principally intended, and who are easily deterred from going to confession when they find the confessionals difficult of access; and (3) the number of confessors being limited, there would not be time enough to hear the confessions of the parishioners satisfactorily, if strangers were also admitted. No exception in favor of any one should be made, as it is apt to serve as an invitation to others to come. Let the missionaries, therefore, be strict in enforcing this regulation, otherwise injustice will be done to the parishioners, and their fellow-missioners will be burdened with additional labor. Speaking of missions in Belgium, Father Van de Kerckhove, S. J., also urges the necessity of confining the Mission exclusively to the people of the parish, adducing fourteen reasons, all of which apply to this country.

7. Separate Mission to the Women and then to the Men of the Parish

St. Alphonsus goes still farther when he says that "the Mission should be divided among the various chapels of the place, if the parish-church is found too small to contain all the people." [8] We have done the same in this country where more than one church was found in the same parish. But this is rarely the case. Generally there is a want of churches. This is the reason why we are accustomed to give a Mission to the women and then to the men of the parish. Many churches in this country are not half large

[8] C. E., Vol. XV. p. 286.

enough to contain the congregation, even if we deduct those who must stay at home. In all such cases we divide the two sexes, giving to each a Mission. This plan has succeeded so well that other missionaries have adopted it. It not only provides for more room in the church, but also produces zeal, if not emulation, among those who are attending the Missions. After the women's Mission is over the women will be of great help to the missionaries to induce the men to attend the men's Mission. Another grave reason for separating the sexes, in this country, is that there are very few churches in which the men occupy seats separated from those of the women. This crowding together is, no doubt, fraught with great danger to morality. St. Alphonsus always provided that the men should be separated from the women when in church,[9] and even when the exercises were performed outside of the church, as, for example, when the Mission-cross was solemnly erected.[10] Such a thing is, however, impracticable in this country. All that we can do is to separate the Mission of the men from that of the women. When, however, the Mission must be given to men and women together, the Prefect of the church should, as far as possible, assign separate places to the men and women who are standing in the aisles.[11] One or two men might be stationed at the entrance of the church to enforce this rule.

It has even happened that we have divided the congregation into four parts by giving a separate Mission, first, to the married women, then to the unmarried women; afterward, to the married men, and then to the unmarried men. This arrangement has met with extraordinary success.

[9] C. E., Vol. XV. p. 250.     [10] Ib. p. 248.
[11] R., n. 107.

## 8. Preaching the Mission in Different Languages

It is difficult to make a Mission successful if it is given in small country towns where the parishioners are of different nationalities and speak different languages. There is, for instance, a small parish, composed of five or six hundred communicants, most of whom speak and understand only English, the rest only German. A thorough Mission should be given to small congregations as well as to large ones. Poor country towns should be preferred by the Fathers of our Congregation.[12] The proper way would be to give a week's Mission to the people of one nationality, and a week to the rest of the people. Yet very few pastors are willing to have the Mission continued for two full weeks, though they may not object to a Mission lasting twelve days. In this case, let a Mission of six days be given to the people of one nationality and another six days' Mission to the rest. This should always be done when the nationalities are about equal. If necessary, a five days' Mission may be given to each nationality. This would be better than to preach in one language in the forenoon and in a different language in the afternoon or evening.

Where the number of the people of the two nationalities is not equal, it will be better to preach to the smaller number in the forenoon, and to the larger in the evening. In this case, instead of the Rosary instruction, one of the usual Mission-instructions should be given, which should, however, not last a full half-hour; then the Rosary should be recited. What subjects are to be preached in the forenoon is left to the

[12] R., n. 6.

option of the missionaries.  We suggest the following:
1, Salvation; 2, Mortal Sin; 3, Penance and its Conditions; 4, Obstacles to receiving Absolution; 5,
Judgment; 6, Hell; 7, Precepts of the Church; 8,
Means of Perseverance; 9, The Blessed Virgin.

Where there are only a few people of one nationality, it will be sufficient to preach two or three
sermons in their own language.  How the instructions for the different states of life are to be distributed, will be treated of in another chapter.

Small Missions of the kind just described are generally more laborious than large Missions, as there is
more preaching in these small Missions.


### 9.   The Penitential Cross and the Pulpit

Before the Mission is begun a penitential cross
should be erected, and a platform or pulpit should be
constructed.  The penitential cross — not the Mission-cross that is to be blessed and erected at or toward the close of the Mission — is to be made of
two planks, nine or ten inches wide, one inch or one
and a half inches thick, twelve to fifteen feet long,
with the cross-piece in proportion; and is to be
painted black or dark-brown; a piece of white mus-
lin four or five yards long should be thrown loosely
over the arms of the cross.  This cross should be
erected before the Mission opens, and placed either
at the altar-railing, or near the high altar in front of
the altar-steps on the Epistle or Gospel side, yet so
as not to hide any part of the altar.  This practice
of erecting a penitential cross has been introduced
with the English Missions into the American Province.  As the sight of such a cross is very impressive, the practice of erecting it should be continued.

In the time of St. Alphonsus it was unknown, nor does the Rule speak of it. St. Alphonsus usually had a large statue of the Blessed Virgin placed on a high pedestal near the pulpit.[13] The Rule also directs that during the sermon a statue of the Blessed Virgin, surrounded by lighted candles, should be placed near the pulpit.[14] In this country we usually have two candles burning on the Blessed Virgin's altar during the sermon.

The question is, In what part of the church should the missionaries preach the sermons? Should they preach from the pulpit, from a platform constructed for the purpose, or from the platform of the altar? The answer to this question will depend on how far the place is suitable to the end that we have in view. This end is threefold: First, the missionary must deliver his discourses in a familiar style; secondly, he must be heard in every part of the church; and thirdly, he must be seen by the people. Now, that place should be chosen which will help us to gain these three ends. St. Alphonsus generally had a platform erected for the reasons above-mentioned.[15] In large churches, however, before a large congregation, he preferred the pulpit.[16] In many churches in this country the platform of the altar admirably serves our purpose; and even the stationary pulpits are well adapted for the preaching of Mission-sermons. Hence, there are very few churches in which a platform need be erected for the Mission. Should it be found necessary to construct a platform, it should not be placed in the center of the sanctuary, nor in the middle aisle, thereby forcing the preacher to have his back always turned toward the tabernacle; nor should it stand in the way

---

[13] C. E., Vol. XV. p. 250.
[14] R., n. 140.
[15] C. E., Vol. XV. p. 250.
[16] Ibid.

of the people when approaching the altar-railing to receive Holy Communion.  Care must be taken that it be made strong, high, and wide, so as not to resemble a mere table.  Strong steps should lead up to it, and on it should be placed a *prie-dieu,* or a small table neatly covered.  If there must be a platform, let it be suitable to the great work for which it is used.

# CHAPTER IV

## OPENING OF THE MISSION

HAVING spoken of the preparation that must be made for the Mission, let us now speak in detail of the work of the Mission itself. The opening of the Mission embraces the invitation that is to be given to the people to attend the exercises of the Mission, and the employment of the best means to secure punctual and regular attendance. Among these means must be especially ranked the introductory sermon and the announcements. The success of the Mission will depend on the manner in which the people come to the exercises. Hence it is evident that the missionaries cannot do too much to secure for themselves and their work the favorable disposition of the people and to attract them to the church.

### 1. THE OPENING SERMON

The time for opening the Mission and preaching the introductory sermon is the High Mass or last Mass on Sundays or holy-days of obligation. To open the Mission on holy-days of obligation is not so suitable. When each of the sexes is to have its own Mission, the introductory sermon is preached but once: at the opening, when the men and the women are together. When the Mission for the women has come to a close, the exercises may be continued for the men on any week-day evening, without any introductory sermon, as the Mission and the conditions re-

quired for making it, may be regarded as having been
sufficiently published. It will, however, be useful to
invite the men to a sermon that is to be preached for
their special benefit during the last Mass, on the second Sunday of the Mission.

The regular introductory sermon should *never* be
omitted. There may be an apparent reason for
leaving it out in Missions of very short duration, to
gain time for an additional sermon on some important subject. But can there be a subject more important than this? Of what use are sermons that
are not listened to, or that are listened to without the
requisite disposition? This is precisely the object that
we wish to attain by the opening sermon. The introductory discourse, delivered in a familiar style, will
at once captivate the people. It will inform them of
the object of the Mission, making them understand
that the missionaries have come to them with an
extraordinary message from God, and that a most
cordial invitation is given to them to be present every
time this message is delivered to them. The same
discourse will also describe the immense benefits which
all will derive from the Mission, and the absolute
necessity that the Mission should be given, as the salvation of many will depend upon it. It will satisfactorily answer the objections that some may feel
inclined to raise against the Mission. It will also point
out what dispositions are necessary to make the Mission successful, and will urge upon the hearers the
acquirement of these dispositions for the love of Jesus
crucified and their immortal souls. It is therefore
quite evident that the introductory sermon forms an
essential part of the Mission. The Rule [1] also prescribes the giving of the introductory sermon. It

[1] R., n. 135.

says: *"Superior, aliusve ab eo designatus, Missionem statuto tempore inchoabit, ejusque* SCOPUM *populo exponet; simulque profitebitur se, aliosque Patres, cor charitate plenum, atque ad* OMNES *juvandos, æternamque* OMNIUM *salutem procurandam, promptos gerere animos. Postea omnes hortabitur ut ecclesiam* FREQUENTARE *ac Missionis exercitiis interesse sibi proponant. . . .* EXERCITA *tempusque iis destinatum singulatim enuntiari poterunt."* St. Alphonsus, as well as others who have written books treating of the Mission, urges the necessity of the introductory sermon.

It will not suffice to join the opening sermon to another sermon, for example, to the sermon on Salvation. We are sometimes, during the latter part of the Mission, compelled by necessity to unite two subjects in one sermon, but this should not be done during the first few days, least of all at the opening of the exercises.

2. ANNOUNCEMENTS THAT ARE TO BE MADE AT THE BEGINNING AND DURING THE MISSION

The announcements that are to be made by the missionaries on the first day of the exercises form another important part of the opening of the Mission. St. Alphonsus [2] urges most strongly the necessity of the so-called *"sentimenti"* or short street-exhortations that are to be made in the different parts of the town or city where the Mission is given, and that have no other object than to announce the Mission and to induce the people to attend it. As a general thing, we may say that half of the success of the Mission depends upon the announcements, and upon the

[2] C. E., Vol. XV. p. 95.

manner in which they are made. For this reason we will here dwell upon them more extensively.

The announcement of the time at which the various exercises of the Mission are to take place, is made at all the Masses on the opening Sunday. It is a well-known fact that often scarcely one-third of the congregation is present at the last Mass. Hence these announcements must serve as an introductory sermon for those present at the other Masses. It is true, it may appear somewhat strange that the missionaries should present themselves to the people, to preach, as it were, to them before they have been formally introduced by the pastor. Yet on this apparent anomaly depends the doing of a great amount of good.

These announcements are to be made by one of the missionaries. His very appearance will produce a good effect. The announcement must be brief and forcible — every word must tell. It should contain the following points: 1, The Mission, previously announced, will be opened with due solemnity at the last Mass; 2, The Mission is the greatest grace that God usually bestows upon a congregation; 3, On the part of the people, an extraordinary correspondence to this grace is, therefore, demanded by God; 4, This correspondence implies, above all, regular attendance at all the exercises, to which they should come with the requisite dispositions; 5, In order not to incur God's anger, no one should despise or treat coldly this extraordinary offer of God's mercy; 6, The people should induce their relatives, friends, and all who need conversion, to come to the Mission; 7, Order of exercises for that day and for the following week; 8, Exhortation to the parents in regard to the Mission for the children, in case this Mission is not to be postponed.

All the other announcements that are to be made during the Mission are of equal importance, and should be made well.

In order to make a good announcement, the following rules should be observed: 1, Wait till the congregation is seated and all are quiet; 2, Speak slowly, distinctly, and loud enough to be heard in every part of the church; 3, Lay particular stress upon the principal point of your announcement; 4, Do not repeat what you have said; 5, Use the plainest language, so as to be understood by everybody; 6, Use the proper expressions that are in common use. For example, in announcing the particular instructions, say "married women and widows," not "married ladies"; "unmarried women," not "young girls," or "young ladies"; "unmarried men," not "young men"; 7, Leave out of your announcement everything that does not belong to it; 8, Make a pause after every announcement that you make.

It is our custom to announce every evening the order of the exercises for the following day, so that those who have come to the Mission for the first time may know the time at which the different exercises take place. Every exercise not included in the order of the day should be announced, morning and evening, on the two previous days. The same thing should be done in regard to such exercises as deserve special attention, as, for instance, the solemn dedication to the Blessed Virgin, or a sermon of special importance, as the sermon on the Church. The name of the preacher, however, should not be mentioned. No announcement should be made at the early instruction, though it may be done briefly on rare occasions. The reason is, because the Father needs for the instruction every moment of the time at his disposal, and the people who come to the early morning instruction, usually come to the evening sermon. The missionaries should avoid making frequent mention of collections, etc. This matter will be treated later on.

### 3. Visits of Invitation and of Civility

Our Rule speaks of visits that are to be paid during the first days of the Mission to the men of high rank of the parish, to the higher clergy and the Religious, for the purpose of inviting them to the Mission.[3] In this country there are no persons of high rank to be found in the parishes. Yet there is usually in every congregation a number of well-known Catholics who never go to church, and who are not disposed to go even during the Mission. A visit which is made to them at their homes and a special invitation which is given to them, have often been blessed with the happiest results. If time permits, such visits should be made by a missionary accompanied by the pastor. If this is not done, let the pastor look after the stray sheep of his flock. Though this may be a disagreeable task, yet it is a meritorious one. The visit to the clergy of the neighboring parishes, particularly to the communities of Religious priests, should always be made by the missionaries in company with the pastor. The object is not precisely to invite them to the Mission, but to keep up a good understanding between these priests and the missionaries. Such acts of courtesy greatly promote the interests of the Mission. In general, the missionaries should leave nothing untried in their efforts to make the Mission known among the people and to induce them to attend it. The example of merchants, of man-

[3] R., n. 136.

ufacturers, and of others in advertising their goods, even in the oddest possible way, may be of service to them. Is it not chiefly to the missionary that these words of the Gospel apply: *"Exi in plateas et vicos civitatis: et pauperes, ac debiles, et cœcos, et claudos introduc huc; — exi in vias et sepes, et compelle intrare, ut impleatur domus mea"?* [4]

## 4. Fixing the Time for the Different Exercises

The great sermons of the Mission constitute the principal exercises, of which all the other exercises are ramifications. Hence great care should be taken that these sermons are preached at the proper time. They are generally preached in the evening, except in places where the people can attend better in the afternoon. We often find that in country towns attendance in the forenoon is better than in the afternoon. The forenoon is, therefore, the proper time for the sermon; and indeed all the discourses of the Mission should partake, in such cases, of the nature of regular sermons. For a time, besides the evening sermon, we usually preached one of the principal sermons, or gave an instruction, in the afternoon of the opening Sunday. But experience has proved that as long as the people are not yet sufficiently warmed up, they will not come to these sermons that follow one another so closely on the same day; least of all can it be expected that those people who especially need the Mission, will come to the first sermons that are preached. On the second or third Sunday of the Mission we generally give in the afternoon, besides the two regular sermons of the day, an instruction on some particular

[4] Luke xiv. 21–23.

state of life. This instruction usually proves successful, owing to the eagerness of the people, at this advanced stage of the Mission, to hear the Word of
God from the lips of the missionaries.

The *Evening Sermon* should always be preached at
an hour convenient for the working-people.[5] In the
cities and large towns of this country we begin the
sermon at eight o'clock. Hence, all that is to precede the sermon, including the hymn and the reading
of the "Daily Acts," should then be over. Our
people cannot leave their work before six o'clock;
then some time must elapse in order to go home, take
their supper, dress, and come to church. To begin
the sermon earlier would deprive many of these people
of the benefit of the sermon. To begin later would
be the cause of great confusion in the order of the
exercises. This sermon should last not much longer
than an hour. *"Concio ad horam, aut aliquanto plus,
protrahatur præter actum doloris in fine concionis eli-
ciendum; nec etiam sit justo brevior."*[6] It should be
neither shorter nor much longer than an hour. Our
manner of making the act of contrition at the end of
the sermon occupies but a short time. There are
special reasons why the Mission-sermons should not
be too long: 1, Our people are apt to regard them
as too tedious, and consequently stay away; 2, They
are already tired from their hard day's work; 3, They
are expected to come back for the early instruction
in the morning. No subject of a sermon, if skilfully
handled, needs more than an hour to treat it to the
satisfaction of the people.

The *Instruction* also should be given at an hour

---

[5] Letter of St. Alphonsus to a Bishop, C. E., Vol. XV. p. 87; and
*Exercises of the Missions*, C. E., Vol. XV. p. 251.
[6] R., n. 88, 138.

that is convenient for the people: *"Hora, qua populus commodissime in ecclesiam venire potest."* [7] The time is to be fixed according to the different circumstances of the place. In this country, it is hardly possible for the entire congregation to come to the same instruction. We have, for this reason, introduced the custom, sanctioned by the Rule,[8] of giving two instructions on the same subject in the morning. The first instruction is given immediately after the Mass, which must begin at five o'clock, and it must be finished at six o'clock precisely. In this case punctuality must be strictly observed, so as to give time to those attending the instructions to go home, take their breakfast, and be in time for their work, which begins usually at seven o'clock. If the people notice that they are not kept beyond that time, they are easily induced to attend regularly the instructions of the Mission. The second instruction is to be given about three hours later, at a suitable time. It may occupy a full hour,[9] though for a good reason it may be shortened, especially at men's Missions. In a few places in the country, where the people can attend the Mission only once a day, the instruction may be advantageously given at the time it was formerly usual to give it, namely, in the afternoon or evening before the sermon. Then it would be best to give it before the Rosary, instead of the Rosary instruction. It should not last longer than twenty-five minutes.

The *Particular Instructions* for the four different states of life should be given at a time when those for whom they are intended can most conveniently attend. Accordingly, the instructions for the married and unmarried men should be given on a Sunday.

[7] R., n. 139.      [8] Ibid.      [9] R., n. 92.

They may be given at the same hour, if there are two places where they can assemble; or they may be given in succession — one in the forenoon, the other in the afternoon, or both in the afternoon. The instruction for the married women is generally given on the afternoon of the first Wednesday of the Mission. If given earlier, it may prove a failure, because religious fervor has not yet been sufficiently awakened. The instruction for the unmarried women is usually given on Thursday afternoons, as they can have that time free, even though they live out at service. Should that time not be convenient, let another that is more suitable be chosen. As these instructions treat of so many things, they cannot be given in less than an hour and a half, yet beyond this they should not be protracted.

NOTE. — In the present arrangement of Missions these instructions are given on Tuesday evening. — [Editor.]

## 5. ARRANGEMENT OF THE MISSION PLAN

The plan of the exercises of the Mission consists in the proper selection of the various subjects for the sermons and instructions; in allotting to them their proper time; and in appointing the Fathers that are to preach them. For various reasons the Superior cannot know at the beginning of the Mission the particular needs of the congregation. He should, however, make his appointments a day or two in advance, so that the Fathers may know in time the duties that they must perform. The hours for the ordinary exercises must, nevertheless, be fixed from the beginning of the Mission.[10] In assigning to the Fathers their duties, the Superior must lay aside all human respect.[11]

[10] C. E., Vol. XV. p. 292.     [11] R., n. 79.

The good of the Mission is the only motive with which he should be animated and by which he should be guided.

According to St. Alphonsus and the Rule, one Father is to preach all the evening sermons of the Mission. For many years we have deviated from this practice for very good reasons. It would be too much labor for one Father to preach all the sermons, since he must, like the rest, be engaged in the confessional. Besides, the duties of the confessional are by far more laborious in this country than on the European Missions. Moreover, our practice gives a pleasant variety to the Mission, and awakens in the people a confidence in the different Fathers. This will prove advantageous for the confessional, and will serve as a preventive of vain-glory. But it will be necessary to appoint only such Fathers as are masters of the subjects on which they are to discourse. Every preacher must also connect his sermon with the sermon that preceded it, so that the sermons of the Mission may form a closely connected whole, and all repetitions may be avoided.

# CHAPTER V

Is there any difference between the Mission-sermon and other sermons? St. Alphonsus [1] says that there is a difference. Others who have written on this subject say the same thing. It would be very difficult to give in one sentence a full and accurate definition of a Mission-sermon, so manifold are the qualities that distinguish it from all other religious discourses. These qualities should be carefully studied by every missionary that wishes to make his sermons profitable to his hearers.

## 1. POPULARITY AND SIMPLICITY

After laying down rules and directions for religious discourses in general, [2] St. Alphonsus goes on to enumerate the qualities of the Mission-sermon. They are as follows:

The Mission-sermon must be *popular*, that is, it must be adapted to the capacity of ordinary people; hence it must be plain, both in *thought* and *expression*. It must be free from lofty thoughts, not necessary for the people to understand or to know, and must present the truths of religion or points of morality in the simplest possible manner, without aiming at the use of high expressions or grand circumlocutions. Hence, no expression should be used that the people

[1] C. E., Vol. XV. p. 94.          [2] Ib. p. 219.

cannot easily understand. However, where the nature of the thought requires it, the language of the speaker must be forcible, and the delivery impressive and vigorous. *"Cuncta simul clara sint et stylo* SIMPLICI *enuntiata, ut ab omnibus capiantur . . . nec omittant Patres loqui vehementer, si id materia postulet."* [3]

"There is no doubt," says St. Alphonsus, "that the sermons prepared for the Missions should be more easy and simple, and less encumbered with Latin quotations, than other discourses. . . . The style of preaching in the Missions must certainly be more simple and popular, that the poor may be persuaded and moved to virtue. The language should be plain and the periods concise, so that a person may understand any sentence without having heard or understood the preceding one, and that they who come to the church in the middle of the sermon may immediately understand what the preacher says.[4]

"The embellishment of a sermon with lofty sentiments and elaborate expressions, to gain a character for one's self, is precisely that adulteration of the word of God which the Apostle avoided; as he writes to the Corinthians: 'For we are not as many, adulterating the word of God, but with sincerity, but as from God, before God, in Christ we speak' (II Cor. ii, 17). On which words St. Gregory observes, that adulterers are not desirous to have children: on the contrary, they abhor them; they propose to themselves nothing else but the gratification of their unlawful passions: such are those who do not preach to gain souls, but to acquire a name and reputation. But let preachers tremble lest God should cut them off, as He threatens by the prophet Jeremias." [5]

---

[3] R., n. 88.     [4] Letter to a Religious, C. E., Vol. XV. p. 34.
[5] Letter to a Religious, C. E., Vol. XV. p. 43.

"I know," says the Saint in another place, "that there are orators who pretend that this is necessary even in sacred discourses in order to attract the people and to induce them to hear the divine word; but I also know that St. Paul protested against it when he said: 'I came not in loftiness of speech or of wisdom. . . . And my speech and my preaching were not in the persuasive words of human wisdom, but in showing of the spirit and power' (I Cor. ii. 1). I grant that preachers who attract the people by the charm of florid discourses have many hearers; but where is the fruit that they derive? 'A sick man,' says Seneca, 'does not ask for a physician that speaks well, but for one that is able to cure him.' Vain preachers may win the praises of some among the learned men, but they will bring no profit to any one. I say, 'Of some'; for, whatever may be the trouble that one takes, one hardly succeeds in making one of those florid discourses in which the learned do not find now this, now that, to criticise." [6]

However, the Mission-sermon must not be allowed to fall into the other extreme. Its language must be *grammatically correct* and free from all *vulgar expressions*. St. Alphonsus says: *"A Mission-sermon is by no means a confused aggregation of vulgar expressions, thrown together without order or art."* Sarcasm and ridicule should never be indulged in. What good can a missionary expect from the employment of such means? The Rule wisely cautions the Fathers against such excesses: *"Abstineant ab omnibus verbis, comparationibus, similitudinibus, quae rusticitatem redolent, vel auditoribus excultis, qui forte adsint, jure ac merito displicere possint."* [7] Yet, as Father Van de Kerckhove, S. J., appropriately remarks, when we

[6] C. E., Vol. XV. p. 200.    [7] R., n. 56.

speak to people so illiterate that they would otherwise not understand us, more common expressions may be proper. St. Augustine, that eloquent preacher of his age, says: *"Melius est ut nos reprehendant grammatici, quam ut non intelligant populi."* [8] St. Jerome also wrote to Nepotian: *"Multo melius est, ex duobus imperfectis, rusticitatem sanctam habere, quam eloquentiam peccatricem."*

## 2. FAMILIARITY OF STYLE

The discourses of the missionary should be *familiar*. When the missionary preaches or instructs from the pulpit, he should never adopt any other tone of voice than that which he uses in *ordinary conversation,* with this difference, that he should speak loud enough to be heard, and modulate his voice according as the subject is more or less important. The discourse should, therefore, be now animated, now calm, now jubilant, now low and subdued. The well-regulated modulation of the voice gives life to the discourse, keeps the audience attentive, and makes the desired impression. To this add *clearness* of expression and *distinctness* of articulation, without haste or *precipitation,* and you will have all the rules that should govern the sacred elocution of the missionary.

The missionary should carefully avoid that irksome sameness of tone which consists in uttering an entire sentence on one note with a slight cadence at the end. He should also shun the so-called *sing-song* tone, uttering one sentence, or a part of it, on one note, and the other on a different note. Let him banish from his mind the notion that there exists a certain *preaching-tone.* If there is such a tone, it must not be adopted by the missionary.

[8] In Ps. 138. n. 20.

With the language of the tongue is closely connected the language of the body, or *gestures*. According to St. Alphonsus,[9] the essential quality of a gesture is that it be *natural,* without affectation or studied gracefulness. The motion of the *hands* should not be vehement; they should not be raised above the head, nor too much extended sideways, nor held too confined. It is a fault always to keep one hand in motion while the other appears to be paralyzed. A still greater fault would be to raise the hand clenched, to strike the pulpit or to clap the hands so as to drown the voice. If the preacher takes the crucifix from his cincture, let him not play with it, but handle it gravely and devoutly. It is also unbecoming to move the *head* too frequently and too violently. It should not be raised too high nor bowed down, nor constantly turned in the same direction. The *eyes* should not be kept closed, nor cast down, nor turned toward one spot. The preacher should not move to and fro on the platform, nor spring forward, nor stamp the feet, nor lean over the pulpit. It is not becoming for the preacher to run from one end of the platform to the other; he should, for the most part, speak from the middle of it. The missionary should always remember that he *represents Jesus Christ,* in Whose work he is engaged. *His language, therefore, his gestures, as well as his entire attitude, should be grave and becoming a representative of Christ.*

### 3. THE MISSION-SERMON SHOULD BE LOGICAL

A Mission-sermon should be logical and free from all *exaggerations*. There should be order in every

[9] C. E., Vol. XV. p. 217.

discourse, especially in the great sermon of the Mission. The *exordium* should be short. After connecting the subject with the one that preceded it, it should at once introduce the new subject, leaving out everything that is foreign to it. The *peroration* should not be tedious. After a brief recapitulation of the main points, excluding every argument, the speaker shall make the application, and pass at once to the act of contrition and resolution which is to be made at the end of every Mission-sermon. The *body of the sermon* should consist of only a few parts, not more than three, and these should follow one another in logical order. Each part should contain few but solid arguments, which are to be followed by logical deductions of their particular applications. At the conclusion of each principal part of the sermon, a suitable application should be made to the spiritual wants of the people. An attempt may be made also to move the will through the affections, but here this should be done briefly, since at the close of the sermon, the will should be, as it were, taken by storm by arousing the emotions of the people. The argumentation must be *true,* that is, without exaggeration. The preacher should never say or advance anything that he cannot prove. Let him not call anything a mortal sin that is only a venial transgression, nor describe as a proximate occasion of sin circumstances that rarely lead people to the commission of mortal sin. He should not mercilessly condemn to hell-fire any class of sinners, nor preach refusal of absolution to any one. It is his business to induce sinners to come to confession; he must not deter them. In the selection of texts of Scripture great discretion should be used. "The quotations from Scripture," says St. Alphonsus, speaking of

Mission-sermons, "should be few, but well explained and well pondered. It will be better to present a single text well pondered by taking care to draw from it suitable moral applications, than to group together several passages which serve more to gratify the vanity of the preacher than to benefit the people." . . . "Only a few examples should be given — two or three, at the most, will suffice for a sermon — and they should not be too long." [10]

### 4. THE PATHETIC PART OF THE MISSION-SERMON — PERSUASION

The object of every sermon, and of every Mission-sermon in particular, is not only to convince the mind, but also to *move the will,* or what is the same thing, to produce a change of heart. To effect this the preacher must work upon the affections. This point is of the greatest importance in the Mission. Each sermon is to attain its peculiar object, and this is attained only when the subject preached makes a deep impression on the hearts of the audience. If the sermon has missed this object, so much of the effect of the Mission is lost. Two kinds of affections are to be moved; those of *fear,* and those of *love.* The movement of the affections of love is the principal end of the sermon. Fear alone will not bring about a true change of conduct. A powerful sermon may, indeed, strike terror into the sinner's heart, and this terror may force him to make a resolution of amendment. It may even drive him to confession. But the fruit of such a conversion is not lasting.[11] That terror will soon subside; it will gradually disappear altogether, and with it all good resolutions. It is, besides, very

10 C. E., Vol. XV. pp. 219, 220.     11 C. E., Vol. XV. p. 302.

doubtful whether a soul that is moved only by terror, is capable of making even a good act of imperfect contrition, such as proceeds from the *"amor initialis,"* and as is required by the Council of Trent for the remission of sins in confession.[12] Finally, it is well known that some terror-stricken souls, after returning from the Mission, give way to despair. "It is incredible," says Van de Kerckhove, "how prone sinners are to despair." [13] And the powers of hell are most eager to turn such occasions to their profit. Their principal aim is to represent God as a cruel tyrant, that it is impossible to serve Him, that He rejects sinners, and that no hope of salvation is left to them. "Hence," says the same great missionary, "after having spoken on some terrible truth, the missionary must give all possible encouragement to sinners."

To the affections of fear, therefore, must always be added those of love. The former are simply the *"initium sapientiæ,"* the latter, *"finis præcepti."* [14] Nor should we ever imagine that the object of some sermons is to create fear and terror only, while the object of others is to beget confidence and love. We are the ambassadors of God, *"cui proprium est misereri SEMPER et parcere."* St. Alphonsus directs that, in *every sermon*, the missionary should principally aim at leaving his audience impressed with the love of God. He quotes the example of St. Peter of Alcantara, who never failed to strike terror into the hearts of his hearers; but who did not omit to reassure them by promising full remission of sins through the great mercy of God and the merits of Jesus Christ. This is "to preach Christ crucified." [15]

The conclusion of the sermon, or the peroration, is,

---

[12] Sess. vi. c. 6.
[13] *Man. miss.* §9.
[14] I Tim. i. 5.
[15] C. E., Vol. XV. p. 302.

above all, the occasion when the missionary puts forth all his efforts to awaken the affections of love. The heart of the preacher and the hearts of his hearers should then be blended in one common act of confidence, love, and contrition.

The preacher must then speak and act as though he were one of the audience, by addressing himself directly to God, to Jesus Christ, to His most sacred Heart, to the Blessed Virgin in their behalf, by asking for mercy and forgiveness, and by forming appropriate resolutions. The people will naturally repeat the same sentiments in their hearts and make them their own. It matters little whether they fall on their knees or not. A few *well-chosen* and *well-prepared* sentences, having a close connection with the subject of the sermon, are sufficient. Long apostrophes lose their force with our people. When the affections of the heart are aroused, it is best to allow them to subside without any further suggestions on the part of the preacher.

It cannot be imagined what consolation the people carry home after such a sermon, and how eager they are to return.

Here it may be well to undeceive some missionaries who are so eager to make the people shed tears. Some few, indeed, have a singular facility in obtaining this result by using certain expressions, modulating their voice in a peculiar manner, etc. They imagine that they have produced an extraordinary effect. But how often are they mistaken! They must remember that tears are often produced without much impression on the heart, while, on the contrary, the heart may be deeply impressed without the flowing of tears. Our principle should be: *"Sermocinantis non est elicere lacrymas, sed quærere animas."*

Which are the most effective means for the missionary to produce contrition in the hearts of his hearers? Not certain expressions or sentences, nor a peculiar inflection of the voice, nor remarkably winning ways, nor any other outward manifestation of the kind, but *being himself deeply impressed with the truth which he preaches, and being full of a truly apostolic zeal.* Of the former of these qualities, even a pagan has written: *"Si vis me flere, dolendum est primum ipsi tibi."* [16] Of the latter, St. Gregory the Great says: *"Qui non ardet, non incendit."* Hence, according to St. Alphonsus,[17] the first and principal rule of a missionary is, *to love God.* He ought to be a man of prayer — a saint.

NOTE. — In his *Exercises of the Missions,*[18] St. Alphonsus calls the act of contrition, which is performed with the people at the close of every Mission-sermon, the most important part of the sermon. It is a most solemn act. The preacher introduces it by making the people kneel down and repeat some short supplications for pardon, *e. g.,* O Lord, mercy! — Then he orders lighted torches to be carried into the sanctuary, while he proposes two or three motives for contrition taken from the sermon. After that the preacher has a large crucifix brought and held up between the lighted torches. Then follow acts of love and contrition suggested by the preacher and repeated by the people, together with some acts of supplication to Jesus Crucified and to the Blessed Virgin Mary. — Our Rule says: *"Actus doloris coram crucifixo, atque ex motivis in concione ipsa expositis, semper est eliciendus."* [19]

This is certainly a most impressive and most effective act. However, in this country it would be regarded as a theatrical performance. We make up for it by a soul-stirring peroration. On some extraordinary occasion, for an extraordinary purpose, this ceremony could nevertheless be performed with great effect, even in this country. It was performed in the past, and there is no reason why it should not be performed in the future, should circumstances permit or require it.

[16] Horace.
[17] C. E., Vol. XV. p. 229.
[18] C. E., Vol. XV. p. 223.
[19] R., n. 138.

## 5.  Apostolic Freedom and Patience

Finally, the Mission-sermon must possess the quality of *apostolic freedom,* as is shown in the lives of all great missionaries.   The missionary must attack vice, no matter where he discovers it, and inculcate virtue, no matter how offensive it may appear to a certain class of people.   He should never feel embarrassed on account of the presence of a few fashionable people, nor shrink from uttering the plain truth for fear of shocking Protestants.   Human respect must be unknown to him.   The example of St. Paul before the Areopagus in Athens, and of St. Peter in the refined city of Rome, are striking illustrations of the apostolic freedom with which the missionary is to speak. Let the missionary treat his audience with the greatest respect, even with that politeness which becomes an apostle.   He should never insult his hearers, nor even shock their feelings, if he can possibly avoid doing so. Proper regard is to be had for the prejudices of some, and for the defective education of others.   Let pastoral prudence be used in our efforts to remove these obstacles.   The missionary should avoid venting his spleen on account of the ignorance of the people and certain abuses prevalent in the parish, thus running the risk of becoming personal.   Does he forget that to remove these evils is the very object of the Mission? Missionaries sent to convert heathen nations expect to find the people given to all sorts of vices and most obstinate adherents of their idolatrous practices, and they apply themselves with all possible patience to eradicate them.   So, likewise, must the home-missionary expect to find in the people to whom he is sent nothing but sin, vice, ignorance, sensuality, sacrilege, etc., to eradicate which is his special vocation. Let him, then, set to work, to fulfil his arduous task with all possible *apostolic patience.* Why should he be surprised to find these evils in the parish? Where is there a place that is free from abuses? The missionary's motto is, *"Argue, obsecra, increpa"* — but *"in omni patientia et doctrina."* [20] Our first missionaries said: *"OBSECRAMUS pro Christo, reconciliamini Deo."* [21]

These, then, are the chief and essential qualities of every Mission-sermon — popularity, familiarity, strict logic, unction, and apostolic freedom united to patience. No sermon should lack any one of these qualities. "Missionaries," says St. Alphonsus, "must always preach as missionaries (even at home or in other places), but particularly on the Missions; otherwise they will have to render a double account to God; since, on the one hand, they produce but little fruit, and, on the other, they give bad example to other preachers." [22]

He who wishes to inform himself still more on this point, would do well to read the work of St. Alphonsus, quoted here so frequently, his Letter to a Religious, and our Mission Rules. With both these treatises, no Redemptorist can be too familiar.

For the conclusion of this chapter we subjoin a most appropriate remark of Canon Oakley: [23] *"The best of all preachers, surely, is he who, while deeply feeling the momentous nature of his office, and distinctly realizing the truth of the announcement he is making, so expresses and so delivers himself, as best to make his auditory share his own convictions in all their force and fulness."* And, speaking of Missions,

---

[20] II Tim. iv. 2.　　　[22] C. E., Vol. XV. p. 206.
[21] II Cor. v. 20.　　　[23] *Priest on the Mission.*

he says: *"At Missions and Retreats, instructions are given in a colloquial, rather than a didactic, form, the preacher not so much haranguing the people as talking to them. This kind of address is quite exceptional. It gives scope for homely illustrations, imaginary dialogues . . . even good-natured satire. But, remember the excellent advice of the poet, 'Be thou familiar, but by no means vulgar.' A bad joke is painful everywhere, but in the pulpit it is like an ugly insect that finds its way into the chalice at Mass, and is at once nauseous to the taste, and offensive to piety. This peculiarly delicate branch of the preacher's duty is to be left to those experienced Religious, who can handle it with judgment, and whose lives of constant prayer and self-sacrifice give a certain point to their spiritual satire, to which seculars must not aspire."*

This shows what is expected of Religious missionaries. Take, then, the advice that St. Paul gives to his disciple: *"Sollicite cura teipsum probabilem exhibere Deo, operarium inconfusibilem, recte tractantem verbum veritatis."* [24]

[24] II Tim. ii. 15.

# CHAPTER VI

## THE GREAT SERMONS OF THE MISSION. — SUBJECTS FOR SERMONS AND THEIR ORDER

### 1. DURATION OF THE MISSION

To lay down a good plan for the exercises of the Mission, special regard must be had to the *object* of the Mission, and to the *time* in which the work is to be accomplished. In this country the object of the Mission is *Instruction, Conversion,* and *Perseverance.* To effect this threefold end, sufficient time is, above all, required. How long a time a Mission is to last, is, therefore, not to be measured by the number of confessions to be heard, but by the spiritual needs of the congregation. In the time of St. Alphonsus many Missions took up a month's time, some were even prolonged for thirty-six days.[1] In this country Missions should be neither too long, nor too short. Not too long, because local pastors are in dread of long Missions, and the people soon become tired of attending the exercises. Very rarely should a single Mission be laid out for two full weeks or fifteen days. A week and a half or eleven or twelve days, are sufficient for any single Mission. We find it difficult to obtain the consent of pastors even to that length. And if pastors find us insisting upon a longer time, they will look for missionaries elsewhere. But, ordinarily, a Mission should not be shorter than ten days, excluding the day for the souls in purgatory. *"Superior*

[1] C. E., Vol. XV. p. 289.

*missiones quas in exiguis locis habebit ad decem saltem . . . dies protrahet."* [2] It is hardly possible to give the necessary number of sermons and instructions in a shorter time. Besides, many hardened sinners do not approach the Mission before the second Sunday. If the Mission be continued for two or three days, it will often happen that they make up their mind to attend, while they will not think of returning, if the Mission closes on that day. When the sexes are divided, it is often difficult to continue the Mission longer than a week for each sex.

### 2. Quality of the Subjects to be Selected for the Sermons

The first thing to be achieved in the Mission is the *Conversion* of the people, some from a life of sin to purity of heart, others from a state of lukewarmness to a life of religious fervor; this constitutes the main work of the first part of the Mission. Even good people need the Mission to open their eyes to the dangers that threaten them, and to put them on their guard against them. *Perseverance* is the work of the second or latter part of the Mission. The *Instruction* of the people must go on both morning and evening, from the beginning to the end of the Mission.

The *Conversion* of the people is effected by the consideration of those very powerful motives which urge man most to work out his salvation. The people must learn to understand the absolute necessity of working out their *eternal salvation* — the dreadful evil of *mortal sin,* the inevitable result of which is *eternal damnation,* unless it be cancelled by *penance,* — the *unhappy death,* the terrible *judgment* that awaits the

[2] R., n. 77.

unrepenting sinner, and the recklessness of *delaying his conversion.* These subjects contain the *motives of fear,* because they fill the heart with the fear of God's judgments and punishment. Besides these, the *motives of love* should be employed to move the hearts of the people. St. Alphonsus says that a conversion effected through the motives of fear only, will not be lasting.[3] These motives are: God's *Infinite Mercy* toward the sinner, the desire of God to forgive the sinner, manifested in the *Passion of Christ,* and in giving us the *Blessed Virgin Mary* as our Refuge, our Advocate, and our Mother.

The *Perseverance* of the people is to be secured by reflection on the chief means to be employed for a truly Christian life. These are: the ready flight from the *proximate occasion of sin,* the constant practice of *prayer,* and the frequentation of the *sacraments.* In order faithfully to put these means in practice, a Christian can do nothing better than secure for himself the constant protection of the Blessed Virgin Mary, looking upon her and invoking her as his Mother. The people must also be warned against the peculiar vices prevalent in the country; and these are with us *drunkenness* and *impurity.*[4] In this order is not included the sermon on *Perseverance,* which is to form the close of the Mission, nor the sermon on the *Mission-cross.*

Our people are, on the whole, much in need of *Instruction,* because, on the one hand, Catholic education still labors under great defects, and on the

[3] *Exercises,* C. E., Vol. XV. p. 302.
[4] Father Benger, in his *Instructions for Missions,* lays down the principle that during Missions no sermons should be preached on particular vices. — In this country, such sermons have become necessary.

other, Catholics are constantly associating with an
unbelieving population. Many are deficient even in
the very rudiments of faith, or at least have not a sufficient knowledge of their meaning. Hence, the
morning instructions, as also the particular instructions for the different states of life, must be given well.
But, over and above this, some instructive sermons
are needed on such subjects as the *Sacrament of Penance, the Precepts of the Church, Faith, the true
Church of Christ,* perhaps also the *Blessed Eucharist,*
and the *Priesthood.* In fact, all the evening sermons
should contain a great deal of instruction.

It is the duty of the Superior of the Mission, with
the advice of the other Fathers, to make such a selection of sermons, and have them preached at such
times and by such Fathers, as will promote most effectually the good of the Mission. He should take into
consideration the time at his disposal, the circumstances of the place, the days on which he may expect the greatest concourse of people, without losing sight, in the sermons, of a logical order which
should be observed in every Mission.

The Rule has the following plan for small Missions: *"In minoribus missionibus, decem vel duodecim
dierum, materia concionum universe hæc erit: invitatio
ad pœnitentiam, salutis operandæ necessitas, procras-
tinatio conversionis, peccatum mortale, mors, judicium,
infernus, æternitas; ac deinde . . . dicetur de oratione
ac necessario de patrocinio Beatissimæ Virginis."* [5]
The Rule evidently leaves it to the choice of the missionaries to preach such other sermons as may be
deemed ncessary; for no fixed standard can be laid
down for all times and countries. We cannot even lay
down a determined plan for a single Mission before

[5] R., n. 90.

we have arrived at the place and acquainted ourselves with the special needs of the people. Were
we to do so, says St. Alphonsus, we would act like
a physician who writes a prescription before seeing
the patient and examining his disease.[6] But, adds
the Rule, *"a concionibus politicis prorsus abstineant
Nostri, et in polemicis maximam adhibeant præcautio-
nem et prudentiam."* [7]

### 3. CONTROVERSIAL DISCOURSES — PUBLIC DISCUSSIONS

Let us add a word on *controversial* or *polemical sermons,* which the Rule requires to be preached *"maxi-
ma cum præcautione et prudentia."* In this country,
we need not fear any interference on the part of the
civil authorities, which the Rule here seems to have
in view. But, with regard to such discourses, let us
ask ourselves candidly, *ad quid?* For the instruction
of the Catholics? Then, let them simply be *instructive sermons,* plain and solid, with an occasional notice
of the most popular objections, and the object is
gained. "But the people need to be told how to defend their religion." They need not so much to be
told how to fight unbelievers, as to be confirmed in
their faith, which is the aim of the Mission. The best
argument that they can use is always the authority
of the Church, whose doctrine can never be called
in question. Are such sermons to convince non-
Catholics? With them the fault is more to be looked
for in their ignorance and early training than in their
malice. Their minds, being prepared by the consideration of the *Eternal Truths,* need only to be instructed. But attack them by a polemical discourse,

---

[6] Letter to a Bishop, C. E., Vol. XV. p. 76.
[7] R., n. 56.

touch the principles that they have cherished from childhood as sacred deposits delivered to them by their forefathers, and the immediate result will be to put them on the defensive. Fight them, and they will fight you, and their self-love will scarcely ever allow you the victory. Such discourses, therefore, can only retard their being convinced, and their subsequent conversion.

The worst practice is to make use of sarcastic language in describing the errors of heresy, to turn into ridicule the religious practices of some sects, to make fun of their preachers, to show up their ignorance, and so forth. Past experience has shown what harm is done to the Mission by such witticisms. In no case should the missionary allow himself to be dragged into a *public discussion or controversy with Protestant preachers*. By this imprudent act he might easily incur the censures of the Church, disturb the public tranquillity of the town, do no good to the Catholics, and leave the Protestants perhaps more opposed to the Church than they were before.

If remarks are made by outside people against the Mission or against the missionaries or against their sermons; if articles appear against them in the public papers; if they are denounced from Protestant pulpits, let them simply bear all in patient silence. *"Principes sacerdotum et omne concilium quærebant falsum testimonium contra Jesum. . . . Jesus autem tacebat."* [8]

### 4.   The Order in which the Sermons should Follow One Another

The various subjects for the great sermons mentioned in this chapter furnish matter for at least nine-

[8] Matt. xxvi. 59–63.

teen sermons: namely, two for the opening and the close of the Mission; nine for the first part of the Mission (*conversion*): Salvation, Sin, Penance, Death, Judgment, Hell, Mercy, Blessed Virgin, Delay of Conversion; six for the second (*perseverance*): Drunkenness, Impurity, Proximate Occasion, Prayer, Sacraments, Mission-cross; and at least two to be given as instructions; such as, Precepts of the Church and Faith, or the Church of Christ. To do full justice to these subjects would require a Mission of sixteen days, two sermons falling on each of the three Sundays. Now, as we have seen, in view of our present circumstances, a single Mission should hardly last over twelve days. Therefore, some subjects must be dropped, others must be united in one sermon. Of the subjects of the first part, that on Mercy may be dropped by treating its main points in the sermon of the Blessed Virgin; Drunkenness and Impurity can easily be united in one sermon. The method of doing so will be spoken of in another place. The three Means of Perseverance may be preached in one sermon; and the erecting of the cross will make a fitting close to the Mission. Thus there would be fourteen sermons which could be preached in a Mission of twelve days.

In a Mission of eleven days one more sermon is to be dropped; in a Mission of ten days, two more; which of them are to be omitted it would be hard to say. The solution of the difficulty depends entirely on the peculiar needs of the place. Still greater solicitude is needed when the Mission is to be finished in eight or nine days. Penance, Death, Delay of Conversion, Drunkenness and Impurity may then be left out, yet so as to make up for them in the other sermons whenever it can be done. The three Means of Perseverance form a beautiful close to the Mission, and they can also be preached in connection with the erection of the cross. Even the sermon on the Blessed Virgin, followed by the solemn act of dedication, makes a grand close to a Mission.

The following subjects should never be dropped, nor united to others at a regular Mission: Introduction, Salvation, Mortal Sin, General Judgment, Hell, Blessed Virgin Mary, Precepts of the Church, Means of Perseverance. At a Triduum or a similar exercise, let the preacher make a selection from these subjects, if so required by the nature of those exercises, and unite them as he may think best. But in the selection of the sermons, let him beware lest he choose only those subjects which are very grave and fear-inspiring. Let the grave be diversified by what is instructive, edifying, encouraging and consoling.

It is customary, in some Provinces, to preach a sermon on *Sacrilegious Communion,* which is followed by a solemn act of atonement before the Blessed Sacrament exposed. We find nothing about this in the Instructions of St. Alphonsus, or in the Rule. Yet this practice has existed for many years. It originated, in the beginning of this century, in the North of Italy; it was thence introduced into France and Germany[9] and then into this country. We find it practised by other missionaries, especially by the Jesuits, but it is not a general custom. Venerable Caspar del Buffalo used to preach this sermon with great effect. It appears somewhat strange that the Fathers who composed the General Chapter of 1855 have not even mentioned it. On the German Missions in this country this sermon, when followed by the atonement, has always been regarded as an affecting

[9] See Prost's written memoirs.

ceremony. In 1860 we introduced it on the English Missions, but soon dropped it (except at some Renewals), because bishops and priests raised objections to it, and because not all the good that was expected from it was always obtained. On the contrary, there is reason to fear that such a sermon is apt to frighten the people and keep them from the sacraments.[10] We gain the end intended by this sermon, by frequently referring to bad confessions, and by a special sermon and oft-repeated instructions on confession and Communion. However, the practice should not be dropped altogether. The sermon with the atonement will do a great amount of good in some congregations. We shall speak of this sermon and of the manner of preaching it in another place.

[10] Even Father Weninger, S.J., who is fond of urging the necessity of great display at Missions, holds the contrary opinion in regard to this ceremony. See his *Practische Winke für Missionäre.*

# CHAPTER VII

## MORNING INSTRUCTIONS

Some books, written for the direction of missionaries, say nothing about instructions to be given, evidently because the subjects of our instructions are embodied in the sermons which they prescribe to be preached in the morning. The reason, in all probability, is to prevent these instructions from being given in a dry, uninteresting manner, so repulsive to the people. Another reason may be a certain disinclination in the people to attend "instructions," owing to that secret pride which makes them imagine themselves not in need of instruction. Some people would think it a most humiliating act to go to a religious instruction. Hence, many missionaries call their instructions sermons, discourses, lectures. It would be well to bear this in mind in making the announcements. The best way is to call every public exercise a sermon.

## 1. Composition of Mission–Instructions

For the most of our people, rich or poor, of the educated or of the working classes, religious instruction is absolutely necessary. Hence, our Mission-instructions are of equal importance with the sermons, and, therefore, they demand the greatest skill on the part of the catechist. Let them be well prepared and written out; or let, at least, a full and clear sketch of all that is to be said, be prepared. *"Catechista rite paratas et elaboratas habeat suas doctrinæ christianæ explanationes."* [1] The instructions must necessarily exhaust their respective subjects, as far as doctrine is concerned. If anything is omitted, the people may easily be led to believe that it does not belong to it: for instance, add to a good purpose of amendment, that we must resolve to avoid the proximate occasion of sin; to contrition, that it must be supernatural; to restitution, that it must be made as soon as possible; or, to forgiveness, that we must exhibit toward our enemies at least the ordinary signs of politeness; and so in many other points.

Besides, the instructor must pay particular attention to a clear division of his subject, following, in this respect, the divisions given in approved catechisms or books of instruction. In sermons, the division need not be so prominent, but in instructions this is necessary in order to assist the weak memories of the people; for instance, Contrition must be: 1, sincere; 2, supernatural; 3, supreme; 4, universal; 5, united with confidence in God. The divisions should be announced in the beginning; then, each point is to be explained distinctly, and supported by a few clear arguments. At the end, all is briefly recapitulated. [2] In the introduction, the connection between the subject of the present and that of the preceding instruction must be established by repeating the main points of the latter, unless there exists no such connection. The principal object to be aimed at by the catechist must be, to leave the audience so instructed on the particular subject of his discourse that he may expect them to retain for the future a sufficient knowledge of that point of our holy religion.

[1] R., n. 92      [2] C. E., Vol. XV. p. 170.

## 2. CHARACTER OF THE INSTRUCTIONS — THEIR DELIVERY

The Mission-instruction, as Father Sarnelli, C.SS.R., remarks, should neither be a dry exposition of the doctrine proposed, nor should it possess the unction and power of a sermon, but it should be kept, as it were between the two, allowing, as the occasion requires, some of the unction of the sermon to flow in to enliven the doctrinal exposition. *"Catechistæ officium erit docere, non autem movere affectus."* [3] The case is different, however, when a subject that should properly be the theme of an evening sermon, *e. g.*, the proximate occasion of sin, the frequentation of the sacraments, is used for a morning instruction.

The instruction should always be given in such a manner as to excite interest, riveting the attention of the audience, rather than making it preferable for them to go home; [4] so that even those whose business is most urgent will say: "I will hear this missionary first, and then hurry a little more to get to my place of business." The poor people often sacrifice their sleep in the morning, remain from their work in the forenoon, come to church on a cold winter's day, in order to hear an instruction to which they have been so pressingly invited, and then they are repaid for all their trouble with a dry, sleepy discourse, in which, according to all appearances, the speaker himself takes very little interest, and seems to work hard to get together a few sentences to fill up half an hour. By such instructions the people are certainly not attracted. For this reason, our Father General says in his Circular, Feb. 2, 1856: *"Superiores missionum*

---

[3] R., n. 92.         [4] C. E., Vol. XV. p. 173.

*nonnisi illos Patres catechistas eligant, qui . . .
omnem operam et diligentiam in solidam populi in-
structionem impendunt, quin perfunctorie grave munus
pertractent"* [5]

The language of the instruction must be pure, and
absolutely free from vulgar expressions. Never
should the catechist imitate peculiarities of pronunciation, or introduce curious expressions made use of by
some people; nor should he ever make use of sarcastic comparisons, or give any class of people op-
probrious names. Such evil habits are unbecoming
in any priest, but in a missionary they are serious
faults that are often followed by deplorable consequences. Regarding jocose language, or expressions
to excite merriment in the audience, the Rule says
that, except once or twice to arouse attention, it
should not be indulged in.[6] In fact, it does a great
deal of harm. Instead of arousing the attention, it
often diverts it, and, what is worse, leaves the people
without the necessary impression. It even causes
some people to doubt whether the missionary really
means what he says, whenever he speaks of some
serious matter. St. Alphonsus says: "I do not know
how that (such conduct) can agree with the respect
due to the church in which one is, and with the pulpit
from which one teaches the word of God, and in which
the catechist appears as the minister of Jesus Christ." [7]

### 3. EXAMPLE TO BE RELATED

St. Alphonsus prescribes that after each instruction an example should be related about the unhappy
result of sacrilegious confessions, whether it be in

[5] Mauron, *Litt. Circulares,* p. 10, II.      [6] R., n. 92.
[7] C. E., Vol. XV. p. 174.

logical connection with the subject or not.[8]   This is
more necessary in Italy, as the German translator of
the works of St. Alphonsus appropriately remarks;
in other countries, the example is made up for by
more complete instructions.   The Rule says that it
need not always be done, but *"plerumque."* [9]   Once or
twice, such examples should be brought into the instructions on the various parts of the Sacrament of
Penance.   But then great care must be taken by the
missionaries, *"ne quid dicant, quod vel non satis fun-
datum, vel secretum sacramentale etsi specie tantum
violare, vel loco, in quo Missionis exercitia habita
fuerunt, injuriam irrogare videatur; et universe non
expedit de se, aut de iis loqui, quæ Nostris accide-
runt."* [10]   There are many books within our reach
which contain a variety of examples suitable for our
Missions.   St. Alphonsus relates a considerable number of such examples in his Mission-instructions.[11]

## 4.  SUBJECTS FOR MISSION-INSTRUCTIONS

Let us now proceed to the subjects of the instructions and their logical order.   St. Alphonsus prescribes that, in the Mission-instructions, there should
be explained: 1, The Mysteries of Faith; 2, The Sacraments, particularly the Sacrament of Penance; and 3,
The Commandments of God and the Precepts of the
Church.[12]   He also gives in detail what should be said
on each of these three points.[13]   Considering our
circumstances in this country, it is hardly possible
to give instructions on all the points contained under
these three heads.   Only in a Mission of two weeks'

[8] C. E., Vol. XV. p. 173.     [11] C. E., Vol. XV. p. 347.
[9] R., n. 93.                  [12] C. E., Vol. XV. p. 172.
[10] R., n. 56.                 [13] C. E., Vol. XV. p. 172.

duration could we speak of them all, by giving, of course, only the essential points of each, as the Saint directs, and by dwelling somewhat longer on those points upon which the people need more explicit instruction. In this country, we generally keep to the subjects indicated by the Rule: [14] *"Materiam instructionis consuetam plerumque constituent præcepta decalogi ac praxis confitendi et communicandi."* As regards the Precepts of the Church, we make a great sermon of this matter whenever we can do so. We hardly ever give special instructions on the *Mysteries of Faith* (although no one disputes their necessity), for the simple reason — lack of time. But we give short instructions on the principal Mysteries of Faith before the Rosary, where we find a special necessity for them. On the Sacrament of Penance and the Most Blessed Eucharist, we are most explicit. The Sacrament of Matrimony and the most essential points regarding Baptism, we explain in our instructions for the married men and women, which include, also, all on the Fourth Commandment that concerns parents. What concerns children, we give in the particular instructions for the unmarried, and in the children's Mission. On Confirmation, we give instructions, when this sacrament is administered during the Mission; on Holy Orders, in the sermon on the Priesthood, where it is needed. Extreme Unction we reserve for the Renewal.

By this it can be seen that we give all the instructions on the *Sacraments* that are or may be needed.

In our instruction on enmity, we comprise the essentials of the Fifth Commandment; in that on restitution, all that belongs to the Seventh and Tenth Commandments. In one or two instructions we give

[14] R., n. 139.

the Second, Sixth, and Eighth Commandments. On the First Commandment we give a particular instruction where it is required. Hence, we give all the instructions needed when we speak on the *Commandments*.

St. Alphonsus asks,[15] whether the instructions on the Sacraments (Penance), or those on the Commandments should be given first. He answers that the instructions on the Commandments should precede those on Penance, because the former recall many things to the minds of the people, of which they did not think before, and, consequently, many want to come a second time to confession, which would involve a great loss of time. Yet, he excepts the case in which the sins committed against the various Commandments are enumerated in connection with the instruction on the examination of conscience. We supply this by making an examination of conscience with the people while the Mass is going on, interposing short prayers at the principal parts of the holy sacrifice. In this country we have to give the instructions on the Sacrament of Penance first. We must begin to hear confessions at least on the third day, and, therefore, we have to prepare the people for them. Our difficulty here consists mainly in this, that almost everything should come first. We follow the order laid down in the following principle: First let the sinner be *reconciled* to God, and then let him be told what Commandments he has to keep to *serve* God.

[15] C. E., Vol. XV. p. 172.

# CHAPTER VIII

UNDER this head we comprise those particular instructions which are given to the married men and widowers, to the unmarried men, to the married women and widows, and to the unmarried women.

## 1. NECESSITY OF THE PARTICULAR INSTRUCTIONS

St. Alphonsus had only two particular instructions given, one to the unmarried women and widows, the other to the married women; and the old Rule does not mention any other. The object of the former instruction was to inspire young women and widows with a great love of the virtue of chastity, even to induce them to profess a life of virginal purity; while it was the object of the latter to instruct the married women in their particular duties.[1] Nothing is said about men, married or single, with the exception of an exhortation which used to be given to the members of the Sodality of the Blessed Virgin, and to those who felt disposed to enter that Sodality.[2]

Times have changed and people have also changed. Particular instructions for each of the states of life mentioned above have become indispensable. Without them, the Mission would be altogether incomplete. This is particularly the case in this country. It is well known how modern society regards matri-

[1] Codex C.SS.R., p. 84. n. 137.
[2] C. E., Vol. XV. p. 255.

mony, and what horrible abuses are made of it, to the great detriment of souls and the ruin of society itself. These false notions have taken possession of the minds of all classes of people. It may be safely said that the abuse of marriage is the chief cause of the other kinds of immorality deluging the world at present. Save the family, and you save the Church and the State. Hence, solid instructions on the sacrament of matrimony, given, however, with the requisite precautions, are not only advisable or useful, but are absolutely necessary, both for the married and the unmarried. For this reason, these four instructions are now prescribed by the Rule.[3] *"Tempore opportuno pro adolescentulis, mulieribus nuptis, juvenibus et viris ad ipsos habebitur concio vel instructio de officiis suo statui adnexis."*

2. SPECIAL REMARKS ABOUT THESE INSTRUCTIONS

1. These instructions are to be given to each class alone,[4] that the preacher may have more freedom in expressing himself on matters which those not belonging to that state of life need not or should not hear. The Rule directs that these discourses be given *"separatim, ubi convenienter fieri potuerit; sed si separatio sexus convenienter fieri non potest, hujusmodi instructio penitus omittatur."* [5] The reason is obvious. If they are omitted, what is wanting should be supplied in the other instructions, in which many points may be included that can safely be mentioned before a mixed audience. Other points must be supplied in the confessional. Still better would it be to preach a special sermon on The Christian Family, in which many

[3] R., n. 143.
[4] Therefore, not even the married men and women are to be taken together.　　　[5] R., n. 143.

of the most important duties of the married and the unmarried can be explained and inculcated.

The simplest method of keeping from the church those who are not to hear a certain instruction, is to take care, in making the announcement, lest too much curiosity be excited by the use of mysterious language, or by stating beforehand the subject of these instructions, or by making so much ado about the non-admittance of other classes of people. Then, at the time when the instruction takes place, let the Prefect of the church open but one or two doors, stationing, within, one or two persons of the class to be admitted, who will politely inform such individuals as cannot be admitted of the nature of the instruction, and request them to withdraw until it is over. This rule of excluding others need not, however, be carried to an unreasonable extent, so as, for instance, to drive from the confessionals a few married women, while the instruction for the unmarried women is going on.

2. The missionary who gives these instructions should be a man of mature age, great experience and gravity of deportment.

Often a younger Father must take charge of the instruction for the unmarried women. Let, then, gravity supply the want of age. He should be well prepared, so as not to bring forth mere *"verba et folia,"* but *"argumenta solida."* He may use his manuscript, lest he forget some essential point. But he should not read from it, except an occasional quotation; otherwise, the instruction will lose greatly in interest and animation. He should not dwell too long on any particular point, in order to have sufficient time for all that is to be said. Nor should he bring in anything that does not strictly appertain to the "particular duties" of the class of people whom he is addressing, in order not to prolong unnecessarily the discourse without doing justice to his subject.

3. He should be careful in the selection of his words and expressions, when he touches on points of a delicate nature, to avoid giving scandal to his hearers, and at the same time to impart sufficient instruction to those ignorant of their most urgent duties. *"In hisce concionibus vel instructionibus Congregati speciatim præ oculis habeant illas præcautiones quas Constitutiones nostræ præscribunt quoad materias ad sextum præceptum spectantes."* [6]

4. In congregations of mixed nationalities the instruction for the unmarried people can generally be given in English, because they all understand it. The instruction for the married is to be given in the language which the majority understand. For the others it must be supplied in some other way; otherwise, four instructions would be required for them.

The particular instructions given in this manner cannot fail to do very great good. Hundreds of the unmarried prepare better for their future state of life; and thousands of the married live more happily together, by bearing their trials more patiently, by educating their children more carefully, and by putting an end to those most horrible practices which are carried on under cover of matrimony, including the most revolting crime — the wholesale murder of unborn children, who are thus excluded from the kingdom of heaven. Thousands of infants, who, in consequence of the words of the missionary, are allowed to live long enough to receive baptism, will forever bless him who deterred their parents from murdering them before birth. *"Ex ore infantium et lactentium perfecisti laudem tuam."* [7]

[6] R., n. 143.  [7] Ps. viii, 3.

# CHAPTER IX

## CONFESSIONS

WE are now approaching that function of the Mission which the Rule calls, *"munus primarium ac præcipuum missionis."* [1]  It is the least in the eyes of men, but the greatest before God; and, without doubt, it is also the hardest.  To give to poor fallen sinners the means of a full reconciliation with God, is the chief object of the Mission.  All the efforts, prayers and hardships of the missionaries tend to that one end.  Without exaggeration, therefore, we may say that confession is *the* work of the Mission.  Now, if it cannot be denied that hell makes every effort to prevent Missions from being given, or, if given notwithstanding its efforts, to destroy the work of the preachers and catechists, to discourage them, to withdraw the confidence of the people from them; it is also certain that the powers of darkness direct all their efforts against confession, in order to frustrate the main object of the Mission at the moment when it is almost gained.  For this reason, it becomes necessary to treat the subject of this chapter with the greatest care and minuteness.

## I.  THE MISSIONARIES ARE TO HEAR ALL THE CONFESSIONS THEMSELVES

Our holy Founder made it a rule that the missionaries should hear all the confessions themselves, to the exclusion of all other confessors.

[1] R., n. 80.

One reason for this is, that the people prefer to go to confession to the missionaries, feeling less embarrassed in doing so. They have more confidence in those who have been sent by God as the extraordinary ministers of reconciliation.

Strong objections may be raised against the admission of other confessors, since they generally lack the necessary experience in dealing with the extraordinary cases to be met with on the Missions. Strangers are often wanting in patience in attending to difficult cases. They are averse to the trouble of hearing general confessions and are apt to hurry through the confessions.

Besides, they cannot stay long enough to attend to unfinished confessions; there is no uniformity of practice between them and the missionaries; they often do not satisfy their penitents in allaying their scruples and troubles of conscience, and they are unsatisfactory in many other ways. Therefore, the Rule of excluding other confessors *"est regula summi momenti."* [2] *"Licebit tamen, si necessitas id postulaverit, confessarios extraneos in auxilium advocare."* [3]

When the missionaries perceive that they cannot possibly get through with all the confessions, the disadvantages enumerated above may be overlooked. Hence, no Mission should be accepted to which a sufficient number of confessors cannot be sent. [4] Such wàs the practice of St. Alphonsus. [5] He would, however, admit other confessors before the general Communions, to hear the few scruples that some might still have on their consciences. [6]

At Renewals the priests of the parish or other con-

[2] R., n. 80.     [4] R., n. 130.
[3] R.. n. 81.     [5] C. E., Vol. XV. p. 287.
[6] Villecourt, *Life of St. Alph.*, Vol. I, ch. 52.

fessors may be asked to assist in hearing confessions. The ordinary difficulties having been settled in the Mission, the people find no obstacle in the way to hinder them from going to their own priests. *"Confessariorum localium opera uti licet."* [7] If there are some who have special difficulties to settle, they have the opportunity offered to them by the presence of the missionaries.

### 2. UNIFORMITY OF PRACTICE

The missionaries should try to be uniform in their practice, especially in their decisions in regard to local difficulties. Such cases may be certain doubtful societies, certain doubtful occasions of sin, a certain kind of amusement, matters of restitution, education, and the like. Let them confer together on any doubtful point, and then follow the decision that they have arrived at. They should be guided in this by what Father General says in the above-quoted circular: [8] *"Exsurgunt nonnunquam quæstiones locales admodum complicatæ, quibus decidendis et ad praxim applicandis summa prudentia et circumspectione opus est, ne conflictus cum auctoritate civili aut ecclesiastica* [9] *exoriantur, vel fidelium admiratio excitetur, vel congregatio nostra vituperationi generali exponatur. Quæstiones hujus generis superiores domuum* [10] *ad quos res spectat, in Academiis, communibus consiliis collatis, examinent, ut de uniformi agendi modo, quem omnes nostri sacerdotes sequantur, conveniant."* Not in deciding cases only, but in every other respect, should the missionaries study to be uni-

---

[7] R., n. 155.     [8] Mauron, *Litt. Circulares*, p. 14.
[9] Local pastors, bishops.
[10] The case is the same on the Missions.

form; otherwise, much confusion will be the consequence, to the great disadvantage of the Mission, and the frequent annoyance of the Fathers.

### 3. When the Missionaries are to Begin to Hear Confessions — Sermons that are to be Heard by the People Before Going to Confession

As a rule, we do not begin to hear confessions before Tuesday afternoon. This does not prevent an exception from being made in favor of one or the other who cannot come at a later time. If, during the course of the Mission, persons present themselves for confession who have not heard any sermons, or only two or three, while they could have attended more, they should be gently admonished, first to attend the Mission, and then to return. But care should be taken lest the number of sermons that we require become known. [11] Many careless individuals would attend just so many and no more.

Here the question arises: What is to be done with those who have heard no sermons and come to confession at the close of the Mission? Some dismiss them at once without mercy. To act thus is not according to the spirit of a true Redemptorist: *"Qui, quasi fame animarum exstimulatus . . . sua retia teneat, nec alteri cedat prædam quam sibi Dominus miserit, sive minor illa sit sive major."* [12] Let it first be seen, whether such an individual could have come to the sermons. If so, let a gentle rebuke be administered, and the penitent be advised to hear one

---

[11] According to an old Statute: *"Regulariter ad confessionem non admittantur fideles, priusquam quatuor vel quinque conciones aut instructiones præcesserint."*

[12] R., n. 82, 84.

or two sermons and return, provided there are one or
two left to be heard. If this be not possible, hear his
confession and do the best that you can for him. It
must, after all, be attributed to the operation of divine
grace that such a person makes up his mind to come to
confession. Experience shows that some of those who
are thus tardy manifest the very best dispositions. In
the Mission, the grace of God works miraculous conversions, sometimes in most extraordinary ways. Yet,
it is also true that many of this class are very poorly
disposed, and seem to come only to get through, and
because others came. These try the patience of the
confessor very much; they do not deserve his assistance. But let him do his best with them. He will
not go unrewarded. If such persons *could not* have
come to the Mission, and perhaps can come no more,
they deserve as much attention, patience and charity,
as the sick who are attended at their homes. Those
who do not belong to the parish, are to be dismissed
without a hearing, as has been already said.

At the Renewal, confessions may begin on the second day, that is, on Monday afternoon, because in the
Renewal it is not required that so many instructions
precede the confessions as in the Mission. Moreover,
the time being shorter, and all in reference to the
Sacrament of Penance having been explained that same
morning, there is no particular reason for further delay.

#### 4. ASSIDUITY IN HEARING CONFESSIONS

When once the confessions have begun, the missionaries should spend all their available time in the
confessional, excepting the time necessary to attend
to their spiritual and corporal wants. St. Alphonsus
had no confessions heard during the sermons and in-

structions, on account of the commotion caused by
those who pass in and out of the confessionals, and
because those who are actually confessing, as well as
the others who are preparing for it, cannot easily
occupy their minds with confession and the sermon
at the same time.[13]   Other missionaries have followed
the same rule; for example, St. Leonard of Port
Maurice, Van de Kerckhove, etc.

In this country, we generally attend at the confessional from 5:15 A.M. till 10 P.M., except the time
for Mass, meals and recreation; nor do we interrupt
the confessions during the sermons, because, owing
to the very limited number of confessors, we cannot
get through with the work in due time, and, chiefly,
because many of the men and women cannot come
at another time.   We spend eleven hours daily in
hearing confessions, while many incidental circumstances add to the usual burden.   Hence it can be
seen that, under present circumstances, the work of
the confessions is most laborious.   For this and other
good reasons, it is customary, at the close of the
first week, to give a day of rest to the Fathers, if the
Mission continues for the greater part of the second
week.

### 5.   The Confessionals

The confessionals are to be erected in a public
place, either in the church, or in a side-chapel, or in
the basement.   They may also be located in a hall
or large school-room, especially when several confessionals are put into the same room.   The sacristy,
or a concealed corner behind the organ, is not a
proper place for them.   An exception might be

[13] C. E., Vol. XV. p. 288.

made in churches where there is in the sacristy a stationary confessional that is used on other occasions. But then let the door remain open, or the penitents wait for confession inside of the place. The confessionals thus stationed in public should be so covered that neither the penitent nor the confessor can be seen. *"Confessiones nonnisi per crates excipiantur."* This prescription does not include the case in which, for good reasons, a number of men, or even one or the other man alone is heard in some place apart from the church. But women are never to be heard in any other way but *"per crates,"* not even the deaf. For these a place must be selected, where they and the confessor can speak loud without being understood by others. At present it is strictly prohibited by the statutes of nearly every diocese to hear women's confessions without a grate. If possible, the men are to be heard alternately with the women. This rule is very essential where the Mission is given to mixed congregations. It is not the custom in this country, as it is in others, to have special confessionals for the men, nor do we generally assign them certain hours, except on two or three evenings. Besides, many of the women, servant-girls for instance, need to be accommodated as well as the men. The observance of this rule will suit all, while it will also prevent the abuse that arises from the excessive shyness of some men to dispute with those forward women who deprive them of their place at the confessional.

It is the custom in all Religious communities, and even among secular priests, to have the name of each confessor fixed over the door of his confessional. This practice has always been kept up among us at home and on the Missions, in this and in the old country. It is needless to say that the people should have equal confidence in all the missionaries. That they have not is a well-known fact. The name over the confessional will enable each one to find the Father to whom he wants to go. The missionaries should, however, never have recourse to certain artifices to attract penitents. Let every one try to be kind to all, neither attract nor repel any one, but simply gather in that harvest which God puts within his reach.

### 6.  ORDER TO BE KEPT AT THE CONFESSIONALS — MEANS TO SECURE A REGULAR ATTENDANCE

For a long time it has been a question among missionaries, by what means attendance at the confessionals could be so equalized that there would be neither too many nor too few penitents; and that the confessors, being always steadily occupied, might comfortably get through the work in perfect order. It is well known that, on some days, there are only a few penitents waiting for confession, while on others the confessionals are so besieged that scarcely half of those coming can be heard; many, after waiting, perhaps, an entire day, have to go home without being heard. And, indeed, it is very hard to tell when they will get an opportunity. This state of things often has very serious consequences. Those who are waiting at the confessionals become weary, are often without food at a late hour, and consequently in a very poor state to make a good confession. Others quarrel before the confessional — another poor preparation for the sacrament. Others, again, wait there for one or two days, yet not long enough to get to confession, staying from their work or their household duties; then they become disheartened, or are not allowed to come any more. Finally, others, seeing the immense throng around the confessionals, make no attempt to come near; and these are perhaps the very persons who need confession most.

St. Alphonsus also encountered this difficulty, and tried to obviate it. Notwithstanding the fact that he generally had from eighteen to twenty Fathers on the Mission in parishes of from two to three thousand souls, this question gave him trouble.[14] He had recourse to repeated announcements [15] inducing the people to come to confession at an early day of the Mission. Others have tried the same without entire success. Some have the practice of distributing tickets to those who remain when the confessor leaves at noon or in the evening. But little relief is obtained from this method. When those with the tickets return, others have already occupied their places, persons who, perhaps, have left their work just for that day. It is the hardest task to drive them away. This constant trouble works upon the mind of the confessor. He is tempted to hurry the confessions, thus giving no satisfaction either to himself or to the penitents. Besides, he is worn out sooner than he would be if he could attend to his penitents with the proper ease of mind.

We have tried the ticket-system; that is, we distributed as many tickets every night as would keep us occupied the next day without being over-crowded. That system also has many disadvantages.

One of the best means for securing a good attendance at the confessionals is to fix a certain definite time for people of the four different states of life, beginning with the married women, — to announce this well, and to enforce it strictly. With some excep-

[14] Villecourt, Vol. I. c. 5.      [15] C. E., Vol. XV. p. 225.

tions those who belong to the class whose time is fixed to be heard, come at the time appointed for them. Toward the end of the Mission there is generally time left to hear the stragglers. Still, a remedy that will perfectly answer every difficulty in this matter is yet to be devised.

## 7. Confessions of the Sick

The missionaries are also to attend the sick who cannot come to church, by hearing their confessions at their homes. It would be too cruel to deprive the suffering and dying portion of the congregation of the consolations that are imparted to all the others. Not unfrequently such individuals are sadly in need of a strange confessor; and even if not, they should not be deprived of the extraordinary indulgences connected with the Mission. The Rule [16] prescribes this act of charity. No one should, however, accept a particular visit, as it is the duty of the Superior to arrange everything in connection with it. St. Alphonsus had two missionaries appointed at every Mission, whose duty it was to visit the sick at any time during the Mission, whenever it was desired.[17] Owing to the small number of confessors, it is our practice in this country to attend to the sick at the end of the Mission, except in a case that suffers no delay. In making these visits, the missionary hears the confession of the sick, grants them the indulgences of the Mission, of the erection of the Mission-cross (if it takes place), and of the Papal benediction, by giving them the simple blessing, saying: *Misereatur* . . . *Indulgentiam* . . . *Benedictio Dei* . . . and enjoining

[16] R., n. 72.        [17] C. E., Vol. XV. p. 295.

some prayer for each. He invests them with the scapulars, if they desire it. In case they do not receive Holy Communion, some other good work is to be prescribed, that they may gain the plenary indulgences.[18]

[18] Decr. 27 March, 1852. (Doc. Auth., p. 239, n. 160.)

# CHAPTER X

### CONFESSIONS (*Continuation*)

THUS far we have spoken of the general arrangements to be made for the confessions. Now we come to the act of confession, or rather to the duties of the confessor. Mission-confessions differ widely from ordinary confessions, and consequently require additional qualities in the confessor, while he is to possess the qualities of an ordinary confessor in an eminent degree.

## 1. QUALITIES OF A CONFESSOR ON THE MISSION — THE TEACHER

Every confessor is to exercise the fourfold duties of *Teacher, Judge, Physician,* and *Father.* In these four qualities, the missionary confessor must especially excel. But, besides these, he must also possess the quality of *Apostle.* Now, in order to be an efficient confessor on the Missions, and to do his duty as *Teacher,* the missionary is in need of

*Solid learning* — He must know Moral Theology well from beginning to end. Nor is it enough for him to be well versed in the *principles* of this sacred science, he must also know how to *apply* them in every case that comes before him. There is hardly a single case in the world that does not come before every missionary for decision. Nor will it suffice to have studied the sacred sciences once, it is necessary to return to them again and again; otherwise, most lamentable mistakes will be the consequence. Let no missionary trust to his own judgment. There is no man in the world that is more exposed to the danger of being guided by mere prejudice than a confessor, to the great ruin of souls. Particularly is this the case in matters of justice, the dispositions required for absolution, the way of dealing with the relapsed, the habituated and those living in the proximate occasion of sin, as well as in regard to the various decisions to be given in many matrimonial cases. *"Non satis est, quod theologiæ moralis scientiam aliquis semel percurrerit, perceperit, et palam etiam docuerit; sed assidue excolenda, ut animo penitus defigantur ea quæ didicerit, et nova semper documenta, quibus ea facultas plurimum affluit, comparentur."* [1] A Redemptorist missionary should be particularly familiar with the Moral Works of his holy Father and Founder, St. Alphonsus, and be guided by his decisions. Besides Moral Theology, let the missionary study the statutes of the diocese where he is giving Missions. He should know our privileges, as well as the ordinary and extraordinary faculties granted by the bishop of the diocese, together with those which our bishops can grant in individual cases; so as to know whether, in certain cases, application can be made to the bishop or not. [2] Nor should he be ignorant of those civil laws which regulate certain cases in matters of justice, where the natural law does not decide. In this point Father Konings' Compendium is a sufficient guide.

## 2. THE JUDGE

Possessed of sufficient learning, let our missionary take his seat *in the place of God* as *a judge* of the

---

[1] Ben. XIV. Inst. 32.    [2] See Putzer's *Commentarium*.

children of God. A judge must not come to the bench with his mind made up beforehand that he will give no hearing to a certain class of people. He must investigate the case before he can pass sentence upon it. Hence, it is wrong for a confessor to say that he will not hear such or such persons, nor give absolution to such individuals, or that a certain business must absolutely be given up, etc., etc. Let the missionary, therefore, first give a kind hearing to every one, try to obtain a full knowledge of any difficult case, examine it in all its bearings, and then let him do what he thinks God Himself would do, since he takes the place of God. *"Videte quid faciatis: non enim hominis exercetis judicium, sed Domini: et quodcunque judicaveritis, in vos redundabit."* [3] *"Nolite secundum faciem judicare, sed justum judicium judicate."* [4] In most cases, he must conduct the examination himself. Nowadays, very few people are sufficiently instructed to be able to make a confession by themselves. It is useless to send away some persons, telling them to examine their consciences. Seeing that they cannot do any better than they have done, they are afraid to return, become discouraged, and give up confession altogether. What good, then, has it done them to be sent away? [5] Father Segneri calls this mode of proceeding, *"errorem intolerabilem."* Let the knowledge given by God to the confessor for the benefit of His people, and his charity supply the wants of the ignorant.

In conducting this examination, let the missionary proceed with his questions: 1, *caste,* so as not to endanger either his own soul or the soul of his penitent in the very act of confession; 2, *prudenter,* not

---

[3] 2 Par. xix. 6.    [4] John vii. 24.
[5] St. Alph., *Prax. Conf.*

wearying his penitents, not terrifying them, avoiding the suspicion of curiosity, and keeping intact the dignity of the sacrament; 3, *sapienter,* proceeding, with a certain astuteness, to discover those sins which penitents are apt to conceal, using expressions that the penitent will understand at once; 4, *sufficienter,* not contenting himself with a few general questions, but inquiring into those sins which the penitent, under his peculiar circumstances, and in his state of life, may most probably have committed. *"Confessarius non interroget de omnibus peccatis quæ ipsi committere potuerint, sed tantum de magis usualibus, quæ ab hujusmodi hominibus committi solent."*[6] Lest some essential point be forgotten, the questions should be proposed in the order of the commandments. Missionaries are in the habit of using certain plans, which they either take from approved authors, or work out themselves. No definite rule can be forced upon a confessor. Each one is free to make or choose a system which accords with his taste and conscience. Still, it is wise to consult our predecessors in this most important matter. We not only possess the plan of our holy Founder,[7] but we have also the plans of St. Leonard,[8] of Father Segneri,[9] Father Schneider,[10] and others. A plan that is especially adapted to our situation in this country may also be found at the end of this chapter.

### 3.   General Confessions

One of the principal points to be settled is, to know whether the penitent is or is not in need of a *general*

---

[6] St. Alph., *Prax. Conf.* n. 19.     [7] *Prax. Conf.*

[8] Van de Kerckhove, § 19.

[9] Haringer, *Buss-Sacrament,* § 36.

[10] *Manuale Sacerdotum,* vel apud Gury.

*confession.* There are many who desire to make a general confession, but not all of them need it; for some, it is even very injurious. There are others who are sadly in need of one, yet they do not dare open their lips about it. It is a well-known fact that sacrilegious and invalid confessions are made to an enormous extent, and that this is one of the chief causes which make Missions so necessary.

If a penitent expresses the desire of making a general confession, let the missionary with a few prudent questions examine, first, whether such a confession would not be injurious to the penitent. If so, let him gently, but firmly, refuse to accept it, explaining to the penitent the reasons why God permits those interior troubles, and telling him that with past sins which have once been duly confessed, we must act as with the dead; that is, we mourn over them, but we do not disinter them lest the stench arising from the grave might infect us with disease. Unless the confessor act with this firmness, these souls will never become tranquil. To rid himself of further trouble, the missionary might be induced to yield this time; perhaps nature, too, has a great deal to do with this yielding; but what good will it effect? Such penitents will only be more uneasy afterward.

In every other case the missionary should allow the penitent to make a general confession. But first he must find out whether such a confession is necessary or not. He will easily discover this by inquiring into the chief troubles of the soul. After he has satisfied himself about the necessity of such a confession, let him conduct the examination with great care as to number and circumstances, making it for the most part himself according to the commandments, and telling the penitent at the end what to do in case some grievous sin has been forgotten. If such a confession is not necessary, let him allow the penitent to state whatsoever burdens his soul, adding perhaps a few questions, and then hear with more minuteness the sins committed since the last confession. So says St. Alphonsus.[11] Such a confession is rather a general review than a general confession. Should one missionary refuse to do this, then the burden falls upon the others, as the saint also remarks. But when a penitent returns afterward with a sin that he has forgotten, how will you know what sort of confession he has made? For if it was a necessary general confession, you have to examine into the number and circumstances of the sin. You should be able to determine this from the penance which you gave him, and which should be a special one, when the general confession is necessary. But if the penitent has been to one of the other missionaries, then for fear of leaving the confession incomplete, take for granted that it was necessary.

### 4. Particular Cases to be Decided

When the confessor is to give his decision in regard to various cases and the obligations to be fulfilled by the penitent, his office of *Judge* demands special discretion lest he give a wrong decision, which, in some cases, may cause the loss of that soul. Let him not exact too much, but let him also beware of laxism. The path to heaven should not be made narrower than it is, nor should any one who is walking on the broad road to perdition be led to imagine himself striving to enter through the narrow gate. Let all prejudice, passion, or peculiar notions be laid aside; let sound reason, enlightened by faith, let the

[11] *Prax. Conf.*

authority of the Church, and the approved decisions of saintly authors be the grounds on which the confessor bases his decision. Such occasions are, when there is question about certain societies, reconciling enemies, making restitution, repairing injuries done to the reputation of another, giving up amusements or friendships, and removing occasions of sin. In regard to this last point, it must first be seen whether, considering all the circumstances, there really exists a *proximate* occasion of sin for this particular penitent; and if so, whether it is *voluntaria* or *necessaria, in esse* or *non in esse:* for then only can a right decision be given. In matrimonial cases, it must be ascertained, whether both of the parties that are living together are not in *bona fide* in regard to the invalidity of their marriage, or only one of them; whether a dispensation cannot or must not be obtained, and how it is to be applied; and if no dispensation can be obtained, whether such parties may not be allowed to live together as brother and sister, especially if a separation cannot be effected without great scandal, since they have grown-up children who know nothing about the matter, or several small children are to be taken care of.[12] Then the case is almost the same as *occasio proxima necessaria.* It is true, there is danger; but is there no danger after separation?

Let it be remarked here, that, after having decided in doubtful cases, the missionary should warn his penitent against ever mentioning the matter in another Mission or on similar occasions, telling him that the case is now settled forever. Otherwise, there will be no end to his troubles.

[12] Cfr. Konings, n. 1638; Benger, Compend., 113, n. 46.

## 5. THE PHYSICIAN

In his quality of *Physician,* the confessor is to restore the life of sanctifying grace to the soul by giving absolution, by administering a salutary penance, and by prescribing the remedies by the use of which the penitent will persevere. The confessor is bound to give absolution, *ex justitia et sub gravi,* to every penitent who has confessed his sins properly and is rightly disposed. But he may, for good reasons, defer absolution, if this can be done *"sine magno incommodo pœnitentis."* This *magnum incommodum* ordinarily exists in the Mission. Hence, the missionary should finish with every penitent [13] who makes his confession as well as he can, and gives sufficient evidence of his good dispositions. It would be asking too much of penitents to wait again for another opportunity of getting to confession, or to compel them to go to others. Many will not again make the attempt. And if, for grievous reasons, they are required to return, let the missionary secure for them easy access to the confessional. He should never tell any one to bring him obscene books, pictures, microscopes and the like, because such action cannot fail to create evil suspicions in the mind of the penitent. Such objects are simply to be destroyed by the penitent, generally before absolution is given. In the Mission, the rule should be: settle all that can possibly be settled, at once, in the confessional. Never, unless absolute necessity demands it, should penitents be required to meet their confessors elsewhere, least of all in the pastor's residence or in the sacristy.

For refusing absolution in the Mission, there must exist very great reasons, because then the penitent has

[13] Van de Kerckhove, § 10; Berardi, I. 224.

everything in his favor.  Attending the sermons, coming to confession, leaving his work, waiting for his turn at the confessional, all of his own accord, after an absence for years from his duties, from Mass, etc., together with many other circumstances, are sufficient proofs of his sincerity.  Even in case he had attended no sermons, the example of others, the conversion of other hardened sinners, may have roused him.  And although his dispositions are deemed yet insufficient, a kind word from the missionary will bring out what is wanting.[14]  Let our missionaries be mindful of the saying of our holy Founder, that he would rather give an account to God for being over-indulgent, than for being too severe with penitents.

### 6.  Penance to be Enjoined

The penance to be enjoined should not consist of a variety of prayers or good works, lest the penitent forget some of them.  Let the penance last a little longer, and consist in one work rather than in a multiplicity of prescriptions to be accomplished in a few days or a week.  In the Mission, there are good reasons for imposing light penances.[15]  Coming to church so early in the morning, sacrificing their sleep, exposing themselves to the cold, the rain, and the snow, the people do a great deal of penance.  They generally have more intense sorrow, pray oftener and with more devotion, frequently make acts of contrition.  Besides, the Mission is a sort of Jubilee, which justifies the lessening of sacramental penance. The penance should always have the character of a remedy against future relapses, especially into sins of intemperance and impurity.  A little prayer said

[14] Van de Kerckhove, § 10.                    [15] Ibid.

in the morning against a certain sin that the penitent is liable to commit during the day is, perhaps, the best penance. Let this be imposed upon him for a certain definite time, and, after that, left to his free-will.

Then, flight from the occasion of sin and the frequentation of the sacraments must be insisted upon. The question arises here, Whether the confessor should compel some to marry, and refuse absolution if they do not wish to make this promise? He should do this only after other remedies have been tried, at least once or twice, and have failed, provided there are no other obstacles in the way. So say Berardi [16] and others. As regards restitution, good advice must be given to the penitent as to the manner of making it. If the restitution can be made at once, it is best to defer absolution until it is done. But let the confessor beware of offering his own services, unless this should be altogether necessary. Let him especially guard against demanding that such restitution-money be brought to himself, when the owner cannot be ascertained.

### 7. The Father

The office of *Father*, which the missionary confessor is to exercise particularly, is sufficiently explained in Moral Theology, especially by St. Alphonsus in his *Praxis Confessariorum*. Let the missionary take as a model the father of the prodigal son, in whom the Father of Mercies is typified. With like charity, kindness, forbearance, he is to bring home the lost child. St. Francis de Sales says [17] that the confessor must bear toward the penitent *"animum vere paternum, recipiendo eum summa cum charitate,*

[16] Vol. II., art. 8.     [17] *Instr. Sacerd.*

*sufferendo patienter ejus rusticitatem, ignorantiam, imbecillitatem, tarditatem, aliasque imperfectiones."* Hence, let him be careful not to show any signs of astonishment or impatience by uttering sighs, shaking his head, gesticulating with his hands, or making remarks that serve to discourage his penitent. Van de Kerckhove [18] says that of the confessor on the Mission, the people should say what is written of Moses: *"Erat vir mitissimus super omnes homines qui morabantur in terra."* [19] But he should by no means be *affectionate.* This would be a great fault. There is an immense difference between kindness and affection, or familiarity. Every one of us knows how much our holy Founder and our Rule warn us against this pernicious fault. All spiritual writers in every age of the Church have severely censured it. From the days of St. Augustine down to the present time, every author that has written on the way of directing souls utterly rejects the idea that tender words are to be used in conversing with penitents. Even to address grown-up persons of the other sex in the second person of the singular number, as is customary in some languages in familiar conversation, cannot be permitted, according to many authors.[20] Nor is it right to call a penitent by name, first or second.[21] Let our confessors constantly and most scrupulously guard themselves against this, and be mindful of what the Rule prescribes: *"Cum mulieribus (illarum confessiones excipiendo) generatim breviores sint, quam longiores, et austeri potius quam concinni et familiares."* [22]

---

[18] *Man. miss.* § 10.      [19] Num. xii. 3.
[20] Berardi, II. n. 278.
[21] St. Alph., *Homo Ap.,* tr. ult. n. 54.
[22] R., n. 289.

## 8. THE APOSTLE

Finally, the missionary is to be an *Apostle,* especially in the confessional. It is much easier to be filled with apostolic zeal in the pulpit than in the confessional. And yet it is here that, properly speaking, the work of the Mission is done. *"Ite, Angeli veloces, ad gentem convulsam et dilaceratam, ad gentem expectantem."* [23] This is the language addressed to the missionaries when they are getting ready for the confessional.

As *Apostle,* the missionary should be filled with an ardent zeal for the promotion of the glory of God and the salvation of souls. This zeal will make him forget the labors and fatigues necessarily connected with the administration of the Sacrament of Penance. He will, therefore, be *prompt and punctual* in going to the confessional, — *"angeli veloces,"* — so as not to make the people wait too long, and thus cause them to become impatient. He will not leave the sacred tribunal as long as he expects a single sinner to come. The Rule forbids any Father to leave the confessional during the time set apart for confessions, without the Superior's permission.[24] He will *hear all* who apply to him without distinction, as God sends them, and will bestow as much care upon a stupid and decrepit old woman, as upon an educated and accomplished young lady. *"Non enim est acceptio personarum apud Deum."* [25] He will try to *reconcile all* to God, giving absolution whenever he can conscientiously do so. Nothing must grieve him more than to be obliged to send anyone away without absolution. But even then he will not simply dismiss the poor sinner, telling him,

[23] Is. xviii. 2.    [24] R., n. 84.    [25] Rom. ii. 11.

"I can do nothing for you," nor send him straightway to hell or to the devil; but he will give him all the advice that he can, thus sowing the seed which may eventually bring about his conversion.

### 9.  PATIENCE WITH VARIOUS PENITENTS

As *Apostle,* the confessor *will have patience* with the many defects of his penitents, which make the work of confession so very difficult on the Missions. If they are ignorant even in regard to the *"necessaria medii,"* he will briefly instruct them, taking their sincere promise that they will procure further instruction afterward.  He should even give to persons of an advanced age the necessary instruction for their First Communion in the confessional, if particular instructions cannot be given to them otherwise.  He may, however, content himself with the few points prescribed by St. Alphonsus for the ignorant, which may be found in the fifth part of this volume.  If such persons are not allowed to make their First Communion during the Mission, they will never make it.  *"Docebo iniquos vias tuas, et impii ad te convertentur."* [26]  There is a host of other defects which tax to the utmost the patience of the confessor. Many penitents come without sufficient preparation. When a question is put to them, they seem not to understand — "Sir, sir?"  They never give a direct answer — "many years ago," "sometimes I did, sometimes I didn't"; give the number in very indefinite terms — "a good many times," "not very often," "often and often," "hundreds of times"; or they simply tell you that they "can't tell," "don't know" "are afraid to tell a lie."  Others can see no harm in what

[26] Ps. l. 15.

they are told is an occasion of sin, and consequently do not wish to give it up. Others, again, go to confession only when there is a Mission, or when the Renewal is given. Oh! how much patience is required in the confessor; how many times must he silently raise his heart to God, asking for this most necessary virtue! *"Impatiens operabitur stultitiam."* [27] Impatience will only confuse him, so that he cannot see his way clearly; and the consequence will be that he will perhaps chase from his presence a poor sinner who could have been saved, and who was sent to him by God. The missionary's patience often gives out on account of having to hear, the entire day and throughout the whole Mission, the same catalogue of sins, sins committed with the same cold indifference, malice, ingratitude. But what is he to do? — Will he, with all his impatient and misguided zeal, be able to say: *"In matutino interficiebam omnes peccatores terræ ut disperderem de civitate Domini omnes operantes iniquitatem"?* [28] How much better would it be for him and the poor sinners that approach him, if he would make the first words of that Psalm his motto: *"Misericordiam et judicium cantabo tibi, Domine"!*

## 10. THE SAVING OF TIME

Finally, as *Apostle*, the missionary should not consume too much time with one penitent while others are waiting for an opportunity of being reconciled to God. *"Ite veloces . . . ad gentem expectantem."* All unnecessary talk, curious inquiry about matters not strictly belonging to confession, is to be omitted. *"Caveat confessarius ne inutilibus interrogationibus quemquam detineat."* [29] The Mission is no time for

---

[27] Prov. xiv. 17.     [28] Ps. c. viii.     [29] *Rit. Rom.*

giving directions to pious souls,[30] or for deciding religious vocations. There is more important work to
be done then. Missionaries who have already acquired some experience and are still extraordinarily
slow in hearing confessions, either have never learned
how to hear Mission-confessions, or they are guilty
of profaning their sacred ministry by indulging in or
allowing useless conversation. A good deal of time
is saved by proceeding in a certain order, from the
deficient confession of the penitent to the examination of other points in which he may probably have
sinned. The shortest way is, to leave his confession
as it is, to proceed at once to the questions according to the commandments, and, when he comes to
the points accused, to ask about their number and
circumstances, settling at once, at the respective commandments, about enmity, restitution, or occasions
of sin.

Here follows the order of those points about which
questions should be asked, although not all are to be
asked of every penitent: —

## II. Schema Quæstionum

*Quæst. prælim.* — 1. *De qua parochia,* — *frequentatio missionis?* 2. *Ultima confessio valida,* — *quot
conf. sacrilegæ, communiones,* — *an sic confirmatio et
matrimonium?* 3. *Pœnitentia impleta?*

*I. Mand.* — 1. *Fides in ecclesiam,* — *cultus acatho-
licus* — *libri contra fidem?* 2. *Oratio, presumptio, de-
speratio?* 3. *Superstitio, spiritismus?*

*II. Mand.* — 1. *Perjurium.* 2. *Blasphema, male-
dictio?* 3. *Vota,* — *promissio jurata?*

*III. Mand. et præcept. eccl.* — 1. *Labor,* — *missa,*

[30] C. E., Vol. XV. p. 288.

— *carnes*, — *jejunium?* 2. *Matrimonium extra ec-clesiam*, — *societas secreta?*

*IV. Mand.* — 1. *Maltractatio alterius*, — *derelictio*, — *debiti redditio* — *onanismus?* 2. *Educatio christi-ana*, — *pueri in lecto parentum*, — *fratres cum sorori-bus in uno lecto*, — *ludorum periculosorum permissio*, — *amasii cum filia vel ancilla sola conversatio?* 3. *Obedientia in mat. gravi*, — *gravis parentum contris-tatio*, — *despectio, derelictio*, — *matrimonium insciis parentibus?*

*V. Mand.* — 1. *Gravis ira, invidia, rixa, inimicitia*, — *homicidium*, — *abortus?* 2. *Scandalum*, — *vestium immodestia?* 3. *Ebrietas*, — *caupones*, — *suicidium?*

*VI. et IX. Mand.* — 1. *Occasionum frequentatio*, — *toleratio?* 2. *Cogitationes*, — *desideria*, — *aspec-tus*, — *lectio*, — *auditio*, — *locutio*, — *amplexus et os-cula*, — *tactus et pollutio sui, alterius, cujus sexus, belluæ?* 3. *Fornicatio* (*onanismus*), — *adulterium simplex vel duplex*, — *incestus*, — *stuprum*, — *sacri-legium*, — *sodomia*, — *bestialitas.*

*VII. et X. Mand.* — 1. *Cujus negotii vel officii ejusque perfunctio?* 2. *Rei alienæ sublatio, emptio, in-ventio, destructio, possessio, desideratio?*

*VIII. Mand.* — 1. *Suspicio non fundata?* 2. *Defa-matio quoad vera*, — *ficta*, — *objurgatio?* 3. *Secreti revelatio?*

*Quæst. fin.* — *Num alia adhuc animæ perturbatio?*

## 12. SIGILLUM SACRAMENTALE

Let a general admonition against the violation of the *sigillum sacramentale* close this long chapter. If Mission Remembrances are given to the penitents, they must be given to all, whether they are absolved or not. Let no remarks be made in recreation about general confessions, hard cases, extraordinary conversions, crimes prevailing in the district, good or bad dispositions, especially in regard to a particular class; or about awkward ways of expressing sins, etc. Let every one thank God for the great good that is effected by the Mission; let him rejoice over the conversion of so many hardened sinners, of whose reconciliation he has been the instrument; but, for the rest, let him observe perfect silence. He has, in the place of God, heard the confession and given the absolution, let him after that also act as God acts in regard to the sins forgiven. He casts them behind His back,[31] even "into the bottom of the sea," [32] and will "remember them no more." [33] The missionaries would do well to come to a common agreement among themselves that they will not, under any circumstances, refer in the slightest degree to matters transacted in the confessional, except for the sake of private consultation in a particular case, always, though, with the necessary precautions. Should any one forget himself so far as to speak of matters belonging to the confessional, all the others should make it a point to interrupt the discourse, and divert it to a different subject.

[31] Is. xxxviii. 17.  [32] Mich. vii. 19.
[33] Jer. xxxi. 34.

# CHAPTER XI

## CEREMONIES OF THE MISSION

WE devote this chapter to the enumeration and description of the ordinary and extraordinary ceremonies which are customary on our Missions in this country, and which have received the approbation of the higher authorities. Missions are the extraordinary ministrations of the Church. It is quite natural that they should be accompanied by extraordinary ceremonies. St. Alphonsus himself had recourse to them; the Rule encourages the use of them. But there is great danger of being carried away by an ill-regulated zeal, and, consequently, of introducing things that border on the profane and burlesque. To guard against this, let it be remembered that, as a general rule, to perform any ceremony opposed to the prescriptions of the Church is wrong at all times. Missions can claim no exception. Then, let particular attention be paid to the regulations established in our Province, as well as to the approved customs.

## 1. ENTRANCE OF THE MISSIONARIES

Circumstances do not as yet permit, in this country, the public reception which St. Alphonsus and the Rule speak of, as given to the missionaries. Yet there should be some solemnity connected with the advent of the extraordinary messengers of God. In this country, the missionaries arrive at the place and proceed to the pastor's residence almost *incognito*. Their solemn introduction to the congregation takes place on the following Sunday or festival at the usual time of High Mass. At a given signal, the missionaries, in their religious habit,[1] each one having his cross on his breast, walk two by two, according to profession, from the Pastor's residence to the front door of the church, and await the Pastor's arrival at the door-way or in the vestibule. At the same time, the Pastor of the congregation — no other priest — leaves the sacristy, vested with surplice (or alb) and stole, and preceded by a number of acolytes with the processional cross, two candlesticks with burning candles, and the aspersorium, moves from the sanctuary to the church-door. At the approach of the cross the missionaries fall on their knees. They remain kneeling until the Pastor has sprinkled them with holy water and has offered them, to be kissed, a large crucifix which he carries from the sacristy, and hands to the Superior of the Mission. This ceremony signifies that the Pastor gives his congregation in charge of the missionaries, especially of the Superior. Such is the traditional explanation of this ceremony.[2]    Other missionaries observe the same ceremony, — some of them at the altar, — and they attach the same meaning to it.[3]    Then the missionaries rise and follow the Pastor, who is preceded by his attendants, to the sanctuary, reciting the canticle *Benedictus* alternately, the Superior carrying the crucifix. During the procession, the choir should sing the same canticle. As, however, they generally cannot sing this, they may substitute the psalm *Lau-*

[1] In cold weather they may wear the zimarra.
[2] See Prost's written memoirs.
[3] See *Life of Caspar del Buffalo.* — Weninger's *Winke,* etc.

*date, pueri.* Wherever the number of missionaries suffices to make up a full choir, they may chant it themselves or alternately with the choir. Arrived at the foot of the altar, they place themselves, equally divided, on each side of the Superior, who stands at the left of the Pastor in the center. Then they make a short act of adoration of the Blessed Sacrament, after which the Pastor ascends to the platform of the altar, where, in a few words and without any other ceremony, he introduces the missionaries to the people, placing the latter under their charge. The Superior, having handed the crucifix to an acolyte to be carried to the side table,[4] begins to recite the prescribed invocations, *Exsurgat Deus,*[5] *etc.,* as far as the first antiphon, *Te Deum Patrem ingenitum.* The other prayers are to be said by each one privately after retiring from the altar. After being thus solemnly introduced to the people, the missionaries take seats in the sanctuary, and assist at the Mass.[6]

If the Bishop of the diocese is present, as often happens in cathedral churches, the missionaries are conducted into the sanctuary by the Rector of the cathedral. After having made a genuflection before the altar, they walk to the throne of the Bishop, kiss his ring, one by one, make a bow together to the Bishop, and return to the altar, where they kneel until the Bishop has finished the introductory discourse. Then they say the prayers, *Exsurgat, etc.*

During the Mass, they should conform to the manner of assisting at High Mass in choir, as prescribed by the ceremonial of the Church.

---

[4] The crucifix may also be fastened on the pulpit for the time of the Mission.

[5] Prayers to be said in approaching the place. R., n. 133.

[6] Prov. Stat. n. 41.

In most of our American parishes people have the bad habit of coming late to the High Mass. Just at the time when the divine service begins, the people come streaming into the church. In most cases, when the missionaries present themselves at the church-door, they are scarcely noticed by anybody, the altar-boys and the priest have to push their way through the crowd without order, some people even stumble over the feet of the missionaries when they are kneeling. Under the most favorable circumstances scarcely a dozen people take notice of the ceremony of presenting the crucifix. It would perhaps have a better effect if the procession would move from the sacristy and the Pastor offer the crucifix to the missionaries to be kissed in front of the altar. But, again the effect of the ceremony is lost, because it is just then that the congregation is gathering. The best and the simplest way under such circumstances would be for the missionaries to move into the sanctuary after the singing of the Gospel, to be introduced to the people by the Pastor and then to say the prayers *Exsurgat Deus, etc.*, without any further ceremony, because it is not allowed to interrupt the Mass by any extra ceremony. But the introduction by the Pastor and the recitation of those prayers is no more of an interruption than any other notice given out from the altar at that time or the silent prayer that every preacher says before the altar. Whenever there are only two or three Fathers to open the Mission, the solemn entrance may always take place after the Gospel.[7] In the beginning of our mission-work in this country there was no public reception given to the missionaries.

NOTE. — Some time ago some of our missionaries introduced the custom of having themselves invested each with a stole by the

[7] Prov. Stat. n. 41.

Pastor after they had entered the church. This practice has no foundation in the tradition of our Missions.[8] Several Superiors of Missions never adopted it; nor does there seem to be any reason for it. The stole is not a sign of jurisdiction, but of the priestly character, and it is to be used only in the administration of the Sacraments and, permissively, on a few other occasions. Besides, the act of giving the congregation in charge of the missionaries is signified by the presentation of the crucifix. The Fathers never wear the stole during the Mission, — why then should they be invested with it?

## 2. SOLEMNITY IN HONOR OF THE BLESSED VIRGIN

The Sermon on the Patronage of the Blessed Virgin Mary and the act of dedication take place on our Missions with great display.[9] The altar of the Blessed Virgin, or, should that altar not be suitable for this purpose, a shrine erected for the occasion, is beautifully decorated with candles and flowers. The people are invited to offer these gifts in advance. Care should, however, be taken that the wishes of the Pastor be consulted in this matter, that no heavy expenses be incurred, and that the poor people be not almost forced to spend considerable sums in purchasing the necessary articles.[10] Let the Prefect of the church take care to give the necessary directions as to a possible danger of fire.

It has been the practice to have little girls dressed in white to assist before and around the altar, or shrine. There should be an equal number of little boys, if they can be had. The object of their presence is to make innocence take the lead in the act of dedi-

[8] Nor does this practice exist among other missonaries. Prov. Stat. n. 41.

[9] How St. Alphonsus had this solemnity performed may be seen in his *Exercises*, C. E., Vol. XV. p. 246.

[10] Prov. Stat. n. 42.

cation, thus inducing the people to dedicate themselves with so much more fervor. This ceremony is most touching, and produces great effect. But it has its difficulties where the sexes are separated. Girls can always be had, but not boys. To have those children for the women only would cause jealousy. To have girls assist at the men's Mission is rather unbecoming. Therefore, if boys cannot be had for the men, this ceremony with the children must be omitted altogether. These children should be at least seven years old, and not over twelve; they should be dressed modestly, and instructed beforehand about the part which they must take in the ceremony. They should not be taken inside the sanctuary, unless this be unavoidable; if they are, they should never be allowed to get among the altar-boys, or sit on the steps of the altar, but they should be seated on benches along the railings. In case these inconveniences cannot be avoided, let them remain away altogether. They should come into the church in procession, but before the recitation of the Rosary, so as not to cause distraction.

Everything being prepared, the ceremony takes place in the following order: — The Rosary is recited without previous instruction. During this time, all the candles on the altar of the Blessed Virgin are lighted. After the Rosary, the usual announcements are made. Then follows a hymn to the Blessed Virgin. It should be of a cheerful character, but not too long. The preacher comes to the pulpit in his usual attire. He begins the sermon without reading the Daily Acts. The discourse should not last more than three-quarters of an hour. After the sermon comes the crowning act of all, the dedication.[11] In other Provinces, and, to a great extent, also in this country, it has been cus-

[11] R., n. 140; Prov. Stat. n. 42.

tomary for another Father to take this part of the ceremony. This adds to the effect, because another Father, not being fatigued by the sermon, performs this important act with more fervor and power. After the sermon, a hymn to the Blessed Virgin is sung.[12] The celebrant and his assistants — most appropriately the parish clergy — proceed from the sacristy clad in their sacred vestments, and go to the altar of the Blessed Virgin. Lighted candles are given to the children. The missionary goes to the pulpit. If he be the same that preached the sermon, he should remain kneeling in the pulpit after his discourse. The hymn being finished, the missionary, in a few brief sentences, announces to the people that the happy moment has arrived, when they shall reëstablish between the Blessed Virgin and themselves the heavenly relationship of mother and children. He explains the nature of the act of dedication to the Blessed Virgin, announcing the most essential qualities of a child of Mary, namely, the renunciation of all sin, having recourse to her in all danger, and placing one's self under her care morning and night. Then he performs the act of dedication, first with the children, but in no more than about two or three sentences, after which he does the same, in a longer form, with the people. He should not ask whether they are willing to do so, much less should he ask a certain class of them, *e. g.,* the young men. He may do this, however, with the children. He pronounces the act aloud and distinctly, making the whole congregation repeat it in the same manner.[13] Having finished the act, he exhorts the

---

[12] Often this hymn is omitted, especially when the preacher performs the act of dedication himself. In that case the clergy come from the sacristy the moment the act of dedication is about to be performed.

[13] C. E., Vol. XV. p. 224; Prov. Stat., n. 42.

people to give thanks to God and the Blessed Virgin for this great privilege, and invites the choir to sing the *Magnificat,* at which all rise, and the altar of the Blessed Virgin is incensed. At the end the celebrant sings *Dominus vobiscum,* and the prayer to the Blessed Virgin, *Defende, quæsumus,* with the long conclusion.

The missionary should not intone the *Magnificat,* unless he is certain that the choir is well versed in taking up intonations of this kind. After the prayer, the clergy proceed to the high altar, where all the candles have been lighted during the *Magnificat,* and the benediction is given with the Blessed Sacrament.

### 3. ERECTION AND BLESSING OF THE MISSION-CROSS

The Mission-cross is erected either inside or outside of the church. If inside, it should be put in a conspicuous place at or near the altar (the penitential cross being removed), and be surrounded with lights and flowers. It should bear an inscription of the date of erection, somewhere near the foot. If the figure of our Lord be attached to the cross, the latter should be plain; if not, it is to be of more elaborate design, and bear another appropriate inscription on the arms.[14] It should be about twelve or fourteen feet high.[15] If it can be done without much inconvenience and delay, it should be raised into its proper position immediately before the blessing, because the people are invited to assist at the "erection" of the cross. Otherwise, it may be erected before or after the ceremony and sermon, or on the next day.

After the Rosary and announcements, the choir

---

[14] There exists no fixed rule in regard to this inscription. It may consist of any pious motto or Scripture text.

[15] A Mission-cross erected outside may be thirty feet high.

sings two strophes of the hymn *Vexilla Regis,* or
*Stabat Mater,* during which the celebrant, — who is to
be one of the missionaries, — with his attendants,
vested as the rubrics prescribe,[16] comes from the sacristy and proceeds to the cross. The hymn being finished, he chants the blessing, taking either the short
formula in our Manual or the long one in the large
Ritual, and observing all the directions of the rubrics.
After the blessing, the indulgences are published and
the prayers for the plenary indulgence to be gained
on that day are recited. The clergy retire to their
seats and the preacher goes into the pulpit, while the
choir sings the usual hymn before the sermon. All
the rest goes on as usual. The sermon is terminated
as directed in the Sketch.[17]

If the Mission-cross is erected outside of the church,
the ceremonies are performed in the same order, with
the following exceptions: — During the procession
from the church to the place where the cross is to be
erected, the hymns mentioned above are continued
until the cross stands in its place. On arriving at the
spot chosen, the celebrant directs the cross to be raised
and fastened. This can be done without much delay,
if everything is prepared beforehand, by means of four
ropes tied to the top of the cross. Then follows the
blessing and the rest, as already noticed. The sermon
may be preached in the church before the procession
moves out, or from a platform outside of the church.
After the sermon follows some appropriate hymn for
the close, during which the procession moves back to
the church.[18]

[16] The Rubric of the Ritual prescribes the red color.
[17] Prov. Stat. n. 43.
[18] It is preferable to erect Mission-crosses inside of the church
for many reasons. Even F. Weninger coincides with this view in his
*Winke.*

We have the indulgences attached to the Mission-cross printed on large cards, one of which should be left with the Pastor, to be framed and hung up in some conspicuous place near the cross in the church, or near the church-door, if the cross is erected outside.

## 4. THE CATAFALQUE AT THE SERMON ON DEATH

A celebrated bishop said, in a circular on Missions: "Man perceives first through the senses, then through reason." St. Alphonsus understood this to perfection. He had recourse to many external representations to move the hearts of the people to repentance,[19] some of which are still retained in Italy. In this country, such external means are not practised, because they would only excite the ridicule of the people, and consequently, they have never been introduced. The use of the catafalque for the sermon on *Death* constitutes the single exception. It is erected before the service, and so placed that it can be seen from every part of the church; six candlesticks with candles are placed around it. The candles are lighted during the Rosary.

Instead of the usual hymn before the sermon, some mournful piece is sung. The best is the psalm *De profundis*, without the *Gloria Patri*. The *Libera*,[20] adopted by some, would be out of place here. It is well to begin the sermon abruptly with the solemn question, Who is dead? Then continue by answering: "The sinner is dead! Dead to God! Dead in his soul! He shall die another death this night at the foot of this catafalque: die *to* sin, lest he die *in* sin sooner than he expects." Then, addressing himself to

[19] See C. E., Vol. XV. p. 244. — R., n. 88.

[20] The *Libera* expresses the humble supplication of the suffering souls in Purgatory for assistance. It should not be used for any other purpose.

all, the preacher asks them, Where their souls would be if their bodies were lying there ready for burial. But how soon may not one or the other be there, etc.

This ceremony never fails to make a very deep impression.

On many Missions this ceremony has been omitted. Yet such means of stirring up the sinners' hearts, after having received the sanction of custom and authority, should not be discontinued.[21]

## 5. THE SINNER'S BELL

It is a custom practised for centuries, and generally adopted on Missions, to have the large bell of the church tolled, during or some time after the evening service, to invite the people to fall on their knees and pray for the conversion of sinners, particularly for those who neglect the Mission. This is called *"the sinner's bell,"* because it is to arouse hardened sinners from the lethargy of sin. The Germans call it *"die Gnaden-Glocke,"* because it represents the call of grace at this extraordinary season.

On our Missions and Renewals in this country, this ceremony is carried out in the following manner: — The Blessed Sacrament being exposed for the evening benediction, after the Exposition-hymn, the celebrant, or one of the missionaries, recites aloud with the people the "Our Father" and "Hail Mary" five times, and "Glory be to the Father" once, beginning with the invitation, "Let us pray for the conversion of sinners, especially for those who neglect the Mission." During the recitation the large bell of the church is tolled, that is, struck about every ten seconds, unless there are peculiar reasons for not doing so. This act is per-

[21] Desurmont, C.SS.R., *Pastoral Theology.*

formed from the first evening of the Mission until the last before the close.

This ceremony should be explained to the people at the opening of the Mission or at some other seasonable time. It should be stated that this bell is to carry to the ears of the wayward sinner the report that the congregation is just now praying for him on bended knees before the Blessed Sacrament; that it calls upon him in the darkness of the night, representing the voice of the all-merciful God Who calls his soul to repentance in the darkness of his sin; that at least the sound of the bell is expected to reach the ears of the sinner who cannot be reached by the voice of the missionary, and that fervent prayers are offered for him, so that he also may come like the rest and be reconciled to God.

### 6. Close of the Mission, Valedictory, Papal Benediction

The Mission very often closes with the Erection of the Mission-cross, the Baptismal Vows, or the Dedication to the Blessed Virgin. Then all is to be observed as has been explained in the proper place. Occasionally it closes with the sermon on Perseverance. In that case nothing special is to be done as far as the sermon is concerned. In all cases, however, the high altar should be beautifully decorated.

The Rule[22] prescribes that the method of St. Alphonsus be followed in the closing ceremonies of the Mission. We follow this method as regards its essential points, adapting the rest to our circumstances. An abbreviated form of the valedictory, for blessing the people, and for giving the Papal benediction, is found after the sermon on Perseverance.

[22] R., n. 149.

Should it happen that the Bishop of the diocese be present at the close of the Mission, the missionary, before giving the Papal benediction, refers briefly to the express command of the Pope, prescribing this blessing at the close of every Mission. He should then add that he imparts this blessing with the kind permission of the Rt. Rev. Bishop, and while saying this, he should bow moderately toward him.

It would be most proper to ask the Bishop to give the Papal benediction. We have the privilege of ceding this honor not only to a bishop, but also *"seniori vel digniori ex clero in missione præsenti."* [23] Immediately after the Papal benediction, the prayers for gaining the plenary indulgence are recited. [24] Then the missionary invites the choir and the people to sing a hymn of praise in thanksgiving for the immense benefits received from God. The *Te Deum* may be chanted in Latin, or in the vernacular. 'If the candles on the altar are not lighted from the beginning of the sermon, they are lit while the blessing is given. At the beginning of the *Te Deum* the celebrant, who should be one of the missionaries, [25] and his assistants come from the sacristy, or the bench where they have been sitting during the sermon, and after making a genuflection, remain standing before the altar. After the *Te Deum*, either all or at least the last (*Domine, exaudi*) of the versicles are intoned by the assistants. The celebrant sings *Dominus vobiscum,* and the following prayers: *Deus, cujus misericordiæ non est numerus, etc.,* to be found after the Votive Mass of

---

[23] Privileg. (Edit. 1909), p. 38. n. 45. *Exercises,* C. E., Vol. XV. p. 242.

[24] *Exercises,* ib.

[25] Prov. Stat., n. 44. This does not exclude the bishop of the diocese or some other distinguished priest, who may be invited to give the benediction.

the Blessed Trinity;  2. *Concede nos famulos tuos,
etc.,* of the Votive Mass of the Blessed Virgin;  3. The
prayer to the Patron of the church, unless it comes
under one of the preceding numbers;  4. *Deus, qui
per B. Alphonsum, etc.,* in honor of our holy Founder;
5. The prayer for the Pope.

Then follows the exposition of the Blessed Sacrament, and the Benediction as usual.  The prayers for
the conversion of sinners are not recited.

Should the Pastor desire to address the congregation, he may do so after the Benediction.

# SECOND PART
# SKETCHES FOR MISSION SERMONS
## FIRST SERIES

# EXPLANATION

## OF THE

# OBJECT AND THE USE OF THESE SKETCHES

THESE Sketches have been compiled principally to serve as a guide to our young missionaries in the composition of their Mission discourses. At the present day, there is certainly no want of matter for Mission sermons and instructions, thanks to the many works at our disposal published for the use of missionaries. But we need a guide to show us the special selection that we must make, and how to dispose of it, for the use of our Missions in this country. An abundance of the most beautiful colors of every desirable variety is of very little use to the artist for the production of a valuable painting, unless his skill know how to dispose of them in the requisite manner, and quantity, and in the proper place. So, likewise, to make a perfect work out of the exercises of the Mission, it is not sufficient to know *what* is to be said, but it is most important to know also, *when*, *how*, and *how much* is to be said. A sermon may be an excellent religious discourse when it is preached by itself, and yet be completely without effect in a course of Mission-sermons. This is a secret that needs to be well understood by young missionaries.

The present Sketches are intended to supply a framework for Mission-sermons. They contain all the subjects ordinarily preached on the Missions by the

Redemptorist Fathers in this country; they follow in the order in which they are generally given on the Missions, and they include those points of doctrine which have been found most essential.

For such missionaries as are well trained in preaching, these Sketches are quite sufficient; others may work them out into complete sermons; while beginners in the exercise of this sacred function should do so, as our Rule prescribes.[1]　In fact, says the aged Father Van de Kerckhove, S. J., it is even more advisable for a missionary to preach from a well-prepared, maturely digested sketch, than from an elaborate, nicely written discourse, because the former makes him more popular in his delivery, more cordial and paternal in his address, and gives his words more unction.

As a rule, adopted by all great missionaries, and especially by St. Alphonsus, a Mission-sermon should not be overcrowded with texts selected from Holy Scripture or the writings of the Holy Fathers.　It should contain but few texts, which should be well applied and, as it were, exhausted.　These Sketches contain many texts, on the one hand, to offer to the missionary a variety for his own selection, and, on the other, to substantiate the doctrine proposed.　A preacher may not always introduce a text which contains the doctrine that he proposes, at least not in full, yet the simple knowledge of such a text gives him more confidence in stating his point.　The texts in the Sketches are mostly given in full, to spare the composer the trouble of searching for them.

Before setting to work to compose a complete sermon from one of these Sketches, it will be useful to read a complete sermon on the same subject by one

[1] R., n. 53.

or two good authors — but not more — in order to see how they have treated the subject, as well as to acquire a greater abundance of good ideas. Care must be taken, however, not to overlook the distinction which is to be made between our times and circumstances and those of the authors whom we consult. Which are the best authors to consult? In the English language, we have hardly any, except the sermons of Father Burke, O. P., and a few of the sermons published by the Paulists. In French, the sermons of FF. Brydaine, Le Jeune, Loriot, Martin, and Mullois are to be recommended. The two last-mentioned are the best. In German, we have hardly one whom we could select as a model. For solidity of matter, Hunolt [2] and Berthold of Ratisbonne may be recommended; Westermeyer, Hillebrandt, Gemminger, Wohlmann, and others have very good sermons, but not solid enough for this country. In Italian, we have the very solid sermons of F. Segneri; and of especial value are the fiery discourses of St. Leonard of Port Maurice. The sermons of both these authors have been translated into French and German.

Those who desire to consult good sketches, will find excellent matter in the sermons of St. Alphonsus,[3] F. Van de Kerckhove, Scherer and Kroenes. The books written by St. Alphonsus for meditations, above all, the *Preparation for Death*,[4] contain excellent matter for Mission-sermons. To furnish his missionaries with such matter was the object that the Saint had principally in view in writing this book, as he tells us in the preface. We shall designate, in their proper place,[5] the particular meditations that contain the requisite matter for the various subjects in question.

---

[2] Recently published in English.

[3] C. E., Vol. XVI.

[4] C. E., Vol. I.

[5] Vol. II, Appendix II.

In undertaking the duties of a missionary we should not endeavor to mould and fashion ourselves altogether after the model of others.   We are, after all, individuals, endowed with individual talent, taste and dispositions, and God will grant us the gift of sacred eloquence accordingly.   We should try to imitate the example of our worthy predecessors; nevertheless, God will fashion His workmen to suit the times and places for which He has called them.   St. Paul wished all his spiritual children to imitate him, yet so as God had given it to every single one: *"Volo enim omnes vos esse sicut me ipsum; sed unusquisque proprium donum habet ex Deo; alius quidem sic, alius vero sic."* (I Cor. vii. 7.)


## MONITUM

A Mission-sermon is not only to be a solid discourse in itself, *i.e.*, framed in good logical order, with its points well defined and supported by the strongest arguments, for the conviction of the understanding and the movement of the heart; but it is also to be brought into close logical connection with the sermons that precede and follow it, and it must contain such matter as the Mission requires in that particular sermon.   The whole Mission depends on each particular sermon.   There must exist perfect harmony among the various sermons, as there is among the members of the human body, each one having its own office, its own work, in its own place, and acting according to its own method.   The failure of one sermon is so much loss to the Mission, and may at times involve the failure of the entire Mission.   What a responsibility for a missionary who neglects his preparation!   Young missionaries should try to understand well the peculiar object of each sermon before they set to work to compose it. The directions placed at the beginning of each Sketch will give the necessary suggestions toward performing this important task.

# SERMONS FOR MISSIONS

## *FIRST SERIES*

## I

## INTRODUCTORY SERMON

THE *object* of this sermon is to induce the people to attend the Mission, and to bring to it the *dispositions* necessary for obtaining its great blessings. To attain this, every effort is to be made to impress upon the people the idea that the sacred exercises are of the greatest advantage by reason of the *immense spiritual benefits* to be derived by all, even the most hardened sinners, no matter how far they may have strayed away from God; and that for some they are a necessary means of salvation. — Next, pains should be taken to remove the *prejudices* which may exist against "Missions" among the class of people to whom the Mission is given, as well as the *objections* and *difficulties* which may be found in this or that particular place, owing to the peculiar situation of the people or to the particular season of the year. — Finally, the missionary should explain and inculcate the *means* to be employed by the people, by the use of which alone they will profit by this extraordinary grace from God. A tender and most pressing invitation must be given to all, and the audience should be asked to invite their relatives and friends who may be in need of the Mission.

This sermon, both in style and delivery, should breathe throughout an air of *holy affability* and *paternal affection,* so as to impress the hearers with a sense of the divine character of the extraordinary message that is about to be delivered to them. This introductory sermon is not to be preceded by the reading of the Gospel or by the publication of any announcements. The notices in connection with the Mission are embodied in the sermon; other notices may be made most appropriately by the pastor himself after the sermon, or at some other time.

It is most befitting the occasion that the missionary introduce himself in a different style from other preachers. His first words should be a certain authorized form of salutation to the people, for instance: "Pax huic domui et omnibus habitantibus in ea," or "Laudetur Jesus et Maria in æternum, amen," or "Pax, benedictio et gratia Dei sit cum vobis omnibus," — to be pronounced in the vernacular.

He may or may not make use of a text of Holy Scripture. If he does, it should be one that at once expresses the idea of the Mission; if he does not, he may take occasion from the penitential cross and the introductory ceremonies, to speak of the Mission, as indicated by them.

## Sketch

Text: "Blessed be the Lord God of Israel, because he hath visited and wrought the redemption of his people." — Luke i. 68.

Introduction. — Such was the expression of joy and gladness of the inspired soul of Zachary, when the first messenger of the Redeemer of the world appeared on earth. Such also should be the expression of your sentiments of gratitude to God on the arrival of His extraordinary messengers, sent to you to bring peace and consolation to your souls. Who are the strange priests here before you, and introduced to you by your Rev. Pastor? They are so many messengers from Heaven, sent to you by God on an extraordinary mission. Through them God comes to you on an extraordinary "visit," to work, through their sacred ministry, "your redemption." They are here to give to the people of this parish (neighborhood) the exercises of an *Apostolic Mission*.

Oh! what an extraordinary grace is a Mission to a parish! And yet, many people draw but little or no benefit from it, because they do not understand the *object* of a Mission, or the *necessity*, or the *advantages* of it, or the *manner* of attending it.

Our first duty, therefore, is to give you a clear idea of all that appertains to the Mission.

## I. Object, Necessity and Utility of the Mission

1. Powerful influence of the three enemies of man — nature, the world, and the powers of hell. Deeper

impression produced by the sensual than by the spiritual. Gradual ascendency of the natural over the supernatural. Eternity lost sight of; present engrossing character of the temporal. Grace, constantly opposed, is lost; sin looms up; supernatural light disappears; spiritual darkness sets in. With purity of heart lost, all taste for virtue is lost, because the heart can have a taste only for what it loves. Immorality, religious indifference, infidelity, enter in its place.

"For my people have done two evils. They have forsaken me, the fountain of living water, and have digged to themselves cisterns, broken cisterns that can hold no water." — Jer. ii. 13. — "Men loved darkness rather than the light: for their works were evil." — John iii. 19. — "The friendship of this world is the enemy of God. Whosoever, therefore, will be a friend of this world, becometh an enemy of God." — James iv. 4.

2. All these evils creep in, in spite of the strong light of the Gospel which illumines the world for more than nineteen centuries.

"The true light that enlighteneth every man that cometh into this world." — John i. 9.

Because people act very much as the heathen nations who fell away from God. They neglect the practice of religion.

"Because that, when they knew God, they have not glorified him as God . . . but became vain in their thoughts, and their foolish heart was darkened. For professing themselves to be wise, they became fools . . . wherefore God gave them up to the desires of their heart, unto uncleanness . . . who changed the truth of God into a lie, and worshipped and served the creature rather than the Creator." — Rom. i. 21–25.

The sad consequence is that, in the course of time, the number of the true servants of God becomes extremely small. A few are kept from a life of sin only by the fear and terror of its awful consequences. The vast majority fear sin no more; some occasionally return for a short time to a life of purity while a much greater number are constantly living in sin, — crime, — religious indifference, — heresy, — apostasy, — infidelity.

And the worst of it is, that they do not even see the evil state in which they are living. Many of them imagine themselves to be good Christians.

"There is a way which seemeth just to a man; but the ends thereof lead to death." — Prov. xiv. 12.

"Who, having known the justice of God, did not understand that they who do such things are worthy of death." — Rom. i. 32.

3. To *remedy* such a state of things the ordinary means of grace — the ordinary ministry of the Church — is insufficient. The evil came in spite of ordinary grace; how can it be banished by it? Therefore, God, Who in His infinite mercy desires by every means to save the souls purchased with the most precious blood of Jesus, and Who never loses sight of those who have abandoned Him, has recourse to extraordinary means — the extraordinary ministry of the Church — *Missions*.

Examples from the Old and the New Testament. On such Missions were sent most of the Prophets — St. John the Baptist, St. Vincent Ferrer, St. Dominic, St. Bernard and others. God sends extraordinary messengers, and accompanies them with extraordinary grace. The Church endows them with extraordinary powers. The result is that the eyes of the wicked are opened, — faith revives, — sin is detested, — confessed, — abandoned, — a full reconciliation between God and His wayward children is effected.

Enumeration of such sinners, generally converted by Missions. Description of their happiness and consolation after the Mission.

4. Crown of all the works of the divine mercy — a

*plenary indulgence,* to be gained twice, or three times, during the Mission; — many *partial indulgences,* to be gained by attending the exercises of the Mission. Seven years and seven times forty days' indulgence for each exercise. Ten years' indulgence for reciting the Rosary together, besides the ordinary indulgences attached to the Rosary.

"I will allure her [Israel] and will lead her into the wilderness [partial retirement from worldly pursuits], and I will speak to her heart. And I will give her vine-dressers out of the same place, . . . and she shall sing there according to the days of her youth and according to the days of her coming out of the land of Egypt." — Os. ii. 14, 15.

5. The same exercises that thus reclaim the wicked, confer immense spiritual benefits upon the good, by removing them more from danger — confirming them more in their good resolutions — detaching them more from the world — uniting them more firmly to God.

It may be said that all these conversions *can* be effected without a Mission. There is no doubt that they *can;* however, they generally *are not* effected without it.

The Mission also gives light to those out of the Church — removes prejudice — makes them think seriously of religion — effects their conversion, or at least puts them on the road to it.

Therefore, gives thanks to God. "Blessed be the Lord God of Israel, etc." Manifest your gratitude by regular attendance at the exercises.

## II. Excuses for not Attending the Mission — Their Origin — The Punishment that Follows

"And he sent his servant at the hour of supper to say to them that were invited that they should come, for now all things are ready. And they began all at once *to make excuse.*" — Luke xiv. 17, 18.

The same thing recurs when a Mission is opened in a parish. Not all, but some, excuse themselves from coming to it.

*"I have no need of a Mission. Let the wicked attend."* Who knows? May you not be greatly mistaken?

"Thou sayest, I am rich, and made wealthy, and have need of nothing; and knowest not that thou art wretched, and miserable, and poor, and blind, and naked." — Apoc. iii. 17.

*"I have no time; I must attend to my business."* Your business is to attend to your eternal salvation.

"Seek first the kingdom of God." — Matt. vi. 33.

You have lost that kingdom. Now it is within your reach.

"The kingdom of heaven is at hand." — Matt. x. 7.

Will you prefer to it a handful of dust? God knew your present occupation when He sent you the Mission. Say not: "I cannot come" (Luke xiv. 20). If God had sent you death instead of missionaries, would you have had time to die?

*"I did not call for the Mission."* — True, you did not, nor would you ever. You have forgotten God — heaven — your own soul. But God has not forgotten you, and He has sent it.

*"I am too far gone; I shall be lost at all events."*

"The wickedness of the wicked shall not hurt him in what day soever he shall turn from his wickedness." — Ez. xxxiii. 12.

Come to the Mission, and you will find salvation not only possible, but even most easy.

The powers of hell are, properly speaking, the true origin of these and many other objections — obstacles — and difficulties. Their opposition is aroused on account of the great loss that they suffer by Missions — their shame and confusion caused by them — and the triumph that heaven will celebrate in consequence of it. God's cause will triumph.

"Let God arise, and let his enemies be scattered. . . . As smoke vanisheth, so let them vanish away." — Ps. lxvii. 2–3.

But, if now you allow your enemies to prevail over you, you cannot evade the *punishment* of God. An extraordinary manifestation of the mercy of God is invariably followed by extraordinary manifestations of His justice.

"I say unto you that *none* of those men that were invited *shall taste of my supper.*" — Luke xiv. 24. — *"Whosoever* shall not receive you, nor hear your words, going forth out of that house or city, shake off the dust from your feet [the greatest act of contempt]. Amen I say to you, it shall be more tolerable for the land of Sodom and Gomorrha in the day of judgment than for that city." Matt. x. 14, 15.

The land of Sodom was not so fortunate as Ninive, which received a missionary and was converted. "Whosoever" — therefore, if there be but one, two, or three, the justice of God shall fall heavily upon them. Examples from other Missions. (Relate one or the other.)

"The kingdom of heaven is at hand." Oh! do not push it away from you! But correspond with this extraordinary grace for the love of God and your own immortal souls!

### III. Manner in which to Profit by the Mission

Extraordinary grace demands extraordinary co-operation. Hence, during the Mission something more than what is ordinary is required of you. To avail yourselves of the great advantages of this season of grace, *three conditions* are to be fulfilled:

1. *Regular attendance at the sermons and instructions.* God sends you an extraordinary message. The least you can do is, certainly, to hear the messenger. The message concerns the most important affairs of your whole being and existence. How reckless, how ungrateful, to disregard it!

Endeavor not to miss a single sermon. Let none stay at home except one responsible person out of each family. But let that one surely have his turn at the next sermon. All the discourses form but one sermon, to which this is only the introduction. The very sermon that you perhaps miss, may be the one particularly intended for you by God.

Attend both mornings and evenings. The morning exercises of the Mission instruct the *mind*, while the evening exercises move the *heart*. Both must go hand in hand. If you attend only mornings, the sermons will lose in interest for you; if only evenings, you will wish to save your soul, but will not know how. For the convenience of the people, the morning sermon will be given twice.

Reading of the order of exercises.

2. *Cease offending God by grievous sins from this hour.* Cease exasperating the anger of God precisely at the time when He is manifesting toward you His greatest mercy. Else, how can you be reconciled to Him?

Therefore, give up sinful habits (mention some of those which are most common), sinful acquaintances, dangerous amusements, books, papers; be reconciled with your enemies; restore as far as possible ill-gotten goods; make reparation for the injury done to your neighbor's reputation, etc.

3. *Offer up fervent prayers for yourselves and others.* No grace without prayer. The air surrounds us in abundance, but it will not benefit us unless we inhale it. "The kingdom of Heaven is at hand," but not yet "within you." The heart must open in holy and fervent prayer, otherwise our sermons will indeed touch your ears, but not your hearts.

Pray, therefore, that you may listen to the sermons as a message from God, that you may derive from each sermon that spiritual profit which God has intended for you, etc. Pray mornings — nights — at your work — at Mass — while reciting the Rosary.

Pray also for others, especially your nearest relatives, friends, all who need conversion; invite, persuade them to come to the Mission.

We missionaries will also pray for you, and we will do so especially for the most obstinate who refuse to attend. Prayers at Benediction. Sinner's bell, — a very old custom on the Missions.

CONCLUSION. — Brief recapitulation.

A season of most extraordinary grace is open for you! Heaven is open to this parish!

"Behold, now is the acceptable time; behold, now is the day of salvation." — II Cor. vi. 2.

General invitation to all — the just — sinners — apostates — infidels—the lowest — the most miserable — the most God-forsaken. . . .

"Come to me, all you that labor, and are burdened, and I will refresh you." — Matt. xi. 28.

Salvation for all without exception; peace to all men of good will!

O good and merciful Father! we thank Thee that Thou hast not forgotten us, that Thou hast not yet abandoned us in our sins! Grant that we may not resist Thee now!

O Mother of Mercy! ever-blessed Refuge of Sinners! I place at thy feet this entire work of the Mission. Bless it! Bless also and protect the good people for whom the Mission is now opened! Bless thy unworthy servants, the missionaries! May this Mission, through thy intercession and assistance, promote the glory of God, and effect the eternal salvation of every soul in this congregation! Amen.

# II

## IMPORTANCE OF OUR ETERNAL SALVATION

The chief cause of the great lukewarmness, the cold indifference in matters of religion, which at the present day is manifested among all classes of people, is, no doubt, a voluntary abandonment of all thought of the supernatural world and of the relation in which we stand to it. Men have lost sight of the eternal, and, therefore, have limited all their interest to the temporal. The spiritual having lost for them all its attraction, they are helplessly hurried away by the sensual. — In order to meet this evil, the minds of men should be forcibly recalled to the fact that there exists another world beyond this present one, and that it is precisely for that world we are created; that time must be followed by eternity; that every human being has to live forever in that eternity; that it is for eternity alone that life is given to man; that every human being is necessarily an endless being in body and soul, and that, *as such,* he will here-after be either in a state of eternal bliss or everlasting suffering. — To induce men to avoid the latter and work for the former is the chief object of the Mission.

The *particular object* of this sermon is to create *a true interest* in the hearts of the people *for their eternal welfare,* and a *firm determination* to save their souls. — This accomplished, a good and *regular attendance* at the various exercises is effected, and half of the success of the Mission is already secured. — Let this sermon, then, be so arranged that the faith of the people in their everlasting existence may be revived to such a degree that they may easily infer for themselves the necessary conclusions which follow, namely, that the work of their salvation is the *most important* affair of life; that they must attend to it *at all costs;* and that they must do so *without the least delay.*

A sermon on the *End of Man,* or on the *Value of the Soul,* will not answer the purpose so well, and will not produce the desired effect, because these subjects must pre-suppose in the hearers a certain degree of lively faith which is wanting in many of them, and because they do not show so plainly the inevitable alternative of either eternal salvation or eternal damnation.

## Sketch

Text: "And the Lord answering, said to her: Martha, Martha, thou art careful, and art troubled about many things. But one thing is necessary." — Luke x. 41, 42.

Exordium. — Martha is a true picture of people in general — busy, troubled, uneasy in regard to their various difficulties, embarrassments, etc. Great mistake committed by thousands in never trying to understand the real and only vocation of life — disastrous consequences of such neglect. The Mission, the great remedy and extraordinary means of arousing the people from their fatal spiritual indifference and lethargy — of opening their eyes to their most precious interests — and of placing them again on the road to salvation. But the work of the Mission will remain without effect, unless the people themselves take a *true* and *lively interest in the work of their salvation.* To create this interest in their souls is the object of the present discourse.

Oh! may it please the Holy Ghost to send a ray of light into your hearts to-night, that you may begin to understand the all-important subject — the importance of your salvation! May the loving heart of Jesus and His ever-blessed Mother Mary give a special blessing to my words! [1]

## I. Man, after this Life, will be either in Heaven or Hell — Forever

There is no alternative. Either of the two — either *heaven* or *hell* — will be the *necessary result* of man's life on earth.

---

[1] A similar invocation should form the close of the introduction of every sermon of the Mission.

1. *A human being is an endless being.* Man will exist for all eternity with body and soul.

"God created man incorruptible, and to the image of his own likeness he made him." — Wis. ii. 23.

"Incorruptible" — *i.e.,* indestructible, imperishable. "To the image of, etc." — man is like unto God, especially in this respect, that the existence which he has received from God will continue as long as God — *i.e.,* forever.

Man consists of body and soul. Death will separate them for a time; but neither will be *annihilated*. The body simply returns into the elements of which it is formed, the soul goes to eternity.

"The dust shall return into its earth, from whence it was, and the spirit shall return to God who gave it." — Eccle. xii. 7. — "Dust thou art, and into dust thou shalt return." — Gen. iii. 19.

On the day of Judgment the body will be formed again and will be reunited to the soul, never more to be separated from it.

"Wonder not at this, for the hour cometh wherein all that are in *the graves* shall hear the voice of the Son of God. And they that have done good things, shall come forth unto the resurrection of life; but they that have done evil, unto the resurrection of judgment." — John v. 28, 29. — "Behold, I tell you a mystery: we shall *all* indeed rise . . . in a moment, in the twinkling of an eye . . . for the trumpet shall sound, and the dead shall rise again *incorruptible* . . . for this *corruptible* [flesh] must put on *incorruption;* and this *mortal* [body] must put on *immortality*. And when this mortal hath put on immortality, then shall come to pass the saying that is written (Os. xiii. 14): Death is swallowed up in victory." — I Cor. xv. 51–54.

To this inflexible law of human existence there is no exception. All the false principles of philosophy, so-called, all the perverse inventions of infidel men, all the ridicule and sarcasm of the impious, cannot alter it or effect a single exception. Impossible for them to make *corruptible* what God has made *"incorruptible."*

Nor will *suicide* put an end to man's existence. The decrees of God cannot be changed by any creature.

"My counsel shall stand, and all my will shall be done." — Is. xlvi. 10.

So, then, *to be once* is *to be always.* Man, once in existence, will exist forever.

But where?

2. *Either in heaven or in hell.* The object of the creation of man is the same as that of the angels, and that again is the same as the object of God's own existence — that is, the infinite glory of God.

"The Lord hath made all things for himself." — Prov. xvi. 4.

God knows, enjoys, and glorifies Himself in an infinite degree. Rational creatures exist for the same end — only in a finite degree. They are made to know and to see God — in this life by faith and after this life by the beatific vision — to the extent to which they have rendered themselves capable of doing so by their fidelity in the service of God on earth. If, while here on earth, they did not serve God as He commanded them, they will then be forever separated from Him, and will exist in eternal misery.

"These shall go into everlasting punishment; but the just, into life everlasting." — Matt. xxv. 46.

The entire human race, then, as it now exists, is moving onward toward eternity, but in two opposite directions; some toward heaven, all the rest toward hell. Of every single individual it can be truly said, that he is either on the road to heaven or on the road to hell.

What a being, then, is man! He is made by God to exist forever! His being is endless! Being made, he can never end — never!   He must move on through this life either into everlasting bliss or into endless despair — either to heaven or to hell — for all eternity!

And what is eternity!   What is the longest life compared with eternity!

This awful thought peopled the deserts of Egypt with holy anchorites; it fills the cloisters with saintly monks and nuns.   It is this thought that strikes fear and terror into the souls of repentant sinners, it even makes the hearts of the just tremble.   To what conclusion will it lead you?

## II. Conclusions Drawn from the Preceding Doctrine

Simply allow reason to speak it will lead you to the following conclusions.

1. *The most important affair of life is to work out our eternal salvation.*   Can there be any conclusion more logical?   Of what benefit can any amount of temporal prosperity be to me, if it must be followed by eternal misery?   If, therefore, I succeed in all my undertakings, but lose my soul, what will my success profit me?   On the other hand, if I should meet with disappointment on every side; find nothing around me but misery, poverty, sickness, etc.; what harm can all this be to me if I save my soul?

"What doth it profit a man, if he gain the whole world, and suffer the loss of his own soul?" — Matt. xvi. 26.

Compare the gain with the loss.   What conclusion, then, will simple reason draw from this?   What else but that the affair of our eternal salvation must be preferred to every other affair of life?   Other affairs must be dropped rather than be allowed to interfere with that of our salvation.   A constant attention to this affair must form the leading feature in all our undertakings.

"In all thy works remember thy last end, and thou shalt never sin." — Eccli. vii. 40.

If we do not allow reason to draw this conclusion, we act *against reason,* we set reason aside, we act unreasonably, we have become *fools* — and the number of such fools is immense.

"The number of fools is infinite." — Eccle. i. 15.

2. *To work out our eternal salvation is the only affair of our life.* Strictly speaking, it is the *only occupation* of life that the Creator has given to man.

"Fear God, and keep his commandments: for this is all man." — Eccle. xii. 13.

*a.* The care about our temporal affairs and that of our eternal welfare are *incompatible.* Man cannot bestow equal care on both. He must neglect either the one or the other.

"No man can serve two masters, for either he will hate the one, and love the other, or he will sustain the one, and despise the other." — Matt. vi. 24.

Thousands of examples prove it. How many say: "I have no time" — "Business prevents me. . . ."

Now, God has promised to take care of our temporal affairs, leaving to us the care of the eternal.

"Be not solicitous for your life, what you shall eat, nor for your body, what you shall put on, . . . for your Father knoweth that you have need of all these things. He feedeth the fowls of the air; . . . He clotheth the grass of the fields; . . . how much more you, O ye of little faith!" "Seek ye first the kingdom of God and his justice, and all these things [temporal goods] shall be added unto you." — Matt. vi. 25–33.

*b.* God could not act otherwise. He could not take the care of man's salvation into His own hands, because this is absolutely man's *own affair.*

No one can pass off into the hands of another the affair of the salvation of his own soul. Man must believe, do good and avoid evil himself personally; no one can do it for him, as may be the case in regard to other business. God Himself cannot do it for him. This, therefore, is exclusively man's own affair.

*c.* Besides, man must *merit* his eternal reward. If God would take it into His own hands, as He has promised in regard to man's temporal support, there would be no merit possible.

All that man can possibly hope for during his endless existence in eternity depends on the solicitude which he bestows on this affair in this life.

"But one thing is necessary." — Luke x. 42.

And yet, men will insist upon caring about their temporal affairs, while they neglect the affairs of their soul. What a sad illusion!

3. *To work out his eternal salvation is man's most urgent affair of life.* We call that most urgent which admits of no delay. The affair of our eternal salvation does not admit of any delay whatsoever, but must be attended to at once. The moment of death will decide for every one his eternal destiny. That decision can never be reversed, or changed, or commuted.

"If the tree fall to the south or to the north, in what place soever it shall fall, *there shall it be.*" — Eccle. vi. 3.

Man dies but once. That one death brings the irrevocable decision.

"It is appointed unto men *once* to die." — Heb. ix. 27.

A man lost once is lost forever.

"Out of hell there is no redemption." — Off. Def.

After hell has seized upon a soul, "there is no one to redeem, nor to save." — Ps. vii. 3.

Now, death is constantly approaching nearer and nearer; its movements are as swift as those of time, as it is passing away. No one knows how much of the time that God in His wisdom has allotted to him, is yet left.

"Watch ye, therefore, because you know not the day nor the hour." — Matt. xxv. 13.

Hence one hour's delay may render salvation impossible for all eternity.

And then, there is no sacrifice that would be sufficient to correct a mistake made in this affair. There are at this moment souls in hell who would sacrifice a fortune, a kingdom, an empire, could they thereby purchase their souls out of hell.

"What exchange shall a man give for his soul?" — Matt. xvi. 26.

With what joy would they hail a Mission! How well would they attend!

4. *The work of a man's salvation is an affair about which he must be most solicitous.*

"With fear and trembling work out your salvation." — Phil. ii. 12.

The reason is because, taking the entire human race into consideration, *there are comparatively but few* who succeed in settling this most momentous affair to their own advantage. The Eternal Truth has said it.

"How narrow is the gate, and how straight is the way, that leadeth to life; and few there are that find it." — Matt. vii. 14. "Many are called, but few chosen." — Matt. xx. 16.

We need not be astonished at this, if we consider the ways of men. Thousands do not even stop to think of the object of their existence. They come and go without having ever seriously inquired about it. Thousands of others never care to know, whether there exists a future world or not.

There are three classes of men in this world:

The *first class* consists of those who *really desire* to *work out their eternal salvation.* Of these some give themselves up to God entirely; as religious, hermits, some of those living in the world. Others give a great deal of their time to temporal affairs, yet without losing sight of their spiritual welfare. Others, again, regard their salvation as a secondary affair. These are fast approaching

The *second class,* which consists of those who do *all* that they can for their *temporal prosperity,* while they do nothing for their souls.

Of the *third class* are those whose thoughts, words, actions, wishes and desires, *directly tend* to the *eternal destruction* of themselves and others.

Enumeration of some of each class. No wonder, then, that but "few are chosen."

CONCLUSION. — Recapitulation.

Christians! every one of you is an endless being — to be either in heaven or in hell forever. To either of these your present path leads, if you persevere in it to the end. My brother, on which road are you approaching eternity now — on that which conducts to heaven, or on that which leads down to hell? Alas! what does your conscience answer?

Does it *assure* you that you are on the *road to heaven?* Then thank God; assure yourself of it still more in this Mission.

"Labor the more, that by good works you may make sure your calling and election." — II Peter i. 10.

Or, is it *doubtful?* Oh! then, make every effort, give yourself no rest until your doubts are removed!

Or, are you *surely* on the *road to hell?* Oh! then, change at once! The least delay may involve you in endless ruin. Thank God for having spared you so long, and for having sent you this Mission for your salvation.

Act of Contrition. — O most merciful Father! We return to Thee our most heartfelt thanks for Thy compassion on our blindness and carelessness. Alas! what would have become of us, had we departed this life before this day! How many have passed away after having lived as we have, and are irretrievably lost! O most loving Father! we come to Thee to-day as repentant children. Forgive us our sins, our attachment to this world, our sinful forgetfulness about our salvation. Forgive us for the sake of the most precious blood which Thy Son Jesus has shed for us, and grant us the grace, that we may henceforth work with heart and soul for our soul's salvation.

And thou, O sweet Mother Mary! — Refuge of Sinners! — assist us at all times, that amidst the dangers of this life we may save our immortal souls. Amen.

Note. — A few acts of contrition like the foregoing are given in full to show how a Mission-sermon should close.

# III

## MORTAL SIN

This sermon has for its *object* to produce in the hearts of the people *true compunction* for the sins of the past, and an *abhorrence* of sin for the future, together with a firm determination to avoid the dangers that lead to it. To effect this, sin must be shown, in all its enormity, as the supreme evil which God must, from the nature of His being, detest and punish, as long as it is not destroyed by an adequate atonement; hence its terrible consequences.

The sermon on Mortal Sin is perhaps the most difficult of all in the Mission, and unless it be handled with the proper skill, it will prove a failure. The world at the present day is too carnal to conceive an idea of this spiritual malady. Most people cannot comprehend why Mortal Sin can be so great an evil, and why its consequences should be so terrible. Others reduce the number of Mortal Sins to a very few cases of rare occurrence. Hence, in this sermon, a clear *definition* of Mortal Sin is to be given, and a *clear explanation* must be added, when and how it is committed, without, however, going through the whole catalogue of Mortal Sins. But, to mention most of the Mortal Sins ordinarily committed, in making short applications of the arguments adduced, is of the greatest benefit. The *arguments* must be solid, plain and effective. The best arguments are those taken from reason, supported by texts of Scripture and sayings of the Fathers. The consideration of the consequences of sin is another powerful means for showing the evil of it, such as the sin of the angels, the sin of our first parents; and then personal sin in its direful effects upon man. Lastly, the great atonement demanded by the justice of God for sin, as shown by the sufferings of Christ, is the most powerful argument. A vivid description of one or the other of the principal events in the Passion of Christ produces great effect, *e. g.*, His agony in the garden, His scourging at the pillar, His death on the cross. A great help in preaching this sermon with success is to be found in good parables and comparisons.

## Sketch

Text: "Cry, cease not, lift up thy voice like a trumpet, and show my people their wicked doings, and the house of Jacob their sins." — Is. lviii. 1.

Exordium. — Why cry so loud? Because, by sin, the people had lost their hearing. Why show them their sins? Because sin had blinded them; they could not see the evil of sin. Thus our people have become deaf — hear not the voice of God — Church — conscience; — blind, so as not to see sin, or not to see it in its grievousness — nor to dread its consequences. Every other evil is understood much better than sin.

"Who can understand sins?" — Ps. xviii. 13.

We can have no adequate idea of the enormity of this evil. But we can and we must have at least such a knowledge as to shun it more than any other evil; and we must suffer everything else, even death, rather than commit a sin. The want of this knowledge is the cause of the damnation of a multitude of souls.

"Therefore is my people led away captive, because they had not knowledge, . . . therefore hath hell enlarged her soul, and opened her mouth without any bounds, and their strong ones, and their people, and their high and glorious ones shall go down into it." — Is. v. 13, 14.

Hence the command given to the missionaries: "Cry, cease not. . . ." I shall lift up my voice this night, and, as far as I can, show you the *enormous evil of Mortal Sin.* Oh! may you understand it!

## I. Mortal Sin in Itself

*Definition:* Mortal Sin is a *deliberate* and *wilful* transgression (in thought, word, or deed) of the *law of God* (or the Church) in a matter of *great importance.* — (Explanation of definition.)

Mortal Sin, therefore, is

1. *A supreme contempt of God,* so much baser on the part of the *offender,* on account of the utter insignificance of a human being.

Who is the *offender?* — A worm of the earth, that dwindles into nothing if compared with God.

"Behold, the gentiles are as a drop of a bucket, . . . behold, the islands are as a little dust. — All nations are before him as if they had no being at all, and are counted to him as nothing." — Is. xl. 15–17. — "The whole world before thee is . . . as a drop of the morning dew, that falleth down upon the earth." — Wis. xi. 23.

And on the part of the *offended,* on account of the infinitude of the Divine Being. Who is *God?*

"Dost not thou think that God is higher than heaven, and is elevated above the height of the stars?" — Job xxii. 12. — "Behold, God is great exceeding our knowledge." — Ib. xxxvi. 26. — "Thousands of thousands ministered to him, and ten thousand times a hundred thousand stood before him." — Dan. vii. 10.

What recklessness! A most insignificant pigmy rises in wilful and deliberate opposition against the infinite God! — and that in a matter of great importance.

Hear the bitter complaint of God:

"Thou hast broken my yoke, thou hast burst my bands, and thou saidst: I will not serve." — Jer. ii. 20.

And God commands no impossibilities.

"My yoke is sweet and my burden light." — Matt. xi. 30.

That same miserable sinner would most willingly oblige a fellow creature, if he could do it, to gain or preserve his friendship; but he refuses to render to God the service that He demands of him. What contempt!

The same sinner hides himself before men, when he wishes to sin, but he cares not that God sees him. What account does he make of God? He completely ignores Him — he despises Him!!

"Who is the Almighty, that we should serve him?" — Job xxi. 15. — "Who is the Lord, that I should hear his voice? . . . I know not the Lord." — Exod. v. 2.

Application to various cases.

Mortal Sin, moreover, is —

2. *An act of the blackest ingratitude.* God commands the fulfilment of His law, not for His own benefit, but for the temporal and eternal happiness of man. Its transgression cannot in the slightest degree diminish the infinite happiness of God nor tarnish His glory; but it must destroy the happiness of man — it aims at the annihilation of the human race. To understand this, examine the object of the various commandments.

"He that seeketh after evil things shall be oppressed by them." — Prov. xi. 27.

The observance of God's commandments brings innumerable temporal blessings upon the obedient child of God (Deut. xxviii. 1–14). But, above all, will the joys of *heaven* be the reward for every act of obedience to God — to be multiplied and increased in proportion to the number of these meritorious acts. God has created man precisely for heaven — has placed him on the road to it — and keeps him in it. How thankful he ought to be!

But by sin man throws heaven, as it were, back into the hands of God; he openly declares to Him that he does not want it.

"The wicked have said to God: Depart from us, we desire not the knowledge of thy ways." — Job xxi. 14.

The sinner does not even care to know the way to heaven.   Like the two old men who tempted Susanna.

"They perverted their own mind and turned away their eyes that they might not look unto heaven, nor remember just judgments." — Dan. xiii. 9.

O shame, sinners! — what have you preferred to the endless joys of heaven? — (Enumeration.)

"They that were brought up in scarlet, have embraced the dung." — Lam. iv. 5.

O degradation! O shameless ingratitude! God has already, in the act of your creation, "made you according to His own image and likeness." But He wants, besides, to unite you most intimately to Himself; He intends to share with you His own Infinite Beatitude, as far as by your own personal merits you render yourself capable of it.   You treat His offer with contempt! You go farther, for —

3. *Mortal Sin aims at the destruction of God.*   The sinner *either* wishes God to approve his act *or* he does not.   In either case, he does all that he can do to *destroy God!*

God, the Infinite Sanctity, is essentially opposed to the transgression of His will and His holy law.

"The way of the wicked is an abomination to the Lord." — Prov. xv. 9.

God cannot but hate sin, else He must cease to exist. He can never excuse it and live.

"Thou thoughtest unjustly that I should be like to thee." — Ps. xlix. 21.

*Or,* the sinner knows that God cannot possibly approve his ways.   In that case, he must also know that his will is opposed to the will of God.   Only one will can reign supreme in one and the same act of volition.   The will of God should certainly predominate. But the sinner sets his will above the will of God, and insists on ruling as supreme master over God in the act of his sin. Here, again, as far as he is concerned, he aims at the dethronement of God, and, consequently, at the destruction of the Supreme Being, as God cannot exist except as Supreme Ruler.

"Thou alone art God in all the earth." — Tob. viii. 19. — "Thou art God alone." — Ps. lxxxv. 10. — "For He is the Lord our God; and we are the people of his pasture and the sheep of his hand." — Ps. xciv. 7.

O sinner! do you comprehend the malice that is contained in your wickedness?

Say not, "I did not mean this." Were you aware that your wicked thoughts, words, or actions were forbidden by God, or not? If not, then you did not commit the evil in question. If you were, then you stand guilty of all.

Your action includes all the malice just described. Do not excuse yourself, but make an humble acknowledgment of your guilt. This is the only way to reconciliation with your offended God. Pray, that you may understand still better the evil of Mortal Sin.

## II. Terrible Consequences of Mortal Sin

God must infinitely hate sin and punish it, even though He discover it in His most noble creatures.

1. *He found sin in His angels, and punished it.* The fallen angels included some who stood next to God — upon whom He had most lavishly bestowed His heavenly gifts.

"In his angels he found wickedness." — Job iv. 18.

They had formed a rebellious design but had not yet carried it out. Immediately they were deprived of their heavenly gifts, changed into most frightful specters, cast out from heaven, and hurled down into the abyss of hell. A special fire was "kindled by the wrath of God to burn them forever." — Matt. xxv. 41.

Nor will they ever have the faintest hope of redemption.

"And the angels, who kept not their principality . . . he hath reserved under darkness in everlasting chains, unto the judgment of the great day." — Jude 6.

When they shall be released for a few moments, only to be put to the uttermost shame and confusion.

Try to fathom the depth of the malice of sin by means of this awful punishment. Either you must say that God's punishment is too severe — which would be a blasphemy, for to be too severe is an impossibility in God, Who is Infinite Justice — or you must admit that such punishment was well merited, and, consequently, that this sin of the angels includes an incomprehensible malice.

The fallen angels committed but one sin; you, thousands! They were God's most noble creatures; you are but a most insignificant worm that crawls in the dust of the earth.

"For, if God spared not the angels that sinned . . . what will befall those who walk after the flesh? . . ." — II Pet. ii. 4, 10 *seq.*

2. *God found sin in our first parents, and punished it.* Consider the state in which they were created. Innocence — union with God — many natural and supernatural endowments. Consider also their condition in Paradise.

They fell into sin by what appeared to be an insignificant act, but which was opposed to the will of God.

What was the consequence? Banishment from Paradise of themselves and their entire posterity —

deprivation of all their endowments — subjection to all sorts of miseries — war — famine — sickness — death — cutting off of all communication with God — closing of heaven against all mankind — ignorance — sins and crimes without number — eternal damnation.

True, they and many of their posterity have been, and will continue to be saved through the merits of the second Adam, Jesus Christ. But for four thousand years the nations of the earth lived in ignorance and sin; many yet remain in this deplorable state; millions of infants who die without baptism will never see God; many baptized adults will be lost on account of their culpable ignorance and sin. The number of the elect will, after all, remain comparatively small. All this is the consequence of that *one* sin committed in Paradise.

What must be the *guilt* of that one sin, which is thus punished by God?

But mark, also, how guilty you may be in the sight of God through sins of similar disastrous consequences, to which you may not attach much importance, as an ill-advised expression, a sinful word, scandalous conduct, immodest dress, etc.

3. *God will punish the sin that He finds in us.* Call to mind the universal deluge by which God destroyed the human race with the exception of eight souls.

"God spared not the original world, but . . . bringing in the flood upon the world of the ungodly." — II Pet. ii. 5.

He burned to ashes the sinful cities of Sodom and Gomorrha.

"Sodom and Gomorrha, and the neighboring cities . . . going after other flesh, were made an example, suffering the punishment of eternal fire." — Jude 7.

Core, Dathan and Abiron, and many others, in all two hundred and fifty men, were swallowed up by fire that burst forth from the earth, for a rebellious act against Moses (Num. xxvi. 10). And similar punishments.

But sinners are not always punished immediately after their sin is committed. God may leave them time for penance; yet no sooner have they given consent to a sin, than all communication between themselves and God is cut off. The soul is dead and in a state of damnation.

"The soul that sinneth, the same shall die." — Ez. xviii. 20.

And this is so, no matter how good and virtuous the sinner may have been before.

"If the just man turns himself away from his justice, and do iniquity according to the abominations which the wicked man useth to work, shall he live? All his justices which he had done, shall not be remembered; in the prevarication, by which he hath prevaricated, and in his sin which he hath committed, in them he shall die." — Ez. xviii. 24.

Oh! how fearful are the consequences of sin! What recklessness on the part of the sinner to consent to it! What utter forgetfulness of self and one's own highest interests!

What a defiant attitude the heart of the sinner must assume in opposition to God! He knows the inevitable punishment of sin — eternal damnation. God must punish it — his conscience reminds him of it — and yet he sins — even in the very presence of God.

"For his eyes are upon the ways of men, and he considereth all their steps. There is no darkness and there is no shadow of death, where they may be hid who work iniquity." — Job xxxiv. 21, 22.

O sinner, reflect! What have you done? How far have you carried your recklessness? You have challenged God's justice, you have defiantly cut off all communication between God and yourself. Let the thin thread of life break asunder, and you are doomed to eternal hell-fire.

## III. The Atonement Required and Made for Sin

All that has been said thus far falls far short of a true description of the immeasurable evil of sin. No tongue can express it, no mind can conceive it, because it is an *outrage* against the *Infinite Majesty of God*.

Who could atone for it? Not the severest penance continued for thousands of years — practised by all men — joined in by all the angels of heaven. The outrage is infinitely greater than such an atonement.

Only a God could adequately atone for an offence committed against God. And this atonement has been made.

The Incarnate Word has offered Himself as an atonement, and the Eternal Father has accepted it.

"For God was in Christ, reconciling the world to himself." — II Cor. v. 19. — "The Lord hath laid on him the iniquity of us all." — Is. liii. 6. — "He was wounded for our iniquities, He was bruised for our sins." — Ib. 5.

Do you wish to know what sin is? Look at the crucifix; behold Jesus dying for sin — consider the immense sacrifice required for it. This tells you what sin is.

"Behold the Lamb of God; behold him who taketh away the sin of the world." — John i. 29.

Therefore, he that commits mortal sin renews the entire crucifixion of Jesus Christ. He does all that was done to Jesus Christ when He was crucified.

"Crucifying again to themselves the Son of God, and making him a mockery." — Heb. vi. 6.

O powerful language! yet so plain, so intelligible, that the most uncultivated mind at once understands it.—*Such is sin.*

Conclusion. — Recapitulation.

Have you ever sinned? Alas! how often! With all the senses of your body — faculties of your soul. Enumeration. And yet you live! Enjoy God's benefits! O infinite mercy of God! And where is the penance? Will you do it now? Oh! resist no longer! Throw yourselves at once before your merciful God, imploring His pardon and forgiveness.

Act of Contrition. — O God of Infinite Mercy! Now I begin to understand what an enormous evil sin is. I thank Thee for the interior light that Thou hast granted me by this sermon. Oh! what have I done! I have outraged Thy infinite goodness, I have lost all right to heaven, I have prepared for myself a place in the lowest hell, I have crucified again Thy Son, Jesus Christ. And I have done so not once, but over and over again.

O my merciful Father! have compassion on Thy wayward child. I return to Thee with grief and contrition in my heart. Pardon me, O Father, pardon me. Through the merits and death of Thy Son Jesus grant me the grace of a true reconciliation with Thee.

O Blessed Mother Mary, pray for me a sinner, that I may obtain a true and hearty sorrow for my sins, that I may humbly and sincerely confess them, and amend my life. Amen.

# IV

## SACRAMENT OF PENANCE

Having become deeply impressed with the consideration of sin and its terrible and inevitable consequences, the sinner will naturally ask: Is there a remedy? — and if there is, what is it, and how must it be applied? — Hence, the sermon on the Sacrament of Penance is next in order. St. Alphonsus [1] absolutely requires this sermon to be preached before the *Eternal Truths,* and to be especially directed against the bad practice of concealing sins in confession.

The special *object* of this sermon is: 1. To revive faith in the Sacrament of Penance, especially in the divine institution of sacramental confession; 2. To encourage the sinner to avail himself of this most consoling remedy; 3. To warn him against an abuse of it, or against sacrilegious confessions. Hence only one part of it is purely dogmatical. If the entire discourse were to be of a dogmatical or polemical character, it would be too dry for the people at this early part of the Mission, and we would run the risk of allowing the little flame of contrition, kindled by the sermon of the previous day, to be extinguished. In the second part, the consoling effects of this sacrament are described. The third part dwells on the horrible state of the soul after a sacrilegious confession, and briefly answers the ordinary difficulties in the way of the sinner in opening his conscience to the priest.

Should this sermon have to be omitted, then it must be supplied in the peroration of the sermon on Mortal Sin, in the exordium of the sermon on the Sinner's Death, and in the morning instructions on confession.

### SKETCH

TEXT: "Now when they had heard these things, they had compunction in their heart, and said to Peter, and to the rest of the Apostles: What shall we do, men and brethren? but Peter said to them: Do penance." — Acts ii. 37, 38.

EXORDIUM. — If the description of mortal sin and its fearful consequences has made an impression on your

[1] C. E., Vol. XV. p. 229.

hearts, your minds will naturally be turned to the question: "What shall we do?" I answer: "Do penance." This is a sure remedy. Ten thousand millions of sins will do no harm to the sinner, if followed by penance, while one without penance will cause his eternal destruction. Proofs for this are found in the Scriptures — the doctrine of the Church — the writings of the Fathers. *But what penance?* — That alone which is prescribed by God, to Whom alone it belongs to lay down the conditions upon which sin will be forgiven. Which is that? How must it be performed? The answer to these questions will form the subject of this sermon.

I. Sacramental Confession, the Condition Prescribed by God for the Forgiveness of Sins Committed After Baptism

1. Penance implies a *full* reparation of the evil of sin — satisfaction — atonement. Hence, to effect a reconciliation, penance must make full reparation to the Infinite Majesty. If our sins involved also an injury to our neighbor, that too is to be repaired; hence, restitution, etc. Penance, therefore, includes: 1, A sincere detestation of sin in the sinner's heart; 2, A firm determination of sinning no more; 3, The preventing as much as possible of the evil consequences of sin; 4, A constant and active desire of making atonement to the majesty of God; 5, Full reparation of the injuries caused to men. For the sinner must do at least what is in his power to make reparation. And what about the immense reparation to be made to God which is not in his power?

Christ has made full atonement for all sins. This must be applied to the sinner, as far as he stands in need of it. It is to be transferred to him — to be made his own — by some means that includes a *voluntary act* on the part of the sinner. Sin is a *wilful separation* from God — reconciliation must be a *wilful return* to God. The great means of applying the atonement of Christ to the sinner are the *Sacraments,* two of which are directly instituted for the remission of sins.

For those who have not yet been raised to a supernatural sphere of life — who are not yet incorporated into the mystical body of Christ — *Baptism* was instituted, by which they begin to exist in the order of grace — regeneration; and in which they receive full forgiveness, provided, if adults, they possess the aforesaid dispositions.

Of this St. Peter speaks, as in the text, because those people were not yet baptized.

"Do penance and be baptized every one of you in the name of Jesus Christ, for the remission of your sins." — Acts ii. 38. — "And there were added in that day about three thousand souls" [were baptized]." — Ib. 41.

For the remission of *sins committed after baptism,* another Sacrament — *Penance* — was instituted by Christ. Baptism cannot be repeated because generation, natural or supernatural, can take place only once.

2. The Sacrament of Penance requires the *Confession* of all *mortal* sins and the Absolution of the priest, besides the above-named dispositions in the sinner's heart.

Confession consists in an *humble accusation* to an authorized priest *of all the mortal sins* of which we are conscious, after a mature examination of conscience, since Baptism, or since the last good confession. Venial sins need not be confessed in order to be forgiven, because there are various other means instituted for the remission of them.

*a.* Confession had been in use before the coming of Christ. See the passages of the Book of Leviticus, in which various offerings are prescribed for various sins — to be immolated by the priest, who, consequently, had to *know* the sins for which he was to make the offering.

"If any one sin . . . let him do penance for his sin, and offer an ewe-lamb . . . and the priest shall pray for him and for his sin." — Lev. v. 1, 5, 6. — "Whosoever shall be guilty of injustice — shall offer for his sin a ram without blemish and shall give it to the priest . . . and he shall pray for him before the Lord. And he shall have forgiveness." — Lev. vi. 2-7. — (See many other texts in the same book.)

"When a man or woman shall have committed any of all the sins that men are wont to commit . . . they shall confess their sin." — Num. v. 6, 7. — "Be not ashamed to confess thy sins, but submit not thyself to every man for sin." — Eccli. iv. 31. — That is, do not confess to everybody. (Corn. à Lap.) "And there went out to him [John] all the country of Judea, and all they of Jerusalem, and were baptized by him in the river of Jordan, confessing their sins." — Mark i. 5.

People were so impressed with the necessity of confession that they did not believe penance of any value without the act of self-accusation.

*b.* The strongest proof that confession is necessary is the doctrine of the *Infallible Church*.

"If any one deny that Sacramental Confession is divinely instituted or is necessary for salvation by divine right, let him be anathema." — Trid. sess. xiv. can. 6. — "If any one say that in the Sacrament of Penance for the remission of sins it is not necessary by divine right to confess all and every mortal sin which one remembers after a due and diligent examination of conscience . . . let him be anathema." — Trid. sess. 14. can. 7.

To this doctrine other Councils of the Church and the sayings of the Fathers throughout all Christian ages bear testimony. For example:

"All the priests to whom people confess their crimes must impose upon them a suitable penance." — Conc. Cabillon. II. a. 813, can. 32. — "Anathema to the priest who breaks the seal of confession." — Syn. Armen. in opp. Dovin. a. 527, can. 20. — "It is necessary to confess our sins to those to whom the dispensation of the mysteries of God has been intrusted." — St. Basil. resp. ad quaest. 288. — "Let every one confess his sins while yet in this life and while his confession can yet be received, while his satisfaction through the priest is pleasing to God." — St. Cypr. de laps.

*c.* The necessity of Sacramental Confession is proved by the *institution of Christ.*

Christ gave *full power* of *forgiving all sins* to the *Apostles.*

"Whose sins you shall forgive, they are forgiven them: and whose sins you shall retain, they are retained." — John xx. 23. — "Amen I say to you, whatsoever you shall bind upon earth, shall be bound also in heaven: and whatsoever you shall loose upon earth, shall be loosed also in heaven." — Matt. xviii. 18.

The same powers He conferred through them on their *lawful successors,* as He did in regard to all the other powers which regard the foundation, the propagation and the ruling of the Church. As the powers which the Constitution of the United States confers upon the first President are thereby likewise conferred upon his lawful successors — so in this case, as regards the powers of the Apostles.

The act of forgiving or absolving necessarily presupposes a full and clear *knowledge* of what is to be forgiven or absolved. Therefore, Confession. Besides, a distinction is to be made between what is to be "forgiven" and what is to be "retained." To do this consistently, a knowledge of the case in all its bearings is requisite. Hence, Confession.

Now, whatsoever the Apostles and their successors do not forgive, but "retain" — remains retained — is not forgiven. Therefore, what the priest does not forgive, *is not forgiven.* Hence, Confession to the

priest, followed by his absolution, is absolutely required for the remission of sins.

NOTE. Of course this sentence is to be understood in a theo-
logical sense. *"De contr. perf. cum voto conf."*

3. *Will it suffice to confess to God alone?* In that
case, the power of the Church would have been
granted in vain, as it would hardly ever be called into
requisition. So says St. Augustine. Besides the
text quoted says the contrary. "Whose sins *you*" —
apostles, priests — "retain, *they are retained*" — not
forgiven. Nor was confession understood in this sense
in the Old Law.

"Be not ashamed to confess thy sins." — Eccli. iv. 31.

Confession to God causes no additional shame, as
He knows the sins already.

Confession means a *disclosure*. We cannot disclose
anything to God.

Nor among the first Christians.

"Confess your sins *one* to *another*." — James v. 16.

Therefore, the sincere confession to the priest of all
the mortal sins committed after baptism, or Sacramental Confession, is the condition prescribed by God
for the forgiveness of those sins — a doctrine always
taught by the Infallible Church, and believed and
practised by all true Christians.

## II. CONSOLATION DERIVED FROM A GOOD CONFESSION

So many and so great are these consolations, that
the brief act of humiliation necessarily included in
that self-accusation, as it must be at confession, appears as nothing in comparison with them. They are:

1. The *assurance* that the *sins are really forgiven*.

*"Remissa sunt."* After days, months, and years spent amid the most fearful troubles of conscience, the sinner has this assurance from the lips of the Divine Truth and from the teachings of an Infallible Church. He has the same consolation as Magdalen, to whom Jesus said: "Thy sins are forgiven thee; go in peace" — the same as the Good Thief, and others. The absolution of the priest is as good as that of Jesus Christ Himself.

2. *Each and every sin is forgiven,* no matter how abominable, or how often committed. Christ possesses *all* power from God the Father.

"All power is given to me in heaven and in earth." — Matt. xxviii. 18.

He has delegated the same to His Apostles and their successors.

"As the Father hath sent me, I also send you." — John xx. 21.

In particular, the power of forgiving sins.

"Amen, I say to you, *whatsoever* you shall . . . loose upon earth shall be loosed also in heaven." — Matt. xviii. 18.

Also those sins are forgiven that have been *forgotten.* But they must afterward be confessed if they are remembered.

"Other sins that do not occur to the penitent are understood as included in the same confession." — Trid. sess. 14. cap. 5.

3. *The sins are completely annihilated.* They are as though they had never been committed. Hence God says that He will forget them.

"If the wicked do penance for all his sins . . . living he shall live, and shall not die. I will not remember all his iniquities that he hath done." — Ez. xviii. 21, 22. — "I am — I am he that blot out thy iniquities for my own sake, and I will not remember thy sins." — Is. xliii. 25.

4. *The sinner will be before God the same that he was before he sinned;* a child of God, therefore, an

heir of the kingdom of heaven, gaining again the possession of all the merits that he had previously acquired and that he had lost by sin.

"I will have mercy on them and they shall be as they were when I had not cast them off." — Zach. x. 6.

Yet the sinner should never cease grieving over his sins; therefore God allows that he can never completely forget them.

5. Even the *body partakes of the consolations* of the soul. Experience. Protestant physicians testify to this, *e.g.*, Tissot, who, on a certain occasion, when a young woman was suddenly cured after confession, said, full of admiration: "What a power confession has among Catholics!"

6. *Heaven rejoices* more over one sinner who is converted, than over ninety-nine of the just who never did anything wrong.

"I say to you that even so there shall be joy in heaven upon one sinner that doth penance, more than upon ninety-nine just who need not penance." — Luke xv. 7.

7. *His sin will never be revealed on earth,* on account of the strict obligation of the sacramental seal. — God watches over it with particular care. He wishes to have what He has forgotten in heaven remembered no more nor spoken of on earth.

8. *The fear of death is removed, because judgment is past.* — Confession has taken its place.

"If we would judge ourselves, we should not be judged." — I Cor. xi. 31.

Oh! how great are the consolations derived from a good confession! — If people would only sincerely reflect on this, would they not all desire to go to confession? — And yet there are millions who dread confession so much that they scarcely dare think of it, in spite of the absolute certainty which they have that they are approaching an unhappy death and everlasting despair. — Others do worse — they make sacrilegious confessions.


## III. WARNING AGAINST SACRILEGIOUS CONFESSION

Whenever one or more of the essential conditions of this sacrament is wanting, the confession is null; and if these conditions be omitted with the knowledge and free-will of the penitent, the confession becomes a *sacrilege*. The greatest number of sacrilegious confessions are made by concealing some grievous sin, the number of times it has been committed, or some notable circumstance connected with it.

The disastrous results of such a confession are:

1. No sin is forgiven.

2. Another sin is added — sacrilege — which exceeds in enormity all the other sins which the penitent may have had to confess.

3. Another sacrilege ordinarily follows the first — an unworthy Communion.

4. It will then be far more difficult to make a good confession. Hence, subsequent confessions are made in the same manner; — Communion is received over and over with the worst dispositions; — Confirmation, — Matrimony, — often Extreme Unction, are received in the same way. — Oh! what an abyss of crimes never known to this world! — Often such unfortunate sinners die in that state; — and then what an awful revelation on judgment-day! What shame, — what remorse for all eternity in hell, — where they will confess everything aloud forever!

Tell me, unfortunate soul, what is it that keeps you from telling your sins?

"Oh! I am so overcome with shame, I cannot bring myself to confess it."

Hear St. Augustine:

"How much better is it for you to put yourself to shame before one man in the secrecy of the confessional, than to be exposed to the myriads of hosts on judgment-day!" — Lib. ii. *De Vis. Inf.*

And there you will appear, as you are here in the church, with all your sins exposed.

"What will the priest think of me?" — He will rejoice with you; he will glorify God for your conversion. As there is joy in heaven over you, so in the heart of the priest.

"The priest may subject me to hard treatment." — Generally not, as soon as he perceives your grief. — But should he do so, did you not deserve much more? — And after all, not a soul in the world will find it out. — The entire transaction of confession goes on, as it were, out of the world.

"The priest knows and esteems me." — He will esteem you much more after that awful confession. By your confidence in him you will have gained his heart and all his affections. — But why not go to a stranger rather than commit so enormous a sacrilege? — For this reason it is even the wish of the Church that all should occasionally have access to strange confessors.

Away, therefore, with all these and other obstacles! Overcome them at once. Trample under foot all human respect. Humble yourself before one man, and you shall be exalted before God and all His creatures.

CONCLUSION. — Recapitulation.

Let us, then, be thankful to the infinite mercy of God for so sure and easy a means of reconciliation! We have not deserved it. It is purely an act of His divine goodness. But, alas! have we not disregarded it, — neglected it, — perhaps treated it with contempt,

— perhaps even most horribly abused it? — And God has borne it all from us!

In sorrow and grief do we, therefore, turn to Thee, O merciful Father! Oh! pardon us all our sins, but in particular our disregard, contempt, abuse of that Sacrament in which Thy infinite mercy displays itself most conspicuously! Grant that we may this time, and for the future, approach this sacrament in all humility and with due respect.

O Mother of Mercy! assist us that we may now enter into judgment against ourselves with all severity; that we may confound ourselves to the very dust of our nothingness; and thus merit, through thy intercession, the infinite rewards of heaven. Amen.

# V

## DEATH OF THE SINNER

In the preceding sermon the way of reconciliation with God was shown to the sinner. If he refuse to accept it, then he must take the inevitable consequences of his reckless perversity. These must be brought to his notice in this and the two following sermons. The sinner has but the alternative, either to die *to* sin by penance, or, by preferring to live *in* sin, to risk the terrible end of the impenitent sinner, — death in sin, — the inevitable consequences of which are a severe judgment and eternal damnation.

The principal *object* of this sermon is to convince the sinner of the vanity of those things which are the object of his ambition, and for which he is sacrificing his eternal salvation; to show him that they escape and disappear like smoke before him, and this much sooner than he expects; that the very idol of his sinful affections, his flesh, must soon crumble into dust, when his proud and sensual soul must depart out of this world in the greatest anguish and despair. To effect this, the absolute certainty and yet most distressing uncertainty of Death are held up to him. Then, the awful death-bed scene of the departing sinner is pictured before him. Finally, is depicted the gradual decay of his body, until nothing remains but a handful of dust.

There are those, and among them Potter,[1] who call it ridiculous to prove the certainty and uncertainty of death, things that are admitted, willingly or unwillingly, by all the world. Our intention is not to prove these points, but to make a serious reflection on them, which hardly ever fails to produce a deep impression, as we learn from experience. We have on our Missions seen men, who after listening to this sermon were afraid to go home without confession. They knew and believed all this before, and yet they did not cease to live in sin.

But it is a mistake, as Potter also says, to take a great deal of pains to describe the anguish, the remorse, and the despair of the dying sinner. However powerfully such a description, taken from books of sermons or meditations, may work upon the imagination of the hearers, it can hardly be said to be founded on facts. Let no more be said about the sinner's death-bed scene than is so in reality.

---

[1] *The Pastor and his People,* p. 1. ch. 5. sect. 3.

Some missionaries prefer to preach on the death of a worldly-minded man; and it may be more appropriate in places where all the people generally frequent the sacraments. A very good sketch of it is contained in the sermon of St. Alphonsus (Dom. xv. p. Pent.) [1] Where, however, the sacraments are greatly neglected, the present subject produces the best effect.

### SKETCH

TEXT: "It is a fearful thing to fall into the hands of the living God." — Heb. x. 31.

Death and Sin are the two greatest evils, because they take from us the two most precious goods. Death takes away the life of the body; Sin, the life of the soul. Yet the former may be only a transition to the greatest happiness, while there is a remedy in Penance for the latter. — But Death combined with Sin — Death in Sin — is the greatest evil of all, because there is no remedy for it.

Man must either die *to* sin or *in* sin. We die *to* sin by true penance. Of that you heard yesterday. Perhaps some will not accept it. Well, then, there remains for them only the alternative. — But then! — "It is a fearful thing, etc." Oh! may they understand this! — Perhaps they will yet change their minds!

### I. CERTAINTY AND UNCERTAINTY OF DEATH

1. *Every man must die.* — This is absolutely certain.

"It is appointed unto men once to die." — Heb. ix. 27.

No one has ever denied it. — No heresy against this doctrine. — The history of the human race proves it beyond a doubt. — Daily experience supports it. — To every human being God has allotted a certain period of life for his trial on earth. The hour, the minute, when it will be ended, is already fixed. As soon as

[1] C. E., Vol. XVI. pp. 448–460.

that moment has come man must die, and no created power can prolong his life.

"The days of man are short, and the number of his months is with Thee. Thou hast appointed his bounds which cannot be, passed." — Job xiv. 5.

Therefore, we all live to die! — How foolish, then, to set our affections upon anything in this world, and, by doing so, to plunge ourselves into endless misery after death!

"This, therefore, I say, brethren: The time is short. It remaineth that they who . . . use this world [act] as if they used it not, for the fashion of this world passeth away." — I Cor. vii. 29, 31.

The more so, because we know not the moment when our lives will end.

2. *Death is likewise absolutely uncertain.* — When, where, how, will you die? — After a long or short sickness? — In the bloom of health? — At home, — in the street, — in your workshop? — While traveling, — at your meals, — during your night's sleep, — in conversation with your friends, — at your amusement, — in church, — while at your prayers? — You know not. No one but God knows.

How many have died, — and die daily, — under similar circumstances! — Sinners and saints, — laymen and priests, — religious, — bishops, —when no one expected it, least of all themselves. — And often so suddenly, that no sacrament could be administered, — that they could not even make an act of contrition, — or invoke the name of Jesus.

About 86,000 people die every day — and of these, says Abbé Ségur, three-fifths die unexpectedly.

You retire in the evening. You may die that night, — and if not then, the next night; — if you survive that, the next night. You rise in the morning. You may die that day; — if not, the next day. You hear the clock strike. It may be the hour of your death; — if not, the next hour. — At every step you may dread, lest the next step be the one into eternity.

"Be you then also ready; for at what hour you think not, the Son of man shall come." — Luke xii. 40. — "Behold, I come as a thief." — Apoc. xvi. 15. — "Watch ye therefore, because ye know not what hour your Lord will come." — Matt. xxiv. 42. — "And what I say to you, I say to all, *Watch.*" — Mark xiii. 37.

What a terrible thought for those who are not ready!

3. The sinner has so much the more reason to fear such a death, because by his sin he has *forfeited the lease of life.* — Life is not granted for sin.

"The years of the wicked shall be shortened." — Prov. x. 27.

If after sin, the sinner is allowed to live, it is to give him time for penance.

"Thou hast granted me life and mercy." — Job x. 12.

If penance is not practised, then the sentence is:

"Cut down this tree; why doth it take up the ground?" — Luke xiii. 7.

And then, sinner, all is over with you forever.

"If the tree fall to the south or the north, in what place soever it shall fall, *there shall it be.*" — Eccle. xi. 3.

Never will you have another chance of saving your soul — never! — never!


II. DEATH-BED SCENE OF THE DYING SINNER

Draw near, sinner; be a personal witness of the dread passage of the sinner into eternity, and see whether this is the kind of death that you desire.

1. You will perhaps tell me that many *infidels, apostates, etc., die with a placid countenance.* — Granted. But what does that prove? God will not

fill their souls with trouble, which, after all, might yet be regarded as a spark of grace.

"He that doth not believe, is already judged." — John iii. 18.

Nor will the powers of hell torment them. They have no reason to fight for the possession of souls which they already securely possess. Besides, the bystanders would perhaps thereby be frightened into conversion. The devil prevents this.

2. *Many others die horrible deaths.*

"A hard heart shall fear evil at the last." — Eccli. iii. 27.

Their last struggle is depicted in Ps. xvii. 5, 6:

*"The sorrows of death surrounded me; the torrents of iniquity troubled me; the sorrows of hell encompassed me; the snares of death prevented me."*

a. *"The sorrows of death!"* Death separates the sinner from all that he loves — earthly possessions, worldly distinctions, pleasures, friends, even his own body. What a "sorrow" for the human heart, to be torn away forever from all the objects of its affections! What a cruel pain and torment!

"O death, how bitter is the remembrance of thee to a man that hath peace in his possessions!" — Eccli. xli. 1.

Such a one cannot bear the thought of dying — and yet he must die. Hence that struggle.

b. *"The torrents of iniquity."* He is in sin. He has done no good, or, if he has, the merit of all is forfeited by sin. As a heavy load the manifold sins of his youth, manhood, old age press upon him; sins in thought, word, action; against all the commandments of God and of the Church; his acts of sacrilege; time — grace — lost, etc.

And these numberless sins fall upon the sinner, not in distinct order, but as a "torrent"; like the terrific confusion of a whirlwind, when in a moment all is consternation and fright.

Death should be a rest after the hard labor of the long day of life. But,

"There is no peace for my bones, because of my sins. For my iniquities are gone over my head, and as a heavy burden are become heavy upon me." — Ps. xxxvii. 4, 5. — "His bones shall be filled with the vices of his youth, and they shall sleep with him in the dust." — Job xx. 11.

Oh! what trouble, what terror shakes his soul to the very center, when he thinks of the inevitable fact that in a few minutes he must fall into the hands of the living God, Whom he has never served — Whom he has despised.

Can there be no hope for him? Yes, indeed, if a priest could yet raise his hand in absolution over him, there would be hope. But there is no priest there. Yet suppose there were, of what use would he be, if there were no true sorrow in the sinner's soul? The dying man could, in such a case, do nothing but add another horrible sacrilege to the multitude of his sins.

However, there is another faint hope. Even in this last extremity the dying sinner might make an act of perfect contrition, which would save him.

"A contrite and humbled heart, O God, thou wilt not despise." — Ps. l. 19.

*c.* But to prevent this last spark of hope from being kindled, *"the sorrows of hell will encompass him."* The efforts of hell are multiplied and increased a thousand times. Hell will show him the wrath of God; his own utter depravity; his total and life-long separation from God; the impossibility of a reconciliation; the certainty of his damnation. He will see hell open its jaws, swarms of furious demons around his bed. Hence his despair.

*d.* The last spark of hope is quenched. *"The snares of death. . . ."* Death will lay its icy grasp upon him. The cold sweat — despair depicted in his face —eyes growing dim — the night of death is upon him — the ears are deafened — the death-rattle is heard in his throat — the breath stops — the last gasp. He is dead! And his soul — *"is buried in hell."* (Luke xvi. 22.)

### III.   His Body shall Crumble into Dust

1. *Cast a last glance* at that mass of flesh before it is enclosed in the coffin. That head which encases the putrid brain (thoughts, schemes, pride, hatred, spirit of independence); those eyes (reading, glances); those ears, that mouth (curses, blasphemies, impure conversation); that throat (imbibing of liquors); those hands (theft, instruments of all sorts of sin); those feet (went to sinful amusements, money speculation, not to church or sacraments). That entire putrid mass (a stumbling-block to man — the ruin of his soul and the loss of his salvation — the object of disgust to Heaven). Away with it into the coffin! Its stench is insupportable. Into the ground with it! There let it lie and be devoured by its own worms!

2. After a number of years, let us pay a visit to that body in the graveyard. Here is the grave. Draw near; read the inscription: "Here lies *the body* of N. N." After reading this, transport yourself in spirit to the gates of hell. Read the inscription over the gate: "Here lies buried *the soul* of N. N."

Come back to the grave; open it. What do you find? A small heap of grayish dust. Take it up; you can hold it in the hollow of your hand. That is now all that is left on earth of that wretched man — of that sinful woman. And for the sake of that the soul is in hell.

For that little dust the soul opposed God — would not submit to the Church — gave itself up to sin and vice — lived and died in sin — and is now given up to everlasting tortures and endless despair!

CONCLUSION. — Recapitulation.

Sinner, hear me! You would not heed the admonition that we gave you yesterday. You could not make up your mind to perform the penance prescribed by God, and thereby obtain full pardon of your sins. Will you allow the voice of death to enter your soul? Who knows but this may be the last time God will speak to you? To-morrow you may have passed through all that I have described. Oh! leave not this church to-night without changing at least your heart! Oh! let me beg of you to throw yourself at the feet of your crucified Saviour, imploring His pardon.

O Jesus! have mercy on me! O Jesus! for the sake of Thy most precious blood, grant me the grace of a true conversion! Help me to break the bonds of sin! Alas! where should I be if I had died in my sins? I thank Thee for Thy patience. I am determined to do penance and change my life.

O dear Mother Mary! pray for us sinners, now and at the hour of our death. Amen.

# VI

## GENERAL JUDGMENT

That which the sinner dreads most, and which is one of the greatest obstacles in the way of his conversion, is confession. But if he will not have recourse to the Sacrament of Penance, to confession to the priest, he will have to make his confession in spite of himself, — only in a far more humiliating form. To show this is the principal *object* of this sermon. The way to do it is, to make the people understand first, that we shall appear before the tribunal of Christ as we are here on earth, with body and soul; hence the resurrection. — Secondly, that there can be no more secrets, and that, therefore, our whole life will be laid bare before the entire rational creation. — Thirdly, that the sentence must follow, according to the demands of Divine justice.

This sermon may easily become a failure, although it may, on the other hand, be a grand and effective discourse. It may become a failure, if the preacher lose sight of the main object to be achieved by it in the Mission, and dwell too long on circumstances not in immediate connection with that object, namely, the necessity of a universal judgment, the destruction of the world, the general meeting, the mutual reproaches, the separation of the elect from the reprobate. All these may receive a passing notice, but no more.

In treating of the General Judgment, the preacher should not draw too much upon his imagination, nor copy the writings of those who have done so. He should build his descriptions and his deductions upon the Word of God, which is his only safe guide in this matter. — Nor is the preacher to confine himself too exclusively to the judgment of the wicked. The judgment of the just is most consoling and full of encouragement to lead a good life. Our Lord Himself, whenever He speaks of this judgment, dwells with great emphasis on the consolations which the just will then experience.

This sermon demands, on the part of the preacher, a tone of severity (but not passion) and the attitude of an inexorable judge. He may even leave out the recapitulation, peroration and act of contrition; finishing quite abruptly, and leaving the audience in suspense. This is done with great effect. The whole idea of this sermon is justice — justice!

## SKETCH

TEXT: "God . . . now declareth unto men that all should everywhere do penance, because he hath appointed a day wherein
he will judge the world in equity." — Acts xvii. 30, 31.

Just retribution of God! The sinner wishes to
escape confession and a temporal satisfaction. He
prefers to die in despair. He will have to confess,
only in worse form. So it is, sin must necessarily be
followed by confession and penance, either before the
divine tribunal of *mercy* or before the divine tribunal
of *justice*. For God "hath appointed a day . . ."
Of this day, and what will happen in it, let us hear
now. On that day we shall all stand face to face, and
shall know all about one another.

"For we must all be manifested before the judgment-seat of
Christ." — II Cor. v. 10.

Therefore this subject deserves our most serious
reflection.

## I. GENERAL RESURRECTION AND MEETING WITH CHRIST

1. This world will come to an end quite unexpectedly.

"The day of the Lord shall come as a thief, in which the heavens
shall pass away with great violence, and the elements shall be
melted with heat, and the earth and the works which are in it,
shall be burnt up." — II Pet. iii. 10. — "Now will I rise up, saith the
Lord. . . . And the people shall be as ashes after a fire; as a bundle
of thorns they shall be burnt with fire." — Is. xxxiii. 10, 12.

2. Then will follow the General Resurrection.

"And he shall send his angels with a trumpet, and a great voice."
— Matt. xxiv. 31. — "The trumpet shall sound, and the dead shall
rise incorruptible. . . . We shall all indeed rise again . . . in a
moment, in the twinkling of an eye." — I Cor. xv. 51, 52.

Foolish sinner! did you imagine that all was over with death? Your body will be formed again "in the twinkling of an eye." It will be the same that it is now, in spite of your unbelief.

"In the last day I shall rise out of the earth, and I shall be clothed again with my skin, and in my flesh I shall see my God." — Job xix. 25, 26.

The shrill sound of the trumpet will be heard, and it will be instantly obeyed, in the highest regions of heaven — in the lowest recesses of hell — in the remotest corners of the earth.

"They shall gather together his elect from the four winds, from the farthest parts of the heavens to the utmost bounds of them." — Matt. xxiv. 31.

3. Although all will rise with the same body that they had on this earth, yet there will be an immense difference as regards the qualities of the body of each one.

"Behold, I tell you a mystery: We shall *all* indeed rise again; but we shall *not all* be changed." — I Cor. xv. 51.

Of the elect, our Lord says:

"Then shall the just shine as the sun." — Matt. xiii. 43. — "Then shall they be as the angels of God in heaven." — Matt. xxii. 30.

While St. Paul says of the reprobate:

"He that soweth in his flesh, of the flesh also shall he reap corruption." — Gal. vi. 8.

Their bodies will rise as a putrid mass.

4. In all probability, the great gathering will be held in the valley of Josaphat.

"I will gather together all the nations, and will bring them down into the valley of Josaphat. . . . Let them arise and let the nations come up into the valley of Josaphat; for there I will sit to judge all nations round about. Nations, nations in the valley of destruction; for the day of the Lord is near." — Joel iii. 2, 12, 14.

And our Lord will preside at the Judgment on Mount Olivet, in the very place where He ascended to heaven, and where His return was announced.

This is the explanation which Cornelius à Lap. gives of the words of the angels:

"This Jesus who is taken up from you into heaven, so shall come, as you have seen him going into heaven." — Acts i. 11. — "Then they shall see the Son of man coming in a cloud, with great power and majesty." — Luke xxi. 27.

He will be surrounded by His entire heavenly court.

"Behold, the Lord cometh with thousands of his saints, to execute judgment upon all." — Jude 14, 15. — "The Son of man shall come . . . with his angels." — Matt. xvi. 27.

In one common act of adoration all will prostrate themselves and worship Him Whom the majority of them treated with contempt in this world.

"We shall all stand before the judgment-seat of Christ. For it is written: As I live, saith the Lord, every knee shall bow to me, and every tongue shall confess to God." — Rom. xiv. 10, 11.

His very look will make the earth tremble.

"From whose face the earth and heaven fled away." — Apoc. xx. 11. — "He looketh upon the earth, and maketh it tremble." — Ps. ciii. 32.

5. The elect will be separated from the reprobate before the Judgment begins.

"And he shall separate them one from another, as the shepherd separateth the sheep from the goats: and he shall set the sheep on his right hand but the goats on the left." — Matt. xxv. 32, 33. — "Then shall two be in the field: one shall be taken, and one shall be left. Two women shall be grinding at the mill, one shall be taken, and one shall be left." — Matt. xxiv. 40, 41. — "There shall be two men in one bed: the one shall be taken, and the other shall be left." — Luke xvii. 34.

The most sacred ties of relationship will be severed — husband will be separated from wife, brother from brother, sister from sister, etc.

## II.  The Judgment and its Awful Disclosures

"The judgment sat, and the books were opened." — Dan. vii. 10.

1. All that has occurred from the beginning of creation until that hour concerning *angels* and *men,* and that till now has been shrouded in deep mystery, will be laid bare to the whole world.

"And the angels who kept not their principality . . . he hath reserved . . . unto the judgment of the great day." — Jude 6.

"Every man's work shall be manifest: for the day of the Lord shall declare it." — I Cor. iii. 13.

The thick veil which in this life covers all will be removed.  No more secrets!  All that ever happened throughout the life of everyone will then be revealed — thoughts, words, actions, with all their circumstances, number, intentions, motives.  All without exception — men, women, children, religious, priests, bishops, popes, princes, kings, emperors, all will be judged.

"And I saw a great white throne, and one sitting upon it. . . . And I saw the dead, great and small, standing in the presence of the throne; and the books were opened, . . . and the dead were judged by those things which were written in the books, according to their works." — Apoc. xx. 11, 12. — "There is nothing covered that shall not be revealed, nor hidden that shall not be known." — Luke xii. 2.

Man's life is a book, in which he writes a page every day.  That page contains his good and evil deeds, thoughts, desires.  At his death the book is finished and closed.  Its contents are a secret to the world.  On Judgment-day, that book will be opened and its contents made known — and he himself will be judged accordingly.

2. Then will appear all his *thoughts,* good and evil.

"When the Lord will come, he will both bring to light the hidden things of darkness, and will make manifest the counsels of the hearts." — I Cor. iv. 5.

(Enumeration of the most ordinary sinful thoughts.)
Likewise all his *words*, their motives and consequences.

"I say to you, that every idle word that men shall speak, they shall render an account for it in the day of judgment." — Matt. xii. 36.

(Enumeration of the ordinary sins of the tongue.)
Then all his *actions,* good and evil, sins of omission and commission. The eye of God has followed man through life. It has seen all.

"And my eye shall not spare, neither will I show mercy." — Ez. vii. 9. — "I will judge thee according to thy ways, and will set all thy abominations against thee." — Ib. 3.

(Enumeration of the most ordinary sins of action and omission, against God, the Church, against particular duties in every one's state or position in life.)

"And they were judged every one according to their works." — Apoc. xx. 13. — "Every one of us shall render an account to God for himself." — Rom. xiv. 12.

3. Then will be made known also the sins that the sinner *caused in others* — or that he did not prevent as far as it was his duty. The elect as well as the reprobate will demand redress and revenge.

"How long, O Lord (holy and true), dost thou not judge and revenge our blood." — Apoc. vi. 10.

(Enumeration of the ordinary sins of direct or indirect scandal.)

4. All will be seen, not as past, as we read it in history, but as *present*. In eternity there is no past nor future, but all is present.

"Are thy days as the days of man and are thy years as the times of men, that thou shouldst inquire after my iniquity and search after my sin?" — Job x. 5, 6.

There is no need of any further inquisition, because all is present.

Moreover, all will judge and be judged, not according to the deceitful balance of their own corrupt nature, but *in the light of the justice and sanctity of God*. All will be seen and judged as God sees and judges it.

"The sons of men are liars in the balances." — Ps. lxi. 10. That is, they weigh things by false weights.

O the shame and confusion that will then come upon the sinner! An exposure before a small assembly of people would be indeed painful. What will it be before the whole world, and in the light of divine justice?

"Then shall they begin to say to the mountains: Fall upon us; and to the hills: Cover us." — Luke xxiii. 30. — "And hide us from the face of him that sitteth upon the throne. . . . The great day of wrath is come, and who shall be able to stand." — Apoc. vi. 16, 17.

5. But then will the just, and those who did penance for their sins, *stand in glory*. Their sins will not appear, because they are already judged, forgiven, forgotten, annihilated. They will even receive glory for their humiliation in confession and penance.

The fact that they have sinned will, of course, be made known, for nothing can remain hidden (Luke xxi. 2); but their sorrow and their penance will then be to their glory. Thus we know the sins of St. Peter, of St. Mary Magdalen, of St. Augustine, but we know likewise their penance. Then too will the good works, words, thoughts, wishes and desires of the just be made known to the world, their acts of love, of charity, of patience, the thousands of temptations overcome, etc.

"Glory and honor and peace to every one that worketh good." — Rom. ii. 10.

They will wonder that so much is made of every

little act of piety, of charity . . . which they performed in life.

"Thy father who seeth in secret will repay thee." — Matt. vi. 18. — "Then shall the just stand with great constancy against those that have afflicted them. These, seeing it, shall be troubled, saying: These are they, whom we had some time in derision; we fools esteemed their life madness; therefore we have erred from the way of truth." — Wis. v. 1–6.

Application to various cases.

6. Judgment will be passed upon all men in general and upon *each individual* in particular, nor will this require even so much time as it takes me to say so.

"He shall judge the world in equity." — Ps. ix. 9. — "And they were judged every one according to their works." — Apoc, xx. 13. — "Every one of us shall render an account to God for himself." — Rom. xiv. 12.

7. *No excuse will be attempted to be made.*

"And another book was opened, which is the book of life." — Apoc. xx. 12.

In this book another history is unfolded — that of the ways of Divine Providence in regard to every man, by which God leads souls to Himself; means of grace, inspirations, secret calls to religion — to penance; and how far every man has corresponded to these attractions or resisted them.

By the revelation of the contents of this book the action of God toward the human race in general — and toward every individual in particular — will stand justified. Poverty, distress, famine, war, persecution, will be seen to be so many means of the conversion of nations and individuals — and to have been permitted for our good.

By this revelation all will likewise understand the numerous and efficacious means placed within the reach of unbelievers, to know the true religion; of sinners, to obtain forgiveness; of the just, to persevere. Side by side will stand their efforts to correspond with those means — or their continued acts of resistance.

"Come, sinner," will the Judge say then, "let us plead together; tell, if thou hast anything to justify thyself." — Is. xliii. 26.

Behold, to your own confusion, *what your brethren have done,* who labored under the same difficulties as yourself!

All excuses, such as "I did not mean any harm," — "I did not know any better," — "I could not be good," — will then fall to the ground.

Every one of the reprobate will see and acknowledge his guilt; the world will condemn them; all will see the infinite justice of —

### III.  The Terrible Sentence and its Immediate Execution

"Let my judgment come forth from thy countenance: let thy eyes behold the things that are equitable." — Ps. xvi. 2.

The Judge now opens His mouth to pronounce sentence.  O terrible moment!  Turning to the small number of the elect — the fruit of all that the Triune God has ever done for man — He will say:

*"Come, ye blessed of my Father, possess you the kingdom prepared for you from the foundation of the world."* — Matt. xxv. 34.

O happiness!  O joy!  Crosses, persecutions, hardships, humiliations — all are now forgotten!

The Judge turns to the left — to that immense crowd of human beings — of ungrateful wretches — whom God has tried thousands of times to bring to a reconciliation — for whom the blood of Jesus has been shed in vain.  He will load them with His *curse,* and cast them off forever.

*"Depart from me, ye cursed, into everlasting fire,*

*which was prepared for the devil and his angels."* —
Matt. xxv. 41.

From this sentence there is no appeal.

"All the judgments of Thy justice are forever." — Ps. cxviii. 160.

The angels will intone a hymn in praise of the
justice of God.

"Thou art just, O Lord, and Thy judgment is right." — Ps.
cxviii. 137.

And the response will be heard from the reprobate:

"*Yea,* O Lord God Almighty, true and just are Thy judgments."
— Apoc. xvi. 7.

And immediately the sentence will be put into execution.

"And these shall go into everlasting punishment; but the just
into life everlasting." — Matt. xxv. 46.

Most painful separation forever! Most heart-rending farewell. The just will triumphantly enter the
"joys of their Lord." Hell will open its jaws and receive its victims. A shriek of despair! and the reprobate in the utmost confusion will be precipitated into
the fiery abyss. Time is no more; there is only *eternity.* The just are in heaven; the reprobate in hell —
both forever! Christians! Have you heard this?
Do you understand it? Tell me, *where will you be
then?*

# VII

# HELL

In this discourse we reach the extreme of the severity of God's justice in punishing sin. It is the greatest and the last effort of the missionary to strike the heart of the sinner with the "fear of the Lord"; and this is its *only object*. To effect this, he gives a description of the pains of the *body* and the tortures of the *soul* of the damned, and dwells on their *endless* duration. Whatever is said must be well supported by the teachings of faith, the Sacred Scriptures, the Fathers, and sound reason. Care must be taken not to advance any proof which is not at once understood, and *ad rem;* or which is only the fruit of an over-excited imagination. Otherwise, the preacher will incur the censure of exaggeration on the part of many in the audience and the effect is lost. It is well known how little people are inclined to believe in the severity of the pains of hell. And if this sermon lose its effect, the effect of the Mission is either entirely lost, or at least considerably weakened as regards the lukewarm and the wicked. It is useless to dwell long on proofs of the existence of hell. It is time lost; since the majority of those to whom we give the Mission believe in it. A few may try to force themselves into the conviction that there is no hell. The doctrine of *Eternal Punishment* concerns one of those *Eternal Truths* that need no proof, because they are deeply engraved on man's spirit. Our Lord and the Apostles did not spend much time in proving these truths, although they lived in an age of unbelief. They simply preached them, and the people trembled. When St. Paul stood before the Roman Governor Felix, *"treating of justice and chastity, and of the judgment to come, Felix being terrified, answered: For this time, go thy way."* [1] — But, it would not be out of place to throw in from time to time a short but powerful reply to the objections that are commonly made. For instance, to the objection that the eternal punishment of the sinner is incompatible with the infinite goodness and mercy of God, the saying of St. Bernard may be quoted, that eternal punishment is precisely what the goodness of God demands. God wants to save the sinner by all means. But, neither the love of God nor the reward of heaven can induce him to give up sin; therefore the terror of ever-

[1] Acts xxiv. 25.

lasting hell-fire must incite him to do so. Yet, such is man's perversity that even this last remedy fails.

The faith of so-called unbelievers is often awakened by the description of the tortures of hell. If not, all arguments are thrown away. — Besides, all the time given to this sermon is needed for the description of the pains of hell, to obtain fully the desired object of the sermon.

Every kind of oratorical embellishment must be far from this sermon. Its style must be simple, and its delivery natural, yet grave and majestic, mingled with sadness. Let the sound of the voice be strong from beginning to end, though never excited or bordering on passion. Occasional exclamations in their proper place produce great effect.

Toward the close of the sermon the preacher must make most strenuous efforts to put an end once for all to the reign of sin, by putting the *fear of God* into the hearts of his hearers.

## SKETCH

TEXT: "Those who know not God, and who obey not the Gospel of our Lord Jesus Christ, shall suffer eternal punishment in destruction." — II Thess. i. 8, 9.

The great event brought to your notice yesterday, you will all witness with your own eyes, be present at, and take a part in. — May you never learn by experience the reality of what it is my solemn duty to speak to you to-day! Sin must inevitably be followed by penance, either in this life or in the next. "Those who know not God, . . ." The unbeliever, the sinner, who will not do penance according to the Gospel, will then have to suffer the pains of hell. It is a special artifice of the devil to remove from the minds of men every thought of hell, to destroy their belief in hell — that they may sin more freely — and thus make sure their damnation. For —

"He that believeth not shall be condemned." — Mark xvi. 16.

Strange, that people can work themselves into a conviction that there is no hell, contrary to the plain teaching of the Church and of Jesus Christ.

But, is it not more strange that those people who believe in hell, walk on the road which directly leads to it? This is owing to a want of reflection on the terrible severity of those endless tortures. Of these I will speak to you to-day. To give a description of them is simply impossible. May you enter with me into this reflection with your whole heart and soul.

O Jesus, crucified to save us from hell, through the intercession of Thy Blessed Mother Mary, enlighten our minds on the terrible punishment of sin, that we may guard against it for the future.

## I. Pains of Sense — or Tortures of the Body

The reprobate are condemned to hell as they lived on this earth, with body and soul. There must, therefore, be tortures for both. Even before the body is re-united to the soul in the resurrection, the soul suffers the pains of sense. The soul retains its sensitive part even when in a state of separation from the body — therefore, also in hell. And the soul will suffer in its sensitive part so much the more because it enjoyed the pleasures of sin through the senses.

1. These pains are without *number* known to us. In hell there is absolutely not the slightest enjoyment, consolation, or relief, because of the total separation from God. Therefore, there is nothing but sheer pain and suffering without intermission.

The rich man, speaking from hell, calls it "a place of torments." — Luke xvi. 28. — "And the smoke of their torments shall ascend up forever and ever; neither have they rest day nor night." — Apoc. xiv. 11.

They are almost infinite in *intensity,* because supernatural — inflicted for an infinite offence — upon a being absolutely indestructible, which no amount of pain of any intensity can destroy. Enumerate all terrestrial sufferings; they are all but as a drop of rain compared with the ocean of the torments of hell.

"Thy malediction and curse is fallen — *stillavit* — upon us." — Dan. ix. 11.

But the tortures of hell are poured out over the reprobate like a *torrent*.

"The nourishment of hell are fire and much wood. The breath of the Lord as a torrent of brimstone kindling it." — Is. xxx. 33.

Hence, hell is absolutely nothing else than

"A land of misery and darkness, where the shadow of death, and no order, but everlasting horror dwelleth." — Job x. 22.

The greater number of those pains are unknown to us, as is indeed the intensity of all of them. Some few are mentioned in the Scriptures. Of these we know the names, but neither their character nor their intensity.

NOTE. — It would make the sermon too long to dwell on all the pains of sense marked here. Let the preacher make a judicious selection.

2. One of the most painful tortures of the body of the damned, mentioned in the Scriptures, is the *perpetual darkness,* in which the reprobate lie buried without being able to move.

"Bind his hands and feet, and cast him into the exterior darkness: there shall be weeping and gnashing of teeth." — Matt. xxii. 13. — "The children of the kingdom shall be cast into exterior darkness. . . ." — Matt. viii. 12.

Never will the reprobate have a ray of light, from the moment of death to an endless eternity.

"Because men loved darkness rather than the light." — John iii. 19.

And because they abused the light of this world for sin. Alas! what misery to be perpetually buried in darkness!

This darkness will fall upon the damned like a heavy storm.

"To whom the storm of darkness is reserved forever." —Jude 13.

Some comparisons. Sick people during long nights.

3. Another torture is that of *hunger*. Hunger in this world causes most terrible sufferings. It has sometimes driven men to such extremes that they devoured their own flesh, slaughtered and ate one another, even the dead carcasses in the graveyard [siege of Augsburg in the Thirty Years' War]; mothers devoured their own children [siege of Jerusalem — also IV Kings vi]. What are the sufferings of a human being left without food after six or eight days? What would they be after one hundred years? And then they would be but small compared with the hunger of the reprobate.

"The people shall be as fuel for the fire . . . and he shall turn to the right hand, and shall be hungry; and shall eat on the left hand, and shall not be filled; every one shall eat the flesh of his own arm." — Is. ix. 20. — "They shall suffer hunger like dogs . . . but thou, O Lord, shalt laugh at them." — Ps. lviii. 7, 9.

Because they refused the Bread of Life in this world, which would have saved them.

"He that eateth my flesh, and drinketh my blood, hath everlasting life." — John vi. 55.

4. A third pain is caused by an excruciating *thirst*. Of this the rich man in the parable is an example. He asked for but a drop of water, yet he could not be gratified with even that little.

"Have mercy on me and send Lazarus that he may dip the tip of his finger in water to cool my tongue." — Luke xvi. 24. — "O that they would be wise and would understand, and would provide for their last things! [Sinners, drunkards.] Their [the demons'] wine is the gall of dragons, and the venom of asps, which is incurable." — Deut. xxxii. 29–33.

5. Another pain of sense is that of an insupportable *stench*. The reprobate, after the General Judgment, fall into hell in utter disorder, some head downward, some backward . . . and as they fall, so they remain piled on top of one another, motionless, forever. The body of each one is like a carcass in a state of putrefaction.

What torture — to be shut up in a dungeon with a putrid corpse near you!

"Instead of a sweet smell there shall be stench." — Is. iii. 24. — "They are laid in hell like sheep; death shall feed upon them." — Ps. xlviii. 15. — "Thy pride is brought down to hell, thy carcass is fallen down: under thee shall the moth be strewed, and worms shall be thy covering." — Is. xiv. 11.

6. To these sufferings are added the tortures to which the reprobate are subjected by the *millions of infuriated demons*.

Man is the very image and likeness of God. The demons will rage against the damned as they would against God. The Christian carries the mark of the blood of Christ on him; that still further excites the fury of the infernal spirits. The torments to which the persecutors of the Church subjected the Christians of the first three centuries are not a shadow to the torments which the devils inflict upon the damned.

"Your adversary, the devil, as a roaring lion, goeth about seeking whom he may devour." — I Pet. v. 8.

How much the more will the devil do so in hell? There his fury is unchained. God gives him full power over the damned, because they were subject to him in life.

"They [the beast and the false prophet] shall be tormented day and night forever and ever." — Apoc. xx. 10.

7. But above all will be the torture of *fire*. What is it to be burnt alive? Some facts.

The fire in hell cannot be compared to the fire in this world; as little as the fire in a foundry to a lump of ice.

"A fire is kindled in my wrath and shall burn even to the lowest hell." — Deut. xxxii. 22. — "The Lord . . . shall show the terror of his arm, in the threatening of wrath, and the flame of devouring fire." — Is. xxx. 30.

That fire is created especially for the torment of the demons (Matt. xxv. 41). Therefore, there must be an immense difference between it and natural fire, because all the fire of this earth would not cause the least pain to a demon of hell.

Into that fire the reprobate are cast alive, with body and soul.

"These were cast alive into the pool of fire burning with brimstone." — Apoc. xix. 20.

They are buried in it (Luke xvi. 22); it shall penetrate them entirely, as "they shall be salted with fire" (Mark ix. 48).

"He will give fire and worms into their flesh, that they may burn, and may feel forever." — Judith xvi. 21.

They will be like so many hot furnaces of fire.

"Let Thy right hand find out all them that hate Thee. Thou shalt make them as an oven of fire, in the time of Thy anger: the Lord shall trouble them in his wrath, and fire shall devour them." — Ps. xx. 9, 10.

*Objection.* How can God, Who is infinitely merciful, inflict such horrible tortures upon a weak human creature, and that forever?

But did that "weak creature" not wilfully oppose the Infinite God — did it not bid reckless defiance to God, in spite of His threats of eternal punishment — did it not deliberately, even scornfully, do those things which were forbidden under the pain of eternal hell-fire? And, then — positively refuse penance and amendment?

"Be not deceived. Neither fornicators, nor idolaters, nor adulterers, nor the effeminate, nor Sodomites, nor thieves, nor the covetous, nor drunkards, nor railers, nor extortioners, shall possess the kingdom of God." — I Cor. vi. 9, 10.

8. The Prophet asks, and I with him:

"Which of you can dwell with devouring fire?" — Is. xxxiii. 14.

Can you — drunkard — thief — adulterer? No! For all the riches and pleasures of the earth you would not endure to be burned alive, to hold your hand on a red-hot stove, to keep your finger in a gas-light for fifteen minutes. No one can. But,

"*Which of you* shall dwell with everlasting burning?" — Ib.

My text gives the answer: "Those who know not . . ." "O thou fool!" (Luke xii. 20.) But "the number of such fools is infinite." — Eccle. i. 15.

## II. Pains of Loss — or Tortures of the Soul

Is this hell? Not the thousandth part of it! So greatly do the tortures of the soul surpass the sufferings of the body.

1. *The loss of God.* The soul was made to be replenished with the presence of God. It naturally longs for Him. At present this innate desire is quenched by the enjoyment of earthly pleasures. After death it cannot be so. The soul is drawn toward Him with all the force of its being. To be kept from Him but an instant, causes infinite pain.

"*Hæc est tanta pœna, quantus ille.*" — St. Aug. de civ. Dei.

Compare the interior or mental sufferings caused by the loss of property, of a child, of a father or mother, which often bring on madness.

The soul's capacity for suffering is limited — the pain of loss is infinite. Therefore it fills the soul to overflowing. Compare an immense quantity of water poured into a small vessel.

Jesus Christ complained of none of His sufferings except His abandonment on the part of His heavenly Father. How terrible must that pain have been!

"I am come into the depth of the sea; and a tempest hath overwhelmed me." — Ps. lxviii. 3.

But Jesus Christ was never truly separated from God — while the reprobate are not only *separated* but also *cast off*.

"A thousand hells are nothing in comparison with the torture of the soul on account of this loss." — St. Chrys. hom. 49 ad pop.

2. And with God lost, *all is lost* — Heaven, salvation, the favor and sympathy of friends and relatives; all consolation, all hope! The soul has incurred the hatred and the curse of God and of all creation.

With God all creatures *curse* the reprobate and turn against them. They have not a single friend, not even among the damned.

"The whole world shall fight with God against the unwise." — Wis. v. 21.

In this world the reprobate still enjoyed the benefit of creatures. They could even abuse them for their base purposes.

"God maketh his sun to rise upon the good and the bad and raineth upon the just and the unjust." — Matt. v. 45.

All this is taken from the damned forever. Therefore, the reprobate are, indeed, dead in the fullest sense of the word. They are continually suffering the pains of eternal death, *i.e.*, separated from everything, and deprived of what constitutes the true light of the soul — God.

"As the soul is the life of the body, so God is the life of the soul. And as the body expires when the soul departs, so the soul expires when it loses God. The loss of God is the death of the soul, as the loss of the soul is the death of the body." — St. Aug. serm 5. de verb. Dom. — "Hell and death were cast into the pool of fire. This is the second death." — Apoc. xx. 14.

Yes, unfortunate souls, where is your God? He told you, *"Depart from me."* But did you not often say the same to Him: *"Depart from us;* we desire not the knowledge of Thy ways." — Job xxi. 14.

Oh! how often will the soul cry out:

"My tears have been my bread, day and night, while it is said to me daily: Where is thy God?" — Ps. xli. 4.

And what was your object? For what did you lose God, the Infinite Good? Enumerate.

3. *Remorse of conscience.* The reprobate cannot blame any one but themselves for their misfortune. *Not God,* Who has done all, sacrificed all, even His only-begotten Son, for their salvation. But they would make no sacrifice.

"What is there that I ought to do more to my vineyard that I have not done to it?" — Is. v. 4. — "He that spared not even his own Son, but delivereth him up for us all, how hath he not also, with him, given us all things." — Rom. viii. 32.

Not *Jesus Christ,* Who came to save all mankind, and shed the last drop of His heart's blood for them.

"The grace of our Lord hath abounded exceedingly . . . which is in Christ Jesus." — I Tim. i. 14.

Not the *Church,* which cried out continually to sinners to be converted — by her ordinary and extraordinary ministry; and had full power for absolving all sins.

"For Christ we beseech you, be ye reconciled to God." — II Cor. v. 20.

But they must blame themselves, because they will know then that —

4. *The commandments of God could easily have been observed.* God commanded no impossibilities. What was difficult to nature would have become easy with grace, which could not have been overcome by the temptations of the whole world and all hell combined, had they not themselves wished for the pleasure of sin. And grace was at their command, had they only exerted themselves a little. And even though they had sinned, no matter how much, reconciliation by penance was easy. A humiliation of a quarter of an hour would have saved them forever. Hear their groanings from the abyss of hell:

"Repenting and groaning for anguish of spirit they say, . . . Therefore we have erred." — Wis. v. 3, 6.

They will recollect that to gain some earthly profit, even to commit sin, they had to make greater efforts than would have been required for their salvation:

"We wearied ourselves in the way of iniquity and destruction, and have walked through hard ways; but the way of the Lord we have not known." — Wis. v. 7.

And what have they gained by it — by those pleasures, money, honors, pride, and ambition? All is gone!

"What hath pride profited us, or what advantage hath the boasting of riches brought us? All those things are passed away like a shadow." — Wis. v. 8, 9. — "Such things as these the sinners said in hell." — Wis. v. 14.

What would those who are in hell now do — what sacrifices would they make, if there were a chance for salvation? Infidels, apostates, drunkards, thieves, adulterers, those who made sacrilegious confessions — what would they do, if they had a Mission? But, alas! no hope! They would at least wish to send a message to this world as a warning for others.

"Father I beseech thee, that thou wouldst send Lazarus to my father's house . . . that he may testify to my brethren, lest they also come into this place of torments." — Luke xvi. 27, 28.

But God has no need of their ministry. Nothing of the kind will be granted them. For them all chance of saving themselves or others is passed.

### III. THE TORMENTS OF THE REPROBATE LAST FOREVER

"And the smoke of their torments shall ascend up forever and ever: neither have they rest day nor night." — Apoc. xvi. 11.

1. O God of Infinite Justice! What is eternity? A moment that lasts forever! And so long will the reprobate suffer! Their tortures will never come to an end, never — never! And no rest — no relief; nor can they ever become accustomed to their situation, nor used to their pains!

*How long is eternity?* It is immeasurable. Imagine one of those who perished in the Deluge — chained down to a fiery bed — making the most strenuous efforts to produce a tear of repentance, hoping thereby to appease the wrath of God. He succeeds in producing one tear every thousand years. He is determined to continue until he has filled with his tears the immense space between the earth and the sky. By this time he has produced *only four.* How long would his task take him? And, should he ever accomplish his object, how much of eternity would then be past? Not a minute!! And if he should go through the same process twice, three, ten, a hundred, a thousand times — what then? Eternity is still in its beginning!

And is there any change in his situation?   Not the slightest!

"As it was in the beginning, so is it now, and so shall it be forever, world without end."

And is there no hope?   Never!   And how long must he suffer? — *Forever!!*

"They shall seek death, but they shall not find it." — Apoc. ix. 6.

They would fain tear themselves to pieces.   In vain!!

"They gnawed their tongues for pain, and they blasphemed the God of heaven because of their pains." — Apoc. xvi. 10, 11.

O tortures!   O despair!!   O eternal damnation!!!

O God of Infinite Justice!   Oh! how terrible to fall into Thy hands!

(No recapitulation.)

CONCLUSION. — I must come to a conclusion.   But how shall I close this discourse?   O merciful Jesus, give strength to my last words to-day!

O Christians!   For the sake of your immortal souls, I entreat you — for the sake of the most precious blood of Jesus, shed for you on the cross, I implore you, *give up sin* — *do penance!*   Away with all your doubts!   Embrace the only saving faith!   Away with secret societies!   Away with the occasions of sin!   Break at once the chains of wickedness!   How soon may you not die?   And then to die in sin! — to be irretrievably lost!   But, not so!   Come!   Begin at once!   Let us all most humbly ask pardon of God.

O God! of Infinite Justice, yet a most merciful Father to all, even the greatest sinners, who come to Thee with a contrite heart, behold me prostrate before Thee in grief and sorrow for my sins!   Oh! despise not the work of Thy hands, for whom the blood of Jesus has been shed!   Pardon my iniquities!

I thank Thee for not having cast me off, as I have so often deserved! Once more receive me as the least of Thy servants! I am determined to do better for the future! Let heaven and earth be witnesses to this my firm resolution.

"I have sworn, and am determined to keep the judgments of thy justice." — Ps. cxviii. 106.

O most merciful Mother Mary! into thy hands I place my sinful soul. Save me, O sweet Mother, from the wrath of God and the eternal flames of hell!! Amen.

# VIII

## MERCY OF GOD

The object of the three preceding sermons is to operate upon the sinner's heart through the *motives of fear*. Fear alone, however, does not affect a permanent conversion. It may effect no conversion at all. Therefore, we now come to such subjects as are likely to arouse within the sinner the *motives of love*. The *particular object* of this sermon is to let the sinner see the infinite goodness of God, manifested in His exceedingly great mercy toward repenting sinners; the consequence of which should be a more perfect sorrow for sins committed, as well as a very great love for God, which is apt to prevent sin in the future. To effect this, the infinite mercy of God is to be explained, as it has been displayed toward this sinful world in general, and as it has manifested itself, and still manifests itself toward the greatest sinners in particular. In this sermon nothing should be said about the abuse of the mercy of God. Everything should inspire confidence and consolation; nothing that might in the least be discouraging should be mentioned.

Instead of the *Mercy of God,* a sermon may be preached on the *Passion of Christ*. St. Alphonsus prefers the latter, because it confirms the audience in the love of Jesus Christ crucified, which, as the Saint says, produces contrition more readily and promotes perseverance more securely.[1] He does not mention it in his enumeration of Mission-sermons, but he desires that for two or three days meditations should be given on the Passion; and this practice is called *Vita devota*. We shall speak of this sermon more in detail in another place.

Another beautiful sermon on this subject is that on the *Prodigal Son*. In the first part, it depicts the sinner's aberration; in the second, it shows the spiritual desolation into which he has fallen; in the third, the dispositions of the repenting sinner, his return and reception at home.

This sermon should be preached in the style of simple narrative, allowing our dear Lord to use His own sweet words, rather than putting forward our own.

[1] C. E., Vol. XV. p. 303.

## Sketch

Text: "And his mercy is from generation to generation, to them that fear him." — Luke i. 50.

Exordium. — Fear and trembling must have seized upon your hearts when you considered the severity of God's justice in judging and punishing sin. If so — the first and chief object of the Mission is attained, which consists in a salutary fear of God.

"The fear of the Lord is the beginning of wisdom." — Prov. i. 7.

If that fear of God and His judgments has brought you to a firm determination to quit sin, your reconciliation is easily obtained. You have every reason to hope in the mercy of God. "For His mercy . . . to them that fear Him."

Under this condition there is mercy for every sinner without exception. What a consoling truth! The severity of God's justice will fall only upon those who do not fear.

O merciful Jesus, send a ray of Thy heavenly light into our hearts, that we may understand the immense love of Thy merciful heart toward the wayward sinner who desires to return to Thee! O Mother of Mercy, bless my words, that they may produce a good effect upon the sinner's heart!

## I. God's Infinite Mercy Manifested toward the Sinner in Protecting and Calling Him

It is a temptation most common among those who have become reckless in sinning, to think that God is merciful and that He will not reject them. But as soon as they have made up their minds to change their lives the very opposite is the case. Then they believe that God despises them and does not desire their reconciliation.   Hell then tries to represent God as a cruel tyrant, who will have no mercy, at least not on certain sinners.   This is not so.

1. God desires to be reconciled with man infinitely more than man desires to be reconciled with God; accordingly, God has done all in His infinite power to save sinful man.

"The Lord is sweet to all; and His tender mercies are over all his works." — Ps. cxliv. 9.

*a.* This is true on the part of *God the Father*.   He has sacrificed more than all creation — to save sinners.

"God so loved the world, as to give his only-begotten Son." — John iii. 16. — "Who spared not even His own Son, but delivered Him up for us all; how hath he not, also, with him, given us all things?" — Rom. viii. 32.

*b.* Again, on the part of *God the Son*.   To save the world,

"He emptied (*exinanivit*) himself, and taking the form of a servant . . . humbled himself, becoming obedient unto death, even to the death of the cross." — Phil. ii. 7, 8. — "Who was a worm, and no man; the reproach of men, and the outcast of the people." · — Ps. xxi. 7.

Who sacrificed blood, life — all — for sinful man, in order to save him.

*c.* The same is true on the part of *God the Holy Ghost.*

"Jesus breathed on the apostles, and he said to them: Receive ye the Holy Ghost; whose sins you shall forgive, they are forgiven them." — John xx. 22, 23.

The Holy Ghost dispenses the means of salvation in abundance to the greatest criminals, inspires the sinner with confidence, contrition and a desire of reconciliation with God, against which *no sin* will be an obstacle.

"*Whatsoever* you shall loose on earth shall be loosed also in heaven." — Matt. xviii. 18.

How, then, can any one imagine that God is unwilling to forgive him?

2. *God loves all His creatures, even the sinner,* so long as he is not yet in hell. He does not exclude him from the common benefits of His providence.

"He maketh His sun to rise upon the good and the bad, and raineth upon the just and the unjust." — Matt. v. 45.

He *protects* him against the *powers of darkness,* who claim him as their own.

"God, to make his power known, endured with much patience vessels of wrath, fitted for destruction, that He might show the riches of his glory on the vessels of mercy." — Rom. ix. 22.

He protects him against *death* in accidents; grants him good health in the midst of a devastating epidemic.

"As I live, saith the Lord God, I desire not the death of the wicked, but that the wicked turn from his way and live." — Ez. xxxiii. 11.

He does so even while the sinner becomes *more emboldened* thereby.

"Say not: I have sinned, and what harm hath befallen me? For the Most High is a patient rewarder." — Eccli. v. 4.

Even while by his sinful acts he *turns* rational and irrational creatures *from and against God;* while after all he can *exist only supported by God.*

"Thou hast made me to serve with thy sins; thou has wearied me with thy iniquities." — Is. xliii. 24.

He protects the *reputation* of the sinner, strictly forbidding those who are cognizant of his sins to publish them to others.

"Hast thou heard a word against thy neighbor? Let it die within thee." — Eccli. xix. 10.

God wants the sins of men to remain secret until Judgment-day if they are not forgiven; forever, if they are forgiven.

O sinner! how much God still loves you after all your sins!

3. Yet all this goodness on the part of God will not induce the sinner to return; therefore *God goes out in search of him*.

Parable of the Lost Sheep. (Luke xv.) God appears to be utterly disconsolate on account of the stray soul; seems to have lost all the joy that the fidelity of the just gives Him. He goes in search of the lost one, and does not rest until He has reclaimed it.

*Means.* — Secret attractions, private and public calamities, ordinary and extraordinary ministry of the Church, Jubilees, Missions.

When He catches a glimpse of the sinner He calls out to him:

"Turn ye, turn ye from your evil ways, and why will you die, house of Israel [O child of my love]?" — Ez. xxxiii. 11. — "God acts toward the sinner as though He depended on the sinner, and as though His happiness depended entirely on his conversion." — (Thom. à Kemp.)

An example of the great mercy of God toward sinners, especially on account of their ignorance, is His action toward Ninive.

"Shall I not spare Ninive, in which there are more than a hundred and twenty thousand persons, that know not how to distinguish between their right hand and their left, and many beasts?" — Jon. iv. 11.

Another, His action before the Deluge. The Lord had determined to destroy the human race, but He gave men a hundred and twenty years for repentance. — Gen. vi. 3. Then yet seven days. — Ib. vii. 4. At last the waters came upon the earth, but not on a sudden. It rained forty days and forty nights — Ib. — all this to leave room for repentance.

II. God's Infinite Mercy toward the Sinner in
his Reception and Pardon

From what we have heard, we can imagine how
the returning sinner will be *received* by God. This
is beautifully shown in the parable of the Prodigal
Son (Luke xv. 18).

The prodigal says: "I will arise and go to my
father." "And rising up, he went home toward his
father's house" — no doubt with a trembling heart —
an object of disgust to all who saw him come. "And
when he was yet a great way off, his father saw him,
and was moved with compassion, and, *running* to
him, fell upon his neck and kissed him." So God
runs toward the sinner when the first movements of
grief make him retrace his steps. He does not make
him stand long at the door and knock, nor give him
a cold reception; but He gives him the kiss of peace
and reconciliation, even before his confession.

"The first robes are put on him, . . .." — a festival
is got up even before the entire family is gathered in,
and there is a general rejoicing over his return.

The ministers of the Church are commanded to
clothe the repenting sinner with the robes of baptismal innocence; he is admitted to Holy Communion;
all share the joy of his soul.

"Even so there shall be joy in heaven upon one sinner that
doth penance, more than upon ninety-nine just who need not
penance." — Luke xv. 7.

Thus is the sinner *received*. What are the *conditions of his full pardon?*

Atonement is already made; it needs only to be
applied. God could prescribe hard conditions; not so
this all-merciful Father.

"Father, if the prophet had bid thee do some great thing,
surely thou shouldst have done it; how much rather what he now

hath said to thee: Wash, and thou shalt be clean. — IV Kings v. 13.

What does God bid the sinner do, and he shall be clean? He requires but that one expression of him: *"Pater peccavi!"* — an acknowledgment of his guilt, made to him whom God has placed over him as a father in His stead, stating with sorrow of heart and the determination to sin no more, the particular points in which he sinned. That is all. And is it too much? Is it too much for you to acknowledge to the priest that you have done wrong; to the one man who is commissioned from Heaven to assure you of your pardon, and who will be the first to share in your joy? And what you have confided to the priest remains with him an everlasting secret.

And if you cannot find a priest, God dispenses even from that condition. But from the condition of contrition and the firm purpose of amendment, God *cannot* dispense. You must detest sin because God detests it, else you cannot be the friend of God. But if you have not these dispositions, "ask and you shall receive."

And if you cannot ask God as you should, ask the Blessed Virgin Mary to obtain these dispositions for you. For this purpose God has constituted her the "Mother of Mercy," the "Refuge of Sinners," the "Hope of the Despairing."

Tell me, then, sinner, is God hard toward you?

"Come, and accuse me, saith the Lord, if your sins be as scarlet, they shall be made white as snow; and if they be red as crimson, they shall be white as wool." — Is. i. 18.

Let every sinner, therefore, take courage and return to his God.

"Come to me, *all* you that labor and are burdened, and I will refresh you." — Matt. xi. 28.

### III. God's Infinite Mercy toward the Sinner after his Reconciliation

1. It is the will of God that the sinner on his part should never cease to be sorry for his sins, and should humble himself before his fellow-Christians. But on the part of God, these sins are *completely forgotten*. God will never reproach the sinner with them, or call him to an account.

"He will have mercy on us; he will put away our iniquities, and he will cast all our sins into the bottom of the sea." — Mich. vii. 19.

The sinner will be the same as he was before he committed sin.

"I will have mercy on them, and they shall be as they were when I had not cast them off." — Zach. x. 6. — *i.e.*, let them have the benefit of all their good works.

If your sorrow is perfect, or if you gain a plenary indulgence, He will *not even* make you undergo *a temporal punishment*.

The *greatest sinner* can yet become the *greatest saint*. Examples are: David, Mary Magdalen, Mary of Egypt, St. Augustine, Margaret of Cortona, etc. So too with you, although the rest of your life may be very short. Examples are: Good Thief — Thais of Egypt, who lived only three years after her conversion.

2. To confirm what I have said, *I call to witness the earth.*

"The earth is full of the mercy of God." — Ps. xxxii. 5.

*The heavens*, where all unite in "singing the mercies of God forever." — Ps. lxxxviii. 2.

*Purgatory*, where the suffering souls cry out:

"The mercies of the Lord, that we are not consumed; because his commiserations have not failed." — Lam. iii. 22.

*Hell,* where every one of the damned must acknowledge that, had he but desired it, God would have had mercy on him.

*The very demons of hell,* who are forced to confess that they have lost every soul who in true repentance turned to God.

*Jesus Christ,* dying for sinners on the cross, calls upon all sinners to return to Him.

"Who is he that shall condemn? — Christ Jesus, who died, yea, that is risen also again, who is at the right hand of God, who also maketh intercession for us?" — Rom. viii. 34.

CONCLUSION. — Recapitulation.

O sinner! may it please God to grant you sufficient light to understand what I have said.

"I bow my knees to the Father of our Lord Jesus Christ, that he would grant you that you may be able to comprehend with all the saints what is the breadth, and length, and height, and depth [of his infinite mercy, his love and compassion for poor sinners]." — Eph. iii. 14–18.

Oh! how could you offend so good a God? But, after you have done so, how can you any longer resist His kind invitation to a reconciliation? No matter what you have done, there is mercy for you. "Come to me all . . ."

Oh! cast yourself, then, on your knees before this all-merciful God, and say from your heart:

O Father of love! O Father of mercy! I am deeply grieved at the many and grievous offences that I have committed against Thy divine goodness. Alas! how could I do it? I trust in Thy infinite mercy, which invites me to return. Else, how could I sum up courage to present myself before Thee? O Father, I will sin no more! No, never! Through the merits of Jesus, my Redeemer, and the intercession of my Mother Mary, let me again be reconciled to Thee. Amen.

# IX

# PATRONAGE OF THE BLESSED VIRGIN MARY

It is well known that no one will ever be lost who, with the proper dispositions, has recourse to the Blessed Virgin and places himself under her special protection, and that we have good reason to fear for the salvation of those who have no devotion to her. To inspire the people with a practical and uninterrupted devotion to her is the ·object of this sermon. It is intended, first, for those who have not yet made up their minds to change their lives. They are, by this sermon, to understand still more the infinite mercy of God, Who has given us the Blessed Virgin as a special advocate that will infallibly obtain for us our conversion, provided we ask her for it. It is intended, secondly, for those who are already converted, as well as for all the rest of the people, that they may at all times have recourse to her — in fact, place themselves under her protection as her children. To effect this, the unlimited intercessory power of Mary, even in behalf of the worst sinner, is to be shown, as well as her never-failing charity and mercy toward all.

This sermon, like others, otherwise excellent, may easily lose in effect, if its proper object be not kept in view and strictly carried out. A dogmatic defense of the devotion of Catholics to the Blessed Virgin against heretics and unbelievers, is out of place here. A handful of Protestants who may chance to be present, should not allow us to lose sight of the main object of the sermon and the needs of our people. It is likewise out of place to speak of the beauty, the grandeur, the glories and graces of the Blessed Virgin. Such a description will give us a great esteem for her, but very little confidence in her. We never call in question the infinite glory of God, and yet we are wanting in confidence in Him. The people will not conceive greater confidence in the Blessed Virgin, because we lead them to contemplate her on her high throne in heaven, but rather when we tell them how near she is to them, and how eager she is to help them. Our Rule says: *Concio habenda est de Patrocinio Beatæ Virginis. Hæc vero concio ad praxim et mores spectet, nec sit nimis theoretica ac multigena eruditione referta."* [1]

[1] R., n. 140.

The solemn act of the dedication of the people to the Blessed Virgin is not a mere peroration. It is an act by itself, although it follows the sermon immediately, according to our present practice.[2] Nor do we simply intend, by this ceremony, that the people should place themselves under the protection of the Blessed Virgin. We intend that more should be effected. From the fact that we are Christians we are children of Mary in the order of grace. Yet, few people care about their Mother; they are wayward children. The Mission is to bring them back to their Mother, and to inspire them with the firm resolution to remain henceforward under her care. It is precisely this idea that the people express when they are made to pronounce the act of dedication.

The style of this sermon is to be as simple as that of the other sermons, although it is generally preached amidst great pomp and splendor. Its delivery must be exceedingly cheerful, hope-inspiring, consoling and encouraging, especially toward the end, when the audience is to be prepared for the act of consecration.

## SKETCH

TEXT: "Behold thy Mother." — John xix. 27.

EXORDIUM. — To-day I come to you with a most cheerful message — a message most consoling for 'all, the just and the unjust, saints and sinners. We have spoken to you of the infinite mercy of God, even toward the most degraded sinners. To make us surely find the way to that divine mercy, God has given us a mother to lead us. "Behold thy Mother." — She is a Mother to the just, to obtain their perseverance; to the sinner, to effect his conversion. She is a most *powerful* and a most *merciful* Mother. Nothing can prevent her from helping and assisting us — nothing will keep her from exercising her office of charity — provided we do one thing — *i.e.*, have recourse to her in confidence. To inspire you to do this is the object of my present discourse.

[2] See Chapter XI. — Ceremonies of the Mission, p. 109.

## I. UNLIMITED POWER OF INTERCESSION OF THE BLESSED VIRGIN MARY

Why should we be wanting in confidence in the Blessed Virgin? Is it because it is not in her power to assist us, or because, though it is, she will not help in certain exceptional cases? No; her intercession is at all times, and in every case, most powerful and efficacious in behalf of the most degraded sinners, even of entire nations steeped in sin and crime.

1. *This privilege was granted to others.* How much more should the Mother of the Redeemer possess it!

It was granted to *Abraham.*

"For Abraham's sake the Lord may bring to effect all the things he had spoken unto him." — Gen. xviii. 19. — "In him all the nations of the earth shall be blessed." — Ib. 18.

Who, through his prayer, would have saved the wicked cities of Sodom and Gomorrha from destruction, had the condition, stipulated by himself, been fulfilled (Ib. 23–32), that is, if ten just persons could be found there.

To *Moses,* at whose prayer God did not carry out His decree of destroying the Jewish nation, which had fallen into the most abominable idolatry.

"But Moses besought the Lord . . . let thy anger cease and be appeased upon the wickedness of thy people . . . And the Lord was appeased from doing the evil which he had spoken against his people." — Exod. xxxii. 11–14.

To *David,* on whose account, notwithstanding his sins, the Lord would not destroy Juda, although that nation had often deserved this punishment for its most horrible iniquities.

"But the Lord would not destroy Juda for David his servant's sake, as he had promised him." — IV Kings viii. 19. — "I will protect this city (Jerusalem), and I will save it for my own sake, and for David my servant's sake." — Ib. xix. 34, and xx. 6.

How much more, then, is this privilege granted to Mary, the *most spotless* of all creatures; whom God has raised *above all men and angels* in dignity; who is *next to God* in heaven?

"The Mother of God has been exalted above the choirs of the angels to the celestial kingdom." — Church *in Festo Assumpt.*

Through whom God has given *the Redeemer* to the world; who truly, and alone, has been made, and is forever the *Mother of God!*

"The merits of the Blessed Virgin are so great with God, that nothing of what she wishes to effect can in any degree fail to be done." — St. Anselm.

2. *Mary is the Mother of Jesus.* A son who loves his mother cannot refuse her anything, provided it is in his power to grant it. Solomon, himself a sinner, said this to his mother, Bethsabee, whose life had been defiled by the crime of adultery.

"And the king said to her: My mother ask, for I must not turn away thy face." — III Kings ii. 20 — *i.e.,* provided thy petition is just, and if granted will do no harm.

But who can call in question the love of Jesus Christ for His Mother? Is it not infinite? Hence Mary can obtain as much as Jesus can grant — all! For this reason is she called by St. Bernard, *"Omnipotentia Supplex."* And St. Antoninus adds: *"Impossibile est, Mariam non exaudiri."*

3. The strongest proofs to substantiate anything are facts. The history of the Church for the last nineteen hundred years abounds with *facts* that show the power of the Blessed Virgin, particularly in regard to the conversion of the most abandoned sinners. The most wonderful and the most extraordinary graces have been obtained through her intercession. Entire nations have publicly acknowledged this. On this account, too,

"*All generations* have always *called her blessed.*" — Luke i. 48.

The prophecy of the Holy Ghost, pronounced by her lips, has constantly been fulfilled, and she is called "Blessed" — "the Blessed Virgin," — not only because she is the Mother of the Redeemer, but principally because God has endowed her with such intercessory power. Thousands of monuments, churches, chapels, altars, erected in her honor, confirm this truth.

4. It is the common opinion of all the divines of the Church that Mary is *the keeper of the treasury of all divine grace* to be given to men (St. Alphonsus, *Glories of Mary, ch. v. sec.* 1). Hence all that God can and is willing to grant to man, according to His infinite power and mercy, is placed in the hands of Mary for her free distribution. This agrees perfectly with her office as Mother. For the mother has the free dispensation of the treasures of the house in behalf of her children. Therefore, the Church calls her *"Mater divinæ gratiæ,"* and applies to her the words of Wisdom:

"In me is all hope of life and of virtue." — Eccli. xxiv. 25. — "In me is all grace of the way and of the truth." — Ib. — "He that shall find me shall find life, and shall have salvation of the Lord." — Prov. viii. 35. — "God has placed in Mary the plenitude of all good, all hope, all grace, all salvation." — St. Bern.

Nor does this in the least derogate from the honor and authority of God, Who wishes thus to honor the Blessed Virgin, as little as it derogates from the authority of the father of a family, to allow the mother to provide the children with all that they need, and on whom the children call for all that they want.

5. The power of the Blessed Virgin is most strikingly illustrated in the fact related in John ii. When there was no more wine for the guests, those people called on the Blessed Virgin to intercede for them with Jesus, although they might have gone directly to Him

— a genuine Catholic practice. To render her power over God and Himself more conspicuous, Jesus first showed the difficulty that was in the way.

"What is that to me and to thee?" — John ii. 4.

It was neither His office nor hers to provide wine.

"My hour is not yet come." — Ib. — *i.e.*, the hour for manifesting His divinity to the world, the hour appointed by the Eternal Father.

Our dear Lord, as He said Himself, never worked any miracle — hence not the first miracle either — except at the command of His heavenly Father.

"I must work the works of him that sent me." — John ix. 4. — "The Father who abideth in me, he doeth the works." — John xiv. 10. — "I do nothing of myself . . . I do always the things that please him." — John viii. 28–29.

Yet her petition could not be refused, and although there was question of removing only a little temporal embarrassment, He worked His first miracle.

"This beginning of miracles did Jesus in Cana of Galilee, and he manifested his glory." — John ii. 11.

Therefore, have confidence in the Blessed Virgin! Nothing is impossible to her, as, for instance, the conversion of the vilest criminal, help in extraordinary temptations, etc.

But is she willing to help every one?

II. Unbounded Charity and Mercy of the Blessed Virgin Mary, especially Toward the Most Abandoned Sinners

We have seen the unlimited power of Mary.

"But what would this power profit us, if she cared nothing about us?" — St. Bonav.

Mary hears and helps the most ungrateful wretch at all times, notwithstanding all his crimes, provided he fulfil two conditions — 1, That he ask her help; and, 2, That he be resolved to change his sinful life. And if the second be wanting, he will obtain it through the first.

1. Because *she loves God infinitely more* than all the angels and saints together love Him.

Hence she desires so much to prevent the loss of even one soul — the image and likeness of God, made for heaven, to glorify God — and redeemed by the blood of Jesus Christ.

2. Because it is *her office to save sinners*. God has made her the refuge of sinners, so that should a sinner, according to the laws of divine justice, be already condemned to hell, he could yet be saved through her. It is her special privilege.

"There is no sinner in the world so lost and sunk in sin, that Mary would abhor him and reject him. Ah! if such would seek her aid, this good mother could and would reconcile them to her Son and obtain for them pardon!" — Blosius, dict. PP. c. 5.

And in her love of God, she fulfills this office wherever she can.

3. Because *she is our Mother*. A mother will do all that she can to save her child from ruin. Our heavenly Mother does the same in regard to her children on earth, with an eagerness infinitely greater.

How is she our Mother? In becoming the Mother of the Redeemer, she became the Mother of the redeemed. Eve is our mother in the order of nature; Mary, in the order of grace. As such she was proclaimed by Jesus Christ Himself when dying on the cross, "Behold thy Mother." Saying this to St. John, He pointed him out to her as one of the many children under her charge — "Behold thy son."

"At the Annunciation, Mary became our Mother — *inchoative;* — under the Cross, where she co-operated for our salvation with the utmost charity — *consummative."* — St. Aug. "She is the Mother of all men." — St. Chrys. "She is the Mother of all the living." — St. Epiph. "She is the Mother of the whole world." — St. Proclus.

Now, it is absolutely against the nature of a mother to see one of her children crying to her for assistance and not to render help while she has it in her power.

"Can a woman forget her infant, so as not to have pity on the son of her womb?" — Is. xlix. 15.

How much more is it against *the very nature of this Mother,* infinitely merciful — *Mater misericordiæ* — to see one of her children in most imminent danger of eternal destruction, crying for help — and not to hear and help him.

Such a thing has *never been heard of.*

"Nunquam auditum a sæculo quemquam ad tua currentem præsidia . . . esse derelictum." — St. Bern. — "If there is any one who has ever invoked thee in his troubles, O Virgin Mother, and thou hast not heard him, let him in future call thee no more merciful." — Idem.

Such a thing is, moreover, *impossible,* considering all that has been said.

"Sooner will heaven and earth go to destruction than that any one who seriously implores the Blessed Virgin for help will be left unaided." — Blosius.

And all this, no matter how great a criminal the one has been who prays to her, provided he desire to amend his life. Mary is not like us, who are accustomed to cast up their past faults to those who apply to our charity for help.

"Mary will not institute an examination into our past merits or sins when we call on her for help." — St. Bern.

(Here should follow an example of a remarkable conversion obtained through the Blessed Virgin.)

Renew, then, your confidence in your Blessed Mother to-day, and, if you have never prayed to her before — if you have even spoken against her — turn to her in confidence. "Behold your Mother." If you are in sin — separated from the Church — on the brink of despair — guilty of the most enormous sacrilege — have recourse to her. In your future trials — temptations — even though caused by yourself — in discouragement — despair — pray to her — and she will help you as a most merciful Mother.

Pray to her also for others — your friends, relatives, sinners of all kinds, the Church, the souls in Purgatory; your prayer will be heard.

### INTRODUCTION OF THE ACT OF DEDICATION

Oh! how thankful ought we be to God for giving us so powerful and so merciful a Mother! How thankful to her for all her motherly care! But have we always been her faithful children? Alas! how few there are who regard the Blessed Virgin Mary as their real Mother! How few who would even call her "Mother"! Have we not been toward her as children who have strayed away from their parents?

Let, then, the old relationship be re-established and confirmed this day! Let us return to her in grief — yet in confidence — and give ourselves to her anew as her children — and remain so for the rest of our lives. Let this be the crowning act of this evening's solemnity. Let the priests of the sanctuary take the lead in coming to the altar of the Virgin Mother, so beautifully decorated with your pious gifts. Yes, let us kneel there at the feet of our Mother, and implore her to forget our past ingratitude, and to receive us again as her devoted children. Let the heavens be witness of our solemn consecration. Yes, O ye blessed spirits of heaven! come and assist at this beautiful spectacle, and pray for us, that from this moment we may always be the truly devoted children of your Queen and our most loving Mother, the ever Blessed Virgin Mary!

## INVITATION TO THE ACT

The solemn moment has arrived when you will consecrate yourselves to the Blessed Virgin Mary as her children. All is ready. There are the priests kneeling at the altar. The angels of heaven are looking down upon you, anxious to see what you will do. "Behold your Mother!" There she is waiting to receive you. Are you ready for this consecration? If you are, *stand up*. So, then, you wish to have the Blessed Virgin Mary for your Mother? Remember, then, that you never again have the devil for your father by committing sin or by seeking the occasion of sin. Whenever you are tempted by him to sin again, quickly have recourse to your Mother, saying, "Mother, help me." Always call her by the sweet name of "Mother," and frequently place yourselves under her protection. If this is your will and determination, then, falling on your knees, repeat after me with a loud and distinct voice the words of the

## SOLEMN ACT OF CONSECRATION

O Immaculate Mother Mary! we, thy servants and children — moved by the thought of thy power and mercy — prostrate before thy altar — and in the presence of the whole court of heaven — return to thee, our most gracious advocate — and our most merciful Mother. We are indeed unworthy — on account of our sins — to call thee Mother — who art so pure and so holy; but thy love and thy mercy — are greater than our sins. And therefore with great confidence — we give ourselves to thy motherly care. We now solemnly consecrate ourselves to thee — as thy children forever.

We promise to love thee — and serve thee evermore — and also to induce others — to serve thee. We pray thee, O Blessed Mother — always to protect us, thy children — in all dangers of body and soul — all the days of our lives. Help us — that we may keep the good resolutions — which we have made — during this Mission. Do not let us offend again — thy divine Son Jesus. Assist us at the hour of death. Save us by thy powerful protection — that we may merit to be with thee in heaven — and with thee and all the celestial court — love, praise, and bless God forever. Amen.

## AFTER THE ACT OF CONSECRATION

You have now consecrated yourselves to the Blessed Virgin. Mary is your mother — you are again her loving children. Let it be so forever! But now give thanks to God and to the Blessed Virgin for this favor. Let the organ peal forth its harmonies, let the voices of the choir burst forth, let your hearts join in the hymn of praise, let Heaven repeat it. Let glory, praise, and thanks be given to God the Father, the Son, and the Holy Ghost, and to the ever-glorious Virgin Mary! Amen.

NOTE. — If children are to take part in this ceremony, the missionary, after making the introduction to the act of dedication for the people, performs that act for the children first. He introduces it in the following (or in a similar) manner:

"My dear Christians, in order that the offering of ourselves to our Blessed Mother may be the more agreeable to her, let innocence go before us and take the lead." — Then, turning to the children, he asks them to stand up and turn toward him. He tells them (changing the tone of his voice suitable for children) that they represent all the children of the parish and that they are to act in their stead. Then he asks them: "Now, my dear children, do you really desire to be the children of the Blessed Virgin Mary? — (Yes, Father!) And will you always remain the children of this good Mother! — (Yes, Father!) Well, then, turn toward the altar of the Blessed Virgin — raise your right hand toward her, and say with me:

"O sweet Mother Mary — receive us — and all the children of this parish as thy children, — protect us as a loving mother, — and lead us always, — on a sure way to thee in Heaven." (Then the children sit down.)

(Turning to the people.) "Now, are you ready to join this band of innocent children? — If so, kneel down, in order to make the offering of yourselves, by repeating aloud the words which I shall say for you."

There are various ways of making this act most effective, the choice of which must be left to the discretion of the missionary.

## ANOTHER SKETCH (*Condensed*)

TEXT: "Hail, Holy Queen, Mother of Mercy, our Hope, hail."

*I. Mary is our Queen* — as long as Christ is our King — "of whose kingdom there is no end." (Luke i. 33.) Mary's kingdom extends over the universe — over heaven and earth.

Over the Church *militant* she rules as a most powerful protectress — "terrible as an army set in array" (Cant. vi. 3); destroying all heresies; crushing the serpent's head lurking in secret societies; the terror of hell; ready to defend the least of her subjects — the moment she is asked.

Over the Church *triumphant* she presides as Queen of glory; surpassing all the heavenly hosts in splendor; uniting in herself the glory of all; and yet most lovingly communicating with the least and the last.

Who should not wish to be her subject?

*II. Mary is the Mother of Mercy.* — All the Fathers, the Saints of all ages, the Church in her Offices, Jesus Christ Himself, call her our *Mother* — not only in name, but in deed, with heart and soul. She has proved it millions of times. "The Mother of God is my Mother" — what encouragement!

But she is pre-eminently the *Mother of Mercy* — placed over men by God, that through her all may receive mercy, who deserve none from God.

Who should not delight in being her child?

*III. Mary is our Hope.* — "It is God's will that we receive everything through Mary." — St. Bern. — "In me is all hope of life and of virtue." — Eccli. xxiv. 25. Through her came the Redeemer — through her comes all the fruit of the redemption. Jesus came to us through Mary, through Mary we must come to Jesus.

Her last title is *"Mother of Perpetual Help"* — at all times, under all circumstances, in all cases — no exception, otherwise this title would be false. "Hope of the despairing" — St. John Dam. "Hope of malefactors." — St. Laur. Just. "Consolation of all in despair." — St. Ephr.

Now, if all hope is in her, then there is none without her. Therefore, confidence — constant recourse — dedication.

# X

# DELAY OF CONVERSION

After the Mission has progressed thus far, and before the next part begins, the slothful and dilatory should be warned against *delaying their conversion,* by showing them, in a fiery discourse, the terrible danger of never being reconciled to God, if they obstinately refuse to do penance during the Mission. The *object* of this sermon, therefore, is to show them the danger of neglecting their salvation, especially at a time when God makes it so easy for them. The missionary must most vividly depict the base ingratitude of careless people, and point out the dreadful consequences with which God ordinarily visits them sooner or later.

It would be well to relate one or two striking examples of those who neglected the Mission, and who were visibly and severely punished by God.

There is one punishment which nowadays befalls such obstinate sinners most frequently, and on which the preacher must dwell particularly, and that is *Spiritual Blindness* and *Obduracy of Heart.* This awful state of the soul may even form the sole subject of this sermon, especially in places in which grace has been abused to a great extent.

The best occasion for this sermon is the second Sunday of the Mission, either in the forenoon or in the evening, when those who have till then neglected to attend the Mission, are supposed to be present. It is to be directed not only to those who have till then neglected to attend, but also to others who, notwithstanding the powerful sermons already preached, remain obstinate in their perversity.

The whole tone of this discourse is that of stern severity and menace.

If, for want of time, this sermon cannot be preached, the missionaries must make up for it in the other sermons. An easy way of doing so is simply to make announcements to this effect; and also publicly to offer the Rosary for the wayward sinners above described, and to throw in one or the other threatening remark about them.

## Sketch

Text: "Delay not to be converted to the Lord, and defer it not from day to day; for his wrath shall come on a sudden, and in the time of vengeance he will destroy thee." — Eccli. v. 8, 9.

Exordium. — We have been laboring for the spiritual welfare of this congregation for an entire week. We have preached the most important truths. (Enumeration). Thus we have pointed out to the sinner the severity of God's justice, and His infinite mercy and compassion for the repenting sinner. Many have heeded the invitation: others have not. Not because they were prevented by sickness or other causes — but *for want of a good will.*

"Thou didst admonish them to return to Thy law, . . . and they withdrew the shoulder and hardened their neck and would not hear." — II Esdr. ix. 29.

To these alone I address myself to-day. Would to God that they would hearken to the words of my text: "Delay not . . ."

If not, then I say to them, in the words of our Lord:

"He that despiseth me and receiveth not my words, hath one that judgeth him." — John xii. 48.

God will judge and dispose of them either in *His mercy or in His justice.* In either case, the judgment will be terrible.

### I. How God Shows Mercy toward the Sinner that Despises His Mercy

The obdurate sinner is accustomed to say: "Oh! God is merciful." Perhaps He will be merciful toward you after all your obstinacy and hard-heartedness in resisting His grace. How?

"He that hath ears to hear, let him hear." — Matt. xi. 15.

*He will let you die in your sins, and cast your soul into the abyss of hell!!* You ask: "Is this mercy?" It is the *only way* in which God *can* show mercy to you, who treat all other mercy with contempt.

1. Because you are *positively unwilling* that God should be merciful to you in any other way. God cannot save you against your will. So far, God has made use of many, and the most efficacious, means to bring about your conversion, such as good inspirations, want, death in the family, sudden death of friends and acquaintances, wonderful preservation of your life, sermons, Jubilees, Missions. But all to no purpose.

"Jerusalem, Jerusalem, . . . how often would I have gathered thy children, as the bird doth her brood under her wings, but thou wouldst not." — Luke xiii. 34.

If such efficacious means of grace remain without effect, then not only God, but every man, must plainly see that your conversion is hopeless. Even now, when you could have come, you have refused; or you did come, but you have not been moved; or you went to confession, and it was a sacrilege. Tell me, in what way can God be merciful to you?

2. This Mission will pass away, and you will continue to *add sin to sin*. For each additional sin your torments in hell must be immensely increased forever. Is it not better that you should die now and receive the punishment due to you so far, than that you be allowed to live and incur, by your additional sins, tortures still further increased in number and severity in hell?

"God will render to every man according to his works." — Matt. xvi. 27.

Hence, the only mercy that God can show you is your immediate death and damnation.

"Behold, these three years I come seeking fruit on this fig-tree, and I find none. Cut it down, therefore. Why doth it take up the ground?" — Luke xiii. 7.

You have not only borne no fruit of good works, but you have committed sin — perhaps caused others to sin — for five, ten, twenty years. Some one, perhaps the Blessed Virgin or your guardian angel, may have asked for a stay of sentence in your behalf.

"Lord, let it alone this year also, until I dig about it, . . . and if happily it bear fruit; but if not, . . . then thou shalt cut it down." — Ib. 8, 9.

Who knows but God wished to have patience until this Mission, which was expected? For this reason you were spared. If it should turn out that this most efficacious grace has been given to you in vain —then we must fear that God, Whom you call so merciful, will show you mercy in the manner described.

3. Examples prove it. Very often one or more such obstinate sinners die suddenly during or shortly after the Mission. (Relate one or two.)

Sinner! it is hard for me to tell you all this; but behold, it is the command of the Most High.

"If, when I say to the wicked: Thou shalt surely die, thou declare it not to him, nor speak to him, that he may be converted from his wicked way and live, the same wicked man shall die in his iniquity; but I shall require his blood at thy hand. — But if thou give warning to the wicked, and he be not converted from his wickedness and from his evil way, he indeed shall die in his iniquity; but thou hast delivered thy soul." — Ez. iii. 18, 19.

I call this whole congregation to witness that I have warned you. Now, see you to the rest!

But very frequently God does not show even this mercy toward the obstinate sinner. And now hear —

II. How God Deals in his Justice with those
who Fear Not His Justice —

1. God has given to man *perfect freedom,* to believe
or not, to do good or evil. . . . He will not interfere
with his liberty, although he constantly abuse it in
opposition to God.  He will *not remove from him His
creatures,* which, for his base purposes he turns against
their Creator.  He will not interfere with him, although by his scandalous conduct he cause the ruin
of so many souls.  Justice will be done him!

2. God will *not shorten his life,* but will give him
every minute that He has decreed for him.  And this,
even though he boast of it.

"How mighty am I? and who shall bring me under for my
deeds? . . . I have sinned, and what harm hath befallen me?" —
Eccli. v. 3, 4.

Some may not be able to comprehend why the
obstinate sinner is allowed to live.  People may pray
for his death; but he will not die before his full time
is up.

"Let both [the cockle and the wheat] grow until the harvest."
— Matt. xiii. 30.

Justice will be done him.

3. The sinner may occasionally do a little good in
the natural order; he may be kind-hearted — generous — benevolent.  For this God will reward him
with earthly prosperity — honors and distinctions
among his fellow-citizens.

People may be astonished at it, and say:

"Why do the wicked live, are they advanced and strengthened
with riches? — Their houses are secure and peaceable, and the rod
of God is not upon them . . ." — Job xxi. 7–12.

4. Justice will be done the sinner.

He will live to an old age — heaping sin upon sin — crime upon crime. His mind is obscured and his heart is hardened. And finally he will die.

"A hard heart shall fear evil at the last." — Eccli. iii. 27. — "They spend their days in wealth, and in a moment they go down to hell." — Job xxi. 13.

And then, *what shall be his hell?*

"Give to them according to their works, and according to the wickedness of their inventions." — Ps. xxvii. 4.

Justice will be done him forever!

I hear the sinner say: "Ah! Father, this saying is hard, and who can hear it? Listen to us, hear us!" Yes, sinner, I will let you speak. "Tell if thou hast anything to justify thyself!" — Is. xliii. 26.

## III. Excuses which the Sinner Alleges for Delaying his Conversion

*"I mean to change my life before I die, but not now."*

My friend, that means *never*. Will God give you *time?* You are not sure of the next hour. Will He give you *grace?*

"Be not deceived, God is not mocked!" — Gal. vi. 7.

You have to be converted when God wants it — and not at your own convenience. Besides, "not now" means a continuance in sin; it is a positive resistance to the Holy Ghost — and sins committed against the Holy Ghost "shall not be forgiven" (Luke xii. 10).

*"I cannot now give up those ill-gotten goods — break off that sinful friendship — forgive my enemies — leave that secret society."*

Fool! Death will come, and you will leave this world without a penny. Death will tear you away

from that man or woman, but your hatred will not
be taken from you. Neither will you be disconnected
from that society, every member of which you will
most likely find with you in hell.

*"But oh! that hateful confession!"*

Will you, then, never make it? You will indeed
make it not only on Judgment-day, but in a few days;
not to the missionary, but to the entire parish. All will
know that there must be something very serious the
matter with you, because all came to the Mission except yourself and a few others. Every one will ask,
"What kept him from making the Mission?"

*"What do I care for the Mission — the Church? I
do not believe in such stuff."*

Now we have it. But hear what the Holy Ghost
says about you:

"These men blaspheme whatsoever things they know not: and
what things soever they naturally know, like dumb beasts, *in these
they are corrupted*. . . . They are raging waves of the sea, foaming
out their own confusion." — Jude 10, 13.

Rest assured there will be a speedy end to your
pride.

"Hitherto thou shalt come and shalt go no further; and here
thou shalt break thy swelling waves." — Job xxxviii. 11.

My friend, there will be an end to your boasted
influence in the world — to your blasphemies; and
then will you cast yourself in shame and confusion
into the abyss of hell, "whence the smoke of your
torments shall rise forever and ever" (Apoc. xiv. 11).

Conclusion. — Such, then, will be the judgment
which God will pass on those who remain deaf to the
warning of His voice, whether He deal with them in
His *mercy* or His *justice*. In either case, their end
will be terrible. O sinners! let me warn you then.

Do not go away as hardened as you came. Repent of your many sins. Call on the ministry of the Church to exercise its beneficent influence over you. But do it soon, lest, if you delay, it may be too late. "Delay not." . . . Text.

# XI

# DRUNKENNESS

After the conversion of the people has been effected by the most powerful motives of fear and love, the whole force of the Mission must be brought to bear on the future, so as to promote perseverance.

It is to be seen, then, whether there are not certain prevailing vices against which the people must be warned. In a great many places in this country dwells the demon of drunkenness, causing immense moral devastation. The Mission must from the very outset declare war against it, and attack it in all its strongholds. Almost every sermon must denounce it. But at this stage of the Mission a special and a most powerful sermon must be given on this vice.

This sermon is not to be a mere temperance lecture, but a Mission-sermon. The utter spiritual ruin caused by this vice to the drunkard and others should be dwelt upon in particular, not the temporal losses and the poverty of the family, which are its consequences. Nor is it sufficient to denounce drunkenness only in so far as it is a mortal sin; drinking to excess in every shape must be proscribed. Perhaps it would be better to use the word *Intemperance* instead of *Drunkenness.* — Finally, the preacher must by no means forget those who are the main cause of this vice — the liquor-dealers — showing them that they will have to account for the fearful extent of the vice of drunkenness.

Let the preacher be unsparing in his language against this vice and its causes, but at the same time very considerate in speaking of persons. Otherwise, he will only arouse their hatred against him; he will never convert them. Let him bear this in mind, particularly in speaking of liquor-dealers, saloon-keepers. An honorable exception should always be made in favor of such as never tolerate excessive drinking in their houses; but their number is exceedingly small.

After this vice has been exhibited in all its hideousness, the means which the people must use to keep from it for the future, must be proposed. Should the pledge be given to the whole congregation? For nineteen hundred years the Church has never spoken of the pledge; she has not adopted it as yet; although there is a strong movement in favor of it. Nor is it likely that she will adopt it in the future. She has other means against drunkenness that have been instituted by God. Experience shows that such wholesale pledgings or similar sweeping prohibitions produce no good, unless they are limited to a certain time. The reason is, so very few keep the pledge. The pledge is even the cause of evil, because those who break their promise believe themselves guilty of great sin the first time they take a drink. Missionaries should not exaggerate, and should, therefore, not exact more than the law of God obliges us to. Nor is it at all necessary for a man who has the fear of God in his heart, to be restrained from evil-doing by any other moral force than the strict commandment of God, issued under the threat of eternal damnation. With this commandment before him, let a man regulate his conduct under all circumstances. If the least touch of liquor will be for him the cause of drunkenness, let him abstain from it entirely; if not, let him take liquor when he needs it, and no more than he needs, and under such circumstances as will enable him to keep himself from the danger of taking too much. Frequent resolutions, repeated every morning, prayer and the sacraments, will furnish him with the necessary strength to observe this rule of life.

The same rule holds good with reference to saloon-keepers. No government-regulations or police-laws, or high license, or heavy fines will effect a reform in this business; but the fear of God and of His judgments must take possession of the man who keeps the liquor-shop, or the saloon. The fear of God will render his business harmless; and to inspire this fear is the aim and purpose of the Mission.

Temperance, or total-abstinence societies do a certain amount of good; the missionaries may promote them, but their principal efforts should be directed to what has just been urged.

NOTE. — When the sermons on *Drunkenness* and *Impurity* are preceded by the sermon on *Delay of Conversion,* the logical connection between them is, that for many the cause of delaying their conversion is that they are addicted to the vice of drunkenness, or impurity, or both.

Even when the sermon on *Delay* is omitted, this idea may be embodied in the exordium.

## SKETCH

TEXT: "Be not deceived, drunkards shall not possess the kingdom of God." — I Cor. vi. 9, 10.

EXORDIUM. — Effects of the Mission, through the many sermons and exhortations, briefly enumerated.

Now, it becomes necessary that you "decline from evil and do good" (Ps. xxxvi. 27) — *i.e.,* keep away from the broad road to hell, and walk in the narrow path to heaven. The two principal roads to hell are *Infidelity* and *Sensuality.* The latter is the one on which most of those Catholics walk who go to their final destruction. It divides into two branches, *Drunkenness* and *Impurity.* Of the former I shall speak to-day. Though one of the most abominable, degrading, destructive of vices, drunkenness is by no means sufficiently detested, and much less guarded against. Let us, then, seriously reflect on its *disastrous consequences.*

## I. Intemperance, the Ruin of the Individual

Food and drink are created by God for the benefit of the body. A certain quantity of each is necessary for the preservation of life. A quantity not exceeding the demands of nature is useful; whatsoever is beyond that does harm rather than good.

"By surfeiting many have perished." — Eccli. xxxvii. 34.

The danger that arises from the unnecessary use of drink is much greater. *Pure wine,* used in moderate quantities, is most beneficial to the human system; yet it is not necessary except in some cases. The excessive use of this beverage does immense harm; and, therefore, the Scriptures warn us against it so emphatically.

"Wine hath destroyed many." — Eccli. xxxi. 30.

*Distilled liquors* are a mere medicine, and must become most injurious as soon as they are used unnecessarily. Whatever little quantity exceeds the actual demand of nature, especially if repeatedly taken, ruins the human system.

*Fabricated liquors* must never be used, as they are deadly poison. And what else are our ordinary liquors?

From this we may judge what harm the man does to his body who frequently and unnecessarily imbibes spirituous liquors, although not to intoxication.

The rule in regard to the use of *wine* should be: *Only when necessary or useful.* As to spirituous liquors: *Never except when necessary.* To overstep this rule is to approach the proximate danger of drunkenness.

But what about him who repeatedly becomes drunk, either on liquors or other strong drinks?

1. He completely disables himself by *ruining his health.* His blood is infected with the strong beverage, and thus all kinds of diseases are engendered.

"Whose constitution is so strong that it can resist so many evils that drunkenness brings on? Who can preserve a body soaked with wine [whiskey], that it will not approach dissolution and become the prey of all diseases?" — St. Basil. "Do you not perceive that, in consequence of immoderate drinking, countless kinds of diseases are contracted? Whence is that abundance of corrupted humors? Whence so much sickness? Does it not arise from intemperance and from immoderate drinking of wine [whiskey]? — St. Laur. Just.

2. The drunkard *commits suicide,* by thus shortening his life. Death must come, perhaps slowly, but surely (Eccli. xxxi and xxxvii, as above). Experience. Many die very suddenly in the state of intoxication.

But, short though the life of the drunkard must be, it is a most miserable and burdensome life to himself and others.

3 The drunkard ruins *his soul* as regards its *natural faculties.* The effects of drunkenness upon the mind are the same as those upon the body. The mem-

bers of the body of the drunkard, when in a state
of intoxication, are paralyzed; so are his mental faculties.   And as the body becomes perfectly useless by
repeated intoxication, so too does the mind.  The
drunkard is useless to himself, to his family; he is
altogether disabled for his ordinary duties — the power
of his mind is impaired — is finally completely lost —
and his home is the mad-house.

4. Much worse are the effects of liquor on the
*moral faculties* of the soul, which thereby are rendered
unfit for the supernatural.  All taste for spiritual
things is lost; faith is obscured; the fear of God, hell,
and eternity disappears; the *lower instincts* of nature
gain the ascendency, and being brought to a more intense degree of excitement by means of strong drinks,
they carry the soul into all sorts of sin and vice.  The
drunkard neglects his *Christian duties* — Mass, prayer,
Confession, Communion; he is guilty of *injustice*
against himself and his family, by squandering the
money given him by Providence; he steals — to obtain
money for drink; his *conduct* becomes *immodest;* he
becomes guilty of impurities of every shape and form,
of *blasphemy* against God and religion, of *murder.*

"Wherever there is drunkenness, there is the devil." — St. Jerome.
"Intoxicating drinks are the poison of the devil." — St. Augustine.
"He that is given to drunkenness is no man: he does not commit
sin, but is sin itself." — Peter of Ravenna.  "Drunkenness deceives him whom Sodom could not deceive." — Origen.

The drunkard often acknowledges this himself.
Not knowing how to account otherwise for his crimes,
he says: "It is whiskey that has made me do all this."

5. A real drunkard is seldom *converted.*  All courage and determination fail him; his nature, thoroughly
infected with liquor, constantly longs for it again.
Fervent and humble prayer would help him.  Of this

he is utterly incapable. Many have tried Confession. They fell back on the day they received absolution.

"Drunkenness is, as it were, the abyss of hell. It keeps back with all force those that have fallen into it. It never more allows them to return to the light of sobriety from the dark abyss into which they have fallen." — St. Augustine. "Many are cured from the effects of the poison of other sins: no one is cured from drunkenness: and this is the reason why wine is compared, not to every kind of poison, but to the poison of dragons, which is incurable (Deut. xxxii. 33)." — St. Ambrose.

We may, then, sum up all that has been said thus far in the words of the text. "Be not deceived. . . ."

## II. Intemperance is the Ruin of the Family of the Drunkard, and an Injury and Disgrace to Society

A. The consequences of intemperance are first of all felt by *his own family*.

1. The drunkard *impoverishes* his family. He throws away for drink the *money* which God has placed in his hands for the support of his wife and children. Not unfrequently he sells or pawns the *property* of the house. He neglects to work for them.

2. The drunkard robs his family of domestic *peace* and *happiness*. What is a drunken husband or father? Description. And this is the man who, when he married, contracted the special obligation of procuring the happiness of his family.

3. He neglects the *spiritual* and *temporal education* of his children. A drunken father cares not whether his children learn and practise their religion, or grow up wild. He cares not whether they learn a trade or art by which they may become useful members of society and earn their living, or not. He brings up a set of vagabonds, who will, as soon as they can

manage to earn a living for themselves, abandon their miserable home — becoming perhaps worse than their own father — a burden to human society.

4. His wicked example induces the children to lead the *same wicked life.* And inasmuch as they have been brought up without any religious principle, they may be expected to give themselves up recklessly to every sin and vice.

5. His wife, unable to practise her religion, and finding no happiness in her desolate home, will finally *give herself up to despair;* will not care to rear a drunkard's children; will give herself up to the same vice; and may in the end possibly be driven to follow a shameful life — simply, perhaps, to make a living.

It is to be feared that the entire family of the drunkard, after dragging themselves through a most miserable existence on earth, will finally find themselves in the torments of hell.

B. The consequences of drunkenness are next felt by *society at large.*

1. In proportion as the drunkard becomes useless, or, rather, burdensome to himself and family, he becomes the same to society at large.

By his immoderate drinking he deprives himself of that which distinguishes him from the beast — *reason* — and becomes *like one,* or, rather, *sinks below the beast.* For all the domestic and wild animals can glory over him that they have never been seen drunk. Besides, an animal retains the use of its limbs and the acuteness of its natural instincts, and is useful for what it is destined. But the drunkard, with the loss of reason, has lost also the use of his limbs and senses, and all control over his natural propensities. He is not only useless, he is a burden to society — a danger to the life of others as well as to public morality —

and he ought to be chained down and shut up in a mad-house.

2. He becomes the *father* of a number of degraded *children* — who from their mother's womb are infected with disease — weak-minded — often idiots; who are either thrown upon the world as a burden, or, what is worse, become in their turn the progenitors of families worse than themselves. Thus one drunkard may be the origin of an entire generation of degraded, immoral human beings — that are a pest to the world.

3. The drunkard is a *disgrace to the Church of God* — as well as the cause of an immense loss to it. Continually is the Church blamed for so many drunkards who belong to it. The Church is despised on account of them. Non-Catholics, on their account, refuse to enter its communion. And while we can give the lie to the infidel world for its slanders against the Church, we cannot deny the fact that many Catholics are drunkards, although the conclusions drawn from it are most illogical.

What harm, then, does the vice of drunkenness bring upon the individual — the family — society! But, alas! what guilt rests upon *those who are the cause* of so much drunkenness; those who lead others into liquor-shops; who have the abominable practice of treating; and, above all, upon those who make a living by selling liquor to drunkards! What awful responsibility rests upon them all, but especially the last-mentioned, it is impossible to describe.

"It were better for him [and for the world] that a millstone should be hanged about his neck, and that he should be drowned in the depth of the sea." — Matt. xviii. 6.

### III.   Remedies against Intemperance

It is of hardly any use to prescribe remedies for the *regular drunkard*.   Over such we can only weep as we weep over the dead whom we cannot raise to life, no matter what we do for them.

But for those who are *not yet regular drunkards,* or who are *not at all given to drinking liquor,* we have a remedy that will surely cure them, or will preserve them from this terrible disease.

Is it the temperance, or total-abstinence pledge? This may be useful, but by itself it is insufficient, because it is devoid of supernatural power.

The total-abstinence pledge is a great help for keeping people out of the proximate occasion of sin.   If it is joined to frequent and fervent prayer and the regular reception of the sacraments, it will do a vast amount of good; otherwise not.

To keep sober — 1. *Avoid the causes* of drunkenness.

*a.* Keep away from the *society* of those who are given to this bad habit.

"Be not in the feasts of great drinkers." — Prov. xxiii. 20. — "I have written to you not to keep company.  If any man that is called a brother, be a  . . . drunkard, with such an one not so much as to eat." — I Cor. v. 11.

*b.* Do not *treat* any one, nor join those who *treat.*

"Challenge not them that love wine." — Eccli. xxxi. 30.

*c.* Stay away from *liquor-shops*.  Do not yield to *human respect,* when you are assailed by others as given to singularity, because you do not drink liquor; nor to *pride,* so as to show that you can drink like others — have money — possess a certain degree of generosity. Do not let yourself be carried away by *your grief* and mortification on account of disappointment — failing in business — family trouble, etc.

*d.* Flee from *idleness* and the company of idlers.

"For idleness hath taught much evil." — Eccli. xxxiii. 29.

*e.* Make use of intoxicating liquors as sparingly as you use *medicine.* Never use any but *genuine liquor* — and *not even that,* although in the smallest quantity, if you have been a habitual drunkard in the past.

2. *Practise holy prayer.* If you have been in the habit of drinking, say one *Pater* and *Ave* every morning to Jesus crucified, with a firm promise to keep from every drop of intoxicating drink that day.

3. *Receive the sacraments* every month — at least every three months; and, for this purpose, join a pious association or a temperance society, the members of which follow this holy practice as a rule.

CONCLUSION. — Recapitulation.

Let me, then, warn you against this terrible and most disastrous vice. To the drunkard I say: pray, if you can; get others to pray for you, that you may understand the greatness of your sin — and that after a good and contrite confession you may again return to a state of sobriety — and carefully employ the means to preserve yourself therein. To those who use liquors beyond necessity, I say: give up this practice before it is too late. To all I say: be sober and watch against the deceits of "the devil, who goes about seeking whom he may devour" [drag into this vice] (I Pet. v. 8).

Oh! may Jesus on the Cross, Who suffered an excessive thirst for our salvation, grant you all the grace of mortifying your palate! For the love of your dying Saviour deny yourselves every drop that may gradually lead you into the fathomless abyss of this sin. May your dear Mother Mary obtain for you this favor, and may you, under her protection, persevere unto the end as sober and fervent Christians! Amen.

# XII

# IMPURITY

The *object* of this sermon is to give a supreme disgust and abhorrence of this vice to a certain class of people, among whom it is not only prevalent to a great extent, but also loved and defended by them, or where the *public conscience* is no longer opposed to it. It should be preached, therefore, only in places where both these perverse dispositions are found together. In other places, it is more advisable to speak of it only when the occasion presents itself in other sermons.

This sermon is to be preached with the utmost precaution. The missionary's horror and disgust for this sin must show itself throughout the sermon. Otherwise, he will tarnish his own reputation and that of his fellow-laborers, and instead of doing good he will only do harm. — The Rule in speaking about this sermon says: *"Cautissimi sint ac castissimi, et memores verborum S. Patris nostri ad confessarios, quod malint in hac re obscuriores esse quam dilucidiores."* [1]

*"When speaking of the sixth commandment,"* says St. Alphonsus, *"we should avoid scandalizing the innocent by awakening their curiosity in regard to the evil of which they are ignorant."* [2]

To this adds Father Sarnelli, C.SS.R.: *"In speaking of this sin, the preacher must put on the wisdom of the serpent and the simplicity of the dove. He should detest this vice in general expressions, but never go into particulars about species and circumstances."* [3] And let it be remarked here, that, according to several authors, the times of St. Alphonsus were more corrupt than ours.

The entire strength of this sermon lies not in the vigor of its delivery, but exclusively in the power of the arguments. A weak voice may produce more effect than a powerful denunciation of the impure. There is no definition, exposition, or explanation to be given of this subject, or of the various species of this sin. Whatsoever the people do not know in reference to this vice they need not and should not *learn* from the missionary.

A considerable part of this sermon must be devoted to the enumeration of the remedies against this vice, which are the same as

[1] R., n. 56.  [2] *Exercises,* C. E., Vol. XV. p. 176.
[3] Note, n. 3, ib.

241

the means of perseverance in general. Owing to special dangers in
certain places, however, some special remedies may be needed,
and these should not be forgotten.

In some places, it may be necessary to preach on drunkenness and
on impurity, when there is not sufficient time for each separately.
In that case, both subjects should be united in one discourse. There
are three ways of doing this: 1. Let the introduction be on the two
main branches of sensuality — drunkenness and impurity. Then,
let the first part be on drunkenness; the second, on impurity, —
employing only the most forcible arguments for each; the third part
will dwell on the remedies against both, some of which are applicable
to both, others to each in particular. — 2. With the same introduction, let the preacher dwell a little while on the subject of
impurity, express, in two or three sentences, his abhorrence of it,
and then dismiss it in disgust, as being too abominable to be treated
before a Christian audience, and to be left to the awful revelations
of Judgment-day. — 3. Let the whole sermon be directed against
both vices, by showing: the abomination of both; their damaging
consequences; and the remedies for their cure.

## Sketch

Text: "Fornication and all uncleanliness, let it not so much as be
    named among you, as becometh saints." — Eph. v. 3.

Exordium. — O great and merciful God! what a
fearful sight reveals itself before me to-day! How
abominable! How disgusting! I see thousands and
thousands of human beings, the very image and likeness of the Eternal God, plunged in a pool of filth
and corruption, carried off into the dark abyss of
hell! Are they heathens — unbelievers — men of no
religion? No! they are Christians — men and women,
children of God through baptism, bearing the mark
and seal of the sacred name of Jesus Christ on their
souls. Were it not for that, never could I open my
lips to speak against a vice that should not be even
so much as "named among Christians." But how
can I allow so many beautiful souls to go to destruction
without giving them at least a warning, without doing
my best to inspire them with a true abhorrence of an

abomination which they seem to love so much? Oh! may the Holy Ghost guide my tongue this day! May the ever-immaculate Virgin Mary assist me, that I may succeed in giving you such a disgust for all sins of the flesh — in thought — word — or deed — that you may keep yourselves free from their contamination forever!

### I. ABOMINATION OF THE SIN OF IMPURITY

How beautiful is the virtue of holy chastity!

"Oh! how beautiful is the chaste generation with glory; for the memory thereof is immortal, because it is known both with God and with men." — Wis. iv. 1.

In the same proportion, the vice opposed to this virtue is detested by God and by men.

1. It is held *in abomination by God,* and, consequently, most severely punished.

*a.* The principal reason is, because the human soul, being so intimately related to God as to be *His own image and likeness* (Gen. i. 26), so far forgets itself as to plunge itself, by this sin, into the filthy mire of the most disgusting abomination, despite all warning and threatening on the part of God. Compare the soul acting thus with the daughter of a king, who, after having cast herself into a disgusting cesspool, although attired in the most costly garments, appears before the king and his court covered with filth.

"Man, when he was in honor, did not understand; he hath been compared to senseless beasts and made like to them." — Ps. xlviii. 21. — "The man that sins by pride and ambition, sins as an angel; he that sins by avarice and covetousness, sins like man; but he that sins by impurity, sins as the beast; and, making a beast out of himself, he deprives himself of that light of soul which distinguishes him from irrational creatures." — St. Bernard.

*b.* Again, God detests sins of the flesh so much because the human flesh has been placed in so intimate a relation with God through the *Incarnation* and the *Ascension* of Jesus Christ, by which human nature, and especially the human body, has been placed at the *right hand of the Eternal Father*. The bodies of Christians form one mystical body with the body of Christ. Through the operation of these mysteries, the human body of every Christian has been so elevated in dignity as to become the *living temple of the Holy Ghost*.

"Know you not that your bodies are the members of Christ? Shall I, then take the members of Christ and make them the members of a harlot?" — I Cor. vi. 15 — or disgrace them by other secret abominations? — "Or know you not that your members are the temple of the Holy Ghost, who is in you, whom you have from God, and you are not your own." — Ib. 19.

What a profanation! what a desecration!

*c*. Therefore, the *severe punishment* of sins of the flesh. This came upon the guilty in a terrible manner in the Old Law — visibly, because those people were of a rude and sensual disposition.

In Numbers xxv it is related that some of the higher classes of the people made themselves guilty of this sin. God spoke to Moses:

"Take all the princes of the people and hang them up on gibbets against the sun, that *my fury* may be turned from Israel." — Ib. 4. "And there were slain four-and-twenty thousand men." — Ib. 9.

Sodom and Gomorrha, with the neighboring country, "with all their inhabitants, and all things that spring from the earth, were destroyed with fire and brimstone," so that nothing was seen "but the ashes rising from the earth as the smoke of a furnace" (Gen. xix. 24–28).

When the entire human race "had corrupted its way upon the earth," God was so grieved over it that

He repented of having created man, and decreed a universal destruction.

"I will destroy man whom I have created from the face of the earth, from man even to beasts, from the creeping thing even to the fowls of the air." — Gen. vi. 7.

Noah alone, with his family, was saved. But the ark was to be closed from the outside (Gen. vii. 16), so that he could not admit any one. Then it rained in torrents for forty days and forty nights without intermission — the waters rose fifteen yards over the highest mountains, and remained one hundred and fifty days, so that not a living being outside of the ark could possibly survive.

Such is the detestation that God has for the sin which you count as a simple human weakness, or a necessity of human nature. How could God detest and punish so dreadfully what is according to human nature which He has created?

*d*. In the New Law similar punishments have been inflicted. Call to mind the terrible destruction of the two cities of Pompeii and Herculaneum, which on November 20, 79, were buried under the burning ashes of brimstone that poured down upon them, covering the former twenty and the latter seventy to one hundred feet deep. The former is now dug out again, while over the latter another city has been built. Many other punishments have befallen the impure. But the New Law is not much older than the Old Law was, when the world was destroyed by *water*. How much longer will it be, before the world shall be destroyed by *fire?*

2. The sin of impurity is *held in abomination by men* of all classes, even by the very sinners who are guilty of it.

*a*. Human nature feels itself degraded under the

guilt of this sin. Hence it is so extremely hard to declare it in *confession*. To mention the species of sin is almost an impossibility to many, and some rather risk eternal salvation than confess it as it is, with its number and circumstances.

*b*. People, including the most impure, prefer to hear any other subject mentioned from *the pulpit* than the one that we are now considering. Everybody feels ashamed when this sin is mentioned. Such is not the case in regard to any other crime, no matter how abominable.

*c*. After having violated her, Amnon hated *Thamar*, more than he loved her before, and he commanded his servants, saying:

"Thrust this woman out from me, and shut the door after her."
— II Kings xiii. 17.

So, likewise, there is no true love, but *mere contempt* for each other, between those who are cognizant of their mutual crimes, even though they be married. Jehu had the lascivious *Jezabel*, who tried to captivate him by her personal charms, thrown from the window into the street, where the dogs devoured her body, leaving nothing but her skull and her hands and feet, so that the passers-by asked: "Is this that same Jezabel?" — IV Kings ix. 37.

*d*. The ancient pagan *Saxons* had so great an abhorrence of this sin, that when a young woman made herself guilty of it, she was forced to strangle herself. Then her body was burned and her seducer hanged near the fire (Berc. *History of the Church*).

The *Emperor Aurelian* had a soldier whom he discovered committing this sin, tied to two trees bent together, and rent into pieces by letting them spring back into their natural position.

So much to show the abomination of impurity on the

part of those who are impure themselves and who might be supposed to care very little about holy purity. I need not adduce the testimony of those who lead lives of sanctity to show the abhorrence in which this vice is held by them.

## II. TERRIBLE DAMAGES CAUSED BY IMPURITY TO THE SOULS OF THE UNCHASTE

Leaving the terrible diseases which this vice brings upon the body to those physicians who profess it as their "specialty" to cure them, let us consider the disease contracted by the soul through this sin.

1. In most cases it is *incurable*. As to virginity lost, there can be no question. That once lost is lost forever. But even the pardon of this sin cannot be obtained, except by means of an extraordinary grace, owing to the want of the necessary dispositions in the penitent.

*a.* The impure soul will not *see* nor *acknowledge* the grievousness of its sin.

"Fornication . . . takes away the understanding." — Os. iv. 11. — "One of the first results of impurity is blindness of spirit." — St. Gregory.

*b.* Consequently, the soul will not *detest* this sin as it should, in order to be pardoned, though it may be ashamed of it.

"I bewail many of them that sinned before, and have not done penance for the uncleanness, and fornication, and lasciviousness they have committed." — II Cor. xii. 21.

*c.* Again, the soul will be wanting in a *firm determination* of avoiding this sin, as well as the occasions that lead to it.

"They will not set their thoughts to return to their God, for the spirit of fornication is in the midst of them." — Os. v. 4.

A habit of this sin produces a hardness of heart that the most extraordinary grace cannot soften. Only look at our young people whom even the Mission cannot bring to repentance, and you have a proof of it.

*d. Confession* is almost impossible, or is possible only in general terms, without number and circumstances.

The greatest number of *sacrilegious confessions* are made on account of this sin.  Sacrilege follows sacrilege, or the *Sacraments* are completely *abandoned.* The sin is continued *without intermission,* in one way or another, up to old age.

"A young man according to his way, even when he is old he will not depart from it." — Prov. xxii. 6.

*e.* He will take these sins with him *into the grave.*

"His bones shall be filled with the vices of his youth, and they shall sleep with him in the dust." — Job xx. 11.

2. This vice *festers frightfully,* it undermines all the powers of the soul, and brings it to a state of *utter spiritual corruption.*

*a.* It takes away all light and understanding.

"The sensual (*animalis*) man perceiveth not the things that are of the Spirit of God, for it is *foolishness* to him, and he *cannot understand.*" — I Cor. ii. 14.

*b.* The Spirit of God cannot dwell in the impure.

"My spirit shall not remain in man, because he is flesh." — Gen. vi. 3. — God leaves them "to shameful affections — gives them up to the desires of their heart, — to uncleanness, to dishonor their own bodies among themselves — they change the truth of God into a lie, and worship and serve the creature rather than the Creator." — Rom. i. 24–26.

*c.* The impure lose their respect for the *other commandments;* they fall into every other sin, even murder and infidelity.  David — Solomon.

Thus the impure soul will live on until it leaves that disgusting lump of flesh and casts itself into the lowest abyss of hell.

"Among a hundred reprobates are ninety-nine who are lost for impurity, and the other one is not quite free from it." — St. Jerome.

3. A most terrible result of this vice is the *ruin of others*. It is like a contagious epidemic that spreads everywhere.

No one can associate with the impure without great danger of being infected by their vice; it spreads like a pestilential disease.

*Empires* have been corrupted and destroyed on account of their impure rulers, such as Chaldæa, Assyria, Persia, Greece, Rome, etc.

*Nations* have been *torn from the Church* on account of it. Germany through Luther — Switzerland through Calvin — England through Henry VIII — Scotland through John Knox, etc.

But what need is there for me to denounce this vice? The verdict has already been pronounced by the two great Apostles, St. Peter and St. Paul.

The verdict of St. Peter is couched in the following words:

"These men, as irrational beasts, shall perish in their corruption. Having eyes full of adultery and of never ceasing sin; alluring unstable souls, having their hearts exercised with covetousness, children of malediction." — II Pet. ii. 12–14.

That of St. Paul is equally severe:

"Be not deceived; neither fornicators, nor idolaters, nor adulterers, nor the effeminate, nor Sodomites . . . shall possess the kingdom of heaven." — I Cor. vi. 9.

Let no one, therefore, deceive himself, but carefully shun this crime in thought, word, and deed. To do so, it is absolutely necessary to employ the

### III. Remedies against Impurity

1. The reason why there is so much impurity in the world at present lies in the numerous causes, now existing, that lead to this vice. These must be carefully avoided.

"Take flight, if you do not wish to perish." — St. Aug.

Such dangers are light literature — improper pictures — indelicate conversation — the stage in general — gymnastic performances in circuses — dressing regardless of modesty — familiarities between young persons of both sexes — close acquaintance with persons of the other sex without lawful excuse — lonely walks and interviews — frequent visits to such persons without a legitimate purpose — want of proper watchfulness over the senses of the body and the affections of the heart, etc.

"Look not around about thee in the ways of the city, nor wander up and down in the streets thereof. Turn away thy face from a woman dressed up, and gaze not about upon another's beauty. For many have perished by the beauty of a woman, and hereby lust is enkindled as a fire." — Eccli. ix. 7–9. — "Behold not everybody's beauty, and tarry not among women." — Ib. xlii. 12.

Modern civilization, it is true, has done away with these principles as superfluous in an enlightened age. The result is obvious.

2. The positive means to be employed are:

*a.* Fervent *prayer* at all times, especially in temptations against the virtue of holy purity. An invocation of the holy names of Jesus and Mary from the heart is sufficient to put the demon of impurity to flight and to render the emotions of man's sinful nature powerless.

"As I knew that I could not otherwise be continent, except God gave it, . . . I went to the Lord, and besought him for it with my whole heart." — Wis. viii. 21.

Happy he who is convinced of this. Temptations will not cease, but they will not overcome him, because God is with him.

"If God be for us, who is against us?" — Rom. viii. 31. — "I thrice besought the Lord that the sting of my flesh might depart from me. And he said to me: My grace is sufficient for thee; for power is made perfect in infirmity." — II Cor. xii. 8, 9.

*b.* Constant, useful *occupation* of the mind, so as to leave no room for thoughts and imaginations of an impure nature to enter, and uninterrupted subjection of the body under the superiority of reason, by a certain degree of mortification (of immoderate nourishment, sensual indulgence, sleep, etc.).

"Behold, this was the iniquity of Sodom, fulness of bread and abundance, and the idleness of her and her daughters." — Ez. xvi. 49. — "While men were asleep the enemy came and oversowed cockle among the wheat." — Matt. xiii. 25.

*c.* The frequent use of the Sacraments of *Penance* and the *Blessed Eucharist;* carefully confessing the slightest sin committed against the proper vigilance over one's self, and receiving Holy Communion with a devout preparation and thanksgiving. Constant union of the flesh of man with the purest flesh and blood of Jesus Christ produces holy purity. This Sacrament is —

"The corn of the elect and the wine springing forth virgins." — Zach. ix. 17. — "As I live by the Father, so he that eateth me the same also shall live by me." — John vi. 58.

CONCLUSION. — Recapitulation.

Such, then, is the horrible vice that undermines our modern society; really the "social evil" — or *the* evil of society, and its ruin. Flee from it — Christians, flee from it! Pray that you may always have a true horror of it, and of those things which must lead to it. Thank God if you have not as yet been contaminated by it, but by no means believe yourselves secure against its contagion. Carefully practise the means indicated, as you may yet fall. On this side of the grave there can be no security except in the constant employment of these means. To those who may have fallen, I have to say: do not despair — there is a remedy in the Sacrament of Penance, to cure the foulest wounds that this vice may have inflicted. But, then, you will require greater fervor — vigilance — and solicitude to overcome future temptations — and a constant penance for the past.

O Jesus! Bridegroom of pure souls, grant us all a true love for the virtue of purity! May Thy most precious blood heal the wounds of the fallen, and preserve them and us all in purity of heart!

O sweet and powerful Mother Mary, protect thy children from the contamination of this vice! Through thy aid, may the guilty do penance, and the innocent pass through this life untarnished, that we all may merit the grace of being one day associated with the pure angels of heaven! Amen.

# XIII

## PROXIMATE OCCASIONS OF SIN

To keep their souls free from the two vices which form the subjects of the two preceding discourses, and from every other sin, — to obtain purity of heart and to persevere in it to the end, — the people must come to a firm determination of faithfully using the means of perseverance instituted by God, without which salvation is impossible. Among these the constant flight from the Proximate Occasion of Sin occupies the first place. To show the importance of fleeing the occasion of sin is the *object* of this sermon.

The Proximate Occasion of Sin is the last stronghold of Satan, by which he keeps sinners in his grasp, and into which, after their conversion, he leads them again in order to secure their relapse. Hence, it is above all necessary to expose this hellish snare by giving a clear and well-defined explanation of its nature. Then, let the necessity of avoiding it be shown by the strongest proofs, taken from the Scriptures, from the teachings of the Church and of the Fathers, from reason and from experience. Let this be done especially when there is question of a *voluntary* proximate occasion. — Let the ordinary objections also be refuted. — This sermon must be preached with great force.

It is the opinion of some that the various proximate occasions should not be enumerated in this sermon, for the reason, perhaps, that the preacher is liable to exaggerate. Let him be on his guard against that excess. To speak, however, of certain proximate occasions in particular, has become almost a necessity, because they are not regarded as occasions of sin by those who love them. — It is also necessary to direct the attention of the audience to the general blindness that prevails in regard to this matter, and to the almost universal habit that reckless people have of claiming an exception, owing to their particular circumstances.

### SKETCH

TEXT: "Watch ye and pray, that ye enter not into temptation. The spirit is willing indeed, but the flesh is weak." — Matt. xxvi. 41.

EXORDIUM. — Thanks to the extraordinary graces conferred upon you during the Mission, you have broken with sin. You detest it from the bottom of your hearts. You have confessed it, or you are anxiously waiting for an opportunity of doing so. "The spirit is willing indeed." You are determined on saving your souls; "but the flesh is weak." It, therefore, becomes essentially necessary to use such measures as will prevent a relapse. One of the most important of these is the one indicated by our Lord Himself — "Watch." *Guard against the danger;* keep, especially, out of such dangerous occasions as generally lead people into sin — *i.e.,* the *Proximate Occasions of Sin.*

## I. The Proximate Occasions of Sin Must Necessarily be Avoided

What are they? They are circumstances in which people will ordinarily yield to sin, either in thought, word, or action; houses — persons — books — a certain business — amusements, etc.

Why must they be avoided so carefully?

1. On account of the *weakness of nature,* in itself so prone to sin. When this human weakness, so hard to be kept within bounds, comes into contact with some *external attraction,* it becomes utterly uncon-trollable, notwithstanding the strongest determination of sinning no more. Thoughts of Death — Judgment — Hell — Eternity — disappear before it like smoke.

"By some exterior voluptuous appearance the devil destroys those whom he could not overcome by means of iron, hunger, and cold." — St. Cypr.

2. He who exposes himself to dangers in which people ordinarily sin, *is proud,* and consequently *left without grace* to resist the temptation. Forgetting his weakness, he believes himself stronger than he

is; stronger than others who fell in them. He refuses to believe those who warn him — whose office it is to know the danger — and who have every opportunity of seeing its ravages — the confessors. But

"God resisteth the proud and giveth grace to the humble." — James iv. 6.

If a man is watchful over himself, God will never allow him to be tempted above his strength.

"God is faithful, who will not suffer you to be tempted above that which you are able, but will make also with temptation issue, that you may be able to bear it." — I Cor. x. 13.

God will not do so for him who carelessly, without real necessity, runs into danger; but He will even *resist* him.

Therefore, it is in itself a sin to expose yourself to such danger, and you will bear the guilt, even though you come out without committing sin; as, for example, going to houses of ill-repute without even consenting to an evil desire — lonely walks with persons of the other sex, etc.

3. He who exposes himself to the proximate occasion of sin *loves neither God* nor His commandments; he *loves sin*. Otherwise, how could he run into the most imminent danger of offending God? We flee from that which we fear.

"Flee from sins as from the face of a serpent; for if thou comest near them, they will take hold of thee." — Eccli. xxi. 2. — "Who will pity an enchanter struck by a serpent, or any that will come near wild beasts? So is it with him that keepeth company with a wicked man, and is involved in his sins." — Eccli. xii. 13.

Do we not keep out of pest-houses and places where there is danger of catching a mortal disease? Do we expose precious treasures to the danger of being stolen? Why, then, expose your soul and salvation to the danger of being lost?

For this reason, no one can *validly receive absolution* who is not determined to keep from the proximate occasions of sin, because, in reality, he has no will of avoiding sin.

4. *Objection:* "My business leads me into it."

Is your business a sinful one? Then give it up. If it is not, then do not make it your business to approach the danger, but do so only in case of necessity, with the proper precautions.

"God has given his angels charge over thee to keep thee in all thy ways." — Ps. xc. 11.

God protects you *in your ways,* but not out of them. And then arm yourself with special watchfulness and prayer.

Example of a traveler on a road infested by robbers, or wild beasts; what care will he take to guard himself against attack; of a fireman who rushes into a burning building to save a child from death.

Parallel between Judith and Dina. (Judith x–xiii, and Gen. xxxiv.)

Judith anointed herself, plaited her hair, etc. Dina went in her usual dress. Judith went into the camp of rough, heathen soldiers; Dina only a short distance from the tents of her father, to see the *women* of that neighborhood. Judith dined, drank and feasted with savage men; Dina did not even want to be seen by men. Judith stayed in the camp for four days; Dina took only a short walk. Judith came home pure and undefiled; Dina fell into an enormous sin, and lost her innocence. Why this? Judith went out because God sent her; Dina out of mere curiosity. Judith prayed and fasted before she went and while out on her important mission; Dina went for amusement only. Application to various occasions of sin.

Is it, then, really your will to avoid sin? Avoid, then, the proximate occasion thereof.

## II. The Proximate Occasion of Sin is to be Avoided at Every Sacrifice

1. Because no sacrifice is too great when our *eternal salvation is at stake;* no deprivation too costly when there is question of losing heaven on the one side, and inevitably incurring eternal damnation on the other; always, however, precluding the case of real necessity, and the employment of precautionary measures.

"What shall it profit a man, if he gain the whole world . . ." — Mark viii. 36 — pleasures, amusements.

2. *Jesus Christ* Himself has taught this doctrine. Speaking of sins of impurity, He says:

"I say unto you, that whosoever shall look on a woman to lust after her, hath already committed adultery with her in his heart." — Matt. v. 28.

Then He goes on to say:

"If thy right eye scandalize thee, pluck it out and cast it from thee; for it is expedient for thee that one of thy members should perish, than that thy whole body be cast into hell." — And the same He says about the right hand, etc. — Ib. 29, 30.

Therefore the occasion of sin is to be removed, even should it be as *near* and *dear* and *necessary,* as is the right eye or the right hand.

It is to be removed, not *gradually,* but *at once;* without mercy, notwithstanding the pain that it may cause you or others. "Cut it off!"

It is to be removed, so as not to *look after it* again. "Cast it from thee!"

There is the *dreadful alternative* before you, either to part with the occasion of sin, or to incur the danger of eternal hell-fire. "It is expedient for thee . . ."

(Application to the various occasions of sin, taking care not to mention other than those which are really *proximate* occasions.)

3. This being so, *Hell does its utmost* to prevent such occasions from being given up — and employs for this purpose the services of a wicked world. St. Leonard relates that the devil, speaking out of a person possessed, and being brought under the influence of the sacred exorcisms, had to confess that of all the sermons on the Mission, he most hates that on the proximate occasion of sin.

For this reason, in asking you to renounce Satan and his works, the Church insisted particularly on your renunciation of *the pomps* of Satan; because, without this renunciation, the other two would have been useless. This makes St. Augustine ask — meaning the occasion of sin — "What has a Christian to do with the pomps of Satan, which he has renounced in baptism?" — (*De. symb. ad. cat.*).

No one will understand this better than those who have been lost in consequence of not keeping from such occasions. (Add here some fearful example.)

## III. Excuses Made and Refuted

How prompt some people are in bringing forth excuses for not putting from them the occasion of sin, or, at least, not so soon. Are they not inspired by hell? But let us hear them:

"*I must mix in society, try to get along with the world as it is, must do as the world does.*"

Hear what St. James says about that:

"He that wishes to be a friend of this world, becomes the enemy of God." — James iv. 4.

"*I have received so many favors from that man — in that house.*"

What did God — what did Jesus Christ, do for you? And what value do you set upon your soul? Would you undergo sickness or death for that man?

*"We are not members of a Religious Order."*

Therefore, must you be so much the more watchful, as you are not surrounded by the protection that religious enjoy.

*"But now I am strong. I feel no temptations in such occasions; the Mission has effected a great change."*

What change? Not in the attraction of the world. All is the same — liquor-shops — theaters — papers —fashions. Your weak nature is the same. But there is indeed a great change in the devil, who,

"When an unclean spirit is gone out of a man he walketh through dry places, seeking rest, and findeth none. Then he saith, I will return into my house from whence I came out. And coming, he findeth it empty, swept and garnished. Then he goeth and taketh with him *seven* other spirits *more wicked* than himself, and they enter in and dwell there." — Matt. xii. 43–44.

That you feel no temptation in occasions in which so many have fallen before you — perhaps yourself — is nothing but a cunning device of the devil, who thereby makes you imagine yourself in security. And you are foolish enough to believe this in the face of all the arguments to the contrary. Proud spirit — you will soon fall!

Anecdote of the bear and the monkey (see Furniss' Tracts) — or some other example.

*"I shall rid myself of the occasion of sin by degrees."*

Why not follow the advice of Jesus Christ — "cut it off" at once, "and cast it from thee"? Who knows better what must be done? In your way, it is much harder for human nature than if it were done at once, and consequently you might just as well say that you will not abandon the occasions of sin.

*"With me the case is different — there is no danger; and if there is, I know where to stop."*

Strange — every one claims an exception in his case; is not this a sign of spiritual blindness?

You know where to stop — why begin at all to play the dangerous game with the devil, when your soul is at stake?

Away with these and all other excuses!

"How long do you halt between two sides? If the Lord be God, follow him; but if Baal, then follow him." — III Kings xviii. 21.

Away with all wavering! If you mean to serve God, serve Him entirely — and not also the devil, the world and yourself at the same time.

CONCLUSION. — Recapitulation.

Well, then, go to work manfully, not like a coward. Behold the extraordinary generosity of God's goodness and mercy, displayed toward you during this Mission. Be generous in your turn. How unworthy would it be of you now, to serve God by halves! Say, then, with a generous heart, "My God and my all." For Thee, O my God, I am determined to sacrifice everything that is calculated to lead me away from Thee again. I thank Thee for Thy goodness and mercy, and I will show my gratitude especially in this, that I will carefully shun all the occasions of sin. O Mother of Mercy! assist my poor human nature and obtain for me that firm determination of avoiding every danger of offending God, which is the first quality of a true servant of God!

NOTE. — The sermon on the "Proximate Occasions of Sin" is, most appropriately, placed after the sermon on Drunkenness and Impurity. — In that case, the introduction should refer to these two vices, to avoid which it is absolutely required to shun the proximate occasions that lead to them. Then in the beginning of the first part the most ordinary of those occasions should be enumerated.

# XIV

## FREQUENT COMMUNION

This is the second great means of perseverance. Holy Communion is as necessary to the soul as nourishment is to the body. It preserves the life of the soul, which is *sanctifying grace.* After the Mission it is a common thing to find almost all the people doing well up to a certain time, when they should go again to the sacraments. If they neglect to go, they invariably fall back into their former sins — if they go, they persevere in their good resolutions. St. Alphonsus used to exact from the people, several times during the Mission, the promise that they would frequent the sacraments after the Mission.

The entire fruit of the Mission is lost, if the people do not frequent the sacraments; and experience proves how slothful people generally are especially in this respect. Therefore, this sermon, if it is to effect any good, must be preached with all possible force of argument. The people must be told in plain words that one Communion a year is not enough to keep the soul in the state of grace; then, how often they should receive.

In places where the faith in the Real Presence has become weak with the greater part of the people, the first part of the sermon should be on the Real Presence, proving it by the most conclusive arguments; because there is generally not enough time for preaching a sermon on that point alone, unless other sermons of great importance be left out. Sometimes it may be sufficient simply to revive the faith in the Real Presence by a few well-arranged sentences in the exordium.

### Sketch

Text: "The bread that I will give, is my flesh, for the life of the world." — John vi. 52.

INTRODUCTION. — By means of this Mission the life of grace has been restored to you through the Sacrament of Penance — a second baptism. It now remains to preserve it. To this end such means must necessarily be employed as are instituted by God for this purpose. Among these the principal one is *Holy Communion*. The flesh of Jesus Christ — His Body — Christ Himself is the spiritual nourishment for the preservation of supernatural life. "The bread that . . ." Very few understand the necessity of it!

May it please God that you understand well what I tell you to-day, because this is one of the chief means of perseverance.

## I. NECESSITY OF HOLY COMMUNION

1. Without Holy Communion supernatural life becomes extinct. A Christian lives in a twofold order, the order of nature and the order of grace. The first makes him a child of man; the second, a child of God, and an heir to the kingdom of heaven. In the order of nature he is born in Adam; in the order of grace he is born in Christ. For the preservation of both lives he stands in need of nourishment. The nourishment for the preservation of the supernatural life is Holy Communion. Go without this food, and supernatural or spiritual death is inevitable.

Twice our Lord spoke of this supernatural life in the same most emphatic words. Both utterances are recorded by St. John. The first refers to the beginning; the second, to the preservation of the life of the soul.

"Amen, amen, I say to thee [Nicodemus]: unless a man be born again of water and the Holy Ghost, he cannot enter into the kingdom of God." — John iii. 5. — "Amen, amen, I say to you: except you eat the flesh of the Son of man, and drink his blood, you shall not have life in you." — John vi. 54. — "He that eateth my flesh and drinketh my blood abideth in me and I in him." — Ib. 57.

He will remain united with Christ. But he will even partake of the very nature of Christ — and consequently live the same life — and stand firm against all sinful attacks.

Without this spiritual nourishment all efforts are in vain. As regards natural life, all care, exercise, air, baths . . . are in vain without nourishment. Go without it, neglect it, and death is certain. The same is true with regard to the spiritual life. Prayer, mortification, retirement . . . are in vain without Holy Communion.

Experience has proved this beyond a doubt. Those who are converted from a sinful life remain good for a time, notwithstanding their temptations. Sometime afterward their will gives way and they fall. What caused the weakness of the will? The want of nourishment. Had they approached the Sacraments after a short interval, they would have remained strong and would have persevered.

When the Assyrians besieged Bethulia they could use no better or more successful means of compelling the city to surrender than the cutting off of the supply of water.

"Holofernes found that the fountain which supplied them with water, ran through an aqueduct without the city on the south side; and he commanded their aqueduct to be cut off." — Judith vii. 6.

Thus the devil acts with Christians, keeping them from spiritual nourishment.

2. But with Holy Communion supernatural life is preserved, and the soul becomes strong. For this we have again the word of our Lord:

"This is the bread which cometh down from heaven [every day at the Mass]; that if any man eat of it, he may not die." — John vi. 50. — "He that eateth my flesh and drinketh my blood, hath everlasting life, and I will raise him up at the last day." — Ib. 55. — "As the living Father hath sent me, and I live by the Father, so he that eateth me, the same shall live by me." — Ib. 58.

All this is most strikingly illustrated by the ceremony of mixing a little water with the wine at Mass. By the water man is represented.

"The waters which thou sawest . . are peoples, and nations, and tongues." — Apoc. xvii. 15.

By the wine, Jesus Christ in His human and divine natures. The little water is lost in the wine; it is not changed into wine, but partakes of its nature. So is man absorbed by the nature of Christ in Holy Communion, while still retaining his own nature and evil propensities, which, however, are thereby made powerless. The prayer of the Church, connected with that ceremony, explains it.

"O God . . . grant that through the mystery of this water and wine we may share in the divinity of him who has deigned to take part in our human nature, Jesus Christ, Our Lord."

Therefore, Holy Communion is the chief means of preserving ourselves in union with Jesus Christ, and, consequently, the principal means of perseverance.

## II. Frequent Communion

To preserve natural life is it enough to take nourishment only once in a great while? Experience proves the contrary, and all agree that nourishment must be taken often. The same is the case with Holy Communion and the preservation of supernatural life.

*How often* must Holy Communion be received? The Church commands us to receive Holy Communion once a year. But in this she regards a rare case in which the preservation of spiritual life may yet be possible. For this reason, she will no longer acknowledge as her child the man who does not go even once a year. It may be possible that a man's life is preserved by one meal a week. This is, in the spiritual life, one Communion a year.

The first Christians went every day (Acts ii. 42, 46); hence their extraordinary fervor and detachment from earthly things. (Ib.)

There is no doubt that they were induced to do so by the Apostles, who, again, had their instructions from the Lord Jesus Himself.

St. Justin, St. Clement of Alexandria, Tertullian, and St. Cyprian say that daily Communion was in vogue at *their* time. St. Jerome says that this was the custom in Rome at *his* time. A synod of Antioch (341, can. 2) ordained that all should be driven out of the church who, while assisting at Mass, do not go to Communion. Hence the heroic strength of those primitive Christians, many of whom became martyrs. St. Alphonsus, who lived a hundred years ago, on all his Missions inculcated the pious custom of approaching Holy Communion every week. And, indeed, this custom is necessary to place our salvation in perfect security and increase in us the practice of virtue. In our own day, the Holy Father has inculcated and encouraged frequent, nay, daily Communion. But here we speak only of the *preservation* of spiritual life.

Experience warrants the following rule:

Persons *settled in life,* not exposed to many temptations, generally preserve the life of grace with four Communions a year — *every three months*. It does not make them very strong, nor does it render them secure; but generally it keeps them from mortal sin. This is the longest time that anyone should stay from Communion.

But for *young* people, and all those who are exposed to many temptations, this would be insufficient.

For such, the rule should be *monthly* Communion; while for some among them even this would not be enough.

Let every one make out for himself or herself a rule of life in accordance with this, and form the firm determination never to deviate from it. For those who do not act thus, I cannot entertain the slightest hope of perseverance.

### III.   EXCUSES

Notwithstanding all that I have said, there are many who will not receive Communion as often as they should. They have their excuses. They act as the guests mentioned in the Gospel, who refused to come to the supper prepared for them by their king.

"And they began all at once to make excuse." — Luke xiv. 18.

Some take delight in their earthly possessions. What do they care about the supernatural life?

"I have bought a farm, and I must needs go out and see it: I pray thee, hold me excused." — Ib.

Others follow their animal nature according to the desires of the senses of the body.

"I have bought five yoke of oxen and I go to try them: I pray thee, hold me excused." — Ib. 19.

Others, again, have plunged themselves into habits of impurity. They disregard the invitation altogether.

"I have married a wife, and therefore I cannot come." — Ib. 20.

Besides these excuses mentioned in the Gospel, there are others.

"I live so far away."

Would any similar objection be made if you were starving for want of food and knew where to obtain it?

"I do nothing wrong." That may be; but we do not go to Holy Communion after we have done wrong, but rather to keep from doing wrong.

"It is so hard to get a chance to go to confession."

Try oftener than once; it is worth the trouble; and go when the throng around the confessionals is not so great. Let each member of the family take his turn.

"I was always accustomed to go to Holy Communion only at Christmas and Easter. Nobody went oftener." And, therefore, you have remained so lukewarm — committed so many sins — you may not even have the grace to know it.

Or, if you kept from great sins, your circumstances or God's special protection may have preserved you from them. It may not be so in future.

It is want of faith — want of appreciation of the Blessed Eucharist . . . that keeps people from Communion. Let them tremble at the warning which Jesus Christ gives them:

"I say to you, that none of those men that were invited shall taste of my supper." — Luke xiv. 24.

CONCLUSION. — Recapitulation.

You have made the Mission. You enjoy peace and happiness of soul. You earnestly desire to save your immortal souls. Let, then, your desire of employing the necessary means be equally strong. Frequent Communion is absolutely required. Make up your mind to go often and to go worthily. It is true, you will find many obstacles in the way. Exert your will, and you will overcome them all.

May the loving heart of Jesus grant you this good will! O Jesus, grant these people Thy love and a true and constant desire often to receive Thee into their souls.  O most loving Mother Mary! often remind these thy children of the promises that they have made in the Mission, and guide them to thy Son Jesus Christ.  May they thus persevere unto the end! Amen.

# XV

## PRAYER

Here we have the last of the three essential means of perseverance. It is scarcely necessary to remind a Redemptorist missionary how much and how often St. Alphonsus insists that this sermon be preached. As *sanctifying grace* is necessary for the preservation of the life of the soul, so *actual grace* is necessary for the acquisition and the preservation of sanctifying grace. But actual grace is obtained only by *Prayer.* — This sermon is, therefore, to be preached in a popular way, but with all possible fervor and zeal. The points to be shown in this sermon are: the absolute necessity of prayer; its efficacy; and the times when we must pray. But above all else, let a clear explanation of prayer, as understood here, be given, and, at the same time, let it be shown how easy it is for everybody — we mean the prayer of the heart. St. Alphonsus wishes missionaries to pay particular attention to this last point.

### SKETCH

TEXT: "Watch ye, and pray that ye enter not into temptation. The spirit indeed is willing, but the flesh is weak." — Matt. xxvi. 41.

EXORDIUM. — Jesus spoke these words to the Apostles shortly after they had received Holy Communion. This proves that something more than Holy Communion is necessary to preserve the life of grace. For the preservation of natural life, something besides nourishment is requisite — *i.e.,* inhaling the air around us. So it is in the spiritual life. We must attract the grace of God by Holy Prayer. This is the last and the most important means to be well understood and practised by you. You have a good will at present. "The spirit indeed is willing." But you are weak as regards your sinful propensities, and your enemies are strong. Therefore, "watch and pray." We have told you how you should watch, when we spoke to you on avoiding the proximate occasions of sin. To-day we shall speak to you on *Prayer*. Oh! may it please God to aid you to understand the absolute necessity of prayer, and to begin at once to practise it!

## I.  Necessity of Prayer

By prayer we understand here the simple asking of God with firm confidence for His assistance. For this no formula is necessary, no words, but only the thought of the heart. Hence, every one can pray, even those who know no form of prayer whatsoever. We can pray in all places and at all times. Prayer, therefore, is the *easiest* of all the *means* of salvation, while it is at the same time the surest and the most indispensable.

1. *Neglect prayer, and you will certainly be lost.* For without prayer no grace, and without grace no salvation.

A body in the state of perfect health is constantly in need of fresh air, which must be inhaled without interruption. Yet the air that fills the lungs must always be exhaled before a new supply can be taken in. Exhalation must always precede inhalation. Thus a man in the state of sanctifying grace is constantly in need of *actual grace,* or the actual assistance of God, to avoid evil and to do good. But this grace will not be given him before his soul is prepared to receive it — *i.e.,* he must be willing to receive it, he must desire it, long for it. This is prayer, which, therefore, must always precede grace.

There is an immense volume of air around us; but neglect to inhale it, and you must die.

There is an infinite treasure of grace at our disposal;

but neglect to attract it, and your soul will lose its supernatural life.

"There is an infinite treasure given to men, which they that use become the friends of God." — Wis. vii. 14.

2. Without the actual grace of God you cannot *avoid evil.* Your enemies are too strong for you. These are, your flesh, the world, and the devil. Explain their power.

Man is like a helpless infant, exposed in a dark forest, surrounded by ferocious beasts, and abandoned to starvation. The infant can do nothing but cry. So is man when abandoned to himself. He can, however, pray, and his prayer is heard.

"Owing to concupiscence," says St. Thomas, "continual prayer is necessary after baptism, in order to enter heaven."

"As I knew that I could not otherwise be continent, except God gave it, and this also was a point of wisdom, to know whose gift it was: I went to the Lord, and besought him for it." — Wis. viii. 21.

3. Without the actual grace of God we cannot *merit* anything for heaven or do anything supernaturally good. With all his natural efforts, man can never effect anything supernatural. But a good work, to be meritorious for heaven, must have a supernatural character. This it cannot have without the aid of God. In the natural order, many good works may be performed, but they merit no degree of supernatural glory.

"Without me you can do nothing." — John xv. 5. — "Not that we are sufficient to think anything of ourselves, as of ourselves, but our sufficiency is from God." — II Cor. iii. 5. — "If any one shall say, that without the previous inspiration of the Holy Ghost and his assistance man can believe, hope, love, or repent, as he ought, in order to obtain the grace of justification, let such a one be anathema." — Trid. sess. vi. c. 3.

4. But no actual grace is received *except through prayer*. As there is no sanctifying grace without the sacraments, so there is no actual grace without prayer.

"It is true that the first graces which come to us without any co-operation on our part, such as the call to the faith or to penance, are granted by God even to those who do not pray. But for all the other graces we have to pray. We believe that no one comes to be saved except by the call of God; that no one who is called, works out his own salvation except by the assistance of God; and that no one merits this assistance except by prayer." — St. Aug.

Reasons: God is indeed most willing to grant us His assistance at all times.

"God will have all men to be saved and to come to the knowledge of the truth." — I Tim. ii. 4.

But, if God should constantly grant it without our prayer, we should be blind and proud enough to ascribe all our good deeds to ourselves, while all glory is due to God.

God would be responsible for our deficiency in virtue — would be accountable for sin and the damnation of the reprobate. For man cannot avoid evil and do good without His assistance. If, then, He gave this assistance without our asking for it, whose fault would it be if we did not practise virtue — if we committed sin, and went to destruction?

There can be no merit on the part of man, and, consequently, there could consistently be no reward, if man is to do not the least thing toward obtaining grace, not even so much as to ask for it.

After this reflection you can explain why so many never understand the truths of faith — why they cannot believe; why so many live in cold indifference; why so few persevere in grace; why others never rise from sin — why they knowingly walk on the road to perdition. It is because they do not pray.

But no sooner do we fulfil this condition than we obtain all.

## II. EFFICACY OF PRAYER

1. *Practise holy prayer, and you will certainly be saved,* because, by it, you obtain all grace for avoiding every evil and doing any amount of good.

A good prayer, *i.e.,* one uttered with humility and confidence, is never left unheard.

"Cry to me and I will hear thee." — Jer. xxxiii. 3. — "Call upon me in the day of trouble, and I will deliver thee." — Ps. xlix. 15. — "Who hath called upon him, and he despised him?" — Eccli. ii. 12. — "Ask and it shall be given you, seek and you shall find, knock and it shall be opened to you." — Matt. vii. 7. — "For every one that asketh receiveth, and he that seeketh findeth, and to him that knocketh it shall be opened." — Ib. 8.

Parable of a son asking bread of his father (Ib. 9, 10), — of the man coming to his neighbor at night at the most unseasonable hour for the loan of three loaves of bread (Luke xi. 5).

2. God hears the prayer of men *without delay.*

"At the voice of thy cry, as soon as he shall hear, he will answer thee." — Is. xxx. 19. — "As they are yet speaking I will hear." — Is. lxv. 24.

Daniel had fasted and prayed for his people three weeks, yet the angel told him afterward:

"From the first day . . . thy words have been heard: and I am come for thy words." — Dan. x. 12.

3. *All things* that are asked for are granted, provided they be not hurtful to our souls, or do not prevent a greater good.

"All things whatsoever you shall ask in prayer, believing, you shall receive." — Matt. xxi. 22.

Even in behalf of the most wicked people. So Abraham was heard, who prayed for the cities of

Sodom and Gomorrha (Gen. xviii); Moses, who prayed for the Israelites (Exod. xxxii).

It is true, it is said,

"God doth not hear sinners." — John ix. 31.

But this is to be understood of them only so long as they want to remain sinners.    But,

"The prayer of him that humbleth himself shall pierce the clouds, and till it come nigh he will not be comforted, and he will not depart till the Most High behold." — Eccli. xxxv. 21.

Often also the effect of prayer is not felt at once, because God wants man to pray with more fervor, and wants to put his confidence to a trial.

Oh! how powerful is holy prayer!    What an easy and effectual means of salvation!

### III.    Frequency of Prayer

We must continually breathe the air around us, because we are constantly in need of a fresh supply.

So we must *always pray,* because we are constantly in need of additional grace.    You overcome a temptation one hour by prayer, it returns again the next; again you must overcome it by prayer.

"We ought always to pray and not to faint." — Luke xviii. 1. — "Let nothing hinder thee from praying always." — Eccli. xviii. 22. — "Pray without ceasing." — I Thess. v. 17.

But there are regular set times when we must pray every day.

1. In the morning.    Then begins a day during which we stand in need of God's help so often — when our passions, the world, the devil, will attack us so frequently.    And yet people generally omit their morning prayer.    Is not this the cause of their frequent falls?

2. At night.    Before going to sleep, prepare for death.

3. Before and after meals. Then remember your God, the bestower of all good gifts.

"The ox knoweth his owner, and the ass his master's crib; but Israel hath not known me." — Is. i. 3.

4. In temptation. Then it will be sufficient to invoke the holy names of Jesus and Mary in your hearts. But omit it — and you fall.

CONCLUSION. — Recapitulation.

On this occasion we have taught you the most important lesson of all. Happy you, if, after studying it well, you put it in immediate practice and never cease from it. Then your salvation is sure. But unhappy you, if this lesson has been taught you in vain. Then your damnation is sure. I call upon heaven and hell to witness the truth of this. Search heaven! All except the innocent children came thither on account of their constant practice of fervent prayer. Search hell! All, without exception, are there because they neglected prayer.

Do you wish now to preserve the fruits of this Mission? Pray! To keep your resolution? Pray! To avoid the occasion of sin? Pray! To overcome temptations? Pray! To reach Paradise? Pray! Pray always — and never cease to pray!

"Lord! teach us to pray!" — Luke xi. 1.

O sweet Mother Mary! obtain for us all the gift of holy, fervent, never-ceasing prayer, and we shall have all that we need, all that we can desire, for time and eternity   Amen.

# XVI

## PRECEPTS OF THE CHURCH

Among the instructive sermons the present one can hardly ever be omitted on any Mission in this country. Our people are extremely ignorant, either of one or the other of these precepts, or of all, or they seem not to know the obligation which they are under of keeping them.

The *object* of this discourse is to show that only those can be true members of the Church who, besides believing her doctrines, observe also her commandments. After a brief demonstration of the principle, the chief precepts of the Church, binding on all Christians, are explained and inculcated by dwelling more at length on those which are generally transgressed, while of the others only a cursory notice is to be taken.

In some congregations more stress must be laid on the duty of hearing Mass on Sundays and Holy-days, and of performing the Easter duties; in others the law of abstinence on Fridays and days of fast needs more attention. But the duty of supporting religion needs to be enforced always and everywhere, and it is our duty as missionaries to speak of this obligation more at length, and to support our doctrine by strong proofs, because local pastors cannot so easily speak of it to their congregations; and if they do, they not unfrequently arouse among the people the suspicion of avarice. And yet, how few of our people fulfil their duty in this regard! Fully one-third of our Catholics do nothing in support of religion; another third do a little, and the remaining third do a good deal — but by no means all that they should do. Very few do so from a purely religious motive, and a man who is unwilling to offer to God the sacrifices which He demands, is not firm in his faith and cannot please God.

This sermon is to be preached at an early part of the Mission, because many are in need of it before they come to confession. It should follow the *Eternal Truths* as soon as possible.

### SKETCH

TEXT: "If any one will not hear the Church, let him be to thee as the heathen and the publican." — Matt. xviii. 17.

EXORDIUM. — The Church is the mystical body of Christ with Himself as the head. She has the Holy

Ghost dwelling in her as her soul. Therefore we must implicitly believe in her; otherwise, we cannot be Christians. But we must likewise obey her commands, her directions, and her ordinances. We must "hear the Church" as regards matters of discipline as well as of faith, or else we are no better than the heathen who know not God — no better than a public outcast of society.

Many seem not to understand this obligation; they regard it sufficient, to believe in the Church. Others look upon it as a slight matter to disobey the precepts of the Church; while others, again, call into question the authority of the Church to issue commands strictly binding on a man's conscience. Therefore:

## I. Why Must we Obey the Church?

1. Because her precepts are *divine,* not human, commandments. The Church is simply the organ of the Holy Ghost, from Whom, properly speaking, proceed all her ordinances.

"The Holy Ghost, whom the Father will send in my name, will teach you all things, and bring all things to your mind *whatsoever I shall have said* to you." — John xiv. 26.

These last words regard not only the doctrine of Christ, but also His precepts. Hence the precepts of the Church are *divine precepts* — the commands of Jesus Christ made known to the world through the Holy Ghost and the Church. Therefore, the Apostles issued their first precepts in the name of the Holy Ghost.

"It hath seemed good to the Holy Ghost and to us, to lay no further burden upon you than these necessary things." — Acts xv. 28.

2. Jesus Christ expressly commanded the Apostles to issue certain precepts, which He made known to them before His ascension into heaven. After commanding them to preach the Gospel to all nations, He expressly adds:

"Teaching them to *observe* all things whatsoever I have commanded you." — Matt. xxviii. 20.

These words mean something distinct from teaching His doctrine of faith, which is contained in verse 19. What are "all (these) things"? They are made known in the form of precepts of the Church. Besides, if Jesus Christ is the head of the Church, then her commandments are, properly speaking, His own.

"He that heareth you heareth me, and he that despiseth you despiseth me." — Luke x. 16.

3. For one and the same reason those who refuse obedience to the Church are placed on an equality with those who have no faith at all. They are to be regarded as no better than heathens — see text — if not worse; because they refuse to acknowledge the authority of God, in Whom they believe, and Whose Spirit they must know rules in the Church. Hence a sin against the precepts of the Church becomes almost equal to a sin against the Holy Ghost, and for this reason we know that those who obstinately transgress the commandments and ordinances of the Church become infidels much sooner, and are converted with greater difficulty, than those who sin against the most sacred commandments of the Decalogue (cf. Matt. xii. 31, 32). King Saul sinned by disobeying the prophet, and David, by adultery and murder; Saul was rejected and died impenitent, while David did penance and became a saint.

We are also bound to obey the commands of other authorities established by God.

"Let every soul be subject to higher powers: for there is no power but from God: and those that are, are ordained of God." — Rom. xiii. 1.

But there is a marked difference between their precepts and those of the Church. Hence, the transgression of them is not so grievous a sin, nor is it followed by so serious consequences, as are transgressions of the Church's law.

The so-called chief commandments of the Church, obligatory upon all Christians, did not appear in the form of commandments in the first ages of the Church, because the first Christians, in their great fervor, fulfilled these prescriptions without being placed under an absolute command. The subsequent decrease of Christian piety made the formal introduction of them a necessity.

*Objection.* — Why did not Jesus Christ issue these commandments explicitly, if He wished them to be so strictly observed?

Most probably He did, although it is not recorded in the Gospel.

But, is it not enough for us that He said: "Hear the Church"?

*Another objection* — In the Old Testament God issued His positive commandment about the most minute observances, and had it carefully recorded in the sacred books. How much more would Christ have done so in the New Law, which is the perfection of the Old, if the obligation was so strict!

The Mosaic Law regarded only a small population, occupying a small territory, living under the same circumstances. The Law of the Gospel is given for all nations, living over the whole earth, under varying circumstances.   Hence, it had to be left to the Church to accommodate these precepts to all times and places, while, in principle, they are always and everywhere the same.

For this reason the Church wants it always to be understood, that the obligation of fulfilling these precepts is not binding upon any one who cannot comply with them, except under the greatest difficulties.


## II.   In What Must we Obey the Church?

In everything, by submitting to all her ordinances — whether given for all Christians in general — or only for the certain class to which we belong; whether given for all times or on account of some peculiar circumstances; for the whole world or only for a limited territory.

But all Christians must submit to the chief precepts, which are binding on everybody.   These are:

1. *To keep Sunday* (instead of the Sabbath of the Old Law) *and certain feasts of obligation.*

*a.* Who is bound by this law?   All — young and old — who have come to the use of reason.

*b.* Why are these days to be kept holy?   Motives for Sunday: one day in the week to be consecrated to God.   Sunday, because on that day Jesus, the Head of the Church, began His life of glory in the Resurrection — because on a Sunday the Holy Ghost descended, united Himself to the Infant Church at Jerusalem, and from that day she began to fulfil her divine mission on earth.

Motives for the feasts to be kept: 1. Christmas, 25th of December, because Christ was born on that day; 2. Circumcision, 1st of January, because He spilled His first blood for the salvation of mankind on that day; 3. Ascension, forty days after Easter, because then heaven was opened, and Jesus Christ entered into it triumphantly with the elect of the Old Testament; 4. Immaculate Conception, 8th of December, when the head of the infernal serpent was crushed through the conception of the Blessed Virgin Mary without the stain of original sin; 5. Assumption of the Blessed Virgin Mary, 15th of August, when she was crowned in heaven as the Queen of angels and men; 6. All Saints, 1st of November, in commemoration of the merits of all the servants of God in Heaven, and the union of the Church triumphant with the Church militant.

NOTE. — The number of feasts of obligation in Canada differs from that in the United States.

*c.* Excuses for not keeping this precept. Enumeration of such as are insufficient, and of such as will exempt from the obligation.

2. *To attend Mass on Sundays and holy-days of obligation.*

*a.* Who is bound? All, from the age of seven years, whenever it is physically possible for them to attend.

*b.* Motives: The greatness of the Holy Sacrifice — its necessity — and the immense benefits derived from it. Therefore, regular attendance is commanded, at least on the days when other occupations are forbidden. The sanctification of Sundays and holy-days cannot be performed in any better way.

*c.* Excuses, false and real. Enumeration. Refutation or approbation.

Nor is it sufficient to attend a part only of the Mass, or to attend without attention. Short explanation of the manner of hearing Mass.

3. *Keep the prescribed days of fast and abstinence.*

*a*. Who is bound to keep the fast? All, except those excused on account of age — infirmity — hard work, or other good reasons. But all must keep the abstinence from flesh-meat on days when no meat is allowed.[1]

NOTE. — It is better not to say anything about those who have not yet come to the use of reason.

*b*. Motives: Penance for past sins — subjection of the unruly flesh — worthy preparation for certain great feasts.

*c*. Which days of fast and abstinence are to be kept? This depends on the particular regulations of the various dioceses in which we actually live. According to the New Code of Canon Law, n. 1252, the following are the days prescribed. Days of fast and abstinence: Ash Wednesday, the Fridays and Saturdays of Lent, the Ember Days, the Vigils of Pentecost, Assumption, All Saints and Christmas. Days of fast only: All the other days (week-days) in Lent. Days of abstinence only: Every Friday. But there is no fast, no abstinence on Sundays and holy-days of obligation.

*d*. How is the fast to be kept? According to the modern discipline of the Church, those who fast are allowed one full meal at mid-day, some warm liquid in the morning, with one or two ounces of bread — and the fourth part of a full meal, or eight ounces of food, in the evening — but no flesh-meat except by special indult.[2] As to the observance of Lent, the particular regulations for every diocese are published annually.

*e*. Objections and excuses. Enumeration. Refutation — or approbation.

[1] Codex Juris Canon., 1254.
[2] See New Code, canon 1250, 1251.

4. *Annual Confession.*

*a*. Who is bound? All who are capable of committing sin.

*b*. Motives: Everyone who has come to the use of reason, is liable to commit sin. To purify one's soul once in a year is certainly not too much for the Church to command. The Church is holy, and consequently she wants her children to be holy. A sacrilegious confession does not satisfy this precept.

*c*. Excuses. There can hardly be any. No one is excused, except those who can neither come to the priest nor send for him. Want of sufficient instruction is no excuse. It must be procured by all means. Parents must either instruct their children themselves, or have them instructed by others, else the sin rests on their own conscience. Nor is it an excuse that they *themselves* know no better, because they are strictly bound to know all about the Christian education of children

5. *Easter Communion.*

*a*. Who is bound? All who have made their First Communion, or who are of an age when they are bound to prepare for it.

*b*. Motives: Preservation of the life of the soul — reunion of all Christians with their Head, Jesus Christ, on the anniversary of the day on which He began His life of glory. The Church regards as separated from her living body those who neglect this duty — and if they die in this miserable state, refuses to bury their bodies in consecrated ground. Hence, an unworthy communion is not sufficient.

*c*. When is this duty to be fulfilled? At Eastertime, the duration of which varies in different countries and dioceses, but in most of the dioceses of the United States it begins with the first Sunday of Lent and closes on Trinity Sunday — fourteen weeks, or more than the fourth part of the year.

*d*. Excuses. As few as for the foregoing precept. The same answers. Any one who has neglected, or who could not fulfil this precept within the prescribed time, is bound to do it at the earliest opportunity.

6. *Support of Church and Pastor*.

Christians are *obliged* to contribute toward the support of religion,

1. By the *law of nature* which commands it as an act of worship to God, as the Creator and Preserver of all things and as man's Benefactor. All things belong to God — man has the simple use of what God gives him; therefore, he is obliged to make an offering of a part of those things as an act of gratitude. For this reason,

"Cain offered, of the fruits of the earth, gifts to the Lord. Abel also offered of the firstlings of his flock and of their fat." — Gen. iv. 3, 4. — "Noah built an altar to the Lord, and taking of all cattle and fowls that were clean, offered holocausts upon the altar." — Gen. viii. 20.

2. From the time of Moses the *positive law of God* made it obligatory that the tenth part of every man's income was to be offered to God.

"All tithes of the land, whether of corn or of the fruits of trees, are the Lord's, and are sanctified to him." — Lev. xxvii. 30. — "Of all the tithes of oxen and sheep and goats that pass under the shepherd's rod, every tenth that cometh shall be sacrificed to the Lord." — Ib. 32.

From that time these offerings were to be given to the priests for their only support.

"And the Lord said to Aaron: You shall possess nothing in their land; neither shall you have a portion among them: I am your portion," *i.e.*, the portion offered to me is yours. — Num. xviii. 20. — "And I have given to the sons of Levi all the tithes of Israel for a possession, for the ministry wherewith they serve me in the tabernacle of the covenant." — Ib. v. 21.

3. In the New Testament the same was observed as in the Old. At first no law was necessary, owing to the extreme liberality of the people.

"They had all things common. They sold their possessions and goods and divided them to all." — Acts ii. 44, 45.

But very soon afterward it became necessary to inculcate this duty.

"Who serveth as a soldier at any time, at his own charges? — Who planteth a vineyard, and eateth not of the fruit thereof? — Who feedeth a flock, and eateth not of the milk of the flock? — Speak I these things according to man? Or doth not the law also say these things?" — I Cor. ix. 7, 8. — See this whole chapter.

Later on it again became a law that *the tenth part of all income was to be offered to God* for the support of the clergy, the churches and all ecclesiastical institutions.

The laws concerning the tithes have been established in many Councils of the Church, and have been proclaimed and inculcated by the Fathers.

"The priest is to despise all that appertains to his living. . . . Instead of this, the firstlings and the tithes are to be given to him by all the people." — St. Theodoret. — "The tithes are a debt, and he that refuses to pay them is guilty of theft, because he keeps what is not his own." — St. Aug. — "The payment of the tithes is due to God, and he that refuses to pay them, takes what does not belong to him. . . . Those who will not pay them, are to be excommunicated, nor can they be absolved from this crime unless they make full restitution." — Trid. sess. 25. cap. 12.

The Church, at present, does not insist upon the payment of the tithes, or the tenth part. Still the obligation remains upon all to support religion, and wherever the Church has made special regulations as to the quantity of these offerings and the manner of making them, these regulations are binding on the conscience of every one.

In the United States there exists no special ecclesiastical law in reference to this matter, except that *all are obliged to contribute to the support of religion according to their means.*

The usual way in which this is done, is by ordinary and extraordinary collections, pew-rents, stipends for Masses, free donations on the occasion of the administration of the Sacraments of Baptism and Matrimony, etc.

4. Special reasons for supporting *the Church*.

1. God *speaks* to us in the sermon. We must at least furnish the place where we can listen to Him with ease. 2. God furnishes us with the *Victim* to be offered to Him, and which is of infinite value — God Himself. We must at least furnish the house wherein and the means wherewith this sacrifice can be offered in a becoming manner. 3. Jesus Christ wishes to *remain with us* at all times in the Holy Sacrament of the Eucharist. We must at least prepare for Him a suitable dwelling. Therefore, are we bound to *build* a church *large enough* for the congregation that is to assemble within its walls to assist at the Holy Sacrifice and hear the Word of God; to *pay the debt* on it; to keep it in *good repair;* and to *decorate* it so that it will deserve the name of "House of God," and be a suitable place for the celebration of the divine mysteries. We are, moreover, bound to furnish *everything necessary* for the *worthy celebration* of the Holy Sacrifice according to the rites of Holy Church, with more or less solemnity, according to the degrees of the various feasts of the Church — altar, vessels, vestments, etc.

Or shall we put our Lord under the necessity of living in a stable? Or make Him rest in a sepulcher not His own — by leaving the church under a heavy debt, or mortgage? Or shall we show our indignation at expenses made for church-decorations, saying with

Judas: "To what purpose is this waste?" (Matt. xxvi. 8).

5. Special reasons for supporting *the Priest*.

1. The priest sacrifices *a fortune,* even before he has any hope of becoming a priest, during his course of studies. His future congregation receives the benefit of this. 2. He sacrifices the very *possibility of making a living* by carrying on some lucrative business. 3. He sacrifices *his time* for the people. 4. He sacrifices *his health* — even *life itself* when the salvation of his flock demands it. 5. He places even his *immortal soul* at stake in assuming such fearful responsibilities. 6. And what does he do for you? He makes you a Christian, instructs, teaches, preaches, offers the Holy Sacrifice, hears your confession, gives you Communion, strengthens you when sick, consoles you in life, reassures you at death, prays for you after death. . . . Is he worthy of the little that you give him?

"The laborer is worthy of his hire." — Luke x. 7.

This holds true of every workman; why not of the priest, of whom our Lord speaks in this passage?

"Know you not that they who work in the holy place, eat the things that are of the holy place; and they that serve the altar, partake with the altar? So also the *Lord ordained* that they who preach the Gospel, should live by the Gospel." — I Cor. ix. 13–14. — "What can we give to this holy man?" — said young Tobias of the angel, who had not done for him the one-thousandth part of what the priest does for you. And he said to his father: "Desire him that he would vouchsafe to accept of one-half of all things that have been brought." — Tob. xii. 1, 4.

Therefore, it is our obligation to support as far as it depends upon us, the priest who will offer the Holy Sacrifice, preach the Word of God and administer to us the Sacraments. Hence we are to support *as many priests as are needed* for our spiritual wants, assist in their *education,* give them a becoming *residence,* and furnish them with a *decent living.*

6. *Punishment* of those who *neglect* this duty.

*a. Temporal punishment.* Such people will never prosper, despite all their efforts to make a living or amass wealth.

Therefore, the ordinary temporal punishment for the neglect of this duty is poverty, famine, etc.

"Beware of defrauding the Lord of the tenth, lest he leave you the tenth, taking away nine." — St. Aug. — "Because you have not given your tithes, therefore are you cursed with famine and starvation." — St. Jerome.

You may have to pay to the physician or druggist what you refuse to give to the Church and the priest; or in State taxes, war costs, etc.

"Hoc tulit fiscus, quod non accipit Christus; dabis impio militi, quod non vis dare sacerdoti." — St. Aug.

Many excuse themselves for not contributing sufficiently toward the support of church and pastor on the plea of poverty. May not this poverty be the punishment for failing in this duty hitherto?

*b. Spiritual punishment.* Those who contribute nothing toward the support of church and pastor, *"graviter peccant."* — Innoc. III.

"They cannot be the servants of the celestial King who refuse to pay him their contributions." — St. Gregory the Great.

They derive no benefit from the services in the church, who do not fulfil their duty in regard to the building, repairing, or ornamenting of the church, even should they enter it. That church for which they have done nothing will benefit them nothing. Neither will the services of the priest avail them anything; his sermons and instructions will not aid their souls, if they do nothing for the education and support of priests. They are unworthy of the sacraments, if they do nothing to provide for their administration. Indeed, a just judgment of God!

7. *Reward* of those who *fulfil* this duty.

*a. Temporal blessings.*

"Give, and it shall be given to you." — Luke vi. 38.

But you must give first — then will you receive in abundance.

"Good measure, and pressed down, and shaken together, and running over shall they give into your bosom. For with the same measure that you shall measure, it shall be measured to you again." — Ib.

It will be given in many different ways — in the shape of health, peace, contentment, etc., a hundred-fold. This is what our Lord means when He says:

"Amen I say to you, there is *no man*, who hath left house, . . . or lands, for my sake, . . . who shall not receive a hundred times as much, now in this time, . . . and in the world to come life everlasting." — Mark x. 29, 30. — "Because our ancestors paid to God the tithes, therefore, they possessed all wealth in abundance. If you pay your tithes, you shall not only receive an abundance of fruit, but you shall also enjoy good health in body and soul." — St. Aug.

*b. Spiritual blessings.* Such people as faithfully do their duty in this repect, invariably make great progress in the spiritual life.

The first Christians sacrificed all. Hence they were so good as to be able to go to Holy Communion daily.

There are still to be found examples of equally generous Christians, who, after making an extraordinary sacrifice of their temporal property, are leading a life of true perfection.

The reason is obvious. The more you are detached from the goods of this earth, the more you will be united to God and gain in supernatural goods.

A proof are the words of our Lord (Mark x) and the saying of St. Augustine, as above.

Therefore, says St. Augustine, "he only is a true Christian who annually pays his dues to the Church and the priest."

Examine yourself now on this last precept. Perhaps you do nothing for religion, because you are single; or perhaps you have not done enough, especially if you take into consideration your *numerous* grown-up *family,* for every member of which the priest must do as much as for yourself; or you have not increased your offerings *in proportion to your wealth.* Or if you have done what you should, perhaps you did so *unwillingly;* or you have given only *what was left* after providing for yourself; or, you wish to have *amusement for it* at a fair, picnic, etc.; or you gave it to *gain by it,* or to earn *praise for it,* etc. In all these cases you have made no sacrifice; consequently you cannot expect a reward for it.

CONCLUSION. — Recapitulation.

These, now, are the reasons why we must submit to the Church, and the particular points in which our obedience must be manifested. Beware of uttering the least complaint against any of them. They are by no means too hard to be observed — and should they become so at any time they will not oblige you under those difficulties.

Instead of reasoning against the authority of the Church, or complaining against her injunctions, thank God that He has called you into her fold; for thereby you are already on this earth a citizen of the kingdom of Heaven. And all that you can do in obedience to the Church is nothing in comparison with what the Church does for you. You should even glory in being obedient children of the Church. For thus you

belong to the most glorious kingdom ever established
— which can never be destroyed by any power —
which makes its subjects truly happy and prosperous
— and which is an infallible pledge of life everlasting.
Amen.

NOTE. — The foregoing sketch, if carried out in full, would make
the sermon too long. Therefore, only those parts are to be preached
in detail which are most needed in this or that particular place. Of
the others a simple statement is sufficient. — If all are needed,
then the more important parts should be given in a sermon, the rest
in an instruction.

# XVII

## MISSION-CROSS

The Mission-Cross is erected, blessed and left in the church where the Mission has been given, or in a conspicuous place outside the Church, to remind the people ever afterward of the Mission, its blessings and the good resolutions they then formed. According to St. Alphonsus, this ceremony should take place on the last day of the Mission. [1] If the Mission close on a Sunday, the afternoon would suit best. It may also form, as it often does, the close of the Mission.

The *object* of the sermon is to show the people in what way the Cross is to remind them of the Mission. The missionary must show that the Mission is another triumph of the Cross over the powers of hell; that the Cross will constantly bring back to them the recollection of the sermons and instructions preached in the Mission; that they must constantly rally around it as the standard of Jesus Christ, to Whom they are solemnly invited to declare their allegiance forever; — and that to induce the people often to visit it, the Church attaches many and great indulgences to it, to be gained by those who thus honor it.

This sermon is pervaded by an air of triumph because of the victory of the Cross in general and at this Mission in particular, and closes with a cheering exhortation to a magnanimous declaration in favor of the Cross and the Lamb of God who was slain on it. If the Mission-Cross is a *crucifix* and not a simple cross, the preacher must make his references to *Jesus Crucified*, excepting what belongs exclusively to the figure of the Cross.

If, for want of time, the sermon on the Chief Means of Perseverance is to be preached at the erection of the Mission-Cross, the following plan will be most suitable: — After pointing out the Cross as a mark of the triumph of grace over sin and hell in the Mission, the preacher presents the Cross as a sign-post with two arms, pointing to the two roads to eternity. Then he tells the people *what they must do* to keep to the road that leads to heaven (means of perseverance). What they will do (the preacher says), he knows not, but Judgment-day will show them placed either at the right or at the left of the cross. From this he makes a transition to the solemn promises mentioned in the sermon on Perseverance.

[1] C. E., Vol. XV. p. 247.

## Sketch

Text: "God forbid that I should glory, save in the cross of our Lord Jesus Christ; by whom the world is crucified to me, and I to the world." — Gal. vi. 14.

Exordium. — Every great event is marked and handed down to posterity by the erection of a monument. So, particularly, is a distinguished and decisive battle commemorated by a monument erected on the battle-field, on which are inscribed the nations that fought, the names of the most valiant officers, the number of slain, etc.

Here, in this church, a great battle has been going on . . . and has come to an end with the victory of Jesus Christ over hell. The contest was a hot and spirited one. Blood flowed in streams — *i.e.*, the blood of Jesus Christ — to wash your souls. In memory of this great event, this Cross is to-day erected and blessed, that by it you may be reminded of the extraordinary benefits bestowed upon you in the Mission. This same Cross also will constantly bring to your memory the sermons that we have preached to you, and will, as long as you love and venerate it, keep you united with Jesus Christ.

## I. Triumph of the Cross in the Mission

1. The cross has triumphed over hell in the *great work of redemption,* accomplished through it. By the cross the power of hell was broken, its pride humbled, its influence paralyzed. For, through the death of Jesus Christ on the cross the sins of the human race have been expiated, human souls have been torn from the grasp of Satan, and all the power that he had gained has been made to disappear like smoke.

"He has blotted out the handwriting of the decree which was against us . . . and the same he took out of the way, fastening it to the cross [sins blotted out by the merits of the cross], and divesting principalities and powers . . . triumphing openly over them in himself." — Col. ii. 14, 15. — "Who his own self bore our sins in his body upon the tree [of the cross]; that we being dead to sins, should live to justice." — I Peter ii. 24.

Therefore, the cross is called by the Fathers the standard of salvation.

"The cross is the standard of salvation, the triumph of Christ, the palm-tree of life everlasting, the sword with which the devil has been killed." — St. Ambrose. — "The cross has saved the world, abolished error, introduced truth, changed earth into heaven, made angels out of men." — St. Chrysostom.

Hence, the glorious triumph of the cross celebrated by the Church.

2. The cross has triumphed over the world and the devil in the *propagation of the Christian religion*.

When men are about to carry out a great design, they make corresponding preparations. If a country is to be conquered, a nation to be subdued, gigantic armaments precede the war, drilling, study, etc.

What preparations were made for the conquest of the world for the religion of Jesus Christ? Twelve poor, unlettered fishermen were taken from their nets on the shores of the Galilean Sea. These were sent into a world full of ambition, pride, voluptuousness. . . . They preached a doctrine in direct opposition to the world's principles . . . without studied eloquence, rhetoric, philosophy . . . and they very soon subdued the world to a doctrine of humility, self-denial, detachment, . . . the Gospel. No sooner did they begin to preach than thousands were converted of every rank and grade of society.

"We are but of yesterday, and we fill your cities, towns, villages, . . . your senates, your armies . . ." — Tertull.

What were the means employed? The cross!

"When I came to you, brethren, I came not in loftiness of speech or of wisdom, declaring unto you the testimony of Christ. For I judged not myself to know anything among you, but Jesus Christ, and him crucified." — I Cor. ii. 1, 2.

Jesus Christ, unknown, the Son of a "carpenter," convicted of crime, sentenced to death, and made to die on a cross, a penalty to which the meanest Roman citizen was never subjected.

"He is accursed of God that hangeth on a tree." — Deut. xxi. 23.

The world revolted, it raised the fiercest persecutions, put to death the believers in the cross. Yet the cross triumphed. The powers of hell, seeing themselves vanquished by it, fear and tremble at its sight.

"The cross is the monument of victory raised against the demons, the sword with which Christ has killed the serpent. The cross is the will of the Father, the glory of the Son, the exaltation of the Holy Ghost, the ornament of the angels, the security of the Church, the wall of the saints, the light of the whole world." — St. Chrysostom.

A dog fears nothing more than the stick with which he has been beaten. At the very sight of it he runs off. So the devil flees at the sight of the cross.

3. The cross has triumphed *in this Mission.* We came to you not with unanswerable arguments of philosophy — not with any particular exterior attraction, "our speech and our preaching were not in the persuasive words of human wisdom, but in the showing of the spirit and power" of the cross (I Cor. ii. 4). That it was which made you set aside all human considerations, cold, inconvenience, business, to come to the Mission. Our simple words penetrated the innermost of your souls. Pride, shame, etc., were overcome. You came to confession, gave up evil occasions of sin, illicit friendships. . . . You have been torn from the grasp of Satan, been made the children of God, . . . to the greatest astonishment of a surrounding world, and even of yourselves.

What is all this owing to? To the cross of Jesus

Christ, or the graces which He merited for you on the cross. . . . Your zeal and fervor in attending the Mission, your redoubled prayers, your holy inspirations and firm resolutions, your reformation of life, . . . all are the fruit of that tree — the cross of Christ.

We have conquered the land — your souls. Therefore do we, in glory and triumph, erect the standard of Jesus Christ here, to proclaim our victory to all future times.

"Tell it to the nations that Jesus Christ is reigning here from the wood of the cross." — Office of the Church. — "Behold the cross of the Lord! Flee, ye adversaries, the Lion of the tribe of Juda has conquered. — Alleluia!" — Ib.

## II. The Mission-Cross is a Continuation of the Mission

It often happens that the good results of the Mission disappear with the sound of the missionary's voice — owing to the powerful influence which the flesh, the world, and the devil exercise over the hearts of men. To produce a lasting effect, the best means is to leave a *missionary* in the parish who will constantly bring to the recollection of the people the sermons preached during the Mission. We do so for you by leaving you this Cross.

1. The Cross preaches to you, *by its figure.* It has *two arms.* These are like a sign-post on the highway. They point out the *two roads* to eternity. They point to the *two divisions of men,* which always exist in the world; those who are *with God,* and those who are *against God.* There is no third division. Man is either in the state of grace or in the state of sin.

"He that is not with me, is against me: and he that gathereth not with me, scattereth." — Matt. xii. 30. — "No man can serve two masters." — Matt. vi. 24.

Nor is any *neutrality* possible. If you do not stand on the side of God by faith and good works, you necessarily are opposed to Him. The Judgment-day will show both classes, the cross between the two divisions, pointing toward them with its right and its left arm. On the first erection of the cross on Mount Calvary, one died at its right and one at its left. The former went to heaven; the latter, to hell. That event foreshadowed what will occur at the end of the world.

With its *top,* the Cross points heavenward; with its *trunk,* toward hell. This preaches to you the incontrovertible truth, that the good shall go forever to heaven; the wicked, forever to hell.

2. The Cross preaches to you by *its mystery:*

*a. The value of the soul,* by showing you the ransom paid for it.

"You are bought with a great price." — I Cor. vi. 20.

It warns you against selling that soul for a trifle — a drink, an impure pleasure, etc.

*b.* It preaches to you the *enormity of sin,* which could not be atoned for except through the sacrifice of the life of the God-man. It warns you against falling into sin again, "crucifying again to yourselves the Son of God, and making him a mockery." — (Heb. vi. 6).

*c.* It shows to you the *severity of God's justice* against the impenitent sinner — death of despair, judgment, hell. It might have been expected that God would pardon His own Son after He had taken the sins of the world upon Himself (Is. liii. 6) — so much the more as Jesus Christ prayed for that favor (Matt. xxvi. 39). — But not so. He had to drink the chalice to the dregs (Is. li. 17).

*d.* The Cross preaches to you the *infinite mercy of God,* Who has spared no sacrifice to effect the recon-

ciliation of the sinner while he lived in opposition to
Him. How merciful He is to the one who returns to
Him in grief and sorrow.

*e.* It preaches the confidence that you should always
have in the *Blessed Virgin Mary,* who at the foot of
the cross was proclaimed "your Mother."

*f.* It confirms you in the *Faith.* Jesus Christ, by
His death on the cross and His resurrection, established His divinity. His doctrine must be true. The
Church which He established is a divine Church. By
the subsequent infusion of the Holy Ghost, that Church
has become infallible. Her doctrine is the doctrine of
Jesus Christ, always the same, and given to the nations
for their guide to heaven.

*g.* By the Cross you learn the *value of the sacraments,* because from it they derive their power and
efficacy.

*h.* The Cross teaches you the *spirit of religion* and
its commandments, humility, obedience, charity, self-
denial, detachment, etc.

It consoles you in your *trials,* sufferings, poverty,
etc. The bitter waters of Mara were sweetened by
a certain wood (Exod. xv. 25).

It *reassures* you after you have *fallen into sin,* as the
Israelites were healed of the bites of the fiery serpents by looking upon the brazen serpent suspended
on the tree (Num. xxi. 9).

Thus the Mission-Cross is an encouragement to the
firm in remaining *steadfast;* a reminder to the *lukewarm* and wavering; a monitor to the *relapsed; a perpetual Mission.*

Like the stone which Josue erected under the oak in
the sanctuary at Sichem, let this Cross be a testimony
unto you — that it may remind you of all that has
been done in the Mission. — (Jos. xxiv. 26, 27).

Visit, then, this Cross often. The Church encourages you to do so by the many indulgences which she, to-day, attaches to it. Before it confirm yourselves in your good resolutions; rouse yourselves from a spirit of tepidity which may have seized upon you; put yourselves to shame; if you have fallen, pray for greater compunction and a stronger determination for the future, and through the merits of the cross seek again for reconciliation.

### III. Enemies and Friends of the Cross

When the standard of a conqueror is planted over the public buildings of a city or country that has fallen into the possession of a foreign power, it may be hated or loved by the inhabitants thereof in proportion to their love or hatred for the new government. Especially dear to a people is their own standard when it again floats in triumph over them, after they have been released from the thraldom of a government which held them in subjection.

When you were baptized, you were enrolled under the standard of the cross. You were afterward conquered by the enemy of Christ — the world and the devil; and, we regret to have to say it, you were conquered pretty much of your own free choice. Now the enemy is driven out of the land that belongs to Jesus Christ. You have seen your great mistake; your dispositions are changed. With joy you have listened to the *word of the cross,* and with free and full determination you have come back to be the friends of the standard of Jesus Christ.

"Christ sent me to preach the Gospel, not in wisdom of speech, lest the cross of Christ should be made void. For the word of the cross, to them indeed that perish, is foolishness; but to them that are saved, that is, to us, it is the power of God." — I Cor. i. 17, 18.

So we have done, and the result is before you. Some indeed have looked upon "the word of the cross as foolishness," and have not listened to it. Such are those given to sins of sensuality, and others.

"Many walk, of whom I have told you often (and now tell you weeping), that they are enemies of the cross of Christ; whose end is destruction; whose god is their belly; and whose glory is in their shame; who mind earthly thngs." — Phil. iii. 18, 19.

But *how will it be in future?* That depends on the fact whether Christ is to reign here or not. We have blessed (and raised) His sacred standard among you; you hail it with joy. Shall we be justified in proclaiming everywhere that Christ reigns in the midst of the Catholics of —— ?

"Tell it to the nations at large that the Lord reigns there from the wood" — of the cross!

Do you say truly, and will you always say: "God forbid that I should glory save . . ."?

Well, let the matter be *decided at once.*

Let us choose between Jesus Christ and the devil — between life and death — salvation and damnation — heaven and hell.

I shall do with you this moment as Josue did with the people of Israel in the desert shortly before their entrance into the land of promise. Having set before them all the benefits received from God, as well as their repeated infidelities, he asked them to declare themselves whether they would serve Him in future or not. They all unanimously declared themselves for God. A stone was erected as a monument of the promise.

On another occasion things turned out differently. Pontius Pilate placed before the same people Jesus Christ and a robber, Barabbas. There Christ was unanimously rejected and the robber preferred.

Here I place before you *Jesus Christ,* while on the other side stands *the devil.* Make your choice! I know that this infernal beast is here, keeping himself hidden in some corner, expecting some to declare themselves for him.

Perhaps some have done so already by staying from the Mission — confession — relapsing into sin. But they can yet change. To others he will insinuate that they must not make any declaration; that they cannot keep it; or, if they make it out of respect for others, they must not mean it.

Well then! Life or death — salvation or damnation? Whosoever will henceforth follow Jesus Christ, and desires to rally under His standard — the Cross — *let him stand up!*

Why! so many! I am astonished! What a joy for Heaven; what a consolation to your pastor; what a glory for this congregation, that so many are determined to serve Jesus Christ and follow the standard of the cross! But let me put you to the test! I shall propose to you certain obligations which, as true followers of Christ, you will be required to keep faithfully to the end of your lives. If you are determined to keep them, answer aloud and with determination that you are.

1. Are you willing to profess the faith of Jesus Christ as taught to you by the Holy Roman Catholic Church? If so — say: *I am.*

2. Are you willing to keep the commandments of God and the Church? If so . . .

3. Are you willing to flee from all sin? If so . . .

But even this alone is not enough — also the occasion must be avoided.

4. Are you then also willing carefully to shun the dangers and occasions of sin? If so . . .

(Here may be mentioned one or two points in particular.)

To carry out these resolutions, the means must be practised. Therefore,

5. Are you willing to practise holy prayer and frequent the sacraments? If so . . .

6. And are you willing and determined to carry out these holy resolutions until the end of your lives? If so, say, once more: *"I am."*

Well done! Now fall on your knees before this Cross and make your declaration:

O Jesus, my crucified Saviour! In presence of this Cross and the entire heavenly court, I choose Thee this day for my Lord, whom I will serve faithfully all the days of my life. Take possession of my heart, and be the Ruler of my entire being. I will be Thine in life; I will be Thine in death; I will be Thine for all eternity — My Jesus and my all! — forever! Amen.

Glory be to God in the heavens! Jesus Christ has conquered, He reigns over the hearts of His people. Ye angels and men, give thanks to the Most High — proclaim the triumphs of the cross. And thou, O sweet Mother Mary! stand at the side of these thy children, protect them in danger, and lead them to their final victory and triumph in heaven! Amen.

# XVIII

## PERSEVERANCE

This sermon forms the close of the Mission. It is, as it were, a recapitulation of the whole Misson, with special reference to the Means of Perseverance and a paternal, almost affectionate, admonition to put them in practice.

This last discourse is to be given in a most familiar and cordial manner. The more it possesses these qualities, the more affecting and efficacious will it be. It should not last so long as the other sermons; if it does it will lose much in effectiveness. The last words of a departing father are short, but impressive. Such should be the parting words of the missionary, as regards both the sermon and the valedictory. Besides, the sermon is to be followed by the Farewell Address and the Papal benediction.

If the chief Means of Perseverance have not been preached before, they will form the three parts of this sermon, which may be developed according to the following plan: —

A Christian exists and lives in the order of nature and in the order of grace. For the preservation of the life of nature, three conditions must be fulfilled. The first may be required rarely; the second needs to be fulfilled often; the third without intermission. The first is, to keep from the danger of death; the second, to take nourishment; the third, to breathe the air around us. The very same is required for the preservation of the spiritual life. The first, keep away from the occasion of sin; the second, frequent the sacraments; the third, practise holy prayer.[1] Then the most essential arguments are adduced for each of these three conditions. Having said all that is necessary on these three points, the preacher appeals to the feelings of his hearers so as to move them to make a generous resolution, which at his suggestion they must pronounce with a loud voice.

Should the Means of Perseverance have been preached before,

[1] St. Alphonsus says: "We should frequently recall to the mind of the hearers the three great means of keeping one's self in the grace of God, namely: 1. to avoid sinful occasions and bad companions; 2. always to recommend one's self to God by prayer; 3. to frequent the sacraments." C. E., Vol. XV. p. 157 and 177.

either singly or together, then this sermon must speak first of the *obstacles* of perseverance; after this, these three means are briefly repeated, and the special method is indicated which everybody can practise with ease; namely, 1, Keep up *courage* by looking only upon the present day and not so much into the future, and by considering the great help that we have at our command; 2, Be faithful in *small matters;* and 3, Discard all *human respect.* — Another division of this subject is to be found in the second series of these Sketches. — Then the final resolution is introduced.

Should the missionary make the people rise and pronounce their resolution aloud? The answer to this question is to be given decidedly in the affirmative. A resolution pronounced aloud is remembered ten times longer than one formed simply in the heart. — If the missionary does not make the people speak, a great part of them may not even know what he has been talking about, and yet, everything will depend on these resolutions. — The solemn manner in which these resolutions are made will bring back the whole Mission to the minds of the people and will not be forgotten so soon. — The Rule prescribes that such promises should be made by the people after their general Communion. *"Tum ab iis* PROMISSIO OBTINEBITUR, *frequenter utendi sacramentis, fugiendi peccata illiusque vitandi occasiones."* [2] We have no general Communions; therefore, we take these promises at the close of the Mission. — The Rule says also that in closing the Mission, *"servetur modus a S. Alphonso præscriptus."* [3] And St. Alphonsus made the people speak aloud at least four times when he closed a Mission. [4] Our missionaries have always done this in Europe; they have done so in this country. Why, then, should it not be done?

The sermon is immediately followed by the *Missionary's Valedictory*.

This last address should be most cordial, and should be short. There is consequently no time for enlarging on points of minor significance; nor should the means of perseverance be dwelt upon again, nor certain points be introduced which the missionary would especially recommend. — Our Rule prescribes that this address, together with the Papal benediction, should be given in conformity with the method of St. Alphonsus. With some little modification, in consideration of the customs of this country, that method will be found in its proper place.

[2] R., n. 142.     [3] R., n. 149.
[4] C. E., Vol. XV. p. 223. — And how many times did not the Saint make the people speak aloud at the act of contrition?

## Sketch

Text: "Therefore, my beloved brethren, be ye steadfast and immovable: always abounding in the work of the Lord, knowing that your labor is not in vain in the Lord." — I Cor. xv. 58.

Exordium. — Once more, and for the last time, do we appear before you, to say to you our last words of admonition and consolation. We must thank the goodness and mercy of God for the great change that has taken place in this congregation. How many hearts are now full of consolation which before the Mission were agitated by the terror of hell! But will they persevere? Before they received absolution, they gave expression to their determination of doing better. I have no doubt that you are all determined to save your souls. It remains now that you always "be steadfast and immovable" in this determination. On this your salvation depends. Let me then admonish you to this holy perseverance. I solicit your special attention to these my last words, which must be few, but which are so much the more weighty.

### I. Obstacles to Perseverance

That there are difficulties to be encountered is sufficiently indicated by the words, "be steadfast and immovable."

Your *enemies* are the same as they have been heretofore. With the exception of one they have not changed.

Your *sinful nature* has not been changed by the Mission. Your soul has been changed, not your flesh and blood. You will have to struggle harder against the demands of your evil propensities, which are not yet accustomed to have their desires refused.

The *world* and *its allurements,* fashions, attractions, theaters, papers, books, liquor-shops . . . are the same. It will cost you some exertion to look upon them as your most dangerous enemies, whom you so long considered your friends. How will you stand the ridicule, the criticism, of that world which you have hitherto feared so much? Some of the very individuals who have made the Mission with you, will turn against you, saying that you take the warnings of the missionaries in too strict a sense.

But there is a great change in your third enemy, *the devil.* This wicked and proud spirit, now banished from the souls which he kept so long in his grasp, will not give up. He will try his utmost to get back what he has lost in the Mission. He has already devised means, snares, traps, . . . the nature of which neither you nor I know, to be employed after the Mission with the skill and vigor of a demon.

"When the unclean spirit is gone out of a man, he walketh through places without water [disconsolate], seeking rest; and not finding, he saith: I will return into my house whence I came out; and when he is come, he findeth it swept [pure] and garnished [acts of virtue]. Then he goeth [seeing himself alone not sufficiently strong] and taketh with himself seven other spirits more wicked than himself, and entering in [if they succeed] they dwell there [for good]. And the last state of that man becomes worse than the first." — Luke xi. 24–26.

Then the relapsed sinner will be kept from prayer, Mass, sermons, Missions, confession, . . . and will be driven to despair.

Our Lord, no doubt, spoke here from His universal knowledge.

God permits all these trials to test the fidelity of the converted soul, and to give it an opportunity of making up for past deficiencies.

This should not discourage you, but only put you

on your guard. Your enemies are strong, but you surpass them by far, in strength, provided you make good use of the —

## II. MEANS OF PERSEVERANCE

They have been explained to you. They are chiefly these three: Flight from the occasions of sin — frequentation of the sacraments — and holy prayer.

How are you to employ them?

1. Be careful and watchful in *small things*. In regard to the occasions of sin, flee from the least danger in conversation, reading, looks, amusements. . . . Never say, "There is no harm" — nor, "There is no danger; I know how to take care of myself." In regard to the sacraments, rather anticipate than postpone your appointed periods of frequenting them. Never say, "Next week." As to prayer, never omit it any morning or night, in the presence of any temptation. Never deem yourself secure without prayer.

"He that contemneth small things, shall fall by little and little." — Eccli. xix. 1.

2. *Do not lose courage* on account of your many temptations, nor even when you fall into a sin, great or small. Your fall should simply rekindle and redouble your fervor — not quench it.

It is an ordinary temptation of hell to make Christians "give up" their endeavors to avoid sin. Yield, and hell has gained the victory. Two contesting armies do not "give up," in spite of their repeated defeats. How much the more should you always begin anew, because the kingdom of heaven is at stake.

"The life of man upon earth is a warfare." — Job vii. 1.

Love God, and He will be with you. Love Jesus Christ, and He will be in you. Love the Blessed Virgin Mary, and she will protect you. Love the angels and saints, and they will proceed into battle with you.

"If God be for us, who is against us?" — Rom. viii. 31.

Thus you will be able to say with St. Paul:

"Neither death, nor life, nor angels, nor principalities, nor powers, nor things present, nor things to come, nor might, nor height, nor depth, nor any other creature, shall be able to separate us from the love of God, which is in Christ Jesus our Lord." — Rom. viii. 38, 39.

3. Keep yourself *under the protection of the Blessed Virgin Mary*. She has crushed the head of the infernal serpent. All the holy writers say that no one who perseveres in true devotion to the Blessed Virgin will ever be lost. Profess yourselves her children, call upon her in temptation. Let her be your guide through life.

"He that shall find me, shall find life, and shall have salvation from the Lord." — Prov. viii. 35.

Follow these directions, and the chief means of perseverance will become easy for you.

### III. Mournful Consequences of the Neglect of these Means — Happy Result of their Use

After the Mission there will be three classes of people in the congregation.

1. Those who know the means of perseverance, but *neglect to do anything*. They resemble a sick man who wishes to recover his health, but refuses all medicine. Such people go to ruin.

2. Those who make use of some means — or use them only to some extent, as it pleases their own weakness and sensual propensities. Neither will they be saved. They resemble the actors on the stage.

who represent emperors, kings, priests, . . . without being such in reality. Such people imagine themselves good Christians, while they are sensual, worldly-minded, self-conceited creatures, who cannot be the friends of God.

3. Those who faithfully employ the means as they are prescribed by God, explained by the Church, and dictated by a sense of sound morality. These only are saved.

"Know you not that they who run in the race, all run indeed, but one receiveth the prize? So run that you may obtain. And every one that striveth for the mastery, refraineth himself from all things." — I Cor. ix. 24, 25. — "Be thou faithful until death: and I will give thee the crown of life." — Apoc. ii. 10. — "He that shall overcome, shall be clothed in white garments . . . and I will confess his name before my Father, and before his angels." — Ib. iii. 5. — "To him that shall overcome, I will give · to sit with me in my throne." — Ib. iii. 21.

O happiness! O glory! to be clothed in heavenly white garments; to sit with Jesus Christ on the same throne; to receive praise from His own lips before God and the angels; to wear the crown of life. Oh! what a blessing!

And the combat is of very short duration — and, after all, very easy — while the reward is without end.

Resolve, then, to employ the means of perseverance in regard to the smaller matters, constantly and courageously, under the powerful protection of Mary! Thus you will certainly gain the victory, and celebrate an everlasting triumph in heaven. Amen.

Note. — The people should be induced, at the close of this sermon, to make the promise of practising the three chief Means of Perseverance, unless this has been done at the erection of the Mission-Cross. A method of proceeding is found in the third part of this volume, at the end of the sermon on the "Means of Perseverance."

# MISSIONARY'S FAREWELL

ABBREVIATED FORM ACCORDING TO ST. ALPHONSUS

THE ADDRESS. — Our work among you being accomplished, the time is come that we must part from each other. Our feelings of joy at the immense good done by this Mission are exceedingly great. Thanks be to God for the blessing bestowed on our labors — for so many souls are now reconciled to God! Yet we are aware that some have not made the Mission. We have preached for them — prayed for them . . . but all in vain. Now we must abandon them; but may the mercy of God not abandon them!

Those who could not receive the sacraments during the Mission may yet gain the indulgences of the Mission during fifteen days after the Mission.

Before leaving this pulpit, I have a threefold duty to perform — 1. To express our feelings of gratitude; 2. To ask a few favors; and 3. To give you the final blessing of the Mission.

1. Let me, first of all, express our thanks to your most respected and most beloved pastor (or bishop). We thank him for having intrusted the work of the Mission to our charge. We also thank him (and his worthy assistants) for the exceeding kindness, brotherly affection, and ready assistance, which he (they) has extended to us during the Mission. We now return to the hands of the Rev. Pastor his dear congregation, renewed and strengthened. May the great Pastor of souls, Jesus Christ, amply reward

him for the kind services rendered to us! May you be in future his pride and consolation on earth.

We also thank you for your regular attendance — your interest in the Mission — your patience with our shortcomings . . . and for all the affection that you have exhibited toward us, and the particular services that you have rendered us during the Mission. May God reward you for all!

2. Then I have three favors to ask: 1. That you will forgive us from your hearts should any of us have given you offence, either in the pulpit, or in the confessional, or on any other occasion. . . . 2. That you will not forget the Mission. When you see this pulpit, remember the sermons. . . . When you see those confessionals, remember the great consolation received there. . . . When you see these railings . . . this Mission-Cross. 3. Do not forget the missionaries in your prayers, as we shall also pray for you. Should you hear of the death of any one of us, pray for his poor soul. . . .

3. And now prepare your hearts for the reception of a threefold blessing. 1. The blessing of the missionaries; 2. The blessing of the Sovereign Pontiff; and, 3. The blessing of Jesus Christ in the Blessed Sacrament.

So then, in the name of the Most Blessed Trinity, of Jesus your Redeemer, of the Blessed Virgin, of St. Joseph, and of all the angels and saints, I raise my hands over you and every house in this parish, imploring heaven to bless every Catholic soul of goodwill within its limits. May God bless the fathers and mothers, the sons and daughters, the innocent children, the sick, the suffering, and the dying! May He bless your various occupations, the food that you eat, the air that you breathe, the ground on which you walk, every day of your life, and the hour of your death. . . . In the name of the Father and (✠) of the Son and of the Holy Ghost.

(To this blessing shall at once be added the — )

PAPAL BENEDICTION. — It is the most ardent desire of the Sovereign Pontiff to give a special blessing to those congregations which have made the Mission, and grant them an additional Plenary Indulgence. He cannot do so in person, so he empowers the missionaries to do it in his name with the crucifix which they wear on their breast. I shall most cheerfully fulfil this commission. To gain this indulgence, excite your hearts once more to true contrition for all your sins . . . promising never to sin again, and to be always fully resigned to the holy will of God. Let us, then, say together a short act of contrition:

O my God! I am heartily sorry for all the sins that I have ever committed, because by them I have offended Thee, the Infinite Good. I am firmly resolved to love Thee in future and never more to offend Thee.

*Confiteor* (said by a priest or the altar-boys). The missionary says: *Misereatur . . . Indulgentiam . . .*

Then making the sign of the cross with his crucifix over the people, the missionary says:

*Benedictio Dei omnipotentis, Patris et Filii* (✠) *et Spiritus Sancti, descendat super vos et maneat semper. Amen.* Translate this for the people — "May the blessing of the Almighty God, Father, Son and Holy Ghost come down upon you and remain with you forever. Amen."

(The papal benediction at the close of our Missions, including all that belongs to it, is pronounced with a loud voice — but not chanted.)

Let us now fulfil the last condition, and devoutly say for the intention of the Holy Father five Our

Fathers and five Hail Marys. (Recitation of the prayers.)

Now let your hearts break forth in acts of holy thanksgiving. Let the organ resound, let the voices of the choir sing a hymn of praise, let your hearts join in the chorus! (Let the bells ring out a joyous peal and announce our joy to the world outside.) Let heaven take it up, and carry our thanks to the foot of the throne of the Most High! Then wilt Thou, also, O Jesus! bless these happy souls. Oh! do bless them, and keep them all united to Thy most sacred heart! As for me, my task is done, my lips must close. But my heart desires to say one single word more, and that is — Farewell! — In heaven we hope to meet again.

# XIX

## SOULS IN PURGATORY

In accordance with the approved custom of all missionaries, of celebrating a High Mass of Requiem for the deceased members of the congregation to which the Mission has been given, and for the relatives of those who have made the Mission, it has always been deemed most useful to exhort the people on that occasion, whenever time and circumstances permit, to a greater fervor in behalf of the poor suffering souls. It is not to be a controversial sermon on the dogma of Purgatory. The audience consists of true believers, whose faith, so shortly after the Mission, is certainly strong enough. The sermon should not be very long, and should be confined to such arguments as will give a new impulse to the audience to advocate the cause of the souls departed. It should be replete with pious sentiment and unction, so as not only to instruct the minds, but also to move the hearts of the hearers. It is the rule of the Church to preach on such occasions immediately before the *Libera and the Absolution*.[1]

St. Alphonsus says nothing of this sermon, nor does the Rule speak of it. But for a long time it has been the custom to preach this sermon, both in' Europe and America. The document by which the Holy See has granted certain privileges to this Mass, and in which also the sermon is mentioned, is dated April 22, 1858.[2]

### SKETCH

TEXT: "Have pity on me, have pity on me, at least you my friends, because the hand of the Lord hath touched me," — Job xix. 21.

EXORDIUM. — Before leaving this church, we would perform an act of charity for the relief of the poorest, the most destitute, the most suffering portion of this community. They are your friends and relatives in Purgatory. They often cry for assistance: "Have

[1] *Rubr. missae. Ritus in celebr. Missae, III.* 3.
[2] Privil., p. 104, n. 132; Doc. Auth., p. 281, n. 193.

pity on me. . . ." But you do not hear them. They could not participate in the indulgences of the Mission, therefore we have given them the benefit of the Holy Sacrifice.

In order that you may never forget them — that your fervor may be even redoubled in their behalf — let me place before your minds the motives which we have for helping them, and the manner in which we should fulfil this duty.

## I. The Sufferings of the Souls in Purgatory are Inconceivably Great

1. Because they are *supernatural*. The least pain endured in Purgatory exceeds all the suffering that can possibly be endured within the limits of nature.

"All imaginable pains in this world are nothing in comparison with the sufferings of purgatory." — St. Bernard. — "Perhaps some one will say, I care not for purgatory as long as I have hope of entering everlasting life. But let all beware of speaking thus, because that fire of purgatory is more painful than any pain or suffering that may be seen or felt in this world." — Cæs. Arel. — "I cannot say what kind of pains these souls suffer, but I can say this much, that each of them would rather suffer all tortures that ever were, are now, and will be endured by men until the end of time, than stay in purgatory but a single day." — St. Cyril of Alex.

2. Because these pains involve *a separation from God*. The state of those souls is that of temporary damnation. The soul is the breath of God. After its time of probation, it longs to be united to God, with a force commensurable with the beauty of God which naturally attracts it. To be kept from a union with God causes, then, a proportionate pain, which is in some respects infinite. Our Lord suffered that pain. It forced from Him the cry: "My God, my God, why hast Thou forsaken me?" — (Matt. xxvii. 46).

3. Because the sufferings of those souls are *equal to*

*those of the damned in hell*. With many, Purgatory is only a temporary hell.

"Who will grant me this, that Thou mayest protect me in *hell*, and hide me till Thy wrath pass, and appoint me a time when Thou wilt remember me?" — Job xiv. 13. — "The same fire that torments the damned in hell, is also the fire that purifies the souls in purgatory." — St. Aug., — St. Greg., — St. Denis Carth., — St. Thomas.

Therefore the Church prays:

"From the gate of hell, O Lord, deliver their souls." — Off. Def. — "Deliver me, O Lord, from the pains of hell . . ." — Lib.

## II. These Most Intense Sufferings are Indescribably Long

1. Because *every single sin, mortal and venial,* not yet atoned for, receives its special punishment. Among these are millions which are committed hourly without being regarded as sinful, *e.g.*, idle talk (Matt. xii. 36). Then those horrible mortal sins, for every single one of which the Church used to inflict in olden times years and years of hard penance. And one day of penance performed in this life is equivalent to years of penance in the next.

2. Because men are most *neglectful in doing penance*. Hardly will they perform the penance prescribed by the priest, and the acts of mortification enjoined by the Church. They even become impatient at the sufferings sent them by a loving Providence.

"The days that are given to us for the purification of our souls we must fulfil, whether we will or not. But, woe be to us if the days are ended, and the intended purification is not ended, because then it becomes necessary that we be purified by that fire than which nothing more excruciating can be imagined." — St. Bernard.

3. Because those souls *cannot do anything for themselves*. They can only suffer, first for one sin, then for the second, the third . . . to the very last one.

"The night cometh when no man can work." — John ix. 4.

How long, then, must they suffer until the long catalogue of sins is gone through?

"Call me, and I will answer Thee: or else I will speak, and do Thou answer me. How many are my iniquities and sins? make me know my crimes and offences. Why hidest Thou Thy face, and thinkest me Thy enemy?" — Job xiii. 22, 23.

No wonder, then, that St. Augustine recommended to the prayers of his friends the soul of his saintly mother thirty years after her death.

Ven. Bede and St. Denis Carth. say that some souls must suffer until the Judgment-day.

4. They *cannot even make known* their sufferings, so as to ask for relief. They would wish to appear to their friends, inspire the preachers. . . . We admonish the faithful to pray for them; we read out the names of the deceased. This is all. Their greatest misfortune is perhaps this, that they are already believed to be in heaven. "Alas!" they cry out, "who will make known my sufferings to my parents, children, friends, . . .? Have pity on me! But you have forgotten me!"

### III. How Can we Assist Them?

In many ways.

1. By helping them to *pay off their debt*. By patience in our trials, daily work, poverty, mortification of the palate in eating and drinking, alms, prayers, Communions. . . . These works offered for the poor souls give them relief, and shorten their time of banishment from God.

2. By having the Holy Sacrifice of *the Mass* offered, which is the great offering of atonement. Especially immediately after the death of our relatives — Requiem Mass — on the third, seventh, thirtieth day and anniversary, instead of "wakes" — expensive fu-

nerals — costly tombstones — customs derived from Protestants, who do not believe in Purgatory.

3. By gaining *indulgences,* plenary and partial, for their relief, for which we have so many opportunities. Enumeration of some.

Notwithstanding so many ways open to us of obtaining relief for the suffering souls, we are guilty of gross neglect in their regard — even toward our own nearest and dearest relatives — father, mother, brothers, sisters, grandparents. Who will help them if not we? "Have pity on me . . . at least you, my friends!" It is possible that our own relatives are among the most abandoned. Many are released, owing to the generosity of their friends on earth — *our* friends wait in vain for help.

And yet it may be that they suffer on our account. The father and mother for cursing their disobedient children — for allowing bad company — amusements — for neglect of proper education — chastisement . . . They worked hard — suffered privations . . . for their children for years; now they are abandoned by them. Their children cannot afford to do anything for their parents. They spend too much for drink, vanities. . . . But God will take revenge on such forgetful children.

"Remember thy father and thy mother . . . lest God forget thee in their sight, and thou . . . wish that thou hadst not been born, and curse the day of thy nativity." — Eccli. xxiii. 18, 19.

CONCLUSION. — Recapitulation.

What have I effected by all this? Perhaps elicited a few tears from the eyes of my hearers, and no more. Shall this, indeed, be all? Oh! forget not, forget not, that you may not be forgotten! Never cease in the exercise of this kind of charity. When you are in the same state of desolation and suffering, you will also find friends who will interest themselves in your behalf. Thus let us go on assisting one another, until we shall all be united with God in heaven, where we shall sing the mercies of God forever.

"Eternal rest grant, O Lord, to all the souls departed and to us all! And let perpetual light shine upon us! Amen."

THIRD PART

SKETCHES FOR MISSION SERMONS

SECOND SERIES

# I

## INTRODUCTORY

TEXT: "Behold, I bring you good tidings of great joy, that shall be to all the people." — Luke ii. 10.

EXORDIUM. — This joyful salutation means the same for this congregation to-day that it meant for the poor shepherds in the fields near Bethlehem, and through them for the whole world. Then this salutation announced redemption, salvation, eternal joy to the world; it announces the same thing to you to-day. What is the meaning of this cross — of the priests, who are strangers, and who are introduced to you? All this means a *Mission,* with all its consolations, graces, and blessings!

Whenever we are about to undertake anything extraordinary, we first ask *what* it is — secondly, *what benefit* we are to derive from it — and thirdly, *how* we are to do it. It is my duty to give you a satisfactory answer to these three questions in regard to the Mission. May Jesus and Mary grant a special blessing to my words!

## I. A MISSION IS THE EXERCISE OF THE EXTRAORDINARY MINISTRY OF THE CHURCH

The ordinary ministry of the Church consists in the usual work of a local pastor; that is, in preaching, in administering the Sacraments, in attending to the spiritual welfare of the people. The extraordinary ministry consists in performing the same work, but in performing it in an *extraordinary manner*.

1. The work of the Mission is performed by *extraordinary persons*. The priests who conduct a Mission have received a special commission for that purpose. They are sent for this special object and for no other; therefore, they are called *missionaries*. They are the special messengers of God.

"For Christ, therefore, we are ambassadors, God, as it were, exhorting by us." — II Cor. v. 20.

The missionaries receive a special training for their extraordinary work. Generally, they are members of some Religious Community, which has received the special vocation from God, to educate and send out priests especially fitted for this work. Though they are not more than other priests, than local pastors, yet they are of extraordinary assistance to them; they are sent to them to undo the devil's work in various parishes, and to uncover the hidden artifices of the powers of darkness.

"He hath made my mouth like a sharp sword . . . and hath made me as a chosen arrow: in his quiver he hath hidden me." — Is. xlix. 2. — "Behold I will send many fishers, and they shall fish them; and after this I will send them many hunters, and they shall hunt them from every mountain, and from every hill, and out of the holes of the rocks." — Jer. xvi. 16.

The fishers, says Cornelius à Lapide, are the local pastors, the hunters are the missionaries.

2. The missionaries come to the Mission accompanied by *extraordinary grace*. The Mission is God's work. He ordains it, although it is brought about through human agency. God gives extraordinary grace to the missionaries — to their work — to the people. This is clear from the extraordinary results produced by Missions, and within a very short time,

results, which without grace so extraordinary would be impossible.

"In an acceptable time I have heard thee, and in the day of salvation I have helped thee." — Is. xlix. 8.

The Mission is such an "acceptable time" and such a "day of salvation."

3. By this grace an *extraordinary blessing* is attached to the work of the missionaries in the *pulpit* and in the *confessional.* The grace of God is imparted to every sermon, but to a Mission-sermon it is given in an extraordinary degree, so that it may, indeed, "show spirit and power" (I Cor. ii. 4), and become "more piercing than any two-edged sword, reaching unto the division of the soul and the spirit, of the joints and the marrow" (Heb. iv. 12).

"For it is not you that speak but the spirit of your Father that speaketh in you." — Matt. x. 20. — "He whom God hath sent speaketh the words of God: for God doth not give the spirit by measure." — John iii. 34.

The Church, knowing the good effects of a Mission-sermon, grants seven years and seven times forty days indulgence to those who hear it, in order to induce the people to appreciate it.

The Sacrament of Penance, so much dreaded at other times, is eagerly sought in the Mission. People who neglected this sacrament for years, are the first at the confessional in the Mission, with the best dispositions, trampling all shame under foot, giving up long-protracted habits of sin, gaining complete victory over their wicked nature and receiving superabundant consolation.

"They are . . . again according to the months past, according to the days in which God kept them." — Job xxix. 2.

4. And that there may be no obstacle in the way, the Church endows the missionaries with *extraordinary*

*power* — so that there may be no sinner, however depraved, who may not receive full remission of his sins during the Mission, provided he be animated with a good will. The missionary can say in truth:

"All power is given to me in heaven and in earth." — Matt. xxviii. 18. — "Whatsoever you shall loose upon earth, shall be loosed also in heaven." — Matt. xviii. 18.

5. Accordingly, *the result* of the Mission is *extraordinary*. The missionaries who give Missions, not among heathen nations but among Catholics, have the same commission that was first given to the Apostles by our dear Lord when He said:

"Go ye not into the way of the gentiles . . . but go ye rather to the lost sleep of the house of Israel. And going, preach, saying: the kingdom of heaven is at hand." — Matt. x. 5-7.

There is, however, this difference, that the Apostles could only announce the coming of the kingdom of heaven, which was not yet established; while their successors, the missionaries of the present day, put the happy people who attend the Mission in possession of it.

They remove all the *obstacles* that stand in the way. Those who make a Mission are never so sure that their past sins are forgiven as they are after a Mission — because their dispositions have all the requisite qualifications. Those who make a Mission gain, more than once, a plenary indulgence, that is, the full remission of all temporal punishment: and at no other time are they surer of this than at a Mission. The kingdom of heaven is theirs; nothing prevents them from taking possession of it, should they die then. And, in order that they may not lose it again, the means by which they can very easily keep themselves in the way that leads to it, are placed in their hands.

How great, therefore, are the consolations that are

derived from a Mission. Was I right when I said: I announce to you "good tidings of great joy"?

And for whom is that joy? "For all the people."

## II. THE BLESSINGS OF A MISSION ARE FOR ALL THE PEOPLE OF THE PARISH

*A. For the good people.*

Do good people need a Mission? Yes, they do:

1. *To guard them against falling into sin.* Does not the number of the wicked increase day after day, owing to the neglect of religious duties on the part of good people, and sometimes of even the very best? The danger, then, is great.

"Wherefore, he that thinketh himself to stand, let him take heed lest he fall." — I Cor. x. 12. — "Howl, thou fir-tree, for the cedar is fallen, for the mighty are laid waste." — Zach. xi. 2.

2. *To correct their errors.* Many are counted among the good, though they are astray. There is a general inclination manifesting itself among so-called good people to explain the law of God and of the Church in a manner that is more agreeable to human nature. There exists a great deal of "private judgment," which finally leads to destruction.

"There is a way which seemeth just to a man: but the ends thereof lead to death." — Prov. xiv. 12.

Among these is to be found the very large number of Catholics who try to do what the Lord Jesus has declared to be impossible:

"No man can serve two masters." — Matt. vi. 24.

3. *To put an end to their sacrileges.* — For some reason or other many of these so-called good people receive the sacraments sacrilegiously. They have not as yet confessed what is buried in the lowest recesses of their hearts. Nobody knows the miserable

state of their souls; perhaps they do not realize it themselves. The Mission will heal these wounds without anybody's becoming the wiser.

4. *To give them the necessary instructions* in regard to their religious duties, both *general* and *particular.* The very best of our Catholics are often in a deplorable state of ignorance; and this cannot be excused.

"God indeed having winked at the times of this ignorance, now declareth unto men, that all should everywhere do penance." — Acts xvii. 30.

5. *To give the necessary exhortations, instructions and directions,* especially to the *growing-up children* and to the *rising generation,* that they may become imbued with sound principles from their childhood, and be put on their guard against the pernicious maxims of the world and of the devil. — Children's Mission. — Invitation to it.

*B. For the wicked and evil-minded people.*

The missionaries are sent principally to the "lost sheep of the house of Israel," *i.e.,* of the true Church.

1. Every congregation has a large share of them. *Who are they?* They are:

*a.* Those who are living, more or less, in sin. The days during which they live in the state of grace are very few. They go to church, to the sacraments once in a great while; they speak of doing better: but they are never in real earnest.

*b.* Those who are not much concerned about the precepts of the Church, and who disregard them for the slightest reasons.

*c.* Those who have separated themselves from the Church by joining some secret society, by a certain marriage, or for some other cause.

*d.* Those who no longer receive the sacraments; who have openly apostatized from the faith; or who have never received any sacrament except Baptism; or who are not known as Catholics.

*e.* Those who openly blaspheme God, who deride religion, who have become confirmed infidels.

*f.* Those who never belonged to the Church — "other sheep that are not of this fold; those must be brought, that they may hear the voice of Christ and belong to the one fold and under the one shepherd" (John x. 16).

All these — and others — it is certain, must have a Mission.

"If, peradventure, God may give them repentance to know the truth, and they may recover themselves from the snares of the devil, by whom they are held captive at his will." — II Tim. ii. 25, 26.

2. The *ordinary ministry* of the Church is for them *insufficient,* because they keep at a distance from the Church, and do not allow themselves to be brought under the beneficent influence of the pastor. The Mission is necessary. God gives them an opportunity to have a Mission.

"Say to them: As I live, saith the Lord God, I desire not the death of the wicked, but that the wicked turn from his way and live." — Ez. xxxiii. 11. — "And he said to them: Go, behold I send you as lambs among wolves." — Luke x. 3.

3. God in heaven, the Blessed Virgin Mary, the Church on earth, Jesus in the Blessed Sacrament, the angels make every effort to bless the labors of the missionaries with success. The missionaries, on their part, act toward those sinners, as Eliseus did toward the dead child whom he raised to life.

"Going in he shut the door upon him, and upon the child (exclusion of every other work), and prayed to the Lord (prayers of the missionaries). And he went up and lay upon the child; and he put his mouth upon his mouth, and his eyes upon his eyes, and his hands upon his hands; and he bowed himself upon him (practical discourses adapted to the needs of the sinner, — the missionary becoming all to all), and the child's flesh grew warm (first effects of the Mission). Then he returned and walked in the house, once to and fro; and he went up and lay upon him (repeated efforts of the missionaries), and the child gaped seven times, and opened his eyes." — IV Kings iv. 32-35.

4. The missionaries *openly attack the powers of darkness,* to force them to surrender the souls held captive by them — souls once bought at the price of the blood of Jesus Christ. Exorcism at the opening of the Mission. Like Moses and Aaron before Pharao, they demand the release of the people of God.

"Thus saith the Lord God of Israel: Let my people go." — Exod. v. 1.

5. Often those poor, deluded sinners are glad to obtain this opportunity of effecting their reconciliation with God. They are tired of their sinful lives.

"We wearied ourselves in the way of iniquity and destruction and have walked through hard ways." — Wis. v. 7.

How consoling for their wayward hearts is the kind invitation to return and the promise of pardon.

"Come to me all ye that labor, and are burdened and I will refresh you." — Matt. xi. 28. — "And if your sins be as scarlet, they shall be made white as snow, and if they be red as crimson, they shall be white as wool." — Is. i. 18.

Some may resist for a time, but grace will finally triumph over their obstinacy. Others may refuse the call of God to the end. So much the worse for them. Their damnation is so much the greater. Therefore,

"We do exhort you, that you receive not the grace of God in vain." — II Cor. vi. 1.

### III. Means to be Employed in Order to Profit by the Mission

When the angel announced the tidings of great joy to the shepherds in the fields of Bethlehem, he added that peace and happiness would be imparted to "men on earth of good will" (Luke ii. 14). So it will be during the Mission. Only those will be benefited by it who have a *good will;* and this good will must show itself by a faithful *coöperation* with the grace offered. But as the grace is something extraordinary, so is the whole work of the Mission; and therefore the co-operation on the part of the people is expected to be *extraordinary* also. This being the case, it is necessary for you:

1. To be *more than usually recollected* as long as the Mission lasts. *a.* By keeping away from even innocent amusements and noisy assemblies, taverns, etc. *b.* By performing no more than your ordinary work, and by having your mind occupied no more than is necessary about business transactions. *c.* By spending more time in the church and in deep reflection on what you hear in the sermons.

"I will lead her into the wilderness and I will speak to her heart." — Os. ii. 14, says the Lord, of His beloved people.

2. To *listen to the sermons* — *a,* regularly, by hearing all of them as far as possible; *b,* with a docile heart, avoiding criticism, giving up false principles, if you find them condemned by the sermons. Say, as did Samuel:

"Speak, Lord, for thy servant heareth." — I Kings iii. 10. — "He that despiseth you despiseth me. And he that despiseth me, despiseth him that sent me." — Luke x. 16. — "And whosoever . . . shall not hear your words, going forth out of that house shake off the dust from your feet. Amen I say . . . it shall be more tolerable for the land of Sodom . . ." — Matt. x. 14, 15.

3. To *pray* — *a,* more fervently — *b,* more frequently — *c,* for yourself and for the members of your family, that this grace may not be given in vain. By prayer you render it, indeed, effectual.

"Pray one for another that you may be saved. For the continual prayer of the just man availeth much." — James v. 16.

4. To *cease committing sin* — and to avoid the occasions thereof; to give up bad habits, enmity, etc. By still adding to the number of your sins, you may make yourself forever unworthy of the mercy of God.

"I expected my vineyard to bring forth grapes, and it brought forth wild grapes . . . therefore I will make it desolate." — Is. v. 2, 6.

CONCLUSION. — General invitation to all. Encouragement to the desponding.

"Look up and lift up your heads [toward this cross], because your redemption is at hand." — Luke xxi. 28.

Thank God for this extraordinary grace — make up your minds at once to profit by it. Oh! may there not be a single man, woman, young man or young woman in this congregation who will neglect the Mission!

Recommendation of the Mission to the Blessed Virgin Mary.

# II

## IMPORTANCE OF SALVATION

Text: "Who can be saved?" — Matt. xix. 25.

Exordium. — Our Lord Jesus had spoken of certain classes of people for whom salvation is most difficult, when the apostles asked this question. We often hear people ask the same question. half in despair, as it were, as though scarcely any one could be saved. Salvation is not impossible, nor even very difficult, if man goes about securing it in the right way. But a vast multitude of people neglect this, and, therefore, they are not, they cannot be saved. With the assistance of God I shall set forth the principles by which a man must be guided, if he wishes to be saved. May you understand then and forthwith put them into practice.

### I. The Work of our Salvation is our own Personal Affair

1. This means that we must attend to it ourselves *personally*. God, the Father, the Son, and the Holy Ghost have done infinitely more for our salvation than is required. The Church, the priests, work for our salvation without intermission — but a few things cannot be done for us by any one else; we have to do them ourselves.

Every other work we may have done by others — the work in the field, in the house, in preparing our food; but the work of our salvation is our *personal* work.

"He that created you without you, will not save you without you." — St. Aug.

2. Salvation is to be to us a *reward*. But how can there be a reward without *merit;* and how can there be merit without personal efforts?

"Strive to enter by the narrow gate." — Luke xiii. 24.

What must become of those who do not "strive" at all? (For further proofs see Sermon in First Series, p. 136.)

3. Therefore, to be saved, a man must have the *will*, the determination, to work out his salvation. When St. Thomas Aquinas was asked by his sisters what they should do to be saved, he answered: "You must have the will to be saved."

Therefore, it is not enough to say: "I would like to be saved" — "I wish to . . ."; you must say, "I will — I am determined to be saved."

Many would like to go to heaven, in fact all people desire to be saved, but for the lack of the will to be saved many are lost. Every one of the damned is forced to say: "I could have been saved, but I had no will to be saved."

"To be saved we have no need of a vehicle or of a sail, not even of hands or feet, but of a will." — St. Aug.

## II. The Work of our Salvation is our Most Important Affair

And therefore, it must go before everything else; everything else must aim at this, *i.e.*, must be directed to this work.

1. There is question not about wealth or poverty, not about high or low position in life, not about honor

or disgrace, health or sickness, but about *heaven* or *hell* — for an *endless eternity*.

"What doth it profit a man . . ." — Matt. xvi. 26. — "My spirit shall be wasted, my days shall be shortened, and only the grave remaineth for me." — Job xvii. 1.

Of what benefit to Solomon is his earthly glory, to Napoleon his fame, to Crœsus his wealth, if they are not saved?

When St. Bernard and his elder brothers left their rich home for the monastery, they said to their younger brother Nivard: "We leave the world; therefore, this magnificent castle and all its wealth are yours." "What!" said Nivard, "you take heaven for yourselves and leave me the earth!" and he followed them to the monastery. Thousands of others would have done the contrary.

2. A man must *sacrifice* everything rather than neglect his salvation — *suffer every loss* rather than the loss of his soul. Then there is no loss; all is gain.

"The kingdom of heaven is like unto a treasure hidden in a field, which a man having found, hid it, and for joy thereof goeth and selleth all that he hath and buyeth that field." — Matt. xiii. 44. — "Know you not that they who run in the race, all run indeed, but one receiveth the prize? . . . Every one that striveth for the mastery, refraineth himself from all things: and they, indeed, that they may receive a corruptible crown; but we an incorruptible one." — I Cor. ix. 24, 25. — "The kingdom of heaven suffereth violence, and the violent bear it away." — Matt. xi. 12.

For this reason all that is in the way of salvation must be sacrificed, pleasures, amusements, certain friendships, a certain business — even our relatives, our own bodies, and the very life of the body, if they oppose our salvation.

"If any man come to me, and hate not his father, and mother, and wife, and children, and brethren, and sisters, yea and his own life also, he cannot be my disciple." — Luke xiv. 26.

Alas! how many are unwilling to make these sacrifices — and therefore how many go to destruction!

### III. Failure in the Affair of our Salvation is Irreparable

The soul once lost is lost forever.

1. We have only one soul — that lost, we have no other to save. If we lose an eye, we have one left, if we lose a hand, a foot, we have another left; not so with the soul.

And even though both hands, feet, eyes, were lost, that would not be the loss of the soul. Even should life itself be lost, that would not be the loss of the soul.

2. A condemned soul can never be saved.

"Out of hell there is no redemption." — Off. Def. — "One soul, one eternity." — St. Theresa. — "In what place soever the tree shall fall there shall it be." — Eccle. xi. 3.

Some short reflection on eternity.

Therefore, said St. Paul to his disciple Timothy:

"Take heed to thyself." — I Tim. iv. 16. — "Yes," says St. Ambrose, commenting on these words, "to thyself, not to thy money, — to thyself, not to thy possessions, — to thyself, not to thy health, — to thyself, that is to thy soul, which is properly thyself."

Application to various cases.

### IV. Success in the Work of our Salvation is Quite Uncertain

Salvation remains uncertain until it is an accomplished fact.

1. Only when death has closed our earthly career can we be certain about our election, or that we are saved. The saint who has already merited the highest crown of glory in heaven and who has but a minute to live, may yet become a reprobate. No

degree of virtue, no amount of good works, renders us sure of heaven.

"Wherefore, with fear and trembling work out your salvation." — Phil. ii. 12. — "If the just man shall scarcely be saved, where shall the ungodly and the sinner appear?" — I Pet. iv. 18. — "Who knows to what end I will come yet?" — St. Bern.

2. We know for certain that most human beings will be lost. May we not be among the lost?

"Many are called but few are chosen." — Matt. xx. 16.

3. We can never have absolute certainty about the state of our souls. For good reasons God does not grant it.

"Man knoweth not whether he be worthy of love or hatred." — Eccle. ix. 1. — "Wherefore, brethren, labor the more, that by good works you may make sure your calling and election." — II Pet. i. 10.

4. There are mentioned in Sacred History the. names of such as gave some exterior signs of amendment, and who were lost. *Saul* repented of his sins, and yet he was possessed by an evil spirit, and he finally committed suicide (I Kings xv. 24. — xvi. 15. — xxxi. 4). *Antiochus* grieved over his evil deeds, and he was rejected (I Mach. vi. 12). *Judas* acknowledged his crime, and he was driven to despair (Matt. xxvii. 4). Who assures you that you are on the way to heaven? You are certain of your sins, are you certain of forgiveness?

CONCLUSION. — Recapitulation.

Alas! what will this careless, indifferent world come to? Awake from sleep, shake off your drowsiness, before it is too late. Be more on the alert for the future! It is the great artifice of Satan nowadays to lull the people to sleep.

"Thou hast drunk even to the bottom of the cup of dead sleep, and thou hast drunk even to the dregs." — Is. li. 17. — "It is now the hour for us to rise from sleep." — Rom. xiii. 11.

What would you do, if your property, if your life were at stake? What, if you could save the life of a poor, beloved child? But, it is your own dear soul that is in danger.

"Have pity on thy own soul." — Eccli. xxx. 24.

Save your soul! man, save your soul!

# III

## MORTAL SIN

TEXT: "This is the fruit (of my work) that the sin of the people should be taken away." — Is. xxvii. 9.

EXORDIUM. — The taking away of sin was the result which God expected from His efforts in behalf of His chosen people: the same is expected to be the fruit of the Mission, namely, that past sins may be forgiven, and future sins may be avoided. But your coöperation is needed, and therefore you must learn to detest sin, if you have loved it in the past. Besides, your salvation is of infinite importance. One mortal sin destroys it. Hence, a wholesome dread of mortal sin is necessary.

Why is mortal sin so terrible? For many reasons, but principally because it is an act of *supreme contempt of God*.

## I. MORTAL SIN IS AN ACT OF CONTEMPT OF GOD'S AUTHORITY

What is a Mortal Sin? — when is it committed? Explanation. —

God has created the universe, and He governs it by wise laws. He cares as much for the smallest insect as He does for the sun in the sky. As He has made laws for animate as well as inanimate creation, and by these laws He leads it to its destiny, so He has made laws for rational creatures, angels and men. Animate creation obeys from instinct, inanimate from nature; rational creatures are to obey from reason and love.

1. God's word is law for all creation, and it is obeyed by all; "for all things serve God" (Ps. cxviii. 91).

God speaks to the angels, and at once they obey.

"Are the angels not all ministering spirits?" — Heb. i. 14. — "Thy will be done on earth, as it is in heaven." — Matt. vi. 10.

The heavens and the firmament obey the voice of God.

"The heavens show forth the glory of God, and the firmament declareth the work of his hands." — Ps. xviii. 1.

The elements submit to God's word.

"Fire, hail, snow, ice, storms . . . fulfil his word." — Ps. cxlviii. 8. — "He sendeth forth light and it goeth and hath called it, and it obeyeth him with trembling. And the stars have given light in their watches, and rejoiced. They were called and they said: Here we are: and with cheerfulness they have shined forth to him that made them." — Bar. iii. 33–35.

God speaks — and the very devils in hell tremble (James ii. 19). God speaks to man — to the sinner, and behold a flat refusal.

"*Non serviam* — I will not serve thee." — Jer. ii. 20.

But behold, all creation serves Me! I will not serve. But your temporal and eternal happiness depend on your serving God! I will not serve . . . What execrable contempt! Who can understand the depth of it? men? angels? the Blessed Virgin Mary? God alone. This contempt is supreme — it is in a certain sense infinite.

And this is what you, sinner, have done, when, against God's express commandment, you blasphemed — profaned the Lord's day. . . .

Do you deserve to live? where, by right, should you be at this moment?

## II. MORTAL SIN IS AN ACT OF CONTEMPT OF GOD'S LOVE

Man is united to God not only through the relationship of subject and creature, but also by the *closest ties of love.* God loves man.

"Yes, I have loved thee with an everlasting love, therefore have I drawn thee, taking pity on thee." — Jer. xxxi. 3.

1. God has given us — *a.* In the order of nature, the members of our bodies — the faculties of the soul. He furnishes us with air, nourishment, good health. What would we be if one of these things were wanting?

"What hast thou, that thou hast not received?" — I Cor. iv. 7.

*b.* In the order of grace, He has given us His only-begotten Son for our redemption — in the crucifixion, a source of all grace — in the Blessed Sacrament with all its blessings.

"God so loved the world as to give his only-begotten Son." — John iii. 16.

God has made us members of His Church, has given us the benefit of the Sacraments, has made our souls the living temples of the Holy Ghost.

"Your members are the temples of the Holy Ghost, who is in you, whom you have from God." — I Cor. vi. 19.

We are the living dwellings of the Triune God.

"If any man love me . . . we will come to him, and will make our abode with him." — John xiv. 23. — "Know you not, that you are the temple of God, and that the spirit of God dwelleth in you?" — I Cor. iii. 16.

2. And now God would like to see some *manifestation of love* toward Himself on the part of man. How does the sinner return that love? With contempt. What God asks of man is not difficult. But man's heart has no love for God — hence sin; man

goes so far as to put away the very thought of God — severs every tie between himself and God, and does that which God has most strictly forbidden. What an outrage on the love of God!

"Hear, O ye heavens, and give ear, O earth. . . . I have brought up children, and exalted them, but they have despised me. The ox knoweth his owner, and the ass his master's crib, but Israel hath not known me." — Is. i. 2, 3.

3. The sinner abuses the very *gifts of God* against God. His *mind* — his *will* — his *memory* — his *affections* and aspirations — in a word, his *whole soul*. (Enumerate the various ways in which these faculties are abused.) His *eyes* — his *ears* — his *tongue* — his *hands* — his *feet* — his *beauty* and complexion — his *entire body*. (Enumerate the abuse of each.)

Comparison. — A poor man sat on the roadside begging for alms. A wealthy man gave him a large piece of gold. The beggar ran and bought a dagger, and, following his benefactor, plunged it into his back, murdering him; then, plunging it into his own heart, committed suicide. Thus does the sinner act toward his loving God.

### III. Mortal Sin is an Act of Personal Contempt of God

Mortal Sin treats God with the utmost contempt.

*A. In His divine perfections,* especially

1. *As the Infinite Good.* God is all perfection — in an infinite degree. Man is to possess the infinite good to his full capacity. The sinner exchanges God for a trifle. Renounce either God or that sinful pleasure. . . .

"Lord, who is like to thee?" — Ps. xxxiv. 10. — "To whom have ye likened me, or made me equal?" — Is. xl. 25. — "Wherefore, hath the wicked provoked God?" — Ps. x. 13. — "They violated me among my people, for a handful of barley, and a piece of bread." — Ez. xiii. 19. — "Thou hast cast me off behind thy back." — Ez. xxiii. 35.

You, sinner, would not have acted thus, had a thousand dollars been at stake, or a much smaller sum. God alone was so contemptible in your eyes as to deserve your disdain.

And in acting thus, the sinner makes his sinful pleasure his last end — his God.

"If you love delights more than God, delights are your God." — St. Thomas.

To prevent the Jews from going to Jerusalem to worship God, Jeroboam had two golden calves made, and presenting them to the worship of the people, said: "Behold thy gods, O Israel." (III Kings xii. 28). The devils act in like manner toward men by presenting sinful pleasure, liquor, enmity . . . to their worship.

Example of the Jews, preferring Barabbas to Jesus Christ — of Judas betraying his master for thirty pieces of silver.

2. Mortal Sin despises God's *omniscience*. God sees and knows everything — nothing can escape His eye.

"Neither is there any creature invisible in his sight, but all things are naked and open to the eyes of him." — Heb. iv. 13.

The sinner is always near to God — he lives in God.

"In him we live, and move and are." — Acts xvii. 28. — "Shall a man be hid in secret places, and I not see him, saith the Lord; do not I fill heaven and earth, saith the Lord." — Jer. xxiii. 24. "If I ascend into heaven, thou art there; if I descend into hell, thou art present. If I take my wings early in the morning, and dwell in the uttermost parts of the sea, even there also shall thy hand lead me . . . And I said: perhaps darkness shall cover me, and night shall be my light in my pleasures. But darkness shall not be dark to thee; and night shall be light as the day; the darkness thereof, and the light thereof are alike to thee." — Ps. cxxxviii. 8–12.

No man would do in the presence of decent people what the sinner is not ashamed to do in the presence of God. It is even most difficult to let one man know the sin in the secrecy of the confessional, that the sin may be forgiven. What contempt of God!

"They provoke me to anger before my face." — Is. lxv. 3.

3. Mortal Sin contemns God in His *omnipotence* and *majesty*. What is God?

"He is the Lord of lords and King of kings." — Apoc. xvii. 14. — "Thy justice is as the mountains of God, thy judgments are a great deep." — Ps. xxxv. 7.

His age is from all eternity — His name is ineffable. His palace is inaccessible light — His ministers the hosts of angels — all nations are before Him as nothing; man is a most insignificant little worm on earth. And the sinner provokes God, the tremendous majesty, at the moment when He can let him drop into the eternal abyss of hell. His life hangs by a weak thread. What recklessness!

"Understand these things, you that forget God, lest he snatch you away, and there is none to deliver you." — Ps. xlix. 22. — "Be not afraid of them who kill the body . . . Fear him, who hath power to cast both soul and body into hell. Yea, I say to you, fear him." — Luke xii. 4, 5.

And yet, how much sin! The world is full of it — it is deluged with it!

*B. Mortal Sin aims at the destruction of God.*

"Sin, as far as it can do so, destroys God," says St. Bernard. God is certainly an indestructible being, nor can the action of the sinner do Him the least harm, or lessen His infinite happiness for a moment. Still, as far as it depends on the sinner, he annihilates God.

1. The sinner does not want God to be *holy;* because he wants Him to approve of his sin; moreover, he wishes God not to be *just;* because he wishes Him to let sin go unpunished; then, he would have God not to be *omniscient,* so that his sin could escape His knowledge; in fine, he is desirous that God were not *omnipotent* and *eternal,* so that He might be unable to punish his sin forever.

But to do away with these attributes of God means to do away with God altogether.

2. What the sinner cannot do to God in reality, as a purely divine being, he actually does to *God incarnate,* to Jesus Christ. For every mortal sin is a repetition of the crucifixion (Heb. vi. 6). It renews the cause of the sufferings and death of Jesus Christ our Lord. It renews the scourging at the pillar, the crowning with thorns. . . . The Jews crucified Jesus Christ but once; the sinner crucifies Him again and again, by his sinful thoughts, words, actions. . . . The Jews crucified Him during His mortal life, the sinner crucifies Him in His life of glory.

Look at the crucifix! Who committed this deed? Jesus Christ could never have been crucified except for sin. Who, therefore, is guilty of this cruel act?

CONCLUSION. — Recapitulation.

Relate what was demanded in the Old Law of the inhabitants of a town in the neighborhood of which a murdered body was found (Deut. xxi. 1–7). (Showing the crucifix) Whosoever is innocent of this murder let him raise his hand! What? — no hand raised? — all guilty? Yes, acknowledge it — but with a repentant heart; acknowledge it, you will be judged guilty — and then? You will be acquitted. You will be cleansed by the very blood that you have shed. Come of your own accord to the tribunal, but soon.

"Come with confidence to the throne of grace, that you may obtain mercy" (Heb. iv. 16). Ask pardon, even now, for all your sinful transgressions, that from this moment you may cease to be sinners. Act of contrition.

## SACRILEGIOUS CONFESSION

Text: "Cursed be he that doth the work of the Lord deceitfully."
— Jer. xlviii. 10.

Exordium. — It is a terrible thing to be cursed by any one, even by an enemy; more terrible to be cursed by a father or a mother — by the priest of God; but it is the most terrible thing to be cursed by God. But this curse falls upon all "who do the work of the Lord deceitfully." This may be done in various ways, but it is done particularly by those who practise *deceit* in confession; deceit against the priest, against God, against themselves. Many are guilty of this, according to St. Leonard of Port Maurice, St. Vincent de Paul, St. Alphonsus, and many other holy and eminent missionaries.

May you understand the grievousness of this sin, and ever refrain from it; or if you have committed it, may you do penance for it. May Jesus and Mary . . .

## I. Sacrilegious Confession is Deceit against the Triune God

1. Against *God the Father*. God, out of love for man, gave up His only-begotten Son, sacrificing Him for the sins of mankind.

"For God so loved the world, as to give his only-begotten Son. . . . that the world may be saved by him." — John iii. 16, 17.

Through Him we receive forgiveness for our sins, no matter how grievous or how numerous; although sin is in a certain sense an infinite offence against His Infinite Majesty.

"Through his name all receive remission of sins." — Acts x. 43.

But the condition laid down by God is that those ·sins must be confessed, that the sinner must acknowledge his guilt.

"When a man or woman shall have committed any of all the sins . . . they shall confess their sin." — Num. v. 6, 7.

Now, this or that sinner goes to confession — but practises deceit against God. Describe several instances of this kind.

The priest believes him to be sincere. He pronounces absolution: "I absolve thee in the name of the *Father*" — "Desist," answers the Eternal Father. "I curse him: he has performed this work deceitfully, and 'cursed is he who doth the work of the Lord deceitfully.' "

2. Against *God the Son*. God the Son took all our sins upon Himself, to make satisfaction for them to God.

"Behold the lamb of God; behold him who taketh away the sin of the world." — John i. 29.

Consider all that Jesus Christ did for the atonement of sin. Sufferings, humiliations, death on the cross. He did it cheerfully, that we might obtain pardon. Now this atonement is applied to us in the Sacrament of Penance. Actually the Most Precious Blood of Jesus is then poured out upon our souls.

"In whom we have redemption through his blood, the remission of sins." — Col. i. 14. — "Without the shedding of blood there is no remission." — Heb. ix. 22.

But the condition is, that we make a sincere confession of the sins which we have committed. On this condition only are the priests allowed to forgive. For this reason did the faithful of Ephesus, "who had followed curious arts, come before the Apostles, confessing and declaring their deeds, and burned their books to the value of fifty thousand pieces of silver." (Acts xix. 19.)

But here comes a man or a woman . . . to confession, and instead of declaring his deeds, he keeps them hidden. The priest is about to give absolution, not knowing the deceit that the sinner has practised. It would not be so great a profanation for the priest to take the chalice from the altar and pour the Most Precious Blood of Jesus on a stone, as it is, to pour it by the act of absolution on that wicked heart possessed by the devil.

The priest, raising his hand, says: "I absolve thee in the name of the Father and of *the Son*." "Not so," replies God the Son. "I curse him, he has made his confession deceitfully, and 'he who doth . . . deceitfully is cursed.' "

3. Against *God the Holy Ghost*. The Sacrament of Penance is administered through the operation of the Holy Ghost. When Christ conferred upon the Apostles the power of forgiving sins, "He breathed on them and said: Receive ye the Holy Ghost." (John xx. 22.)

He, therefore, who makes a bad confession by concealing a sin, lies to the Holy Ghost. And what happens to those who lie to the Holy Ghost, you may learn from the dreadful example of Ananias and Saphira. Acts v. 1–10. Relate example in full.

Apply to various instances. There comes a young woman; she has finished her confession, but has concealed that night's walk when sin was committed. "Is this all?" says the priest. "Yes." "No more?" "Certainly no more." He gives absolution: "I ab-

solve thee in the name . . . and of the *Holy Ghost.*"
"Cease," interrupts the Holy Ghost. "She has lied
to me; I curse her, for 'he who doth . . . deceitfully is cursed.'"

What a disastrous crime is not a sacrilegious confession! And yet so many make bad confessions!
Enumerate those of ordinary occurrence.

What is the difficulty? What excuses have those
sinners? Let us hear them.


## II.  DIFFICULTIES IN MAKING A CONFESSION

1. "I am ashamed to confess certain sins that I
have committed." Yes, and everybody knows what
those certain sins are, before you tell them.

Do you think you are the only one that has committed those sins? Perhaps they are very common.

You are ashamed to confess them to a priest, who
will forget them as soon as you have told them.
There would be some excuse for you, if you had to
tell them before the whole congregation. But, unless you endure this momentary shame now, you will
have to endure endless shame before the whole world,
on the day of General Judgment and in eternity. You
will then feel this humiliation a thousand times more,
because your sins will appear as God sees them.

St. Chrysostom says (Prœm. in Is.), that God has
attached shame to sin, but inspires confidence to confess it. The devil reverses this order of things; he
arouses confidence and boldness to commit sin, but
shame to confess it.

2. "I am afraid of the priest." Has the priest ever
hurt anybody in confession?

At the secular tribunal the crime of a culprit is ascertained, and then punished. At the tribunal of

penance the sin is laid bare, and then pardoned. Even when absolution is deferred or refused, the penitent has nothing to suffer. But conceal your sin, and a fearful punishment will be the necessary consequence.

What would a criminal who is condemned to death do if he were promised full pardon provided he acknowledged his crime, not in public, but to one man in secret? And you will be sentenced to eternal death for your sin; yet you are assured of full pardon, if you secretly confess it to a priest. And you refuse to do so!

3. "My sin might be made known if I confess it." Explain the obligation of the sacramental seal.

4. "But, would not the priest think ill of me?" Does the priest know you? If so, go to one that does not know you. But does the priest think ill of you? Yes; if he knows your sin before confession, but not from the moment you have sincerely confessed it. Your humiliation covers all. The priest will rejoice with you, as the angels in heaven rejoice over your conversion. Instead of giving the priest a bad opinion of you, you gain his esteem. No one but confessors understand this.

5. "I shall confess my sin on my death-bed." Will you be able to do so then, when your strength is almost gone? Will it be easier outside the confessional? Will you have time? Will you have the use of your mental faculties? How many, alas! thought of doing so, and are now in hell.

Unfortunate sinner! You have committed that shameful sin — perhaps many times — perhaps you have already made so many bad confessions — the sin is committed — cannot be undone — heaven is closed against you — your name is stricken from the book of life — it is written in hell. You have it in your power to repair all this — within five minutes — by whispering your sins to a priest — and they will be buried forever. What foolishness to neglect this!

Go to your room, get into a corner, and whisper your sins to the wall. Can you do this? They are not so secret there as in confession — but they are not forgiven. Can you not just as well tell your sins to the priest in a corner of the confessional?

And if, notwithstanding, you find it difficult to tell your sins — can you not ask the priest to assist you, stating that something burdens your soul, and you feel ashamed to tell it?

Add an example of a person that made bad confessions and was lost. See St. Alphonsus' *Exercises for Missions*, and *Catechetical Instructions*.[1] A good example is found in Furniss' Tracts, Book xi. p. 21.

CONCLUSION. — Recapitulation.

My dear Christians, examine yourselves on this subject. If guilty — prepare for a general confession. So many make general confessions in the Mission. Be not ashamed to do so. Then, you will again obtain peace of soul; perhaps you have not possessed it for a good while. How happy will you then be again — how thankful to God for the Mission! But, in future serve God better, persevere unto the end, and when you enter heaven, you will gratefully sing the mercies of God forever. Amen.

[1] C. E., Vol. XV, passim.

# V

## THE SINNER'S DEATH

TEXT: "Woe to you, ungodly men, who have forsaken the law of the most high Lord . . . if you die, in malediction shall be your portion." — Eccli. xli. 11, 12.

EXORDIUM. — Immense number of "ungodly men" and women; though only a minority of them "have forsaken the law of God" — holy faith and its teachings of morality; the most of them have never cared about it; have, on account of too much business, or for other reasons, never thought of it. They will come to die too. How will such people die?

They will die either *calmly* and *quietly*, without showing the least sign of disturbance; or all of a *sudden*, without any of the usual forebodings of death; or after some *lingering disease.*

The first case is the most terrible — in the second case there is scarcely any hope — in the third case there is some hope, which will not be realized.

### I. THE SINNER'S CALM AND QUIET DEATH

Is it true that some close a life of sin in perfect calmness? This is a frequent occurrence in the case of men .who have never given a thought to religion, such as politicians, high officials, business-men . . . who have considered religion as a kind of outward form . . . who have openly apostatized from the true religion. . . .

These men are never troubled about God, religion,

353

their spiritual welfare; neither in life nor at death.
Who should trouble them?

1. *Not God,* because He has completely abandoned
them. Judgment is passed on them. God will plead
no more with them.

"He that doth not believe is already judged." — John iii. 18.

The disturbance of conscience, the terror of soul,
in the dying sinner would be a grace of God. But
even that grace, if given at death to those who in life
have completely ignored God, would be despised.

"I will destroy . . . those that have not sought the Lord nor
searched after him." — Soph. i. 4–6. — "Seek the Lord, while he may
be found." — Is. lv. 6.

2. *Not their own conscience.* They have hushed
their conscience to silence, when it tried to speak;
they have drowned its voice in the din of worldly
pleasure and occupation. In punishment, it does not
speak at the most critical moment.

"All these curses shall come upon thee . . . till thou perish,
because thou heardst not the voice of the Lord thy God." — Deut.
xxviii. 45.

3. *Not the powers of darkness.* Why should they
disquiet those who are their own? By terrifying these
sinners at the point of death, the demons would run
the risk of losing them. They would lose the bystanders, who would be terrified at so terrible a death.
Therefore, the devil does everything to soothe their
minds at that dreadful hour; he fills them with a false
confidence, he may even paint a smile on their dying
lips, to deceive those who want to be deceived.

"The way of the wicked shall deceive them." — Prov. xii. 26.

When, therefore, you see men who have led wicked
lives and have refused to do penance, preserve great
calmness at a moment when even the just are terrified,

you may conclude that their damnation is certain; while the terrors of the just will be changed into joy.

"The wicked man shall be driven out in his wickedness, but the just hath hope in his death." — Prov. xiv. 32. — "Woe to you, ungodly men . . ." — Text.

## II. THE SINNER'S SUDDEN DEATH

1. No man is certain about the moment of his death. The sword of death is suspended over the head of every one. We know not the moment it will drop and strike the fatal blow. The hand of God holds man suspended over the infinite abyss of eternity; it may let him fall into it any moment. Abbé Ségur says that three-fifths of those who die pass out of this life suddenly and unexpectedly.

The sinner has special reasons to fear such a death in punishment of his prolonged enmity with God, and of his continued abuse of life.

"Let not the days of the wicked be prolonged, but as a shadow let them pass away that fear not the face of the Lord." — Eccle. viii. 13. — "The years of the wicked shall be shortened." — Prov. x. 27.

2. Will those who lead a life of sin and who are overtaken by a sudden death, think of conversion? Will they sincerely return to God by an act of perfect contrition? There is a slight possibility that they may, but there is little or no probability. In most cases of sudden death the dying person loses all consciousness at once, and does not recover it. Enumerate several instances. In such a case there can be no question of a sincere conversion.

Or consciousness is not lost at once. Still the mind is then so bewildered that conversion is the last thing it thinks of. Death comes like a terrific cyclone, when all of a sudden the air turns black, is rent every moment by thunder and lightning, when houses and trees are blown to atoms; everything is terror and consternation. If there is any thought of God then, it is apt to fill the soul with despair.

"Behold the whirlwind of the Lord, his fury going forth, a violent storm, it shall rest upon the head of the wicked . . . in the latter days you shall understand these things." — Jer. xxx. 23, 24. — "I will laugh in your destruction . . . when sudden calamity shall fall on you, and destruction, as a tempest, shall be at hand." — Prov. i. 26.

Therefore, if God should let the sinner die suddenly, there is very little hope for his salvation. "Woe to you ungodly men. . . ." (Text.)

Take an account. In forty years quite a number of the present audience will have died suddenly. May their death not be unprovided!

## III. The Sinner's Death after a Lingering Sickness

There is yet hope for the dying sinner, in case his death is preceded by a protracted sickness. It is the last grace from God. But this hope is frustrated by several causes.

1. The Fathers of the Church have not much faith in a death-bed conversion.

"He who never thought of death is unworthy of any consolation in death." — St. Cypr. — and he would not allow them to receive Holy Communion. — "We can administer penance but we can give no security. A penance asked by a sick man is sick; if asked only at the point of death, I fear it is dead." — St. Aug. — "The sins have abandoned you, you have not abandoned sin." — St. Ambr. — "Scarcely one out of a hundred thousand who have always led a sinful life, deserves pardon from God." — St. Jerome.

2. The sinner on his death-bed remains a sinner to the end. Let us suppose the dying sinner under the most favorable circumstances. Suppose he has the priest in due time. The sinner is unwilling to make his confession; he may be persuaded to make

it. Is this penance? He is scarcely able to summon up sufficient strength for so important a transaction. Has he the necessary sorrow for his sins, a firm resolution to sin no more? Let him become well again, and you will soon find out what it amounts to. He receives the three Sacraments, Penance, Viaticum and Extreme Unction. Is their reception a reconciliation with God, or a threefold sacrilege? To receive the sacraments worthily in such a case, requires an extraordinary grace. Will that be granted to one who has always resisted grace?

"You have despised all my counsel, and have neglected my reprehensions. I also will laugh in your destruction and will mock, when that shall come to you which you feared." — Prov. i. 25, 26. — "Where are their gods in whom they trusted; let them arise and help you and protect you in your distress." — Deut. xxxii. 37, 38.

Or the priest is called so late that he finds the sinner just in his last agony. He is scarcely justified in administering a sacrament, unless the dying man has asked for it. Perhaps he had nothing to say about it. The sacraments are conditionally administered. Of what use will they be?

3. But perhaps no priest is called, and this is the case most frequently. Still there is hope in an act of perfect contrition. But what contrition has the dying sinner?

In life the sinner presumptuously thinks only of God's goodness and mercy, in death he thinks despondently of God's justice. The dread of judgment, the terror of hell, his innumerable sins, past ingratitude, may crowd upon the mind of the dying sinner, and utterly confuse him. Fear and trembling seize upon his heart.

"This day of the Lord is darkness and not light. As if a man should flee from the face of a lion, and a bear should meet him; or enter into the house, and lean with his hand upon the wall, and a serpent should bite him." — Amos. v. 18, 19.

The sinner looks upon his *life* and he is frightened; he looks up and beholds an angry *Judge;* he looks for his friends and sees *demons;* he holds on to life and the yawning abyss of eternity opens before him. No guardian angel, no priest, no religious consolation. *"Proficiscere,"* depart! this life is at an end for you.

"A hard heart shall fear evil at the last." — Eccli. iii. 27.

As the fisherman laughs at the bouncing and bending fish that he has caught, so the devils laugh at the remorse of the dying sinner.

"The wicked shall fall in his net." — Ps. cxl. 10.

Thus the dying sinner is tormented from within; bewildered from without; the minutes pass rapidly away; the sweat of death gathers on his brow; the last moment is come; death has done its work.

"Woe to you, ungodly men . . ." — Text.

CONCLUSION. — Recapitulation.
Hear the words of the Prophet.

"Seek ye the Lord, while he may be found, call upon him, while he is near." — Is. lv. 6.

He is near now; He is in search of you, His lost sheep. At another time you may seek Him but not find Him.

"I go, and you shall seek me, and you shall die in your sin." — John viii. 21.

May the all-merciful God keep this calamity from you! May the Refuge of Sinners, the Blessed Virgin Mary, obtain your conversion!

# VI

## GENERAL JUDGMENT

TEXT: "The heavens shall reveal the iniquity of the wicked, and the earth shall rise up against him." — Job xx. 27.

EXORDIUM. — The General Judgment will be preceded by universal destruction. Description. Why?

"For these are the days of vengeance." — Luke xxi. 22.

How often would the sun have rather been obscured than shed its light on the iniquitous actions of man; how often would the moon . . . the air . . . the water . . . have denied their services to man, had God permitted it! But now the days of vengeance have come. "The earth shall rise. . . ." (Text.) All creatures are indignant and rise in revenge.

"The whole world shall fight with him against the unwise." — Wis. v. 21.

Now, what must the Day of Judgment itself be, if its approach is so terrible! For the just it will be a day of triumph, but for the sinner it will be

"A day of wrath, a day of tribulation and distress, a day of calamity and misery, a day of darkness and obscurity, a day of clouds and whirlwinds." — Soph. i. 15. — "For the day of the Lord is great and very terrible; and who can stand it?" — Joel ii. 11.

Why so terrible? I shall explain the reason. Oh! may you comprehend it, for it concerns you all! May Jesus and Mary . . .

## I. THE APPEARANCE OF THE WICKED ON THE DAY OF JUDGMENT

After the earth and all creatures have taken their revenge on the wicked, God appears in the heavens.

"The heavens shall reveal . . ." God will make the wicked appear as objects of horror and disgust before the whole world.

1. In the resurrection the just will appear as bright as the sun, as beautiful as the angels. Hence their bodies will undergo a wonderful change.

"The body is sown in corruption, it shall rise in incorruption; it is sown in dishonor, it shall rise in glory; it is sown in weakness, it shall rise in power; it is sown a natural body, it shall rise a spiritual body." — I Cor. xv. 42–44.

The bodies of the wicked will not share in this wonderful change, but they will rise as *living carcasses,* which cannot be placed among the angels in heaven.

"Now this I say, brethren, that flesh and blood cannot possess the kingdom of God, neither shall corruption possess incorruption. Behold, I tell you a mystery. We shall all indeed rise again, but we shall not all be changed." — Ib. 50, 51. "For what things a man shall sow, those also shall he reap. For he that soweth in his flesh, of the flesh also shall reap corruption." — Gal. vi. 8. — "Thy pride is brought down to hell, thy carcass is fallen down, under thee shall the moth be strewed, and worms shall be thy covering." — Is. xiv. 11.

2. How painful is it not for a person of distinction to appear in rags, with torn shoes, tattered clothes, before a respectable assembly! . . . What will it be to appear before Jesus Christ, the angels, the blessed, with *a body covered with rottenness and worms?* . . . And the wicked will all be well known — their position in the world . . . And it is most likely that their bodies will bear distinctive marks of the crimes committed by them. One can tell even now the vain, the drunkard, the impure . . . by their appearance. How much more so then!

"The day of the Lord shall declare every man's work." — I Cor. iii. 13.

What shame covers a person fallen from virtue, when his crime is made known! Such a person avoids appearing in public. And yet we live in an age of corruption and moral darkness. What will it be when all around us is the heavenly light of God's splendor and majesty!

3. Sinner, you may now put on the *appearance of innocence,* while you are steeped in immorality; frequent respectable society; cover your guilty flesh with the tinsel of vanity; assume a dignified exterior; hold a prominent position in society — in church. . . . Soon the day will come, and "the heavens shall reveal your iniquity." Further application.


II. THE AWFUL REVELATION OF THE LIFE OF THE
WICKED

Nothing is more painful to the human soul than to be found guilty of sin. And there is reason for it. For nothing is so base, so degrading, even in the eyes of mortal man, as the degrading shame and guilt of sin, because of its utter contempt of God, our loving benefactor. Man often refrains from sin for fear of being found out.

1. Hence, that great difficulty in confessing one's sins — hence, the thousands upon thousands of bad confessions — hence, also, so many stay away from confession altogether. Now, if it is so hard to appear as a sinner before a priest, what will it be to have your sins exposed to the gaze of *myriads of holy souls* and of *angels* in the clear light of heavenly justice; who will all judge as God judges; in whose eyes sin and the sinner appear alike most degrading? And in the presence of that vast assembly there will be no possibility of hiding, of excusing, of palliating anything.

When the soldiers of an army are led prisoners through a city, deprived of their arms, gazed at by

thousands of spectators, they feel their shame and
degradation keenly.   The officers cast off their insignia.
What will Christians do among the reprobate?   Can
they cast off the mark of Baptism?

"What will you do in the day of visitation and calamity . . .
where will you leave your glory?" — Is. x. 3. — "I will change
their glory into shame." — Os. iv. 7.

2. But what will it be to appear as a sinner *before
the all-seeing Judge?*   Who will stand His wrathful
countenance?   Adam and Eve "hid themselves," after
their sin, "from the face of the Lord God, amidst
the trees of paradise." (Gen. iii. 8.)   The two wicked
judges, tempting the chaste Susanna, gave as an excuse,
"Nobody sees us" — (Dan. xiii. 20); and yet "they
were ashamed to declare to one another their lust"
(Ib. 11) until they were rendered shameless by that
lust.   But "they had turned away their eyes that they
might not look unto heaven nor remember just judgments." (Ib. 9.)

"The Lord shall be known when he executeth judgment." —
Ps. ix. 17.

God is known to the sinner as he believes in His
existence — but He is not known to him, because he
thinks not of His presence and justice.   God is ignored by this sinful world, but He will be *known* in
His judgment, when He will show sin as it is in reality, together with the punishment which it merits;
when He will show also that He knows all, including
the most minute circumstances.

"I am the judge and the witness." — Jer. xxix. 23.

King Baltasar, feasting with his nobles and sacrilegiously abusing the sacred vessels taken from the
temple of Jerusalem — saw "fingers as it were of the
hand of a man, writing over against the candlestick
three words; then his countenance changed and his

thoughts troubled him, and the joints of his loins were loosed, and his knees struck one against the other." (Dan. v. 5, 6.) What terror will seize the sinner when he will see not the *fingers of a hand,* but the *eternal Judge* in His majesty, in the *light of heaven,* not of a *candlestick,* exposing the whole life of the sinner, not in three indistinct words, but by a clear manifestation well understood by all rational creatures!

3. What crushing terror and consternation will come upon the sinner, when, with all his sins laid bare, he appears face to face *before the angry Judge?* Queen Esther "sank down and her color forsook her, when she appeared before King Assuerus, who was terrible to behold and who with burning eyes showed the wrath of his heart." (Esth. xv. 10.)

When Joseph of Egypt made himself known to his brothers, saying, "I am Joseph, your brother, whom you sold into Egypt — his brethren could not answer him, being struck with exceeding great fear." (Gen. xlv. 3.) Daniel "fell on his face trembling" when the angel Gabriel appeared to him (Dan. viii. 17). The soldiers who came to make Jesus Christ their prisoner fell back to the ground when He said, "I am he" (John xviii. 6). When the beloved disciple, St. John, saw Jesus Christ on the island of Patmos, "he fell at His feet as dead." (Apoc. i. 17.)

What will happen when the divine Judge will appear; "from whose face the earth and heaven flee away" (Ap. xx. 11); "Who looketh upon the earth and maketh it tremble" — (Ps. ciii. 32); "in whose sight the heaven and the heavens of heavens, the deep and all the earth, and the things that are in them shall be moved; the mountains also, and the hills, and the foundations of the earth shall be shaken with trembling when God shall look upon them" (Eccli. xvi. 18, 19)? How will the troubled heart of the sinner be shaken, how will his bones shake? Will he then assume his former boldness, put on a brazen face, as he used to do, when he bade defiance to God and His Church?

4. And then that crushing *revelation of his sins,* each one of which suffices to annihilate him in the presence of the divine Judge. Behold the just and terrible Judge removing the veil which has so long covered that soul — a sink of iniquity!

Sins *against God,* infidelity, contempt of God, hatred of God, blasphemy, superstition, sacrilege, perjury, violation of the Lord's day, ridicule of piety, of holy things and practices —

Sins *against yourself,* neglect of instruction, neglect of grace, impenitence, pride, vanity, drunkenness, impurity — Sins *against your neighbor,* parents, children, priest, — enmity, calumny, theft, seduction —

"O man, who art thou that repliest against God."— Rom. ix. 20. — "What shall I do when God shall rise to judge? and when he shall examine, what shall I answer him?" — Job. xxxi. 14.

O you helpless, insignificant worm of the earth! What chance is there for you?

"And they shall say to the mountains: Cover us; and to the hills: Fall upon us." — Os. x. 8. — "Hide us from the face of him that sitteth upon the throne, and from the wrath of the lamb." — Apoc. vi. 16.

III. Execution of the Just Judgment upon the Wicked

Terror and despair will reach their climax when the irrevocable sentence of damnation will be pronounced upon the wicked. A criminal before a secular tribunal may be pardoned — no pardon here; his sentence may be lenient — the severest sentence here; it may be commuted — no commutation here; there may be an appeal — no appeal here; at all events, the punishment will one day come to an end — this punishment is eternal, it can never be revoked.

1. All communication between God and the sinner is cut off forever. "Depart from me." No reconciliation possible — at any sacrifice.

"Your iniquities have divided between you and your God." — Is. lix. 2.

2. The reprobate are loaded with the curse of God. If "a mother's curse rooteth up the foundation" (Eccli. iii. 11), what effect will the curse of God have upon the damned?

Without mercy they are left to the fury of the demons; they are consigned to the same tortures with them.

3. They will be hurled into the everlasting fire of hell, in the sight of the blessed and the angels (Apoc. xiv. 10).

The angels and the saints will praise and adore the just judgments of God.

"And these" (the damned) "shall *go* into everlasting punishment" (Matt. xxv. 46) — of their own accord; for in that hour, says St. Chrysologus, it will seem easier to them to suffer the torments of hell than to behold the wrathful countenance of the Judge.

See them throwing themselves, amid the most terrible shrieks of despair, headlong into the abyss of hell — see the earth closing on them!

And there will be a new heaven and a new earth (Apoc. xxi. 1), after all the wickedness has been swept away. The holy city, the new Jerusalem, will come down from heaven, the tabernacle of God with men, and He will dwell with them. And they will be His people, loving and praising Him and doing His holy will amidst infinite happiness.   In their unspeakable joy and gratitude they will give glory to God and say: "To the king of ages, immortal, invisible, the only God, be honor and glory forever and ever. Amen."   (I Tim. i. 17).

NOTE. — This short description of the glory of the Saints with God has a twofold object: 1, to show the *glorification* of the elect, and 2, the still greater *confusion* of the reprobate because they are utterly forgotten.

# VII

## HELL

Text: "Depart from me, ye cursed, into everlasting fire, which was prepared for the devil and his angels." — Matt. xxv. 41.

Exordium. — Example of St. Francis Borgia, who daily for five hours meditated on hell and trembled. Why do you not tremble when you think of hell? Is there no hell?

*There is a hell;* so says reason — so says faith — so says the Omnipotent God — so says Holy Writ — so says the Holy Ghost in the Church — so says Jesus Christ — so say all the Fathers of the Church — and who are you, that say, there is no hell?

Sinner, unless you do penance, you will be burning in hell before the people surrounding your death-bed are certain of your death.

Reflect on it now — perhaps you will yet change your life.

### I. Pains of the Body

"Everlasting fire," which includes all that the senses of the body, with its highly susceptible soul, can suffer.

1. *The sight.* From the day of their death the reprobate will never have the benefit of a ray of light.

"Cast him into exterior darkness." — Matt. xxii. 13. — "A land of misery and darkness, where the shadow of death, and no order, but everlasting horror dwelleth." — Job x. 22.

But they will see what is most torturing to the sight. The damned see a *fearful prison.*

"They shall be gathered together as in the gathering of one bundle into the pit (cf. Matt. xiii. 30); and they shall be shut up there in prison." — Is. xxiv. 22.

They see *fire* — the infuriated *demons* — those whose damnation they have *caused* — their *companions* of sin — the *hideous members* of their own bodies.

Ah! they would fain tear their eyes from their sockets, because they have deserved this by their unguarded looks!

2. *The hearing.* The damned will hear the *infernal howlings* of the demons — their hellish sarcasm and yelling — the curses, maledictions, execrations of the millions of reprobates — the terrible reproaches of the victims of sin, of husbands against wives, of wives against husbands, of children against parents, of parents against children.

"There shall be weeping and gnashing of teeth." — Matt. viii. 12. — and in six other passages of the Gospel.

3. *The smell.* The damned will be tormented with the offensive odor of *sulphur* and *brimstone* — with the pestilential exhalations of the damned bodies, and the stench of their rotten carcasses, as they are piled upon one another, "gathered into a bundle."

"Their slain shall be cast forth; and out of their carcasses shall rise a stink." — Is. xxxiv. 3.

4. *The taste.* The damned will suffer a hellish *hunger.*

"Woe to you that are filled, for you shall hunger." — Luke vi. 25.

Zeno, the emperor, was buried alive while drunk by his wife Ariadne, and was found with his arm gnawed away. They suffer a *hellish thirst* — not a drop of cooling water.

"Father Abraham, have mercy on me and send Lazarus, that he may dip the tip of his finger in water, to cool my tongue, for I am tormented in this flame." — Luke xvi. 24. — "Their wine is the gall of dragons, and the venom of asps." — Deut. xxxii. 33. — "Behold I will feed them with wormwood, and will give them gall to drink." — Jer. xxiii. 15.

5. *The touch.* The damned will burn in the fire kindled for the devils.

"For every one shall be salted with fire." — Mark ix. 48.

Therefore, fire in the flesh, the bones, the veins, the mouth, eyes, ears.

They will suffer the incessant tortures of the demons.

## II. Pains of the Soul

1. *The mind.* The damned will see at once all the fearful pains in body and soul, and their mind — conscience — will tell them: "To this you are condemned forever." The mind will comprehend, feel and realize the immeasurable loss of everything good and beautiful which it has inflicted upon itself. It will recognize sin as the cause of all this — will detest it supremely — and it will be convinced of the extreme folly of having yielded to sin.

"Therefore we have erred from the way of truth." — Wis. v. 6.

2. *The memory.* The damned will remember the favorable advantages that they had to save their souls — the numerous graces — the opportunities for doing penance — they will remember father, mother, priest, who are now in heaven. Eternal separation!

"What hath pride profited us? . . . All those things are passed." — Wis. v. 8, 9.

3. *The will.* The damned will be tortured by an ardent desire to be saved; they will call for help and

rescue; they will ask, amidst the most pitiful lamentations, to be released — to be given another trial. But they are abandoned, cast off. Then extreme sadness will seize them — fury — despair.

"For the hope of the wicked is as dust which is blown away with the wind . . . and as smoke that is scattered abroad by the wind." — Wis. v. 15.

4. The *entire soul* will be deprived of the *possession of God*. The soul of the damned is left empty. As the hungry cannot be satiated but by food, so the soul cannot be happy without God. How terrible is that word, "Depart" — it means everlasting separation!

"Thy inner parts were filled with iniquity and thou hast sinned: and I cast thee out from the mountain of God, and destroyed thee." — Ez. xxviii. 16.

In vain will be their howling and gnashing of teeth — in vain their blasphemies; God has forgotten them, and so have all the friends of God.

The state of the damned may be compared with that of a man buried alive six feet under the surface of the earth. He knocks against the coffin, he screams . . . no one hears him, no one cares about him.

"I am become as a man without help, free among the dead. Like the slain sleeping in the sepulchers, whom thou rememberest no more: and they are cast off from thy hand." — Ps. lxxxvii. 5, 6.

### III.  Eternity of Hell

To save us from eternal hell, the Infinite God became man, suffered most cruelly, and died a most ignominious death. It is something that God alone can comprehend.

"He hath cast the lot for them; and his hand hath divided it to them by line; they shall possess it forever." — Is. xxxiv. 17.

*What is eternity?* As many years as there are grains of sand on the sea-shore — as there are drops

of water in the ocean — atoms of dust in the air . . .
All these do not make a minute of eternity.

Human life may be compared to a clock — which
is wound up at birth — goes during life; the hands
point to 10, 20, 30, 50 years; death approaches —
already is the hammer raised to strike the last hour —
it falls — it strikes the hour of death; the clock is
run down — it stops; the hands point to *ever — never*.
Existence    forever — redemption    never!    Eternal
death!

CONCLUSION. — Is there any sinner here who intends to live on in sin; who refuses the grace of reconciliation with God?    Let him look down into the abyss
of hell.    Then say, do you really want to become a
reprobate?    Then, bid farewell to Jesus Christ, to the
Blessed Virgin, to your friends, to heaven, to your
own salvation.    O no!    I hear you say.    O no! my
Jesus, do not condemn me!    Forgive me!    I will do
penance, sin no more, and persevere to the end.    O
Blessed Mother Mary! obtain for me the grace of a
true conversion.

# VIII

## THE PASSION AND DEATH OF CHRIST

TEXT: "He was wounded for our iniquities, he was bruised for our sins: the Lord hath laid on him the iniquity of us all." — Isaias liii. 5, 6.

EXORDIUM. — To-day I have to relate to you a mournful yet most consoling fact — unique in history; the like never happened before nor will it ever happen again. It is represented by a well-known object, the crucifix. I mean the Sufferings and Death of Jesus Christ. How sad to see the Son of God, made man, atone for our sins in so cruel a manner; yet how consoling, since He did it out of love for every one of us!

"He loved me and delivered himself up for me." — Gal. ii. 20.

This fact I shall bring before your minds to-day, hoping thereby to produce in your hearts *sincere sorrow* for your sins and a *true love of Jesus Christ*. Let it be understood that time and space are nothing before God. Hence it is the same as if Christ were suffering and dying now and in our presence.

1. Let us, then, place ourselves in spirit in the ancient city of Jerusalem, crowded with people that have come from every part of the country to celebrate the Pasch.

Behold, an uproar in the streets in a certain direction! Crowds of people are running about in utter confusion. Their shouts and cries indicate something extraordinary. They have just now taken from his cell a prisoner whom they arrested last night, and they are hurrying him to the governor's palace to have him sentenced and executed before to-morrow. No delay! A most dangerous man, secured by ropes tied around his waist; yet his look is not that of a criminal. It is *Jesus of Nazareth*. He is brought before Pontius Pilate. The false accusations.

See Jesus Christ, fallen into the hands of His enemies and dragged from tribunal to tribunal. Jesus suffered this in order that you might not fall into the hands of the demons and be dragged by them into the eternal damnation of hell.

2. Jesus is brought to Herod, because no fault was found in Him by Pontius Pilate, who thought thus to free himself from a disagreeable task. Jesus is followed by an immense crowd of people, with constant insults and mockeries.

Herod mocked Him as a fool, and had Him clad in a white garment, presenting Him thus to the surrounding crowd as a man bereft of reason.

Learn from Jesus to bear insults, ridicule and mockery for the sake of your holy religion; acts of injustice, because you are a Catholic. Suffer willingly to be contemptuously decried as a fool, for the sake of your holy religion.

3. Jesus is brought back to Pontius Pilate, who, seeking to release Him, had recourse to the ancient custom of delivering a prisoner on the feast of the Pasch. He proposed Jesus. But Jesus is unanimously rejected, and a robber, Barabbas, is preferred. Why did not Pontius Pilate use his authority and pronounce Jesus innocent? Oh! that detestable human respect!

You act in the same manner whenever you betray the cause of religion, in order not to displease men. Alas! how often do you not prefer a robber to Jesus Christ; yes, the robber of robbers — Satan himself!

This outrage is repeated by man whenever he prefers sin to virtue. God is thus cast aside, and Satan takes possession of his heart.

4. Pontius Pilate had declared Jesus innocent three times, and yet he condemned Him to be scourged.

"I, having examined this man, find no cause in those things wherein you accuse him. No, nor Herod . . . I will chastise him, therefore, and release him." — Luke xxiii. 14–16.

Chastise him! and innocent! what justice is this?

Behold, Jesus is led to the pillar — stripped in presence of a vast multitude — unmercifully scourged for an hour; forty soldiers, two at a time, took their turns (Rev. to St. Bridget); blood flowing profusely — skin cruelly torn — pieces of flesh hanging down (Rev. to St. Theresa) — ribs laid bare. (Ps. xxi. 18.)

With our bodily eyes we might then have beheld the cruel soldiers beating and cutting most deplorably the sacred body of Jesus; but to the eyes of our soul are shown, by the light of faith, men of all ages, of all nations and ranks, guilty of the cruel and bloody scourging of Jesus, the innocent Lamb of God, by their violations of holy chastity.

Sinner, behold how your loving Redeemer allows His innocent body to be lacerated, in order to atone for your immodest liberties and acts of impurity! Do you see how He loves you?

5. The ropes are loosened. His clothes are put on the wounded body of Jesus. He is led off a short distance. His clothes are violently torn off again, and an old red cloak is thrown over His shoulders; He is seated on a bench; a bundle of thorns, twisted into a crown, is placed upon His head — and the thorns driven into His sacred head. Mock genuflections, to deride His royal dignity, together with many other insults.

Compare your attire of vanity with the cruelly stripped and bloody body of your Jesus — with the old and shabby garment hanging from His shoulders — your head-dress with His — your face with His, covered with spittle and blood. Examine the thousands of wilful thoughts of pride, envy, enmity, which you entertain in your head and heart. These are the thorns penetrating the head and brain of your Jesus. See, He had to atone for you, to save you! How many thorns will you still drive into His head?

6. When Pontius Pilate saw Jesus in this condition, he surely thought the people on seeing Him would demand His release. Therefore, he brought Him out on the balcony. Description of Jesus and the motley crowd below. The stones of the street might have been expected to show sympathy at such a sight; but no compassion could have been expected in the hearts of those fiends in human form. "Away, away with Him! To the cross with Him!" they cry aloud.

This is the cry of those worldly-minded souls who do not wish a king that gives them the example of humiliation and sufferings; who do not wish to be ruled by His doctrine of self-abnegation — Christian simplicity. . . . "Our king is Cæsar" — the world — its lusts — pleasures — and vanities. And they effectually crucify Jesus by their sins.

Now the act of the basest injustice ever perpetrated on earth takes place. Jesus Christ, the Son of God, though most innocent, is condemned to the death of the cross. The sentence of condemnation is published, and Jesus is publicly proclaimed an impostor, a criminal — who must be put to death.

The crowds of people that had come into the city were stirred up by the enemies of Jesus; they are made to believe that Jesus had acted as an impostor in every part of the country. The indignation of the strangers was aroused, and they, sympathizing with their seducers, joined in the death-cry of Jesus. At home they spread these false impressions among their friends.

Jesus did not defend Himself, though He could have done so with the greatest ease and success.

O poor sinners! Jesus Christ is rejected by the people and sentenced to death, that you may not be cast off and doomed to eternal perdition!

And you, guilty of thousands of crimes, are ashamed to acknowledge your guilt in secret to a priest, in order to obtain pardon!

7. In haste was the sentence carried out. Other criminals are allowed a few days or weeks; not so with Jesus the Redeemer of the world. Contrary to all custom, He was burdened with His cross. The cross was a load too heavy for the strongest man. But what would malice not do? Jesus takes it on His shoulders, although He sees that it is too heavy for Him. What could love refuse?

And you complain of the heavy yoke of the commandments of God and of the Church! You have broken them with the meanest recklessness, and Jesus Christ must atone for your transgressions by carrying His heavy cross.

Jesus falls repeatedly under the weight of the cross. No sympathy for him — but pulling — dragging — kicking — and beating, until He manages to rise.

And when you fall sick or suffer something, you become impatient if everybody does not sympathize with you.

8. The meeting with His sorrowful Mother.

What grief must have penetrated the maternal heart of Mary when she saw her Divine Son with the cross on His shoulders! What pain must have filled the loving heart of Jesus at the sight of His dear Mother!

He does not speak, but He casts a sad look on her. What mother would not feel it? He must leave her stand there plunged in grief, and struggle on to Calvary. She follows.

Let us pause here and learn from Jesus not to regard those near and dear to us, when we find them in our way on the road to heaven — not to be carried away by human respect, so as to omit for the sake of pleasing others the least thing that we are obliged to do for the love of Jesus Christ.

9. Jesus finally reaches the top of the hill. His garments are cruelly torn from His body; his wounds begin to bleed again. A surgeon, removing the bandages from an open wound, takes all possible care not to cause unnecessary pain. No regard for Jesus!

This is the work of every vile, impure sinner, who, with utter disregard to modesty, casts off nature's shame and surrenders himself to the iniquities of sin!

And now begin the cruelties that none of the four evangelists could summon up courage to describe, except in these two words: *"Crucifixerunt eum."* Description of the crucifixion; fastening the hands and feet to the cross with iron nails; the harrowing sounds of the hammer pierce the soul of His Mother. The raising, adjusting and wedging of the cross. What sufferings! The three hours' agony — condolence of nature — constant mockery of the chief priests — the soldiers — the Jews — even of those who happened to pass by.

Sinner, you have made your hands the instruments of sin, you have walked on the broad road to hell, you have surrendered yourself to the work of darkness, and have laughed at those who warned you. See,

Jesus Christ allowed Himself to be crucified and mocked in order to atone for those sins and to save you. Have courage, then, fear not that God will reject you, if only you wish to amend.

10. His interior desolation. The martyrs experienced a most indescribable interior joy in their sufferings. Not so Jesus Christ; He was abandoned by men and by His heavenly Father. He saw innumerable sins committed at the very time of His sufferings; and in all future ages; even by those who ought to love Him most. He saw that the majority of those for whom He suffered would after all be lost.

Imagine the feelings of one who makes every possible sacrifice to obtain a certain object, but in vain. — Jesus, dying on the cross for the salvation of men, foresees His efforts, for the greatest part, frustrated. Men will not even thank Him for what He has done for them, much less love Him in return. This thought filled Him with the deepest desolation.

"I am come into the depths of the sea; and a tempest hath overwhelmed me." — Ps. lxviii. 3.

Hence that plaintive cry:

"My God! my God! why hast thou forsaken me?" — Matt. xxvii. 46.

New insults followed. The sight of men's ingratitude was so great a suffering that it broke His heart. Bowing down His head, He yielded His soul into the hands of His Eternal Father.

At that moment the earth shook — the rocks were rent — the graves opened — the dead arose and appeared to many. Many went away in deep silence — striking their breasts out of compunction. Thus suffered and died Jesus Christ, the Redeemer of the world.

CONCLUSION. — And what impression does all this produce in your heart, sinner? Perhaps you will continue the work of sin, thus "crucifying Jesus Christ again and again and make him a mockery" (Heb. vi. 6)? Or, will you not leave Calvary in spirit with compunction in your heart?

If so, then carry home as a memento: 1. The strongest confidence in the mercy of God; 2. The greatest and most generous love for Jesus Christ; 3. The highest esteem for your soul, purchased at so great a price; 4. The greatest horror of sin; 5. The strongest determination to avoid sin and every occasion of sin — giving up human respect — vain pleasures — and suffering everything for the love of Jesus Christ.

Oh! may the love of Jesus Christ henceforth dwell in your souls! may it increase from day to day; may you also have a true compassion for His sorrowful Mother — may the sufferings and death of Jesus so penetrate your hearts that you will say with St. Paul:

"God forbid that I should glory, save in the cross of our Lord Jesus Christ, by whom the world is crucified to me, and I to the world." — Gal. vi. 14.  Amen.

# PROTECTION OF THE BLESSED VIRGIN MARY

TEXT: "Behold, from henceforth all generations shall call me blessed."
— Luke i. 48.

These words were pronounced at the dawn of Christianity by the prophetic lips of the Blessed Virgin Mary. And from the foundation of the Church to the present day the prophecy which they contain has been fulfilled. Where is there a true Christian that does not call Mary the "Blessed Virgin"? Devotion to the Blessed Virgin Mary has always been on the increase in the world, and it will ever more increase to the end of time. The more the world abounds in wickedness, the more must the devotion to the "Refuge of Sinners," to the "Help of Christians," be on the increase.

As for you, during the Mission and after it, nothing is more necessary than a true filial devotion to the Blessed Virgin; during the Mission, that you may all make it well; after the Mission, that you may all persevere. What are the chief reasons for this devotion?

## I. VENERATION OF MARY

*Veneration* is not *adoration;* adoration is due to God alone. The veneration of Mary consists in the *honor* which we pay her. The Saints are to be honored. But there is no greater saint than Mary.

1. *Mary's sanctity was prepared by the greatest graces.* —

*a.* It was due to the position and dignity of Mary as Mother of God, and in proportion to the exaltation of that position. The earthly paradise was made so beautiful because it was to be the home of the first Adam — a mere human being. Mary was chosen to be the dwelling-place of the second Adam — the God-man. The temple of Solomon was richly adorned because in it the Ark of the Covenant was to be preserved. How much more should Mary be adorned, who was selected to become God's living tabernacle, of which the Ark was only a figure?

Therefore was she styled "full of grace" by the Angel Gabriel just before she became the living Sanctuary of the Incarnate Word. Then she began to harbor within herself the source and giver of all graces. From that moment she was also destined to become the channel and depository of all the graces that God wished to communicate to mankind.

"In me is all grace of the way and of the truth; in me is all hope of life and of virtue." — Eccli. xxiv. 25.

*b.* The *nearer* a thing approaches its *cause,* the more it participates in the nature and perfections of that cause. Compare a child to its parents — a brook to its spring. Angels possess more of the divinity than man. Jesus Christ, as God, is the source of all grace; as man, He is the distributor of all grace.

"The word of God on high is the fountain of wisdom." — Eccli. i. 5. — "The grace of God, life everlasting, in Christ Jesus our Lord." — Rom. vi. 23.

Now, who is nearer to Christ than Mary? He was nine months enclosed in her chaste womb — thirty years under the same roof with her.

"And, therefore, was it necessary that she received a greater plenitude of grace." — St. Thom. — "As all rivers flow into the ocean, so all rivers of grace into the heart of Mary." — St. Bonav.

The Fathers of the Church call her *"pelagus gratia-rum"* — "ocean of grace."

2. *Grace effects sanctity through our coöperation* — by the *practice of virtue.*

*a.* In ordinary men coöperation is seldom equal to grace.  In Mary it was.

"Among the blessed she shall be blessed." — Eccli. xxiv. 4. — "My abode is in the full assembly of saints." — Ib. 16.

St. Bonaventure and St. Bernard say that she possessed the sanctity of the Archangels, the love of the Cherubim and the Seraphim, the zeal of the Apostles, the fortitude of the Martyrs, the innocence of the Confessors, the purity of the Virgins, the patience of all the Saints; but in a far higher degree.  Of her purity you have a proof at the Annunciation, when she asked: "How shall this be done?" (Luke i. 34.)

*b.* Therefore, the Church honors her with the title of *"Beatissima Virgo"* — a title given to no other; "Queen of Angels — of Patriarchs . . ." because as queen she is above all her subjects.  The Church tells us that she is raised far above the angelic choirs. "The holy Mother of God is raised above the choirs of angels to the celestial kingdom." (Off. in Assumpt.)

3. *Mary is adorned with the greatest privileges.* God does not always make known the sanctity of His saints by special, celestial gifts.  But oftentimes He does, and He did so in a special but invisible manner with regard to Mary.  We do not read much of her in the Scriptures, but had she not the gift of miracles? (visit to Elizabeth — Cana) — the gift of prophecy? (see text) — in common with other saints? And she possessed what no other saint had:

1. Immaculate Conception.  2. Immunity from all sin.  3. Maternity and virginity at the same time.

4. Mother of God.  5. Death from love.  6. Assumption with soul and body into heaven.

Therefore is Mary to be honored more than any other saint or all the angels.  After God and the Humanity of Christ, she is to be honored most. *Hyperdulia.*


## II.  INVOCATION OF MARY

We ordinarily invoke the help of those who are able and willing to assist us.

1. *Mary is most powerful to help us,* because,

*a.* She is the *Mother of God.*  What is a mother's power?  Examples: the sanctification of St. John the Baptist at the mere sound of her voice (Luke i. 41) — the inspiration of Elizabeth (Ib.) — the miracle at Cana, obtained by a single expression of her desire (John ii. 3).

*b.* She *loves God* so much; therefore, God does her will.

"The Lord will do the will of them that fear him; and he will hear their prayer." — Ps. cxliv. 19.

*c.* She is the *treasurer of all graces.*

"All power is given thee in heaven and on earth." — St. Damian. — "The same power belongs to the Mother that the Son possesses; through the omnipotent Son she has become omnipotent." — Idem. — "It is believed that Mary opens the abyss of the Divine Goodness for whom she wishes, how she wishes, and when she wishes." — St. Bern.

2. *Mary is most willing to help us,* because,

*a.* She is a *saint.*  What did the saints do — Abraham, Moses, Judith? . . .

*b.* She loves God more than any other creature loves Him.  But the love of our neighbor is in proportion to our love of God.  Compare the labors of the saints in behalf of their fellow-beings.  Mary can do all this, and infinitely more, without hard work.

*c*. She saw the *example of Christ*.  Could she forget what Jesus did for men?

*d*. She is *our spiritual Mother*.  What will a mother not do for her child?

"Woman, behold thy son. . . . behold thy mother." — John xix. 26, 27. — "Can a woman forget her infant, so as not to have pity on the son of her womb?" — Is. xlix. 15.

Therefore, invoke her in spiritual and temporal needs, for light, for strength, for help, for consolation. . . . now in the Mission, that you may all make it; and after it, that you may persevere.

### III.  Love of the Blessed Virgin Mary

1. We *love* those whom *we honor*.  We love those who possess eminent qualities, just because we feel compelled to honor and respect them: all the more when those eminent qualities are to our benefit.

Should we not love the Blessed Virgin Mary, full of grace and virtue — the Queen of angels and saints — that immaculate dove — that virginal heart — the Mother of God — the greatest benefactress of mankind? . . .

2. A *child* certainly loves its mother.  It is a duty commanded by nature.  Now Mary is our spiritual Mother, who brought us forth to the life of grace on Calvary in the sufferings and death of Jesus, her Son and our brother, after she had conceived us in the mystery of the Incarnation; who gave birth to us, not without pain, as to her divine Infant; through whom we have so often been delivered from sin, and preserved from hell; who has obtained for us so many graces; who invites us to have recourse to her in all our wants; a Mother upon whom we never call in vain.

Conclusion. — Recapitulation.

Do you love the Blessed Virgin Mary? Prove your love, give evidence of it — *sinners,* by carefully shunning sin; for every sin is a sword piercing your spiritual Mother's heart; the *just,* by persevering, offending her Son no more; *all,* by glorying in being her spiritual children, by practising certain devotions in her honor every day.

But show your love especially at this solemn moment by publicly declaring yourselves her children, and by placing yourselves under her constant protection.

### ACT OF DEDICATION

# X

## DELAY OF CONVERSION

TEXT: "Except you will be converted, he will brandish his sword."
— Ps. vii. 13.

EXORDIUM. — Great good accomplished in this Mission — Enumeration. "This is the finger of God" (Exod. viii. 19). Some have remained hardened, obstinate. "This is the finger of the devil." Hear God's warning, like the roar of thunder approaching from a distance.

"His wrath shall come on a sudden, and in the time of vengeance he will destroy thee." — Eccli. v. 9. — "Except you. . ." — Text.

My words do not concern the converted, because not needed; nor the perverts, because not heeded; but the believing and yet delaying; Catholics as well as non-Catholics.

## I. DELAY OF CONVERSION IS MOST INJURIOUS TO GOD

1. It is an outrage to *God's majesty*. It is an outrage not to forgive an inferior, and to refuse reconciliation when he asks it, even though he be the offender — a greater outrage if he be an equal — still greater if he is the offended party — still greater if the offended party is of very high rank. What is it to refuse reconciliation with God, Who now seeks it most emphatically through the Mission? Describe God, the infinite Lord, Who is the offended party. Describe the sinner, that insignificant worm of the

earth. What an outrage to refuse reconciliation — to tell God to go away!

"If a man put away his wife . . . and she marry another man, shall he return to her any more? . . . Nevertheless, return to me, saith the Lord, and I will receive thee." — Jer. iii. 1. — "For Christ, we beseech you, be reconciled to God." — II Cor. v. 20. — "Say not to thy friend: Go, and come again, and to-morrow I will give to thee, when thou canst give at present." — Prov. iii. 28.

2. It exhausts *God's mercy*. The mercy of God is infinite in itself, but limited in its acts. He that says, I will repent later on, is, as St. Augustine says, not a penitent but a scoffer. But "God is not mocked" (Gal. vi. 7).

The mercy of God abounds in wealth, but if it be abused, God's wrath abounds in equal wealth.

"Despisest thou the *riches* of his goodness, and patience, and long-suffering . . . But according to thy hardness and impenitent heart, thou *treasurest* up to thyself wrath." — Rom. ii. 4, 5.

3. It provokes *God's justice*. In warnings of this kind the Holy Scriptures abound.

"We would have cured Babylon, but she is not healed; let us forsake her." — Jer. li. 9. — "Because thou hast not known the time of thy visitation . . . Thy (Jerusalem, a figure of the soul) enemies shall cast a trench about thee, and compass thee round, and straiten thee on every side (prevent the influence of grace), and beat thee flat on the ground (steep in sin), . . . and they shall not leave in thee a stone upon a stone (destroying all good dispositions)." — Luke xix. 43, 44. — "And now I will show you what I will do to my vineyard. I will take away the hedge thereof (fear of God) . . . I will take down the wall thereof (restraint), and it shall be trodden down. And I will make it desolate. It shall not be pruned, and it shall not be digged (ministry without effect) . . . I will command the clouds to rain no rain upon it (no grace)." — Is. v. 5, 6. — "Woe to thee that spoilest, shalt not thou thyself also be spoiled." — Is. xxxiii. 1.

## II. DELAY OF CONVERSION IS MOST DANGEROUS TO THE SINNER

Those who delay their conversion say, and perhaps they mean it, that they will attend to this work later on.  To do so, they must have time, the will, and grace.

1. Will they have *time?*  They may be snatched away by a sudden, unforeseen death.  Many examples prove this.  But even though they may live a good while, when their last sickness binds them to their death-bed, they may not think of settling the affairs of their soul before it is too late.  Nobody dares break the opinion of the physician to them.  Many have died without the priest, while several priests were in the house.

"Thou hast granted me life and mercy." — Job x. 12.

Soon neither may be granted any more.  He that has promised to the sinner forgiveness, says St. Augustine, has not promised him to-morrow.

2. Will they have the *will*, that is, a will penetrated with sorrow and a determination to amend, conditions absolutely required to merit pardon?

"A good life is generally followed by a good death; a bad life by a bad death." — St. Aug. — "A death-bed conversion is a theater conversion." — St. Chrys. — "Out of a hundred thousand who have delayed their conversion till death, scarcely one is converted." — St. Jerome. — "They who begin on their death-bed to do penance continue to do it in hell." — St. Greg. — "I gave her (a harlot) a time that she might do penance, and she will not repent of her fornication." — Apoc. ii. 21.

But, you will say, I have seen sinners converted on their death-beds.  So have I.  It is a miracle of grace.  But,

3. Will you have that *grace?*  Miracles of grace are rarely bestowed on ungrateful, inveterate sinners.  God gives grace to all "at the acceptable time" (II Cor. vi. 2); afterward no more.

"You shall seek me, and you shall die in your sin." — John viii. 21.

The grace of a happy death is the greatest grace given to man.  *What a mockery,* if God would say to the sinner, who never cared to serve Him: "Well done, good and faithful servant . . . enter thou into the joy of thy Lord" (Matt. xxv. 21); to those who were ashamed of their faith: "You have confessed me before men, I will confess you before the angels of God" (Luke xii. 8); to the impure: "Come, blessed are the clean of heart" (Matt. v. 8); to the drunkard: "Blessed are they that hunger and thirst after justice" (Ib. 6); to the thief: "Blessed are the poor in spirit" (Ib. 3)!

No, God is not mocked. *"Sicut vita — finis ita."* As life so death!

CONCLUSION. — Recapitulation.

What a reckless game does the sinner play with God! But he will be the loser, losing not his property, nor his life, but his soul and salvation. Therefore, hear the voice of your conscience, of your friends, of the Church, of God in the Mission, "Lazarus, come forth." Come out of the sinful habits in which your soul is buried. Come back to life. Allow not this "acceptable time" to pass away without putting it to good use. You may never have it again!

# XI

## DRUNKENNESS AND IMPURITY

TEXT: "Do not err. Neither fornicators . . . nor adulterers, nor the effeminate, nor liers with mankind . . . nor drunkards . . . shall possess the kingdom of God." — I Cor. vi. 9, 10.

EXORDIUM. — It was revealed to St. Bridget of Sweden that so many souls fall into hell as to outnumber the sands on the sea-shore, or the flakes of snow falling from the clouds in winter (Lib. 2. c. 6). What is the cause? The numerous sins which are so wantonly committed, especially those of *Drunkenness* and *Impurity*. St. Paul excludes from heaven all those who are guilty of these two sins, not because salvation is absolutely impossible for them, but because those who are addicted to either or to both, fall so low that it costs them superhuman efforts to rise again, and because they neglect the means required for a life of purity or sobriety.

May it please the all-merciful God, through the intercession of the Blessed Virgin Mary, to help you to understand the heinousness and the abomination of these two vices.

I. DRUNKENNESS AND IMPURITY ARE HELD IN SUPREME ABOMINATION BY GOD

God detests every sin. There are sins even more injurious to the divine Majesty than these two. But there is no sin that so degrades man and so disfigures the image and likeness of God in him as these two crimes.

1. *Drunkenness and Impurity make brute beasts out of men.* Man addicted to either of these vices sets aside *reason,* which distinguishes him from the brute beast, and makes himself like it. He prefers to follow his brutish instincts and allows himself to be carried away by them, because he gives the unbridled appetites and passions of his flesh full sway. Thus the intemperate and the impure aim at nothing higher than the gratification of the flesh.

"Whatsoever they naturally know, like dumb beasts, in these they are corrupted." — Jude 10. — "Walking according to their own desires in ungodliness . . . sensual men, having not the spirit." — Ib. 18, 19. — "And all the earth was in admiration after the beast . . . and they adored the beast, saying: Who is like to the beast?" — Apoc. xiii. 3, 4.

2. In following these two vices *man degrades himself below the brute beast.* By drunkenness, because the irrational beast will not drink what is injurious to its nature — it never drinks to excess — by drink it never renders itself useless or unfit for what it is made — nor does it commit other excesses to which man is carried by drink. How man degrades himself below the brute by acts of impurity, is too abominable to mention.

"Hear these things, all ye nations . . . man when he was in honor did not understand, he hath been compared to senseless beasts and is become like to them." — Ps. xlviii. 1-13. — "The Lord knows . . . how to reserve the unjust unto the day of judgment to be tormented, especially them who walk after the flesh in the lust of uncleanness. . . . These men, as irrational beasts, naturally tending to the snare and to destruction, . . . shall perish in their corruption. Having eyes full of adultery and of sin that ceaseth not, alluring unstable souls, children of malediction." — II Pet. ii. 9-14.

3. *The drunkard and the impure prefer the mire of immortality* — in beastly lust — *to the kingdom of heaven.* How vile, to exchange the kingdom of heaven, the possession of God, for a momentary gratification of the depraved appetites of the body! But that both

the intemperate and the impure do so, there cannot be the least doubt. "Do not err." (Text.) The Apostle repeats the same thing again and again.

"The works of the flesh are manifest, which are fornication, uncleanness, immodesty, luxury . . . drunkenness, . . . of which I foretell you, as I have foretold you, that they who do such things, shall not obtain the kingdom of God." — Gal. v. 19, 21. — "For know ye this and understand, that no fornicator, nor unclean . . . hath inheritance in the kingdom of Christ and of God. Let no man deceive you, for because of these things cometh the anger of God upon the children of unbelief. Be ye not partakers with them. . . . For the things that are done by them in secret, it is a shame even to speak of . . . And be not drunk with wine wherein is luxury." — Eph. v. 5–18.

Those who give themselves up to these vices do not deserve that the earth should bear them any longer. Hence, the severe punishment that God has inflicted upon the whole world, upon Sodom and Gomorrha, and numberless individuals.

"Mortify your members, (keeping them from) fornication, uncleanness, lust, evil concupiscence . . . for which things the wrath of God cometh upon the children of unbelief." — Col. iii. 5, 6.

## II. Drunkenness and Impurity are the Cause of Numberless Other Sins

*a. In regard to the drunkard and the impure himself.* And this in regard to the *same sin.* The drunkard and the impure, who break the precepts of sobriety and purity, know not where to end. The reason is, that, on the one hand, sensual nature impels them to a continuance of sin, and on the other, God despises and abandons them, so that they have not the grace to resist.

"A young man according to his way, even when he is old he will not depart from it." — Prov. xxii. 6.

This is true to the letter in regard to every young drunkard, every young debauchee.

*b.* In regard to *every other sin*. No commandment is sacred to those who give themselves up to sins of sensuality. Show this by going through the commandments of God and the Church.

"Where there is drunkenness, there is the devil." — St. Jerome. — "One of the first results of impurity is blindness of spirit." — St. Gregory.

Therefore, the impure and the intemperate will rush like madmen into every sin and vice.

*c. In regard to others.* Who is secure in the company of the intemperate or the impure? To come into contact with them is certain ruin. One drunkard makes ten — ten make a hundred, etc. The same with the impure. "Tell me your company and I will tell you what you are," is a proverb. One wicked youth . . . corrupts a whole school, academy, factory, etc. Drunkenness and Impurity are the two most powerful machines of hell.

"I have written to you not to keep company, if any man that is named a brother be a fornicator . . . or a drunkard . . . with such a one not so much as to eat." — I Cor. v. 11, — on account of the imminent danger of contagion.

III. The Conversion of the Drunkard and the Impure is Next to Impossible

1. Because these sinners *will not change their minds* for the better.

"They will not set their thoughts to return to their God, for the spirit of fornication is in the midst of them, and they have not known the Lord." — Os. v. 4.

2. Because they *neglect the means* of correcting their evil habits. These means are fervent prayer, the frequentation of the sacraments, the careful shunning of every occasion of sin. They will hardly ever pray, they have lost all respect for the sacraments, they

are the slaves of their beastly passions. They yield to
the first wicked thought.

"For, that of the true proverb has happened to them: 'The
dog is returned to his vomit, and the sow that was washed, to her
wallowing in the mire.'" — II Pet. ii. 22.

### 3. Because all *religious feeling has left them*.

"Fornication and wine and drunkenness take away the understanding." — Os. iv. 11. — "The sensual man perceiveth not the
things that are of the spirit of God, for it is foolishness to him, and
he cannot understand." — I Cor. ii. 14.

Such people ridicule the idea of changing their
lives. The most serious thoughts of Death, Hell,
Eternity, produce no impression on them. Their souls
are buried in the flesh.

4. Because they have already partly *lost the faith,*
and they finally give it up completely.

"Wine and women make wise men fall off (apostatize)." — Eccli.
xix. 2.

They live and die in their sins.

"His (the wicked) bones shall be filled with the vices of his
youth, and they shall sleep with him in the dust." — Job xx. 11.

5. *Daily experience* proves what I say. Will this
sermon cause the drunkards and the impure of this
place to change their lives? Some few may take it
to heart. But the majority of them? What can we
do for them? We may weep over them, as we weep
over the dead, who cannot be brought back to life.
St. Paul wept over them, calling them enemies of the
cross of Christ.

"For many walk, of whom I have told you often, and now tell
you weeping, that they are enemies of the cross of Christ; whose
end is destruction; whose God is their belly; and whose glory is
in their shame." — Phil. iii. 18, 19.

To all this, and in conclusion, I shall let a voice be
heard from the depth of hell. "He that hath an ear
to hear let him hear." One of those who had passed

their lives in the enjoyment of sensual gratification —
"who had feasted sumptuously upon this earth" — sent
a message of warning to his brethren, begging to have
it delivered: *"Father, I beseech thee, that thou wouldst
send Lazarus to testify unto my brethren, lest they also
come into this place of torments."* (Luke xvi. 27.)

The message was never delivered. I have delivered
it to-day to all the drunkards and the impure that
have listened to me. "He that hath an ear to hear
let him hear." Let him take it to heart, and let him
put in practice at once the means of a thorough conversion and of holy perseverance.

Sinner, wake up from your dangerous sleep! To-
day God speaks to you — the Church speaks to you —
even hell speaks to you in warning. But, alas! is it
perhaps too late?

# XII

## CHIEF MEANS OF PERSEVERANCE

Text: "Be thou faithful until death, and I will give thee the crown of life." — Apoc. ii. 10.

What wonderful changes have taken place in this congregation since the opening of this Mission! You are all now the beloved children of God, heirs of the kingdom of heaven. Your hearts are full of joy and gratitude toward God for His love and mercy toward you. But you are not yet saved. Many temptations are to be overcome. The powers of darkness are even now preparing their snares for you. God permits this to test your fidelity toward Him. Having proved yourselves faithful until death, you will receive the crown of life.

But to be faithful to the end, you must always put in practice the *three chief Means of Perseverance*. If you neglect but one you cannot persevere.

The present discourse treats, therefore, of the three chief Means of Perseverance, and how you must employ them.

Imprint deeply on your minds the words which I address to you to-night.

There is a twofold life in man; the life of nature, and the life of grace. The one begins with man's existence, the other, with Baptism; the one is derived from Adam, the other, from Jesus Christ; the one makes you a human being, the other, a Christian. Each must be preserved by the respective means which God has decreed for it.

For the preservation of the natural life three conditions must be complied with: first, that we breathe pure air; secondly, that we take healthy nourishment; thirdly, that we avoid every unnecessary danger of death.

Similarly three things are required for the preservation of the spiritual life: first, breathe the spiritual air of actual grace, by *Prayer;* secondly, take spiritual nourishment, by receiving *Holy Communion;* thirdly, keep from the danger of death, by avoiding the *Proximate Occasion of Sin.*

## I.   PRACTICE OF PRAYER

1. Prayer is *most easy,* because it requires no exertion on the part of the body; it is a simple act of the soul, an act of the will.

2. Prayer is *most necessary,* because without it we shall be left without the actual help of God, which we constantly need, to avoid evil and to do good.

3. Prayer is *most efficacious,* because God cannot resist prayer.   He has promised to hear it, and He is faithful to His promise.

4. We must *pray constantly,* because God grants us the help that we need for the time being only; we must ask again and again for what we need again and again.   We can inhale only as much air as we need for the moment; the next moment we must inhale again.

(For a further development of these points, see Sermon on Prayer, in the First Series, page 269.)

## II.   FREQUENTATION OF THE SACRAMENTS

1. *Necessity of Holy Communion* for the preservation of the life of the soul.   The life of the soul must

be preserved by the means instituted by God for that purpose, which is nothing less than the body and blood of Jesus Christ Himself.

"Amen, amen I say unto you: Except you eat the flesh of the Son of man, and drink his blood, you shall not have life in you." — John vi. 54.

The flesh and blood of man are constantly inclined unto evil.

"For the imagination and thought of man's heart are prone to evil from his youth." — Gen. viii. 21.

The body and the blood of Jesus Christ are most pure. When His divine body is communicated to our body, and when His soul is united to ours, our whole being is elevated, purified and sanctified. When we eat of this tree of life, "we shall be as God" — Jesus Christ (Gen. iii. 5).

Without Holy Communion we are, generally speaking, unable to resist corrupt nature. Living examples are all those adults who cannot or will not approach Holy Communion because of their being either outside of the Church by heresy and apostasy, or careless and lukewarm Catholics. They all profess openly that they cannot be good, cannot be chaste.

2. *Holy Communion must be received frequently.*

As we must take food daily to preserve the life and strength of the body, so we must frequently receive Holy Communion to preserve the life and strength of the soul. Examples of the first Christians — the advice of the Church — sayings of the Fathers, especially of St. Alphonsus, who at the close of his Missions used to exact from the people the promise to receive every week.

*How often must we receive Holy Communion?*

Experience teaches you how often you must take nourishment for the preservation of the strength of your body. Experience teaches you, likewise, how often you must receive the sacraments. No one should wait longer than *three months*. But, *monthly Communion* should be the rule for young people, because they are more exposed to sin.

(For further explanations see Sermon on the Frequentation of the Sacraments, in the First Series, page 261.)

### III. Proximate Occasion of Sin

*Definition.* Such circumstances in which people *ordinarily* fall into sin. These may be:

*a. Things;* such as intoxicating drinks, irreligious books and papers, novels, plays, games, etc.

*b. Places;* such as public houses and bar-rooms, dance-houses, houses of doubtful character, of ill-fame, bad theaters, wakes, parties, Protestant service, etc.

*c. Persons;* such as drunkards, those who speak against religion, chastity, loose company-keeping, close acquaintance with persons of the other sex without a good purpose, or if for a good purpose, in a wrong way, having lonely interviews, walks, etc. Regarding this last point the rule is: *Never alone.*

"Missionaries are too severe." It is not we that warn against and condemn the committing of one's self to the occasion of sin. *God* Himself has most emphatically forbidden it; the earth bears testimony of this divine prohibition; innumerable voices from hell and from heaven most solemnly caution us against the proximate occasion of sin.

1. God. *a, By word:*

"He that loveth danger shall perish in it." — Eccli. iii. 27. — "Watch ye; the spirit indeed is willing but the flesh weak." — Matt. xxvi. 41. — "Flee from sins as from the face of a serpent." — Eccli. xxi. 2. — "Who will pity an enchanter struck by a serpent, or any that will come near wild beasts?" — Ib. xii. 13. — "If thy right eye scandalize thee, pluck it out and cast it from thee. For it is expedient for thee that one of thy members should perish rather than thy whole body be cast into hell. And if thy right hand . . ." — Matt. v. 29.

*b. By examples:* Dina ravished, Gen. xxxiv. Samson betrayed by Delilah, Judg. xvi. David sins for not guarding his looks, II Kings xi. Solomon gives himself up to idolatry, III Kings xi. St. Peter's denial of Christ, Matt. xxvi.

2. EARTH. *a.* The *Church* through her Fathers, theologians, confessors, missionaries, etc.

*b. Reason.* Not only is sin wrong, but it is wrong also to love it, and to wish for it. But he who puts himself into the occasions of sin without necessity, loves sin, wishes for sin, and is, therefore, guilty of sin. You flee from the pest-house, infected districts, for fear of contagion. Flee, therefore, from the occasion of sin. Where there are two or three gathered together in the devil's name, he is among them.

*c. Voices from the hospitals.* Men and women with loathsome diseases — drunkards suffering from delirium tremens . . . why? -Occasion of sin.

*d. Voices from the mad-house.* Maniacs, idiots . . . the result of evil habits. People acting against reason are deprived of the use of it. Why this? Occasion of sin.

*e. Voices from the prison — from the gallows.* Thieves, robbers, murderers confess that they became depraved by not avoiding the occasion of sin.

*f. Voices from the civil and criminal courts.* Divorce resorted to, prolonged lawsuits, criminal proceedings, etc. — all the result of frequenting the occasions of sin.

*g. Voices from the offices of physicians,* where the most disgusting diseases are examined — *from the graves — from the river sides — from the waters —* which are the silent witnesses of suicides committed to hide shame, to end the sorrows caused by disappointment, etc. — all the fruit of the occasion of sin.

*h. Voices from the tribunal of Christ* — hear the appeals against seducers — the cries of the murdered innocents against unnatural mothers, who committed murder to hide their shame — all brought on by the occasion of sin.

3. HELL — *a.* Thence arise the *cries of despair* of the damned, their curses, their execrations against the occasions of sin that caused their ruin; their threats of *revenge* against those who led them into the occasion of sin; their *maledictions* against those whose duty it was to keep them from these occasions of sin.

*b.* The *open avowal of the demons,* who confess that in the occasions of sin they have their best and most successful allies in leading human souls to hell.

Example related by Blessed Leonard, of the devil's confessing out of a possessed person that of all the sermons preached at a Mission he disliked most that on the proximate occasion of sin.

Therefore, away with all excuses. They are inspired by hell. You have before you the fearful alternative: *Either give up the proximate occasion of sin or your eternal damnation is certain.*

NOTE. — The third part of this Sketch is enough for one sermon. As a part of a sermon it has to be considerably shortened.

CONCLUSION. — Recapitulation.

Here you have before you the means of perseverance, without which salvation is simply impossible. What do you intend to do? You constantly put in practice similar means to preserve the life of your bodies. Will you do less for your souls — for God? Whose infinite mercy has again dealt with you in so

fatherly a manner in putting you once more on the
road to salvation?    Do you still hesitate?

"How long do you halt between two sides?   If the Lord be God,
follow him, but if Baal, then follow him." — III Kings xviii. 21.

Your choice is between God and the devil, between heaven and hell, between salvation and damnation, between eternal life and eternal death.    Come,
then, to a generous resolution, to a firm determination
to practise the three chief means of perseverance as
I have explained them to you.    Make this resolution
*aloud* before God, before the world, and in contempt
of the devil.    Make it *together* for your mutual encouragement.    Arise, then, and courageously answer
three questions which I shall ask you.

My dear Christians, I ask you, before God and in
the holy name of Jesus Christ:

1. Will you in future constantly practise holy
prayer?   If so, then answer aloud: I will.

Note. — If the answer to the first question is somewhat remiss,
the question must be repeated.   St. Alphonsus did the same.

It is necessary to demand an expression of the *will, of resoluteness*,
and *of determination.*

2. Will you receive the holy sacraments as frequently as I have told you?   If so . . .

3. Will you carefully shun the proximate occasion
of sin?   If so . . .

And now let me add one more question:

Will you try your best to carry out these three
resolutions until death?   If so, then answer once
more:   I will.

Thanks be to God — the victory is gained!    Religion will triumph in this congregation.    Oh! may the
Blessed Virgin Mary, to whom you have dedicated
yourselves as children, guide you and assist you through
all the difficulties of life, and help you to be faithful

to your resolutions until death, that you may receive the crown of life everlasting! Once more let me say with the Apostle:

"Thanks be to God, who hath given us the victory through our Lord Jesus Christ. Therefore, my beloved brethren, be ye steadfast and immovable, always abounding in the work of the Lord, knowing that your labor is not in vain in the Lord." — I Cor. xv. 57, 58.

# FOURTH PART
# INSTRUCTIONS FOR MISSIONS

# A. — Instructions on the Sacraments and the Commandments

## I

## CONFESSION. — EXAMINATION OF CONSCIENCE

This instruction should be brought into connection with the sermon preached the evening before, namely, on the importance of salvation. No man can be saved who is in the state of mortal sin, and mortal sin can only be forgiven by a *good* confession. The necessity of confession need simply be stated, not proved at any length, to the audience present on the first Monday morning. — Now, how is a good confession made? — The answer to this question forms the subject of the instruction.

Confession is an *accusation* of ourselves to the priest; — and this accusation must be — 1, *sincere;* 2, *brief;* 3, *humble,* and 4, *entire.* — It is entire, when we accuse ourselves of all the *mortal* sins, together with their *number* and necessary *circumstances,* that we committed since our sins were forgiven us the *last time.*

To make such a confession a due *examination of conscience* must go before it. Then explain how that is made.

Finally (if there is time), the ordinary difficulties which some people find in making a confession should be cleared away in the manner described.

### SKETCH

EXORDIUM. — You have heard the sermon on the importance of saving our immortal souls. A soul cannot be saved so long as it is in the state of mortal sin. There is a remedy, but only one — true penance. Will any kind of penance be sufficient? No, only that which God has instituted for the remission of sins — sacramental confession. Confession is necessary for the remission of sins committed after baptism. No forgiveness without it.

Let me tell you to-day how to perform this most

important act of religion, so that through it you may be assured of the remission of your sins.

## I. Qualities of Sacramental Confession

Confession is an *accusation* of ourselves to the priest. The object of this accusation is to place ourselves before the priest as *guilty* as we know ourselves to be before God. It should be accompanied with an earnest desire that the priest may see us as guilty as we are before God.

You should proceed against yourself as you would against one with whom you have a law-suit.

You lay your case before the judge as clearly as you can, and desire in all earnestness that the judge shall find your opponent guilty. The same you must do against yourself before the priest at confession.

1. This accusation must be *sincere*. No excuses, no accusation of others, no enumeration of our good works. "They took the curse out of me" — "I said angry words, but I could not help it" — "They make me do it" — "It's rum that did it," etc., etc., are expressions not to be used in confession, because they destroy the most essential quality of it — self-accusation.

Let the penitent also avoid cloaking or dressing up his sins by giving them a different name, *e.g.*, confessing deeds as bad ·thoughts. Let him rather present them to the priest as they are before God, yet as modestly as possible.

2. The accusation must be *entire*. The penitent must tell:

*a.* Every *mortal sin* of which he knows himself to be guilty since his last good confession.

*b.* He must mention the *number*, how often he has

committed it — the exact number, if he can; about how many times, if the number is uncertain. But if he cannot at all come near the exact number, let him find out, *a,* how long he has been addicted to the sin; *b,* how often he has generally committed it in a day, in a week, or in a month; *c,* whether at certain times he did not cease to commit it — how long and how often this has happened.

Enumeration of abuses in this respect; as, "I don't know" — "Can't tell" — "Often and often" — "Millions of times" — "I wouldn't tell a lie," etc. There is no excuse for these and similar evasive expressions, because men know how to express themselves at once and to the point in the transaction of business of temporal importance.

*c.* The penitent must confess such *circumstances* as change the nature of his sins.

3. The accusation must be *simple.* All unnecessary conversation is to be omitted. Make a clear statement of your sins, and no more; by acting otherwise the validity of the sacrament is in danger, as unnecessary talk destroys contrition. Besides this, there are two other faults committed against simplicity: *a.* Waiting too long after telling a sin, expecting another question from the priest. Tell all your sins as you know them before you expect the priest to speak. *b.* Wasting time in enumerating irrelevant circumstances, *e.g.,* mentioning streets, houses, etc.

4. The accusation must be *humble.* The penitent should present himself as a criminal before the tribunal of Christ, guilty of the fire of hell, seeking for pardon and absolution. He should take the advice and direction of the confessor as though it came from Christ Himself, especially in regard to reconciliation with enemies, giving up dangerous acquaint-

ances, visits to theaters, or other dangerous amusements, books, the restitution of ill-gotten goods, or the reparation of an injured reputation. Never dispute or argue with the priest, because he must know best what is to be done, and your salvation depends *on his decision.*

5. *Encouragement* for those who are afraid to tell their sins in confession: 1. The priest can never tell what he has heard in confession so as to betray the penitent. If you tell your sins to the walls in the corner of a lonely room, they are less secret than when you tell them to a priest in confession. The priest must rather die than reveal your sins. Bury them, therefore, in the heart of the priest, and they are hidden forever. 2. Do not heed the temptation: what the priest might think of you. Your conversion is the greatest consolation to him. "There shall be more joy over one sinner" . . . (Luke xv. 7). The priest usually does not know his penitents, nor does he care to know them; but if he knows you, he does not know your sins out of confession. 3. Think of the General Judgment, when all sins not forgiven in time will be published to the whole world, and will be known in heaven and in hell for all eternity. 4. Be not afraid of the priest, who is in the confessional not to hear virtues, but sins; and remember that, having received absolution, your sins are really judged, forgiven, and settled forever. 5. Should you not be able to express yourself, ask the priest to assist you, but then answer every question truthfully and to the point.

In order to make a confession as here stated, it must be preceded by the

## II. EXAMINATION OF CONSCIENCE

This consists in making use of ordinary diligence in calling to mind all the mortal sins that we have committed since our last good confession — "Ordinary" *i.e.*, such diligence as we use in any business of importance. "Mortal sins," because we are not strictly bound to confess venial sins, except when there is a doubt whether they are mortal or not.

He certainly cannot be said to be truly sorry for his sins, or determined to make a good and sincere accusation of them to the priest, who does not even take sufficient care to recall them to mind.

He who goes before a civil magistrate with an accusation against another will certainly try to recollect the case as it is, in order to be able to make a clear statement of it. Thus must the penitent act toward himself.

This condition is not fulfilled by those who leave all to the priest, depending on his questions, who say that they are no scholars, etc.

Therefore, prepare for your confession in the following manner:

1. Examine your conscience, as though you were to die immediately after your confession.

*Pray* to the Holy Ghost for light. The soul in the state of mortal sin is in darkness. We need the light of God to see our sins. Have firm confidence; for God desires nothing more earnestly than that you should know your sins.

2. Find out the *exact time* of your last confession. Examine whether that confession was good or bad. If good, begin your examination from that time. If bad, go back to your last good confession. If doubtful, do the same, if you have good reason for believing it

was bad; if you have no good reason, leave it to the decision of the confessor.

3. *Ask* yourself what mortal sins you have committed since that time. As soon as you have discovered them, find out their number, as stated before, and whether some particular circumstance was not perhaps connected with them, changing the nature of the sin.

Take special care to find out all your sins in thought, word, deed, omission, and in your particular state of life.

4. In examining your conscience, follow the order of the *commandments* of God and of the Church, not forgetting your special duties of life, the capital sins and the sacraments. The very best way is to go through the table of sins found in the prayer books, the mission-book to be preferred. If you cannot do either, then go over your life from your last confession, trying to recollect what you have done wrong, and in that same order you may afterward make your confession.

The examination need not be made all at one time, nor need it be made immediately before confession, nor in the church. All that is necessary is that you try to know all your sins, so as to be able to confess them properly.

*Precaution* should be taken lest penitents give way to scrupulosity, spending too much time in their examination, while they hardly think of true contrition and of amending their lives. Grievous sins do not easily escape our memory, and about venial sins we are not bound to be so exact.

## III. Manner of Confession

1. Practically explain how a confession is to be made — "Bless me, Father." "I confess" (to be said before coming in, when there are many waiting), as far as "through my fault." Last confession — good or bad — absolution — penance performed — enumeration of sins without interruption. Then, "For these and all my other sins which I cannot remember, I am heartily sorry," etc. Listen attentively to the admonition given by the priest. Say all that you may wish to say before he comes to the absolution. Then do not interrupt him before he is finished. While the priest gives you absolution, make an act of contrition.

2. After confession retire to a quiet place and give thanks to God for His goodness and mercy.

If you have forgotten to confess a mortal sin, return to the same priest or another to confess it — before going to Holy Communion, if you can conveniently do so; if not, tell it in your next confession.

Remember also that there still rests upon you the obligation of making some *satisfaction* for your sins. This consists: 1. In the exact performance of the penance that the priest has imposed upon you. A penance imposed for grievous sins obliges under grievous sin. Should you therefore think yourself unable to perform the penance that the priest gives you, you should tell him so at once. You cannot change it afterward on your own authority. The penitent should desire hard penances; otherwise he must make up for insufficient satisfaction either in purgatory or by sufferings in this world. 2. In imposing upon yourself and performing voluntary penances. St. Mary Magdalen practised hard penance for thirty years; St. Mary of Egypt for forty-seven years; St. Peter shed tears every night until his death over his sin of denying Christ, etc.   3. In bearing patiently all the sufferings that Divine Providence allows to befall you.   4. In making up for your want of fervor in this point by gaining the indulgences of the Church.

NOTE. — If time does not permit, the third part of the foregoing instruction may be left out.

# CONTRITION AND FIRM PURPOSE OF AMENDMENT

First show the *absolute necessity* of contrition for the forgiveness of sin. — Then explain the *qualities* of contrition. It must be 1, *sincere;* 2, *supernatural;* 3, *supreme;* 4, *universal;* 5, united with *confidence* in God. — Show also the difference between *perfect* and *imperfect* contrition and the effect of each.

Explain also the *qualities* of the *purpose of amendment* which must necessarily be united to contrition. It is to be: 1, *firm;* 2, *universal;* 3, *efficacious.* Lay special stress on the necessity of shunning the proximate occasion of sin.

Lastly, point out the means by which a hardened sinner can obtain true contrition.

## SKETCH

EXORDIUM. — What we said on the Sacrament of Penance yesterday constitutes the outward part of it. Now we come to the interior dispositions which must of necessity accompany the exterior acts of penance. They consist in true contrition for our sins and a firm purpose of amendment.

## I. NECESSITY OF CONTRITION

1. No sin can possibly be forgiven without true contrition and a firm purpose of amendment, no sin ever has been, ever will be, because this is an impossibility before God.

No sinner can be reconciled to God who still loves what God hates and detests and who is not determined to abandon it. Now God absolutely detests sin, as it is directly opposed to His will and sanctity, and as it is a violation of His most holy and just law. Therefore, He cannot be reconciled to one who does not hate it from his heart — and who, consequently, does not sincerely regret having committed it — and who is not firmly resolved to avoid it in future.

2. A confession most exact, most humiliating, repeated over and over, but without true contrition, is worthless. Such a confession must be re-made in order to obtain forgiveness.

3. Sometimes forgiveness can be obtained without actual confession. *Confessio desiderii* has the same effect as *baptismus flaminis*. Example of a man struck down in mortal sin and no priest at hand. But never without true contrition, which in this case must be perfect.

The great work of redemption is lost to those who have no contrition.

"I came to heal the contrite of heart." — Luke iv. 18.


## II. Qualities of Contrition

It must consist —

1. In a *sincere interior regret,* grief, sorrow for what has happened. Exterior manifestations of it are not required, yet they may indicate its intensity. Examples.

2. It must proceed from *supernatural motives*. God cannot forgive the sinner who is sorry for his sins only on account of some loss sustained in the natural order. Examples.

3. It must be *universal* — *i.e.,* it must include all mortal sins committed by the penitent, whether he remember them or not, because one cannot be the friend of God in one respect while one is opposed to Him in another.

4. It must be *supreme, i.e.,* we must regret our sins more than any other evil that we may have or could have sustained. The penitent must not be alarmed if he have not the same *feeling* of regret for his sins that he has for temporal sufferings or losses. We have not always command over our feelings.

5. It must be united to a firm *confidence* in the mercy of God.

6. Such contrition may be *imperfect,* and this is sufficient for a good confession — or *perfect;* according as the principal motive of sorrow proceeds from *fear* of God's punishments, or from *love,* on account of having outraged the Infinite Good.

Take, as an illustration, two children who have disobeyed their parents in a serious matter, and who are about to be punished for their misbehavior. Both are sorry, and regret what they have done. But there is a difference in their motives. The one is sorry because he fears the punishment, the other, because he has grieved his parents.

As soon as God sees perfect contrition in the sinner's heart, He pardons him at once, provided he be determined to make his confession as soon as he can. How valuable, therefore, is an act of perfect contrition. Learn by heart a short act of perfect contrition and say it often.


III. Qualities of the Purpose of Amendment

True regret necessarily includes a firm purpose of avoiding in future what we regret. The purpose of amendment, included in contrition, must possess the following qualities:

1. It must be *firm* — *i.e.,* not easily shaken, so that the penitent be determined not to sin again, no mat-

ter how violent the storms of temptation may be that
rise against him.

2. It must be *universal* — *i.e.,* the penitent must be
determined to avoid not only one or the other sin,
or those which he has confessed, or is about to confess; but every sin, so as to offend God no more, at
least not grievously.

3. It must be *efficacious* — *i.e.,* the penitent must be
determined to put in practice the ordinary remedies
against relapse, especially *holy prayer* — flight from
*dangerous occasions* — and the reception of the *sacraments.* He must likewise be willing to do his best
toward repairing the damages caused by his sins, by
making restitution, by repairing the reputation of his
neighbor which he has injured, and by giving up the
enmity and ill-feeling which he may have borne against
his neighbor. Finally, he must begin at once to follow the good advice given him by his confessor.

Some people at times feel very scrupulous about
their past confessions, fearing that they were made
without true contrition or a firm purpose of amendment. They may easily settle this point. Let them
ask themselves in all sincerity whether they went
to confession out of a supernatural motive, in order
to obtain forgiveness from God, and whether they were
at the time determined not to sin again grievously. If
so, let them be satisfied about their past confessions,
notwithstanding their subsequent relapse; if not, the
validity of their past confessions must be questioned.

If you have not true contrition nor a firm purpose
of amendment in your heart, what must you do to
obtain it? 1. Pray for it in confidence. God wishes
nothing more sincerely than to be reconciled with you,
and He will therefore certainly grant it. 2. Cast a
look *up* toward God, Whom you have offended, and

toward heaven, which you have lost; *down* into hell, which is open under your feet, and where your name is already written in letters of fire; *before you,* toward Mount Calvary, where Jesus Christ suffered death on account of your sins.

If you can say the act of contrition devoutly, and really mean from your heart what you say, then you have true contrition.

# III

## GENERAL CONFESSION

Neither St. Alphonsus nor the Rule mentions anything about this instruction, although St. Alphonsus desires that in every instruction the people should be warned against sacrilegious confessions.[1] — A General Confession is the only means of salvation for thousands, and yet they know not how to go about it. In this instruction state plainly *who* those are that *must* make a general confession, and then explain the *method* of making it. Then mention those *who must not* make a general confession, and for what reasons. Those *who are free* to make a general confession should receive no more than a passing notice.

This instruction is *not to precede* the two instructions mentioned above. It is *to follow* them. The people must first be told how a good confession is to be made, and consequently what makes a confession bad, before they are told of the remedy.

### SKETCH

EXORDIUM. — If the penitent sinner have made his confession as explained in the two foregoing instructions, his sins are *surely* forgiven. If, however, he have omitted a single essential point, his sins are *surely not* forgiven. If he have done so wilfully, he has even added by his bad confession the dreadful crime of *sacrilege*. The only remedy left him for salvation is to confess all the mortal sins that he has committed since his last good confession. If several confessions have been bad, he is obliged to make what we call a *General Confession*.

[1] C. E., Vol. XV. p. 172.

## I. For Whom is a General Confession Necessary?

It is necessary for all those who have made bad confessions:

1. For want of a conscientious *accusation* of all their mortal sins — by making a careless examination of conscience, or none at all; by cloaking sins — trying to give them a different color from what they have in reality; by maliciously excusing them — lessening their guilt — excusing the intention; by purposely confessing them to a priest who is deaf or who does not understand the language; by purposely telling them in an obscure manner — with a low voice, quickly hurrying over them, so that they may escape the notice of the priest; by wilfully omitting certain mortal sins altogether, which have never been confessed, or about which it is at least very doubtful whether they have been told; by not telling the sins that were forgotten in past confessions; by omitting such circumstances as change the nature of the sin; by not stating the exact number as far as possible; by confessing as doubtful a sin which is certain, or giving the number or circumstances as doubtful when they are certain about them; by confessing thoughts for actions — to say, for instance: "I had bad thoughts," when in reality they committed bad actions.

2. For want of *true contrition* — by going to confession through routine; or only because sent or forced to confession by parents, wives, friends, rules of society; or only to fulfil one's Easter duty, though but outwardly; or perhaps out of an affection for the priest, etc.; being at the same time very little concerned about the offences committed against God, and having very soon relapsed again.

3. For want of a *true resolution,* or purpose of amendment; by not abandoning the proximate occasion of sin, dangerous company, sinful society, places of sinful amusement; by taking no pains whatsoever to become better; never having a real determination to avoid sin.

4. For want of due *reparation of injuries* done to one's neighbor — by retaining ill-gotten goods; by omitting restitution, not paying long-standing debts; by not repairing the damages done to the neighbor's property; by keeping up hatred — by not forgiving injuries received; by omitting to repair the damage caused to the neighbor's reputation; by not repairing the harm done by public scandal.

In case of *doubt,* whether a general confession is necessary or not, lay the matter before the priest in confession, and in following his decision you may rest secure.

For many people a general confession is *not necessary* but of great *utility.* With the priest's permission they may make one by going through a general review rather than an exact confession.

There are others to whom a general confession would only *do harm.* They feel most anxious to make it, owing to their constant troubles of conscience. They should know that God permits their interior trials, *a,* as a penance; *b,* as a preventive against future sins; *c,* as a constant monitor to interior sorrow. Their state of mind will not be changed by a general confession. It will last as long as God wills it.

Unless a person of this description is sure that his past confessions were bad, he should not be allowed to make a general confession.

It is a great consolation for us all to know that — if we did what we thought was required for a good confession, even though perchance there were no true contrition in our hearts, without our being aware of it — though some other essential condition were wanting in our past confessions, of which we have no positive knowledge — those confessions need not be re-made until we are positively certain about these deficiencies, because our sins are forgiven in Communion — in the subsequent good confession — or by an act of perfect contrition which we have since made.

## II.  Manner of Making a General Confession

1. In the first place, make up your mind to do the work *yourself*.  Do not leave all to the priest; although, in his charity, he will assist you whenever he finds it necessary.  Be firmly *determined* to make this confession as well as you possibly can.

2. Begin by invoking the *Holy Ghost* to assist you. Put all your confidence in Jesus and Mary, who will certainly come to your assistance.

3. *Examine* your conscience as though you had never been to confession from the time that you made your last good confession.  Find out the exact time, if possible.

4. Find out the number of *bad confessions* and *unworthy Communions* which you have made since, and also whether you have received any other sacrament in the state of sin, as Confirmation, Extreme Unction, Matrimony.  But, if you went to confession for some time, not thinking of the bad confessions that you made before, and being perfectly willing to tell all your sins, then those intermediate confessions were not bad, nor the Communions unworthy.

5. The *easiest way of examining your conscience* is to begin from the time you made your last good confession

— or from your childhood, in case all your confessions have been bad. Go through your entire life slowly in your mind, trying to recollect the places you lived in — your daily occupations — your company — your amusements. . . . In the same order you may confess your sins to the priest. Thus you will easily remember everything, without having recourse to writing.

As soon as you have discovered a mortal sin, ask yourself how many times you committed that sin on an average in a year, a month, or a week, and how long you were addicted to it. Examine also whether there was not a particular circumstance connected with it, which is to be stated in confession.

6. When you come to the priest in the confessional tell him at once that you have come to make a general confession; tell him why you deem it necessary to make a general confession — and from what time you have to start. Then make your confession as you prepared it, mentioning the time when you made the last good confession, how many bad confessions you have made, etc., as stated in number 4. Then tell all the mortal sins which you committed during that time, whether you have confessed them before or not. Confess them all as though you had made no confession at all during that time, stating at the same time, as well as you can, the number and the necessary circumstances of each.

In a general confession that is not necessary or that may be called a review of your life or of a part of it, it is not necessary to be so particular in enumerating the number and kind of sins. It is enough to make a general statement of them.

7. *Answer every question* of the priest in the best and clearest way possible; answer directly — not in an evasive manner; for all the questions ordinarily put

to persons at a general confession are of such importance that the salvation of their souls depends on the answer.

8. It is quite natural that you should forget one or more of your grievous sins at a general confession. Be not uneasy on this account about the validity of your confession.

Tell *whatever* you may have *forgotten* to your confessor or to any other priest as soon as you remember it — or at least in your next confession. If you think of it before Communion, confess it, if you can conveniently do so; if you cannot conveniently do this, make an act of contrition for it and go to Communion, resolving to confess it the first time you go again to confession.

9. Expect some hard *penance* from the priest and accept it cheerfully, because you have deserved many and severe punishments which the justice of God must lay on you, especially for your great abuse of the sacraments.

# IV

## ENMITY

This is for many persons one of the great obstacles in the way of receiving pardon. They are most unwilling to forgive. Great difficulties are thereby caused in the confessional. — Therefore, this subject is to follow immediately the instructions on the Sacrament of Penance, although it properly belongs to the commandments.

The catechist is not to dwell long on the love of our neighbor or of our enemies, but he shall point out most forcibly — 1, the *necessity* of pardoning our enemies, and 2, the *manner* of doing so. He must severely castigate those who refuse to forgive, and show how unworthy they are of receiving pardon from God. It would even be well to cite an example of the fearful judgment of God that befell those who refused to forgive their enemies.

### SKETCH

EXORDIUM. — We have told you all about the Sacrament of Penance; also how bad confessions are repaired. Two obstacles, however, may exist which prevent a full reconciliation between God and the sinner. It is useless to attempt confession before these are removed. The one is *enmity;* the other is the *possession of ill-gotten goods*. Of the former I shall speak to-day; the latter I shall explain on another occasion.

### I. NECESSITY OF FORGIVING

No one *can receive forgiveness* from God unless he forgive all his enemies from the heart.

1. God commands us to love our neighbor as ourselves, no matter who or what he may be.

"Beloved, let us love one another. . . . He that loveth not, knoweth not God, for God is love." — I John iv. 7. — "If any man say, I love God, and hateth his brother, he is a liar." — Ib. 20. — "A new

426

commandment I give you, that ye love one another. . . . By this shall all men know that you are my disciples, if you have love one for another." — John xiii. 34, 35. — Also Matt. xix. 19; — Id. xxii. 39; — Rom. xiii. 9; — Gal. v. 14; — James ii. 8.

Directly opposed to this commandment is *enmity*. Enmity consists in a protracted anger against our neighbor.

"In consequence of enmity we have an aversion for certain persons; we even abominate them." — St. Aug. — "We speak with them and of them with detestation; cannot bear the sight of them; wish them evil; do them harm; rejoice over their misfortunes, etc." — St. Thomas.

*Who are our enemies?* Not those who have offended us by accident, through thoughtlessness, in the heat of passion, without intending thereby a direct offence; but those who hate — envy — afflict — persecute — oppress us, etc.; and these God commands us to forgive.

"Bless those who persecute you." — Rom. xii. 14.

2. There is no forgiveness of sin possible for you, so long as you live in enmity with your neighbor and refuse reconciliation.

"Forgive thy neighbor, if he hath hurt thee, and then shall thy sins be forgiven to thee when thou prayest." — Eccli. xxviii. 2. — "If you will forgive men their offences, your heavenly Father will forgive you also. But if you will not forgive men, neither will your Father forgive you your offences." — Matt. vi. 14, 15.

3. *Parable* (Matt. xviii. 23). The wicked servant spoken of owed ten thousand talents (about fifteen million dollars) to his lord, and when he asked his lord to have patience with him, his lord was moved by pity and he forgave him the whole debt. After going out this servant found one of his fellow-servants who owed him one hundred shillings (a little over twelve dollars). He, too, asked for patience. But the other had no pity on him, etc. The lord of the wicked

servant had him called back, reprimanded him most severely, demanded the entire amount, and had him cast into prison until he paid the entire debt. By this immense sum our sins are represented; by the small amount the offences committed against us by our neighbors. And then Jesus adds: "So also shall my heavenly Father do to you, if you forgive not every one his brother from your hearts."

4. In the *prayer* which our Lord has taught us, He makes us pray that God may not forgive us our sins, except on condition that we forgive our enemies.

"Forgive us our trespasses *as* (in the same manner, to the same extent) we forgive those who have trespassed against us." — Matt. vi. 12. — "How can you extend your hands toward heaven, or move your tongue, or ask pardon; for if the Lord would wish to forgive you your sins, behold, you do not permit it, since you retain in your mind the offence of your fellow-servant?" — St. Chrys. — "When you pray you bring a malediction down upon you, because you pray, forgive us our trespasses as we forgive . . ." — St. Athan.

5. None of your *good works* is acceptable to God, because you are an object of abomination to Him as long as you do not effect a reconciliation between yourself and your enemy. God turns away from those who turn away from their neighbor.

"If, therefore, thou offer thy gift at the altar, and there thou remember that thy brother hath anything against thee, leave there thy gift before the altar, and go first to be reconciled to thy brother, and then coming thou shalt offer thy gift." — Matt. v. 23, 24.

## II. How Must we Forgive?

As God forgives us. And this is expressly what we mention in the Lord's prayer, when we say: "Forgive us *as* we forgive."

"Let all bitterness and anger and indignation . . . be put away from you, with all malice, and be ye kind one to another, merciful,

forgiving one another, *even as God* hath forgiven you in Christ." —
Eph. iv. 31, 32.

Therefore:

1. Forgive *all offences,* no matter how grievous, or
how frequently committed.

St. Peter asked: "Lord, shall I forgive my brother till seven
times?" — Jesus said to him: "I say not to thee, till seven times,
but till seventy times seven," — to any number. — Matt xviii. 21, 22.

2. Forgive *unconditionally,* without requiring satisfaction, or looking for revenge. However, it is not
required to give up just claims.

"He that seeketh to revenge himself shall find vengeance from
the Lord; and he will surely keep his sins in remembrance." —
Eccli. xxviii. 1.

Remember that you could never make satisfaction
to God, were He to require it of you.

3. Forgive, even if your enemies *continue to hate
you.*

"Bless them that persecute you: bless, and curse not." — Rom.
xii. 14.

4. *Make the advance* toward a reconciliation, especially if you are the offender: *a.* By speaking in a
friendly manner to the person whom you have
offended; *b.* By asking pardon, if you are an inferior,
or the offence was very grievous.

*Objection.* "I will speak to him if he speaks to me
first."

To be friendly toward those who are friendly
toward us requires no Christian virtue.

"If you love them that love you, what reward shall you have?
Do not even the publicans this? And if you salute your brethren
only, what do ye more? Do not also the heathens this?" — Matt.
v. 46, 47.

Generally speaking, the other person says the same.
Who, then, is to speak first? That one will do so

who is filled with a Christian spirit; another cannot do it, and therefore refuses.

"I spoke in my mind." That is not speaking, but thinking.

"I have nothing against him." Why not speak, then?

5. *Forget all,* so that you can easily exhibit the ordinary signs of politeness, and do a work of charity to your enemy. God also forgets the sins which He forgives.

"Their sins and iniquities I will remember no more." — Heb. x. 17.

*Objection.* "I can't help thinking of it." Banish such thoughts as you must other temptations. Your merit before God is so much the greater. God permits them as a reparation for the repeated acts of aversion indulged in before.

Example of some terrible punishment inflicted on such as would not forgive.

# V

## RESTITUTION

The ignorance of people in regard to this obligation is incredible. As eager as people are to grasp their neighbors' goods, so unwilling are they afterward to make restitution, and hence the difficulties met with in the confessional.

Here also the catechist is — 1, to show the *necessity* of restoring ill-gotten goods, and 2, he must answer the questions, *who* must restore, — *to whom,* — *what,* — *when,* — *how* — and who is *free* from the obligation. On short Missions this and the foregoing instruction are often united in one.

The catechist, in treating on this subject, should guard against false assertions and decisions, and not overstep the teachings of Moral Theology.

### Sketch

Exordium. — As eager as people are to grasp their neighbors' goods, so unwilling are they afterward to make restitution. And thereby they incur eternal damnation for the sake of earthly goods.

### I. Why Must Restitution be Made?

1. Because *injustice excludes* man from the *kingdom of heaven.* And a man is guilty of injustice so long as he has not made reparation for his acts of injustice.

"The unjust shall not possess the kingdom of God." — I Cor. vi. 9.

2. Restitution is demanded by the *law of nature.* Man must give to every one his due. *Unicuique suum.* There must be order in society. It is disturbed by acts of injustice; repaired by restitution.

Common sense would be shocked, if the sins of injustice were forgiven and no restitution exacted. Shown by some examples.

3. It is demanded by the *Scriptures:*

"When a man or woman shall have committed sin . . . they shall confess their sin, and restore the principal itself, and the fifth part over and above, to him against whom they have sinned." — Num. v. 6, 7. — "If any man steal an ox or a sheep, and kill or sell it, he shall restore five oxen for one ox, and four sheep for one sheep." — Exod. xxii. 1. — "The curse shall come to the house of the thief . . . and it shall remain in the midst of his house and shall consume it, with the timbers thereof and the stones thereof." — Zach. v. 4. — "Woe to him that heapeth together that which is not his own! — How long also doth he load himself with thick clay." — Hab. ii. 6.

4. It is demanded by the *Fathers:*
"If those go to hell who did not clothe the naked, what about those who stole and thereby rendered others naked?" — St. Aug. *Non remittitur peccatum, nisi restituatur ablatum.* "There can be no absolution without previous restitution." — St. Aug.

5. It is demanded by the *Church.* She strictly forbids confessors to give absolution to those who are unwilling to make the requisite restitution.

Some think that restitution is a simple *penance* imposed upon them by the priest. But should the priest even forget to remind them of the restitution to be made, they are bound to make it nevertheless. This obligation goes so far, that even the confessor is bound to make restitution, should he unlawfully pronounce his penitent free from it.

*Objection.* "What would become of me and my family, if I were to make restitution?" But what will become of you, if you do not make it?

Example of a father of a family, who made his will before he died, bequeathing to the devil, his wife, children, priest, his soul and body — related by St. Alphonsus, *Exercises*.[1]

## II.  Who Must Make Restitution?

Every one who has wronged his neighbor in his temporal property, no matter by what means, in what manner, and to what extent.  If the injury is but a trifle, restitution is to be made under the penalty of venial sin.  But many small thefts make the obligation of restitution grievous, because no one is allowed to enrich himself unjustly.  The chief classes of those who must make restitution are:

1. Those who have stolen their neighbor's goods.

2. Those who have culpably caused damage to their neighbor's property, or by fraud deprived him of some gain.

3. Those who have cheated their neighbor in business transactions, in buying, selling, in weight, in measure, in making out bills, in not keeping their contracts, passing bad money.

4. Those who do not pay lawful debts, take unjust recompense, make overcharges, defraud their servants or workmen of their just wages.

5. Those who accidentally come into the possession of their neighbor's goods by finding things lost, receiving overpay, overchange.

6. Those who have influenced others to commit some act of injustice by buying stolen goods, encouraged or assisted others in doing damage, or in engaging in some unjust dealing.

In these days it becomes necessary to be on one's guard.  For many an unjust transaction passes under the specious name of "business," "smartness"; and

[1] C. E., Vol. XV. p. 486.

many excuse themselves on the plea that everybody else does the same.

Injustice can never become lawful.

"Thou shalt not have divers weights in thy bag, a greater and a less . . . a greater bushel and a less . . . Thou shalt have a just and true weight . . . The Lord God abhorreth him that doth these things, and he hateth all injustice." — Deut. xxv. 13–16. — "Neither thieves, nor covetous, nor extortioners shall possess the kingdom of God." — I Cor. vi. 10.

### III. How is Restitution to be Made?

In regard to this question the various conditions to be complied with in making restitution must be explained.

1. *What must be restored?* The stolen article itself, together with its natural increase in value; an equivalent, or its value, if the thing stolen cannot be had, so as fully to indemnify the owner for the loss that he has sustained by your act of injustice.

Zacheus restored fourfold for what he had defrauded (Luke xix. 8); you are simply to repair the damage that you have caused.

2. *To whom?* To the owner, if known; if not, to God, *i.e.*, for pious causes; however, not for pew-rent, etc. If the owner is dead, to his heirs. In doubtful cases, consult the confessor.

"But if there be no one to receive it (the ill-gotten treasure), they shall give it to the Lord." — Numb. v. 8.

3. *In what manner?* Without *danger to your reputation,* which is more valuable than any material thing. But there are hundreds of ways to avoid that danger, as restitution may be made by proxy, letter, express, the confessor, etc., etc.

4. *When?* If possible *before* confession, or *immediately after,* as soon as possible; in proportion to

your means — by installments, if it cannot be done all at once without great damage to yourself and family. Some delay is allowable in every case when your reputation is at stake.

5. *To what place?* To the place and address of the owner, sent to him free of expense, and so that it surely comes into his possession. Otherwise restitution cannot be said to have been made.

### IV. Causes which Free from the Obligation of Restitution

1. If impossible on account of poverty. But in that case it is advisable for the unjust man to offer up good works for the owner, that the Lord may bless him the more in a temporal or spiritual respect.

Otherwise the thief will have to suffer in purgatory until he has paid the last farthing.

2. If the owner has remitted the debt.

3. If the owner has caused damage to the thief to the same amount, or did not pay him what was just and due.

But it is no excuse that you suffered damages from others; that you do a great deal in charity or piety; or that such acts of injustice are ever so common — or that you cannot make a living, or carry on business without defrauding others.

If you find restitution hard, remember the saying of our Lord: "What doth it profit a man . . ." (Matt. xvi. 26.) Example.

# VI

## ENMITY AND RESTITUTION COMBINED

EXORDIUM. — The same as in the Instruction on Enmity.

### I. NECESSITY OF PARDONING OUR ENEMIES

1. *Who* are our enemies? (Ib. Part I. n. 1.) — *Why* must we forgive them? Because we cannot be pardoned until we have pardoned our enemies. (Proved, Ib. in n. 3, 4, and 5).

2. *How* must we forgive? As God forgives us, namely, *a*. All (Ib. Part II. n. 1.) — *b*. By making the advance (Ib. n. 4.) — *c*. By forgetting the past (Ib. n. 5).

### II. NECESSITY OF MAKING RESTITUTION

1. *Why* must restitution be made? (Instruction on Restitution, Part I. n. 1, 2, 4 and 5.)

2. *Who* must make it? (Ib. Part II. Introductory part only.)

3. *How* is restitution to be made? (Ib. Part III. — all that part.)

4. Excuses from restitution. (Ib. Part IV., all to the end.)

CONCLUSION. — Be on your guard against these two obstacles that shut out souls from heaven. Should you be entangled in them at present, remove them while it lies in your power, and then come to receive pardon from your offended God.

# VII

## HOLY COMMUNION

The Sacrament of Penance *restores* spiritual life to the soul —
Holy Communion *preserves* it. This point is, therefore, next in
order. In reference to this Sacrament the people must know
— 1, *what* they receive, and 2, *how* they must receive it. —
If the sermon on the Real Presence is preached, a few sentences in regard to it will suffice here; otherwise, a few of
the strongest proofs must be adduced here to confirm the
people in their faith. — Then let the catechist mention the *principal
effects* of Holy Communion. — In regard to the second point, the
people must learn to understand, that if they wish to draw any
benefit from Holy Communion, they must receive it — 1, *worthily;*
2, *devoutly;* 3, *frequently.* — Let the catechist, therefore, denounce
in the strongest terms sacrilegious Communion. Then let him show
that to receive devoutly, due *preparation* and a good *thanksgiving* are
required. Let him dwell particularly on thanksgiving, because that
is generally neglected, and let him insist especially on acts of
petition after Communion.

As to the outward attitude of the body in going to Communion
and the way of acting at the altar-railings, it suffices to give
these matters a passing notice, because other points of far greater
importance need more attention.

Nothing need be said here about *frequent* Communion, because
that point is treated in a sermon.

### SKETCH

EXORDIUM. — After explaining the Sacrament which
*restores* spiritual life to the soul — Penance — we now
proceed to the explanation of the Sacrament which
*preserves* that life — Holy Communion.

## I. BENEFITS DERIVED FROM HOLY COMMUNION

The blessings bestowed upon the soul by Holy
Communion are easily understood from the consideration of

1. *What we receive.* In Holy Communion we receive the true body and blood, soul and divinity of Jesus Christ — or Jesus Christ entirely. His body is blended with our body, His soul with our soul, His divine nature with our human nature. His mind enlightens our mind, His will invigorates our will, His senses purify our senses . . .

"He that eateth my flesh, and drinketh my blood, abideth in me, and I in him." — John vi. 57.

2. *Jesus Christ is our food.* As food assimilates with the flesh and blood of man, if he be in a healthy condition, and imparts to them the nourishment which it contains, so Jesus Christ becomes united with the communicant, bestowing upon him His own strength, vigor and life.

"My flesh is meat indeed, and my blood is drink indeed." — John vi. 56. — "As the living Father hath sent me, and I live by the Father; so he that eateth me, the same also shall live by me." — John vi. 58.

Many other effects are produced by Holy Communion.

3. He that neglects Holy Communion destroys the life of the soul in the same manner as the life of the body is destroyed, when it is left without food.

"Amen, amen I say unto you, except you eat the flesh of the Son of man, and drink his blood, you shall not have life in you." — John vi. 54.

## II. Worthy Communion

In order that Holy Communion may produce its wonderful effects, it must be received *worthily, devoutly,* and *frequently.* About the frequency of Communion we shall speak some other time.

*A worthy Communion* is one that is received in

the state of grace, that is, the state of a soul which is free from mortal sin. Therefore,

1. If you are in the state of mortal sin, make a *good confession* before you approach Holy Communion. Even if you remember only venial sins, it is better to go to confession before Communion, lest they should be mortal. Only those who go to Communion oftener than once a week, need not go to confession each time.

If you have forgotten to confess some mortal sin, make an act of contrition for it, and tell it to the priest afterward, at least in your next confession.

2. *An unworthy Communion* — *a,* can do no good; as little as food that is put into the mouth of a corpse; *b,* it does an immense deal of harm, because it is a wanton profanation of the holiest of holy things; it forces Jesus Christ into a soul that is in the possession of the devil — that unhappy soul eats and drinks its own damnation (I Cor. xi. 29).

## III. Devout Communion

Holy Communion is received devoutly, when it is preceded by *due preparation* and followed by *devout thanksgiving.*

1. The preparation is *remote* and *proximate*. *Remote preparation* is made: *a*. In the *body;* the communicant must be fasting from midnight — have no inclination to vomit — and be decently dressed, as he usually is on Sundays. *b*. In the *soul;* the communicant must be sufficiently instructed — be in the state of grace — and have a great desire to receive Jesus Christ.

2. *The proximate preparation* consists in the various acts of devotion which immediately precede the act

of receiving Holy Communion. If you receive at Mass, you may make this preparation from the elevation of the Mass; if outside of the time of Mass, spend at least fifteen minutes in devout prayer before receiving.

What prayers should you say then? Any prayer will answer, either from a book or on the beads. But the best method is to put to yourself three questions which you should answer yourself. These are:

*a. Who* comes to me in Holy Communion? Answer: *Jesus Christ.* Make acts of faith; say that you believe this firmly — that you are ready to lay down your life in defense of this doctrine. *b. To whom* does He come? Answer: To a *sinner.* Make acts of contrition, resolution, humiliation, by expressing your unworthiness. *c. Why* does He come? Answer: For the purpose of *helping* me — to be one with me — to strengthen me — to console me. Make acts of love — of confidence — of desire.

To remember this, keep in mind the three questions: Who? To whom? Why?

Invoke the Blessed Virgin, your guardian angel, your patron-saints, that they may accompany you when you receive Jesus Christ.

3. When it is time, approach the altar-railing without *delay.* The strong faith in your mind and the ardent devotion in your heart should prompt you to approach the altar in a *devout manner.* When you have come to the railing make a profound *genuflection* — kneel at the railing — hold the *cloth* stretched out before you — raise your *head* so as to see the top of the tabernacle — open your *mouth,* put out your tongue — receive the Sacred Host devoutly — *swallow* it at once — make an interior act of profound *adora-*

*tion — leave* the railing immediately — *genuflect* devoutly — and *return* to your place, knowing that you carry within you the greatest treasure that is in heaven or on earth, and hence conduct yourself exactly as the priest does when he carries the Blessed Sacrament through the church in procession. Keep from spitting out for a good while. Should the sacred particle adhere to the roof of your mouth, do not remove it with your finger, but with your tongue. Never chew or masticate it with your teeth.

Having returned to your place, collect all your thoughts, have no care about anything around you — but begin at once to make a *devout thanksgiving,* which again is *proximate* and *remote.*

4. *Proximate thanksgiving* consists in the devout reflections and prayers which immediately follow the reception of Holy Communion. These prayers may be taken from the prayer-book or may be said on the beads. But must we read out of a book what we have to say to our Lord when He has come to us? The best method is again to make use of the three questions mentioned above — *Who has come? to whom? why?* — to give the answers, and to add appropriate interior acts.

*a. Who* has come? Answer: Jesus Christ, Who is now within you — Whom the angels around you adore. Make acts of profound adoration and thanksgiving. *b. To whom* has He come? Answer: To a most *unworthy creature.* Make acts of profound humility before Him, of holy joy on account of this great privilege, acts of contrition and of a firm determination to sin no more. *c. Why* has He come? For the purpose of becoming one with you, to impart to you His divine strength and power, to grant you all the graces that you may ask for yourself and others.

Think of all your spiritual and temporal needs and earnestly supplicate help. This is your most precious time. Pray for your relatives and friends. Jesus says to you: "What wilt thou that I should do to thee?" (Mark x. 51.) Do not lose your opportunity.

Add the prayers for the plenary indulgence, if any may be gained on that day. Finally, put yourself into the hands of the Blessed Virgin Mary, that she may help you henceforth to remain united with Jesus Christ.

5. *Remote thanksgiving.* Spend the day devoutly, remembering the immense privilege that has been granted you. Keep the house of your soul clean — watch over yourself — pray more — and resolve to go to Holy Communion soon again.

6. What a sorry sight to see people receive Holy Communion with so little devotion; who seem not to know what to do after Communion; who leave the church immediately after receiving! Have they faith? No wonder that Holy Communion profits them nothing.

# SINS AGAINST FAITH — SUPERSTITION

This life is to be succeeded by the *life eternal,* to obtain which man must *keep the commandments.* — The Mission is principally directed against sin. For this reason the instructions on the commandments regard more the negative than the positive side, that is, the sins committed against them. — In the present instruction the sins against *faith, hope,* and *charity* are to be explained, but particular attention must be paid to *superstition,* because it is so common and hardly any one believes it to be a great sin. — Next in importance are the *dangers to faith,* which must be exposed in their proper light. However, let the missionary proceed with great prudence in giving his warnings.

In short Missions this instruction is omitted.

## SKETCH

EXORDIUM. — We have told you how the *life of the soul* is to be *restored* if lost (Sacrament of Penance); and how it is to be *preserved* (Blessed Eucharist). Now we have to show you how it is to be *regulated,* according to the laws laid down by God's commandments.

Had we time, we should explain all the commandments, drawing your attention to all the sins committed against them. But, as it is, we can point out only those sins which are most usually committed, and which have not been considered in the other sermons of the Mission.

To-day I take up two classes of sins against which I must particularly warn you. These are the sins against *Faith* and the sins of *Superstition.*

## I. SINS AGAINST FAITH

1. The law of faith commands us *to believe in God* and in all that He makes known to us *through His Church* on earth.

Every man must know and believe under the penalty of eternal damnation the following three points: 1. There is one God in three Divine Persons, the Father, the Son, and the Holy Ghost. 2. God rewards the good in heaven and punishes the wicked forever in hell. 3. The Son of God became man, suffered and died on the cross, to redeem us from sin and hell.

Besides this, every Christian must have himself instructed in, and must believe all the doctrines contained in the *Creed*, the *Our Father*, the *Ten Commandments* and the seven *Sacraments*.

Faith is the most precious gift of God, because it is the foundation of all the other virtues and of all supernatural merit. Hence, the sins against faith are the most detrimental.

2. Sins against faith are committed: by *denying* any article of faith — by wilful *doubt* about any doctrine of the Church — by being *ashamed* of one's faith or by denying it — by exposing one's self to the *danger* of *losing the faith*, by getting entangled in a *religious dispute* without being sufficiently instructed to defend the sacred truths of religion — *reading* heretical books, tracts, sermons, Bibles, or keeping them in the house, — *listening* to infidel discourses, sermons, lectures — *associating* without necessity with infidels — joining non-Catholics in their worship, in public or in private — attending the *celebration* of their worship by active co-operation — showing one's self *indifferent* toward religion — yielding to *indifferentism*, thinking it all

the same what religion a man may hold or practise, that all religions are good — being a so-called *lib-
eral Catholic* — neglecting to receive the *necessary
instruction* . . .

When *doubts* about matters of faith arise, oppose
them by simple acts of faith in the doctrine of the
Church, which cannot fail. Do not *scrutinize* divine
truths, but believe them in a childlike spirit, without
desiring a *clear understanding* of them, as they are beyond the reach of the human mind here on earth.

## II. Sins of Superstition

1. *What is Superstition?* According to St. Thomas
it consists in giving divine honor to creatures, or in
honoring God in an unbecoming manner. Therefore,
he is guilty of superstition who, to obtain a certain end,
makes use of those means which are not ordained for
that purpose, either by *nature*, or by a special ordi-
nance of *God*, or through the institution of the *Church*.
Such acts are:

*a*. To *wear* certain articles, amulets, writings, etc.,
against dangers, to keep them in the house against
fire — to put faith in these or similar things said to
have fallen from heaven, to have been found in the
Holy Sepulcher, to have been approved by Urban
VIII, etc.

*b*. To *do* certain things, at certain hours, on certain
days, with certain observances, in a certain manner. . . .

*c*. To effect *cures*, by certain prayers and ceremonies, repeated a certain number of times.

*d*. To cut *cards*, or have them cut — to tell for-
tunes or have them told, in order to recover things
lost, obtain information about persons absent, find out

who did this or that harm, unfold future events. . . . (Key in the Bible — wedding-cake, etc.)

*e.* To ascribe *power* to certain *articles,* such as horse-shoes, etc. . . . and to wear them or put them up in certain parts of the house.

*f.* To believe in certain *unlucky days,* unlucky occurrences . . . and to act accordingly. To believe in *dreams* and to be guided by them.

*g.* To believe in *spiritism,* to assist at the meetings of spiritualists. . . .

2. *How great a sin Superstition is.* Superstition is for the most part a very great sin,

*a.* Because it is *contempt of the means* that God has instituted for certain purposes — it sets aside Divine Providence.

"Is there not a God in Israel, that ye go to consult Beelzebub the god of Accaron? Wherefore, from the bed on which thou art gone up, thou shalt not come down, but thou shalt surely die." — IV Kings i. 3, 4. — "The soul that shall go aside after magicians and soothsayers, I will set my face against that soul, and destroy it out of the midst of its people." — Lev. xx. 6.

*b.* Because it is direct or indirect *worship of Satan.* It ascribes to the devil certain attributes which God alone possesses. It is the aim of the devil to receive divine worship from Christians.

*c.* Because it leads to *blindness of spirit.* The superstitious are seldom converted; they defend their practices, nor can they see any harm in them. Let us hear their

*Excuses:* "In performing cures only sacred words are used — it is done in the name of the Most Blessed Trinity." Satan also can use sacred words and he often does so. "Satan transformeth himself into an angel of light" (II Cor. xi. 14).

"It helped; it effected a cure." That may be — Satan knows more than any physician — God permits it for the punishment of those who make use of such means, to blind them still more — God helps when, and where, He sees that His interposition will produce a good effect in the soul — Satan helps in order to lead finally to evil.

"Satan gives a little honey to instil his hellish poison, he uses holy things to ruin souls." — St. Chrys.

CONCLUSION. — Therefore, give up all those evil practices, trust in Divine Providence, and in the saints, in the prayers of the Church, and rather suffer every evil for the love of Jesus Christ, than commit sin. Repent, that God may forgive you; like the Christians of Ephesus. "And many of them who had followed curious arts, brought together their books, and burnt them before all, and counting the price of them, they found the money to be fifty thousand pieces of silver" (Acts xix. 19).

# IX

## BLASPHEMY — PERJURY — CURSING

The chief sins to be attacked in this instruction are *perjury, blasphemy, cursing* and *the breaking of vows.* — All these sins, except, perhaps, the last, are very common, just because people are very ignorant in regard to their grievousness. — Let the catechist have his points well supported by solid arguments, and denounce these vices with due severity.

### Sketch

God is to be honored in Himself, in His attributes, in His saints, in holy things, and in His creatures. Sins committed against this obligation are most grievous.

### I. Blasphemy

This horrible sin consists in using injurious language against God and things consecrated to God. It is committed by

1. *Imprecations* against God, wishing evil to God. This is of all sins the most grievous; it is a diabolical act.

2. *Insulting language* against God and His holy attributes. It is committed by denying that God possesses a certain perfection, accusing God of injustice, too great severity; by attributing to God a certain defect; by attributing to creatures divine qualities; by turning into ridicule the praise of God, acts of divine worship; by speaking with contempt of Jesus Christ, or using His Holy Name in vain; by uttering holy words in the excitement of anger.

"Bring forth the blasphemer without the camp, and let them that heard him put their hands upon his head, and let all the people stone him." — Lev. xxiv. 14. — "I have delivered Hymeneus and Alexander up to Satan, that they may learn not to blaspheme." — I Tim. i. 20. — "On account of blasphemies there arise earthquakes, famine and pestilence." — St. Chrys. — "The blasphemer lends his tongue to the devil, and the devil gives him his spirit and rage." — St. Chrys.

## II. Perjury

This crime consists in taking a false oath.

An oath consists in calling God to witness, either in private or in public, to the truth of an assertion. If the assertion for the truth of which God is to vouch, to our knowledge, is *true*, the oath is lawful, and even a meritorious act, provided it concern a matter of *importance*. It is a great act of irreverence to call God to witness for a *trifle*. If the assertion, to our knowledge, is *false*, then the oath is false, and is *perjury*, a most grievous sin, because it is calling upon God to *bear witness to a lie*. In *doubtful* matters the statement is to be made as doubtful, or to the best of our knowledge. Witnesses before a court and on oath do not commit sin, if they make their statements and answer questions to the best of their knowledge.

Perjury, connected with *injustice* or injury to the reputation of others, binds to *restitution* and due reparation.

*Promissory oaths*, if taken deliberately, are still binding after being broken — once or repeatedly — *e.g.*, a pledge taken under oath. A simple *pledge* is neither an oath nor a vow, but a simple resolution. Oaths to do something evil are illicit and not binding.

## III. Cursing

This sin is next to blasphemy, because it is directed against the image and likeness of God, or the works of His hands. It consists in *imprecations* — maledictions — praying prayers . . . either in thought or in word — against one's self or others — irrational or inanimate creatures.

1. *Its malice.* — It is a most abominable practice; it is the language of the damned.

"Ye are of your father the devil, and the desires of your father ye will do." — John viii. 44.

It manifests most wicked dispositions. The curser raises himself above God, and imperiously dictates what God must do, and on the spot. He positively commands God to send sickness, misfortune, hell and damnation upon a fellow-creature — and that, instantly, to satisfy the curser's wrath.

It violates charity in the highest degree by treating our neighbor with the utmost contempt, and wishing that the greatest possible punishment should befall him. What wickedness if the members of a family curse one another!

2. *Its consequences.* The curse will fall upon the head that uttered it.

"He loved cursing, and it shall come unto him; and he would not have blessing, and it shall be far from him, and he put on cursing like a garment; and it went in like water into his entrails, and like oil in his bones. May it be unto him like a garment which covereth him, and like a girdle with which he is girded continually." — Ps. cviii. 18, 19.

It is the source of so many evils that befall others.

"The prayer of him that curseth thee in the bitterness of his soul shall be heard: for he that made him will hear him." — Eccli. iv. 6. — Therefore St. Chrysostom says: "If any one curse, let all run to him, in order with united force to close up his mouth, because it is the source of so many evils."

And what an *awful account* will follow such evil habits, if even every idle word must be accounted for!

3. *Excuses:* "My children put me into a pas-

sion." This is not the way to correct their faults. "I mean no harm by it." Then do not use language at which the angels shudder. "I pay no attention to it." So much the worse. "I do it in joke." Fine joke, that outrages God and man! "I do it in anger, but I am sorry immediately." Check it, as it is your duty.

4. *Remedies:* *a*. When angry, say nothing; pray for patience. *b*. At every curse in future make an act of contrition, imposing upon yourself a small penance, making a cross on the floor, or kissing it: give money to the poor; deprive yourself of some palatable food — sugar, milk, etc. *c*. Consecrate your tongue to Jesus Christ in Holy Communion.

# X

## IMPURE THOUGHTS, LOOKS, READING, CONVERSATION

This instruction does not explain these sins; it simply warns against them in general terms, and, in particular, against impure *thoughts, reading* and *conversation*.

Special attention is to be paid to the general custom of *light and bad reading* and of *immodest conversation*. The latter must be attacked in the severest terms.

With regard to sins of action the catechist may say, that he will leave that sink of iniquity covered until the Day of Judgment.

### SKETCH

In these days of general moral corruption thousands of sins are committed in the matter of impurity, which are not considered as wrong by many; yet they are, almost without exception, grievous sins. It is the object of this instruction to open your eyes to them, that you may guard against them in future.

These sins are committed:

### I. IN THOUGHT AND IMAGINATION

A distinction is to be made between simple temptations and thoughts wilfully entertained. The latter are wrong, and *great sins*. It is wrong

*a.* To *delight* interiorly in what is sinful exteriorly.

"He that is *delighted* with wickedness shall be condemned." — Eccli. xix. 6. — "But they that are Christ's have crucified their flesh, with the vices and *lusts*." — Gal. v. 24. — "Mortify your members . . . *lust*, evil *desire*, and *covetousness*." — Col. iii. 5.

452

*b.* Interiorly *to approve of past sins,* which is a repetition of the sins committed, or of sins in general against purity.

"Lust hath perverted thy heart." — Dan. xiii. 56. — "When concupiscence hath conceived, it bringeth forth sin." — James i. 15.

*c. To desire* to commit it, whether the action follows or not. The sin may begin from within or from without. If the latter, the sin is not yet accomplished, so long as the consent is wanting from within: if from within, the sin is committed regardless of the action from without.

"I say to you, that whosoever shall look on a woman to *lust* after her, hath already committed adultery with her in his heart." — Matt. v. 28.

## II. In Looks

They are sinful, when cast upon sinful objects with deliberation and reflection. It is a want of watchfulness that must lead to sin. Such a look induced David to commit adultery and murder. (II Kings xi.) Therefore Job made a covenant with his eyes, that they should not look upon a virgin. (xxxi. 1.) The Scriptures are full of warnings against the too free use of the eyes.

"Turn away thy face from a woman dressed up and gaze not about upon another's beauty. For many have perished by the beauty of a woman, and hereby lust is enkindled as a fire." — Eccli. ix. 8, 9.

## III. In Reading

A. *Obscene books, or papers.*

Reading is worse than listening to bad conversation: 1. Because the book speaks more unblushingly. 2. Repeats it again and again; there it stands. 3. It is listened to with more reflection and with less shame, or none at all. 4. We easily make our own what we read.

The proverb says: "Tell me with whom you go and I will tell you what you are."

B. *Books and papers of a doubtful character,* such as novels, story papers, etc.

Those publications which do not describe sin so unblushingly are as bad as the more indecent ones, because they insinuate what they do not express, and it is that meaning which is drawn out of them. Besides, they leave a great deal to the imagination, which is guided by the book. Again, to buy such books, etc., is a support of sin.

But those readers have their specious excuses:

1. "These books are not bad." Chastity is considered very little by them. They contain the language of sinful lust. Does not your conscience feel uneasy when you are occupied with such reading? Would you like to die while reading that story?

2. "I want to improve my style of language." We have good books for that. Do you wish to improve yourself in the use of doubtful language? The style of many of those books is very common, even low and vulgar. Who has ever elevated his mind by reading novels; is not the very contrary the result?

3. "These books, papers, contain many beautiful things." We go for good things to good books; there are enough in the market. Does it make poison less dangerous that it is made to glitter? These books give you a distaste for work, for all good reading, for acts of piety. They teach you to form acquaintances behind the back of your parents, to slight the laws of the Church, and many other evils.

4. "I know how to discriminate. I take only what is good out of that reading, passing over what is

bad." If you knew how to discriminate, you would not read those stories at all. Where is there a good director of conscience that approves such reading? Which makes the deeper impression, good or evil? And as a general thing, evil is gathered from it.

5. "This reading has made no bad impression on me." Do you understand what a bad impression means? You may have received the evil impression long before you knew it. The passion which you have for such reading is an evidence that an impression has been made. Who ever drew any blessing from such reading?

### IV. In Immodest Conversation and in Listening to It

Were there none to listen, there would be few that would use immodest language. Listening, especially when accompanied with laughter, encourages them.

1. Immodest conversation shows a *more wicked heart* than impure deeds; it shows that the heart is full of impurity.

"How can you speak good things whereas you are evil? for out of the abundance of the heart the mouth speaketh . . . an evil man out of an evil treasure bringeth forth evil things." — Matt. xii. 34–35.

When the stomach is overloaded, its contents are apt to come out of the mouth; so likewise, if the heart is overfilled with impurity, it flows over and comes out of the mouth; and there are people enough most eager to catch up what flows from mouths so filthy.

2. Immodest conversation meets with *universal condemnation*. It is condemned.

*a. By reason.* Nothing spreads the general corruption of morals more than this: As 1. It *sows* the seeds of evil in souls not yet acquainted with this vice. 2. It *encourages* it in those acquainted with it. 3. It *confirms* old sinners in their habits, all in consequence of the knowledge that others do the same.

*b. By Scripture:*

"They are corrupt and become abominable in their ways." — Ps. xiii. 1. — "Their throat is an open sepulchre; with their tongues they acted deceitfully; the poison of asps is under their lips; their mouth is full of cursing and bitterness. Destruction and unhappiness are in their ways. Judge them, O God." — Ps. v. 11; Ps. xiii. 3. — "If there be a sin with thee, disclose it not." — Eccli. xix. 8. — "Fornication and all uncleanness let it not . . . so much as be named among you, as becometh saints." — Eph. v. 3.

*c. By the Church* — which warns even confessors to be cautious, and to leave confession somewhat deficient rather than speak too plainly about this matter; not to question children imprudently. (Rit. Rom. de Pœnit. quoad conf. 6.) Grown people are to express themselves in a becoming manner, and not to enter into indecent details; and after confessing these sins once, they are not to confess them again explicitly, unless it be necessary. Teachers of catechism and preachers are to express themselves in regard to this sin only in general terms. *"In hac ipsa re explicanda cautus admodum sit parochus et prudens et tectis verbis rem commemoret, quæ moderationem potius desiderat, quam orationis copiam"* (Cat. Rom. de Sexto).

*d. By the heathen.* Aristotle asked the legislators of Athens to expel from the city all those who used impure language (7 Eth. c. 6). Diogenes punished severely two of his disciples who talked in this manner with each other. Clitomachus rose from the table when he heard such conversation there.

3. It is a source of the *most disastrous scandal.* By wicked insinuations, snares, temptations, continued

for years, the devil is not able to do what such a foul mouth effects by one unclean speech.

Two boys were playing innocently together; innumerable devils were about them blowing into their faces, giving them temptations. But they resisted. A third boy came. The devils left. This boy began to jest improperly. Soon all three committed sin. (Vis. of a Servant of God.)

Father Cataneus relates of a young man who was about to take the religious habit in the Society of Jesus. A party was given at his departure. Improper language was used. The young man was tempted the next night — gave way to a bad desire — died and was damned that night.

Impure talk is not one sin, but as *many sins as there are persons present,* listening to it. Its baleful effects *spread* most rapidly and continue to spread even after the death of the evil talker.

It is a sure sign of *damnation.* For the foul-mouthed never repent, never acknowledge their sin, do not amend, but continue the same vile practice.

"They are not confounded with confusion, and they have not known how to blush, therefore shall they fall . . . they shall fall saith the Lord." — Jer. viii. 12. — "They receive the punishment of the scandal-giver." — Matt. xviii. 6.

The same is to be said of *immodest songs,* of *language of double meaning,* or veiled under all sorts of *comparisons;* this is as bad, if not worse, because it is listened to with less shame; it shocks less; absorbs the thoughts more — gains its end more securely. Compare it to a poisoned cup, a sword hidden under a cloak.

CONCLUSION. — What must you do if you have to be present where such conversation is carried on? If it comes to your ears let it not go into your heart;

pray in your heart that you may take no pleasure in what you cannot help hearing. And in no manner take part in it.

How terrible! Thousands are guilty of this sin, even such as go to Holy Communion. Of these St. Augustine says:

"Consider, brethren, whether it be right that out of the mouth of Christians, where the body of Christ enters, should come forth a lustful song, the poison of Satan."

# RASH JUDGMENT — DETRACTION — CALUMNY

The instruction on this commandment comprises the sins of *rash judgment, tale-bearing, backbiting, detraction* and *calumny,* — all of which are most common and hardly ever considered grievous.

In Missions of shorter duration the last three instructions are united in one or two by mentioning only the sins committed by the tongue. This instruction comes under the title, *"Sins of the Tongue."*

If more instructions than those here indicated are needed, the *Sacrifice of the Mass* and *Human Respect* should be taken as subjects. Notices of these are found elsewhere. [1]

## SKETCH

Everyone has a right to his good name so long as he has not lost that right by public misdeeds, *i.e.,* he has a just claim upon all that all should *think* and *speak* well of him. A good reputation is more valuable than wealth.

"A good name is better than great riches." — Prov. xxii. 1.

The preservation of the good name of all is also demanded for the welfare of *human society,* that scandals may be avoided.

To violate another's good name, particularly in a serious matter, is, therefore, a great sin. This sin is committed in various ways. All the sins of this kind come under the following heads:

## I. RASH JUDGMENT

1. This consists in giving up our good opinion of our neighbor without sufficient reason, and judging him

[1] Vol. II. Renewals.

guilty of evil without sufficient evidence. If we have sufficient reason for thinking evil of him, no sin is committed, as we cannot go against our convictions. But in this case let us make all the allowances that we possibly can.

2. Rash judgment arises — *a*, from an evil inclination to *believe the worst* of our neighbor — *b*, from a bad habit of *believing every report* without discriminating between the people who spread them — *c*, from the habit of judging others *according to ourselves* — *d*, from *envy*, that cannot bear the success of others.

3. The *malice* of this sin appears from the condemnation that it receives from our Lord Jesus Christ.

"Why seest thou the mote that is in thy brother's eye, and seest not the beam that is in thy own eye? Or how sayest thou to thy brother, let me cast the mote out of thy eye, and behold a beam is in thy own eye? Thou hypocrite, cast out first the beam out of thy own eye, and then shalt thou see to cast out the mote out of thy brother's eye." — Matt. vii. 3-5. — "With what judgment ye judge, ye shall be judged." — Matt. vii. 2. — "Judge not before the time; until the Lord come, who both will bring to light the hidden things of darkness, and will make manifest the counsels of the heart." — I Cor. iv. 5.

## II. Detraction

1. This sin consists in publishing the faults of others that are *true* but *not known* — or in a country where they are not known. It is called *detraction*, because it unjustly lessens the reputation of one's neighbor. To the same class of sins belong *backbiting*, which consists in secret fault-finding with our neighbor's conduct, in a depreciation of his merits, his motives, etc., and *tale-bearing*, which is committed by carrying disagreeable reports from one to another, and which is often the cause of enmity and quarrels.

2. This entire class of sins is severely condemned in the Scriptures.

"Hast thou heard a word against thy neighbor? let it die within thee, trusting that it will not burst thee." — Eccli. xix. 10. — "All things whatsoever you would that men should do to you, do you also to them. For this is the law and the prophets." — Matt. vii. 12. — "The detractor is the abomination of men." — Prov. xxiv. 9. — In the Epistle to the Romans (i. 30) St. Paul enumerates, among a number of evil-doers, "detractors," of whom he says in particular "that they are hateful to God," and "that they who do such things are worthy of death; and not only they that do them, but they also who consent to them that do them," *i.e.,* those who listen to them. — "The whisperer and the double-tongued is accursed, for he hath troubled many that were at peace." — Eccli. xxviii. 15.

### III. CALUMNY

1. This sin consists in publishing faults that are *not true*.

It is also called *defamation* — and is committed in various ways. It is calumny and defamation to originate an evil report concerning an innocent man — to spread what others have originated — to make a great fault out of a small one — to put a bad construction on what others say or do — to confirm what others say and to add more to it — to depreciate the merits of others — to disparage the good that others mention as having been done by your neighbor — to remain silent with a significant look, which means that you know better — to praise a man and then enumerate his faults.

2. That calumny is a grievous sin is evident from common sense, as well as from the sayings of the Scriptures.

"False calumny is more grievous than death." — Eccli. xxvi. 7. — "The death (caused) by a wicked tongue is a most evil death and hell is preferable to it." — Eccli. xxviii. 25.

3. Calumny becomes still more grievous when it is committed by open *reproach* — by reviling others to their face, or by *libel*, which is calumny in print or in

writing. For this is the same as robbery, as it forcibly wrests from men their honest reputation.

4. Those who *listen* to *calumny,* . . . are just as guilty as the calumniators, because they supply the occasion, without which the harm could not be done.

"My son, have nothing to do with detractors." — Prov. xxiv. 21. — "Hedge in thy ears with thorns, hear not a wicked tongue." — Eccli. xxviii. 28. — "It is not easy to say which is the more damnable, to detract or to listen to detractors." — Pope Eugene. — S. Francis de Sales, speaking of detraction, says: "It is a threefold murder in one act: it kills the soul of the detractor, and of the listener, and takes away the civil life — reputation — of the detracted."

Therefore, remember that it is your duty to correct those who talk against others, if you have authority over them; if not, you should at least call their assertion in question — show yourself indifferent toward the conversation or even displeased with it — turn it to something else — say something good of the one calumniated — try to excuse him, etc.

5. But it would certainly be worse to *inquire* about the conduct of others, knowing already what will be said — or inquire about certain suspicions without sufficient reason, and thus become the occasion of slander, etc. — acting thus particularly with children, who suspect no evil.

"The heart of the wicked seeketh after evils." — Prov. xxvii. 21.

6. To *obtain pardon* for the sins committed by slander and calumny, besides a sincere confession, *restitution* is required for the injured reputation, as well as reparation for all the material damage caused by the defamation.

This is extremely hard on account of the great confusion that it causes the sinner, and very few have the courage to undertake it. It is hard also on account of the extreme difficulty connected with taking back all that has been said — and preventing it from spreading. Example of St. Philip Neri, who, for a penance, made a lady who had committed this sin buy a chicken and pull out the feathers while carrying it home, and collect them afterward.

For publishing secret faults the offender is obliged to efface the bad impression produced by his uncharitable talk, and, if possible, to induce the parties who have heard it not to believe it. For spreading false reports or belying others, the lie must be positively retracted. For public reproach or libel, the pardon of the offended party is to be asked.

CONCLUSION. — Let all take to heart the admonition of the Wise Man:

"Hedge in thy ears with thorns, hear not a wicked tongue, and make doors and bars to thy mouth. Melt down thy gold and silver, and make a balance for thy words and a just bridle for thy mouth." — Eccli. xxviii. 28, 29.

# XII

## SINS OF THE TONGUE

EXORDIUM. — The tongue is the *most useful* member of the human body. What is a man who is deprived of the use of his tongue? You can realize this on a visit to a deaf and dumb institute. The tongue is the *most honored* member of the body. It alone is allowed to touch the Blessed Sacrament. With it man communicates with the rest of mankind; with it man will join in the praise of God in heaven.

The abuse of the tongue causes most harm in the world.

"The tongue is a fire, a world of iniquity." — James iii. 6.

It deprives a man of all the blessings of religion.

"If any man think himself to be religious, not bridling his tongue, but deceiving his own heart, this man's religion is vain." — James i. 26.

While the good use of the tongue brings a man to a state of perfection.

"If any man offend not in word; the same is a perfect man." — James iii. 2.

The sins of the tongue are, for the most part, committed against the Second, the Sixth and the Eighth Commandment of God, the most grievous and yet the most ordinary of which we intend to speak of here.

### I. SINS OF THE TONGUE AGAINST THE SECOND COMMANDMENT

These are *blasphemy, perjury,* and *cursing.* See Instruction IX, Parts I, II, III.

## II. Sins of the Tongue against the Sixth Commandment

These are: *immodest conversation, obscene songs,* and *language of double meaning.* See Instruction X, Part IV.

## III. Sins of the Tongue against the Eighth Commandment

These are *detraction* and *calumny.* See Instruction XI, Parts II and III.

Conclusion. — "Blessed is he that hath not slipped with his tongue." (Eccli. xxv. 11.) "I said: I will take heed to my ways, that I sin not with my tongue." (Ps. xxxviii. 2.) "Hedge in thy ears. . . ." (Concl. to Instr. XI.)

# B. — Particular Instructions

## I

## FOR MARRIED MEN AND WOMEN

### A. For Married People

The instruction for the married men differs very little from that for the married women. — After a brief introduction on the necessity of every man's knowing and fulfilling the special duties of his particular state of life, to save his soul, — the missionary speaks for some time on the way of *entering married life* according to the law of God and the Church, showing which marriages are *sinful* and which are *invalid*. This point is of great importance, owing to the too great recklessness of people contemplating marriage.

Then follow the *duties* of the husband *toward his wife* and, in the instruction for the women, of the wife *toward her husband*. These consist — 1, in living together for life, this being a most practical point in this country; 2, in promoting each other's *temporal happiness;* and 3, in assisting each other in the work of their *eternal salvation.* In this point the shocking abuses of married life are to be severely dealt with, but only in *general* expressions, particularly selected, and supported by the instructions given by the Archangel Raphael to young Tobias. — Here the women are to be told about their special duty, or so-called *marriage-debt* toward their husbands.

The second part of this instruction deals with the duty of parents *toward their offspring,* in rearing their children principally for the kingdom of heaven. This duty begins with the beginning of the child's life. *Onanism, foeticide, craniotomy* (this last point before men only) are to be chastised with all severity. This part requires good study and most exact preparation on the part of the missionary. Speaking of it superficially is tantamount to saying nothing; saying too much gives scandal. — Then follows *temporal* and *spiritual education* in all its requirements in regard to the three stages of the life of the child, *infancy, school-age, youth.* — Lastly, the solicitude of parents about the *future vocation* of their children is to be spoken of, be it to the religious or the married life.

In preparing this instruction it would be well for the missionary to keep before him the golden words of Most Rev. Father General Mauron, as recommended by the Provincial Statutes, p. 51, n. 27.

## Sketch

The welfare of society, of the Church, and of the world in general depends on the good or evil state of the family. The state of the family, in turn, depends on the manner in which each member of it fulfills his respective duties. On the fulfilment of these duties depends the salvation of each and every individual. A married man (woman) can go to heaven only as a married man (woman). Therefore, besides fulfilling his duties as an ordinary Christian, he must fulfil his duties as a married man. If he does not, he cannot be saved at all.

Now, there exists among our married people nowadays a great deal of ignorance concerning their matrimonial duties — hence the neglect of them. Moreover, modern society exercises a terrible influence for evil upon the state of matrimony. Hence the importance of this instruction.

Married men (women) have duties to perform: 1. toward their wives (husbands); 2. toward their children.

## I. Duties of Married People toward Each Other

Matrimony is the most important state of life. Therefore has God established certain laws in reference to matrimony; Christ, raising it to the dignity of a sacrament, added a few more. So also the Church. Hence,

1. It is the first duty of those who marry *to enter* that state according to the law of nature, of God and of the Church.

According to the legislation of the Church at present, dating from the publication of the Decree *"Ne temere"* (Easter, 1908, April 19), and contained in the New

Code (published Pentecost, 1918, May 19), only those marriages are valid which are entered into without diriment impediment and according to the form prescribed, *i.e.,* in the presence of the parish priest, or his delegate, and two witnesses. Wherefore, a marriage contracted before a civil magistrate, justice of the peace, or alderman is invalid. A marriage contracted before a minister is also invalid, and furthermore the Catholic party incurs excommunication.

Where an impediment exists, it must be removed by dispensation before the marriage can be valid. The principal impediments which render a marriage invalid are the following:

Consanguinity, or Relationship by blood, to the third degree inclusive (collateral). Canon 1076, § 2.

Affinity, or Relationship by marriage, arising only from a valid marriage, to the second degree inclusive (collateral). Canon 97, 1077.

Spiritual Relationship, arising from Baptism only, between the person baptizing and the person baptized, and the latter and his sponsors. Canon 768, 1079.

Disparity of worship, between a baptized Catholic and one that is not baptized. Canon 1070, § 1.

Crime, between parties who were engaged to each other before the former wife or husband of either party was dead; which engagement was either followed or preceded by an act of adultery between them. Canon 1075. (This before men only.)

*Ligamen,* between parties, one or both of whom have a lawful wife or husband still living — although not heard from for a long time, or divorced by civil law. Canon 1069, § 1.

There are many other impediments of matrimony, although they are not of so frequent occurrence as the foregoing.

Married persons implicated in an impediment of matrimony must bring their case before their pastor or their confessor, to have the difficulty settled. In secret cases nothing will be made known.

2. The second duty of married people demands of them *perpetual* living together, no matter how their circumstances may change. The wife is to follow the husband (except in case of too great inconvenience), wheresoever he goes. The evil results of the desertion of a husband or a wife are enormous. Hence, beware of giving cause to such an unhappy separation.

There is absolutely no possibility of dissolving the matrimonial tie between married people who have lived together.

"Whosoever . . . shall marry another wife, committeth adultery, and he that shall marry her that is put away, committeth adultery." — Matt. xix. 9. — "The woman, whilst her husband liveth, shall be called an adulteress, if she be with another man; but if her husband be dead, she is delivered from the law of her husband." — Rom. vii. 3.

We have nothing to do with "divorce," introduced and believed in by Protestants.

However, the Church allows husband and wife to *live apart* from each other for four reasons: 1. Mutual consent; 2. Imminent danger of life; 3. Danger of salvation; 4. Adultery. But they are not allowed to separate on their own authority. They must abide by the decision of their pastor or the bishop. They must also come together again as soon as the cause ceases, except in the case mentioned last.

3. God has provided against the evil of separation. Husband and wife loved each other before marriage by the impulse of nature. The Sacrament of Matrimony purifies, elevates, and strengthens this love. They must do their share to keep it up, and there will never

be a cause for separation — on the contrary they will promote each other's happiness.

To promote each other's *happiness for time and eternity* is, in fact, a part of their matrimonial contract. Love will impel them to fulfil this contract.

*A*. They promote each other's *temporal prosperity and happiness*.

1. By avoiding everything that is calculated to grieve the other or disturb his happiness — *in thought* — suspicions, want of respect, jealousy; *in words* — harsh expressions, cutting remarks, calling names, passionate corrections, curses, maledictions, tale-bearing; *in deed* — brutal treatment, neglect in assisting each other, drunkenness, adultery.

2. By taking every opportunity to show *esteem* and *love* for each other.

Love is inventive. Married people who love each other will know a thousand ways of fulfilling this duty.

3. By making *sacrifices* for each other. The husband (wife) should forget his (her) own comforts, and look only to those of the wife (husband).

The mutual relationship between husband and wife is clearly defined by St. Paul in Eph. v.:

"Let women be subject to their husbands, as to the Lord in all things." — 22, 24. — "For the husband is the head of the wife, as Christ is the head of the Church." — 23. — "Husbands, love your wives, as Christ also loved the Church, and delivered himself up for it." — 25. — "So also ought men to love their wives as their own bodies." — 28. — "No man ever hated his own flesh." — 29. — "Let the wife reverence her husband." — 33.

What is frequently the cause of misery in families? Apart from the neglect of the mutual duty here stated, they married consulting their carnal passion and misguided fancy. It may be, too, that their unhappiness is a just punishment for their excesses before marriage, or in marriage.

Let them take their misfortune as a penance, and strive to obey God's holy law in future.

*B.* Husband and wife must co-operate in each other's *eternal welfare;* and in this respect, more than in any other, they are to each other a *"helpmate."* They effect this,

1. By consoling, encouraging, advising each other; by good example — family prayer — assisting each other in their attendance at divine service — sermons — in attending to their Christian duties — praying for each other — assisting each other at and after death.

2. By carefully attending to their so-called matrimonial duty.

The passion of the flesh cannot be overcome except by the means established by God. These are prayer, the sacraments, mortification, retirement. Very few, however, are inclined to make use of these means. For the majority of men God has instituted a remedy more agreeable to corrupt nature — marriage.

"For fear of fornication let every man [who cannot otherwise be pure] have his own wife, and let every woman have her own husband." — I Cor. vii. 2.

The very essence of marriage consists in the mutual grant by married persons to each other of certain privileges and rights over their bodies. This begets the matrimonial duty, which is binding on both, under the strictest obligation, under all circumstances and at all times. An obstinate refusal of these rights is often the cause of many sins and crimes.

"Let the husband render the debt [thus contracted] to his wife, and the wife also in like manner to the husband. The wife hath not power of her body [so that she could refuse at pleasure], but the husband [by virtue of his marriage to her]. In like manner the husband also hath not power of his own body, but the wife." — I Cor. vii. 3, 4.

Note. — "Mulieres quæ debitum denegant multoties propter *hoc solum* damnantur, et in causa sunt, cur etiam viri damnentur." — Hom. Ap. tr. ult. n. 22.

3. By positively excluding from their marriage-bed all *sinful abuses*.

The evil suggestions of corrupt nature must, therefore, be positively refused and suppressed. Those who abandon themselves to sinful excesses are left by God, and are abandoned to the powers of hell.

"Hear me, and I will show thee who they are, over whom the devil can prevail; for they who in such manner receive matrimony, as to shut out God from themselves, and from their mind, and to give themselves to their lust, as the horse and the mule, which have not understanding, over them the devil hath power." — Tob. vi. 16, 17.

Men ought to be satisfied because, in consideration of human frailty, God allows them, in a certain respect, more than the animal — and they may, without sin, do what the animal, from instinct, will never attempt. (This for men only.)

To know what is right and wrong in reference to this point, consult your own conscience; in case of doubt — the priest in the confessional, but in the proper terms.

## II. Duties of Married People toward their Children

Example of an engineer who out of ignorance or malice causes an accident on the railroad. Who is to blame?

1. The first and principal object of marriage is to raise a family for the kingdom of heaven. Besides the salvation of their own souls, married people have

no other object to pursue than the rearing of children for God.

Therefore fathers and mothers, in entering upon the state of matrimony, have taken upon themselves the greatest responsibilities — the education of children. They have laid down their own immortal souls as a pledge that they will procure the temporal and spiritual welfare of every child that Divine Providence is willing to place under their charge (step-children included). If, on account of their ignorance, neglect, or malice, one of them is lost, the pledge — *i.e.,* their souls, is lost too.

2. The sins that are committed against the chief end of married life are simply enormous.

Married people begin to live in a bad state as soon as they begin to wish to have no more offspring, or not so soon, or not in so rapid succession; and yet continue to live as usual in regard to their marriage privileges.

But this perverse disposition goes farther and shrinks from nothing, no matter how criminal.

*a.* A shocking crime in this respect is the direct exclusion of offspring, or the limiting of its number, by positive means; by positively preventing the course of nature (Gen. xxxviii) — or in any way impeding the generation of children.

*b.* But a worse crime is the wilful murder of the poor child before it is born, by procuring an abortion — or by bringing on a miscarriage — a crime which is worse than murder under ordinary circumstances, because the child thus killed is deprived both of temporal and spiritual — eternal — life.

And let it be understood that the child has life and a soul from the first moment of its existence in its mother's womb.

*c.* A similar crime is the ill-treatment of the mother in a state of pregnancy on the part of the father; or the want of sufficient care for herself and child on the part of the mother.

What idea must such men and women have of the holy state of matrimony? They must look upon marriage simply as a state of legalized lust. Still they have a few sickly, emaciated children. What must we think of such children who are, nevertheless, born of such a marriage, as it were *by accident?* They are already given to most unnatural excesses of lust even in their infancy — one of the causes of the corruption of morals in the present age.

Note. — Constat ex quotidiana experientia omnes conjuges onanistas onanismi malitiam omnino cognoscere; et quamvis ex eorum responsis prima fronte aliquando appareat eos de peccati gravitate nullo modo dubitare; nihilominus, si confessarius statum suorum pœnitentium onanistarum maturuis perpendat, facile perspiciet atque intelliget, quod ignorantia in qua illi versantur est vincibilis et culpabilis, quia saltem quamdam notitiam in confuso de onanismi malitia semper habent. Ideo, quoties tanti criminis malitiam se ignorare affirmant, audiendi non sunt, quia se ipsos decipiunt.

*Aliquando concionatores,* præsertim si conjugatos alloquantur, onanismi malitiam ac damna explicare et exponere *possunt,* modo summa prudentia et quasi, ut ita dicam, per transennam hoc faciant.

*Confessarius* autem *tenetur plerumque* de hac re interrogare quia ex centum conjugiis vix quinque et sex immunia sint, etiamsi sint in bona fide, quia agitur de damno in rempublicam et Ecclesiam redundante. — Nardi de onanismo, p. ii, art. I.

*Objections:* "We cannot support a numerous family." Have faith; cannot God, Who creates those children, support them? Who gives you your daily bread?

"The woman is sickly; physicians have pronounced her incapable of bearing any more children." Physicians are not infallible in their decisions. Yet, if this is really so, what would you do if the woman were dead? Perhaps this very sickness has been brought on by former excesses. Take it as a chastisement.

(The foregoing Objections for men only.)

"We do not want to be burdened with many children." But, to have many children and bring them up for heaven is the very object of married life.

"Yet the woman shall be saved through childbearing." — I Tim. ii. 15. — "I will that the younger (widows) should marry, bear children, be mistresses of families." — Ib. v. 14.

3. Instead of giving themselves up to these iniquitous practices, let Christian parents consider themselves highly privileged, if God gives them a numerous offspring, no matter what the world may say.

"Children's children are the crown of old men; and the glory of children are their fathers." — Prov. xvii. 6.

Especially should the mother thank God as soon as she becomes aware that she is blessed with an additional child; she should pray for it, and take the best care that it may come into the world in safety. As the time of confinement approaches let the mother receive the sacraments and arm herself with great confidence in God and in the Blessed Virgin.

4. Not only *generation* but also *education* belongs to the office of father and mother. Hence,

Children must be brought to *baptism* shortly after their birth. In case of danger of life, private baptism is to be administered by the priest or a lay person, or, in extreme necessity, by the parents.

Parents, especially the mother, must baptize the child, in case of a miscarriage — in all cases in which the child, thus prematurely born, is probably living, no matter how young that child may be. Hence parents must know the method of administering private baptism.

Hence, also, the necessity of employing the services of a skilful and conscientious physician or midwife, who will have a proper regard for the spiritual and temporal welfare of the child.

In no case are parents allowed to permit the attending physician to take the life of the child, in order to save the life of the mother. In these extreme cases recourse must be had to fervent prayer and to some votive offering in the event of a happy delivery. (This for men only.)

5. *Spiritual* and *temporal education* of the child, the former to have the preference in all cases.

Christian education begins with the infancy of the child.

First rudiments of religion — prayers — keeping from evil company — from the bed of their parents — not letting them sleep together without distinction of sex — eradicating their faults by mild chastisements.

One of the principal duties of parents consists in giving their children a *good, Catholic school education*. Therefore, they must work for good parish schools. Efforts of priests, bishops, and Popes to that effect. Efforts of hell and its emissaries against Catholic schools.

Let parents be especially solicitous in sending their children to the sacraments — in having them prepared for first Communion and Confirmation, at the proper age. Should they get sick, call the priest for them, even at the age of seven years.

6. When the children leave school, they are again thrown on the exclusive care of the parents.

It is generally looked upon as a most difficult task to lead growing-up children on the path of Christian duty. But if the parents have reared the children well from infancy, this task becomes easy, because they fear God and will, therefore, submit to their parents.

"In the fear of the Lord . . . there shall be hope for his children." — Prov. xiv. 26. — "Hast thou children? — Instruct them, and bow down their neck from their childhood." — Eccli. vii. 25. — "Lest he regard thee not and so be a sorrow of heart to thee." — Ib. xxx. 12.

The good education of grown-up children requires,

*a.* The good example of the parents, which serves as a model to the children. To learn a thing well, it is necessary to see it done by others.

*b.* Parents must send them regularly to church — make them receive the sacraments at proper intervals — and insist on their saying their prayers daily.

*c.* They must watch over their morals — keeping them from the company of the other sex — from visiting certain dangerous houses and families; forbidding them dangerous books — papers — amusements — plays — staying out after dark, etc.

*d.* They should correct their faults, but they should never curse them, nor act in a fit of passion; they should even administer salutary chastisement, yet so that the children are not provoked, but see the justice of the punishment.

"You fathers, provoke not your children to anger, but bring them up in the discipline and correction of the Lord." — Eph. vi. 4.

Example of neglecting the chastisement of wicked children seen in Heli and his punishment (I Kings iv.)

7. Particular care is demanded from the parents when their children are about to choose a *new state of life.*

If God calls them to the religious life, or to the ecclesiastical state, place no obstacle in their way; thank God rather for thus favoring your family; and give them every assistance in your power.

Parents who resist God in calling their children to the religious life, forget that the children belong to God. God will punish them through those very children.

If they wish to be married, allow no company-keeping before the time of marriage; let it not be protracted too long; allow no private interviews, or lonely walks. Prevent every marriage that will make them unhappy in this world and imperil their eternal salvation — mixed marriage — or marriage with a bad Catholic. Give them all the necessary instructions for their new state of life.

These now include all the chief duties of your particular state of life, on the fulfilment of which depends your eternal salvation. Begin anew by making the Mission well, sincerely repenting of the faults committed in the past against the duties of your state of life, and confessing them; and live for the future as though you were married this very day.

# II

# FOR YOUNG MEN AND YOUNG WOMEN

## B. For Unmarried People

The instruction for unmarried men differs in a few points from that for the unmarried women. — The special duties of unmarried people are twofold, 1, those which they have to fulfil in order to be what their *present age* requires of them, and 2, those which regard their *future state* of life.

*As to the present,* they have special duties toward their *parents,* toward their *brothers and sisters,* and toward *themselves.* After briefly but forcibly speaking of the first two, let the missionary deal more in detail with the last. — Young people must above all else preserve the *faith,* by learning always more about it, and by avoiding the ordinary dangers of losing it. Then, they must practise the virtue of *chastity,* by employing the positive and negative means necessary for the preservation of that virtue. Young men must also be warned against excess in *drinking* and against *gambling.*

*As to the future state of life,* the *vocation* to a higher life must first be considered; then *marriage,* in regard to which young people are most liable to make serious and irreparable mistakes that may involve their temporal and eternal welfare. They must be told *whom* to marry — which point includes mixed marriages and some other impediments; *when* to marry — which includes so-called old bachelors, but it is very wrong to denounce women of an advanced age for not marrying; *how* to marry; and what *preparation* is to be made for marriage. In this last point company-keeping is spoken of; *how long* and *in what manner* it is to be kept. Young people must also be warned against inconsiderate and secret *engagements* of marriage.

If there exist any particular abuses in certain places, they are to be duly noticed.

## Sketch

Particular instructions are absolutely needed for young people, because they are most exposed to the dangers of the world, and yet they very often do not see them. Further, because their future state of life is still to be settled, in the determination of which they may make serious and irreparable mistakes.

They are in the same situation as a traveler in a strange country, arriving at a point from which many roads diverge, and who needs some one to tell him which road to take to lead him to his destination.

Young people have a *twofold duty* to fulfil; that which regards their *present* state of life, and that which concerns their *future*.


## I. A Young Man's (Young Woman's) Duty for the Present

1. A young man (young woman) must, above all, be a *good Catholic;* hence, sound in faith. Firmly believe in the Church — constantly obey her — avoid human respect — be not ashamed of your faith.

"He that shall be ashamed of me, and of my words, in this adulterous and sinful generation (Protestants and infidels), the Son of man also will be ashamed of him, when he shall come in the glory of his Father with the holy angels." — Mark viii. 38.

Therefore, shun the *danger* of losing your faith. Keep away from infidel associations, irreligious books and papers, etc. Strengthen yourselves more and more in your faith, attend sermons, read good books of instruction, so as to understand your faith, and to be able to defend it.

2. Young men (young women) generally have still *their parents*. Toward these they are to fulfil the duty of

*a. Respect,* in word and action.

"Honor thy father and thy mother, that thou mayest be long-lived upon earth." — Exod. xx. 12. — "The eye that mocketh at his father, and that despiseth the labor of his mother . . . let the ravens of the brook pick it out, and the young eagles eat it." —

Prov. xxx. 17, *i. e.*, he shall die a miserable death and his corpse be devoured by the birds of prey. — "Cursed be he that honoreth not his father and mother, and all the people shall say: Amen." — Deut. xxvii. 16.

### *b. Obedience,* as long as he is at home.

"If a man have a stubborn and unruly son, who will not hear the commandments of his father or mother . . . they shall bring him to the gate of judgment . . . and the people of the city shall stone him." — Deut. xxi. 18–21.

### *c. Love,* which must reach even beyond the death of the parents.

"He that afflicteth his father, and chaseth away his mother, is infamous and unhappy." — Prov. xix. 26.

What ingratitude to afflict the parents who have worked hard and made the greatest sacrifices for their children!

3. Young men (women) are to be adorned with *purity of body and soul.* Virginal purity is their most precious ornament. For this reason they must preserve themselves *undefiled,* especially from the sin of impurity; hence make good use of the necessary means.

*a. Positive* — *esteeming* holy chastity and virginal purity as it is seen by the light of grace. *Examples:* Joseph of Egypt, Susanna, St. Joseph, the spouse of the Blessed Virgin, Mary herself, and many saints; practising *holy prayer,* especially in temptation; particular *devotion to the Blessed Virgin* (three Hail Marys morning and evening, scapular, sodality) — frequenting the sacraments, *monthly communion.*

*b. Negative* — avoiding all *light reading,* romances, love-stories, etc.; despising *immoral conversation; not staying out* after dark; keeping from such *public plays* as have no regard for common decency; avoiding all such *amusements,* at which young people of both sexes recreate themselves together — no matter what sort of pious face they assume, especially certain parties, dances, etc.; avoiding a regular acquaintance with a person of the *other sex;* not keeping *company* before the time for getting married has arrived. To a young woman in particular the advice should be given to avoid all freedom in her *looks and manners;* to study a certain simplicity in *dress,* notwithstanding the ever-changing fashions of the world.

"Whosoever will be a friend of this world, becometh an enemy of God." — James iv. 4.

## II. A Young Man's (Young Woman's) Duty for the Future

1. God assigns for every individual a *certain state of life* — giving him certain dispositions for that state. He will make it known to him in time. It is the duty of a young man (young woman) to find out his vocation in life and follow it. God will give him the grace of salvation only in that state to which He calls him.

A man may lose his true vocation by selecting one more congenial to his sinful inclinations. This mistake may involve his eternal damnation, because God will not give him the graces prepared for him in the state of life to which He had called him.

There is a *threefold vocation* in the Church of God: the ecclesiastical — the religious — the secular state of life.

As regards the first, God always provides His Church with a sufficient number of priests. Whenever there is dearth of priests, it is an evident sign that some young men do not follow their vocation.

In regard to the second, if a young man (young woman) feels himself (herself) called to that sort of life, let him (her) find out which particular Order God wants him (her) to join. A prudent confessor will decide. Beware, however, of mistaking a momentary motion of piety for a vocation.

The third state of life is twofold — single and married. Single life is the more perfect, but very few are called to it.

"All men take [understand] not this word, but they to whom it is given." — Matt. xix. 11.

There is a certain class of people who desire to remain single, but whose own sad experience teaches them most plainly that they are not called to this kind of life. They do very wrong in remaining single, because they neglect the principal means of their salvation, matrimony.

*Excuses:* "Cannot find a good wife." Anyhow, you can find one as good as you are. "Cannot support a family." God will provide the daily bread for yourself and family. Let young women give up their excessive extravagance and their too free conduct, and there will be less ground for such objections.

If it should really be impossible to marry, let the proper means be employed for leading a pure life.

2. Most of our young people are called to the state of matrimony. Many begin a life of misery with marriage. Infidel State laws have invented as a remedy the iniquitous practice of granting divorce. This will not cure the evil, but increase it. The evil is the result of an injudicious choice, and a sinful preparation.

God will provide the future partner in life. For if God provides for mankind in general and for every individual in particular, He will certainly provide a suitable companion in life for the young man (the young woman); because on that selection entirely depends their temporal and eternal happiness. Moreover, on the state of matrimony depends the good or evil state of society and of the Church.

The same principle is taught in the Scriptures: "House and riches are given by parents, but a prudent wife is properly from the Lord" (Prov. xix. 14). Marriage of Isaac and Rebecca (Gen. xxiv); of Tobias and Sara (Tob. iii. 3–6).

To secure for themselves the guidance of Divine Providence in this most important matter, let young people faithfully serve God in their youth. Obedience to parents, to which a special blessing is promised (Tob. iii. 17, 18). God punishes a dissolute life in youth by allowing young people to enter into an unhappy marriage.

Accordingly, avoid husband (wife) *hunting* by going into company; having recourse to certain attractive ways — stylish fashions; fortune-telling — and other superstitious practices.

On the contrary, obey the laws of God and the Church in this matter — and especially have recourse to prayer.

3. Certain marriages are *forbidden* by God and the Church — *impedimenta dirimentia*. Explanation of some — especially the prohibition of mixed marriages.

Reasons for avoiding mixed marriages:

*a*. Because they originate from a cold indifferentism in regard to faith — and from other unworthy motives.

*b*. Because such marriages are never happy; there can be no true union of heart and soul so long as the parties differ in regard to the most sacred things.

*c*. Because the faith of the Catholic party is in danger, first in practice, then in itself, as experience proves, and this on the principal ground, "to have peace."

*d*. Because the matrimonial tie is not believed to be indissoluble on the part of the Protestant party.

*e*. Because the education and salvation of the children are at stake. It requires the teaching and example of both, the father and the mother, to educate good children. Experience shows what becomes of the children of mixed marriages.

For these reasons mixed marriages were forbidden in the Old Law — Deut. vii. 3; in the New Law — II Cor. vi. 14; by the Fathers of the Church, especially by St. Ambrose and St. Augustine, by many Councils and Popes. The Church never permits them; she only tolerates them under certain restrictions, and then they are to be celebrated without any sacred ceremony. Canons 1060, 1061, 1062. Explanation.

How a Catholic young man (young woman) can think of entering a mixed marriage — or keep company with a Protestant with a view to marriage, in the face of all this, is hard to explain, except on the supposition that in his heart he has ceased to be truly Catholic.

4. When a young man (young woman) contemplates marriage, let him (her) proceed in the following way:

*a.* Never form an acquaintance before the time of marriage is come. This time is to be determined by your age and your circumstances.

*b.* Before you take any steps, receive the sacraments, to propitiate the anger of God for your past sins and to obtain light to make a good choice.

*c.* Make your choice with prudence and circumspection, investigating whether this or that person will make you happy in life, and help you on the way to salvation. For this investigation an acquaintance must be formed, company must be kept, until full satisfaction is obtained.

*d.* As soon as you discover that the person to whom you pay your attentions does not suit you, give up the acquaintance; if the contrary, form an engagement — and make preparations for carrying it out immediately. *Sponsalia*. Canon 1017, §§ 1, 2, 3.

*e.* During the time of acquaintance avoid private interviews — lonely walks — and everything that may lead to sin; pray more and receive the sacraments oftener, that God may assist you in making the right choice. A neglect of this may be the cause of your everlasting misfortune, as it has been and is for many others.

*f.* Give timely notice of your intended marriage to your pastor — receive his instructions in reference to your new state of life — and have everything done before and at your wedding, as the Church prescribes. In regard to your household duties and other matters of importance in connection with temporal prosperity, take the advice of your parents or nearest relatives.

*g.* Your wedding-feast should be celebrated principally in the church. Have a Mass said or sung for yourselves, at which you should go to Holy Communion. Recommendation of the Nuptial Mass. Exclude from your wedding-feast everything objectionable to morals — indecent jokes, plays. Avoid all unnecessary expenses; get nothing for mere show. Enter your new state of life with the fear and the love of God in your souls, and with Jesus in the Blessed Sacrament in your hearts.

These, now, are the particular duties of Christian young men (young women) — duties by no means in accord with the principles and views of this present perverse world. But they are the maxims of the Gospel, and of the Church, and the absolute condition on which depend the present, the future, the temporal, and the eternal prosperity of our young people.

# FIFTH PART

# MINOR EXERCISES

I. ROSARY
II. MISSIONS FOR CHILDREN
III. APPENDIXES

# I

# ROSARY

# I

## DIRECTIONS FOR GIVING OUT THE ROSARY

The practice of saying the Rosary as a preparation for the evening sermon, has been kept up in our Congregation since the time of St. Alphonsus. Some other missionaries have the same practice. There are two reasons for it. The first is, to keep the congregation occupied, while the people are still coming in; the other, to obtain the grace from God, through the intercession of the Blessed Virgin Mary, that all may profit by the sermon which is to follow. On our Missions, as a rule, the recitation of the Rosary is the work of one of the missionaries, whenever there are at least two; otherwise, another priest may say it, or even a layman, should there be no priest at hand. It is our practice to introduce the Rosary by a short discourse, tending to lead the people to greater love and devotion for this most efficacious prayer. As regards both the introduction and the recitation of the Rosary, the Rule *obliges* us to follow the method and prescriptions of St. Alphonsus — *"a qua deviare Nostris nullatenus permittitur."* [1] This method is given by St. Alphonsus in his *Exercises for Missions*, chap. II.[2]

### 1. Rosary Instructions — Their Subjects and Delivery

The *Rosary Instruction* is not, properly speaking, an instruction nor an exhortation, but simply a

---

[1] R., n. 137.     [2] C. E., Vol. XV. p. 334.

few words of introduction. According to St. Alphonsus, it should be a "narration of an authentic fact or incident, by which it is practically shown how the Blessed Virgin Mary protects those who love to say the Rosary." [3] To this Father Sarnelli, C.SS.R., adds, that it may also consist of a short exposition of the excellence of this prayer, of its component parts, of the manner of reciting it, of the indulgences attached to it; to which may be added a refutation of the objections ordinarily made against it. In general, let it be said here, that in all cases in which a departure is made from the method laid down by our holy Founder, no subject should be introduced which is not in close connection with the Rosary. If some of our missionaries have, for good reasons, deviated from this rule in time past, their action is not to be taken as a standard.

The only exception that has met with general approval in this Province is to give one or two instructions on blessed articles in general and in particular, and also one or two on the scapulars. These bear a close relation to the Rosary, because the beads are one of the articles which we bless; and also the devotion to these articles, at least for the greater part, is simply an extension of the devotion to the Rosary. But care must be taken that these latter instructions do not exceed the limits of the former.

From the nature of the Rosary instructions, it can easily be seen that they are not to be composed nor delivered in the style of an instruction, much less in the style of a sermon. They are to be simple, familiar, and short conversational discourses, yet so delivered that they be heard and understood by the whole congregation.

[3] *Exercises*, C. E., Vol. XV. p. 130.

## 2. How Long the Instructions are to Last

The time allowed for them is about eight or, at most, ten minutes. That they should not take up more time, may easily be seen from the model of one which St. Alphonsus gives in full in his Instructions. In our present situation there are, besides, other reasons why they should not be longer. The evening service generally begins at half-past seven. The great sermon should positively be finished by nine o'clock, or not much later; otherwise, the congregation would be kept too late in the night to be expected back again early in the morning. Still, a full hour must be given to this sermon. Hence, a little before eight o'clock, the introduction, Rosary and announcements should be over, as nearly five minutes will still be needed to sing the hymn, and to read the Daily Acts of a Christian life. The more the Rosary instruction is prolonged, the shorter the sermon will be. Now, which is of greater importance? Moreover, the minds of the people should not be wearied by long reflection before the sermon begins. They need the full vigor of their minds for the latter. How hard is it not to keep the audience attentive during a sermon of an hour! A prolonged Rosary instruction would make it still more difficult.

## 3. When to be Omitted

The Rosary instruction is sometimes to be omitted altogether. St. Alphonsus says "that this introduction should be given only when there is time for it, and when it becomes necessary to keep the congregation occupied, which is rarely the case." Accordingly, the saint had the instruction omitted altogether, sometimes during the entire Mission.[4]  On our Missions in this country, the ordinary occasions on which the instruction should be dropped, are: before the sermon on the Blessed Virgin, followed by the act of dedication; the erection of the Mission-Cross; the closing exercise; and when the blessing of the articles of devotion takes place before the sermon; otherwise, the service would be too long on these evenings.  Besides, on some Missions, the church is crowded with people, often long before the service begins.  Whenever this is the case (even should it be during the entire Mission), the instruction should be left out, or at most only a few words — three or four short sentences — should be said.  At such times the people are most uncomfortably packed together, are already tired waiting, and find it difficult to hold out.  All that the instruction does, then, is to diminish the effect of the sermon.  In such cases, the articles of devotion should be blessed as briefly as possible.

## 4.  MANNER OF GIVING OUT THE ROSARY

After the introduction follows the recitation of the Rosary.  In some countries it is the custom of the people to recite the Rosary alternately, in the same manner as the Psalms are said or chanted by two choirs.  And, in fact, the Rosary is nothing else than a Psalter.  When recited in this manner, the priest who conducts the recitation begins with the *Deus in adjutorium,* in Latin or in the vernacular, as in the beginning of a canonical hour.  Then, those on one side of the church say the first part of the Creed, of the Our Father, the Hail Mary, the Glory be to the Father; and those on the other side answer the second

4 C E., Vol. XV. p. 130.

part. Before each decade, the leader reads the mystery and the short consideration. This is the method that St. Alphonsus refers to in his Instruction; but he prescribed that all should be said in the vernacular.

It is the general usage in this country, as also in some other countries, for the leader to take one part throughout, and for the people to respond with the second part. Of those who use this method, some interpose the mystery between the first and second parts of the Hail Mary throughout the decade, while others mention it only once in the beginning of the decade, adding a short reflection and a prayer. This last method approaches nearest to that of St. Alphonsus, and is the one to be followed on the English and French Missions. Three short sentences will suffice. For example:

Before the first decade say: "Let us meditate on the five joyful — sorrowful — glorious — mysteries. First mystery, the Incarnation of the Son of God. Consider that the Son of God was made man to become our Redeemer. Let us pray that the fruits of the Redemption may not be lost on our souls. Our Father, etc." Then for the second decade, second mystery . . . consider . . . let us pray . . . and so forth, for all the rest. These little considerations and prayers may be different, according to the needs of the people. A Father who possesses the spirit of prayer will have them at his command, as Father Sarnelli remarks. St. Alphonsus himself had the explanation of the mysteries abbreviated in this manner, as may be seen in the old Rule.[5] He would even sometimes have one or the other decade omitted, when there was no time left for the recitation of the whole Rosary. This may still be done, if it should happen

[5] Codex. n. 126.

that, in giving the introduction, the Father should forget himself and exceed his appointed time.

It has become customary with us during the Mission simply to mention the mysteries between the decades.

On German Missions, the second method is followed, namely, that of mentioning the mysteries between the first and second parts of each Hail Mary. As regards the order of giving out the mysteries, they should be made to follow one another according to the days of the week. The joyful mysteries should be taken on Mondays and Thursdays, the sorrowful on Tuesdays and Fridays, the glorious on Sundays, Wednesdays and Saturdays. No attention is to be paid to Advent, Lent, or Paschal time on the Missions, in order that the people may hear all the mysteries mentioned. On the Sunday of the opening of the Mission the joyful mysteries are inserted to avoid confusion. The explanation of the manner of meditating on these mysteries during the recitation will form a Rosary instruction. The time required for the Rosary, if recited with devotion, varies according to circumstances. When the mysteries are simply mentioned between the decades, it takes ten minutes to say it well. When the mysteries are inserted in the Hail Mary, it takes four or five minutes more. Nor could the recitation be finished in less time without great injury to the devotion and edification with which this sublime prayer is to be offered.

### 5. Abuses to be Abolished

Our English-speaking Catholics have the bad habit of answering in an almost inaudible tone to the prayers that are publicly recited in the church.

Some mutter a few words in a most indistinct and scarcely audible manner; the most of them do not answer at all. Then, again, they begin with the answer when the leader is not yet half through with his part. No wonder, then, that a whole congregation can finish the beads in five minutes! But whether any indulgences are gained by this kind of recitation is a great question. One thing, however, is certain, that the Rosary recited thus is said only by a few who are near the altar; the rest do nothing. Our missionaries should, by gentle means, induce the people to say the beads according to the approved custom in the Church. Let our Fathers endeavor, in general, by the explanation and the recitation of the holy Rosary, to give edification to the people. They should induce them, by word and example, to love and cherish this devotion, not only during the Mission, but ever afterward; and a great share of the merits of the Mission will be their reward.

## II

# SHORT INSTRUCTIONS BEFORE THE RECITATION OF THE ROSARY

### ROSARY INSTRUCTIONS

REMARK. — Every little paragraph may make an instruction by itself.

### I. REASON WHY WE SAY THE ROSARY ON THE MISSION

In preaching no effect is produced without grace. There is no grace without prayer. The most efficacious prayer is that to the Blessed Virgin. The best method of obtaining her intercession is the Rosary, on account of its intrinsic value — and the repeated invocations — fifty times, multiplied by one thousand or fifteen hundred voices — which makes fifty thousand or seventy-five thousand invocations, addressed to the Blessed Virgin. Will she remain deaf to this? Therefore let *all* join in the recitation of the Rosary, say it with a *loud voice,* and with *deep devotion.*

### II. ORIGIN OF THE ROSARY

1. Counting prayers on beads or pebbles was practised by the ancient hermits — St. Bridget of Ireland in the fifth century — St. Gertrude in the seventh — the Crusaders, etc.

2. In the year 1208, St. Dominic was sent to convert the Albigenses. After three years of fruitless labor, he retired to the chapel of N. D. de la Pouillé, where, after a fast and prayer of three days, the

Blessed Virgin revealed to him the Rosary as the most powerful means of converting sinners. He put in execution at once what he had heard, with most wonderful effect. (See Scheerer, vol. v, p. 886.)

3. Fifty years after the introduction of the Rosary, a hundred thousand heretics had already been converted by it, and thousands of sinners brought to penance. The Arch-confraternity of the Rosary was established and approved 1261. Twenty-five Popes have approved the Rosary and enriched it with indulgences. Many chapels have been built in honor of the Rosary. "Queen of the Most Holy Rosary" was added to the Litany of the Blessed Virgin.

### III. Intrinsic Value of the Rosary

1. It is composed of the most sublime *prayers,* as the Sign of the Cross — the Creed — the Our Father — the Hail Mary — Glory be to the Father.

2. The consideration of the *mysteries* is entwined with these prayers, as the chain with the beads. They are, as it were, a compendium of instruction on all the principal mysteries of faith — a book which contains the life, death, and glory of our Lord and the Blessed Virgin.

3. The mysteries are divided into the *joyful,* the *sorrowful,* and the *glorious.* The first show us the love of God in the Incarnation, the love of Jesus Christ, the life that He led, the example that He gave to men, the obstacles of our salvation which He removed.

4. The sorrowful mysteries show us the effects of sin, its malice, its punishment; the value of our souls; how much we should love Jesus Christ and His sorrowful Mother; how much we should be inspired with love of suffering.

5. The glorious mysteries reveal to us the reward of heaven; the dignity of our souls as the living temples of the Holy Ghost; they greatly increase our confidence in Mary, next to her Son in heaven.

6. The joyful mysteries confirm us in the *faith;* the sorrowful enkindle our *love;* the glorious increase our *hope.*

7. The mysteries of the Rosary include the entire time between the Incarnation and the Ascension of Our Lord; between the Annunciation and the Coronation of the Blessed Virgin Mary in heaven.

### IV. MYSTICAL SIGNIFICATION OF THE ROSARY

1. The full Rosary consists in the recitation of one hundred and fifty *Hail Marys.* These represent the one hundred and fifty *Psalms* recited in the Church of God, and through which God receives so much honor and praise. By saying the Rosary we honor God through the Blessed Virgin Mary, whom we ask to offer to God, in our behalf, that part of the life of the Redeemer on which we meditate — and we do so by each Hail Mary. Therefore the Rosary is also called the Breviary of the Laity.

2. A rosebush produces green *leaves, thorns* and *flowers.* The joyful mysteries of the Rosary are the green leaves — the sorrowful mysteries are the thorns —the glorious mysteries are the flowers.

3. The third part of the Rosary is said, to gain the indulgences attached to the recitation of it. It consists of *fifty Hail Marys.* Fifty years had to pass before the Lord granted to the Jewish people the year of Jubilee. Fifty days after the day of the glorious Resurrection of Jesus Christ, the Holy Ghost communicated Himself to the Church.

4. The whole Rosary is divided into *fifteen decades*, corresponding to the fifteen mysteries, which are, as it were, fifteen steps. Each begins with an Our Father and ends with a Glory be to the Father. Fifteen steps led up to the Holy of Holies in the temple of Jerusalem, and the fifteen so-called "Gradual Psalms" were chanted by the people of God in going up these steps.

5. Each decade is composed of *ten Hail Marys*. Ten just souls would have saved Sodom and Gomorrha from destruction; ten commandments are to be kept in order to be just; the wages of the laborers in the vineyard consisted in a *denarius*.

### V. ORDINARY INDULGENCES ATTACHED TO THE ROSARY

Brief explanation of the meaning of indulgences — if deemed necessary.

1. Plenary indulgence on the last Sunday of every month for those who recite it together at least three times a week (12th May, 1851).

2. Plenary indulgence at the hour of death for saying it at least once a week (15th Jan., 1714).

3. One hundred days' indulgence for the Creed, each Our Father and Hail Mary of the Bridgetine Rosary (10th July, 1515), and the same for the Dominican (1726). Five hundred days' for the Crozier beads.

4. Ten years and ten quarantines are granted to those who say the Rosary with others (12th May, 1851).

To gain these indulgences a person must *own* the beads on which he recites; [1] numbers of beads may be blessed and given away afterward; the *first owner* is

[1] Those who answer, when two or more say the beads together, need not have a rosary to gain the indulgence. Canon 934, 3.

entitled to the indulgences. Broken beads can be repaired, the whole chain be renewed, new beads be put in; the indulgences remain as long as the beads are not utterly destroyed or sold. (New Code, Canon 924, 2.)

### VI. Power of the Holy Rosary

Pius V ascribed to the Rosary the great victory gained by the Christians at Lepanto, 7th Oct., 1571, over the Turks, who threatened Europe; Clement XI attributed to it another victory which Charles VI gained over the Turks in Hungary, in 1716; and shortly after, the delivery of Corcyra from Turkish power; Leo XIII prescribed the recitation of the Rosary for the whole month of October and for every Sunday throughout the year, to free the Church from her oppressors; many millions of souls have been delivered from sin and eternal destruction through the Rosary; an immense amount of good is done by it on every Mission, as experience proves.

### VII. The Rosary a Very Easy Prayer

1. The Rosary is a most sublime and a most powerful prayer; yet it is a very easy prayer. All that is required is the recitation of the most ordinary prayers, in the prescribed order, united with the meditation on the mysteries. Those who do not know all the mysteries may meditate on one or two; and those who do not know even that much may simply recite the prayers.

2. Manner of saying the Rosary: Sign of the Cross — Creed — Our Father — three Hail Marys — Glory be to the Father. Then for each decade: Our Father, ten Hail Marys, Glory be to the Father, meditation on the mysteries.

3. Way of meditating on the mysteries: Consider what the mystery means; pray for a particular grace in connection with it. Do this either before the Our Father of each decade, or while saying the Hail Marys.

4. We say the *Creed* to strengthen our faith, and to enliven it. In this firm and unshaken faith we address ourselves to God, offering the seven most comprehensive petitions of the *Our Father* — confiding in the merits of Jesus Christ, Who has gained all for us — *the mysteries* — but we ask all through the Blessed Virgin Mary, through whom all graces are given — *ten Hail Marys:* all to the glory of the Triune God — *Glory be to the Father*.

This is the most effectual way of praying, and at the same time it is very easy.

## VIII. The Rosary a Prayer for all — Practised by all Classes of People

1. It is a sign of genuine *Catholicity;* for no one but a good Catholic says the beads. It preserves the faith and restores it. Examples. *"Tu sola omnes hœreses interimisti."*

2. Distinguished persons of *royal rank* have said the Rosary: Emperor Charles V — Frederick III, of Germany — King Francis II — Henry II — Charles IX, of France — Alphonsus II — and Henry I, of Portugal; many of the princes of England, Bavaria, Saxony, Naples, Savoy, Sardinia, etc.

3. Great *statesmen* and distinguished *artists:* Daniel O'Connell — Radetzky — Joseph Haydn.

4. Great and holy bishops have said the Rosary: St. Francis de Sales — St. Charles Borromeo — St. Alphonsus Liguori. All founders of religious orders said and prescribed it.

5. The Rosary should, therefore, be made a regular *family devotion*. It should be said in every house at night-prayers, and the whole family should take part in it. This practice will keep the faith alive in the house. Every attempt is made to weaken the faith, and to lower the sense of morality by intruders. Oppose them with the Rosary. They will either keep away or pray with you. The Rosary will in all cases gain the victory.

## IX. OBJECTIONS AGAINST THE ROSARY

1. "Constant repetition." *"Sanctus" in heaven;* (Ps. cxxxv.); the Canticle of the three young men; Prayer of Jesus in the Garden of Olives; "My God and my all" of St. Francis.

2. "It gives more honor to Mary than to God." Through Mary we know and worship God.

3. "It is too tedious." Yes, for those who do not love to pray, and have no love for the Blessed Virgin.

4. "It is no prayer for the educated" — who at the same time are full of pride; not so as regards the humble.

5. "We should not use many words." (Matt. vi. 7.) We use very few words, but knock repeatedly, as the Lord commands. (Luke xi. 8.)

6. If a little child that just begins to articulate a word or two, says nothing but "Mamma," the mother is delighted with it — and the oftener the child utters that sweet expression, the more the mother is pleased.

## X. ARTICLES OF DEVOTION

1. Moses sweetened the waters of Mara by throwing wood into them (Exod. xv. 25). Eliseus healed the unhealthy spring of waters at Jericho by casting

salt into it (IV Kings ii. 21). The Church blesses various articles, and imparts to them certain graces in favor of those who use them.

The articles of devotion which we bless confer upon their owners all those graces which are expressed in the prayers uttered by the priest in blessing them. Besides, the usual Papal indulgences, which include many plenary and partial indulgences, are attached to most of these articles, and a plenary indulgence at the hour of death. Then some special indulgences are attached to them. The indulgences are gained by those only in whose favor these articles are blessed.

2. Blessed crosses and crucifixes increase our love for Jesus crucified, for sufferings, etc. Special indulgences of the Stations of the Cross; for kissing the crucifix, seven years' indulgence.

3. Blessed medals are most powerful against temptations — effect the conversion of sinners — protect against corporal dangers. General Conrobert at Alma.

4. Sacred pictures secure for their owners the special protection of the saints who are represented by them. Make them the friends of your house.

5. Blessed wax-candles are used at prayers in time of danger — thunder-storms, etc.; when you wish to pray with particular fervor; when a sacrament is administered in the house; during the last agony; near the body of a deceased Christian.

## XI. The Scapulars

1. Their nature. A religious habit entitles to a participation in all the merits of those religious communities to which it belongs.

2. There are five generally blessed in the Mission: 1. Of the Order of Mt. Carmel, the brown; 2. Of the

Blessed Trinity, the white; 3. Of the Order of the Immaculate Conception, the blue; 4. Of the Order of Servites, the black; 5. Of the Passion, the red.

3. They are a protection for soul and body in life — assure us of a happy death — secure for us a speedy deliverance from purgatory.

4. Many indulgences are attached to them, among others a plenary indulgence to the brown Scapular after each confession, visiting the church; and to the blue scapular, by reciting six Paters, Aves, Glorias, in honor of the Most Blessed Trinity and of the Immaculate Conception, *toties quoties;* with the usual intentions, the wearer gains all the indulgences of the Holy Land, of Rome, of Portiuncula, and of St. James in Compostella.

5. The conditions are: 1, to be duly invested, and, 2, to wear them. The Sabbatine indulgence (explanation) requires either the recitation of the Office of the Blessed Virgin or abstinence on Wednesdays and Saturdays; but this can be changed by any priest in this country, in or out of confession.

Scapular prayers never oblige under sin, mortal or venial.

6. To be invested in the scapulars persons must be personally present. Once invested with them, you are invested for life, unless you lay them aside with the intention of wearing them no longer. The scapulars may be worn over the undergarments. When torn they may be mended; or new ones may be procured and worn without being blessed again. They may also be worn sewed up in little cases or bags.

# II

## MISSIONS FOR CHILDREN

# I

## DIRECTIONS FOR CONDUCTING THE CHILDREN'S MISSION

### 1. Necessity

For many important reasons it has always been our rule and custom to give a Mission to the children, apart from that for the grown people. If this is not done, the Mission will be of no use to the children. They are, indeed, most eager to come to the sermons, but as St. Alphonsus remarks: [1] "Understanding only a little of what is preached, they pay but little attention and spend the time in talking, playing, and pushing one another; this is a source of constant trouble to the preacher and to the hearers. It has therefore been thought expedient . . . to assemble them in another place, where, after they have received an instruction in catechism, we address to them a short discourse." This little Mission should always be given, if it be in any way possible. For the children also should be impressed with the *Eternal Truths,* and be practically instructed in what concerns the reception of the sacraments, and the way of leading a truly Christian life. Often they have already committed grievous sins, have even loaded their tender souls with the most horrible sacrileges, for which their Mission is the most opportune remedy.

### 2. Who Should Attend

The class of children to whom this Mission is to be given consists of those who are ten years old, and not

[1] *Exercises,* C. E., Vol. XV. p. 165.

yet over fourteen. Children who are younger only cause trouble and distraction, while they profit nothing by the instructions. Older children should attend the Mission of the grown people, as they are very badly in need of these sacred exercises, while those for the children would be insufficient.[2]

### 3. When it Should be Given

St. Alphonsus had the exercises for the children given every afternoon throughout the entire Mission, while the services for the grown people were going on in the church.[3] In Europe, at the present day, the Fathers give them for three or four days only, from the beginning of the Mission. They make a great display at their general communion, producing thereby a deep impression upon the grown people, who are generally in attendance, and thus preparing them for the Mission. Our peculiar circumstances in this country will hardly allow the grown people to attend; so this object cannot be attained. Moreover, many children show no eagerness at all to come during the first days of the Mission, nor do the parents as yet take a sufficient interest in the spiritual welfare of their children to send them. Hence, to obtain the desired success by these exercises, the last days of the Mission are often the best. Wherever a division of the sexes is made, the few days between the women's and the men's Mission is a most suitable time for the children's Mission.

### 4. The Most Convenient Hours of the Day

The greatest difficulty is generally experienced in assigning an hour for the exercises which will suit

---

[2] Prov. Stat. p. 60, n. 29.
[3] *Exercises*, C. E., Vol. XV, p. 165.

all the children who ought to come. In many places, many of the older children are living out, or are employed in factories, etc., and therefore cannot come during working hours without losing their places. If such children are in the majority, it would be better to give their exercises in the evening, while the grown people are attending the sermon in the church, provided there is a place where they can assemble. But, if they are in the minority, let them attend the exercises for the grown people, while the others have theirs during the day. In other places, again, most of the children, if not all, attend the public schools. It would not be very prudent to interfere too much with their school time. They generally can come to church at 7.30 A.M., when they may attend a Mass and an instruction of half an hour or so, or receive an instruction without the Mass. Then let them assemble again at 3.00 or 3.30 P.M. The superintendents of schools, if kindly requested by the pastor, ordinarily show some generosity in allowing the Catholic children to leave school earlier for such purposes. Where all the children attend the Catholic schools, the missionaries can have everything their own way. We cannot force circumstances; we have to take things as they are, and do the best we can for the poor children, giving the benefit of the Mission to as many as possible.

5. SEPARATION OF THE GIRLS FROM THE BOYS

In two places our Rule makes mention of the children's Mission. First, general directions are given to the Father who conducts it,[4] and then particular regulations are laid down regarding their confessions,

[4] R., n. 94.

Communion, and the closing exercises.[5] The Rule prescribes that great care be taken that the girls be kept separate from the boys, and it therefore prescribes that each sex assemble in a separate place. Our limited number of missionaries does not always admit of this separation; let, then, the Father in charge pay special attention to it. But circumstances will sometimes make a separation absolutely necessary. No missionary can successfully give these exercises to more than three hundred children. A larger number cannot be kept under proper control by one Father. If the number, then, be too great, a division of the sexes should be made. In some places we have given the exercises to the girls in connection with the women's Mission, and to the boys with the men's Mission. In other places we have had them at the same time, but in two different places and in charge of two Fathers.

## 6. First Communicants

"With respect to the boys and girls who are to make their First Communion, the missionary who gives the instruction in Christian doctrine shall prepare them for a considerable time before they receive Communion, and as a rule, admit only those who are ten years old and over." [6] With us this passage can mean nothing else than that particular care should be bestowed upon those who have been already selected and instructed by the pastor for First Communion.

When Missions lasted two and three weeks there was time enough to prepare children for their First Communion. In shorter Missions it has its difficulties.

[5] R., n. 144, 145, 146.     [6] R., n. 144.

The admission of children to their First Communion is not, *strictly* speaking, an act reserved to the respective pastors of parishes.[7]   Still, many claim it as an exclusive right belonging to them, and on the Mission prudence forbids us to interfere with this claim.   But when there is question about children fifteen years old or more, we are allowed greater latitude.   Such children ought by all means to be prepared for their First Communion; otherwise, how will their souls be saved?   They are very often not even known to the pastor, or, if they are, no objections against preparing them are made.   Younger children ought to be told to frequent the parish Sunday-school, and try to be admitted into the First Communion Class.   To act otherwise would rather be an indirect approval of the carelessness of some children in frequenting Sunday-school.

### 7. Manner of Preaching to Children

It is not an easy task to give these Missions for children with success.   *"Hoc opus, hic labor, ut instructiones pro parvulis bene fiant. Facilius est concionem ad populum habere, quam instruere parvulos, ut cum fructu fiat."* [8]   St. Alphonsus understood how difficult this was, and hence he charged two of the best missionaries with this duty.[9]   Fathers, not yet sufficiently experienced on the Missions, are unfit for this task.   The manner in which the missionary should perform this important work cannot be better expressed than in the words of Father Van de Kerckhove, S. J.[10]

---

[7] Damen, *Theol. Mor. II:* n. 135, qu. 2, and Codex Juris Canon. n. 854, § 4.

[8] Van de Kerckh. *Man. Miss.* § 20, n. 4.

[9] Villecourt, I, ch. 52.

[10] *Man.* § 20, n. 4.

*"Eliseus suscitans filium mortuum Sunamitidis* (IV
Reg. iv. 34) *posuit os suum super os ejus, et oculos suos
super oculos ejus, et manus suas super manus ejus, et
incurvavit super eum, et calefacta est caro pueri et vixit
puer. Sic debet missionarius cum parvulis quasi par-
vulus agere; non tono concionatoris, sed simplicissimo
modo, in parabolis, comparationibus et historiunculis,
penetret intellectum parvulorum, ut capiant veritatem
et amplectantur. Tali modo etiam se amabilem reddit,
et parvulorum corda lucratur."*

The perusal of Father Furniss's tracts cannot be too
strongly recommended to those who are to give Missions or Retreats for children.

## 8. Duration of These Exercises

These exercises should last at least three days, beginning on an afternoon, continuing for two full days,
and closing on the fourth day with general Communion
and the final exercises. During these days the children
should be induced to keep from playing in the streets,
to say their morning and night prayers, with an additional Hail Mary for the success of the little Mission,
and to attend Mass in the morning if possible.

## 9. Discipline to be Enforced

During the instruction good order is, above all,
necessary. The children should not be allowed to
talk in church; they should be made to come in and
take their places in silence and with reverence. In
going out, they should not be allowed to go from
their seats in disorder, rushing to the door with shouts
and cries, but they ought to be shown how to leave
their places quietly, one after another, and to make
a genuflection on going out. It is useless to use

harsh words, and worse to pull them by the hair or ears, or slap them in the face,[11] as there are more gentle means to keep them in order. Let the missionary, above all, be grave, yet gentle,[12] and keep his eyes fixed on them during the instruction in such a manner that every one believes that the Father is always looking at him; yet he should not allow his eyes to rest upon one or several in particular: *"Maximopere caveat ne oculos in faciem puellarum intendat."* [13] It is a great help to preserve order, if, at the first exercise, the missionary places a certain number of children in every pew, beginning with the youngest. It makes them remember the number of the pew and their respective places, and they will keep them at all the exercises. By this means the Father can easily count them, and see immediately, at the next exercise, how many are absent. The first in the pew is constituted overseer, or head. He is every day at recess to report the absentees. This also serves as an additional motive to attend every exercise.

## 10. Nature and Order of the Exercises

Each exercise, according to St. Alphonsus, consists of two parts: an instruction and an exhortation, or a short sermon on one of the *Eternal Truths*. Experience proves that it is better to give the exhortation first. The minds of the children are not yet fatigued; they are therefore better able to pay attention to the subject of meditation. Besides, they take more interest in the instruction afterward, seeing, by the exhortation, the necessity of learning to understand their religious duties. Between the two parts, about five

---

[11] *Exercises,* C. E., Vol. XV. p. 157.     [12] Ib.
[13] R., n. 94.

minutes' rest is given. Neither of them should last over half an hour. One or two verses of a hymn [14] may be sung in the beginning, in the middle, and at the end, if the children know them well; otherwise not, because it would only cause distraction. The missionary should recite with them aloud, slowly, distinctly, and with short pauses, the ordinary prayers, the commandments and the sacraments, making them all join in with their hands folded devoutly. If the greater part do not know some of these prayers, the missionary should say them word for word alone, and make them repeat them after him together. In this way they will learn them. Many children do not even know how to say an act of contrition. The catechist should teach them the abbreviated form by St. Leonard. The catechist should not ask questions except in general. Children of advanced age are afraid to come, if they are liable to be asked questions which they cannot answer. Our children in this country are very sensitive on this point.

[14] *Exercises*, C. E., Vol. XV. p. 334.

## II

## EXERCISES OF A CHILDREN'S MISSION

According to St. Alphonsus,[1] every exercise at a
children's Mission consists of two parts; the instruction and the exhortation, or little sermon.

### I. THE INSTRUCTION

The instruction comprises: 1. The explanation of
the *mysteries* of *faith*. 2. The explanation of the *Sacraments*, especially of *Penance* and *Holy Eucharist*.
3. The explanation of the *Commandments* of *God*
and of the *Church*.

#### 1. MYSTERIES OF FAITH

Motives of faith are, because God, Who can neither
deceive nor be deceived, has revealed these truths.
There is but *one God*, infinitely good and all perfect —
the infinite beauty — the Creator of all things — omnipotent — immense and everywhere present — exists
from eternity to eternity. God is *Infinite Justice*.
He will reward the good forever in *Heaven,* purifying
them first, if necessary, in *Purgatory*, and will punish
the wicked forever in *Hell*. There are *three Divine
Persons*, though but one God, because these persons
possess but one nature and one essence, the same
divinity and the same divine perfections; they are in
every respect equal to one another; the Son proceeds

[1] This entire treatise is taken from St. Alph., *Exercises*, C. E.,
Vol. XV. p. 156.

from eternity from the Father, the Holy Ghost from the Father and the Son. The Son of God assumed *human nature,* body and soul, in the immaculate womb of the ever *Blessed Virgin Mary,* through the Holy Ghost, and is called *Jesus Christ,* true God and true man; Who *suffered* and *died* on the cross under Pontius Pilate, to save us from sin and hell; Who *arose* from the dead on the third day — *ascended* into heaven — and *sits* at the right hand of the Father, *i.e.,* possesses the same power in heaven as the Father — Who will *judge* the soul of every man after death, which is called the particular judgment, and on the last day, after the general resurrection of the body, when the souls are reunited again with their bodies — He will come in great majesty to judge all mankind, the living and the dead. The living (the good) He will reward forever in heaven and the dead (the bad) He will punish forever in hell. There is but *one true Church,* instituted by Jesus Christ, the Roman Catholic, outside of which there is no salvation. There is a *Communion of Saints.* All those who are in the grace of God belong to it.

## 2. THE SACRAMENTS

There are seven Sacraments, instituted by Jesus Christ, through which we receive the grace merited for us by Jesus Christ in His sufferings and death. *Baptism,* which cleanses man from original and personal sins. *Confirmation,* which imparts strength to overcome temptations, and to profess the faith without fear. In *Extreme Unction* we receive assistance against our own moral weaknesses and against the temptations of the devil at the hour of death — it remits the sins which we cannot then confess and wipes out every trace of sin — health is often restored to our bodies if its restoration benefits our eternal salvation. *Holy Orders* impart to those who are ordained the powers of the priesthood and the grace to exercise them in the manner required. *Matrimony* unites a man and a woman for life in a holy union. It gives them a supernatural love for each other and the grace to bear each other's burdens till death; also to bring up their children in the love and fear of God.

The sacrament of *Penance* is to be explained more in detail. Before confession a careful examination of conscience is to be made. Contrition, to be excited before entering the confessional, must be sincere — supernatural — universal — sovereign — and full of confidence. The difference between perfect and imperfect contrition is to be explained. To contrition must be united the purpose of amendment. It must be firm, universal, and efficacious. These qualities should be explained well. Confession of all mortal sins and of all doubtful venial sins committed since the last good confession. . . . Sins forgotten must be confessed in the first confession in which you think of them. (Difficulties which children meet in confession to be removed.) Penance to be performed in the manner imposed by the priest and without delay.

The Sacrament of the *Blessed Eucharist.* Explain: 1. What it is, namely, the body and the blood, the soul and the divinity of Jesus Christ, or Jesus Christ entirely, under the appearances of bread and wine. Explain what is meant by "appearance." 2. That Jesus Christ is entire in each little particle, when the sacred host is broken, and remains present till the sacramental species are consumed. 3. That as material nourishment preserves and strengthens the life of the body, so this spiritual food preserves and strengthens the life of the soul. 4. What preparation is to be made for receiving Holy Communion, in regard to the body and the soul.  5. Lastly, explain the way of approaching Holy Communion, of making a proper thanksgiving, and inculcate the necessity of frequent Communion.  If time permits, an instruction on the *Holy Mass* should be given.  Very few children have an idea of what the Mass is.

### 3. THE COMMANDMENTS

The explanations are to be brief.

By the *first Commandment* we are obliged to *believe* in God, and to believe all the truths of our holy religion — to *hope* in God, trusting to obtain heaven and the means of reaching it, according to His promises and through the merits of Jesus Christ; to *love* God above all things and our neighbor as ourselves.  This commandment enjoins also the duty of *prayer,* and forbids all *superstitious* practices.

The *second Commandment* forbids us to *blaspheme* God and holy things, and to *swear* a false oath.  It enjoins upon us to keep vows.

The *third Commandment* forbids *servile work* on Sundays.

The *fourth Commandment* commands *reverence, obedience,* and *love* to parents, Superiors and pastors.

The *fifth Commandment* forbids us to *wish evil* to others, to rejoice over their misfortune, *envy, jealousy, enmity, murder.*

The *sixth and ninth Commandments* forbid all that is *immodest* in thought, imagination, desire, reading, looks, listening, speaking, touches, actions, alone or with others.

The *seventh* and *tenth Commandments* forbid the *taking and the keeping* of what does not belong to you, or the *damaging* of your neighbor's property.

The *eighth Commandment* forbids *rash judgment, tale-bearing, detraction, calumny,* speaking or listening to it, abusive language, and revealing secrets.

The *Precepts of the Church* command us: 1. To keep Holy-days of obligation like Sundays. 2. To hear Mass on all Sundays and Holy-days. 3. To keep the days of fast and abstinence. 4. To go to confession and Holy Communion once a year, at Easter time. 5. To contribute toward the support of religion. 6. Not to solemnize marriage at forbidden times.

## II. THE EXHORTATION

The exhortation consists of a little sermon on the same subjects that we preach to the grown people; but we select such ideas, proofs, and illustrations as are more adapted to the capacity of children. Each exhortation should embody some striking example, and should close with the recitation of an act of contrition.

## III. GENERAL PLAN OF THE CHILDREN'S MISSION

REMARK. — The following plan is laid down for three full days, with an introduction for the opening in the evening prior to the first day, and the closing exercises, with Holy Communion, in the morning of the fourth day. Circumstances often make it necessary to limit these exercises to a shorter time. Below may be seen a shorter plan, adapted to our ordinary Missions.

Before the instruction let the director recite, with the children, the Our Father, the Hail Mary, and the Creed; — at the end, the Commandments of God, Precepts of the Church, and the Sacraments, — or the Acts of Faith, Hope, and Charity.

### INTRODUCTION

*Anecdote* of St. Anthony and the fishes at Rimini. *Necessity* of Missions for children. They think so little of their souls and eternity; they are surrounded by wicked companions; they are liable to receive the sacraments unworthily. *Extraordinary grace* of God — love of Jesus Christ for children.

*Punishment* of those who neglect it. God may abandon them; the boy that died cursing; excuses refuted. *Means:* Regular attendance; keeping from sin; prayer, recollection, daily Mass.

### FIRST DAY

*Morning Exercise.* A. *Sermon.*—On the *Importance of Salvation.* Man an *endless being* — either forever in heaven or in hell, with body and soul; the work of our salvation the *most important business;* to be attended to without delay; few succeed in it; why?

B. *Instruction.* Cursory explanation of the mysteries of Faith with special reference to the Church.

*Afternoon Exercise.* — A. *Sermon. Sin, how wicked in itself;* how *injurious* to the soul; how disastrous in its *consequences;* the fallen angels; Adam and Eve; the child that blasphemed, died, and was damned, as related by St. Gregory the Great.

B. *Instruction.* Cursory explanation of the *Commandments* of God and the *Precepts* of the Church; the *Sacraments,* except Penance and Eucharist.

### SECOND DAY

*Morning Exercise.* — A. *Sermon.* — *Death* of a *good child;* of a *bad child;* the body in the *grave;* the doves that accompanied the funeral of a good child.

B. *Instruction.* — *Confession,* its *necessity;* its *difficulties; manner* of making it; the *penance* imposed.

*Afternoon Exercise.* — A. *Sermon.* — *General Judgment;* the *resurrection;* the public *examination,* which must include a catalogue of the sins that children usually commit; *sentence* and its execution.

B. *Instruction.* — *Examination of conscience,* how

to make it; *contrition,* its qualities. *Purpose of amendment,* what it must include. *The woman* that vomited *snakes* during confession, kept one, and then died.

### THIRD DAY

*Morning Exercise.* — A. *Sermon. Hell;* the tortures of the *body, darkness, hunger, fire;* the tortures inflicted by the *devils.* Pains of the *soul, facility* of salvation, *remorse. Duration,* for all eternity. Catharine of Naples.

B. *Instruction.* — *Holy Communion,* worthy and unworthy; manner of receiving it; preparation and thanksgiving. Some fact from history of an unworthy communicant.

*Afternoon Exercise.* — A. *Sermon.* — *Heaven.* The religious that heard the little bird sing. Paraphrase of the words: "No *eye* hath ever seen, nor *ear* heard, nor hath it entered *into the heart* of any man, what God hath prepared. . . ." We are the *heirs* of heaven; its possession will never be taken from us.

Instead of this may also be preached the *Sufferings* and *Death of Christ,* stopping at the most important points and making the proper application, with a view of producing a horror of sin and a true love for Jesus Christ. The *agony* in the garden — the *flagellation* and the *crowning with thorns* — the *carrying of the cross* — the *nailing to the cross* — the *death on the cross.*

B. *Instruction.* On the Holy *Mass.* What it is; how it should be heard; when. The young man that was sent to the iron-works and heard Mass on the way.

### FOR SHORTER MISSIONS

It frequently happens that the children's Mission opens on Sunday afternoon, and closes on Wednesday noon. In this case the matter for the sermons and instructions may be abbreviated in the following manner:

*Sunday P.M.* — After an exhortation to attend well comes the *sermon* on the importance of salvation — and the *instruction* on the mysteries of faith.

*Monday A.M.* *Sermon* on sin and death — *instruction* on the Commandments and Sacraments.

*Monday P.M.* *Sermon* on judgment and hell — *instruction* on the Sacrament of Penance.

*Tuesday A.M.* *Sermon* on the Passion, or on Heaven — instruction on Holy Communion.

*Tuesday P.M.* Preparation for confession in the following manner:

## IV. Confession of the Children

Before the children go to confession they assemble in their usual place. The director admonishes them to make a good confession, and says a prayer with them to the Holy Ghost and to the Blessed Virgin for the grace of a good examination of conscience, as follows:

"Come, Holy Ghost, enlighten my mind and strengthen my heart, that I may know all my sins, detest them from my heart, sincerely confess them, and amend my life." Hail Mary.

Then the director goes through an examination of conscience with the children, pausing a little after each point — mentioning those mortal sins, and the more grievous venial sins, against the various commandments, which children are wont to commit. He concludes by making the long act of contrition with them. Then the director divides the children equally among the different confessionals; he admonishes them to say some prayers after confession, in thanksgiving, and then to go home and remain more than usually recollected, in order to prepare well for a worthy Communion.

## V. Communion of the Children

Considering all the circumstances of our position in this country, it is best to avoid all extraordinary display, such as processions, burning candles, dressing in white, veils, etc. The greater the simplicity, the more fervent is the devotion of the children. The missionary should be present to preserve order, and direct the children in the various acts of devotion.

The children assemble in a hall near the church, and thence go in procession to the church, the boys preceding the girls. If this be impracticable, they assemble at once in the church. Being arranged in their proper places, they make an *act of adoration*, the missionary admonishing them thereto, and suggesting it to them as follows: My children, you are now assembled in the presence of Jesus Christ, Whom you are to receive to-day. Make an act of profound adoration, and say: "O Jesus! in Thy most holy presence I fall on my knees and adore Thee from the bottom of my heart. I adore Thee in union with all the angels that surround the altar of this church."

"Blessed be Jesus in the most holy Sacrament, now and forever!"

### AT THE BEGINNING OF THE MASS

"Dear children, make an offering of this Mass to the Eternal Father, in union with the priest at the altar, and say:

" 'O Eternal Father! in this most holy Sacrifice of

the Mass I offer Thee Thy Son Jesus Christ, together with all His merits. I offer this Mass to the honor and glory of Thy infinite majesty.

" 'I offer it in thanksgiving for all the benefits that we have received from Thee, and I thank Thee especially to-day for having given us Thy Son Jesus in the most holy Sacrament.

" 'I offer it in atonement for all my sins, and for the sins of all the living and the souls in purgatory, to satisfy for all the outrages committed against Thy infinite majesty.

" 'I offer it to obtain the grace of a worthy Communion, holy perseverance, and eternal salvation.' "

Then the children may sing a hymn or say prayers in silence.

#### AT THE OFFERTORY OF THE MASS

"The priest now offers to God bread and wine which are to be changed into the body and blood of Jesus Christ. Unite yourselves to the offerings of the priest to God the Father, saying:

" 'O my God! I offer myself entirely to Thee, and I promise to spend my whole life in Thy most holy service. I unite this offering to the offering of the priest at the altar.' "

*After the elevation of the Sacred Host:* "O Jesus! I most profoundly adore Thy sacred body; have mercy on me, O Jesus!"

*After the elevation of the chalice:* "O Jesus! I most profoundly adore Thy most precious blood. O Jesus! cleanse me from all my sins."

*After the consecration* the director has the children repeat the following acts, pausing before each to tell the children the nature of the act, so that they know what they are saying.

*Act of faith.* — My beloved Jesus, I firmly believe that Thou art really present in the most holy Sacrament, and for this my faith I am willing to lay down my life.

*Act of hope.* — My loving Redeemer, I hope in Thy goodness that, coming to me to-day, Thou wilt inflame my soul with Thy holy love, and grant me all those graces which I need for my eternal salvation.

*Act of love.* — O my Jesus! the love of my soul, I love Thee above all things with my whole heart. It is the most ardent desire of my soul to spend my entire life in serving and loving Thee.

*Act of contrition.* — O my Jesus! how can I dare approach Thy holy altar to receive Thee into my heart? I know that I have offended Thee. I have deserved hell, and to be abandoned by Thee. Pardon me, O Jesus! and forgive me all the sins that I have ever committed, and grant me the grace never more to offend Thee.

*Act of desire.* — Come, then, O Jesus! come into my soul; it longs to receive Thee. O Jesus! come and unite Thyself to me, and do not let me be separated from Thee again.

*Act of humility.* — O Lord! I am not worthy that Thou shouldst enter under my roof; speak but the word, and my soul shall be healed. (This sentence should be repeated when the priest says the first *Domine non sum dignus.*)

May the body and blood of our Lord Jesus Christ preserve my soul unto life everlasting. Amen.

O Blessed Virgin Mary, my holy Mother, my dear Guardian Angel, and all ye, my blessed Patron Saints, come now and guide me to Jesus, my love and my all!

The catechist should recite the *Confiteor* himself

with a loud voice, and answer the *Misereatur* and *Indulgentiam.*[2]

### ACT OF COMMUNION

The children should go to the altar-railing and return in good order. During Communion the choir may sing some pious hymns.

### THANKSGIVING AFTER COMMUNION

The following acts are recited with pauses and explanations, in the same manner as the preparatory acts.

*Act of adoration.* — O Jesus! I firmly believe that Thou art really present within me. I adore Thee, I cast myself at Thy feet, I embrace Thee, I press Thee to my heart. O Jesus! may I ever be united with Thee.

*Act of thanksgiving.* — O Jesus! I thank Thee with all my heart for having deigned to enter my soul to-day. Oh! what happiness for me to have Jesus Christ within my breast! All ye angels and saints of heaven, help me to thank Jesus for His love and condescension.

*Act of love.* — O divine Love! Thou art come to visit me with so much love. I give Thee my will, my liberty, my whole self. Henceforth I desire to live only for Thee. May my body and my soul, my powers, my senses, all be employed only in serving and pleasing Thee.

*Act of petition.* — O my Jesus! I beseech Thee to grant me all the graces necessary for my salvation. Give me a constant sorrow for my sins; give me light to see the vanities of the world, the deceits of the devil, and the strength to avoid them. Grant that I may always love Thee and never more offend

[2] *Exercises,* C. E., Vol. XV. p. 151.

Thee. Grant me the grace of holy perseverance to the end of my life. Grant me a happy death and life everlasting.

I also recommend to Thee my parents, relatives, and friends, all those who are living in sin, and the souls in purgatory.

#### RECOMMENDATION TO THE BLESSED VIRGIN MARY

O sweet Mother Mary! take me to-day under thy special protection, that henceforth I may always remain a worthy dwelling for thy divine Son Jesus Christ, and that my soul may never be defiled again by a single sin.

*To gain the plenary indulgence,* recite together six [3] *Paters, Aves, Glorias,* and one *Credo.*

## VI. CLOSING EXERCISE

This exercise comes either in immediate connection with the thanksgiving, or a later hour of the day may be selected for it. It consists of the following:

1. *The closing exhortation,* which comprises the means of perseverance. These are for children: *a.* Strict *obedience* to parents, guardians, pastors; *b.* Constant *prayer,* especially morning and evening, before and after meals, and in temptation; *c. Monthly Communion; d.* Flight from *danger,* evil companions, books, amusements, etc. *e.* Constant devotion to the *Blessed Virgin Mary,* confraternity, medal, scapulars, etc., especially professing ourselves as her children. For this purpose follows here the

---

[3] This extra *Pater, Ave* and *Gloria* was added by St. Alphonsus to the number usually required to gain the indulgence, for the Bishop, the civil authorities, the parish priest and all priests, and for the missionaries. — C. E., Vol. XV. p. 155.

### ACT OF DEDICATION [4]

O most holy Mary, my Mother and my hope! on this day I dedicate myself to thee; after God, I wish to belong to thee, and to spend the rest of my life in serving thee. Be thou my Mother! May I always be thy child. I place under thy maternal protection my body and my soul. To thee I give my mind, my will and my memory, that I may never indulge in any sinful thought. Into thy hands I place my eyes, my ears and my tongue, that I may never look upon, listen to, or say anything displeasing to God. To thee I give my hands and my feet, that they may never become the instruments of sin. O most blessed Lady! let me not become again the slave of hell. Assist me in every temptation. Never forsake me until thou seest me before thy glorious throne in heaven, where I shall love, praise, and thank thee for all thy tender mercies toward me, thy poor child, for all eternity. Amen.

Then may follow a hymn to the Blessed Virgin; after which the Papal benediction is given and the prayers for the plenary indulgence are recited. Finally, the articles of devotion are blessed, and those who wish may be invested with the scapulars.

If this children's Mission be given by itself, after the Papal benediction the missionary makes an appropriate farewell address, which is followed by the benediction with the Blessed Sacrament.[5]

---

[4] The candles on the Blessed Virgin's altar should be lighted for this act.

[5] St. Alphonsus used to close this exercise with a beautiful ceremony. He had the benediction given with the ciborium, and while the tabernacle was being closed, he exhorted the children to lock up their hearts with Jesus in the tabernacle; then he took out the key, and placed it into the hands of the statue of the Blessed Virgin. — *Exercises*, C. E., Vol. XV. p. 155.

# APPENDIX I

## PRAYERS BEFORE AND AFTER THE INSTRUCTIONS

*Our Father — Hail Mary — I believe in God*

### THE TEN COMMANDMENTS OF GOD

(According to the Catechism of the Third Plenary Council of Baltimore.)

1. I am the Lord thy God, who brought thee out of the land of Egypt, out of the house of bondage. Thou shalt not have strange gods before me. Thou shalt not make to thyself a graven thing, nor the likeness of anything that is in heaven above, or in the earth beneath, nor of those things that are in the waters under the earth. Thou shalt not adore them, nor serve them.

2. Thou shalt not take the name of the Lord thy God in vain.

3. Remember thou keep holy the Sabbath day.

4. Honor thy father and thy mother.

5. Thou shalt not kill.

6. Thou shalt not commit adultery.

7. Thou shalt not steal.

8. Thou shalt not bear false witness against thy neighbor.

9. Thou shalt not covet thy neighbor's wife.

10. Thou shalt not covet thy neighbor's goods.

## The Chief Precepts of the Church

1. To hear Mass on Sundays and holy-days of obligation.

2. To fast and abstain on the days appointed.

3. To confess at least once a year.

4. To receive the Holy Eucharist during the Easter time.

5. To contribute to the support of our pastors.

6. Not to marry persons who are not Catholics, or who are related to us within the third degree of kindred, nor privately without witnesses, nor to solemnize marriage at forbidden times.

## The Seven Sacraments

Baptism, Confirmation, Holy Eucharist, Penance, Extreme Unction, Holy Orders and Matrimony.

## The Christian Acts

*Act of Faith.* — O my God! I firmly believe that Thou art one God in three Divine persons, Father, Son and Holy Ghost; I believe that Thy Divine Son became man, and died for our sins, and that He will come to judge the living and the dead. I believe these and all the truths which the Holy Catholic Church teaches, because Thou hast revealed them, who canst neither deceive nor be deceived.

*Act of Hope.* — O my God! relying on Thy infinite goodness and promises, I hope to obtain pardon of my sins, the help of Thy grace, and life everlasting, through the merits of Jesus Christ, my Lord and Redeemer.

*Act of Love.* — O my God! I love Thee above all things, with my whole heart and soul, because Thou art all-good and worthy of all love. I love my neighbor as myself for the love of Thee. I forgive all who have injured me, and ask pardon of all whom I have injured.

*Act of Contrition.* — O my God! I am heartily sorry for having offended Thee, and I detest all my sins, because I dread the loss of heaven and the pains of hell, but most of all because they offend Thee, my God, who art all-good and deserving of all my love. I firmly resolve, with the help of Thy grace, to confess my sins, to do penance, and to amend my life.

### Short Act of Contrition by St. Leonard of Port Maurice

O my God! I am very sorry for having sinned against Thee, because Thou art so good; and I will not sin again.

# APPENDIX II

## CARE OF THE IGNORANT AND OF CONVERTS

### I. INSTRUCTION OF THE IGNORANT AND OF CONVERTS

In connection with the children's Mission, is also to be mentioned the *extraordinary instruction* given to the ignorant and to converts. In many places, especially in large cities, there are numbers of adults of both sexes entirely destitute of religious instruction, and therefore wholly incapable of receiving any sacrament. The Mission is the only occasion on which they are found out, and when they, for the first time, manifest a real desire of saving their souls. For these, the instructions and sermons of the Mission are insufficient. Hence a Father is generally appointed to give them special instructions, unless one of the priests of the place is willing to take charge of them; this, however, is rarely the case. To this instruction are admitted also those who manifest a desire to join the Church, if the pastor does not wish to take them under his special care.[1]

These instructions comprise the same subjects as the instructions given to the children, with this difference, that they must be more explicit. They generally begin on the third or fourth day of the Mission, or with the men's Mission, if the sexes are

[1] The most practical advice to missionaries with regard to the instruction and reception of converts on the Mission in this country is found, at great length, in Father Weninger's *Winke*.

divided. They are begun in the evening when the Rosary instruction begins, and close in time to let those in attendance go to the evening sermon. They should be continued almost to the close of the Mission, so as to give these people the most necessary knowledge of their Christian duties, and yet give them time to receive the sacraments before the Mission closes.

In places in which many adults are found who have not received Confirmation, we ask the bishop of the diocese to administer this sacrament to them during or at the end of the Mission. We give them the necessary instructions in the evening instead of the introduction to the Rosary, once or twice. This instruction must be duly announced.

## II. Short Catechism for the Ignorant

A Christian should know, at least, how to make the sign of the cross, to say the Our Father, the Hail Mary, the Apostles' Creed, and a short act of contrition. He should also know the Commandments of God and of the Church, at least what is commanded and what is forbidden by them, and the most essential points about those sacraments which he has received and is to receive. All this is contained in the foregoing instructions for children.

Every one should be able to answer the following questions, which are taken from the works of St. Alphonsus:

1. Who created the world and everything in it?
A. God.
2. Is there more than one God?
A. There is but one God.
3. How many persons are in God?

A. Three: the Father, the Son, and the Holy Ghost — equal to one another in everything. Each of the three persons is God — yet there is but one God.

4. Who is Jesus Christ?

A. God the Son, the true God and true man, who through the Holy Ghost assumed human nature in the immaculate womb of the Blessed Virgin Mary.

5. What did Jesus Christ do for men?

A. He died on the cross, to redeem us from hell, and to merit for us life everlasting.

6. Where will the good go after death?

A. To heaven, to enjoy forever the happiness of God.

7. What will become of the wicked?

A. They will be cast into hell, to suffer eternal torments.

8. What must a Christian believe?

A. He must believe all that the Holy Roman Catholic Church teaches.

9. What must a Christian do?

A. He must keep the commandments of God and of the Church.

10. How does a Christian obtain pardon for his sins?

A. By a good confession.

11. What do we receive in Holy Communion?

A. The body and the blood of Jesus Christ.

12. Is Holy Communion necessary?

A. It is as necessary for the soul as nourishment is for the body.

More explicit instruction is to be given about the manner of going to confession and to Holy Communion.

## III. Useful Remarks about Ignorant People

The number of ignorant persons, even among Catholics, is alarmingly great in this country. They generally consist of those who have never received any other sacrament after baptism, because their religious training was utterly neglected from childhood. The Mission is the only opportunity when these poor souls can be gained to God. Therefore, they are a special object of the missionary's apostolic charity and solicitude.

It is not necessary, however, that such persons, in order to be admitted to the sacraments, know how to *express* themselves in clear words in regard to what they have heard and learned in their special instructions. It is enough that they can be reasonably supposed to *know* and to *believe* what they have been taught.

In reference to this matter Frasinetti says: "There are many who, if questioned in the ordinary manner on the mysteries of faith, remain confused and silent; but if asked in a different form, they give quite satisfactory answers. If you ask what is meant by the *Unity* and *Trinity* of God, the *Incarnation,* the *Passion* and *Death* of Jesus Christ, they fail to give an adequate reply. Ask, on the contrary: *Are there several Gods or only one? Are those Christians or unbelievers who adore the Father, the Son, and the Holy Ghost as one God? Was Jesus Christ born of the Blessed Virgin Mary or St. Elizabeth? Was it on the cross that Jesus Christ died or elsewhere? etc.* — and you will in most cases receive the correct reply." [2]

Nor is everybody so ignorant in reality as he may

[2] *Parish Priest's Manual,* p. ii, c. vi.

be regarded when met with the first time. The same author says: "It would be extremely difficult to find a Christian ignorant of the Unity of God, who has never heard God spoken of in the Plural. The same must be said of the Trinity, when we reflect that he has heard it mentioned thousands of times, and has been taught to make the sign of the cross. Times without number a Catholic sees the image of Mary with the infant in her arms, the crucifix, etc. Therefore, he is after all not so ignorant as at first supposed. This may tranquilize those confessors who insist on having a general confession made, because of the ignorance of the mysteries of faith which they discover in their penitents." [3]

Cardinal Gousset says the same: "In a Catholic country, where the exercises of religion are publicly practised; where the sign of the cross is continually made; where the cross and the crucifix are to be met with in the churches, in the houses . . . it is difficult for Catholics to be ignorant of the great mysteries of faith to such an extent that the absolution given to them would be invalid. It is certain that they may know and believe these mysteries, without being able to give expression to their knowledge." [4]

## IV. Some Remarks about Converts

Although it is more advisable to leave converts to the care of the local pastors, yet there are many reasons why it is better that the missionaries instruct and receive them into the Church.

Many pastors are too much occupied with other work, or find the instruction of converts too labo-

[3] Ibidem.
[4] *Theologia Moralis,* v. 2, n. 573. See St. Alph., *Prax. Conf.* n. 22. — Konings, *Mor.* n. 259.

rious — or they prefer to have the missionaries do this work. Those converts themselves wish to benefit by the Mission. For a long time, perhaps, they have desired to take this step, but have not had sufficient courage to do so; they would prefer to make their confession to a missionary, for which the opportunity is now offered; or there is some other reason why such people should be received before the close of the Mission. Once they have made their confession and Communion, the chief and the most difficult task is fulfilled, and they find it easy to practise their religion afterward.

But this precaution should be taken, namely, to leave them in the care of some practical Catholic, who at the same time could be their god-father, and who will assist them with timely advice and direction; and to make them acquainted with the pastor, to whom they must in future entrust themselves as to their spiritual Father.

Let the missionary, therefore, into whose hands such converts happen to fall, either instruct them himself, or, after giving them the necessary encouragement, introduce them to the Father who is in charge of this instruction.

The chief points in which they must be instructed are: the Infallible Church, in which they must implicitly believe and which they must obey; the Sacraments of Baptism, Eucharist and Penance; especially the Mass — and devotion to the Blessed Virgin Mary. They hear all the practical points of religion in the sermons and instructions.

# APPENDIX III

## EXAMINATION OF CONSCIENCE

*Explanation.* — To assist the people in the examination of their conscience, the following catalogue of questions is read to them during each of the two Masses that immediately precede the morning instructions on one or more of the first few days of the Mission. The reading must be slow, distinct, and with short pauses, interposing at the principal parts of the Mass appropriate acts of devotion.

### PRAYERS TO BE SAID AT THE VARIOUS PARTS OF THE MASS, FOR WHICH OTHERS MAY BE SUBSTITUTED

*At the beginning of the Mass.* — O Eternal Father! we offer to Thee this Mass in atonement for our sins. Send Thy Holy Spirit into our hearts, that through His divine light we may know, detest, and sincerely confess all our sins.

*At the Offertory.* — Receive, O Eternal Father! through the hands of the priest, these sacred offerings; grant us full pardon of our sins, and all the graces necessary for our eternal salvation.

*At the "Hanc igitur."* — Let us renew our faith in the Real Presence of Jesus Christ in the most Blessed Eucharist, and most humbly adore the sacred body and the precious blood of Jesus, now to be present on the altar. (Kneel in silence.)

*At the Communion.* — O most loving Jesus! come to me, poor sinner that I am; enter my soul with Thy purifying grace, that, being cleansed from my sins by the Sacrament of Penance, I may become worthy to receive Thy sacred body and blood in Holy Communion.

*Concluding Prayer.* — O my God! I thank Thee for having made known to me my sins. Grant me the grace of a sincere sorrow for all the sins that I have ever committed, and a firm resolution to sin no more and to avoid the occasions of sin. Assist me also in making a sincere and contrite confession. This I most humbly ask of Thee through the merits of Jesus Christ and the intercession of the Blessed Virgin Mary. Amen.

## EXAMINATION

### PRELIMINARY QUESTIONS

When did you make your last good confession — fulfil the penance? Did you make a sacrilegious confession? How many times? Did you make an unworthy Communion? How many times? Did you receive Confirmation or Matrimony in the state of mortal sin?

### FIRST COMMANDMENT

1. *Against faith.* — Did you wilfully remain ignorant of your religion? — deny your faith? — doubt an article of faith? — speak against your religion or any point of doctrine? — read Protestant or infidel books? — join non-Catholics in their worship, public or private? — neglect to receive Confirmation? Have you been ashamed to practise your religion? If guilty in any of these points — how many times?

2. *Against hope.* — Did you presume on God's mercy? — despair of salvation? — lose confidence in

God in times of trial — neglect prayer altogether, or for a considerable time? If guilty — how many times?

3. *Against the love of God.* — Did you conceive an actual hatred against God? — look upon God as a tyrant? — desire that there were no God? If guilty — how many times?

4. *Against the worship of God.* Did you commit sacrilege by violating persons or things consecrated to God? — believe in superstitious practices? — perform them, or have them performed by others? — take part in meetings of spiritualists? — give love-drinks? — invoke the devil? — perform acts of witchcraft? If guilty — how many times?

Ask pardon of God for all your sins committed against this Commandment, and firmly resolve not to commit them again.

## Second Commandment

1. *By blasphemy.* — Did you make use of insulting language against God? — Jesus Christ? — the crucifix? — the Blessed Sacrament? — the Blessed Virgin Mary? — the saints? — sacred relics? — pictures? — sacred ceremonies? — speak in mockery of them? — murmur against Divine Providence? — ridicule piety or religious practices? — misbehave during divine service, thereby disturbing others? If guilty, how many times?

2. *By perjury.* — Did you swear a false or rash oath? — in doubtful matters? — committing thereby an act of injustice? — habitually swear by the name of God or Jesus Christ? — make a false promise under oath? — break a promise made under oath? — induce or cause others to commit perjury? If guilty — how many times?

3. *By the violation of vows.* — Did you break a

vow? — delay its fulfilment? — illegally break a matrimonial engagement, or unreasonably delay its fulfilment? If guilty — how many times?

4. *By cursing.* — Did you utter an imprecation against yourself or others, prayers, etc.? Are you in the habit of using profane language, without making efforts to get rid of it? If guilty, how often — how long have you had this bad habit?

Ask pardon of God for all your sins committed against this Commandment, and firmly resolve not to commit them again.

### Third Commandment and the Precepts of the Church

1. *Servile work.* — Did you, without lawful excuse, perform servile work on Sundays or Holy-days of obligation? — how often? Did you have it done by others? — how many?

2. *Hearing Mass.* — Did you, without lawful excuse, miss Mass on such days entirely? or a considerable part of it? — how often? — keep others from it? — how many? — purposely stay from sermons and instructions? — how long?

3. *Fast and abstinence.* — Did you, without lawful excuse, eat flesh-meat on Fridays and days of fast? — how often? — give it to others? — how many? — violate the prescribed fast? — how often?

4. *Easter duties.* — Did you miss your duty of annual confession and Easter Communion? — how many years?

5. *Support of religion.* — Did you contribute your share in supporting church and pastor? How long have you neglected it? — prevent others from doing it? — how many?

6. *Secret societies.* — Did you join or favor a secret society prohibited by the Church?

7. *Christian marriage.* — Did you marry out of the Church? — ask for dispensations in this matter without good reasons? — marry with some impediment known to yourself, without dispensation? Are you at present living in a marriage which you know to be null? — how long? Did you encourage others to do so? — how many?

Ask pardon of God, etc.

## Fourth Commandment

1. *For husband and wife.* — Did you in any way sin against the sacred laws of matrimony? — cause or give way to jealousy? — ruin the temporal or spiritual happiness of your partner of life? — abandon each other or cause an unhappy separation? — If guilty — how many times?

2. *For parents.* — Did you endanger the life of your children before, at, or after birth? — neglect their bodily welfare? — let them grow up without sufficient religious training? — neglect or delay too long their Baptism? — confession? — First Communion? — Confirmation? — Extreme Unction when sick and dying? — neglect to instruct them in the most essential points of religion? — their prayers? — to send them to Mass? — catechism? — endanger their morals by bad example? — allow them bad company, sinful amusements, dangerous reading? — let them work in places dangerous to their faith and morals? — unreasonably prevent them from a certain marriage? — force them to another? — keep them from following a higher vocation? — neglect to correct their evil habits? — curse them? — give way to prejudice against step-children? If guilty — how many times?

3. *For children.* — Did you always respect, love, and obey your parents in all matters of importance? — keep seasonable hours? — promise or contract marriage without their knowledge and advice? Did you curse — threaten — strike — despise — ill-treat — ridicule them? — use harsh words toward them? — behave rudely toward them? — publish their faults? — revile them? — refuse to speak to them? — wish them misfortune, sickness, death? — refuse to work for them? — abandon them? — neglect to pray for their souls? Have you been ashamed of them? If guilty — how often?

4. *For masters and employers.* — Did you overburden your servants or employees with work? — refuse them the necessary nourishment? — their due wages? — discharge them without just reason? — before the appointed time? — to their great disadvantage? Allow them to keep dangerous company and frequent places of sinful amusement? If guilty — how often?

5. *For servants and employees.* — Did you treat your masters and employers with the proper respect and the obedience due to them? — diligently perform the work for which you were hired, without wasting or stealing their property? — without absolute necessity, remain in the service of those who endangered your morals or would not allow you to comply with your religious duties? If guilty, how often, or how long?

6. *For parishioners and subjects in general.* Did you show great disrespect toward your bishop or pastor? — disregard their ordinances? — destroy the confidence of others in them? — raise factions, or take part with the seditious and disaffected? Did you show the proper submission to the civil authorities? — take part in mobs — lynching-parties? — offer vio-

lent resistance to the law? — practise fraud in elections? If guilty — how often?

Ask pardon of God, etc.

## Fifth Commandment

1. *Against yourself.* — Did you, without necessity, considerably impair your health or recklessly expose yourself to danger of death? Had you an intention of destroying yourself or did you wish for your own death? — curse yourself? — give way to violent anger and passion? Have you been guilty of drunkenness? If guilty, how many times?

2. *Against your neighbor.* — Did you give way to envy— hatred — desire of revenge — contempt for others? How many times, and how long? Wish your neighbor evil? — rejoice over his misfortune? Did you grossly abuse others? — injure them by blows, wounds? — intend to commit murder? — carry out your nefarious design? Were you in any way accessory to such a crime?— cause the death of an innocent child? If guilty — how many times?

3. *Sins of scandal.* — Did you cause others to sin by your conduct or conversation? — by wearing immodest dress? — by making lascivious presents? — writing improper letters? — getting up sinful amusements or leading others to them? — causing others to become intoxicated? — did you lead, drive, or show any one to places of sin? — dissuade others from changing their sinful life? If guilty — how often?

Ask pardon of God, etc.

## Sixth and Ninth Commandments

1. *Sins of the heart.* — Did you wilfully dwell on impure thoughts, imaginations, desires? — think of

carrying them out? — what was their object? If guilty — how often?

2. *Sins of the eyes.* — Did you gaze at immodest objects? — of what kind? — read dangerous, obscene papers, books? If guilty— how many times?

3. *Sins of the ears.* — Did you delight in listening to impure songs and conversation? If guilty — how many times?

4. *Sins of the tongue.* — Did you use immodest language? — of double meaning? — sing immodest songs? How many and what persons were present? If guilty — how often?

5. *Sins of action.* — Did you frequent sinful amusements? — keep up a sinful acquaintance? — take or permit sinful familiarities? Did you commit an impure act? — alone? — with others? — with relatives? —with those whose position would considerably change the nature of your crime? with an irrational creature? If guilty — how many times?

Ask pardon of God, etc.

## Seventh and Tenth Commandments

1. *By dishonest acquisition.* — Did you commit theft? — of what value? — of things consecrated to God's service?— from rich or poor? If guilty — how many times?

2. *By causing damage.* — Did you ruin your neighbor's property? — to what extent? — carry on unjust lawsuits? — try to gain by unjust means? — engage in reckless speculation? — ruin the interests of others by defamation? If guilty — how often?

3. *By retaining ill-gotten goods.* — Did you neglect to pay your debts? — profit by bankruptcy? — retain things found? — keep things borrowed from others or

deposited with you? — neglect to satisfy parties whom you injured by wounds? — rape? — fornication? — adultery? — murder? — refuse alms to the needy? If guilty— how often?

4. *By unjust co-operation.* — Did you influence — command — advise — encourage —assist others in stealing or doing damage? How often?

5. *By contracts.* — Did you, without just cause, break a contract — refuse, delay, unjustly lessen the wages due to your servants? — take a legacy to which you were not entitled? — execute a will contrary to the wishes of the testator? — have it annulled without just reason? Did you charge exorbitant prices — interest — sell adulterated articles? — buy stolen goods? — cheat in weight and measure? — make out false bills? pass counterfeit money? — cheat at games? — negligently perform the work for which you were hired? — neglect to correct mistakes in receiving over-change or money paid above your due? — take remunerations — obtain insurance-money, without being entitled to them? in dealing with others, take advantage of their ignorance or their distress? If guilty — how often?

6. *By public officials, lawyers, physicians, etc.* Did you qualify yourself for your position? — conscientiously attend to your duty? — unnecessarily prolong your services? — protract lawsuits? — do justice to all? — spend extravagantly the public money or put it to your own use? — make unnecessary, exorbitant charges? If guilty — how often?

Ask pardon of God, etc.

### Eighth Commandment

1. *By rash judgment.* — Did you entertain rash suspicions against others? — form a rash judgment against

any one? — entertain, without good reason, contempt for others? — communicate your suspicions to others? If guilty — how many times, and how long each time?

2. *By detraction.* — Did you make known the secret faults, defects, sins of others? — inquire into their faults? — make known the crimes of others in a country in which they were yet unknown? — speak disparagingly of your neighbor? — try to lessen his merits in the eyes of others? If guilty — how often, of how many and to how many?

3. *By calumny.* — Did you belie any one? — spread false reports against his character? — put an evil construction on what others said or did? — distort their intentions? If guilty — how often, and to how many?

4. *By listening to evil-talkers.* — Did you give a willing ear to slander or calumny? — enjoy it? — laugh at it? — add something of your own to it? If guilty — how many times?

5. *Under aggravating circumstances.* — Did you speak against men of ecclesiastical dignity? — religious? — against other men in high positions? — or listen to such language against them? If guilty — how often?

6. *By contumely.* — Did you insult others? — privately or publicly? — or speak insultingly of them in their absence, yet so that they should or could hear it? If guilty — how often?

7. *By violating secrets.* — Did you, without just cause, reveal secrets committed to you? — open your neighbor's letters? If guilty — how often?

Did you repair the injury thus caused to your neighbor's reputation, as far as it lay in your power?

Ask pardon of God, etc.

# THE REDEMPTORIST ON THE AMERICAN MISSIONS

## Vol. II

# THE REDEMPTORIST

ON THE

# AMERICAN MISSIONS

## VOL. II

CONTAINING THE DIRECTIONS AND SKETCHES FOR
THE VARIOUS EXERCISES GIVEN BY THE
REDEMPTORIST FATHERS IN THIS
COUNTRY ON

## RENEWALS

BY

## JOSEPH WISSEL, C.SS.R.

THIRD REVISED EDITION

PRIVATELY PRINTED

1920

THE PLIMPTON PRESS
NORWOOD·MASS·U·S·A

# CONTENTS

## FIRST PART

### DIRECTIONS FOR RENEWALS AND KINDRED EXERCISES

## SECOND PART

### SERMONS FOR THE RENEWAL OF THE MISSION

#### (First Series)

## THIRD PART

### SERMONS FOR THE RENEWAL OF THE MISSION

#### (Second Series)

## FOURTH PART

### INSTRUCTIONS FOR RENEWALS

## FIFTH PART

### SERMONS FOR MISSIONS AND RENEWALS GIVEN ON CERTAIN OCCASIONS

# FIRST PART

# DIRECTIONS FOR RENEWALS AND KINDRED EXERCISES

# THE REDEMPTORIST

## ON THE

# AMERICAN MISSIONS

## CHAPTER I

### RENEWAL OF THE MISSION

#### 1. Object and Necessity of the Renewal

Before the time of St. Alphonsus Renewals of Missions were unknown. He was the first to see the necessity of a repetition of the exercises of the Missions, as well as of a renovation of the good spirit produced by them.[1] The Renewal of the Mission, a special fruit of the apostolic zeal of our holy Founder, has been kept up in the Congregation, and has been highly appreciated as a special inheritance by all our missionaries ever since his time.[2] The character of the Renewal differs in some respects from that of the Mission. This is clearly seen from its peculiar object, which is threefold: 1. To give more solidity to the work of the Mission, and to bring it nearer to perfection. 2. To encourage the relapsed, to reconcile them again, and to render their perseverance more

---

[1] Villecourt, vol. i. ch. 53.

[2] Redemptorists are the only missionaries that give Renewals, properly so called. The Jesuits call Renewals the Missions that they give in places in which they have given missions some years previously. See Van de Kerckhove, *Manuale Missionum*, and Weninger, *Die hl. Mission*. Still, F. Weninger speaks of a different course of sermons for his Renewals.

secure.   3. To give another opportunity to those
who neglected the Mission, or who were prevented by
some obstacle or other from attending it.

In reference to the first object, it is to be remarked
that the many and extraordinary conversions produced by the Mission are very rarely so permanent
as not to be followed by a relapse. The deep impressions made by the sermons are gradually effaced,
old sinful nature gains strength in proportion, the
will becomes weaker, the attractions of the world
stronger, and the attacks of hell more violent. A repetition of the exercises of the Mission restores the
good spirit, and fills all with a stronger determination
to make good use of the means of perseverance. Besides, the final object of every Mission is to put the
true love of God into the hearts of the people. Now,
all that the Mission proper can effect is to fill their
hearts with the fear of God and His judgments. To
lead them directly to the love of God, then, is the
special object of the Renewal. *"Finis præcepti est
charitas de corde puro."* [3] So, likewise, is it the work
of the Mission to deter from sin, while the Renewal
tends more toward implanting virtue.

The second object often makes the Renewal a real
necessity. Those who have fallen back into their
old sins are generally afraid to appear before their
own priests for confession. They are, therefore, again
exposed to the greatest danger of letting years pass
by before they approach the sacraments. The return
of the missionaries gives them courage. They try
again, take greater precautions, and they are more
successful.

The third object for which the Renewal is given
is to reach certain classes of people. They are: those

[3] I Tim. i. 5.

who, at the time of the Mission, were absent from home, or who were kept away by sickness; the neglectful, the wicked, the abandoned, who, of their own accord, stayed from the Mission or the greater part of the exercises; and, finally, those who made bad confessions at the Mission.

From all this it is evident that the Mission should invariably be followed by the Renewal. It is precisely for these reasons that Renewals are more readily accepted by us than Missions, and that the former are to be given even in preference to the latter. Hence, it becomes an important duty for the missionaries to give the Mission with which they are charged, in such a manner as to induce the pastor of the congregation to ask for the Renewal of his own accord.

Father General says: "*Superiores . . . non acceptent missionem pro eo tempore, quo alibi Renovatio acceptata est . . . quinimo, superveniente Renovationis petitione, Missionem acceptatam, si commode fieri potest differant.*" [4]

## 2. Conditions Required to Make the Renewal a Success

In order to make the Renewal successful, three conditions, particularly mentioned in the Rule, are to be fulfilled.[5]

The first is, that it be not *delayed* too long: "*Redeant infra spatium ad summum quatuor aut quinque mensium.*" The Mission must still be fresh in the minds of the people. They should still recollect the principal sermons and instructions. This is the foundation on which the edifice of the Renewal is to be built. In

---

[4] Mauron, *Litt. Circulares*, VII. iii, p. 10.
[5] R., n. 153; Prov. Stat. p. 82.

case of a longer delay this foundation has to be laid again, and, beyond this, nothing can be done; consequently, the work of the Mission never reaches any degree of perfection. Besides, in case the Renewal be delayed, most of the people relapse into their old sins, and it requires double the amount of work, of patience, and of endurance to convert them again. Experience proves that the majority of those converted at the Mission remain steadfast for about four or five months, then they begin to neglect the means of perseverance, and consequently fall into sin again. It is precisely at this time that the Renewal should come to their assistance, support their weakness, and fortify them for the future.

The second condition is, that *the same missionaries* give the Renewal that gave the Mission, at least in great part. "*Spiritus renovationes iidem Patres, si fieri potest, instituent, qui missioni interfuerunt.*" [6] It is astonishing what effect is produced by this. The work is already half done. The same confidence exists among pastor, missionaries, and people; so also the same love, the same fervor. Everybody feels at home from the very beginning, which is not the case when strange missionaries come. " If this condition be overlooked," says Father Desurmont, C.SS.R.,[7] " the Renewal is deprived of one of its most essential elements, one singularly beneficial in gaining the object of these exercises." Our experience in this country proves the truth of this.

The third condition is, that the exercises of the Renewal *differ from those of the Mission*, in all that regards form, and at least the half of them as regards matter. "*Peracturi aliquod aliud exercitium publicum ser-*

[6] R., n. 155.
[7] *Pastoral for Redemptorists*, lib. 18, c. 22.

*monum.*" [8]    Should the people discover that the exercises are the same as those of the Mission, they will easily excuse themselves from attending regularly.    Yet, special regard must be had to the time which has elapsed between the Mission and the Renewal, and to the moral state of the congregation during that time.    In general, let it be understood that it requires more prudence, tact and skill to give a Renewal with proper effect, than a Mission.

[8] R., n. 153.

## CHAPTER II

THE Renewal is divided and subdivided in the same manner as the Mission. It treats: 1. On man's last end and his *Conversion*, which is to be effected through motives of fear and love; to the latter, however, more prominence is given in the Renewal. 2. On *Perseverance* through positive and negative means. The selection of the various subjects depends, in a great measure, on what was preached during the Mission, by whom, in what manner, and with what effect. Whatever deficiency had to be permitted at the Mission, owing to want of time or good preachers, is to be remedied and supplied in the Renewal. Also the time which has elapsed since the Mission is to be taken into consideration, as well as the change which may have taken place in the congregation. If, for some grave reasons, more than six months have elapsed since the Mission, or if the greater portion of the congregation is new, the Renewal should not differ much from the Mission; it may be a simple repetition of the same exercises. That this is properly no "Renewal" is evident.

It is said above that the object of the Renewal is man's *Conversion*. This word has in some respects a different meaning here from what it has in the Mission. Here it means conversion from a life ordinarily free from mortal sin to a life of true piety, from a life wavering between God and sin to a life of determination in the service of God, and it also includes conversion from relapse and from a life of sin in regard to those who did not make the Mission or did not make it as they should. All this must be kept in view in arranging the plan of sermons and in composing and preaching the sermons. *Sin* must again be denounced as the greatest evil, this time the sermon including also venial sin. The people are again to reflect on the *Eternal Truths;* but the consolations derived from the consideration of them are now to be made more conspicuous. The motives of *love* must also occupy a more prominent part in the Renewal than at the Mission. With reference to *Perseverance*, it is necessary to warn against *Relapse*, by pointing out the ways of the powers of darkness in drawing away again from God souls that are converted. Finally, such subjects are to be preached as may be needed for the *Instruction* of the people.

The Renewal is to be shorter than the Mission. "*Exercitium brevius . . . per paucos tantum dies.*" [1]

At the time of St. Alphonsus [2] Renewals did not last a week. The old Rule confines them within the limits "*trium quatuorve dierum.*" [3] With us they should last a full week, but not go beyond that. Our Missions are shorter, therefore the Renewal should be longer, to make up for the deficiency of the former in regard to certain matters that had to be curtailed in the Mission.

---

[1] R., n. 153, 155.

[2] Villecourt says that the Fathers preached on the same subjects at the Renewal as they did on the Missions. Tannoja says the contrary, that they preached more on the abuse of grace, the danger of relapse, etc. The latter deserves more to be believed, as he was a contemporary of St. Alphonsus. The Saint also directed that the sermons at the Renewal should be shorter and less frequent than at the Mission.     [3] Codex C.SS.R., n. 149.

The order of sermons at the Renewal may be arranged in the following manner:

1. *Introductory Sermon*, which explains the object of the Renewal, refutes the objections supposed to be made, and gives the means for making it well.

This sermon can scarcely be omitted, because many people cannot understand why another Mission should follow so soon. Many of the less fervent do not feel inclined to attend the Renewal, and, therefore, absent themselves, either on account of a certain indifference which induces them to think that one Mission is sufficient for them, or because they have relapsed into sin, and are, therefore, completely discouraged to attempt another.

2. *The End of Man*. In the Mission the "Importance of Salvation" was preached, because that subject speaks more forcibly to the soul in the state of sin. In the present discourse, the real object of man's creation is explained, namely: To know and to serve God for His own sake, and thereby to work out our own salvation.

3. *Sin in general*, as in direct opposition to man's last end. This subject includes venial and mortal sin. The love of God and the love of sin, although the sin be only venial, yet deliberate, are incompatible. To give the people a horror and detestation for both is the main object of this sermon. For special reasons that prevail in certain places, this sermon may be altogether on mortal sin.

4. *Death of the Just*, which describes the happy end of such as have endeavored to carry out in life the end for which God has placed them upon this earth. It forms a contrast to the death of the sinner. The death of the just is full of sweet consolation, while about the death of the sinner there is nothing but

terror and despair. As such, the description of the death of the just is a most powerful means for the conversion of sinners, especially if some comparison be instituted between this death and that which they have to expect, if they do not amend.

5. *Particular Judgment,* at which it is decided for every man individually, whether he has fulfilled the end of his creation while on earth or not. At one glance the soul departed will see its whole life as it is before God. That judgment, therefore, depends entirely on ourselves. The object of this sermon is to move the people to a greater sincerity in all their thoughts, words, and actions, so that they may endeavor to spend their lives as they want them to be before God. Another object is to make clear to the people that all duplicity and hypocrisy will not avail them anything; that they will be rewarded or punished according to the real value of their deserts. A third object is to strike terror into the sinner's heart by showing him that all his misdeeds will be weighed in the balance of divine justice.

Care should be taken lest anything be said in this sermon which cannot be proved by good authority, so as to give no chance for doubt to the audience, or give them the suspicion of exaggeration.

6. *Happy and Unhappy Eternity.* The object of this sermon is to show the final end to which those come who live according to their destiny, as well as those who do not. It is an encouragement to the good, and a terror to the wicked. It is intended for both classes, to serve the principal object of the Renewal, namely, the confirmation of the good in their holy resolutions, and the conversion of the obdurate and relapsed from their evil ways.

After these sermons something should be preached

to console and encourage those who may need some soothing remedy for their wounded hearts. Hence,

7. *The Prodigal Son.* This subject may be selected for congregations, a great part of which live in sin. For others the *Passion of Christ* is more suited, giving great prominence to the description of the excessive love of Jesus Christ. But if this sermon was preached in the Mission, it is not to be repeated here.

After the foregoing subjects, either all or a selection of them, have been preached, *Perseverance* must engage the attention of the missionaries. For this purpose comes:

8. *Relapse,* its malice and fearful consequences. This sermon is to warn the people against another relapse into a state of mortal sin, which is so much the more dangerous on account of the two preceding Missions. It is but too frequently the case that a relapse after the Mission and the Renewal is followed by the saddest consequences. Hence, let this sermon be preached with all energy and fervor.

Yet care must be taken against going to extremes — which is very easy — in this sermon. We should not call every fall into sin a relapse. Nor should we, in all cases, call into question the validity of the absolution which the unfortunate sinner received before. Least of all should we, by the way in which we present our subject, leave the impression on the audience that a relapsed sinner can nevermore be converted.

9. *Human Respect,* one of the ordinary causes of relapse. The object of this sermon is to strengthen the audience against one of the most fearful influences that bear upon those converted from a sinful life, and often most successfully.

If this sermon cannot be preached, let this point be

given so much the more prominence in the first part of the foregoing sermon.

10. *Scandal,* given directly or indirectly, is another most powerful agent to snatch souls from the hands of God. This sermon is to be a warning to those who so soon after the Mission undo the great work which the Mission has effected.

11. *The Blessed Virgin Mary,* in whose honor the Rule obliges us to preach a sermon, not only on Missions, but also during other public exercises,[4] is not to be forgotten at the Renewal. A practical discourse is that on "The Child of the Blessed Virgin Mary." To inspire the hearts of the people with this devotion was the object of the sermon on the Blessed Virgin at the Mission, when the people publicly dedicated themselves to Mary, declaring themselves her children. Now it becomes essentially necessary to give a new stimulus to that good disposition, and, as far as possible, perpetuate it. In this sermon we take the people as already dedicated to the Blessed Virgin, and tell them how happy they ought to consider themselves as children of so great a Mother, and how they should conduct themselves so as to make themselves more and more worthy of her.

The act of dedication is not repeated, except in case a great part of the people, say one-third, are new-comers; for it is better not to make them think that, owing to their infidelities, the act of dedication has lost its value, otherwise their next mortal sin will make them think the same again, and make them give up all confidence in Mary. Let it be understood, on the contrary, that they are always the children of the Blessed Virgin. This thought will, from time to time, serve them as an impulse to render themselves

[4] R., n. 140.

more worthy of her. Should the act of dedication be repeated, it should be stated that this is done principally for those who did not make it in the Mission, and that the repetition serves the others only as a confirmation of their declaration made at that time.

The sermon on the "Sorrows of the Blessed Virgin" would also form a most appropriate subject.

12. *Heaven*, man's true and final destination. The object of this sermon is to encourage the people to keep their good resolutions and to serve God cheerfully, by showing them the infinite reward with which their holy endeavors will be crowned. No more beautiful or efficacious subject could be brought to their consideration toward the close of the Renewal.

This sermon must be full of unction, life and joy. These qualities are easily obtained through the conviction that the description of the joys of heaven can never be exaggerated, that a Christian is an heir of heaven, and that the joys will never end.

It is evident that not all these sermons can be preached within the limited compass of a week. A proper selection, therefore, is to be made according to the special needs of the people to whom the Renewal is given.

Should it be deemed necessary to give a special exhortation for such as again delay their conversion, a sermon on the "*Abuse of grace,*" or some similar subject, may be preached after the sermon on the Blessed Virgin. The sermon on the "*Qualities of prayer*" may in like manner be introduced.

13. *Renewal of Baptismal Vows*, by which the faithful, "*quasi modo geniti infantes,*" begin life anew. In this sermon the hearers are brought back to the day of their baptism. Not having lived in accordance with the destiny that they received at their regener-

ation, but being now purified from their sins, and having learned their Christian duties to perfection by means of the Mission and the Renewal, they are now bid to commence anew, and live up to the grace received in baptism more faithfully for the rest of their lives. To produce these sentiments in their hearts is the main object of this sermon. The so-called "Baptismal Vows" are contained in the six questions proposed immediately before the administration of that sacrament. These, then, form the subject of the sermon. It would be too tedious to enter into an elaborate explanation of the ceremonies and prayers used in the administration of Baptism, nor would it be directly to the point. After a plain and concise explanation of the vows, they are renewed publicly and aloud. This sermon is also the close of the Renewal; hence, it is followed by the *Valedictory Address*, given in full, similar to that at the close of the Mission.

It is not customary to celebrate after the Renewal a Requiem Mass or preach a sermon for the souls in Purgatory.

# CHAPTER III

### 1. Instructions to be Given at the Renewal

The main point to be attended to by the missionaries is the worthy reception of the sacraments on the part of the people. It is a deplorable fact, that even during the Mission many confessions are made badly. For this reason we begin our instructions again with the Sacrament of Penance.

1. *True and False Penance*, which comprises in one instruction all that was said on the Sacrament of Penance in the Mission. But we add the happy results of a good confession and the evil consequences of a bad confession.

2. *Worthy and Unworthy Communion;* benefits or evil consequences, as they follow from either one or the other.

3. *Mass*, and the manner of attending it with profit.

4. *Word of God*, or the necessity of hearing sermons and instructions. This is the ordinary means through which God makes known to us His will and inspirations, and by which religion is kept up. This instruction is so much the more important as the people become careless in hearing the Word of God.

5. *Temptations and Crosses*, which are the inseparable companions of every man's life — their benefit, and the means to overcome the former, and to bear the latter with patience.

16

6 *Rule of a Christian Life* for every day, every week, every month, and every year.

7. *Manner in which a Christian should meet Death.* This instruction includes *Extreme Unction*, the immediate preparation for death, and the manner of assisting the dying. The people hardly ever receive an instruction on these matters, which, after all, are most important. For this reason the missionaries should supply this great want.

Only six instructions are needed at the Renewal. Let those, therefore, be selected that are the most needed.

During the Renewal the instructions may take up as much time as during the Mission.

In the Renewal no separate instructions for the *particular states of life* are given. Should it, however, be deemed necessary to speak on these special duties, the sermon on the *"Christian Family"* may be preached toward the close of the exercises.

## 2. THE SOLEMN ATONEMENT BEFORE THE BLESSED SACRAMENT

In regard to this ceremony, practices were adopted in times past, some of which were actually turned into ridicule by priests and people; while others were in direct opposition to the Rubrics; for instance, giving Benediction in dead silence without the *Tantum ergo* and the prayer preceding it. In this country we may perform this most touching ceremony in the following manner:[1]

The altar is decorated as on the greatest festivals. The candles are lighted during the recitation of the Rosary. After the Rosary, the clergy come to the

[1] Prov. Stat. n. 45.

altar while the preacher goes to the pulpit, on this
occasion with surplice and stole,[2] out of respect for
the Blessed Sacrament. The Blessed Sacrament is
exposed, and the exposition-hymn is sung. While the
clergy and the people are still kneeling, the preacher,
also on his knees, begins the sermon with an excla-
mation expressive of the immense love of Jesus in the
Blessed Eucharist; or by an act of most humble
adoration on his part and on the part of the people.
From this he gradually passes over to the coldness
of the hearts of men toward Him, their acts of irreverence, their sacrileges. As soon as he begins to speak,
the candles on the altar may be extinguished one by
one, leaving only the prescribed number, namely,
twelve,[3] burning, the six large candles and six near
the ostensorium. The preacher may take occasion
from this circumstance to direct the attention of his
hearers to the fact that there are but few hearts left
(which are represented by .the lighted candles) that
have the love of Jesus in the Blessed Eucharist burning within them. Having introduced the subject of
his sermon, namely, the enormous ingratitude of men
exhibited by their sacrilegious acts and other sins of
irreverence and profanation toward the Blessed Sacrament, he directs the ostensorium to be veiled [4]
until he has finished his description of human ingratitude, and produced greater love for Jesus Christ

[2] Cf. Old Rule about closing sermon. — But the preacher is not
to take off these vestments at the act of atonement, as is the custom with some while they are making a public confession of their
own sins. Such a confession would cause great surprise in the minds
of our people. Nor should the missionary ask the clergy to beg
pardon for their sins.

[3] *Instr. Clem.* § vi, n. 8. — *Rom. Cerem.* ch. iv, art. 1.

[4] There exists no positive prescription of veiling the Blessed Sacrament during a sermon. But it is the general practice.

in the congregation. Then the preacher rises, and the clergy and the people sit down.

Toward the close of the sermon, the preacher must do all in his power to produce in the hearts of his hearers deep compunction for their want of love, acts of irreverence, etc., to exhort them to ask pardon of Jesus Christ, and to dispose them for the act of reparation. He may say that he will leave them for a few moments to their own feelings and the emotions of their hearts. The choir sings the *Agnus Dei*, as at High Mass, or some other hymn to the Blessed Sacrament. During the singing, the priest remains kneeling in the pulpit,[5] and the candles are lighted again.[6] At the end of the *Dona nobis* the veil is removed, the clergy go to the altar, and the preacher rises to introduce the act of atonement. Having invited the congregation to follow him in silence and contrition, he pronounces the act with deep piety and feeling. This act should consist in a fervent prayer and in nothing else.

Then follows the *Tantum ergo* and the rest, as usual at Benediction. The prayers for the conversion of sinners are said immediately after the Benediction.

Circumstances may require that this solemnity be performed without the exposition of the Blessed Sacrament. In that case let the preparations be made as if there were exposition. The preacher after the hymn of the Holy Ghost preaches the sermon in the usual attire. The sermon is followed by a hymn to the Blessed Sacrament, the Blessed Sacrament is exposed with the usual ceremonies, then the preacher,

---

[5] In European Provinces the practice prevails that some other missionary performs the act of atonement. During the change the *Miserere* is sung.

[6] In case they had been extinguished.

who is still in the pulpit, after a short introduction,
makes the act of atonement, as mentioned above.
No one can raise the least objection to this, as there
is no prescription or decree against such *"ferverine"*
before the Blessed Sacrament exposed.


### 3. The Renewal of the Baptismal Vows

This ceremony forms the close of the Renewal.
In preparation for it, the baptismal font should be
most beautifully decorated, if it occupies such a
position in the church that it can be easily seen by
the congregation, or if it can be moved to such a
place without much inconvenience.  If the baptismal
font cannot be used, then some other vessel resem-
bling a baptismal font may be taken and decorated
in its stead.  In case nothing of this kind can be done,
let the Baptismal Vows be renewed before the altar
on which the Blessed Sacrament is exposed.   St.
Alphonsus [7] always preached the closing sermon before
the  Blessed  Sacrament  exposed — and  the  Rule [8]
allows it.   On a table near the baptismal font there
should be a large candle on a candlestick of considerable size.  This also should be decorated.  The candle
is to burn during the ceremony.  Then the white
garment, consisting of a large veil, is to be so attached
to the font that it, as it were, flows out of it.  Finally,
the book of baptismal records is to have a prominent
place on the table.   These emblems have a deep sig-
nification, and should, therefore, be seen by the entire
congregation.  The attention of the people should be
directed to the font in the exordium of the sermon,
and the emblems explained.

It is the custom with certain confraternities after a

[7] *Exercises*, C. E., Vol. XV. p. 235.        [8] R., n. 149.

Retreat to renew the Baptismal Vows with burning candles in their hands. This may be allowed where the members of such confraternities occupy their places in the pews in perfect order and do not over-crowd the church. To do so at the close of a Renewal with a promiscuous crowd in the church, though there were only men, is a perilous under-taking, which, for the sake of prudence, should be avoided.[9] All that can be allowed is to place a row of children on each side, or around the baptismal font, with candles lighted only for the act of renewal. If the font occupies a place in the center of the sanc-tuary, these children are placed in two rows, one on each side of the font, with the smallest children nearest to it. This represents innocence flowing from the font, and preserved during the successive years of youth.

The Pastor may be invited to stand at the side of the font, facing the congregation, when the act is about to be performed, because he, as the representa-tive of the Church, is to receive the vows of the people in her name.

During the act of the renewal of these solemn en-gagements the people are to stand and extend their right hands toward the font or altar, to carry out, to some extent, the idea of touching the font, which they should do were they near it.

This ceremony has greater effect, if the act of re-nouncing the devil, etc., is performed before the vows of the profession of faith are explained. The vows

[9] This practice was forbidden in this Province by the Provincial on Nov. 26, 1878. If the ceremony is performed for men only, they may use lighted candles; but they should not light the candles them-selves and throw away the burning matches. One or two altar-boys should light the candle of the first man in every pew. Prov. Stat. n. 46.

are renewed with the greatest fervor when the explanation is still fresh in the minds of the people.

If this ceremony takes place before the Blessed Sacrament exposed, the veil may be placed on the altar, and it is to be taken away at the end when the vows have been pronounced.

### 4. The Simplest Way of Constructing a Temporary Confessional

Temporary confessionals are needed at almost every Mission. Carpenters are often at a loss to know how to make them, and it is very difficult to give them a description that they will understand. The following plan will answer the purpose:

Put together three simple boards, fastening them on both ends with a strip of wood nailed over them, so as to have a table of five by four feet. The center board to be shorter to leave room for the grate.

Two small pieces, twenty by four inches each, are nailed, one on each side, to the edge of the lower end of this table, allowing them to reach out fifteen inches on the one side and four inches on the other. This serves as a pedestal.

Over the two longer ends of these two pieces is nailed a board nine inches wide, for the penitent to kneel on.

Two feet and four inches above this kneeling-board the opening for the grate is to be made, a foot and a half square.

Two inches below the grate, on the side of the kneeling-board, a strip of board, two feet by four inches, is to be fastened, on which the penitent can rest his elbows. On the other side, but four inches below the grate, a strip of the same size is to be fastened for the confessor.

About half an inch above the grate a narrow strip is to be fastened, reaching across the three boards, to hold them together.

The grate is to be made of round staves not over a quarter of an inch in diameter, crossing one another in lattice-work form, an inch and a half apart, and fastened at the intersections. It is to be fastened in the opening by two narrow frames nailed against it on both sides.

On the top-end toward the people, a strip of four feet in length is to be fastened, to which a piece of calico of a dark color is to be tacked, to hide both priest and penitent from the view of the people.

### 5. THE MISSION REMEMBRANCE

This is either a picture especially selected for this purpose, or a card with some pious sentences printed on it, or a leaflet containing some prayers, etc. The last form, with the picture of the Most Holy Redeemer on the first page, is at present adopted in this country.[10] It contains the Daily Acts of a Christian Life, which are read before the great sermon. The Rule says nothing about the Mission Remembrance, but it is at present distributed on all our Missions in every Province. The right to modify it, or to adopt a different form, seems to be understood as reserved to the Provincial, because there must be uniformity in this matter, which otherwise could not be obtained. At least the "Daily Acts" are not to be changed without

[10] See Prov. Stat. p. 84. The Renewal Remembrance has the picture of Our Lady of Perpetual Help on the first page.

the Provincial's approbation. [11] It is customary in this Province for the confessors to hand a Remembrance to each penitent, and by this means we count the confessions. As it is given in the confessional, it must be given to every one, whether he is absolved or not. It is given also to the children.

### 6. ARTICLES OF DEVOTION

These consist of such objects of piety as we generally bless and indulgence. We may advise Pastors to have the sale of these articles conducted in their own name; we may indicate in particular what they should provide, and where they can obtain the best selection; we may assist in fixing the prices: but we should never charge ourselves with their purchase, their transportation, nor guarantee payment. After the store is open for the public, we should keep away from it, in order to avoid the suspicion of drawing the profit from the sale of these articles, as well as of too close familiarity with those in charge. We should at the proper time announce to the people that they should provide themselves with these articles, telling them where they may purchase them. But we should not carry these announcements to such an excess as to create a suspicion of money-making, nor directly denounce others who sell similar articles in the neighborhood.

The Rule prescribes that the articles of devotion be blessed during the last two or three days. [12] This gives sufficient opportunity for all to provide themselves with such articles, especially if the blessing takes place twice a day, as is the custom with us. Hence, they need not be blessed during the first part

[11] R., n. 87.                    [12] R., n. 147.

of the Mission, nor is there any necessity for the people's besieging the priest's parlor for this purpose after the Mission is closed.

In blessing the articles of devotion, the Father simply puts on the stole of the prescribed color.[13] He should not introduce more blessings than have been customary, namely, of pictures and statues, crosses and medals, the ordinary rosary, wax-candles and the five scapulars. Bibles and other books are blessed with the simple sign of the cross, and then sprinkled with holy water. The Father should not commute the conditions for gaining the Sabbatine Indulgence into other prayers from the altar, because this faculty is given only to confessors, to be applied to each one individually and for good reasons.

### 7. CONFRATERNITIES

Our Rule prescribes that we should direct our particular attention to the confraternities that are already established in the congregations to which we give Missions.[14] We should give a new impulse to those already existing, reorganize those about to be dissolved, and establish one or the other where none exists. Confraternities are a most efficacious means for promoting the frequentation of the sacraments, prayer, and mutual charity. They are, therefore, a most powerful aid to preserve the fruits of the Mission. We should assist the Pastor with our advice in preserving such sodalities in their fervor, especially in reference to the things to be done in presiding over their meetings, and the frequentation of the sacraments. As to new associations to be established, we may propose especially the Sodality of the Blessed Virgin, so

---

[13] Prov. Stat. n. 47. — White is sufficient for all.  [14] R., n. 152.

strongly recommended by St. Alphonsus,[15] if there is a priest who is willing to take it in charge; the Rosary Society, the Purgatorian Society, the Conference of St. Vincent de Paul, and others mentioned in the Rule.[16]

Should we promote Temperance or Total Abstinence Societies? Experience proves that such societies have become a necessity for a certain class of people, and that, as an encouragement, they should also be joined by men otherwise of temperate habits. But they should be based on the principles laid down by the Holy See for such associations. The remedy against intemperance should be found in supernatural rather than in natural means.

## 8. Mission Plans to be Kept

At every Mission and Renewal, a plan of all the exercises is to be written out, so that every one may know his particular duties. This plan, which must be filled up completely, at least toward the end of the exercises, should be kept for future reference in the house which gives the Mission. It is necessary for the Renewal, because the Renewal is to be arranged according to the exercises of the Mission. It is also necessary for a future Mission, because then it is important to know who preached, and what was preached. The same sermon should not be given to the same Father; if it is, he should treat the subject in a different manner and style. These plans are, moreover, most useful for various other purposes.

## 9. Renewal for the Children

During the Renewal something extra is also to be done for the children. The reasons are the same

[15] *Exercises*, C. E., Vol. XV. p. 255.    [16] R., n. 152.

as they were during the Mission. Two exercises for the children are sufficient during the Renewal.

Each of these exercises should consist of an instruction and an exhortation. The choice of the subjects depends entirely on circumstances, as it is to be made according to what is most needed and most appropriate.

In general the following subjects may be proposed for the *exhortation* — How much God loves children, and how much they should love Him. — The joys of heaven. — The sufferings of Christ.

For the *instruction* the first two subjects of the instructions for grown people suit best: — Good and Bad Confession. —Worthy and Unworthy Communion. — Holy Mass and how to hear it. — Love of the Blessed Sacrament, visits, divine service, etc.

In a word, the catechist should have the future of these children in view, and give them such instruction, advice, and direction, as to secure their perseverance.

The confessions of the children should again be heard apart from those of the grown people. They again receive Holy Communion in a body, and with the same ceremony as during the Mission.

10. Minor Observances during the Mission and the Renewal

The success of the Mission depends a great deal on good order, which demands that every exercise be performed with strict regularity, uniformity, and punctuality. In relation to this matter, we subjoin the following points:

*a.* The first morning-instruction is always preceded by a *Low Mass*, except in places where circumstances demand an inversion of this order. The second instruction is likewise preceded by a Low Mass.

A High Mass takes up too much time, tires the people, and causes other inconveniences. It should be avoided, if possible. There may, however, be singing at either of the two Masses, or at both.

*b.* At the first Mass Communion is given by another priest, who should begin when the celebrant is reading the Epistle or Gospel, so as not to be in his way. The celebrant does not interrupt the Mass while the other priest opens the tabernacle, says *Misereatur*, and performs the rest at the altar. The latter continues giving Communion, but stops at the Consecration, standing with his face turned toward the altar.[17] He does not give the blessing after replacing the ciborium on the altar; he leaves it there to be put into the tabernacle by the celebrant after consuming the Precious Blood. If the number of communicants is extraordinarily great, another priest may assist in giving Communion at the last Mass, to prevent delay. Without a most urgent reason Communion should not be given at a time of the day when it is not allowed to say Mass.[18]

*c.* St. Alphonsus had the *Benediction* with the Blessed Sacrament given only at the close of all the exercises.[19] In this country, we have it every day of the Mission. Special permission need not be asked of the Ordinary, because it is permitted all over the United States.[20] In Canada the rules of every diocese are to be consulted.

[17] O'Kane, n. 693; De Herdt, II. n. 28.
[18] Decr. 7. Sep. 1816.
[19] *Exercises*, C. E., Vol. XV. p. 235.
[20] II Plen. Council, n. 375.

*d.* On the Sundays included in the Mission no *Vespers* are sung, the time being taken up by other exercises.

*e.* After the morning-instructions, the missionary recites with the people the acts of *faith, hope, charity,* and *contrition.*[21] We should take those contained in the Catechism of the III Plen. Council, because they are now generally prescribed. St. Alphonsus directs[22] that the act of contrition should be a longer one for grown people, while it may be short for children. After the acts, a pious canticle may be sung.

*f.* The *director of the choir* should be properly instructed; otherwise, a great deal of disorder in the exercises will be the result. The director must be told — *a.* What is to be sung at the evening services, namely, the hymn before the sermon; the *Miserere* or *Stabat Mater* after the sermon, for about five minutes; the hymns for benediction; the changes to be made on the evening of the dedication to the Blessed Virgin, of the Erection of the Cross, the atonement before the Blessed Sacrament, the Baptismal Vows, the close of the Mission, and, perhaps, before the sermon on Death. Before the sermon on Judgment part of the *Dies iræ* may be sung.[23] *b.* What peculiar character the various pieces must possess, namely, gravity and devotion. The choir should not be allowed to substitute motets for the *Miserere.* *c.* That the various pieces must not occupy more than the allotted time; and that, in particular, the Masses selected for High Mass on Sundays must be short. The choir should

[21] R., n. 139. The *Ave* may be omitted, since the prayers prescribed by Leo XIII are to be said after Mass.

[22] *Exercises*, C. E., Vol. XV. pp. 143, 177.

[23] The Rule gives no special direction as regards singing. At every exercise St. Alphonsus had something sung that bore a relation to the discourse which preceded or followed.

be kept from exhibiting their musical knowledge at the expense of the Mission.

*g.* The *Daily Acts of a Christian Life,* as found in the "Mission Remembrance," are to be read by the preacher of the great sermon before beginning.[24] No other reading is to be added. The people should not be made to repeat them. We begin to read these acts from the second day of the Mission, but omit them whenever the nature of the sermon or of the ceremony to be performed requires it.

*h.* For several most important reasons we do not celebrate any *general Communion* on our Missions or Renewals except for the children. Should there be any, it is to take place in the same manner as the Communion of the children. St. Alphonsus gives directions how to do it.[25]

[24] R., n. 138.     [25] C. E., Vol. XV. p. 146.

# CHAPTER IV

## SECONDARY MISSION EXERCISES [1]

BESIDES Missions and Renewals, there are other public exercises, which include a series of sermons and instructions, to be performed by our missionaries. These are Missions on a small scale. According to circumstances, these exercises may either approach the Mission-sermon in style, or resemble ordinary parish-sermons. Under this head come Jubilees, Lenten sermons, Novenas, and Triduos.

### 1. GENERAL REMARKS

According to the words of St. Alphonsus, a missionary is always to preach as a missionary. The same spirit that guides us on the Missions, is to be followed at these secondary exercises. So, also, with certain modifications according to circumstances, is the end aimed at by the former the end of the latter, namely, conversion and perseverance in the practice of the Christian virtues. The sermons preached on such occasions should be replete with power and unction, and practical in their application, yet within the proper limits of moderation, as far as extraordinary efforts, exclamations, etc., which are proper to Missions, are concerned. Very rarely should a certain prevailing vice form the chief subject of any single sermon, although the sermons are to be directed in the appli-

[1] Cf. R., n. 166–174.

cation against certain local abuses. The instructions given on such occasions have for their object the worthy reception of the sacraments, and the reformation of morals in the community. No particular instructions for different classes of people are given, because they properly belong to the Missions. If the Rosary is recited, it is not preceded by an instruction. Confessions are mostly heard by other priests, yet the missionary is also to spend his free time in the confessional. There is hardly any occasion for extraordinary ceremonies at these exercises, except at the close, when some display is allowable.

At Jubilees the missionary should make his appearance as on the Mission, in his habit and with his cross, because they approach nearest to Missions; also, and for the same reason, at Novenas or Octaves which are not of the Blessed Sacrament. At other exercises he may preach in surplice and stole, as this seems to be more in accordance with the customs of this country.

## 2. THE JUBILEE

If the exercises of a Jubilee consist in a regular Mission or Renewal, the regulations laid down for Missions are to be followed; with this exception, that in one instruction the conditions for gaining the Plenary Indulgence of the Jubilee must be explained. It is best to take this first, and then give the instructions on the Sacrament of Penance. If no regular Mission or Renewal is given, these exercises are to be regulated in accordance with the object of the Jubilee, and with reference to local vices and abuses. The object of the Jubilee is the conversion of the world, principally through the motive of love on account of the extraordinary manifestation of the mercy of God, and the complete union of man with God by means of the plenary indulgence. Hence, the usual succession of sermons may be arranged in the following order:

1. *Mercy of God*, manifested especially in the Jubilee.
2. *Salvation of Man*, the chief object to be gained.
3. *Sin*, absolutely to be abandoned.
4. *Abuse of this Extraordinary Time of Grace;* the fearful consequences of this abuse; consequences which often follow immediately after such seasons of grace; and then the
5. *Terrible Judgment* immediately after death; and the
6. *Awful Punishment* of the sinner *in hell*.
7. Parable of the *Prodigal Son*, with special application to this season of grace. During the Jubilee all men are invited to return to the Church; therefore,
8. *Faith* in the Church, and *Obedience* to her commandments.
9. *Means of Perseverance*, which consist in avoiding the proximate occasion of sin, fervent prayer, and the frequent and worthy reception of the sacraments. To make use of these means, the people are exhorted to place themselves under the
10. Most powerful *protection of the Blessed Virgin Mary*, to whom they should devote themselves, as her children, by a *solemn act of dedication*.

In accordance with the same end of the Jubilee, the following instructions may be given:

1. *Confession*, its necessity and essential qualities, as the first condition required for gaining the indulgence of the Jubilee. This subject may be divided into two or three instructions.
2. *Holy Communion*, the second condition. Worthy Communion and its effects. Unworthy Communion and its consequences. This subject may also be divided.

3. The *other conditions* of the Jubilee. — Although
the Church grants a plenary indulgence, she, nevertheless, wishes her children to lead a

4. *Life of Penance.* This demands a spirit of mortification and self-denial, as expressed in the Gospel;
hence, no useless amusements, no vanities. Holy
submission under

5. *Crosses, Trials, Temptations,* which are the inheritance of all Christians. In a word, all should commence to regulate their conduct by the

6. *Rule of a truly Christian Life,* as laid down in the
Gospel and in the spirit of the Catholic Church.

### 3. Lenten Sermons

The tenor of these sermons is the same as that of
Jubilee sermons. A course of Lenten discourses
consists of no more than five or six sermons, that is,
one for every week in Lent, according to the custom
prevailing in this country. Wherever we have two
sermons in a week, there are two different courses,
neither of which includes the ordinary sermon at the
High Mass on Sundays. The nature of the subjects
chosen for these sermons varies between the moral,
the dogmatic, and the instructive, yet so that each
course follows up one idea, and that the sermons
follow one another in logical order. Care should be
taken in regard to dogmatical or instructive discourses,
that they do not become too dry; hence they should
always close with some practical applications.

### 4. Novenas, Octaves, Triduos

Courses of such sermons may be preached in honor
of some great mystery of our holy religion, in honor
of the Holy Ghost, of some saint, or for the souls in

purgatory. This determines the subject of the discourses. As a general rule, all the sermons of a Novena or Octave must be directed to one end. We may be allowed to indicate the subjects of some of them.

While preaching in honor of the Blessed Sacrament, we may show the various ways in which Jesus Christ manifests His love in this august mystery; then again, how we may show our love and devotion toward Him; or we may simply explain the various points of faith in reference to this sacrament.

In a Novena in honor of the Holy Ghost, we may explain the seven gifts of the Holy Ghost, — the sins against the Holy Ghost, — the ways in which the Holy Ghost works upon earth, etc.

During the Octave of All-Souls, we may explain the various motives why we should assist them, — the means by which we can help them, — the profit that we derive from this devotion for ourselves, etc.

In a Novena or Octave in honor of some saint, we may preach on his most remarkable virtues, — on the means that he chiefly employed to acquire sanctity, — on his chief works for the benefit of the Church, etc. In a Novena of this kind the main point is to be left for the great sermon to be given on the feast itself; for instance, the greatest privilege of the saint, as *Doctor Ecclesiæ*, etc. — his most prominent virtue, his greatest work, etc.

In Triduos the same rule is to be observed, only the subjects must be more contracted, so as to completely exhaust them. This is particularly the case with the *Forty Hours'*.

During Novenas, etc., sermons may be preached either in the evening only, or morning discourses may also be added; the proper time for which is the High Mass, which should be sung every day.

### 5. May Devotions

These do not differ much from the Rosary instructions given on the Mission, but they include a sermon for the introduction, and another for the close. The short exhortations may be on the Litany of the Blessed Virgin, her virtues, the mysteries of the Rosary, some famous pilgrimages, miraculous pictures, wonderful conversions obtained through her intercession, etc.

### 6. Erection of the Stations of the Cross

If, during the Mission, the stations of the cross are to be erected, the missionary may perform the ceremony, provided he has received the special faculty for it from the Bishop or the Provincial. The Manual contains all the prayers, as well as a description of the ceremonies. The following order is observed in the performance of this solemn act:

After an appropriate hymn, the missionary explains, in a brief discourse, the origin of the Way of the Cross, its extension over the whole world, its privileges, its indulgences and the conditions for gaining them. Then the pictures and crosses are blessed. After that, they are hung up on the wall in the prescribed order. While the first station is being raised, the choir sings a strophe of the *Stabat Mater*, after which follows a short reflection on what is represented by that station, with some special application, prayer, and act of contrition; finally, one "Our Father, Hail Mary, and Glory be to the Father," to be recited with the people. All this is done by one missionary from the pulpit, while another, or the Pastor, performs the ceremony of erection. After the "Glory be to the Father," another strophe of the *Stabat* is sung, during which the second station is hung up. Then follows again the reflection, etc., as at the first. This order is followed throughout the entire ceremony. All the rest is found in the Manual, together with the *actus formalis*, to be written and to be left in the Church.

On some Missions, instead of the sermon on the Passion, the Way of the Cross is performed. This is done in the same order as the erection, leaving out the blessing and erection of the stations. Instead of speaking of the Way of the Cross as above, the missionary should make the introduction on the Passion of Christ in general, gradually leading his discourse to the stations. The procession around the stations is conducted by one Father, while the reflections should be made by another from the pulpit. At the close, the people should be invited to visit the stations often, on account of the many indulgences attached to this devotion and the immense profit that they derive from it for their souls.

# CHAPTER V

## MISSIONARY'S SPIRITUAL GUIDE ON THE MISSIONS [1]

*"Attende tibi, et doctrinæ: insta in illis. Hoc enim faciens, et te ipsum salvum facies, et eos qui te audiunt."* [2] The object of the first and principal care of the missionary must be himself, if he desires to preserve the good spirit in himself while he is working for the welfare of others. Nay, the success of his apostolic labors depends, in a great measure, on the care that he takes of himself.

The work of the Missions differs from the administration of the sacraments in that the sacraments produce their effect *"ex opere operato,"* while the effect of the Missions depends *"ab opere operantis."* The good result of the Missions is generally in proportion to the qualities of the instruments which Divine Providence uses for the salvation of souls through this extraordinary ministry. "Outside of the sacraments," says Father Desurmont, C.SS.R., "Jesus Christ ordinarily communicates efficacy to the instrumentality of His ministers in proportion to their supernatural, as well as natural dispositions." [3] Now, extraordinary work requires extraordinary dispositions. It is for this reason that our young missionaries receive special training for the Missions during their years of

---

[1] The quotations in this chapter are too numerous to be recorded in full. The citations are sufficient for any one who desires to consult the sources, which are in the hands of every Father.

[2] I Tim. iv. 16.  [3] *Past.* lib. xxi. c. 1.

38

study, and later in the second novitiate. How our missionaries should prepare for this extraordinary work, as well as the manner of executing it, has been shown in detail. There remains now something to be said about the missionary's conduct while engaged in giving Missions.

### 1. The Spirit of St. Alphonsus, our Guide on Missions

Our missionaries are to be guided by the spirit of our great Father and Founder, St. Alphonsus. If this constitutes our principal rule when at home in our cells, or when engaged in the ordinary ministry of the Church, it should in a special manner be the ruling spirit of our actions when on Missions. Now, the spirit of St. Alphonsus consists in a great love of Jesus Christ as the Redeemer of the world. This love will produce in the missionary a proportionate zeal as well for his own sanctification as for the salvation of souls. According to our saintly Founder, personal sanctification always goes before the work of the apostolic ministry, or *"opus ad intra"* precedes *"opus ad extra."* Even while engaged in exterior work, our principal attention should be directed to our own sanctification. These two kinds of work may seem incompatible. But the missionary life of St. Alphonsus, the directions that he has given to his children, the rules that he has laid down for Redemptorist missionaries, the approved customs of the Order, and the Provincial Statutes, clearly prove that the exterior and the interior work are in perfect harmony with each other.

It remains now to be seen how our missionaries are to act in accordance with the directions derived from these sources: When setting out for the

Missions; While engaged on the Missions; When returning from the Missions.

## 2. Leaving Home for the Missions

Having received their appointment for certain Missions, the Fathers leave home as the Apostles did when they set out for their missions among the heathens. They should not carry with them more luggage than they need for the time being, nor ride in carriages without a real necessity.[4] Some inconvenience does not make a necessity. The entire band of missionaries repair at a seasonable time to the oratory, where they recite the *Itinerarium* together. Then they receive the Superior's blessing, and leave the house *in nomine Domini*.[5] All are subject to the Superior of the Mission. On the journey, without the Superior's permission, no Father is allowed to separate from the others, or to stay at any place. In case no Procurator[6] has been appointed, the Superior shall keep the money given them at home for their traveling expenses. He is not allowed to hand small amounts to his subjects "*ad usum arbitrarium*,"[7] but only when necessity requires it, "*ad usum determinatum*." After their return, the Superior of the Mission is to give an exact account of all their expenses, as well as their receipts, since they left home.[8] According to our Privileges, our missionaries are not bound to say the Divine Office of the day on their journey to and from the Missions or during the Mission (see below, n. 4. I). Yet, they are aware that they are not obliged to use this privilege in case of sufficient time.

"*Iter faciant collecto ac devoto animo, tempusque*

---

[4] R., n. 71.  
[5] Ib. n. 133.  
[6] Ib. n. 109–111.  
[7] Ib. n. 228.  
[8] Ib. n. 227.

*impendant absolvendis consuetis pietatis exercitiis: Deo
quoque commendent felicem Missionis exitum.*" [9]  Accordingly they should spend some time in pious reading,
mental prayer, saying the Rosary, etc.  Their conversation should not attract the attention of those around
them; it should be modest and becoming to Religious.

Our vow of poverty obliges us in traveling, to
refrain from all luxuries, as, for instance, riding in
parlor cars without necessity, buying useless literature,
be it the daily papers or magazines, etc.  The virtue
of holy poverty should be our guide and companion
on our apostolic travels from Mission to Mission, as
it was the faithful companion of Jesus Christ, the
Model and Prince of all missionaries.

### 3. Arrival of the Missionaries

Having arrived at the place where the Mission is
to be given, the first and principal thought of the
missionaries should be to make a favorable impression
on all whom they meet, the Pastor, his assistants, the
servants of the house, the people in the neighborhood;
for much depends on the first impression that the
missionaries make, and it takes a great deal to change
first impressions.  It would be rather rude in a missionary to ask for his room immediately on his arrival,
to ask the housekeeper and other servants their names,
to overwhelm them with all sorts of orders, to find
fault with the room assigned him, to have the furniture
or bedding changed, etc.  The missionaries should not
forget that they are simple guests at the priest's
house.  The spirit of mortification and the love of
poverty should not allow them to notice the lack of
certain conveniences.

[9] R., n. 133.

As soon as convenient, the missionaries should repair to the church to make a brief visit to the Blessed Sacrament,[10] in order to thank our Lord for their safe arrival and to pray for a special blessing upon their apostolic labors in the parish.

### 4. CONDUCT OF THE MISSIONARIES DURING THE MISSION

The duty of giving edification, as well as of preserving their religious spirit, requires of our missionaries the careful practice of certain virtues as laid down in our missionary rules,[11] and as explained more in detail by St. Alphonsus.[12]

They are the following:

I. *Prayer and recollection.* The first days of the Mission ought to be specially devoted to holy prayer. The Rule even prescribes a day of recollection [13] *"ut optime fieri poterit."* It would be very difficult to carry out this rule here to its full extent. But we can make up for it by spending a good deal of time in the church, by hearing some Masses in the morning, devoutly assisting at the High Mass, at the evening services, and by employing all our spare time in useful reading or study.[14]

Let what little of the Divine Office is to be said, be said well. During the time of the Mission, local Superiors or the Superiors of Missions, by virtue of a Rescript of Benedict XIV, dated July 13, 1745, have the faculty of commuting the Divine Office for their subjects into other vocal prayers.[15] They may assign them what, according to another priv-

---

[10] Cf. R., n. 135.
[11] Ib. n. 59–74.
[12] *Exercises*, C. E., Vol. XV. p. 297.

[13] R., n. 116.
[14] Prov. Stat. n.22.
[15] Privilegia. n. 53.

ilege, local Superiors can give to their subjects that are, for a length of time, engaged in home-work, namely, a certain number of Psalms (not less than seven), seven times *Pater noster* and the *Credo* twice, by which they satisfy for the whole Office.[16] For a long time such has been the practice in this Province.

Mass should be preceded by a short preparation,[17] and be followed by a thanksgiving of half an hour, unless a Father has to give an instruction immediately, which then takes the place of thanksgiving. However, unless the work of the confessions in the morning is particularly pressing, or for some other good reason, the same Father should not say the Mass and give the instruction which follows. After confessions have begun, the thanksgiving after Mass lasts only a quarter of an hour.[18] And when people are waiting at the confessionals, it would be wrong to protract it beyond that time.[19]

In the morning our missionaries make half an hour's meditation together.[20] This lasts but a quarter of an hour on days on which confessions are heard from early morning. The meditation must always be in common, yet, for a good reason, it may be made somewhat later than usual, to allow more rest to the Fathers.

St. Alphonsus prescribes that in spring the Fathers should go to the confessionals immediately after ris-ing, and make the meditation in the afternoon after *siesta*.[21] Very frequently we have to go to the con-fessionals in this country as early as possible, to hear the men that cannot come during the day. We omit

---

[16] Ibidem.
[17] R., n. 115.
[18] R., n. 115.

[19] *Exercises*, C. E., Vol. XV. p. 300.
[20] R., n. 114.   Prov. Stat. n. 20.
[21] *Exercises*, C. E., Vol. XV. p. 292.

the meditation in common on those days, but every one should make up for it privately.

Besides this, every one is to make a visit to the Blessed Sacrament and to the Blessed Virgin, and to say the Rosary.[22] From these two exercises our missionaries are not dispensed.

It is most strongly recommended to spend half an hour, or at least fifteen minutes, in prayer, before preaching the great sermon.[23]

In order that all these exercises of piety may be performed with the proper devotion, they should not be postponed till evening, but should be attended to earlier in the day. A half hour before 3 P.M., and another half hour at 7 P.M., would suit all for these exercises.

But the spirit of prayer cannot exist without recollection. To promote this, silence is to be kept to a certain degree. When two or three are in one room, they should not disturb one another by protracted conversation. They should stay no longer than necessary in the common-room, in the rooms of the Pastor or his assistants, or in the parlor. From the time of rising to the close of the meditation,[24] and from half-past ten at night,[25] silence is prescribed, as at home during the three hours of silence in the afternoon.

Our Rule does not expressly mention that particular examen should be made on the Mission, which signifies that it is not to be made in common, nor does it mention the *Angelus*. But, as a good Christian will never omit the *Angelus*, so a fervent Religious will never spend a day without performing this little, indeed, but most important exercise of the particular examen.

[22] R., n. 114.　　　　[24] R., n. 507.
[23] R., n. 91.　　　　[25] Prov. Stat. p. 34, 19.

When a missionary has lost the spirit of prayer it can be said of him: *"Comederunt alieni robur ejus."* [26]

II. *Humility.* No Father should ask a favorite exercise for himself, but should cheerfully accept those charges with which the least human glory is connected, such as the Rosary, the instruction of the children, sick-calls, etc.[27] Every one should be satisfied with the confessional assigned to him.[28] Our missionaries should excel in love of the confessional, accepting without distinction all classes of persons, even preferring the poor, the ignorant, the most degraded, etc.[29] The humble missionary makes no display of his past achievements, former success, vast experience; much less will he boast of his noble birth, nationality, or distinguished ancestry.[30]

In the same spirit of humility will the missionaries bear contempt or ill-treatment from the clergy or the people, nor will they let a word of complaint escape their lips with regard to it.[31] They should also cheerfully bear the trifling inconveniences and humiliations which every day brings to the poor followers of the poor Jesus.

III. *Obedience.* This virtue, so necessary for good order on the Missions, requires that the Superior be Superior, and the others be subjects. Let the Superior understand his responsibility, and fulfil the directions laid down for him in the Rule.[32] Let him, above all things, act without being influenced in the least by human respect,[33] because, otherwise, he will rob the work of the Mission of the blessing of Divine Providence.

---

[26] Os. vii. 9.
[27] *Exercises*, C. E., Vol. XV. p. 298.
[28] R., n. 84.
[29] Ibidem.

[30] R., n. 59.
[31] R., n. 50 and n. 60.
[32] R., n. 75-79.
[33] R., n. 79.

The subjects, on their part, must act with perfect submission, and work hand in hand under the Superior's direction, from the time they leave the house until they return. It is by no means wrong to make representations to the Superior, but it is very wrong to raise opposition, to show unwillingness to comply with certain charges, to murmur and complain to other missionaries, and, what would be the worst of all, to the Pastor or his assistants; or to confer with the latter about certain arrangements to be made, without being authorized to do so. Holy obedience requires, above all, from Superiors and subjects that they carefully keep the rules laid down for Missions. Submission of judgment and will is a sacrifice required of a Religious at all times, but it is indispensably necessary on the Mission.[34] Without it there is no blessing of God to be expected, the work becomes an insupportable burden for Superiors and subjects, and the Mission bears no fruit.

IV. *Mortification and self-denial.* This twofold virtue is to be the constant companion of the missionary on account of the numberless difficulties and hardships which he necessarily encounters almost daily.[35] Suffering saves more souls than work. In particular, let the missionary be on his guard against discouragement, if he meet with no success in saving the souls for whom he works. To labor without satisfaction or consolation, to toil without seeing any fruit, requires the virtue of an apostle, of a true follower of the Redeemer.

The missionary must also be a lover of hard work, without looking for ease and comfort. He must sacrifice sleep, rest, health, even life itself, to win souls to God.[36]

[34] R., n. 62.    [35] R., n. 49, 50.    [36] R., n. 49.

For the sake of edification, the missionaries must mortify curiosity,[37] by refraining from visiting places where curiosities may be seen,[38] such as museums, galleries of art, factories, etc., except objects of piety. Their outdoor recreation should be becoming and edifying. The people believe the missionaries to be saints, and consequently every action of theirs that does not correspond with this standard will create surprise.[39]

The missionaries ought to practise mortification especially at table. They should be satisfied with the meals served them. They should guard most carefully against the use of liquor.[40] Only in case of necessity should the Superior permit the moderate use of it, and take care that the Fathers contract no habit for it. Nor should the subjects forget that they need the Superior's special permission to eat or drink anything out of the regular time for meals.[41]

Another species of mortification which the missionaries must practise consists in moderation of zeal. They should not take upon themselves more than their strength permits, nor should they give to work the time set apart for bodily rest; they should not omit their usual acts of devotion, nor perform them in haste. Otherwise, the work allotted to them will in the end suffer and their strength of body and soul fail them.

V. *Modesty*. This virtue is a powerful safeguard against the many dangers to which we are exposed on Missions, and an effective means to win the hearts of the clergy and the people. The one as well as the other is essentially necessary for the success of the

[37] R., n. 68.
[38] *Exercises*, C. E., Vol. XV. p. 299.
[39] R., n. 65.
[40] R., n. 118, 119.
[41] Prov. Stat. p. 125.

Mission. With regard to the former, this virtue should keep us from familiarity with priests [42] and people.[43] There should, indeed, be a certain freedom and cheerfulness in our conversation with seculars; yet it must be kept within proper limits, so that we do not lose due respect for them, nor they for us. We should be accessible to all; our very appearance should inspire confidence; yet so that we at the same time command reverence and respect. This is especially required in our conversation with the female servants and other women about the house, ladies occupied in the sacristy, and others with whom we may be thrown in contact.[44]

It is not becoming that any one, except the Superior, or the one authorized, give them small presents in acknowledgment of their services. No other, therefore, should do so.

In regard to persons of the other sex the missionaries should conscientiously observe what the Rule enjoins on this point.[45] Useless correspondence should not be kept up after the Mission.

Apostolic modesty includes also a certain religious simplicity, which gains the hearts and confidence of priests and people. Simplicity is one of the chief characteristics of our Institute, and one which makes our Missions so fruitful. People feel themselves attracted by simplicity, while they are kept at a distance from those in whom they notice much ceremony and reserve. We must be men without pretensions, learned without a desire of showing it, wishing to impart instruction without letting the people feel their ignorance, and ready at any moment to undertake the conversion of the most wicked and degraded without subjecting them to too much humiliation.

For the priests of the parish the missionaries should

[42] R., n. 108.    [43] R., n. 68.    [44] R., n. 66.    [45] R., n. 78.

always show the utmost respect in their absence as well as in their presence. We should never criticize their administration, find fault with their ways, or overwhelm them with our suggestions. We should, indeed, endeavor to exercise great influence over them, so as to make them instrumental in continuing the great good which the Mission has produced. This should be done, however, by example rather than by words. Our example will invariably be to them a most striking and effectual lesson, if we have gained their affections.

Furthermore, modesty must be the distinguishing mark in our general bearing, at church and in the Pastor's residence. We should not put ourselves forward for the performance of certain ceremonies or the direction of them. Neither should we take the lead in the choir, nor preside at the organ. Least of all should we stand among the members of the choir, taking a part in the singing. In a word, our entire conduct should everywhere and at all times manifest the apostle of Jesus Christ, the extraordinary messenger of heaven.

VI. *Politeness.* There are virtues which make us agreeable to God, and there are virtues which make us agreeable to our neighbor. The latter are the offspring of the former, in the same manner as the love of God begets the love of our neighbor. They are comprised under the head of "Christian politeness." The most zealous, virtuous, and prudent missionary will effect no good, if he is a man of unpolished manners. For such Religious as never or rarely come into communication with the people, the study of good manners may be in a manner superfluous; but for us who, by our vocation, are brought into all sorts of society, the case is different. For this reason, our

novices are instructed in the general rules of politeness, which it would be well for us to read over again
even in our advanced age.[46]  Besides these, we should
try to acquire a knowledge of the customs of the
country;[47] among others, the particular points to be
observed at table.

There is much danger of contracting a certain
rudeness of behavior under our present circumstances.
The class of people with whom we have to deal, the
great neglect of good manners in general, excessive
freedom and familiarity among ourselves, which not
rarely degenerate into rudeness, — all affect our
conduct, and tend to deprive it of its agreeableness.

Let it be again observed, that politeness positively
excludes undue familiarity.  It commands a certain
reserve in conversation, in the manner of shaking
hands, in the use of jocose language, etc.  Nor is it
necessary to transgress our Rules, in order to be polite.
We can be most affable toward children, without
yielding to a certain proclivity to patting them on the
head or shoulder, squeezing their arms, taking them
on our knee,[48] etc.

VII. *Holy indifference about health.*  "The health of
an apostle," says Father Desurmont, C.SS.R., "is, like
the life of poor Religious, subject to extraordinary
laws of Divine Providence."  The health of missionaries is protected by, we may say, preter-natural
means.  They sacrifice themselves to God, simply
"seeking the kingdom of God, and His justice," —
propagating the one and enforcing the other — "and
all these things" (health, food, raiment) "are added
unto them."[49]  "*Nolite timere, ne propter regnum Dei
militantibus hujus vitæ necessaria desint.*"[50]  But a

---

[46] *Rule of Novitiate, appendix.*  [48] R., n. 293.  [50] Ven. Bede.
[47] *Excelsior*, by Howard.  [49] Matt. vi. 33.

missionary that will not leave the care of his health to God, cannot count upon that special protection which Divine Providence extends to those who blindly abandon themselves to their good Father in heaven. God will allow all sorts of infirmities to come upon him, which will more or less disable him for the apostolic work. In fact, God will not use him any longer in the execution of a work for which he is unworthy. The same is the case with those who make use of remedies, either directly forbidden by the Rule, or at least restricted to certain limits, such as, "*Liquores non citra necessitatem concedendi.*" [51]

Resting on this principle, the Rule [52] prescribes to our missionaries a holy abandonment into the hands of God, and forbids an over-solicitous care about their health. Nevertheless, it does not prohibit ordinary care to be taken to preserve our bodily strength on the Missions. We are, consequently, allowed to use ordinary precautions on the Missions, especially such as the Rule sanctions, and which have always been found beneficial.

## SANITARY REGULATIONS FOR THE MISSIONS

A. *Work with a certain calmness and ease of mind.* We should take proper care lest we work ourselves into an unnatural state of mind, which necessarily creates a derangement of the system. Let mind and body be kept in their normal state. Hence, avoid interior trouble and anxiety about your sermons and instructions, or other matters connected with the Mission. Do what you can, according to your strength, leaving the rest to God, in Whom you should confide with childlike simplicity. Moreover, avoid undue

[51] R., n. 119.  [52] R., n. 63, 64.

excitement when you meet with difficult cases in the confessional. With the greatest possible calmness of mind reflect and decide according to your knowledge, acting as you think God would act in each case. Never hurry the confessions on account of the multitude of penitents. Hear each confession as quietly and deliberately when a hundred penitents surround you, as you would if you had to hear only two or three. Do not lose the equilibrium of your mind when extraordinary difficulties arise during the Mission; rather pray more fervently, and strengthen your confidence in God.

B. *Beware of excess in eating and drinking.* Brainwork is said to require a good deal of nourishment. This is true, but it is the quality, rather than the quantity, of the food, which furnishes it. It is certainly injurious to health to take a heavy breakfast, consisting of meat, vegetables, etc., which, within four hours, is followed by a sumptuous dinner; and add to it a heavy supper, with a collation before retiring, and be engaged almost the entire day in mental work, which absorbs the vital powers of the body. The necessary consequence is that the excessive quantity of food remains undigested in the stomach. Recourse is then had to stimulants, appetizers, etc., which may procure a momentary relief, but which will not cure the evil. Besides, these artificial aids to digestion, being somewhat agreeable to the palate, are after a while no longer taken as medicine, but in large quantities and at short intervals. And having once accustomed ourselves to them, we can hardly do without them. They derange the system by instilling into the blood unhealthy secretions which are the germ of other diseases. Let your rule, then, be the following: Take a light breakfast, somewhat more than at home, so that you come hungry to the dinner-table; take a good dinner, without entirely satisfying your appetite; do the same at supper; take very little before going to bed, no more than, perhaps, a refreshing drink and a morsel of food. According to the advice of hygienists, three hours should intervene between the evening meal and bedtime. Keep this rule, and you will preserve your strength in the midst of work, besides performing many acts of mortification for the sanctification of your soul.

C. *Take your regular sleep.* The ordinary time for sleep in this country is from 10.30 P.M. to 4.30 A.M. together with an hour from 1.30 to 2.30 P.M. [53] This makes seven hours in all, enough to refresh the body, yet altogether necessary after a hard day's work. Every one should co-operate that this amount of sleep may be enjoyed by all, by observing punctuality at night prayers, by retiring at the proper time, and by keeping the prescribed silence.

D. *Allow yourself the ordinary recreation.* It is the custom in this country to have a full hour's recreation, including breakfast, in the morning, and an hour and a half, including dinner, at noon, and the same, including supper, in the evening. The last half hour of the evening recreation may be employed in private devotion. It is for this purpose that it has been added; formerly the evening recreation lasted only an hour. Every one should try to shorten the meal-time, and, consequently, be punctual in coming to table, not too slow in eating, nor prolong the conversation. Singing, or other musical performances immediately after meals, is injurious to health. Parlor-business should be settled briefly, or, if it should take some time — as, for example, when instructions are

[53] Prov. Stat. n. 19.

to be given — it should be postponed, as has been said before.

Whenever our recreation takes place in company with the clergy of the place, we do not say the *Ave Maria*, etc., publicly, on our knees, but privately without any outward ceremony, as that would embarrass strangers.

The practice of these virtues will not only preserve the religious spirit of our missionaries, but will at the same time give them a great delight in prosecuting with fervor the work of their apostolate, and always assure them of success.

## 5. The Missionaries' Return After the Mission

As soon as the work of the Mission is finished, the missionaries should leave the place.[54] They should make no visits except to the sick, take no unnecessary rides, accept no invitations to dinner in the houses of seculars, or allow themselves to be detained by anything not in connection with the Mission. In returning home, or going to another Mission, they should not go by circuitous routes for the sake of recreation, nor visit convents or other places. After their arrival at home, they are allowed some bodily relaxation, but they should also repair by the prescribed recollection the loss that their souls may have suffered.[55] Then, they should spend the time until they go out again, as usual, following the regular order of the day.

[54] This rule was laid down and followed by all saintly missionaries, as Segneri, St. Leonard, etc., and was enforced by St. Alphonsus. See C. E., Vol. XV. p. 291; also, Old Rule, Codex, n. 146.
[55] R., n. 126, 127.

### 6. Expenses of the Missions

That Missions are expensive, both for the Pastor and the missionaries, is certain. It is expected that the Pastor will see to the indemnification of the missionaries, and pay them something additional for their support. As a rule, we never ask anything, should it even happen that we do not receive enough to cover our expenses, or that we receive nothing at all, as has already occurred. Our reputation for disinterestedness is worth more to the Congregation than any amount of money. This is a point of the first importance, says Father Desurmont. However, the missionaries should modestly accept what is offered, unless it is clear from circumstances that the amount offered is not intended by the giver, or would impoverish the Pastor, in case he pays it out of his own pocket.

The question here arises, Since we have not as yet any foundations for Missions in this country, by what means may the expenses of the Mission be covered? Pastors should be prevailed upon not to mention this subject to their congregations before the close of the Mission. The usual collection may, however, be taken up at the principal services of the day. The night before the close of the Mission, the Pastor may draw the attention of the people to their duty of defraying the expenses of the Mission, but he should avoid speaking of the missionaries, "to whom the congregation is greatly indebted, and who should be handsomely rewarded," etc. Should the Pastor insist very much, one of the missionaries should make that announcement in his stead, using, however, the most moderate expressions.[56]

[56] In fact we even prefer to do it ourselves, because some Pastors say too much on this point, making the Mission appear as a money-making business. Prov. Stat. p. 130, n. 3.

## 7. Rules for Missions given by Fathers from Different Houses

Wherever any of our houses has a number of Fathers sufficient for the Missions of the district assigned to that house, the Provincial may leave it to the Rector of that house to accept and give Missions as far as his means will allow. The Rector of that house may also ask the Rector of another house to send him one or two Fathers to help at one or the other Mission. At present, this is generally done through the Provincial. Other Missions are accepted and arranged by the Provincial himself or under his immediate supervision, and the Fathers for giving them are selected from different houses.[57]

Whenever Fathers from different houses give a Mission together they must regulate their conduct as though they belonged to the same community from the time they meet until they separate, and not for the precise time of the Mission only. In regard to this point there exist here the following regulations:[58]

1. "Fathers, leaving the house for Missions, are subject to the Superior of the Mission, no matter who he is or from which house he may be. They are, if not recalled, subject to him as long as the course of Missions lasts, be it in *actu missionis* or during the intervals between one and the other Mission or on the journey outward or homeward. Hence, they are obliged to ask permissions from him, and to show letters — *exceptis excipiendis* — to him just the same as they are bound to do at home under their respective Rectors." As regards letters in particular, the Superior is not merely to glance over them, but "con-

---

[57] R., n. 130, 131; also n. 889, vii.
[58] Letter of Fath. Prov. Nov. 28, 1882.

scientiously to read the letters that come to and go from the Fathers under his charge." [59]

However, if subjects of a local Superior are with him on a Mission, they send and receive letters or other mail directly from their local Superior. Mail matter between missionaries and their own local Superiors does not pass through the hands of the Superior of the Mission.

II. "Every Father, no matter what his position at home may be, is in conscience obliged to give immediately all donations, Masses, *restitutiones incertas* to the Superior of the Mission.[60] At the end of the Mission, after deducting all expenses incurred on account of the Mission itself, that is, Mission Remembrances, etc., all the money received directly from any source whatsoever, save for Masses, is equally divided, regardless of any one's personal expenses, among the respective missionaries." [61]

But in regard to Missions given in our own churches by our own Fathers replaced by substitutes from the house of the Mission, the following regulations are to be observed: [62]

1. The traveling expenses to and fro are paid by the respective Rectors for their subjects.

2. The respective subjects say Mass to the intention of their respective houses.

3. The Rector of the church in which the Mission is given is to pay to the missionary for whom he sent a substitute *one-half* of the sum that he pays for every other missionary to the Superior of the Mission.

4. The missionary replaced by a substitute shall

---

[59] Prov. Stat. p. 46, n. 10.
[60] R., n. 129, 282.
[61] Prov. Stat. n. 76, iii.
[62] Letter from Fath. Prov. Jan. 17, 1886.

share *equally* with the other missionaries in all the accidental income of the Mission.

III. "Masses received of the ordinary stipend shall be divided equally among the missionaries. Masses received of a higher than the usual stipend shall be sent to the Provincial by the Superior of the Mission.[63] But if such Masses are to be said immediately by this or that Father, let him say the Masses and have the full benefit of the stipend." [64]

IV. "Donations of precious articles or other valuable goods shall be sent to the Procurator of the Province by the Superior of the Mission. Articles worth less than three dollars may be divided equally or sent to the Procurator of the Province." [65]

[63] Letter from Fath. Prov. Apr. 12, 1878.
[64] Letter, Dec. 4, 1880.
[65] Letter, Apr. 12, 1878.

# SECOND PART

# SERMONS FOR THE RENEWAL OF THE MISSION

## FIRST SERIES

# I

## OPENING OF A RENEWAL

TEXT: "And after some days Paul said to Barnabas: Let us return and visit our brethren in all the cities wherein we have preached the word of the Lord, to see how they do." — Acts xv. 36.

EXORDIUM. — The Apostles had the world before them to convert. — Nevertheless, they returned to those places in which they had established the faith and had placed the faithful under the care of good and zealous priests. They did so, not only to pay a simple visit, but

"Confirming the souls of the disciples, and exhorting them to continue in the faith." — Acts xiv. 21.

We do the same. Although overwhelmed with work, we return to those congregations to which we have preached the Mission, to renew these sacred exercises. This way of acting has been found so useful, so necessary even, that we prefer to drop a Mission rather than omit the Renewal of a Mission already given. This assertion may, at first, appear to be somewhat exaggerated. Listen, therefore, to the reasons for it, the statement of which forms the subject of the present discourse.

### I. THE RENEWAL IS TO FINISH THE WORK BEGUN IN THE MISSION

A tradesman is perfectly free to take an apprentice or not. But after he has taken him, he is bound to

teach him the trade to perfection. We were free to
accept the Mission that we gave you or not. But
after we had accepted it, we were bound to do our
best to complete the work. Now, our work was left
in an unfinished state. There are two causes for this:

1. The object of a Mission, as designed by God
and the Church, is to lead the people from the road
of perdition to the true and *perfect* service of God.
This includes a true hatred of sin, penance and absolution, reunion with God, and a love for virtue, not
merely out of fear of eternal punishment, but out of
love for the Infinite Good.

The Mission has done only the half of this work.
All that it could possibly effect, at least in the majority
of you, was a hatred of mortal sin, sorrow for the
past, a sincere confession, and a will to make good
use of the essential means of perseverance; and all
this, principally, *out of fear* of *eternal damnation*. We
had to be satisfied with this result.

Now we have come to bring our work to perfection.
Our object will be to inspire your souls with more
noble dispositions, to endeavor to make of you *truly
loving children of God*, provided we find your hearts
willing to follow our instructions.

"The end of the commandment is charity, from a pure heart." —
I Tim. i. 5.

Only after having produced this charity in your
souls, have we gained the full object of the Mission.

2. The fear of God is a strong motive for serving
Him; but it soon disappears, and with it all the good
resolutions produced by it. The love of God alone
confirms man in grace. St. Paul prayed for the
Ephesians that they might be "rooted and founded
in charity" (iii. 17).

Owing to their lack of the true love of God, many

who make the Mission become rather careless and lukewarm very soon after the Mission is over, in proportion as the impression produced by the meditation on the *Eternal Truths* disappears, — as boiling water cools when removed from the fire. They become less careful in shunning the danger of sin; less fervent in their prayers. . . . On the other hand, their passions are at work; the world attracts, the devil urges them. . . . They are already *sinking;* they would again fall most miserably. But the Renewal of the Mission comes to their relief just in time to prevent such a misfortune.

By attending the exercises, they will not only renew their resolutions, but, strengthening them with better and higher motives, they will make them lasting, so as to ensure their perseverance unto the end.

"Call to mind the former days wherein, being illuminated, you sustained a great fight" (Heb. x. 32), — and carried off the victory over sin and hell.

Oh! how important, how necessary, then, is the Renewal of the Mission!


## II. The Renewal is to Raise again those Who have Relapsed into their Former Sins

But some may have already relapsed, and they are now perhaps utterly discouraged, thinking it impossible to persevere in the service of God. What we had reason to fear has unhappily occurred. Hell has gained the victory again over them, and is now celebrating a malignant triumph over the most extraordinary grace of God. — But there shall be an end to your triumph, ye infernal demons!—Your momentary success shall be turned to your greater confusion!

1. It is true the sin of those weak souls is now much greater, their ingratitude much baser . . . than it was before the Mission. Let them acknowledge it! By the Mission they were enlightened on the grievousness of sin and its fearful consequences, their duties, etc. God forgave them all their sins. He manifested to them His infinite love and mercy. . . . And yet, where is the fruit? Sin, and sin again!

Do they deserve pardon again? Indeed, they do not *deserve* it. But God has once more manifested His mercy toward them in sending the Renewal. They will be forgiven again, provided they return with *deeper contrition*, with a *stronger determination* to avoid sin and the occasions of it, — and especially if they strive to appease the wrath of God by some *voluntary penance*, before they approach the sacred tribunal on this occasion.

God forgave the Israelites again and again, after their repeated falls into the sin of idolatry and other crimes. St. Paul absolved the incestuous Corinthian who had fallen into sin after his reception into the Church. St. John admonishes his children not to sin, but not to despair of forgiveness after they had sinned (I John ii. 1, 2). The Church grants absolution to the relapsed, — but only under the above-mentioned conditions.

2. After all, we are constrained to say a great deal *for the consolation* of such relapsing sinners. They certainly meant well at the Mission, and for some time afterward. For a time they fought manfully, and only after a struggle they foolishly yielded. They did some good in their first fervor. Their relapse has taught them a most wholesome lesson. They know now by their own sad experience that we did not exaggerate when we insisted so much on careful flight

from the occasions of sin, on fervent prayer, and on the frequentation of the sacraments.

They fell because they did not believe us. They believed their own judgment, the persuasions of the world, and the suggestions of the devil. And the greatest lie that hell makes them believe is the constant persuasion that for them there is no remedy; that it is useless to try; that they cannot be good.

After another reconciliation, these poor deluded souls will believe us more firmly, and will not fail to put in practice those means so strongly inculcated by the Church for holy perseverance.

There is also reason for supposing that they did not attend the exercises of the last Mission well, missing some, or not giving the proper attention to them. Seeing now the necessity of attending those exercises in a different spirit, they will, no doubt, attend this Mission better than the last, thus trying to supply past deficiencies.

Therefore, do not lose courage. Try again, but with more energy, in a different spirit, especially in a spirit of humility, knowing your own weakness and your utter insufficiency without the prescribed means of grace.

"Thou hast given occasion to the enemies of the Lord to blaspheme." — II Kings xii. 14.

Wicked men cry down the Missions on account of your bad example. They proclaim the greatest graces from heaven to be powerless to make the people serve God. The demons of hell glory in their pretended strength over God's grace. But so far and no farther shall the swelling waves of their boasted pride proceed. You will make the Renewal, begin once more, and thus by your redoubled fervor shut the mouths of your enemies and frustrate the designs of hell.

III. The Renewal Gives an Opportunity to Participate in the Graces of the Mission to those who did not Make the Last

The last Mission was a great success, but not for all. There were some

1. *Who could not* participate in its blessings, on account of sickness, absence from home, or some other legitimate cause.

They also are God's beloved children. He will not withhold from them those extraordinary spiritual benefits which He granted to the rest of the congregation. When Jesus appeared to the Apostles the first time after the resurrection, Thomas was not with them. He appeared to them again when they were all assembled together, and then He paid a special regard to the spiritual infirmities of Thomas. But there are others in the congregation

2. *Who would not come* to the last Mission. Every means to induce them to come remained ineffectual. They indeed have justly deserved to be abandoned by God. Perhaps some have already died in their sins. Others may have been struck with spiritual blindness, or may have been placed beyond the reach of God's extraordinary grace in some other way.

But others are here. God calls them once more by this most extraordinary method, inviting them to a reconciliation. Oh! the depth of the mercy of God!

May they acknowledge in this the finger of the Most High! Let them hear in spirit the prophetic words of Jesus over Jerusalem, and apply them to themselves:

"O Jerusalem, Jerusalem! how often would I have gathered together thy children, as the hen doth gather her chickens under her wings, and thou wouldst not. Behold, your house shall be left to you, desolate." — Matt. xxiii. 37, 38.

Let them fear lest that curse of God befall them.

"These men have not known my ways, so I swore in my wrath that they shall not enter into my rest." — Ps. xciv. 11.

CONCLUSION. — Recapitulation.

You fully understand, now, the object to be attained by this Renewal, and the reasons which make it so important. It was for these reasons that we greatly desired to return to you, and that your Rev. Pastor has so kindly gratified our desires. Now, it remains for you to second our wishes by your punctual and regular attendance, as well as by your docility of heart, of which you gave us so striking a proof during the Mission.

The indulgences are the same as in the Mission. Repetition. Order of exercises.

Well, then, unite your minds and hearts to ours in holy prayer and in fervent supplication that God may bless our humble work. We, on our part, placing no confidence whatsoever in our unworthy efforts, place this Renewal at the feet of the Queen of Heaven, our most powerful protectress and most loving Mother. May she direct these holy exercises, and obtain for them the blessing of the Eternal Father, for the conversion of sinners, the confirmation of the good, the joy of heaven, and the greater promotion of the glory of God. Amen.

## II

## THE LAST END OF MAN

Text: " Tell us, what is thy business? — of what country art thou? and whither goest thou? " — Jonas i. 8.

Exordium. — History of Jonas — his flight to Joppe — embarking for Tharsis — the storm — questions asked by the mariners. Jonas answered:

"I am a Hebrew, and I fear the Lord the God of heaven." — Jon. i. 9.

Were I to ask these same questions, people would tell me the country of their birth, their business, their plans, their movements in the immediate future.

"These things they thought, and were deceived, . . . and they knew not the secrets of God." — Wis. ii. 21, 22.

Men are full of earthly thoughts; hence they do not even know their real origin nor the end and object of their existence. And yet, this is the first thing a man must know, if he wants to live as a human being.

My object, in the present discourse, is to teach you this most important and salutary lesson. —May it please the Holy Ghost. . . .

### I. The Last End of Man is the Possession of God

1. *Whence* do you *come?* Did you come into this world by chance? You were born of your parents; but who formed your body, and who gave it a soul?

"God made us and not we ourselves." — Ps. xcix. 3. — "Thy hands have made me and formed me." — Ps. cxviii. 73. — "Thy hands have made me and fashioned me wholly round about." — Job x. 8.

2. And *for what object* did God create you? Every creature exists for a certain purpose, whether it continue to exist in the state in which God has made it, as the sun, the stars, the herbs, the animals; or whether it have been shaped into various forms by the hand of man, as a hammer, a pen, a knife, etc.

Does man exist for a certain purpose, or does he come and go without a particular end? Man, certainly, is created for some special end.

St. Augustine says that, at his time, there were two hundred and eighty-eight opinions in regard to the object of man's existence (De civ. Dei, lib. xix. c. 1). How many different opinions are held now by men in relation to this point?

3. Are we to look for man's end in this world? That end necessarily must consist in something which is within the reach of everybody, otherwise God would have acted irrationally; in something which will make man really happy, — for to create man for a miserable existence would have been cruel on the part of God.

Now, what can the world give to man?

"All that is in the world is the concupiscence of the flesh, and the concupiscence of the eyes, and the pride of life." — I John ii. 16.

Examine, whether all can possess the three things mentioned here, and whether, when they possess them, they are really happy.

*a.* The full gratification of the flesh cannot be obtained by all, so as to satisfy their desires completely; many are utterly incapable of carnal desires. And are those who wallow in the flesh happy? And if they are, how long?

*b.* Earthly possessions, which are the object of the concupiscence of the eyes, are within the reach of but very few. With life-long work and toil they cannot be obtained. And are those happy who have the good fortune of possessing wealth?

*c.* As to honors and distinctions — the object of the pride of life — very few can belong to the highest ranks of society; and those who enjoy the privilege are often more miserable than the lowly and the poor.

There existed one man who succeeded in procuring for himself all that his heart could desire, — Solomon, — and hear what he says about it:

"And I surpassed in riches all that were before me in Jerusalem . . . and whatsoever my eyes desired, I refused them not; and I withheld not my heart from enjoying every pleasure, and delighting itself in the things which I had prepared . . . and I saw in all things vanity and vexation of mind." — Eccle. ii. 9–11.

If man's last end is to be looked for in this world, then the beasts are better off than he, because they have on earth all that makes them happy.

4. But what a sad delusion, if this is a general mistake!

Man's last end cannot be found on this earth, because he is not to remain here, except a very short time.

"Man shall go into the house of his eternity." — Eccle. xii. 5. — "For we have not here a lasting city, but we seek one that is to come." — Heb. xiii. 14. — Jacob, asked about his age by Pharao, said: "The days of my *pilgrimage* are one hundred and thirty years." — Gen. xlvii. 9. — "While we are in the body, we are absent from the Lord." — II Cor. v. 6.

We are endless, interminable beings, existing for all eternity. But time is nothing in comparison with eternity, not so much as a second compared with a million of years. Consequently, we must look for our last end in the world to come.

Divine revelation enlightens us on this point.

5. Man exists *for God.*

"The Lord hath made all things for himself." — Prov. xvi. 4. — "And every one that calleth upon my name, I have created him for my glory, I have formed him, and made him." — Is. xliii. 7.

And how could it be otherwise with man, since God has endowed him with a close similarity to Himself?

"To the image of his own likeness he made him." — Wis. ii. 23.

God places man on this earth for trial, giving him some terrestrial happiness, and afterward, if he has been found faithful to God's holy will, He raises him into the celestial kingdom. He there unites man to Himself, to give him an insight into His infinite perfections, to behold them as far as he is capable, and, beholding God as He is, to admire, praise, and love Him as God loves Himself, for an endless eternity.

"We see now through a glass in a dark manner; but then face to face. Now I know in part, but then I shall know as I am known." — I Cor. xiii. 12. — "This is eternal life: that they know Thee, the only true God, and Jesus Christ, whom thou hast sent." — John xvii. 3.

And there in heaven man is to *possess* and to *enjoy* God, the Infinite Good, and to be one with Him.

"I am thy reward exceeding great." — Gen. xv. 1. — "That they all may be one, as Thou, Father, in me, and I in Thee; that they also be one in us." — John xvii. 21.

6. And then man is to *glorify* God forever.

*The glory of God* is the grand end of all creation, the grand object of all the actions of God. This is the great and harmonious chorus in which angels and men, animate and inanimate creatures, are to take part, with God as the center.

"To the King of ages, immortal, invisible, the only God, be honor and glory forever and ever. Amen." — I Tim. i. 17.

A higher destiny God could not give to man. It is the end and destiny of God Himself.

Alas! how small is the number of men who understand their last end and destiny! And among the few who know and understand it, how few there are who live and act in keeping with it!

## II. How must a Man Live on this Earth According to his Last End

The Wise Man says:

"Fear God, and keep his commandments: for this is all man."
— Eccle. xii. 13.

By this fear is not understood that terror of the divine judgments which is "the beginning of wisdom," but a true love, which causes a constant solicitude, lest we do anything displeasing to the divine goodness. He that loves God keeps His commandments.

1. The true love of God arises from a *true knowledge* of Him. For knowing God and esteeming and loving Him are one and the same thing. If we know a man who possesses all good qualities, we naturally love and esteem him, and we cannot understand why others do not do the same. Hence, we should constantly grow in the knowledge of God.

This is done by the study of nature, in which God displays His greatness in an eminent degree.

Then this knowledge is acquired and increased by reflection on the doctrines of revelation. These show us God as the Infinite Good, infinite in every perfection, love, beauty, power. . . . They explain to us His ever-watchful Providence, His constant presence near, around, and within us, His love in our creation, preservation, destiny, in the Incarnation and Redemption, in the sanctification of men by means of the Sacraments. . . .

Therefore, a man's first and chief duty is to know

his religion and to perfect this knowledge more and more.

2. The knowledge of God begets *love,* and love makes the observance of the commandments easy. If we love God, we want but to know His will, and we shall carry it out to perfection, even in the minutest details.

"He that hath my commandments, and keepeth them, he it is that loveth me." — John xiv. 21. — "If any one love me, he will keep my word." — Ib. 23. — "He who saith that he knoweth him, and keepeth not his commandments, is a liar, and the truth is not in him." — I John ii. 4. — "To know Thee, is perfect justice: and to know Thy justice, and Thy power, is the root of immortality." — Wis. xv. 3. — "Fear God, and keep his commandments for this is all man." — Eccle. xii. 13.

Love does not regard so much the punishment of sin nor the reward given to virtue. It simply has the good pleasure of God for its motive and aim.

Hence, the colder our love of God becomes, the more we shall disregard His commandments. And if it simmers down to a mere fear of His judgments, we shall not care any more about smaller offenses.

All the temptations of the passions, of the world, and of hell fall to the ground before a soul that loves God, as an arrow fired against a rock of granite.

3. The love of God produces *zeal* in the exercise of virtue, in promoting the service of God among men. It urges the soul to spend every minute of free time for God; to perform its daily task well, in order to please God by it; to use every opportunity for doing good.

"Whether you eat or drink, or whatever else you do, do all for the glory of God." — I Cor. x. 31.

4. Love never *thinks hard* of God. It knows that

"His wisdom reacheth from end to end mightily, and ordereth all things sweetly." — Wis. viii. 1. — "The very hairs of your head are all numbered." — Matt. x. 30.

Hence arises *perfect resignation* to the holy will of God. A good Christian is, therefore, always calm and serene, hoping and trusting in God under all circumstances. Even when he has fallen into sin he does *not despair*, knowing the infinite goodness and mercy of God. He cheerfully performs the prescribed penance; but then he never ceases to offer works of atonement to His infinite justice and sanctity.

Thus, such as live according to their last end are always happy, even on this earth, — precisely what God wants them to be even after the fall of our first parents.

Alas! how few are there, nowadays, who know God, love Him and serve Him, or who even care about doing so!

"God looked down from heaven on the children of men: to see if there were any that did seek God. All have gone aside, they are become unprofitable together, there is none that doth good, no not one." — Ps. lii. 3, 4.

All men have become earthly-minded.

"The ox knoweth his owner, and the ass his master's crib; but Israel hath not known me, and my people hath not understood." — Is. i. 3.

What will be the final result? Deeply reflect on the

### III. Consequences of Not Living According to our Last End

Far from being happy, those who live not according to the end for which God has destined them, are most miserable, even *here on earth*.

1. Because they have turned away from the true source of happiness, which is God. No sweetness is to be found in vinegar and gall; no light, in darkness.

"My people have done two evils: they have forsaken me, the fountain of living water, and have digged to themselves cisterns, broken cisterns, that can hold no water." — Jer. ii. 13.

God has communicated His perfections in a slight degree to created things. They are enjoyed by such as do not place their last end in them. For others they contain bitterness and disappointment.

"Know thou and see that it is an evil and a bitter thing for thee, to have left the Lord thy God." — Jer. ii. 19.

2. Because they look for happiness in themselves. The moment God is put aside, the faculties of the soul, the senses of the body, in which happiness is sought after, become prolific sources of misery. A knife for cutting wood becomes dull if you cut stones with it. So the soul of the sinner is never happy— depression, despair. . . . The body becomes subject to a variety of diseases, and is hurried to the grave. Explanation. Particular cases.

"The sinner's glory is dung and worms." — I Mach. ii. 62.

3. Because sinners make creatures their last end. Thus they make creatures serve against God. They are to assist man in living according to his destiny, and by being abused they are made to serve man against his destiny.

"All things serve thee [God]." — Ps. cxviii. 91.

They take revenge by causing the sinner's unhappiness. St. Thomas says that the multiplication of crime is the cause of so many irregularities in the atmosphere, the air, ocean, . . . yet God compels them, as it were, for the inscrutable purposes of His mercy, to continue in the service of man.

They sigh over this.

"We know that every creature groaneth, and travaileth [laboreth] in pain, even until now." — Rom. viii. 22.

But toward the end of time they will break forth in their fury.

"The whole world shall fight with him [God] against the unwise." — Wis. v. 21.

4. Finally, they are doomed to eternal misery. A thing that does not serve the purpose for which it was made, is cast aside as useless, especially after being tried repeatedly.

They reject God, as they care not for Him nor His service. God rejects them in turn.

"The unprofitable servant cast ye out into the exterior darkness. There shall be weeping and gnashing of teeth." — Matt. xxv. 30.

CONCLUSION. — Recapitulation.

You understand, then, in what consists your real happiness on earth and in heaven. How easy it is to procure it! Why have you been unhappy thus far? You comprehend the cause.

"Turn, then, turn from your evil ways: why will you die, O house of Israel?" — Ez. xxxiii. 11.

Pray that you may know your end, to see how far you have deviated from it.

"Lord, make me know my end, that I may know what is wanting to me." — Ps. xxxviii. 5.

God is most willing to let you understand it, since He has destined you for it.

O Blessed Mother of Jesus! do not allow us to walk any longer on any other road but the one destined for us by God; lead and protect us on it until we have reached the end for which we have been created. Amen.

# III

## SIN IN GENERAL — VENIAL AND MORTAL

TEXT: "Flee from sins as from the face of a serpent." — Eccli. xxi. 2.

EXORDIUM. — "Love is not loved," cries out St. Mary Magdalen of Pazzi. Hence, so very few carry out the end of their creation. Men love rather what is directly opposed to "love" — sin. Perhaps they fear great sins, because these deprive them of their eternal salvation; but as to smaller sins they are utterly indifferent. And yet

"He that is unjust in that which is little, is unjust also in that which is greater." — Luke xvi. 10.

To carry out, as much as possible, our destiny as men and Christians, we must "flee from *all* sins as we flee from a serpent," which we find hidden in the grass. To effect this, let us consider the evil of sin, whether small or great, in itself, and in its consequences.

## I. EVIL OF SIN IN ITSELF

Speaking of smaller transgressions, we do not include simple imperfections, nor the mere result of human weakness or forgetfulness; we mean sins committed with *open eyes*, with *free* and *deliberate consent*, although they are not mortal sins.

1. All sin is *an act of opposition to the will of God*.

"This is the will of God, your sanctification." — I Thess. iv. 3. — "He predestinated us to be made conformable to the image of his Son." — Rom. viii. 29.

It is God's will and command that we not only keep from such acts as must separate us from Him completely, but that we be free from everything sinful, taking, as far as possible, the life of our Saviour as a model. Hence, avoid such sins as uncharitable remarks, telling falsehoods, acts of impatience, every unnecessary indulgence of the taste, the eyes, the body in general. . . .

Say not, "this is but a small affair." Therefore, it is so much the easier to observe it, and so much the meaner not to care about it; and it betrays a cold indifference toward the Infinite Good, for whose love we do not care to do even what is so easy.

"The smallest acts of neglect are a stain in your conduct, so much the more shameful the easier it was to avoid them." — St. Bonaventure.

Everything that is great in the physical and moral world is composed of small parts. A palace, a steamboat, a farm. . . . So in regard to the moral world.

"Amen I say unto you, till heaven and earth pass, *one jot*, or one tittle shall not pass of the law, till all be fulfilled." — Matt. v. 18.

Hence, he who loves God will also fulfil his part in this magnificent work, and not pass over with indifference "one jot or one tittle" of the law.

"He that feareth God, neglecteth nothing." — Eccle. vii. 19.

2. All sin is an act of *great ingratitude toward God*. You fear mortal sin. You try to keep out of hell. But you care nothing about increasing your glory in heaven by avoiding smaller transgressions. And God, in His infinite love, has prepared it for you. Jesus Christ has purchased it back for you at the cost of His life. And you, blind creature, simply wish to keep from hell; whether you shall possess happiness in heaven in a higher degree or not, you care not, — nor

whether you shall love and glorify God more there. . . .
You esteem as *nothing* what has cost God *all*.

How much God abominates such ingratitude He
has expressed in His message to the bishop of Laodicea:

"I know thy works, that thou art neither cold nor hot [neither
guilty of great sin nor fervent]. I would that thou wert cold, or
hot [mortal sin might terrify thee into a life of fervor]. But because thou art lukewarm. . . . I will begin to vomit thee out of
my mouth." — Apoc. iii. 14–16.

God here compares Himself to one who has swallowed something at which the stomach turns, and who
is about to vomit it out. Such is the disgust of God
against those ungrateful beings who are still to some
extent united to Him by grace, but not by true love.

The principal cause of the disgust of God is, in
such men, a *latent pride* which God cannot bear.
They esteem themselves far above what they are.

"Thou sayest, I am rich, and made wealthy, and have need of
nothing; and knowest not, that thou art wretched, and miserable,
and poor, and blind, and naked." — Ib. 17.

3. The smallest sin is, therefore, *a greater evil than
any other evil in the world*. A wilful lie is worse than
all sickness, famine, war, destruction by fire or water.
An ordinary curse is worse than the death of the
entire human race. A wilful distraction at Mass or at
your prayers is worse than the damnation of the
whole world. . . . No matter, therefore, how great
the good is that might be expected to come from one
sin, although but venial, — or how great the evil to
be prevented by it, it must never be permitted. The
evil which you cause by your sin affects the Infinite
Good, while all other evils affect only creatures.

What should you, then, not do and suffer rather
than commit a single wilful sin! Rather let the body
be given over to the possession of a demon, tortured

day and night, lie sick in bed, emaciated by starvation, . . . than be given to worldly ornaments,
the indulgence of the palate, idle talk, sloth. . . . And
yet, looking down into the bottomless sink of your
corrupt heart, what do you discover there?

## II. Evil Consequences of Sin

1. *Consequences produced by sin itself.* A bad
fruit carries in itself the seed of other bad fruits. So
with sin. One sin begets another; thus, one may be
the father of a thousand. One venial sin, the cause of
many mortal sins.

Reasons: God abominates a lukewarm soul. That
soul will have severe temptations. These it will
not overcome without the actual assistance of God.
But God will treat the soul with the same indifference
with which it treats Him. Hence, a miserable fall.

Fervent prayer would help the soul. Of this a
lukewarm soul is incapable. Therefore . . .

Pride will not allow the soul to humble itself before
God, acknowledging its misery and its utter depend-
ence on God. And He even "resists the proud"
(James iv. 6), instead of assisting them. Therefore. . .

In its blindness, which is assisted by hell, the soul
will not even acknowledge its guilt to be of any serious
nature after it is fallen. Hence, no repentance, no
sincere confession, and therefore sacrileges without
end.

2. *Venial sins, unscrupulously committed, soon become mortal sins.* Thus, thoughtless cursing will soon
become serious imprecations; slight· acts of disobedience will soon bring on grievous acts of opposition;
slight familiarities with the other sex will soon change
into sinful freedoms; unchecked passions will bring on

enmity; small thefts will lead to great ones; frequent lies, to calumnies, etc.

A spark of fire may cause an immense conflagration; a small hole in a ship, its destruction; a little slight cold, not attended to, the death of a man. So a sin of so-called little account may cause the eternal ruin of one, ten, a thousand souls. Explanation.

The five foolish virgins had only forgotten to bring oil along with their lamps (Matt. xxv), and they could not enter with the bridegroom. The wicked servant had simply neglected to work with the talent intrusted to him by his master (ib.), and he was cast into exterior darkness. . . .

Alas! how many, after leading a worldly life, not wishing to believe themselves so bad as they are, may one day knock at the gates of heaven, saying, "Lord, Lord, open to us"; and to their utmost terror they will hear the words, "Amen, I say to you, I know you not" (Matt. xxv. 11, 12).

3. *The punishment of sin, small or great.* Consider, first, the *temporal punishment in this world.* The wife of Lot allowed herself a forbidden look of curiosity upon the burning cities of Sodom and Gomorrha. For this she was instantly turned into a pillar of salt.

"Save thy life; look not back . . . and his wife looking behind her, was turned into a statue of salt." — Gen. xix. 17, 26.

Sudden death for a curious look! Think of your manifold sins of curiosity!

Moses struck the rock twice out of which God wished water to spring forth to quench the thirst of His people, thus giving way to distrust in God's mercy toward a wicked people. For this, although a man so much beloved by God, so pure, and so holy, he was not allowed to lead the people into the Promised Land.

Moses and Aaron (who was guilty of the same want of confidence) were to die in the desert.

"The Lord said to Moses and Aaron: Because you have not believed me . . . you shall not bring these people into the land, which I will give them." — Num. xx. 12.

Remember your distrust of God, — neglect of prayer, — giving all your time to business, lest you should be in want.

Oza only stretched out his arm to prevent the ark of God from falling when it was brought through the land of Cariathiarim. For this he was struck dead on the spot.

"And the indignation of the Lord was enkindled against Oza; and he struck him for his rashness: and he died there before the ark of God." — II Kings vi. 7.

Call to mind your little care about supporting the Church; your acts of irreverence in the Church. . . . Many lose their faith in consequence. Their souls are struck dead.

Saul committed an act of disobedience for which he had a good excuse (I Kings xv); David, an act of vanity (II Kings xxiv); the prophet sent to Jeroboam, an act of disobedience (III Kings xiii); and yet how terrible was the punishment that followed upon each. Reflect upon your omissions of duty in your state of life.

Consider, secondly, the *punishment of sin in purgatory*. Terrible is the punishment that befalls the soul that is saved, but must still suffer a long time in purgatory.

"All imaginable pains in this world are nothing in comparison with the sufferings of purgatory." — St. Bern. — "Perhaps some one will say, I care not for purgatory, as long as I have hope of entering life everlasting. But let all beware of speaking thus, because that fire of purgatory is more painful than any pain or suffering that may be seen or felt in this world." — Cæs. Arelat. — "I cannot tell what kind of pains these souls suffer, but I can say this much: that each of them would rather suffer all the tortures that ever were, are now, and will be endured by men until the end of time, than to stay in purgatory but one day." — St. Cyril Alex.

What a great evil is that which is to be expiated by such unheard-of suffering!

### III. Application to Mortal Sin

Now, if all this has to be said of minor transgressions, called venial sins, what must a grievous offense against God — a mortal sin — be! If a venial sin dishonors God to such a degree, what is it to provoke the wrath of God, with full and free deliberation, in a matter of the highest importance? If a simple lie is so great an evil, what is theft, injuring our neighbor's character, enmity, etc.? If such is the evil of an act of vanity, slight self-indulgence, what about impurities, drunkenness, etc.? All possible evils should rather be permitted to befall the world, including the eternal damnation of the human race, than to offend God by a small sin, *e.g.*, irreverence in the house of God. . . . What is it, then, to commit sacrilege, lose the faith, desecrate feasts and the Lord's day. . . ?

Compare the punishment of a venial sin with that of a mortal sin, — as eternal darkness, hunger, fire, demons, endless despair.

If these things inevitably befall those who are yet united with God by grace, what shall happen to those who are completely separated from God, cast away forever, condemned to hell? O Christians, reflect! St. Mary Magdalen of Pazzi justly exclaims: "If men rightly understood what sin is, they would never commit it."

Conclusion. — Recapitulation.

Did you "rightly understand what sin is," even such as is hardly regarded as an evil, which people generally pass over unnoticed?

Alas! how many millions of sins may you not have committed, for not one of which you have even done so much as to be truly sorry! How surprised would your souls be, had they to pass out of this life now, and see themselves in the light of divine justice! Oh! pray that the light of God may fall upon you now before you die, so that you may see the many sins which defile your souls!

But what shall I say to those who wilfully and deliberately have committed grievous sins, the penalty of which is, and must be, eternal hell-fire, unless they be atoned for by true penance? Have not some of you committed them again since the last Mission, when we warned you so earnestly against them? Oh! repent of it ten times, a hundred times, more than you did before! Impose upon yourselves even now some voluntary penances, before you approach again the tribunal of penance. Firmly resolve to keep from the dangers of sin after this, and to suffer death a thousand times rather than commit again a grievous sin.

Oh! may it please our dear Mother Mary to obtain for you this great grief and firm purpose of amendment! May you all serve God faithfully in future, so as to avoid the smallest wilful sin, and to lead a life truly pleasing to God until your last breath. Amen.

## IV

## DEATH OF THE JUST

TEXT: "With him that feareth the Lord it shall go well in the latter
end, and in the day of his death he shall be blessed." —
Eccli. i. 13.

EXORDIUM. — You will best find out the sweetness
experienced in fearing and serving God, when the
hour of death arrives. All is fear, terror, and despair
for the sinner when he has arrived at the gates of eternity; all is confidence, peace, and consolation for the
just. What is death for the just? Properly speaking,
not the end of life, but rather its beginning; transition
from temporal to eternal life; or, also, the end of all
misery and the beginning of real happiness. It is no
happiness to live in joy, but it is true happiness to die
in joy. Let us, then, witness the moment when the
pious soul is about to leave this miserable world, to be
united with its heavenly bridegroom in eternity.

## I. THERE IS NOTHING IN THE PAST THAT SHALL DISTURB THE PURE SOUL AT ITS DEPARTURE

There lies one who never possessed much of the
goods of this world, or if so, was truly detached from
them. Sickness has done its work. The place of the
physician is taken by the priest, who has always
stood in the closest relation to that soul in life. The
last rites of the Church have been administered.
Death is momentarily expected. But death has
nothing fearful to that soul as regards its past career.

1. On the contrary, it is an occasion of joy. Now there will very soon be an *end to all troubles,* sufferings, cares, solicitude. . . . Life is nothing but a period of suffering, for the rich as well as the poor.

"Man, born of a woman, living for a short time, is filled with many miseries." — Job xiv. 1.

The approach of death is like the coming of the night to the man who has worked hard during a hot (cold) day. He longs for rest. It is what the end of a long, tedious journey is to the traveler who approaches a beautiful city in which he expects to meet his friends, to live in the midst of them in the greatest happiness.

2. It is *the end of all temptations* and dangers of losing one's soul and salvation.

"The life of man upon earth is a warfare." — Job vii. 1.

These temptations have attacked the pious soul often fifty, a hundred times in the day, and have been the cause of constant fear and anxiety in life. Now they are over.

How happy does a traveler feel, after passing over an ill-constructed, badly-managed railroad, through a country where the malice of men is a great cause of fear to the passengers, when the last signal is given and the train has arrived safely at the terminus! How great is the happiness of a soldier after all the battles are fought and the war is over, and he can return to his home!

What constant watchfulness, what prayers and sighs, what care and solicitude, does it not require to keep the soul from sin in the midst of all the attacks of nature, the world, and the devil!

For this reason God often hastens to take a soul out of this wicked world, to keep it from contamination.

"He pleased God . . . and living among sinners he was translated (into Heaven) . . . lest wickedness should alter his understanding, or deceit beguile his soul." — Wis. iv. 10, 11. — "For the bewitching of vanity obscureth good things, and the wandering of concupiscence overturneth the innocent mind." — Ib. 12. — "His soul pleased God; therefore he hastened to bring him out of the midst of iniquities." — Ib. 14.

Well may that soul say: "For me to die is gain" (Phil. 1. 21).

The just man is not frightened when he is given up by his physicians, nor terrified at the prayer of the Church: "Go forth, Christian soul, from this world; to-day thy dwelling shall be with the angels in Paradise!"

## II. Nor is there Anything in the Present that can Terrify the Soul at its Departure

1. *Not its sins.* Either this man has led a life of innocence and purity, or he has had the misfortune of committing sin. If the latter, these sins have been confessed and annihilated by penance. God has forgotten them (Ez. xviii. 22). They may for a long time have caused him interior trouble. God permitted that for good reasons. The Sacrament of Extreme Unction has taken it away. His conscience enjoys a peace "which surpasseth all understanding" (Phil. iv. 7).

2. *Not the want of good works.* It is true he will see that he might have done much more good for God, for himself, and his neighbor. Still, his life is not empty. There are the many temptations overcome, the many fervent little ejaculations, aspirations, . . . prayers night and morning, acts of sorrow and contrition, prayers for a happy death, . . . Masses heard, confessions, Communions, little alms, crosses and trials borne patiently.

"And patience hath a perfect work." — James i. 4.

None of these good works is lost, but they all follow the soul to eternity.

"Blessed are the dead, who die in the Lord. From henceforth now, saith the Spirit, that they may rest from their labors: for their works follow them." — Apoc. xiv. 13.

3. *Not the separation from their dearest friends and relatives.* Fathers and mothers are torn away from their children. God knows what He does and what He will always do for men. Fathers or mothers do more for the children when in heaven, or even in purgatory, than they can do here. They understand better their real needs, and their prayers in their behalf are far more fervent and, therefore, more powerful. They also know that the separation is only temporary.

4. But what about *the fearful night of death* that the soul must pass through? True, it is fearful; but God will never, nor at this time, allow a temptation to come over the soul for which it has not sufficient strength.

"God is faithful, who will not suffer you to be tempted above that which you are able." — I Cor. x. 13.

Some have no temptations at all; others have terrible attacks to encounter, but the Last Sacraments give them sufficient strength against them. Nor is *the last struggle* so very hard, as is often imagined. In many cases the body is so prostrated that dissolution is rather a relief than a pain. Then death is no harder than falling asleep when the body is very much fatigued. For others the last struggle is greater. But the true Christian knows well how to suffer, and he will, therefore, most willingly offer this last sacrifice in union with the sufferings and death of Christ.

"The souls of the just are in the hands of God, and the torment of death shall not touch them. . . . Their departure was taken for misery, . . . but they are in peace. . . . And though, in the sight of men, they suffered torments, their hope is full of immortality, . . . because God hath tried them, and found them worthy of himself." — Wis. iii. 1–5.

### III. Nor has the Future Anything Terrible for the Departing Soul of the Just

1. *Judgment* is already *passed* for that soul. That soul has often judged itself with all severity in the tribunal of penance. Sin is judged but once.

2. *Jesus Christ* is coming, not in the capacity of Judge, but rather as a tender bridegroom who comes to lead home his faithful spouse. His sweet voice is already heard from afar.

"Well done, good and faithful servant; because thou hast been faithful over a few things, I will place thee over many things; enter thou into the joys of thy Lord." — Matt. xxv. 21.

3. *Heaven is approaching.* The Eternal City is even now becoming visible. A ray of light, coming from the other world, is reflected on the countenance of the dying Christian.

"I rejoiced at the things that were said to me: We shall go into the house of the Lord." — Ps. cxxi. 1.

This world passes away. The eyes grow dim; the ears have closed to earthly sounds; the night of death has set in. But just where the most awful despair of the dying sinner begins, there opens for the soul of the elect the new joy of supernatural bliss. The light of this earth is gone; earthly creatures have passed away; friends and relatives he sees no more. But already do the beams of heavenly splendor shine upon him; the dazzling beauty of Heaven's glory rises before him; there come to meet him friends and relatives from the other world; his guardian angel, his Patron Saints, St. Joseph, the Blessed Virgin

Mary, stand at his bedside. Presently the last ties are severed, he breathes his last — that *beautiful soul is gone* — to its eternal reward.

"Precious in the sight of the Lord is the death of his saints." — Ps. cxv. 15.

How different is such a death from the death of the impenitent sinner! Mark the contrast.

RECAPITULATION, with reference to the death of the sinner at every point.

Will you not say, then, with Balaam when he saw the Israelites in the desert,

"Let my soul die the death of the just, and my last end be like to them"? — Num. xxiii. 10.

Well, then, lead the life of the just; for death is the echo of life. You have it all in your own hands. *"Sicut vita, finis ita."*

Cancel by prayer and penance the guilt of your past lives, and then spend the rest of your days in such a way as befits a good Christian. Live detached from earthly goods, pleasures; . . . bear all your trials with Christian patience; watch over your soul, overcome your temptations, be devout to the Blessed Virgin, love God above all things, . . . then you are ready at all times.

"Blessed are those servants, whom the Lord when he cometh, shall find watching; and if he shall come in the second watch, or come in the third watch, and find them so, blessed are those servants." — Luke xii. 37, 38.

# V

## PARTICULAR JUDGMENT

Text: "It is appointed unto men once to die, and after this the judgment." — Heb. ix. 287.

Exordium. — How few there are who fear the judgments of God! Hence that universal indifference and forgetfulness of duty. At the moment the soul departs from the body, its whole life, including the most minute circumstances thereof, will be laid before it as it is before God, and then will it receive reward or punishment accordingly. As regards that judgment, even the just live in painful uncertainty; how much more should the lukewarm Christian, the sinner, fear!

"[At the judgment of God] if the just man shall scarcely be saved; where shall the ungodly and the sinner appear?" — I Pet. iv. 17,18.

Let us, therefore, enter deeply into a consideration of that solemn transaction.

### I. The Tribunal and the Judge

When the last tie that holds the soul united with the body is severed, there reigns about the death-bed a momentary stillness which involves a world of mysteries. That is the moment of judgment, of an *irrevocable decision*. According to all probability, judgment will be held in the very place in which the soul departs. Our Lord said repeatedly that He will *"come* to judge" (Matt. xxiv. 44). Consider then,

1. *Who shall be the Judge? — Jesus Christ*, a moment

before a most merciful Father, now a Judge with *Divine severity*.

*As God*, — *a*, *Who knows all* — every step, movement, look, word, innermost thought, imagination, plan, design, and understands the value of each; Who has closely observed the prayers, aspirations, forbearance, charities, confessions, Communions, of that man, as well as his sins, no matter how hidden. The Wise Man says of the adulterer:

"Every man that passeth beyond his own bed, despising his own soul, and saying: Who seeth me? Darkness compasseth me about, and the walls cover me, and no man seeth me: whom do I fear? the Most High will not remember my sins. And he understandeth not that his eye seeth all things, . . . and he knoweth not that the eyes of the Lord are far brighter than the sun, beholding round about all the ways of men, and the bottom of the deep, and looking into the hearts of men, into the most hidden parts." — Eccli. xxiii. 25–28. — "These things hast thou done, and I was silent, . . . but I will reprove thee, and set before thy face. Understand these things, you that forget God." — Ps. xlix. 21, 22.

*As God*, — *b*, *Who must punish* or *reward* according to the *eternal laws of Divine justice*. He cannot give reward for what deserves none, cannot grant heavenly glory for what was done from earthly motives, to please men, for outward show, for self. . . . He must punish sin as it is in His sight, not as it is before men, who weigh things in the deceitful balance of their passions. Nothing but the severest justice!

"The Son of Man shall come, . . . and then will he render to every man according to his works." — Matt. xvi. 27.

Jesus Christ will be the Judge also,

*As man*, — *a*, *Who practised everything Himself* that He required man to do, obedience, poverty, humiliations, etc.

*As man*, — *b*, *Who sacrificed everything* for that creature — honor, wealth, comforts, blood, life; and for Whom that creature would make no sacrifice.

2. *Who shall be judged?* — *Every man* that passes out of this life: emperor, king, magistrate, lawyer, priest, bishop, pope; every man, woman, child, of every grade of society, of every occupation.

"We must all be manifested before the judgment-seat of Christ, that every one may receive the proper things of the body [what he has done during his life in the body] according as he hath done, whether it be good or evil." — II Cor. v. 10.

There is the *pure soul*, with all its virtues, prayers, mortifications, Masses, Communions. . . . Its sins are atoned for, the penance performed. *What Judgment* shall be passed upon this soul? *None at all.* That soul has already judged itself with all severity. For it is laid up the crown of justice. . . . It will enter at once into the joys of the Lord.

Others will appear in the *state of grace*, but, with *many* debts yet to be paid, or in a state of *imperfection*, not yet fit for heaven. There are yet thousands and millions of sins to be atoned for, many of which they would not even acknowledge as sins. Enumeration. All their *temporal punishment* is yet due. To their greatest surprise will they hear that all their little sufferings, crosses, trials, . . . were so many occasions granted by a loving Providence for their purification; things which they regarded as their greatest misfortune, and which were, perhaps, their greatest grace.

But a vast majority will appear there *as enemies of God.* For them now

"It is a fearful thing to fall into the hands of the living God!" — Heb. x. 31.

Baltasar was terrified at the three words written on the wall (Dan. v. 6). Daniel withered away and lost all strength at the archangel's coming (Ib. x. 8). The three apostles became frightened at our Lord's transfiguration (Matt. xvii. 6). How shall a soul appear before Christ, Whom it despised, Whose commandments it trampled under foot? And now that soul appears covered with sins, sullied, defiled with a filth that makes it a more disgusting object to Jesus Christ than a putrifying carcass is to man. And all this for that *miserable lump* of flesh that is lying at its side, dead and falling into decay.

## II. THE STRICT EXAMINATION

1. The examination of the life of man after death is not performed in the way of a *regular trial:* the *light of God* falls upon the soul, and in that light it sees its *whole life*, including the minutest circumstances, *present* before it, *as God Himself sees it.*

"In thy light we shall see light." — Ps. xxxv. 10. — "Every man's work shall be made manifest: for the day of the Lord shall declare it, because it shall be revealed in *fire*, and the fire shall try every man's work, of what sort it is." — I Cor. iii. 13. — "In the end of a man is the disclosing of his works." — Eccli. xi. 29. — "All things that are done, God will bring into judgment for every error, whether it be good or evil." — Eccle. xii. 14.

Hence, all the works of man will then appear before him, no better, no worse than they are in reality, before God.

"Weight and balance are the judgments of the Lord." — Prov. xvi. 11. — "We know that the judgment of God is according to truth." — Rom. ii. 2. — "Every way of a man seemeth right to himself; but the Lord weigheth the hearts." — Prov. xxi. 2.

2. A strict account will then have to be given in regard to the use of the senses and the members *of the body*, the eyes, ears, tongue, hands, feet, etc.

"We must all be manifested . . . that every one may receive the proper things of the body, . . ." — II Cor. v. 10.

3. Then, in regard to the use of the faculties *of his soul*, the mind, the will, the memory, talent, etc.

" To one he gave five talents, and to another two and to another one, to every one according to his proper ability. . . . But after a long time the Lord of those servants came, and reckoned with them." — Matt. xxv. 15, 19.

4. An account will be asked of the *time* that God granted to every one.

"God created man of the earth . . . he gave him the number of his days and time . . . and all their works are as the sun in the sight of God . . . and afterward he shall rise up, and shall render them their reward." — Eccli. xvii. 1, 3, 16, 19.

5. An account will be demanded of the *wealth* that God gave to man for doing good.

"Honor the Lord with thy substance." — Prov. iii. 9. — "Give alms out of thy substance." — Tob. iv. 7. — "Give an account of thy stewardship." — Luke xvi. 2.

6. A severe account must be rendered of God's most precious gifts *of grace* and the many *opportunities of doing good.*

"That servant who knew the will of his lord . . . and did not according to his will, shall be beaten with many stripes. . . . And unto whomsoever much is given, of him much shall be required." — Luke xii. 47, 48.

7. The good deeds of man will be weighed in the balance of the sanctuary, as prayers, alms, fasts, Masses, Communions, etc. And how shall they appear?

"I will judge justices." — Ps. lxxiv. 2. — "Often our justice appears as injustice when it is examined by divine justice, and what shines as gold in our estimation, appears as dirt under the examination of the judge." — St. Greg., lib. 5. Mor. c. 6.

Alas! how shall our good works dwindle down when they are exposed to the piercing light of God!

"If any man's work abide which he hath built thereupon [the foundation, Christ] (i.e. his faith in Christ) he shall receive a reward. If any man's work burn, he shall suffer loss." — I Cor. iii. 14, 15.

8. Then, there will appear in its true light all the evil that a man has done. In particular,

His *thoughts:* Murmuring against God, doubts against faith, interior blasphemies; . . . rash judgment, hatred, envy, contempt, revenge; . . . self-love, sinful attachments, sensual imaginations, delights, desires. . . .

His *words:* Speaking against faith, the Church, commandments, admonitions, ordinances; . . . false oaths, defamations, tale-bearing, lies, curses, maledictions; . . . impure language, instigations to evil, seductive conversations, all kinds of idle talk. . . .

His *actions:* Looks, reading, violation of Sunday, feasts, abstinence, fast, . . . acts of irreverence, acts of revenge, seduction, intemperance, theft, . . . sins of impurity, alone, with others. . . .

His *omissions:* Neglect of instruction, prayer, Mass, support of church and pastor, restitution, reconciliation with enemies, of particular duties, advice, correction. . . .

*Souls ruined:* One's own children, brothers, sisters, servants; . . . some of whom may already be in hell, or on the way to it, or have amended, or did not yield to you; . . . by immodest dressing, keeping taverns, getting up dangerous amusements, leading others to them, the sale or compilation of dangerous literature. . . . What an account!

And what can the poor soul say to all that rises up before its eyes now?

"Indeed, I know it is so, and that man cannot be justified compared with God. If he will contend with him, he cannot answer him one for a thousand." — Job ix. 2, 3.

And now in strict accordance with the account will be —

### III. The Final Sentence

1. Unfortunate soul! what will you do now?

"What shall I do when God shall rise to judge?" — Job xxxi. 4.

*Who* shall *defend* you? Where are those whom you were afraid of here, who encouraged you in your sins? Will they now take the sentence upon themselves for you? Foolish human respect!

Will you bring up in your defense, *your weakness*, your *temptations*, the attractions of the *world?* You will know that the proper and frequent use of the Sacraments, as well as fervent prayer, would have made you stronger than all hell and the world combined.

"Tell if thou hast anything to justify thyself." — Is. xliii. 26.

Or will you *return into your body?* Oh! how would you know, in that case, how to subdue that unruly flesh, keep it from danger, mortify and chastise it! But this is impossible.

"Shall man that is dead, thinkest thou, live again?" — Job xiv. 14.

But already is *the decision* about to be given on which depends your fate forever. Hear it!

2. Imagine a criminal tried for several days for a crime that deserves death. The jury have been out for deliberation; they return; the foreman rises; all are in suspense; he speaks: *"Not guilty!"* Oh! what joy for the criminal! Most willingly does he pay for the services of the men employed in his defense. But if the verdict is the opposite, *"Guilty!"* Oh! the thunderbolt that crushes him to the floor! Still, there is some faint hope of obtaining a commutation of sentence. And if not, his death on the gallows may turn out to be his salvation.

Your Judge speaks now. How you watch His lips, His first words! *"Come, thou blessed child of my Father*, possess and enjoy the kingdom of heaven prepared for thee from the beginning, and well deserved by thy virtuous life!" Oh! what joy for you! Now all is gained forever. How little will you think of your poverty, sickness, tribulations! . . . With what holy resignation will you go into the flames of purgatory, to be purified for your final entrance into the kingdom of Heaven!

But of such as will be favored with this consoling sentence there will be comparatively few. The greater number will hear the sentence: *"Depart from me, thou accursed wretch;* go into that everlasting fire well deserved by thy sinful life and impenitent death!" Oh! what terror and dismay will befall the condemned soul! Now all is over! From this sentence there is no appeal. What now are honors, pleasures, power, and wealth? What can the soul say? It is struck dumb. In despair it casts itself into the abyss of hell.

CONCLUSION. — Review of the picture.

Christians! sooner or later we must all appear before that tribunal, go through the examination, and we shall all inevitably receive one or the other sentence. Prepare for it! You have it in your own hands. All depends on your penance and your future life.

"God has placed it in our power what judgment we shall receive."
— St. Aug. serm. 47 de sanctis.

Take this matter into your hands at once, for the judgment may come upon you at any moment, and attend to two things:

*a.* Judge yourself with all severity about the past;

*b.* Do everything in future as though you were to render an account for it immediately.

Oh! make sure of your election! You will never

be sorry for it.   But neglect it, and you will grieve
over it forever.

O Eternal Judge! through the intercession of Thy
ever-glorious Mother, grant us the grace of true
compunction of heart and full forgiveness for our sins.
"*Juste Judex ultionis. . . .*

"O Just Judge of retribution,
Grant us pardon, absolution,
Before the hour of dissolution!"   Amen

# VI

## HAPPY OR UNHAPPY ETERNITY

TEXT: "Man shall go into the house of his eternity." — Eccle. xii. 5.

EXORDIUM. — These words will become true in regard to every one of us. Of every one it will be said, one day, "He is dead and gone," and some few people will mourn over us. He is gone — where? Into Eternity. For no one will be annihilated. *Eternity* — what a significant word! Who can fathom its depth, or measure its width and length?

What is the cause of so much religious indifference among men? What the cause of so much sin?

"With desolation is all the land made desolate: because there is none that considereth in the heart." — Jer. xii. 11.

No one reflects on Eternity. For this reason Moses complains:

"O that they would be wise and would understand, and would provide for their last end." — Deut. xxxii. 29.

Let us enter that unknown region in spirit, explore it as far as we can, before we enter it in reality. With Jesus and Mary as our guides, let us enter, deeply reflect on all that we shall see there, and turn it to our spiritual profit.

### I. MAN IS ON THE ROAD TO ETERNITY

1. "Man shall go into the house of his eternity." He is actually going, — moving onward. In this there is no freedom, as there is in other respects. "He *shall* go."

He cannot turn to the right, nor to the left, — nor stand still, — nor go back. As time passes, he moves onward. He cannot go back an hour or a minute. "He shall go."

Imagine yourself on a fast train on a railroad that leads over an abyss of a depth of about 400 to 500 feet, with the bridge left open, the engineer not knowing it, nor able to see it before he approaches, on account of the darkness of the night. Every second you are approaching nearer the awful spot where you and all on board of the train will be plunged into the deep. In such a position is man on the road to Eternity.

And how fast does time pass away! Once in a year the earth makes a circuit around the sun of 600 millions of miles, or 68,000 miles an hour. And this is the calculus of time, so fast it passes away.

How careful ought we, then, to be in putting our time to good use, so as to be prepared for Eternity!

And there are people for whom time does not pass away fast enough. They need amusement, even of a sinful nature, in order to "kill time" ! !

2. Time is given to man as a preparation for Eternity. Every moment of time he can increase his glory in heaven to an immense degree. He may also abuse it for his deeper damnation. The amount of time is fixed for every human being. Every day, every hour, it becomes so much shorter, until the last moment is come, perhaps quite unexpectedly.

The entire life of man, in comparison with Eternity, is but a moment.

"A moment on which eternity depends." — St. Bernard.

How soon will it be over! In fifty years hence all of us here will be in Eternity. And where? That depends on the way we spend life.

What would we do if for one hour we were allowed to be in a gold-mine and gather up as much as we could grasp? We would come out possessed of a fortune. And what do we do with the time allowed us to gather treasures for Eternity?

3. Man is at all times placed on the brink of Eternity. When shall he enter? Eternity is invisible, and is, therefore, approaching invisibly.

Imagine a man walking within a foot of a deep abyss without perceiving it. Such is man moving along the precipice of Eternity. He may topple over at any time, at any age, with or without previous sickness, whenever it will please God.

"If the master of the house knew at what hour the thief would come, he would certainly watch." — Matt. xxiv. 43.

Therefore, "be ye ready"; watch constantly over your soul, that nothing may happen which would be its ruin forever, were you to pass into Eternity in that state.

After having considered the road and the entrance to Eternity, let us step in, and there see, first:

## II. THE TWO ETERNITIES

"Man shall go into the house of *his* eternity," *i.e.*, that Eternity which he has prepared for himself in life.

1. There is the *Eternity of heaven,* — forever happy, full of joy without interruption; and the *Eternity of hell,* of endless misery, torment and despair. Some prepare for themselves a house in heaven by their faith, hope, charity, mortification; others are building their house in hell by infidelity, sin, human respect, sensuality, pride.

You are surely on the way to the one or the other

Eternity. And you know not with positive certainty on which, that you may strive always to "make sure your election." II Pet. i. 10.

"Man knoweth not whether he be worthy of love, or hatred." — Eccle. ix. 1.

In this matter there exists perfect freedom. Each one can do as he pleases. But into that house which he has built for himself, into that he *shall* go, and into no other.

"I call heaven and earth to witness this day, that I have set before you life and death, blessing and cursing." — Deut. xxx. 19.

2. There is a difference, however, in the reward, and in the punishment of every one in particular.

"The Son of man will render unto every man according to his works." — Matt. xvi. 27.

There are not two in Heaven who enjoy the same degree of glory. Take, for an example, one child that dies shortly after baptism, and another that lives until it has performed a few meritorious acts; a man that simply dies in the state of grace, with a certain amount of merits, on the one side, and a saint on the other. One good deed more increases immensely the glory in heaven already merited; one more prayer, one more act of mortification, of patience, of flight from sin, one more temptation overcome. . . .

What a blessing, then, is a long life spent well! How precious every moment of time; how inestimable every opportunity of doing good!

"In doing good, let us not fail; for in due time we shall reap, not failing. Therefore, whilst we have time, let us work good." — Gal. vi. 9, 10.

The same difference exists in hell in regard to the punishment of the damned.

The man guilty of one mortal sin, and dying impenitent, is lost, and will suffer the thousands of tortures heaped upon him. An additional mortal sin would increase his sufferings twofold. . . . What will be the punishment of a hundred, a thousand, a million mortal sins! . . . What will be the hell of one that lives in sin from childhood to death, which occurs in old age!

How foolish is it, therefore, to imagine, that it is all the same, whether you are lost with one mortal sin or a thousand; that you may as well "enjoy life," because you will be condemned to hell anyhow!

### III. Essential Qualities of the Two Eternities

1. Eternity is *supernatural*. Eternity not only exceeds the limits of nature, but it is also infinite.

Hence the least degree of glory in heaven exceeds all that has ever been felt, heard, seen . . . on earth.

"Eye hath not seen, nor ear heard, neither hath it entered into the heart of man, what things God hath prepared for them that love him." — I Cor. ii. 9.

So it is, likewise, with the tortures of hell. From some passages of Holy Scriptures we know the names of some of the tortures which the damned endure. But the real nature of those pains, their number, their intensity, is beyond all description and imagination. Hence, they can never be exaggerated. The most frightful description of the least pain of hell continued for hours would be far short of the reality.

2. Eternity is *immutable*. It is always the same. There is no getting accustomed to anything, either in heaven or in hell. After thousands and millions of years the blessed and the damned still say, "*Sicut erat in principio.* . . ."

In this world you get used to pleasure, so that it is

no longer pleasure, — even to acts of piety, to hardships, to sickness, to poverty. Not so in eternity. Ask a man that has been raised from poverty to affluence. . . . He will tell you that in the beginning he enjoyed it exceedingly, but now. . . . Ask a prisoner, chained to the ground in a dark, underground dungeon. . . . He will say that in the beginning it was frightful, but now. . . . Contrast this with the joys of heaven and the tortures of hell, where it is always as it was in the beginning.

The reason is, because time is a succession of moments and hours, . . . while Eternity is but a moment, and that lasts forever. Millions of millions of centuries are there but a moment.

"Of this one thing be not ignorant, my beloved, that one day with the Lord is as a thousand years, and a thousand years as one day." — II Pet. iii. 8.

Oh! consider, then, what it is to be *forever happy* in Eternity; and what it is to be *forever unhappy!*

3. Eternity is *endless*. — Suppose all the waters of the earth were changed into ink, the sky into parchment. The sky is lowered, so that we can reach it with our hands. All men over the whole earth lay aside all other business. They begin to write figures, and continue writing for weeks, months, and years, until they have used up the last drop of ink. By that time they have arrived at a figure that cannot even be imagined. Yet that does not yet designate the number of the years of Eternity.

What happiness, then, to enjoy the glory of heaven for Eternity! What are poverty, misery, hunger, . . . if through them we reach heaven, and merit by them a constant increase of glory!

"The sufferings of this time are not worthy to be compared with the glory to come, that shall be revealed in us." — Rom. viii. 18.

Oh! what consolation for the soul when, after departing from this world, it hears from the lips of Jesus Christ: "*Come*, blessed child of my Father. . . ."! It *comes* to God to behold Him in all His glory, and to be made one with Him.     It will seem to it — and who knows but it is so in reality? — that it is always penetrating deeper and deeper into this infinite abyss of glory, seeing always more and more of God, and loving Him always with a new impulse, without the slightest apprehension of ever being separated from Him, while the "torrents of pleasure" are pouring upon it from the heart of God.

"Such shall be that pleasure with which you will be always filled, and yet you will be longing for it while you are filled with it.  What I say, I do not understand, but God knows how to do it." — St. Aug.

But, alas! how shall this interminable duration appear to the reprobate? They are told to *depart*, to go away from God, with His curse upon them.  No hope of any reconciliation, no end to their tortures. It will seem to them as though they were always going further and further away from God.

Oh! what a heart-rending thought! To be cast off forever! To be abandoned forever to the fury of the demons, and the most terrible despair!

How, then, will appear to the reprobate the wealth of this earth, the honors that they coveted, the pleasures that they enjoyed, on account of which they never thought of working for their last end and destiny! Ah! Christians, if you could see hell but for a moment, you would suffer yourselves to be cut into a thousand pieces rather than commit a single mortal sin!

CONCLUSION. — Recapitulation.

Let us, then, go to work sincerely in preparing for that Eternity which we are constantly approaching, and which we *must* surely enter.

Settle the affairs of your soul *without delay*, lest, when you are willing to think of it, it be too late. Let these be settled before any other business.

Settle them *effectually*, radically, removing what must be removed, giving up what must be given up, practising what must be practised.

Settle them *securely*, leaving nothing in a doubtful state. We cannot afford to leave in doubt matters on which depends our all. This would be a most sinful neglect.

"Make your calling and election sure." — II Pet. i. 10.

But this is not effected by doing nothing. Time is given us for work; an entire Eternity will be given us for rest.

"Then, saith the Spirit, they may rest from their labors." — Apoc. xiv. 13.

While those who do not work now, will have no rest forever.

"And the smoke of their torments shall ascend up forever and ever: neither have they rest day nor night." — Apoc. xiv. 11.

O merciful Jesus! open our eyes, that we may see whither we are going. Oh! let us know our defects and our sins, and assist us in speedily amending our ways! Grant us a true sorrow for the past and a firm determination for the future. Grant us Thy love and a hatred for everything that is against it.

O Blessed Mother! take pity on thy children, who grieve over their sins. Protect us, that we may never offend God again; that we may love Him above all things, now here on earth, and hereafter forever in heaven. Amen.

# VII

## PRODIGAL SON

Text: "I will arise, and will go to my Father." — Luke xv. 18.

Exordium. — Strange delusion! When the sinner is about to offend God, he thinks of God's great mercy. He expects to be forgiven again. But after his fall, he thinks of God's infinite justice, and fears that there is no forgiveness for him. Are there not such deluded souls among you? Why did some not make the Mission? Perhaps they were afraid to return to God. Why have some others relapsed since then? Because they were not afraid of God, and now they are afraid of approaching God again. Let them take courage and say: "I will arise . . ." (text). These words were the first step that a wayward son took in coming back to his father. For the encouragement of all sinners our Lord relates this beautiful parable. I shall let Him speak Himself — that is, relate the parable in His own words — and only make an occasional remark of my own. Let all sinners pay attention.

### I. The Prodigal's Aberration

Our Lord relates that "a certain man had two sons. And the younger of them said to his father: Father, give me the portion of substance that falleth to me. And he divided unto them his substance. And not many days after, the younger son, gathering all together, went abroad into a far country: and there wasted his substance, living riotously" (Luke xv. 11–13).

1. *Causes of sin.* — The sinner is young. Youth is full of ardor, illusion, ambition. It wants to live as the world does, without any restraint. It pants for pleasure. It loves an idle life, worldly amusements; above all is it longing for independence.

This son demands *his* portion, although nothing as yet is his. So the sinner calls the faculties of his soul, the senses of his body, *his* property, his own portion; demanding from God the independent right of using them according to his pleasure. And yet all these belong to God, and must be used to His honor according as He prescribes.

The word "father" should tell him that he is God's creature, and hence God's property.

But all these goods, once in the hands of the sinner, are soon dissipated. To enjoy them more freely, he goes abroad, away from all exercises of piety, the Sacraments, church, good Christian society, priests; in order that not a word from them, nor the sight of them, nor the remembrance of them may disturb his conscience. The sinner goes into the sinful, boisterous world.

2. *Work of sin.* — There he wastes his substance, the immense treasures of grace, baptismal innocence, merits already acquired, the glory of heaven already merited, his pious inspirations, the benefits of a good early education, of good example, good natural dispositions, taste for virtue and decency, uprightness of heart, delicacy of conscience; his talent, which he prostitutes to sin; faith, respect for religion; he wastes even the vigor and strength of his body in the service of sin.

3. *Consequences of sin.* — "And he [the Prodigal]

began to be in want, and he went and cleaved to one of the citizens of that country. And he sent him into his farm to feed swine" (Ib. xv. 15).

The world has nothing to offer to the soul. It is reduced to starvation. Those vain pleasures are only for the body. And those hungry passions cry incessantly: "Bring, bring" (Prov. xxx. 15). Man becomes their slave. He has lost all power over them. He dare not refuse them anything, even at the sacrifice of his conscience and soul. He becomes a slave to the world, the judgments and maxims of which he must respect. He is under the power of Satan, who has full control over his mind, will, imagination. . . .

"And he would fain have filled his belly with the husks the swine did eat; and no man gave unto him" (Ib. 16).

Such is the degraded state of the sinner that there is no pleasure, no matter how beastly, that he does not covet. He envies even the stupid condition of the brute beasts of the field, wishing that, like them, he had no law but brute instinct, no other destiny than the gratification of sense and of the flesh.

"Man when he was in honor did not understand: he hath been compared to senseless beasts, and is made like to them." — Ps. xlviii. 21.

What degradation, what slavery, instead of the independence looked for!

"Such is the fate of one who refuses obedience to his Heavenly Father." — St. Chrys.

Examine whether this is not the sad state of soul in which many of you must acknowledge yourselves to be; and whether there are not the same causes for it. But, courage! Observe the happy change in the Prodigal.

## II. The Prodigal's Reflection and Return

"And returning to himself, he said: How many hired servants in my father's house abound with bread, and I here perish with hunger" (Ib. 17).

1. *Pious reflection.* — If the sinner would only stop to reflect on his miserable situation! But, alas! many do not even do this much. They prefer to be undisturbed. They will not listen to admonition. Their conscience is hushed into silence. Thus they are driven to a miserable end.

Others, however, enter into themselves. They reflect on their sinful life, the unhappiness of their soul, the causes which have brought them into it. They recollect the peace of soul which others enjoy who serve God, although not to perfection; the happiness which they enjoyed in their innocent days.

"Who will grant me, that I might be according to the months past, according to the days in which God kept me?" — Job xxix. 2.

In taking this sad view of his state the sinner does not despair, but he reflects on the infinite mercy of his Heavenly Father. He is encouraged by it. He arms himself with a —

2. *Courageous resolution.* — "I will arise, and will go to my father" (Ib. 18).

It is not a vague wish, a faint desire, but a will, a determination, a resoluteness, that animates his soul. Nor does he shrink from acknowledging his sins, and he most humbly craves forgiveness; not as though he wanted to dictate to his father, but being willing to be received back under any condition, even as the lowest in the house.

"And say to him: Father, I have sinned against heaven, and before thee; I am not worthy to be called thy son: make me as one of thy hired servants" (Ib. 18, 19).

He desires not to be excused, but to be looked upon as guilty of the scandal that he has given, as well as of the offense offered to God.

3. *Efficacy of his resolution.* — "And rising up he came to his father" (Ib. 20).

So must the sinner act. He must not wait long, — until the devil blinds him again, — or until he commits more sin. But, corresponding with the good inspiration, let him rise at once and go. Let him rise, trampling under foot all human respect and all other considerations, and go, — away from wicked companions, — away from the occasions of sin. Let him go, and present himself famished and ragged as he is; let him go to his father.

With these and no other dispositions must the sinner return to his God. But then, let him be consoled. He will surely obtain forgiveness.

### III. The Prodigal's Reception and Pardon

"And when he was yet a great way off, his father saw him, and was moved with compassion, and running to him fell upon his neck, and kissed him" (Ib. 20).

1. *God encourages the returning sinner.* — When He sees him corresponding with the first good inspiration and beginning to retrace his steps, He hastens to meet him, overwhelming him with grace to complete his conversion. He embraces and kisses him even before a full reconciliation is effected. He does not wait till he comes, nor does He allow him to wait at the door; He does not cast up to him his former ingratitude, the injury and insult received at his hands, . . . although He owes it to His divine honor, which demands

some reparation; to His sanctity, which cannot encourage sin; to His justice, which has rejected others less sinful. He seems to think of nothing but His mercy. Animated by grace, the sinner makes his humble confession.

"And the son said to him: Father, I have sinned against heaven, and before thee, I am not now worthy to be called thy son" (Ib. 21).

2. *God forgives the sinner*, and reinstates him in his former position.

"And the father said to his servants: Bring forth quickly the first robe, and put it on him, and put a ring on his hand, and shoes on his feet" (Ib. 22).

The priests are placed under an obligation to absolve the repenting sinner as soon as they are fully satisfied about his good dispositions.

They are to clothe him again with the first robe of baptismal innocence. Before God and the angels he is no more seen in his rags, but pure and ornamented with grace. He wears on his soul the sign of union with God — the ring; and he receives strength — the shoes, to walk with a firm step on the thorny road to heaven.

3. *God nourishes him* with the strong food of heaven.

"And bring hither the fatted calf, and kill it, and let us eat and make merry" (Ib. 23).

That soul which could not be nourished with the "husks" of sin, and which was, consequently, abandoned to starvation, now, purified by grace, is at once admitted to Holy Communion, and all who see it rejoice over it.

"So I say to you, there shall be joy before the angels of God upon one sinner doing penance" (Ib. 10).

There may be those who will call into question the

propriety of making "so much ado" over the conversion of a sinner.

"And he [the elder son] was angry, and would not go in." . . . (Ib. 28).

But they do not understand the mystery of the mercy of God.

"It was fit that we should make merry and be glad, for this thy brother was dead, and is come to life again; he was lost, and is found" (Ib. 32).

CONCLUSION. — Recapitulation.

Now, poor and wayward sinner, . . . here you have before you an exact description of your own aberrations, the causes of your sin, . . . given by our divine Redeemer Himself. Does it not exactly answer your case? Examine how you were led into sin. . . . Are not the spiritual misery and desolation described here also your own? Examine. . . . Well, then, let your return be also like that of the Prodigal. But that now depends on yourself. That God calls you is evident. Do not reject the call. It may be the last. You have already repeatedly deserved the severest chastisements. Say, then, in confidence: "I will arise, and will go to my Father." And all that the sequel of the parable relates will be realized in your regard.

O eternal and merciful Father! may all poor and abandoned sinners give ear to Thy sweet invitation, that they may rise and return to Thee!

O Refuge of Sinners! Mother of Divine Mercy! obtain full pardon and forgiveness for us all, and then, holy perseverance unto the end. Amen.

# VIII

## RELAPSE

TEXT: "Behold thou art made whole: sin no more, lest some worse thing happen to thee." — John v. 14.

EXORDIUM. — The Prodigal, after his return to his father's house, did not leave it again. He had learned a salutary lesson, and he profited by it. Besides, who knows whether his father would have received him a second time with the same kindness as before? Our Lord never gives so much hope to a relapsed sinner as He does to the sinner at his first conversion. On the contrary, He warns him most earnestly against falling back into sin: "Sin no more, lest . . ."

And yet, how many relapse into their former state of sin, even after two successive Missions! Let me warn you against this, principally on account of the fearful consequences which generally follow.

### I. CAUSES OF RELAPSE

Who relapses into his former state of sin? Not those who are assailed by most violent temptations, nor those who fall into smaller transgressions;

"For a just man shall fall seven times, and shall rise again." — Prov. xxiv. 16.

Nor those who may unhappily fall into one or the other grievous sin. But the relapse of which I speak is that of one who falls back into the same old sins very soon after his conversion, without much or any resistance, without prayer; . . . and falls back in

115

the same manner as before; and the same number of times, or even oftener. Examples. — Of such I speak in the present discourse.

The ordinary causes of this relapse are:

1. *Doubtful penance.* It is very probable, at least in many cases, that these unfortunate souls made bad confessions. Perhaps they were not in earnest about it, concealed some sins, or some notable circumstances, or the number of their sins. Perhaps a total change of heart did not take place; for how could the heart change so soon again? Especially if we consider those most powerful motives which produce the change of heart in true penance, as the offense of God, the loss of heaven, eternal damnation; how can we believe so speedy a relapse possible?

"He does true penance who so deplores his past offenses that he will not sin any more in the future." — St. Isid. — "There is a penance by which the soul is indeed accused, but not healed." — St. Aug. — "I say to the penitent, What does humiliation profit you, if it be not followed by a change?" — St. Aug.

2. *Want of the spirit of penance.* This spirit is required not only for the atonement of the past, but also for a precaution against a future relapse. Constant sorrow for the past prevents the commission of additional sins, especially because it is essentially united to a firm purpose of sinning no more. This spirit necessarily produces self-abnegation as regards pleasure, amusement, company of a dangerous character. . . . It therefore does away with the occasion, and thereby excludes a certain facility of falling back into sin.

"I chastise my body, and bring it into subjection: lest perhaps, when I have preached to others, I myself should become a castaway." — I Cor. ix. 27.

3. *Neglect of the three essential means of perseverance:* flight from the proximate occasions of sin,

frequentation of the sacraments, and holy prayer. Neglect the means, and the end cannot be reached. It would be easier for a stream of water to run uphill than for a soul to persevere in grace without the use of these means. (See obstacles to be overcome, — the sermon on Perseverance, First Part, — which make the application of these means absolutely necessary.)

4. *Human respect.* — This is a most powerful agent of hell. He that is guided by it is abhorred by God and His saints, and is, consequently, left without supernatural aid. The world will always be opposed to God and the maxims of religion.

"If I yet pleased men, I should not be the servant of Christ." — Gal. i. 10.

Some examples to show the influence of human respect upon the newly converted.

## II. Malice of Relapse

The repeated prevarication of the relapsed sinner contains a much greater malice, and includes, therefore, a much greater offense against God. It includes —

1. The *blackest ingratitude* toward God, Who granted the sinner so much grace for his conversion, so much strength for overcoming the obstacles in his way; Who dealt with him so kindly in his reconciliation. The Mission! what an extraordinary grace, and yet followed by a relapse! Now the Renewal! Shall another relapse be the result?

2. The *grossest infidelity* to God. The most solemn promises made to God, in private as well as in public, are disregarded and set aside. The judgment passed by the repenting soul in favor of God and His holy law, and against itself, is thus reversed against God;

the sentence of mercy declared void, and His justice challenged. The sinner, by his relapse, *de facto* repents of his repentance. Some years ago such a wicked man was heard to say: "I am sorry for the tears that I shed in the Mission."

3. The most *outrageous contempt* of God. The relapsed sinner is tired after a few days of the sweet yoke of Jesus Christ; the service of God has no attraction for him; he finds it loathsome; hence, he sets it aside. He prefers his sinful pleasures to the joys of heaven, his illicit friendship to the friendship of God, hell to heaven, the devil to God. He, as it were, asks the pardon of Satan for having abandoned his service, although only for a few days.

"The relapsing sinner, instead of rendering satisfaction to God, offers satisfaction to the devil." — Tertull.

In his temptations such a sinner does not pray, because he does not want the assistance of God. Alas! who can describe all the contempt of God that is included in the relapse into one's former state of sin? Therefore, God also abhors such a sinner.

"How exceeding base art thou become, going the same ways over again." — Jer. ii. 36.

### III. Evil Consequences of Relapse

I would not wish to say that the conversion of the relapsed sinner is absolutely impossible, but I must say that it is, at least, extremely difficult.

1. On the part of *human nature.* — Frequent relapses into sin induce a habit, which becomes a second nature. Nature will not overcome nature.

"He that washeth himself after touching the dead, if he toucheth him again, what doth his washing avail? So a man that fasteth for his sins, and doth the same again, what doth his humbling himself profit him?" — Eccli. xxxiv. 30, 31.

There is, indeed, the medicine of grace. But medicine repeatedly applied remains without effect. As the body gets accustomed to material medicine, so does the soul to the medicine of grace.

"For if, flying from the pollutions of the world, . . . they be again entangled in them and overcome, their latter state is become unto them worse than the former. For it had been better for them not to have known the way of justice, than after they have known it, to turn back from that holy commandment which was delivered to them." — II Pet. ii. 20, 21.

2. On the part of *hell*. After having forced an entrance again into the soul, the evil spirit will "dwell there" (Luke xi. 26). He will stifle every good desire, — keep it from prayer, sermons, good friends, and will lead it into utter despondency.

"And the last state of that man becomes worse than the first." — Ib.

The sinner will give up confession and all efforts, saying: "Of what use is it to me? I have tried it; it did not help me." He will call sermons "useless things," and, therefore, he will not assist at them any more.

3. On the part of *God*. Only some extraordinary grace would avail anything, for ordinary grace is ineffectual. Will God grant this to one who treats Him with so much ingratitude and contempt?

Will a father clothe again and again in beautiful white garments, the child that every time throws itself with them into the mud in the street, and seems even to delight more therein than in cleanliness? Neither will God clothe again and again with graces the soul that delights in sin and crime.

God forgives up to a certain number of sins; and gives His grace only in a limited degree to those who abuse it. How soon may the relapsing sinner reach the last sin, which, committed, may nevermore be forgiven! This is so much the more to be feared after God has shown such extraordinary mercy. So in regard to the last grace, which may be given very shortly after the Mission and the Renewal. Who knows but this may be the last?

"Thou hast ordered all things in measure, and number, and weight." — Wis. xi. 21.

After the last grace follows that terrible curse mentioned by S. Paul:

"It is impossible for those who were once illuminated, have tasted also the heavenly gift, and were made partakers of the Holy Ghost, and were moreover tasted the good word of God, and the powers of the world to come, and are fallen away; to be renewed again to penance." — Heb. vi. 4–6. — "The earth that drinketh in the rain which cometh often upon it, . . . but which bringeth forth thorns and briers, is reprobate and very near unto a curse, whose end is to be burnt." — Ib. vi. 7, 8.

CONCLUSION. — Recapitulation.

Oh! how important is this point for all of you! Be determined, then, to preserve yourselves from a relapse into your former sins. You will find it easy if you employ the proper means. Nor are these difficult to practise, if you have a will. Say, then, to God with David: "I have sworn, and am determined to keep the judgments of Thy justice." (Ps. cxviii. 106.)

But do not even trust your firm determination; trust rather in God, Who is your salvation. Do not abandon God, and He will not abandon you.

## IX

## HUMAN RESPECT

Text: "He that feareth man, shall quickly fall." — Prov. xxix. 25.

Exordium. — Nothing is more true than this sentence, inspired by the Holy Ghost. One of the principal causes of a speedy relapse into sin is *Human Respect*. Let us try to know this evil well, and to understand its abominable qualities, so that we may hate and detest it from our hearts.

### I. Human Respect the Greatest Dishonor to Man

In what does it consist? It consists in words, or actions, or omissions against one's own conscience, for fear of displeasing man. Such are conversations against faith or morality; supporting or encouraging acts of injustice or other sinful transactions; denying the faith, dressing in a scandalous manner; omitting one's Christian duty, — some good work; omitting timely correction of inferiors, or of others to whom a correction would be profitable, etc.; and all this in order not to incur the displeasure of men.

1. Such conduct shows a man to be a great *coward*. To deny the truth and assert falsehood, to call false what the Infinite Truth has revealed, to call right wrong and wrong right, to incur the indignation of God, to forfeit salvation, simply in order to avoid the censures of man, what a disgrace! what cowardice!

"Who art thou, that thou shouldst be afraid of a mortal man, and of the son of man, who shall wither away like grass? And thou hast forgotten the Lord thy Maker, who stretched out the heavens, and founded the earth; and thou hast been afraid continually all the day at the presence of his fury who afflicted thee." — Is. li. 12, 13.

2. It exhibits him who yields to it as a most contemptible *slave*. Certainly no one can be called free who serves the views, the wishes, the ignorance, the caprice, of others; trying to accommodate himself to them. Examples.

"You are bought with a price; be not made the bond-slaves of men." — I Cor. vii. 23.

How foolish! Will those people go to judgment, to hell, for you? Or if by Human Respect you suffer the loss of one degree of glory in heaven, who shall recompense you?

The world is not fond of acting thus when some temporal interest is at stake. What does it care for the opinions or the ridicule of others when money is at stake, or some high position among men?

3. It is the greatest *disgrace* to a Christian. What does a man of education care about the censures of the ignorant? But in matters of religion the world at large is most ignorant.

"The wisdom of this world is foolishness with God." — I Cor. iii. 19. — "The word of the cross to them that perish, is foolishness." — Ib. i. 18.

Should, then, a Christian care about what the world says or thinks about his principles or actions? And as regards the science of religion, the education of the Christian is infinitely superior to that of any man educated only in worldly sciences.


II. Human Respect the Greatest Injury to God

1. It *respects God less* than a miserable man, who is but to be the food of worms.

Peter and John, answering, said: "If it be just in the sight of God, to hear you rather than God, judge ye." — Acts iv. 19. "Fear not them that kill the body and are not able to kill the soul; but rather fear him that can destroy both soul and body in hell." — Matt. x. 28.

2. It includes the *blackest ingratitude* toward Jesus Christ. What has that man on whose account you fear to profess and practise the religion of Jesus Christ, done for you? And what has Jesus Christ done for you? He exposed Himself to the ridicule and scoffings of the world for you.

3. The authority of Jesus Christ is practically *ignored* by those who are led away by Human Respect.

"Do I seek to please men? If I yet pleased men, I should not be the servant of Christ." — Gal. i. 10.

Some ordinary examples in which this point is practically exhibited.

Should these considerations be insufficient to make you strong against Human Respect, then reflect on the

### III. Evil Consequences and Subsequent Punishment of Human Respect

1. Human Respect carries man to the *greatest excesses*. Thus Aaron had the golden calf made and adored (Exod. xxxii). Solomon, to please his wives, built temples in honor of false gods and worshipped them (III Kings xi. 7, 8). St. Peter denied Christ. Pontius Pilate, to please the Jews, condemned Jesus Christ to death against his own conscience and all the rights of justice. So, likewise, many amongst our people lose their faith, swear false oaths, neglect their Christian duties, commit all kinds of sin, theft, detraction, impurity . . . on account of Human Respect.

2. But the just punishment will follow immediately.

Such people earn the contempt of their fellow-men, whom they endeavored to please. How can a coward, or a man that dares not assert the truth, command respect? An independent man is honored and esteemed, although his principles may be abhorred; not a man of a slavish mind. They earn the just contempt of God.

"He that shall be ashamed of me and of my words, of him the Son of Man shall be ashamed, when he shall come in his majesty, and that of his Father and of the holy angels." — Luke ix. 26.

## IV. REMEDIES AGAINST HUMAN RESPECT

To cure yourself of this evil, or to protect yourself against it, consider

1. The example of the saints of the Old Testament. David did not care for the mockery of his wife Michol when he danced before the ark, manifesting his joy (II Kings vi). Tobias went alone to Jerusalem, while the other Jews did not. He feared God, and served Him, keeping the law in spite of the apostates around him, and in the midst of a heathen neighborhood (Tob. i. 5, 6). Daniel, in spite of the royal decree prohibiting the worship of the true God, went home, and opening his window, prayed toward Jerusalem (Dan. vi. 10, 11).

2. The example of the saints of the New Testament. The Blessed Virgin Mary, St. John, and the holy women were not afraid to follow Jesus to Mount Calvary, notwithstanding the ridicule of the people. The Apostles preached and proclaimed the doctrine of Christ, although they were hated, persecuted, and put to death for it. The holy martyrs intrepidly professed their faith in Jesus Christ and the Church, although it cost them their blood and lives. How little does it take to overcome you! . . . Examples.

Encouraged by these noble examples, trample under foot all Human Respect; professing your faith without fear; and practising it without being ashamed.

CONCLUSION. — Recapitulation.

After burying these reflections in the depth of your hearts, look up to that beautiful heaven which is at stake, and where you behold the long lines of heroes who have won the victory over Human Respect by their courage and magnanimity; cast a look down into that dreadful hell which will be your home forever if you do not set aside Human Respect; behold those numberless human beings, piled on one another, who lost their faith, or never professed it, or who were dragged into sin, because they were afraid to displease men. Seeing all this, say with the Apostle, adopting his words for your own:

"I am sure that neither death, nor life, nor angels, nor principalities, nor powers, nor things present, nor things to come, nor might, nor height, nor depth, nor any other creature, shall be able to separate us from the love of God, which is in Christ Jesus our Lord" (Rom. viii. 38, 39).

# THE CHILD OF MARY

TEXT: "If I forget Thee, O Jerusalem [mother], let my right hand be forgotten, let my tongue cleave to my jaws, if I do not remember thee." — Ps. cxxxvi. 5, 6.

EXORDIUM. — A great solemnity took place during the Mission, the solemn dedication of this congregation to the Blessed Virgin Mary. It was then that you chose her for your Mother, and gave yourselves to her as her children. I trust that this beautiful relationship has not been broken since. Let us confirm it to-day, and let your love and veneration for this great Mother be still more increased; for thus you render your salvation absolutely secure.

"He who is devoted to the Blessed Virgin Mary is as secure of heaven as though he were in heaven already." — Abb. Guerric.

Let us, for this purpose, consider, first, the excellence of this great Mother, and, then, the noble qualities that should adorn her children in order to render them more and more worthy of her.

## I. EXCELLENCE OF MARY

1. The ideal of this great *masterpiece* of the Creator occupied the mind of God from all eternity.

"I was set up from eternity, and of old before the earth was made." — Prov. viii. 23.

God even then adapted her to the great end that He had in view, and prepared the ornaments of body and soul that were to adorn her in time. Nor did He foresee any resistance on her part; on the contrary,

He foresaw the most faithful co-operation with His grace. Hence, from all eternity she has been the most beloved Daughter of the Father, the Mother of the Son, and the Spouse of the Holy Ghost: beautiful relationship with the Triune God.

2. As such she was selected to be the *great means of reconciliation* between God and man. In the great work of the Incarnation, she was again most intimately united with the human nature of the Redeemer. The Word was made flesh in her most spotless womb. She merited the extraordinary privilege of hearing herself called "Mother" by the Lord of heaven and earth.

3. To fit her for this extraordinary dignity, God prepared her from the first moment of her existence, *Immaculate Conception*. He endowed her soul from that time with supernatural ornaments, of which we mortals on this earth can have no idea.

"She alone surpassed heaven and earth in greatness." — St. Chrys. — "Mary is a work which is surpassed only by the Master himself." — St. Pet. Dam. — "Above thee is only God, and below thee all that is not God." — St. Ans. and St. Bern. — "God could create a greater heaven and a greater world, but he could not create a greater and a higher mother than the Mother of God." — St. Bonav.

Hence, when the time came that her Creator was to rest in her tabernacle (Eccli. xxiv. 12), the Angel Gabriel called her "full of grace" (Luke i. 28); and thus we have a witness from heaven to testify to her greatness.

"She possessed the plenitude of grace." — St. Jerome. — "Her grace was ineffable." — St. Aug. — "It was immense." — St Epiph. — "So much grace was given to Mary as it is possible to confer upon one and a pure creature." — St. Bernardine. — "The Lord was with her; she was blessed among women." — Archangel Gabriel.

4. Not only was Mary ever free from the slightest sin (Trid. sess. vi. can. xxiii), but she most faithfully

*co-operated* all her life long with the inspirations of grace. She went beyond every other creature in her sufferings, which she bore so heroically, to the immense increase of her merits.

5. Therefore, after her death she was assumed into heaven with soul and body, and exalted *over all the choirs of the angels*. God has made her the Queen of angels and men, of heaven and earth; the Mother of mercy, the refuge of sinners, the help of Christians, the dispensatrix of all graces. Heaven, purgatory, and earth unite in her constant praise; and yet they can never fully sing her praises.

"If the members of all of us were changed into tongues, we could not give her sufficient praise." — St. Aug.

And this great Lady is our Mother! Truly our Mother, and we are her children. What a privilege, what a joy, what a consolation! Let us glory in this, but let us also endeavor to be children worthy of her.

## II. Qualities of a Child of Mary

1. A good child does *not work against* the interests of his mother, nor does he promote the interests of those who bear his mother a mortal hatred. As a child of Mary, a Christian must not promote the interests of the wicked spirits of hell, whose power she has crushed. Hence, he must admit of no sin, mortal or venial, which is the work of hell. Nor can any one have the Blessed Virgin for his Mother who has the devil for his father in promoting his desires (John viii. 44), following sinful fashions, amusements, scandal, advocating principles detrimental to her honor.

2. A good child always remains in close *communication* with his mother. So the child of Mary. Prayer, ejaculations, sighs, pious glances toward her pictures,

invoking her in temptation. . . . Three Hail Marys after rising and before retiring to rest.

3. The true child of Mary frequently strives to do something in *her honor*. What happiness that we have every facility for doing some little thing that gives pleasure and joy to her pure heart in heaven!

*a.* As regards *prayer*. The Hail Mary whenever the clock strikes, at the beginning and end of every work, the Angelus, the Litany, the Rosary. . . .

*b.* As regards acts of *mortification*. Turning our eyes from objects of vanity, avoiding useless conversations, abstaining from a cooling drink, innocent amusements; mortification at table, doing away with some useless article of dress, bearing heat, cold, hunger, thirst, fatigue, calumny, slander.

*c.* Celebrating her *feasts*, whether of obligation or devotion, by hearing Mass, receiving Communion, making little offerings in the shape of some alms to the poor, . . . observing Saturday by some special acts of devotion or self-abnegation.

*d.* Practising the devotion to the Blessed Virgin without interruption by wearing a medal, the *scapulars*, joining some pious *confraternity* that promotes the glory of God, the honor of Mary, the salvation of souls.

4. The true child of Mary tries to *imitate* the virtues of his Mother. There must be a similarity between the Mother and the child. The most conspicuous of the virtues of Mary are: her humility, manifested on all occasions, in lowering herself below others, although she stood higher than the angels in dignity; her simplicity in her poverty, in her dwelling, dress, furniture, ways, manners, general bearing; her love of retirement, avoiding all public display, except for charity's sake; her obedience, in most minutely fulfilling the law of God, in submitting to St. Joseph, who was

far beneath her; her spotless chastity, for which she was willing to forego the privilege of being the Mother of the Redeemer; her extraordinary love for sufferings and her perfect resignation to the holy will of God in everything.

The more a Christian excels in the exercise of these virtues, the more he will be like his Mother, the Blessed Virgin Mary.

5. The true child will not only strive to please his mother himself, but he will also endeavor to *induce others* to do the same. So, then, the child of Mary will strive to promote and spread her devotion everywhere, especially among those under his charge, his friends, relatives, and all over whom he has any influence. Your desire should be to see her loved and praised by all men. Example of St. Ildefonsus, who was rewarded by her with a chasuble (Surius, tom. I), and of St. John Damascene, to whom the Blessed Virgin restored his right hand, which the Emperor Leo had ordered to be cut off, because by his writings he defended the veneration of pious pictures.

Such efforts merit for you the grace of perseverance. St. Bernard calls it a most infallible sign of salvation.

"Those that explain me shall have life everlasting." — Eccli. xxiv. 31.

To acquire these qualities of a child of Mary does not require many and extraordinary efforts. A good will and a true love for this good and great Mother are all that is necessary.

CONCLUSION. — Recapitulation.

What a glorious act was it, then, when you dedicated yourselves to this great Mother as her children! But have you ever since tried to be her worthy children? Did you not, perhaps, displease her often by your careless conduct? Have you not been a disgrace to her? Beg pardon, then, promising to do better for the future. Offer yourselves to her anew and with more sincerity. Once more declare and profess yourselves her children, and continue to be so in reality to the end of your days. Then rest assured that you will gain a glorious victory over your passions, over this wicked world, over hell, and you will triumph over them forever in heaven. Amen.

## XI

## THE JOYS OF HEAVEN

TEXT: "Be glad and rejoice, for your reward is very great in heaven." — Matt. v. 12.

EXORDIUM. — The sweet yoke of the law of God becomes most easy for us when we consider that every little act which we perform for God will meet with an infinite reward. Oh! if we could understand but a little the joys of Heaven, which will infallibly crown our good works, no suffering and no sacrifice would be too great for us, were it only for one degree of glory more to be gained by it! Let us, then, reflect on the Joys of Heaven which are in store for us, and thereby animate ourselves to holy perseverance.

### I. JOYS FOR THE BODY

1. There will be no more suffering or affliction for the body, no sickness, no pain, nor the slightest possibility of anything of the kind.

"God shall wipe away all tears from their eyes, and death shall be no more, nor mourning, nor crying, nor sorrow shall be any more; for the former things are passed away." — Apoc. xxi. 4.

2. The recollection of past sufferings, temptations, trials, pains . . . will add to the happiness of the blessed, if they have been endured for the pure love of God. Soldiers delight in recounting their battles, hardships; . . . mariners glory in the storms and shipwrecks that they have gone through. And so much the more because the bodies of the blessed are especially rewarded for their sufferings on earth.

"If we suffer with Christ, we shall also be glorified with Him. And the sufferings of this time are not worthy to be compared with the glory to come, that shall be revealed in us." — Rom. viii. 17, 18.

3. The bodies of the blessed will be endowed with the same qualities that the glorified body of Christ possesses; impassibility, subtlety, agility, brightness. Explanation.

"Our Lord Jesus will reform the body of our lowness, made like to the body of his glory." — Phil. iii. 21. — "This corruptible must put on incorruption; and this mortal must put on immortality." — I Cor. xv. 53. — "Then shall the just shine as the sun, in the kingdom of their Father." — Matt. xiii. 43.

4. The entire body (every part of it) will be overwhelmed with an abundance of pleasure.

"They shall be inebriated with the plenty of thy house, and thou shalt make them drink of the torrent of thy pleasure. For with thee is the fountain of life." — Ps. xxxv. 9, 10.

### Pleasures for the *eyes:*

"Eye hath not seen." — I Cor. ii. 9. — "In my flesh I shall see my God." — Job xix. 26. — "That city hath no need of the sun nor of the moon, to shine in it; for the glory of God hath enlightened it, and the Lamb is the lamp thereof." — Apoc. xxi. 23.

### For the *ears:*

"No ear hath heard" (I Cor. ii. 9) such music, such singing, as will be the angelic music. A slight touch of an angelic harp, heard by St. Francis of Assisi, transported him into ecstasy.

### For the *heart:*

"Nor hath it entered into the heart of man." — I Cor. ii. 9. — "Then shalt thou see and abound, and thy heart shall wonder and be enlarged." — Is. lx. 5. — "As you have drunk upon my holy mountain, so all nations shall drink continually; and they shall drink, and sup up, and they shall be as though they were not." — Abd. i. 16, *i.e.,* shall be completely absorbed in pleasure.

And the least of the pleasures in heaven will by far exceed all that has ever been seen, felt, heard, or imagined on earth, put together, because it is supernatural.

Now compare with this the foul pleasures of the flesh enjoyed in this world, but momentarily, for which heaven is bartered away forever, and which must be followed by eternal torments.

## II. JOYS FOR THE SOUL

1. Happiness of the *mind*. It consists in the acquisition of the most extensive knowledge of all terrestrial and celestial science. Nothing that God has made will be unknown to man in heaven; for all is made for the knowledge and enjoyment of man. To this is added the knowledge of God.

"We see now through a glass in a dark manner; but then face to face." — I Cor. xiii. 12. — "We shall see him as he is." — I John iii. 2.

2. Happiness of the *will*. It consists in loving and enjoying God in proportion to the knowledge that we have of Him. The soul is made for the possession of God. It has a boundless desire of enjoying God. God will satisfy this by allowing the soul to enjoy the abyss of His divinity to the full extent of its capacity. The soul will be absorbed in God.

"As the hart panteth after the fountains of waters; so my soul panteth after thee, O God." — Ps. xli. 2. — "I shall be satisfied when thy glory shall appear." — Ps. xvi. 15. — "We shall behold, love and possess." — St. Aug.

3. Happiness of the *memory*. It consists in recollecting all the various and harmonious ways of Divine Providence in regard to the government of the whole world, the salvation of the human race in general, of every individual in particular, in regard to ourselves. . . . We shall then see that what we looked upon as a misfortune, was in reality a great blessing. The recollection of our sufferings, humiliations, hardships,

. . . and the reward gained by them, will add greatly to our celestial happiness.

"Blessed is the man that endureth temptation, for when he hath been proved, he shall receive the crown of life, which God hath promised to them that love him." — James i. 12.

### III. The Society of Heaven

Man is a social being also in heaven, and he will, therefore, delight in company there as well as he does on earth. As the misery of the reprobate is increased by their wicked company, so is the happiness of the blessed augmented by the pleasant company of the inhabitants in heaven.

1. There will be true friendship and love, true familiarity between all, without distinction, high or low, angel or saint, without disguise, envy, ambition, suspicion. . . . Charity will never be weakened. God Himself will be most familiar with the very lowest.

2. And how many are they? Of the saints?

"I saw a great multitude, which no man could number, of all nations, and tribes, and peoples, and tongues, standing before the throne, and in the sight of the Lamb, clothed in white robes, and palms in their hands." — Apoc. vii. 9.

How beautiful, glorious, holy, cheerful, and blessed will each one be! Members of families will find one another. The loss of one or the other will not disturb their happiness in the least, because they will glorify God in His justice.

The angels will associate with men as their brethren, congratulating them on their victory. How many?

"Thousands of thousands ministered to him, and ten thousand times a hundred thousand stood before him." — Dan. vii. 10.

To these are added the Blessed Virgin Mary, Jesus Christ, God in the three Divine Persons.

Between all there will be a perfect union.

"I pray . . . that they all may be one, as thou, Father, in me and I in thee; that they also be one in us." — John xvii. 21.

This prayer of Jesus will be fulfilled to perfection in heaven.

### IV. Eternity of Heaven

All this happiness will never come to an end, nor will there be the slightest fear of losing it.

"Of his kingdom there shall be no end." — Luke i. 33. — "The just shall live forevermore, and their reward is with the Lord. . . . They shall receive a kingdom of glory at the hand of the Lord." — Wis. v. 16, 17. — "Better is one day in thy courts above thousands." — Ps. lxxxiii. 11.

Some comparison by which the duration of eternity is illustrated; for example, so many centuries as atoms of dust over the whole earth, and yet no end! !

Oh! what joy, what happiness, to live as long as God, to be as happy as God, to reign with God, without interruption, without diminution, without end! To be *forever one with the Infinite Good!!!*

Conclusion. — Recapitulation.

What a consoling thought, that we have a place in heaven already! Heaven belongs to us! it is our inheritance. Jesus Christ has purchased it for us with His own blood and life. Baptism has made us the heirs of heaven. If we lost it by sin, we have regained it by penance. Heaven is not for the wicked; it is for the pure, the just, the humble, the suffering for the love of God. Persevere, then, in doing good, in resisting temptations, in loving God, and in suffering for his sake. Through the merits of Jesus Christ and the intercession of the Blessed Virgin Mary, may you remain faithful to the end.

"Be thou faithful until death, and I will give thee the crown of life" (Apoc. ii. 10).

# XII

## RENEWAL OF BAPTISMAL VOWS

TEXT: "And I said; now I have begun." — Ps. lxxvi. 11.

EXORDIUM. — The time is at hand that our work among you must come to a solemn close. Let it be crowned by a most august act of religion, *i.e.*, the solemn Renewal of your Baptismal Vows. The Psalmist gives us the example. After having "thought of the days of old, and having had in his mind the eternal years," he felt a change in his soul, and he made up his mind to begin, as it were, life anew. "And I said . . ." (Text).

So have you spent a number of days, during the Mission and its Renewal, in reflecting on the judgments and mercies of God, grieving over your sins, and making atonement for them. To-day you appear "as newborn babes" (I Pet. ii. 2) before God. What could you do better than to say also, but with determination, "I have said it, and already have I begun"? For this reason we bring you back to the baptismal font (at least in spirit), bid you consider the solemn engagements that you then made with God — make them anew — keep them more faithfully than in the past, for the rest of your lives.

## I. RENUNCIATION OF SATAN, SIN, AND THE OCCASIONS OF SIN

"Decline from evil and do good" (Ps. xxxvi. 27), is the grand principle of a Christian life. The young postulant for Baptism must solemnly engage himself to carry it out; and only on this condition is the Sacrament of Regeneration administered to him. Three questions are asked which relate to the evil to be avoided, and three which refer to the good to be done. Let us, then, consider the first:

1. From the beginning there exists a sworn enemy of God, — *Satan*, with his fallen angels, — who with all his might tries to bring all creatures under his dominion. Unhappily, through the sin of our first parents, he has gained power over the human race. All are under his control until they are regenerated in Christ, born in the supernatural order, adopted as children of God.

No man is adopted as a citizen of a country unless he *renounce all foreign allegiance*. Thus must the new Christian renounce every power outside of God. But there exists only the one — Satan. Therefore.

And this renunciation must be *absolute* and *complete*.

"No one can serve two masters." — Matt. vi. 24.

Therefore the Church asked you before your baptism: "*Do you renounce Satan?*" And you answered readily: "I DO RENOUNCE HIM."

2. Nor was this sufficient. We do not effectually renounce a certain power so long as we *do its works*, promote its interests. Neither can we renounce Satan so long as we do his work and promote his interests. Satan stands in opposition to God. Hence all that is opposed to the will of God is his work — *sin*. As long, therefore, as we are given to sin, we stand on the side of Satan, in opposition to God.

To renounce Satan means nothing so long as we do his work.

"By their fruits you shall know them." — Matt. vii. 16.

Therefore we must also, and most emphatically, renounce all sin.

For this reason, the Church asked you a second question: *"And do you renounce all his works?"* And you answered again with determination: "I DO RE-NOUNCE THEM."

3. Nor is this all. Satan ruled supreme over the world, until, through the Redeemer, his power was broken; still, the greater part of that world voluntarily remains in his service, and by means of it he perverts governments, rules the fashions, amusements. It is through the world and its enticements that he rules and gains over to his service millions and millions. These, then, are his pride, his triumph, *his pomps*, because through them he glories over God. Hence, a true Christian can have nothing to do with them.

These include all worldly principles, sinful amusements, in a word, all that is dangerous to pure morality, or that is called the occasions of sin. To be a friend, a child, of God, and at the same time a friend of these things, is simply impossible.

"Whosoever will be a friend of this world, becometh an enemy of God." — James iv. 4.

Nor can we be said to have effectually renounced Satan or his works so long as we allow ourselves to be captivated by his pomps.

For this reason the Church asked you a third time: *"Do you renounce all the pomps of Satan?"* And you answered, a third time, with true Christian courage: "I DO RENOUNCE THEM."

After these three questions had been answered, the Church anointed you on the breast and between the shoulders, signifying *the strength* to be conferred upon your soul in Baptism against all the attacks of Satan and the world. The Church laid aside the violet, and put on the white stole, to denote *her joy* over your fortitude.

But how have you used this strength, and how have you corresponded with the joyous expectations of the Church? A look into your lives will tell you. Might it not be said of you that, judging from your conduct, you had sworn allegiance to Satan, so eagerly have you pursued his pomps, so sedulously have you carried out his works and promoted his interests?

But all this is now past and ought to be forgotten. You have grieved over it.

Now (here, in the presence of the baptismal font), I ask you to begin anew, to renew that part of your engagement which refers to the evil to be avoided. It is useless to proceed any further before we have again, and effectually, and with determination, renounced the powers of darkness.

Are you determined, then, to renew your engagements thus far explained? If so, rise from your seats.

I shall now ask you the same questions that you were asked before your baptism, and I expect you to answer aloud with a will and determination that will put hell to flight.

*Christians! do you renounce Satan?*

If so, say: I do renounce him.

[ (If they answer rather timidly) Is that the way you renounce this infernal beast? That will not put hell to flight. Therefore, once more:

*Christians!* I ask you, in the name of the Holy Church, *Do you renounce Satan?*

That is better.]

Now, let me proceed to the other two questions.

*And do you renounce all his works?*

If so, say: I do renounce them.

*And do you renounce all his pomps?*

If so, say: I do renounce them.

Well done! Let hell be confounded at this! Satan shall have no part in you any more. You shall henceforth be his *sworn* enemies, enemies to sin, and enemies to all that may lead you into sin.

## II. FAITH IN GOD, JESUS CHRIST, AND THE CHURCH

One part of our Baptismal Vows is now renewed and confirmed; now we can safely proceed to the other part. Turning away from the enemies of God, we come to God Himself.

1. A true Christian must believe that there is but *one God*, the Creator, Preserver, Supreme Ruler of all that exists; must likewise hold as *absolutely true* all that God has made known to man; must implicitly *obey* all God's commandments, and place in Him *all his confidence*. All this means *to believe in God*.

"Without faith it is impossible to please God. For he that cometh to God, must believe that he is, and is a rewarder to them that seek him." — Heb. xi. 6.

For this reason the Church asked you: *"Do you believe in God, the Father Almighty, the Creator of heaven and earth?"* And you answered: *"I do believe."*

2. But how do we know the truths which God has revealed, and the commandments which He has prescribed? For this purpose the *Word was made flesh*, to make known to us all that God wants us to believe, do, and avoid; and He showed us, by His own example, how to carry out the prescriptions of the will of God; those in particular which are hard for human nature, as poverty, contempt, obedience, meekness.

He also effected our reconciliation with God, meriting by His passion and death the atonement for our sins and our reunion with God. He proved His divine mission and character by the many miracles that He wrought, especially by His resurrection. In Him we must believe, and Him we must imitate. This is *to believe in Jesus Christ.*

"This is my beloved Son; hear him." — Luke ix. 35.

For this reason the Church asked you a second question — "*Do you believe in Jesus Christ, His only Son, our Lord, who was born into this world, and who suffered for us?*"; And you answered: "*I do believe*"; meaning thereby that you would believe and do all that Jesus Christ has taught, hoping in Him and taking Him for your model.

3. And how do we know the doctrine of Jesus without any danger of deception? After the ascension of our Lord, *the Holy Ghost* came down, inseparably uniting Himself with the Church which Jesus Christ had founded, and of which, as His mystical body, He is Himself the head. In this Church the Holy Ghost acts, directs, and speaks in the same manner as the soul does in the human body. This Church, then, teaches divine truth, gives divine directions, prescriptions, well understood and cheerfully received by all who are united to her; and who are consequently under the direct influence of the Holy Ghost. The faithful, united to the Church, form thus a Communion of Saints; through her ministry they obtain the forgiveness of their sins on entering her bosom, and afterward, if they do penance after falling; they will rise glorious from their graves at the end of time, and will have life everlasting.

"The Paraclete, the Holy Ghost, whom the Father will send in my name, he will teach you all things, and bring all things to your mind whatsoever I shall have said to you." — John xiv. 26. — "He shall abide with you forever." — Ib. 16–17.

This, then, is *to believe in the Holy Ghost and the Holy Catholic Church.*

Hence, the Church asked you a third question: *"Do you believe in the Holy Ghost, the Holy Catholic Church, the Communion of Saints, the forgiveness of sins, the resurrection of the body, and life everlasting?"* And you answered: *"I do believe."*

Then, in the name of the Most Blessed Trinity, to Whom you had vowed faith, confidence, love, and obedience, the Church, trusting that you would carry out your solemn promises, administered to you the Sacrament of Baptism, thus making you a child of God and an heir of the kingdom of Heaven.

Christians! your conscience will bear me out when I say that you have fulfilled these promises very poorly. Examine your faith and obedience to the Church, love and imitation of Jesus Christ, confidence and love of God. Does it not seem as though you had renounced God, instead of vowing to Him love and obedience? But all this is forgiven.

Renew, then, in your new fervor, your promises as though you began to live this day. Say again: "Now I have begun."

Are you ready to renew your engagements to God? Rise again from your seats.

Well then, Christians, *"Do you believe in God, the Father Almighty, the Creator of heaven and earth?"*

If so, say: I do believe.

*And do you likewise believe in Jesus Christ, His only Son, our Lord, who was born into this world, and who suffered for us?*

If so. . .

*And do you believe in the Holy Ghost, and in the Holy Catholic Church?*

If so. . .

*And do you, finally, believe in the Communion of Saints, the forgiveness of sins, the resurrection of the body and life everlasting?*

If so. . .

Now let me add one question:

*And are you willing and determined to keep these engagements until death?*

If so, then say with firm determination; I am.

O great God! Who art witness of these solemn promises of Thy people, mercifully receive them, and grant that they may be kept faithfully! O Blessed Mother Mary! protect these people from sin, and lead them safely to heaven.

# VALEDICTORY

And now, Rev. Father, pastor of this congregation, we return into your blessed hands and to your pastoral charge this congregation, pure and holy and reunited to God, which you entrusted to our care for the time of the Mission and the Renewal. May it prosper under your watchful care! May it henceforth turn to better profit the constant and unweary efforts of your pastoral solicitude and apostolic zeal! May all your parishioners, by their truly Christian life, strive to repay you, at least to some extent, for the labor and fatigue undergone for them in the past, thus softening the hard yoke of a pastor of souls!

And you, dear Christians, I most heartily congratulate you on this occasion for the good will which you have again manifested during this Renewal. May God bestow upon you a most abundant blessing! O most merciful Father! extend Thy all-powerful hands over this congregation! Be Thou indeed their Father in all their temporal and spiritual necessities! Grant them, through the merits of Jesus and the intercession of the Blessed Virgin Mary, a steady increase in every virtue, holy perseverance, a happy death, and the crown of eternal glory — in the name of the Father, and of the Son, ✠ and of the Holy Ghost.

In addition to this receive now again, as you did at the close of the Mission, the *Papal Benediction,* or the Blessing of the Holy Father the Pope, so well merited by you for your untiring efforts in behalf of your salvation, and the worthy reception of the Sacraments. Renew, then, your sorrow for all your past sins, detesting even every attachment to sin, no matter how small, and adding an act of perfect resignation to the holy and most adorable will of God.

O my God! I am most heartily sorry for all my sins. It grieves me that I have so often offended Thee, the Infinite Good. I firmly resolve, with the assistance of Thy grace, never more to offend Thee. I love Thee, O Infinite Love! and for the love of Thee I resign myself entirely to Thee. Do with me according to Thy pleasure in time and eternity.

*Confiteor.* — *Misereatur.* — *Indulgentiam.* — *Benedictio Dei omnipotentis.*

(Five *Our Fathers* and *Hail Marys* for the intention of the Pope.) It remains for you, now, to give thanks to God for all that His goodness and mercy has done for you during the Renewal. As for us, we have, with God's grace, now finished our work among you. May His blessing be upon it forever! — *Farewell!*

# THIRD PART

# SERMONS FOR THE RENEWAL OF THE MISSION

## SECOND SERIES

# I

## OPENING OF THE RENEWAL

Text: "I will go and return to my brethren, that I may see if
they be yet alive." — Exod. iv. 18.

Exordium. — Like Moses we return to you to see
whether you are yet alive, in *body* and *soul*. Several
may have died since the Mission the death of the
body; others, the death of the soul, others, both. For
those who have passed out of this life we can do nothing
but pray for their souls. For those who have lost the
life of the soul, we can do more; with God's grace, we
can resuscitate them again. But for those who are
dead, body and soul, we can do nothing. To those
who are still alive, and who have so far persevered,
preserving the life of the soul, we want to administer
additional strength. In a word, we want to renew the
work of the Mission, and establish firmly the good
effected by it.

## I. What is the Renewal of the Mission

The Renewal is a repetition of the Mission.

1. In regard to the *exercises*. Although the sermons are not all the same as in the Mission as regards
their subject-matter and their character, yet they are
all of the nature of Mission-sermons, and aim at the
same object. These excerises will not take up so many
days as the Mission, but they will take place in the
same order.

2. In regard to the *extraordinary blessings* attached
by God to the exercises of the Renewal. We know

this from the great results achieved by the Renewal, conversions that surpass even those of the Mission. Enumeration.

3. In regard to the plenary and partial *Indulgences*, gained by those who attend the exercises and receive the Sacraments.   Announce them.

4. In regard to the *amount of work* that the missionaries will bestow upon the congregation.   If we are not all the same persons, we are the same in zeal and in good will to promote the spiritual progress of the people.

5. From this allow me to conclude that the Renewal will also be a repetition of the Mission, as far as your *zeal* and *fervor* and *eagerness* are concerned in attending the exercises and frequenting the Sacraments.   State order of exercises.   And, to animate you to this, let me tell you in particular:

## II. For whom the Renewal of the Mission is Given

1. For all those who *did not make* the Mission, *a*, because they could not make it, or *b*, because they did not care to make it.   For these it is an act of the most extraordinary mercy of God.   Let it not be abused.

2. For those who *made the mission badly*, *a*, by not attending it as they should, *b*, by receiving the Sacraments unworthily.   For these the Renewal is an occasion of making reparation to God for abusing His greatest generosity toward them.

3. For those who have *relapsed* into their former sins.   Need we be astonished, considering the difficulties that they had to encounter on the part of weak nature, on the part of the devil, and on the part of their surroundings?   Unfortunate souls, you have lost every-

thing that the Mission had brought you, with the exception of two things: 1, the mercy of God, and 2, our sympathy! A proof for the one and the other is our return to you. If God did not wish to forgive you again, He would not have sent us back to you. As for us, we act as St. John the Evangelist, who came back to look for a young man whom he had converted and entrusted to the care of a priest, but who had become a robber. "Where is my treasure?" asked the Saint. He went in search of him, found him, and did not give him up until he had gained him back. We missionaries will do the same thing here. Apply to various cases.

Let them all return again. But,

"Be mindful from whence thou art fallen; and do penance, and do the first works." — Apoc. ii. 5 [which you did in the Mission].

4. For those who since the Mission *have lost their first fervor*, and are giving way more or less to their sinful propensities. These are leaning now to one side, now to the other. They do not wish to break with the friendship of God, but at the same time are they greatly attached to sin or to the things that must lead to sin.

"Woe to them that are of a double heart . . . and to the sinner that goeth on the earth two ways . . . woe to them that are faint-hearted . . . who have gone aside into crooked ways." — Eccli. ii. 14-16. — "How long do you halt between two sides? — If the Lord be God, follow him." — III Kings xviii. 21.

We have come back to encourage them anew, to raise their hearts and minds to what constitutes their true happiness. And we had to return so soon, for fear, if we delayed, it would be too late.

"We, brethren, being taken away from you for a short time, in sight, not in heart, have hastened the more abundantly to see your face with great desire." — I Thess. ii. 17. — "To confirm your hearts without blame, in holiness, before God and our Father." — Ib. iii. 13. — "Lest, perhaps, he that tempteth should have tempted you, and our labor should be made vain." — Ib. 5. — "For you are our glory and joy." — Ib. ii. 20.

We say all this to you. Every word of this applies to the Renewal and the necessity of it.

5. For those who have *persevered* in the good resolutions which they made at the Mission. We come to *confirm* them in their good dispositions.

"They [Paul and Barnabas] returned again to Lystra, and to Iconium, and to Antioch, confirming the souls of the disciples, and exhorting them to continue in the faith." — Acts xiv. 20, 21.

We return to these good and faithful souls, to strengthen and enrich them still more in heavenly grace. A strong man does not object to becoming stronger; a rich man, to greater wealth.

"He that is just, let him be justified still; and he that is holy, let him be sanctified still." — Apoc. xxii. 11. — "Woe to him who says: it is enough. As soon as you say, it is enough, you perish." — St. Aug. — "Fire never says, it is enough." — Prov. xxx. 16.

Love is a fire which always wants more, and extends farther.

CONCLUSION. — Recapitulation.

Jesus Christ is the same in the Renewal as in the Mission; the Blessed Virgin Mary, the same; the grace of God, the same; the missionaries, the same; may you also be all the same. — Invitation.

O great God of heaven, Creator of mankind, give a special blessing to our work!

"Turn again, O God of hosts, look down from heaven, and see, and visit this vineyard; and perfect the same which thy right hand hath planted; and upon the son of man whom thou hast confirmed for thyself." — Ps. lxxix. 15, 16.

## II

## THE END OF MAN

Text: "I spoke with my tongue: O Lord, make me know my end . . . that I may know what is wanting to me." — Ps. xxxviii. 5.

Man is placed here upon this earth to carry out the end for which God created him. Not to carry out that end means not to live as a man. Hence, it is above all necessary to know that end; then only can we know whether we have deviated from it, and how far. Alas! how many men live and die without ever having known their end, and are consequently cast off as useless things that have not served the end for which they were made.

The Psalmist prayed for a knowledge of his end, that he might thereby know what was wanting to him. May this same prayer be in your hearts, and may you attentively listen to my words while I explain this end to you. May Jesus and Mary. .

### I. Man's Last End is God

1. The catechism asks the question: "Why did God make you?" And it gives the answer: "God made me to know Him, love Him and serve Him in this world, and to be happy with Him forever in heaven."

Our end can be nothing else than God, for

"The Lord hath made all things for himself." — Prov. xvi. 4.

Therefore I am not made for this world, nor for men, nor for myself, but for heaven.

"And now what is my hope? — Is it not the Lord? — And my substance is with thee." — Ps. xxxviii. 8. — "Arise ye, and depart, for there is no rest here for you." — Mich. ii. 10. — "For we have not here a lasting city, but we seek one that is to come." — Heb. xiii. 14.

For this reason God never permits the human soul to find true rest and real happiness in this world, that it may not forget to look for its rest beyond the grave.

"The soul is restless until it rests in God." — St. Aug.

3. Now, if God be our end, we are obliged to *know* Him, and to know as much about Him as we can.

If we are to work for a certain end, we necessarily must know that end, and love it. One who works for money, wealth, etc., necessarily knows its value and loves it. If God is our end, we must not only know but also *love* God. And in reality this is the chief commandment given to man:

"Thou shalt love the Lord thy God with thy whole heart, and with thy whole soul, and with thy whole mind. This is the greatest and the first commandment." — Matt. xxii. 37, 38.

If we aim at a certain end in all sincerity, we work for it, we give our time and talent to it, we *serve* it; just as everything else, to be what it is made for, must *serve the end* for which it is made.

"The Lord thy God shalt thou adore, and him only shalt thou serve." — Matt. iv. 10. — "Fear God, and keep his commandments: for this is all man." — Eccle. xii. 13.

To these three acts of the soul, performed on earth, correspond the three chief features of its happiness in heaven. In proportion to its knowledge of God on earth, it will *see* God; in proportion to its love of God here, it will be *united* with Him there; in proportion to its service rendered to God here, it will *share* in His *happiness* there.

"We see now through a glass in a dark manner; but then face to face." — I Cor. xiii. 12. — "We all beholding the glory of the Lord with open face, are transformed into the same image from glory to glory, as by the spirit of the Lord." — II Cor. iii. 18. — "As thou, Father, in me, and I in thee; that they also may be one in us." — John xvii. 21.

The tendency of all things is toward unity, — final unity in God. In God everything finds rest. For this reason the Psalmist says:

"One thing I have asked of the Lord, this will I seek after; that I may dwell in the house of the Lord all the days of my life." — Ps. xxvi. 4.

## II. Means to be Employed to Reach our End

1. *The knowledge of God* is acquired by the contemplation of His great work *in nature*.

The world has not come into existence by accident, nor has it existed from all eternity. Who made it? Who keeps order in it? Who rules the immense universe? Who provides for all living creatures, great and small? The answer to these questions shows you the greatness, the power, the magnificence of God. Who can produce a single flower and give to it its peculiar beauty? Who fills a drop of water with so many living beings? Only give it a thought, and you must see the immense greatness of God.

From nature pass over to *the mysteries of our holy religion*, to the teachings of faith. There you see God as your Creator, your Father; you see in what close relation you stand to Him; you see His immense love toward you, etc.

Oh! how easy is it to know God! But, it is to the humble and the simple that this knowledge is given, not to the proud.

"I confess to thee, O Father, Lord of heaven and earth, because thou hast hid these things from the wise and prudent, and hast revealed them to little ones. Yea, Father; for so hath it seemed good in thy sight." — Matt. xi. 25, 26. — "I know mine, and mine know me." — John x. 14.

The knowledge of God is not given to the carnal.

"The sensual man perceiveth not these things that are of the spirit of God." — I Cor. ii. 14.

Nor to the proud, nor to the curious, who want to understand what is above human reason.

"Seek not the things that are too high for thee, and search not into things above thy ability; but the things that God hath commanded thee, think on them always, and in many of his works be not curious." — Eccli. iii. 22.

2. *The love of God* is a natural offspring of the knowledge of God, of His greatness, of His infinite perfections, and of His excessive love toward us, who are so closely connected with Him. Simple reflection on the various truths of religion cannot but produce in us a great love of God, which by every successive reflection will be wonderfully increased.

"The Lord hath appeared from afar to me. Yea, I have loved thee with an everlasting love." — Jer. xxxi. 3. — "The Father himself loveth you." — John xvi. 27. — "For God so loved the world, as to give his only-begotten Son." — John iii. 16.

Add to this the great love of Jesus Christ toward men, the sacrifice that He has made for them; the love of the Holy Ghost, Who is pre-eminently called the spirit of love, and what He constantly does for you in the Church. Must you not love God, then, too?

"He that loveth not, knoweth not God." — I John iv. 8. — "The charity of Christ presseth us." — II Cor. v. 14. — "The charity of God is poured forth in our hearts, by the Holy Ghost, who is given to us." — Rom. v. 5.

3. He that loves God, *serves God*. Love likes to please, is careful not to offend, looks for opportunities to render services, inquires what may please most, etc.

"If any man love me, he will keep my word." — John xiv. 23. — "He that loveth me not, keepeth not my words." — Ib. 24. — "Let us love God, because God first hath loved us." — I John iv. 19.

Love not only tries to please, but it is *not displeased* at what the beloved does, especially if it is certain that the beloved always acts from a motive of love. And this is the case with God in regard to us.

"Think of the Lord in goodness, and seek him in simplicity of heart." — Wis. i. 1. — "Many waters cannot quench charity, neither can the floods drown it." — Cant. viii. 7.

4. An *infallible means* to increase our knowledge, love, and service of God consists in *acts performed out of pure love for God*. God rewards such acts most generously. For every act of this kind He gives you a greater knowledge of Himself, which in turn produces a greater love for Him and a greater fidelity in serving Him. This greater service of God merits again a deeper knowledge of Him, etc. And so it goes on increasing, until you do and suffer everything for God, and finally wish to do nothing more except to work for God. Then you have accomplished your end here on earth.

"Therefore, my beloved brethren, be ye steadfast and immovable; always abounding in the work of the Lord, knowing that your labor is not in vain in the Lord." — I Cor. xv. 58. — "God is good to the soul that seeketh him." — Lam. iii. 25.

What glory in heaven, what union with God will follow a life spent in this manner!

After this consideration you will be able to tell whether you have lived according to your end or not, and if you have not lived according to your end, you can tell "what is wanting to you." — Examine

### III. The Causes why Men Neglect their Last End

1. *Because they do not know it.* People generally know what the end of the various objects around them is; they know the object of houses, of chairs and tables, of clothing and food, of various tools, of plants and trees, of the various kinds of domestic animals, etc.; but they do not know what the object of their own existence is.

They do not know it, because they do not care *to learn it.*

It is in man's nature to learn, to acquire knowledge. The learned are held in high esteem. Men make great sacrifices of time and money to acquire a high degree of proficiency in the various sciences. They study machinery, agriculture, mathematics, geometry, mental philosophy, astronomy; they study most minutely the system of their own bodies. But the question of all questions, "Why do I exist?" is left unheeded.

Young people have their arms full of books while walking in the streets; everywhere your eye meets a magnificent structure called a school-house, an academy, a lyceum, etc. Yet this one great question is never studied. And, therefore, are the people led astray by their own folly.

"Therefore is my people led away captive, because they had not knowledge, and their nobles have perished with famine, and their multitude were dried up with thirst." — Is. v. 13.

The souls of men are famished for want of the nourishment of religious knowledge, their hearts are dried up for want of religious consolation.

Men try to feed their souls and replenish their hearts with what is not suitable for their nourishment.

"He would fain have filled his belly with the husks the swine did eat." — Luke xv. 16.

But, people *do not* even *want to know* their last end. When such knowledge is offered them, they repel it.

"Depart from us, we desire not the knowledge of thy ways." — Job xxi. 14.

2. Because *people keep away from the source of true knowledge.* The knowledge of our last end and of the means of reaching it, is imparted by the ministers of the Church.

"The lips of the priest shall keep knowledge . . . because he is the angel of the Lord of hosts." — Mal. ii. 7. — "Going, teach ye all nations." — Matt. xxviii. 19.

But, alas! the priests of the Church are shunned, their instructions are avoided, their sermons are not listened to. The young are reared with scarcely a smattering of religious knowledge; no religious books or papers are kept and read, but novels and irreligious trash.

"O children, how long will you love childishness, and fools covet those things which are hurtful to themselves, and the unwise hate knowledge." — Prov. i. 22.

3. *Because those who know a little of their last end do not reflect on what they know.* We are in the habit of seriously reflecting on what concerns our highest interest. We think of it at all times, and in all places. We want to know all about it. We even, if needs be, set aside the thoughts of all other affairs.

Why do so few people follow up the affairs connected with their eternal destiny?

"With desolation is all the land made desolate, because there is none that considereth in the heart." — Jer. xii. 11.

Have they no thoughts? They have, indeed, without intermission, but for money, pleasure, amusements, worldly affairs, etc. Therefore, what few instructions they receive are of no benefit to them.

"We speak the wisdom of God in a mystery, a wisdom which is hidden . . . which none of the princes of this world knew." — I Cor. ii. 7, 8. — "It is foolishness to him (the sensual man), and he cannot understand, because it is spiritually examined." — Ib. 14.

4. *Because men fail to act according to the knowledge that they possess.* He that has an affair at heart beyond all others, never thinks he has done enough to insure its success. Is this done by men in regard to their last end? "I know enough," "have no need of sermons, Missions," etc., are expressions very common, even among Catholics. Why is that boy, girl, not sent to Catechism? "They know enough." Do we hear that in regard to knowledge profitable for this life?

"The children of this world are wiser in their generation than the children of light." — Luke xvi. 8.

CONCLUSION. — Recapitulation.

The time given to you for carrying out the end of your creation is short, very short, and it becomes shorter every day. Spend well the remainder of your days. Try to know your last end, reflect on it, act according to it. Begin with this Mission. Do not care what others do, worldlings, wayward Catholics. . . . "However it be with others, neglect not thyself." — Imit. lib. i, c. 25.

# III

## MORTAL SIN, THE DEATH OF THE SOUL

TEXT: "Who will give water to my head, and a fountain of tears to my eyes? And I will weep day and night for the slain of the daughter of my people." — Jer. ix. 1.

EXORDIUM. — Hell is not the greatest evil that can befall a man. Mortal sin is the greatest evil. To be put to death for murder is not so great an evil as is the murder which deserves it.

"It is no evil to be punished, but to deserve punishment." — St. Aug.

God, though He be God, cannot inflict upon man so great an evil; man inflicts that evil upon himself and upon God. A million of men have not tears enough to bewail this evil. "Who will give water . . .?"

And those who have brought this evil upon themselves do not bewail it, do not repent.

Let me, therefore, as far as I can, explain to them the evil that Mortal Sin brings upon the soul. May Jesus and Mary . . .

### I. MORTAL SIN IS THE DEATH OF THE SOUL IN THIS WORLD

For this reason it is called *Mortal* Sin.

"The soul that sinneth, the same shall die." — Ez. xviii. 20.

1. Mortal Sin *deprives* the soul of *life*. That life is sanctifying grace, which is God Himself residing in the soul.

"The gift of grace surpasses all the faculties of created nature, because it is a participation of the divine nature." — St. Thom. — "All things of his divine power which appertain to life and piety are given to us . . . that by these you may be made partakers of the divine nature." — II Pet. i. 3, 4. — "He who is joined to the Lord, is one spirit." — I Cor. vi. 17. — Cf. John xiv. 23.

Hence, says St. Augustine, as the soul gives life to the body, so does God give life to the soul. And consequently, as life in the body becomes extinct when the soul departs, so life becomes extinct in the soul when God is driven from it by sin.

"Sin, when it is completed, begetteth death." — James i. 15.

By Mortal Sin all communication between God and the soul is cut asunder, because it is a direct opposition to God, malice to sanctity, darkness to light, error to truth . . .

"Thou wast the spouse of Christ; thou wast the temple of God, thou wast the dwelling of the Holy Ghost. And as often as I say, *thou wast*, I must grieve, because thou art no longer what thou wast." — St. Aug.

2. The dead soul is what the dead body is — *a corpse.* The dead soul, the soul in Mortal Sin, possesses all the quality of a corpse.

*a.* It has lost its beauty and has become hideous.

"How beautiful art thou! — How beautiful art thou!" — Cant. iv. 1. — "The noble sons of Sion were clothed with the best gold . . . her Nazarites were whiter than snow, purer than milk, more ruddy than the old ivory, fairer than the sapphire." — Lam. iv. 2, 7.

This applies to the soul in the state of grace. But hear what is said of the soul in Mortal Sin.

"From the daughter of Sion all her beauty is departed." — Lam. i. 6. — "How is the gold become dim, the finest color is changed? The face of Sion's Nazarites is now made blacker than coals and they are not known in the streets" (of the city of God). — Ib. iv. 8. — "Thou wast the seal of resemblance (of the likeness of God), full of wisdom, and perfect in beauty, until iniquity was found in thee." — Ez. xxviii. 12, 15.

Therefore, be well dressed exteriorly, sinners, — in your interior you are a hideous corpse; glory in your beauty, you are a corpse. . . .

*b.* The soul in sin has lost its *activity;* it can merit no more for heaven by good works, as little as a dead body can do anything for its living.

"If I should distribute all my goods to feed the poor, and if I should deliver up my body to be burnt, and have not charity, it profiteth me nothing." — I Cor. xiii. 3.

All that the sinner can merit by his good works is the grace of conversion, and for this he should work, that he find mercy.

The soul in Mortal Sin has lost also *all its merits,* gained in the past, just as the body by death is deprived of all its possessions. And should these merits have accumulated as much as those of a St. Peter, a St. Francis . . . sin has swept them off.

"If the just man . . . do iniquity . . . all his justices which he hath done, shall not be remembered." — Ez. xviii. 24. — "Thy enemies have opened their mouth against thee; they have hissed and gnashed with the teeth, and have said: We will swallow her up: lo, this is the day which we have looked for; we have found it." — Lam. ii. 16.

Such a soul is like a shipwrecked vessel (describe); like a wheat-field destroyed by a hail-storm (describe); like a burnt-out beautiful palace (describe).

"To what shall I compare thee . . . for great as the sea is thy destruction: who shall heal thee?" — Lam. ii. 13.

*c.* The dead body *sees no more.* Neither does the dead soul. It does not see the terrible abyss of eternal damnation open before it.

"Thy prophets (your passions, the devils) have seen false and foolish things for thee; and they have not laid open thy iniquity, to excite thee to penance." — Lam. ii. 14.

*d.* The dead body *hears no more.* Neither does the

dead soul, it has become insensible. It is deaf to the voice of conscience, of the priest, even of the warnings and chastisements of God.

"Blind the hearts of this people, and make their ears heavy, and shut their eyes: lest they see . . . hear . . . and understand . . . and be converted and I heal them." — Is. vi. 10. — "And I became as a man that heareth not." — Ps. xxxvii. 15.— "Thou hast struck them, and they have not grieved." — Jer. v. 3.

*e.* The dead body spreads a *deadly stench,* — it *infects* the living. The dead soul will soon infect others that are yet pure, and instil into them deadly disease.

"He that joineth himself to harlots, will be wicked. Rottenness and worms shall inherit him." — Eccli. xix. 3.

The dead must be buried. If the dead soul be not raised to life again, where is it buried?

"The rich man died; and he was buried in hell." — Luke xvi. 22

## II. HELL THE GRAVEYARD OF THE DEAD SOUL

"Hell and death were cast into the pool of fire. This is the second death." — Apoc. xx. 14, *i.e.,* hell shall forever devour the damned and death shall forever kill them. — "*Eternal death.*"

When a murderer is sentenced to death, he is handed over to the sheriff, who will drag him to the gallows and there hang him up by the neck until he is dead. When the soul that has murdered itself and has taken the life of God out of itself, comes to depart from this life, it is dragged out of the foul prison of its body, placed before the tribunal of the all-just God, found guilty and cast off into the abyss of eternal death.

The state of the human soul, "buried" in hell is similar to the state of the body buried in the grave.

1. The body in the grave is deprived of *all delights* congenial to its inclinations. So is the soul in hell.

Man's soul is created for the *true,* the *good,* and the

*beautiful*. To find and enjoy these constitute the
natural happiness of the soul. In hell the soul will
find none of these three goods; it will find nothing
but *falsehood* and *lies*. Sin was represented as not so
disastrous in its consequences. It is found all false — a
lie.

"You have ploughed wickedness, you have reaped iniquity; you
have eaten the fruit of lying." — Os. x. 13.

And what is there *good* and *beautiful* in hell, where
there is nothing but horror, abomination and perpetual disorder?

"A land of misery and darkness, where the shadow of death,
and no order, but everlasting horror dwelleth." — Job x. 22. —
"But the unbelieving and the abominable, and murderers, and
fornicators, and sorcerers, and idolaters, and all liars, they shall
have their portion in the pool burning with fire and brimstone;
which is the second death." — Apoc. xxi. 8.

2. The body in the grave is devoured by *worms*
generated by itself. The soul in hell is filled with
worms, the stings of its conscience, because it sees
clearly how easy it was to be saved. It was saturated
with sin, it fattened on it; this fat is now changed into
worms that gnaw on it forever.

"For the worm shall eat them up as a garment, and the moth
shall consume them as wool." — Is. li. 8. — "Their worm shall not
die." — Ib. lxvi. 24. — "When a man (a soul) shall die, he shall
inherit serpents, and beasts, and worms." — Eccli. x. 13.

3. The body in the grave is *banished* from *all society*.
The soul, naturally fond of society, finds none in hell;
hence, no consolation, but everlasting despair. A
reprobate soul has no friends among the angels, the
blessed in heaven, or the damned in hell, not even
among the devils. It is hated, abominated, cursed
by all. It cannot find a resting-place even in the
lowest recesses of hell.

"Because they forsook the covenant of the Lord . . . therefore he hath cast them out . . . and hath thrown them into a strange land." — Deut. xxix. 25–28. — "My kinsmen have forsaken me; and they that knew me, have forgotten me." — Job xix. 14.

4. The body in the grave is *dissolved* and turned into earth, because the principle of life that kept it together has gone out of it. The reprobate soul is constantly, as it were, torn asunder, and is become like hell itself, full of confusion, full of horror and despair, because God, its life and inheritance, has left it, cursed it, and cast it off forever.

"My wrath shall be kindled against them; I will forsake them . . . they shall be devoured; all evils and afflictions shall find them, so that they shall say: In truth, it is because God is not with me, that these evils have found me." — Deut. xxxi. 17.

They may cry to God, He will not hear them, because they did not hear God when He called out to them.

"Because I called and you refused . . . you have despised all my counsel . . . I also will laugh in your destruction." — Prov. i. 24–26. — "Know thou and see that it is an evil and a bitter thing for thee, to have left the Lord thy God." — Jer. ii. 19.

Compare with the soul in hell a man buried alive, six feet in the earth. He calls, he shouts, he knocks . . . no one hears him, — no one cares about him.

CONCLUSION. — Recapitulation.

Alas! how many are in this mournful state of soul now, — perhaps some, — many of you! — And they do not see, do not perceive it, because they are dead. — Have I reason, then, to lament over them? "Who will give water . . . ?" Dead bodies seldom come back to life. Dead souls oftener, and at any time they sincerely wish and pray for it.

Well, then, hear my voice: "Return, return . . . why will you die?" — (Ez. xxxiii. 11), — die the eternal death? "Jerusalem, Jerusalem, — be converted to the Lord thy God."

O most loving Jesus, raise these souls from the dead, as Thou didst raise Lazarus, — these men, women, young men and young women . . .

O Mother of Mercy, pray for them!

## IV

## DEATH THE TEACHER OF A GOOD LIFE

Text: "In all thy works remember thy last end, and thou shalt never sin."— Eccli. vii. 40.

Exordium. — Everybody wishes to die a happy death. The best means to do so is to have death constantly before our eyes, and to consider that it may come upon us at any moment. Now, to die well, we must live well. If I may die any moment, I must live well every moment. Strange illusion! Nothing can be more certain, and yet a great number of people, even of those whom we call good, live and act as though this were not so.

Death is a most powerful teacher. It tears from our minds a *threefold illusion* that blinds us in life, and it lets us see the naked truth. The first is life itself, which we imagine will last yet a long time. The second is the estimation of the goods of this earth. The third is the idea of our own greatness. Death teaches us the very opposite.

O Death, come, stand before us, be our teacher, let us be thy pupils!

### I. Men Promise Themselves a Long Life

There is not a single living individual, unless he be completely bereft of reason, that does not know that man must die. It is a punishment inflicted upon the whole human race. St. Bernard says: "As the soul is the life of the body, so is God the life of the soul. The soul could not be separated from God except by sin. The body could not be separated from the soul except by death. But sin came, and therefore death comes." And yet people live as though there were no death.

No one denies the certainty of death. Faith, reason, daily experience make impossible an assumption to the contrary. But, in reality, we make out for ourselves a sort of everlasting existence on this earth. We do not believe that we shall die to-day, this week, this month, this year. If we did, we would act differently. Thus lives the sinner, thus the ordinary Christian.

No one denies the uncertainty of death as to the time, the place, the manner, in which it may occur. There are a thousand causes that may bring it on at any moment. Thousands of examples prove it. Yet men live and act as though this could never happen to them.

"There is one that is enriched by living sparingly . . . he saith, I have found me rest, and now I will eat of my goods alone. And he knoweth not that death approacheth, and that he must leave all to others, and shall die." — Eccli. xi. 18–20. — "I will say to my soul: Soul, thou hast much goods laid up for many years; take thy rest, eat, drink, make good cheer. But God said to him: Thou fool, this night do they require thy soul of thee: and whose shall those things be which thou hast provided?" — Luke xii. 19, 20. — "Nothing deceives man so much as the expectation of a long life." — St. Cypr.

We all believe the uncertainty of life, — we see it. Yet we all act as though it were not so! The evil spirits of hell add their share to this illusion by using the same deception that Satan practised on Eve: "No, you shall not die the death" (Gen. iii. 4), "you have time enough to do penance," "after some time you may change your life" . . . Illustrate by examples.

Death takes away this illusion and forcibly teaches us that EVERY MOMENT OUR LIVES MAY COME TO AN END.

Whether we are old or young, whether sick or well, the thin thread that holds body and soul together may part any moment. Death teaches this truth more forcibly than all the texts of Scripture, than all the sayings of the Fathers, than all the exhortations of priests and missionaries. Thousands of causes may produce an instantaneous, unforeseen, unexpected death. Thousands of facts prove this. No rank of society, no age, no part of the world, no year or century has any security against death.

"Man knoweth not his own end; but as fishes are taken with the hook . . . so men are taken in the evil time, when it shall suddenly come upon them." — Eccle. ix. 12.

What lesson does this teach us! Why be so solicitous about next year, since you may not live another week? Why defer penance, confession, till next month, since you may die the next hour? Why dally with this or that wicked imagination, since you may drop dead with that thought still in your mind? And so forth.

"In all thy works. . . ." — TEXT. — "Watch ye, therefore, because you know not the day nor the hour." — Matt. xxv. 13.

## II. "THE GOODS OF THIS WORLD ARE OF GREAT IMPORTANCE"

Who does not labor under this illusion? And who can divest himself of it? True, these goods are perishable; we know that we cannot possess them forever; the Gospel denounces wealth, and praises poverty; still we must have them. The pleasures of life pass away, the vanities of the world are but worthless tinsel; still we must go along with the world. And am I not to enjoy life while I have it? Why should we not love honor and esteem? After all, those who enjoy the esteem of men get along best. And so forth.

Do you wish to know what real value all these things possess? Death will teach you that ALL IS VANITY.

Let death come before the lapse of another hour, and what are all these things worth?

What is wealth to the dead man? He cannot use a penny of it. One Hail Mary, said with devotion, is then worth more than a million of dollars. Of what use are garments, fashionable dresses? They are all left behind. What has become of bodily beauty? Of what benefit is hair-dressing in the grave? What are honors and the esteem of men? Very soon you will be forgotten, and others will receive those honors. After all the honors that you received on earth, before God and in reality you are no more than the state of your soul entitles you to.

And what about pleasures, sinful or not? Tell me would you go to that dance, party, theater, company, walk, if you were sure that you should die that same night? And who assures you that you will not?

"Lo I die, what will the first birth-right avail me?" — Gen. xxv. 32. — "Naked came I from my mother's womb, and naked shall I return thither." — Job i. 21. — "We brought nothing into this world: and certainly we can carry nothing out." — I Tim. vi. 7. — "The memory of the dead is forgotten." — Eccle. ix. 5.

### III. MAN BELIEVES HIMSELF TO BE SOMETHING GREAT

Notwithstanding the teachings of the Scriptures and of sound reason, man has a more or less exalted idea of his own greatness, and therefore claims to be entitled to the admiration, the honor and esteem of others. Some take pride in their external appearance, others in the splendor of their earthly possessions, others in their talent, in their gift of being great speakers, others in their political career. In principle they will admit the nothingness of man, in reality they do not believe it, and they make every effort to appear great before the world.

Death, however, teaches them that — "ALL MEN ARE EARTH AND ASHES." — Eccli. xvii. 31.

How soon does death remove the illusion of corporal beauty! First, man is stripped of all outward pomp. Decorate the corpse as you please, it is a ghastly mass of decaying human flesh. It is deprived of life, of motion; the eyes closed for the rest of time; the mouth shut, the tongue stiff; the entire body becomes a disgusting mass, it is eaten up by worms; the frame falls into ashes. Where is that superior mind, that elated heart, those lofty thoughts? All has disappeared like a vapor.

To have a still clearer idea of this, stand at a man's death-bed.

*See him dying.* — His hands and arms become powerless, the breast scarcely able to draw breath, the head unable to raise itself, the lips foam, the eyes grow dim, the face bathed in the cold sweat of death. Add to this the anguish of soul at the near approach of dissolution, that cannot be prevented by any medical art; the horror at the thought of having to pass into eternity; the awful fear when on the point of falling into the hands of the living God. Who knows anything about that last moment, when the last tie between body and soul is rent asunder!

*See him after death.* — Come and see yourself as you are laid out for burial. Gone is all that beauty of which you thought so much, which you so often and so long admired when standing before a mirror; the body stiff, beginning to emit an insupportable stench;

the cheeks fallen in, the eyes sunk in their sockets, the lips pale; the people come, cast a silent look at the corpse, then go. They may even surround your corpse with exterior splendor, it cannot last long. The burial cannot be delayed. Earth must be given to earth.

*See him in the grave.* — Behold the words of Job verified:

"I have said to rottenness: Thou art my father; to worms, my mother and my sister." — Job xvii. 14.

Multitudes of worms and similar insects are engendered in the body, crawling through the eyes, nose and mouth, eating holes through the breast and stomach, and devouring all the flesh that is on the bones. For a time the body is a flowing ,mass of putrefaction, until all is devoured by the millions of worms, which finally devour one another; the bones crumble into dust and finally disappear in the earth.

"Thou shalt return to the earth, out of which thou wast taken; for dust thou art and into dust thou shalt return." — Gen. iii. 19.

What now has become of that imaginary greatness? Compare what a proud, vain, self-conceited man or woman is on earth with what he or she will be then.

One question more: What about the soul? What has become of it? The answer to that will remain shrouded in mystery as long as time will last. Over that many men labor under another illusion which death alone cannot remove.

"I saw the wicked buried: who also when they were yet living were in the holy place, and were praised in the city as men of just works." — Eccle. viii. 10.

CONCLUSION. — Recapitulation.

Behold the important lessons which death teaches you. To draw the proper fruit from this meditation resolve: 1. By all means and without delay to prepare your soul for death, if, in the state in which you are now, you would be afraid to appear before God. 2. Be completely detached from earthly goods. 3. Lay aside all vanity and extravagance. 4. Shun all those things most carefully after doing which you would not like to die immediately. 5. Begin each day as though you were not to see the end of it.

"In all thy works. . . ." — TEXT.

# V

## PARTICULAR JUDGMENT

Text: "Wherefore hath the wicked provoked God? — For he hath said in his heart: He will not require it." — Ps. ix. 13.

Exordium. — Why is there so much sin committed? Whence this cold indifference about religion? People do not think of the Judgment to come. They do not reflect that they will have to give an account of all that they do.

"Wherefore hath the wicked . . ." — Text. — "All things that are done, God will bring into judgment for every error, whether it be good or evil." — Eccle. xii. 14.

God has given to man full liberty to do as he pleases. He will never interfere with him. But in the end man will be called to an account, that it may become manifest what use he has made of his freedom, and that he may receive what he has deserved, reward or punishment.

There is this terrible future about the Particular Judgment, that no one knows the moment when it will come upon him.

Let us seriously meditate on it. May Jesus Christ, our Judge, grant us the necessary light!

### I. How the Soul will Appear Before Christ

Picture to yourself the human soul a few moments before its final separation from the body. The dying man is surrounded by his friends, who can render him no more help. The soul is penetrated with terrible anguish, it has entered the dark night of death, it is but a minute distant from eternity, the Great Judge is approaching.  A minute more — and it finds itself in an unknown region, in eternity;  it stands before Jesus Christ — all alone.  It sees those who gaze at its lifeless body, but they do not see the soul, nor what is passing directly before them.

1.  A *supernatural light* surrounds and penetrates the soul, so that it sees itself and its whole life as distinctly as God sees it.  Every thought, word, and deed of its entire life will be manifested in the clearest light.

"Power is given you by the Lord and strength by the most High, who will examine your works, and search out your thoughts." Wis. vi. 4. — "In the end of a man is the disclosing of his works." — Eccli. xi. 29.

2.  In this light will be cleared up all *affected ignorance*, by which a man did not know the true religion, certain points of faith to be believed, certain duties to be fulfilled, sins committed, which man did not want to believe to be wrong, occasions of sin not regarded as sinful.

"The way of a fool is right in his own eyes; but he that is wise hearkeneth unto counsels." — Prov. xii. 15. — "There is a way which seemeth just to a man: but the ends thereof lead to death." — Ib. xiv. 12.

Among these are the *doubts* which man neglected to clear up, until he forced himself into a sort of conviction that he was doing right; so-called *"formed consciences,"* with reference to enmities, acts of injustice, sins against charity, sins against purity (especially in married life).

"Every way of a man seemeth right to himself: but the Lord weigheth the hearts." — Prov. xxi. 2.

## II. Scrutiny of all the Good and the Evil Done in Life

1. The *good deeds* performed in life will then be scrutinized, and it will be seen what they were worth before God.

*a.* The good deeds performed *for the pure love of God*, together with all the holy desires, aspirations, acts of patience, resignation, self-abandonment. These are like pure gold found among stones. But how much of it shall be found in man's life?

*b.* The good deeds performed out of a supernatural motive indeed, but more *for the sake of the reward* than for the honor and glory of God; partly also *for the sake of gaining by them the esteem of men*. These are like gold mixed with foreign ingredients.

How much, deserving of a heavenly reward, will remain for the soul, that light will show.

"The fire shall try every man's work, of what sort it is." — I Cor. iii. 13. — "Our justice compared with God's justice is injustice." — St. Greg. l. 5. mor., c. 6. — "I will judge justices." — Ps. lxxiv. 3.

*c.* The good done, *to avoid evil*, or *to atone for evil committed*, will be of greater or less value, according to the dispositions and intentions of the soul. Among these good acts are prayer in temptation, acts of mortification and self-denial.

Many a little act of piety, many a work of charity, etc., will then be very great, while on earth it is looked upon as little. And many a good deed that is looked upon as great, will dwindle into almost nothing.

2. *The evil deeds*, as a rule, will appear by far greater than they are regarded upon earth, because the least sin is an offense committed against the Infinite God. Under this head will be judged:

*a.* *The good left undone,* to which the soul was bound in duty, such as its duties as a Christian, as a Catholic, as a parent, as a man in office.

*b.* The *good done badly,* in the state of mortal sin, or done in such a way that God was offended, others scandalized. For instance, attending Mass, sermons, with wilful distractions, with evil thoughts, while talking to others, with evil designs, such as going to evening services with bad intentions.

"My soul hateth your new moons and your solemnities; they are become troublesome to me, I am weary of bearing them." — Is. i. 14.

*c.* All *evil thoughts, words, actions* of the entire life, not expiated by penance.

"I say unto you that every idle word that men shall speak, they shall render an account for it on the day of judgment." — Matt. xii. 36. — "For every one shall bear his own burden." — Gal. vi. 5.

*d.* All the *evil caused in others,* on account of duty neglected or scandal given.

"Give an account of thy stewardship." — Luke xvi. 2. — "Life for life, eye for eye, tooth for tooth, hand for hand, foot for foot." — Deut. xix. 21.

### III. THE WITNESSES

The Lord has no need of any witnesses to establish a good or evil deed. Nevertheless, for the greater glorification of His saints and for the greater confusion of the reprobate, we may presume that the Lord will admit the presence of accusers, of defenders and of witnesses at this Judgment.

1. The chief accuser will be *the devils of hell,* who by the permission of God intrude themselves before this tribunal. They have surrounded the death-bed during the last few hours. They will not depart into hell before they have tried their utmost to see that soul condemned.

"The accuser of our brethren . . . who accused them before our God day and night." — Apoc. xii. 10.

What will this accuser not bring up? How will he not plead for his right to possess that soul?

2. The *guardian angel* of that soul may do everything to defend it, but can he make evil good, or an act of virtue out of a sin? May he not have to confirm the accusations of the evil one?

"Take notice of him and hear his voice . . . for he will not forgive when thou hast sinned." — Exod. xxiii. 21.

3. The *souls of the ruined* will demand revenge on their seducers. If those in heaven cry for revenge, how much more those in hell.

"And they cried with a loud voice, saying: How long, O Lord, dost thou not judge and revenge our blood on them that dwell on the earth?" — Apoc. vi. 10.

4. The souls of those who *are still living*, perhaps still in sin, will be represented at that tribunal by their guardian angels.

"See that you despise not one of these little ones: for I say to you, that their angels in heaven always see the face of my Father who is in heaven." — Matt. xviii. 10.

5. The last witness will be your own *conscience*. And what will it say, what can it say in its own defense? How often did that conscience warn the soul? But it was not heard.

"Let us plead together: tell if thou hast anything to justify thyself." — Is. xliii. 26. — "Let my judgment come forth from thy countenance: let thy eyes behold the things that are equitable." — Ps. xvi. 2.

## IV. Final Sentence

The justice of this sentence can never be questioned. Nor is there any appeal from it; for the highest tribunal has rendered its decision. The sentence is an act of the mind of God, which clearly understands the exact value of good works and the depth of the malice of sin. It is an act of God, Who cannot be deceived, Who cannot deviate from justice, Who is incapable of being influenced by respect of persons, by the art of eloquence or by other similar motives. No sooner is the sentence pronounced than it will be put in execution.

The sentence will be either for *eternal glory*, to be imparted without any delay, or after a shorter or longer *expiation in purgatory*, or for *eternal damnation*. Describe the joy of the soul saved at once; the resignation of the soul sent to purgatory; the consternation of the soul condemned to hell.

CONCLUSION. — What judgment would you have to expect, were you to die now?

"If judgment is first (most severe) with the house of God (members of the true Church), what shall be the end of them that believe not the Gospel of God? — And if the just man shall scarcely be saved, where shall the ungodly and the sinner appear?" — I Pet. iv. 17, 18.

Awful are the revelations of that Judgment.

On May 25, 1321, a man named Gottfried died in the town of Bruchsall. After about seven hours he returned to life again, but did nothing but moan and weep. Pressed by the priest, he told what he had seen of eternity. Among other things he said that so many souls came to be judged with him, that it seemed the whole world had died. All of these were condemned to hell except twelve; of these, two went to heaven, nine to purgatory, and himself was permitted to expiate his sins on this earth. He lived twelve years afterward, and practised the most severe penance. After his death he was buried in the parish church before the altar of St. George. (Chronicles of Hirschau.)

Prepare for judgment by passing a severe judgment on yourself before the priest. And after that lead such a life, from day to day, from hour to hour, as to hold yourself in readiness for this Judgment. Fear no man, but fear God and His judgments. "Fear ye him, who after he hath killed, hath power to cast into hell. Yea, I say to you, fear him." (Luke xii. 5.)

# VI

## ETERNITY

Text: "I thought upon the days of old, and I had in my mind the eternal years." — Ps. lxxvi. 6.

Exordium. — Nothing is better calculated to make us reflect on our past conduct, and to induce us to make good and firm resolutions for the future, than the thought of *Eternity*. St. Augustine called it *the great thought*, for it is greater than man can comprehend. Eternity is something that has no end, is not subject to any change, cannot be counted by numbers, and cannot be described by words. There is only one Eternity, but we distinguish a twofold eternity, in its relation to God and to man. We are all most closely connected with eternity; for man is an endless being. But, alas! how seldom do we think of it. Let us deeply meditate on it to-day. May Jesus and Mary be our guides, that we may draw great profit from our reflection.

### I. The Eternity of God

1. *God is eternal.* — His Eternity has no beginning nor end. If God had a beginning, He must have come into existence from nothing. But, nothing cannot produce anything. He must, therefore, have produced Himself. If so, then He should have existed before Himself. Who would say this? Therefore, He existed always, forever, without a beginning, before all creation; for an endless eternity, before anything existed outside of Himself.

God will never come to an end, because God is a being of infinite perfections. The least defect is incompatible with God. Therefore, there never can be an end to His existence. God will exist forever.

God is a being without limits. Transport yourselves into boundless space, and God is there. He is not limited by either space or time.

"God is from eternity to eternity, and to him nothing may be added, nor can he be diminished." — Eccli. xlii. 21, 22. — "Before the mountains were made, or the earth and the world was formed; from eternity to eternity thou art God." — Ps. lxxxix. 2. — "He seeth from eternity to eternity, and there is nothing wonderful before him." — Eccli. xxxix. 25.

2. *The thought of the Eternity of God is terrible for the sinner.* — He that has incurred the enmity and hatred of a man, has the assurance that it will not last forever; for no matter how powerful the latter may be, he must die and pass away. But God will never die, and therefore He will detest sin and punish the sinner forever.

"His justice remaineth forever." — II Cor. ix. 9. — "And the smoke of their torments shall ascend up forever and ever." — Apoc. xiv. 11.

The punishment of crime in this world is short; at most it can last only as long as the life of the culprit. But God punishes forever. He casts into an eternal prison, and chastises the wicked with an everlasting fire.

3. *The Eternity of God is an object of the greatest consolation to the just.* — Even here on this earth, He most abundantly remunerates the faithful services rendered Him. Those who enter the service of the mighty ones of this earth and who are richly rewarded by them must always fear that they may die soon. But God can never die.

Man is made to share in God's own happiness.

What a consolation that this happiness can never come to an end!

"The mercy of the Lord is from eternity and unto eternity upon them that fear him." — Ps. cii. 17. — "The saints of the most high God shall take the kingdom; and they shall possess the kingdom forever and ever." — Dan. vii. 18.

What folly, then, to serve the world, to serve man, and thereby lose sight of God! St. Francis used to say to his brethren: "Brethren, we have promised God great things, but greater things He has promised us. The labor and the trouble are short, but the Eternal Remuneration gives us an eternal reward." And St. Ignatius said: "If I possess gold and silver what have I? and for how long? But if I possess God, what have I then? and possession without end!"

## II. The Eternity of Man

Man has a beginning but no end. God has made him for Himself, to exist with Him forever. And, therefore, his existence can never terminate. Man is placed here on this earth only for a very short time, to show his fidelity to God. He is like a man who is to dwell in the rich and commodious palace of a powerful king, and who is made to wait a little in the vestibule until he is called in.

"God created man incorruptible." — Wis. ii. 23. — "Man shall go into the house of his eternity." — Eccle. xii. 5.

1. Man shall go either into endless joy or endless torture. All men shall be assembled before the tribunal of Christ. There they will stand in two divisions, the just and the reprobate. The former go to heaven, the latter to hell.

"These shall go into everlasting punishment: but the just into life everlasting." — Matt. xxv. 46.

Travelers in an unknown region look for sign-boards, that they may not miss the right road. On your journey to Eternity you always have two roads before you, one leading to eternal happiness, the other to eternal torments. The cross is the sign-board; it points to the right and to the left, up and down. Follow the road to the right and you will go upward to heaven. You are fully aware of it whenever you take the wrong road.

"The king shall say to them that shall be on his right: Come ye blessed of my Father. . . . Then he shall say to them that shall be on his left: Depart from me . . ." — Matt. xxv. 34, 41.

Whithersoever you will go, there you will be forever.

2. *How long is that Eternity?* Denis the Carthusian says: "Imagine the whole universe to be an immense globe of steel. Every hundred years a little bird comes flying alongside of this globe and touches it with its wing. How long would it take, until the whole globe would be worn away by these slight contacts? And those millions of millions of years and centuries are nothing in comparison with eternity."

What a fool is he, who for the sake of a sin deprives himself of heaven and plunges himself into hell!

"But the number of fools is infinite." — Eccle. i. 15.

Man works and suffers many privations in order to have something upon which he can fall back in his old age, and he acts wisely. What do you do for Eternity? If to gain heaven you did but half of what you do to amass a little fortune, you would enjoy forever the glory of a Saint.

A man that does not work for heaven has lost either his faith or his reason.

3. Unfortunate men, that are too much taken up with the world, that never think of Eternity, as though

it did not concern them! When in Eternity, they *will think of time,* and that forever. All time will then appear like a little speck far away. Their own lifetime will scarcely appear longer than a minute when compared with a thousand years. How foolish to have misspent it for pleasure, to have thrown it away, when by using it well they might have procured for themselves a high degree of glory in heaven! What remorse!

"This, therefore, I say, brethren; the time is short; it remaineth . . . that they that use this world, (act) as though they used it not." — I Cor. vii. 29, 31. "Our time is as the passing of a shadow." — Wis. ii. 5.

CONCLUSION. — Recapitulation.

O Eternity! how soon will I stand at thy gate, when I cannot retrace my steps, when I must enter. Oh! how much would I wish then to have but a few hours left to prepare my soul for Eternity! Perhaps the eternal God will still give you a few days. We cannot be certain about this, but we hope He will do so. Perhaps He will give you more. If He does, what will you do? Will you squander this precious time as you have squandered the time that God has given you thus far? It happened in the city of R. in the year 1857, in the month of February, that on a Saturday evening in a store an elderly man jokingly asked a young married man which of the two would pass into eternity first. The older man left the store to go home. While crossing a bridge he fell from it into the river and was drowned. His friends searched for his body on Sunday morning. They drew up a body. Whose was it? That of the young man. He had been murdered that night and his body thrown into the river. When will you go into Eternity?

# VII

## MOTHER OF SORROWS

TEXT: "Son, forget not the groanings [sorrows] of thy mother."
— Eccli. vii. 29.

EXORDIUM.— When the three friends of Job heard
what had befallen him, they came to sympathize with
him.  As soon as they saw him they wept, rent their
garments, sprinkled their heads with dust, and sat
with him on the ground seven days and seven nights,
condoling with him on account of his sufferings.  The
Mother of Jesus suffers, but finds no sympathizing
friends.

"Weeping she hath wept in the night, and her tears are on her
cheeks; there is none to comfort her among all them that were
dear to her." — Lam. i. 2.

Are you not the same?  To arouse some sympathy
in your hearts for your suffering Mother, let me propose to your consideration the sufferings which she
underwent in union with her divine Son for the redemption of mankind.

### I. MOTIVES OF COMPASSION FOR OUR BLESSED MOTHER

1. *Nature* demands it of us.  We must have put off
all feelings of human nature if we can see people suffer
without at least sympathizing with them.  Example
of the good Samaritan, who, although a perfect stranger
to the one who had fallen among the robbers, was
moved with compassion toward him (Luke x. 33);
of the daughter of Jephte, whose companions went with

her into the mountains to condole with her, and ever afterward, "from year to year, the daughters of Israel were accustomed to assemble together to lament the daughter of Jephte for four days." (Judges xi. 38–40.)

2. *Gratitude* and *justice* compel us to it.    The Mother of Sorrows suffered for our sake.

"For your sake Mary suffered unspeakable tortures; for your sake she shed the most bitter tears.    Would it not be ingratitude beyond comparison if you would not return thanks to her for all her sufferings of love with a single expression of sympathy and compassion?" — St. Ambr.

We have been the cause of those sufferings to her. We have caused the sufferings of Jesus by our many and grievous sins.    And these were the swords that pierced her heart.

And now, is it not cruelty above all cruelty to inflict severe and painful wounds upon a loving and unoffending friend, and, when weltering in his blood, to show him no sympathy?

What, then, is to be said of a Christian who has caused so much suffering to the Mother of Jesus, and who feels altogether unconcerned about her?

3. She is our *Sorrowful Mother*.    This one word tells all.

How can a child be without sympathy for his suffering mother?    This motive becomes most powerful when we consider that she sacrificed her most beloved son Jesus precisely in order to receive us as her children. "Son, forget not . . ."    (See text.)    By her sufferings she protects us against the rod of justice, as Rebecca protected Jacob against the wrath of Esau (Gen. xxvii. 42, 44).

"Why shall I be deprived of both my sons in one day?" — Gen. xxvii. 45.

She saved us, as the wise woman, called by Joab from Thecua, saved the life of Absalom, who had been sentenced to death by his father, King David (II Kings xiv. 5, 11). Does she, then, not deserve our sympathy?

When Clotilde was held captive and most cruelly tortured by Amalric, she sent a cloth saturated with the blood of her wounds to her brother Hildebert, asking, "Can you look at this, and still remain indifferent to my sufferings?" Hildebert found no rest until he gathered an army and took her away by force.

Mary shows you the wounded and bleeding body of her Son resting on her lap, asking you, "Can you look at this, and remain cold to my sufferings?" How can you if you are a Christian, if you are my child?

We are moved to tears when we read of the overwhelming grief of a mother who sees her son whom she once loved and still loves, led to the place of execution to expiate with his death some great crime. How is it that we have no tears of compassion for Mary, who sees her divine son Jesus led out to be crucified, although most innocent, as a victim for the sins of the world!

## II. The Sorrows of Mary in Particular

The sorrows of our Blessed Mother lasted throughout the life of her son Jesus; but there are seven principal ones especially selected by the Church for our consideration. They are called "The Seven Dolors," represented in some pictures by seven swords piercing the heart of Mary. Let us make a short reflection on each.

1. *Presentation of Jesus in the Temple.*

*a.* Mary gave up Jesus to God's anger as a sacrifice for the sins of the world. What an offering for a mother! For Jesus was to die as a victim to the justice of God. To be the Mother of God meant, therefore, to be the Mother of Sorrows.

*b.* Would men honor, revere, love Him? No! He should be contradicted before and after His death, until the end of the world. The world would never appreciate the offering of Mary.

*c.* "This child is set for the ruin of many in Israel" (Luke ii. 34). So, then, Jesus was to be the ruin of many souls. The very brightness of His light, the very fact of His coming, was to be the cause of the destruction of some of those on whose account He had come.

*d.* And therefore God would, after all, not receive all the glory for which Mary had prayed so long. Men would even ridicule the very fountain of grace. What sorrow, pain, and affliction did these considerations cause to the soul of Mary!

2. *The Flight of Jesus into Egypt.*

*a.* This sorrow was caused by the wickedness of man. Jesus is to flee, at night, through unknown regions, to an unknown country; is to sojourn in a strange land, where there is no society for this good mother except that of heathens. She is exposed to the privation of the very necessaries of life. What harm had Jesus done? And yet He is hated and driven from His country.

*b.* On the return journey from Egypt He is too young to walk, too old to be carried. No traveling accommodations as in modern times. There is, besides, the fear of Archelaus. Wherefore they went to Nazareth. The Creator flees from the creature. He is welcome in heaven, but not on earth.

*c.* Jesus is now on earth, in the Blessed Sacrament, among the monuments of wealth, as He was in Egypt among the gods of the Gentiles, not known, — despised, made to flee by a wicked, material world. What sorrow did not all this cause His good Mother!

3. *The three days' loss in Jerusalem.*

*a.* The Blessed Virgin lost her son Jesus, and did not know why. What painful uncertainty! Had she done anything wrong, who feared nothing more than the slightest offense to God, or the smallest neglect in the discharge of her duty in regard to the infinite treasure committed to her care?

*b.* She knew not where He was, nor what He might be suffering.

*c.* There was perfect darkness around her soul, as though God had abandoned her. So great was her sorrow on this occasion that she gave utterance to it: "Son, why hast thou done so to us?" (Luke ii. 48.)

The loss of Jesus (the grace of God) is the greatest evil. Pray to this sorrowful Mother, that you may comprehend it.

4. *Meeting with Jesus on His way to Calvary.*

In connection with this sorrow consider

*a.* Jesus taking leave of His Mother. What a sorrowful interview, what a painful separation, united with perfect resignation on both sides!

*b.* Her affliction when she heard and saw what was done to Jesus; when He was scourged at the pillar, crowned with thorns, rejected by the unanimous cry of the people; when the sentence of death was pronounced upon Him and heralded through the streets of the city.

*c.* But her sorrow reached its climax when she stood by the wayside and saw Him with the cross on His shoulders. He does not speak, but only casts a sad look at her. What mother would not feel it? He leaves her stand there plunged in grief, and struggles on to Calvary. She follows. Let us follow also.

5. *The Nailing of Jesus to the Cross.*

*a.* When she reaches the summit of Calvary, she hears above the clamor of the people the sharp sound of the hammer that drives the iron nails through the sacred hands and feet of Jesus. She sees Him raised on the cross, — mocked, suffering most intensely. She witnesses the division of His garments, those garments which she had made with her own hands. She hears Him complain of thirst, and she cannot reach Him a cooling drink. Vinegar and gall are given Him amid the jeers of the bystanders.

*b.* Her second motherhood, that over us, is then proclaimed. The first was full of joy ("Hail Mary"); the second, full of sorrow. The first was made by an angel; the second, by her dying Son. In the first she was made the Mother of God; in the second, of wicked, ungrateful men.

*c.* She hears Jesus complain of interior desolation: "My God, my God . . ." She suffered with Him. Neither had she any consolation.

"Therefore have I said: Depart from me, I will weep bitterly: labor not to comfort me." — Is. xxii. 4.

6. *The Descent from the Cross.*

When Jesus was dead, while she still remained plunged in sorrow, there took place

*a.* The piercing of His side. This act of cruelty was felt by Mary alone. Here was literally fulfilled the prophecy of Simeon: "Thy own soul a sword shall pierce." — Luke ii. 35.

*b.* When the body of Jesus was taken from the cross, it was laid on the lap of His blessed Mother. What a sad spectacle! With tearful eyes she looks upon that lacerated body, contemplating wound after wound, trying to extricate the thorns from His head, replacing the skin over the bleeding wounds, where it is still hanging to the body, and embalming it with her tears. Sinner! this is your work. But have confidence, praying to her that this immense sacrifice may not be lost to you.

"O all ye that pass by the way, attend and see if there be any sorrow like to my sorrow." — Lam. i. 12.

7. *Burial of Jesus.*

*a.* Jesus is carried to the grave — the most illustrious dead that was ever buried; yet how simple, and at the same time how solemn, is that funeral. Mary casts a last mournful look upon the body; then she retires from the grave. O sweet Mother! how hard for thee to go home this evening without thy Son! Mary without Jesus! Never was there an anguish so awful; never woe so superhuman.

*b.* She goes back by the way of Calvary, thus making the way of the cross for the first time after the death of Jesus, but in reversed order, beginning with the last station and ending with the first. Her heart was full of grief. It was an ocean of sorrow.

"To what shall I compare thee, or to what shall I liken thee, O daughter of Jerusalem? To what shall I equal thee, that I may comfort thee, O virgin daughter of Sion: for great as the sea is thy destruction" [sorrow]. — Lam. ii. 13.

Mary did not close her eyes that night, but spent the time weeping.

"Weeping she hath wept in the night, and her tears are on her cheeks; there is none to comfort her among all them that were dear to her." — Lam. i. 2.

CONCLUSION. — Having reflected on the seven principal Sorrows of your dear Mother, ask yourselves how many of these sorrows have been caused by your sins, committed even since the Mission. It was then that you came back to her like a sorrowful child, acknowledging her as your mother and placing yourselves under her protection.

But have you not plunged a sword of sorrow into her heart since? For, remember that every sin causes a wound in the body of Jesus and a pain in the heart of Mary. Her altar is not decorated to-day as it was at the Mission. She appears before you in sorrow, in deep affliction over your sins. Ask her pardon, then, and promise her, this time, that there shall instantly be an end to your sinful career, and that by your faithful co-operation with God's grace, under her most powerful assistance, you will be to her a cause of joy and consolation. Resolve also "to comfort her," — *a*. By not increasing her pain by the commission of new sins. Let us cease adding to her sorrow. — *b*. By loving to suffer with her and for the love of Jesus.

"Sancta Mater, istud agas crucifixi fige plagas, cordi meo valide; tui nati vulnerati, tam dignati pro me pati, pœnas mecum divide."

*c*. By propagating devotion to her. *d*. By often reflecting on her Sorrows.

"Blessed are they that mourn; for they shall be comforted." — Matt. v. 5.

She will "comfort" us in our sufferings, at death, and after death.

"Flammis ne urar succensus, per te virgo sim defensus, in die judicii."

# VIII

## THE CHRISTIAN FAMILY

TEXT: "As for me and my house, we will serve the Lord." — Jos. xxiv. 15.

EXORDIUM. — When we see the oldest and most sacred ties of human society approaching dissolution, we have every reason to fear that the end of time is nigh. The oldest, the strongest, and the most sacred ties are those of the family. They are becoming weaker and are fast dissolving; husbands separate from wives; children, from parents; . . . and with the family the whole human society is threatened with ruin. For on the state of the family depends the welfare of the city, of the state, of the Church, and of mankind in general.

To save the family it must be placed on the basis of Christianity; it must be a *Christian Family*.

What do we understand by a Christian Family, and by what means will it become such?

### I. IDEA OF THE TRUE CHRISTIAN FAMILY

Matrimony was instituted by God in Paradise; Christ raised it to the dignity of a Sacrament — which made it "a great Sacrament, but in Christ and in the Church." (Eph. v. 32.) — The union between Christ and the Church is the true type of the matrimonial union. In the Christian family the relationship between husband and wife must, above all, be based on truly Christian principles. Hence,

1. How must *husband and wife* act toward each other? They have become "two in one flesh" (Matt. xix. 5), and they must become one heart and soul. They must make every effort to promote each other's welfare.

*a.* By making their *"marriage honorable* in all things" (Heb. xiii. 4).

*b.* By diligent work and *economy*. The husband is to procure the necessary support for the family, while the wife is to dispose judiciously of the earnings of the husband for the benefit of the family. Let them beware of squandering the money with which God has provided them and their children for their support.

*c.* By *patiently bearing* with each other's faults. We discover faults in others, and others in us. They are a mutual burden. Mutual patience and forbearance are the only remedy.

"Bear ye one another's burdens; and so shall you fulfil the law of Christ." — Gal. vi. 2.

*d.* In giving mutual *good example*, each one modeling his conduct according to the virtues exhibited by the other.

*e.* By gentle admonition and *friendly correction*, to be taken in the same good spirit. This is a duty which husband and wife owe to each other. Any one left without timely correction is liable to fall into great sins.

*f.* But, above all, by *loving each other*, so as to make every sacrifice for each other's temporal and spiritual happiness.

"Husbands, love your wives, as Christ also loved the Church, and delivered himself up for it." — Eph. v. 25. — "Because the husband is the head of the wife, as Christ is the head of the Church; therefore as the Church is subject to Christ, so also let the wives be to their husbands in everything." — Ib. 23, 24.

*g.* By *living together* for life.

"To them that are married, not I, but the Lord commandeth, that the wife depart not from her husband. . . . And let not the husband put away his wife." — I Cor. vii. 10, 11.

2. Father and mother must co-operate in the promotion of the *spiritual* and *temporal prosperity of their children:*

*a.* By giving them a good religious *education.* The children are created for heaven. They must be led to it by the road which religion points out. This road must be made known to them. Instruction, catechism, school.

"If any man have not care of his own, and especially of those of his house, he hath denied the faith, and is worse than an infidel." — I Tim. v. 8.

*b.* By keeping them *from evil* and its various occasions — reading, associations, acquaintances, amusements, etc.

*c.* By *eradicating their defects,* chastising them, even when yet quite small as well as when grown up, but with the proper discretion and out of a sense of duty, not in a fit of passion, nor, as it were, out of revenge.

"He that spareth the rod hateth his son; but he that loveth him correcteth him betimes." — Prov. xiii. 24. — "And you, fathers, do not provoke your children to anger; but bring them up in the discipline and correction of the Lord." — Eph. vi. 4.

*d.* By instructing them or having them instructed in some *honest business,* so as not to leave them a burden or perhaps a danger to society. Accustoming them to honest labor from their childhood, but without prejudice to their mental education. Idleness is the source of all evil. Special care to be taken in the education of daughters, who are to become industrious mothers of families.

In all this, parents must act *in concert*, and be free from all prejudice, especially against *step-children*.

3. *The children are to promote the spiritual and temporal happiness of their parents:*

*a.* By scrupulously fulfilling their duty of *reverence, love,* and *obedience;* when small as well as when grown up; knowing that their parents will have to render a severe account of them.

*b.* By *praying* for their parents before and after their death, remembering that they may have to suffer for the sins which they have caused them to commit by their misconduct.

*c.* By helping to *support* their *parents,* in doing their best to render their old age pleasant and comfortable. There is a time when children can do nothing for themselves, and there is another when parents are entirely helpless.

*d.* Brothers and sisters among themselves should make *home pleasant* by cultivating true love and harmony among themselves, assisting one another in every way, and encouraging one another to a life of piety.

This, then, is the idea of the Christian Family.

Such a state in the family transforms their house into a little heaven upon earth. But do you generally find it so?


## II. The Deplorable State of the Modern Family

Most of our families are unhappy. Everything seems to be out of joint there. What is the cause?

1. *Husband and wife* render each other miserable for a time and eternity,

*a.* By neglect of economy, by idleness, and dissipation. The scanty earnings, hardly sufficient for the support of the family, are squandered away for drink, articles of vanity, and vain amusements. There is no mutual love, interest, sympathy, etc. All that they ever possessed of these was a temporary — but most impetuous carnal affection, which is soon extinguished.

*b.* By their unreasonable impatience with each other's faults, — their curses, — maledictions, — their hatred and detestation of each other.

*c.* By their utter neglect of their religious duties, their prayers, and the respect due to God and His holy commandments. Hence the grossest violations of the sanctity of marriage, sin after sin, crime after crime, no matter how destructive, until they have completely ruined their health, extinguished the last spark of their soul's life, blunted their consciences, and have made themselves fit for nothing but the fire of hell.

*d.* By becoming unfaithful to each other, and finally separating. They part as regards house and home, after they have parted for a good while in heart and affection, to surrender their bodies and souls to adultery, sanctioned or not by the civil law. Should shame, however, keep them together, they lead a life that resembles hell upon earth.

2. *Parents make their children unhappy.*

*a.* By neglecting their religious education, rearing them for their temporal interests, sometimes only to flatter their instincts of pride and vanity, incurring heavy expenses, for which in return they receive nothing but affliction.

*b.* By allowing their children to spend their youthful days in idleness, or by using them to make a little money; thus neglecting their early training, to the prejudice of their virtue and religion. Such parents seem not to know why God has given them children, or what a precious treasure they are.

*c.* By neglecting necessary correction, being over-indulgent with them on account of their tender or advanced age; by one contradicting the other, when either administers a correction, uprooting thereby the last trace of reverence for a father or a mother.

*d.* By permitting them dangerous amusements, company, reading, free association with the other sex at any hour or place, as long as they please, and by giving the example themselves perhaps, by living "free and easy."

Many parents find it difficult to rear a numerous family. A large family is reared more easily than a small one, provided Christianity is made the basis. All that the parents have to do is to bring up well two or three.

These will, by their example, lead the younger ones in the right path, teach them their religion, and by their work help to support them.

3. *Children make their parents (as well as themselves) unhappy for time and eternity,*

*a.* By their utter want of love, reverence, respect, and obedience, manifested in word and action, almost every hour, and in the most shocking manner. Thus parents are paid back for what they have done for their children — or rather not done. Parents do not teach their children the fear of God; God allows the children to grow up without the fear of their parents.

*b.* By refusing obedience and submission altogether as soon as they think it no longer necessary or advantageous to themselves; a just punishment for the parents who refuse obedience and submission to God and the Church.

*c.* By abandoning them as soon as they can make a living for themselves, leaving their parents to toil and labor as long as they can do so, then to utter destitution, and finally to the almshouse — another just punishment for having reared children for the world, not for God. Neither shall *they* have any benefit from their children.

Such, to a great extent, is the deplorable state of the family in our days. There are very few families that do not suffer from one or the other of these evils.

What is the cause of this? These families have been begun and continued without God and the blessings of the Christian religion.

### III. Means of Making the Family Truly Christian

1. The Christian Family is to be *prepared* with God, and according to the laws of Christianity. Hence, young people, contemplating marriage, should above all,

*a.* Make themselves worthy of the protection of God by a life of Christian piety from their early days.

*b.* When the choice of a partner of life is to be made, let them not consult their own fancy and evil inclinations, nor make their choice according to the dictates of blind passion; but let them consult God and pray to Him Who alone scrutinizes the hearts and souls of all men, and Who knows best which persons suit each other for a happy matrimonial alliance; let them ask the advice of their parents and their spiritual director.

*c.* Let them form no close acquaintance with young persons of the other sex before the time, against the prohibition of the Church, without a good deal of forethought, and when formed, keep it according to the laws of sound morality, without protracting it to an unreasonable length of time. Such persons will scarcely keep company with more than one, because God directs them aright.

*d.* Let them enter into their new state of life with due preparation, and according to the prescriptions of the Church.

Then they will lay the foundation of their new family with the blessing of God.

2. The Christian Family is to be *continued* with God.

The house of the Christian Family ought to be a little chapel, in which the father is the pastor, the mother the assistant, the children the congregation.

In the little chapel at home all is to be done that is done in the church. Family service is to be held twice or at least once a day. Morning and night prayers in common; instructions and exhortations, corrections to be administered. Every Christian home is to be a house of prayer.

Alas! how many families make their home a "den of thieves." No religion, no fear of God, immoralities, misery, a hell on earth, from which there is a direct transition into the hell of the next world.

Great are the blessings which God has promised to the truly Christian Family. "God keeping his covenant and mercy to them that love him, and to them that keep his commandments, unto a thousand generations." — Deut. vii. 9.

CONCLUSION. — Recapitulation.

Examine the state of things in your family, the cause of the evil that exists there. Penance. Resolution. Perhaps you have begun without God; have thus far continued without Him. Do not end without God!

Let every member of the family take it to heart, father, mother, son, daughter, even the growing child. Let each one do his share in making the family what it ought to be, no matter what others do. Let this be the firm resolution of each one:

"As for us, and our house, we will serve the Lord." — TEXT.

## SCANDAL

Text: — "Woe to the world because of scandals. For it must needs be that scandals come: but nevertheless woe to that man by whom the scandal cometh." — Matt. xviii. 7.

Exordium. — We have labored among you to banish sin from your hearts, to destroy the reign of Satan. With God's grace we have succeeded. But how soon may it not be that sin is brought back! From what source? From *Scandal*. Therefore, "Woe to you because of scandals." Some of those who have made the Mission will, perhaps, be among the first to bring back sin.

For this reason must we raise a warning voice against the scandal-givers that may rise up among you, and put you on your guard against their poisonous influence. May Jesus and Mary bless my words.

### I. How is Scandal Given

1. *Definition of Scandal.* — Scandal is a word or act that is calculated to cause sin in others, whether the sin of others is intended or not, or whether that sin really follows or not. "Whatsoever teaches you evil is scandal." — St. Aug. Scandal is a greater sin, if the person who gives it exercises a greater influence over the one scandalized, such as parents in regard to their children, influential persons in a community, or such as by their actions give the tone among others.

2. *Scandal is given by words* against *faith* and religion, expression of doubts about certain doctrines, censures

pronounced against the Church, criticism of her ordinances, finding fault with her discipline, boasting about not believing all that priests say, etc.

By words against the teachings of sound *morality*, advising perjury, approving or counseling immoral conduct, acts of injustice, of disobedience, of revenge, inducing to intemperance, keeping from Mass, etc. By ridiculing piety, religious practices, modest behavior, etc. By denying that certain evil deeds are wrong, because "everybody does it"; by scoffing at the warnings of the priest regarding the occasions of sin as too severe, etc. By improper conversation, or language of double meaning, etc.

3. *Scandal is given by actions*, such as evil behavior in the presence of others, by improper dressing, by impure gestures and loose manners, by keeping a house open to drunkards and to all sorts of unprincipled individuals, by leading others into it, by taking young people away from the eyes of their parents, to lonely walks, by getting up or leading others to sinful amusements or sinful pastimes, theaters, dances, etc. By showing by your actions that you despise the authority of the Church, of the parents of others, telling them not to mind them, etc. By composing, publishing, selling, lending impious books, papers, pictures, etc.

4. *Scandal is given by acts of omission*, by parents who neglect the duty of educating their children; allow them dangerous company, night-walking, lonely interviews; fail to correct their faults. Scandal is also given by those who neglect their Christian duties with the knowledge of others, etc.

## II. Grievousness of the Sin of Scandal

Scandal does an immense injury to God.

1. *The Father.* — It defaces the image and likeness of God in the person scandalized. It tears from the hands of God souls for which He has sacrificed His only-begotten Son; for which God has appointed an angel as guardian and companion; the loss of which is greater to God than if the whole universe were destroyed; which are the object of the eternal and infinite love of God.

2. *The Son.* — Scandal renders the work of the redemption fruitless in regard to the scandalized; it destroys all that Jesus Christ has done for those souls, all His teaching, all His sufferings, His death on the cross; it tramples under foot His most precious blood shed for those souls; it renders useless the institution of the Church, of the Sacraments, the many beautiful doctrines of the Gospel; it adds immensely to the sufferings and agony of Jesus Christ; it breaks His heart on the cross. When our Saviour warned against scandal, He added:

"For the son of man is come to save that which was lost." — Matt. xviii. 11.

3. *The Holy Ghost.* — Scandal destroys all that the Holy Ghost has done for the souls of the scandalized from their infancy through the teaching and the fostering care of the Church, through the administration of the Sacraments of Baptism, Confirmation, etc. It puts those souls in opposition to the Holy Ghost and the Church, estranges them from the priesthood, and renders them insensible to the impressions of divine grace.

"Nowadays the Church is not persecuted by heretics or pagans, but by her own children, that is, by Christians that give scandal." — St. Bernard.

4. Scandal is the *most powerful ally of the devil*, it helps him to do what he cannot do alone; it seconds and carries out his hellish designs; it is a most powerful agent in filling hell with human souls.

The scandal-giver is an *incarnate devil;* his hands, his feet, his tongue are at the disposal of the devil; they become the devil's hands, feet, etc. The devil has not these members to do evil with, he avails himself of the members of men who gladly give them up.

And what earthly gain can the scandal-giver expect? Nothing but a satanic joy.

Sinner, reflect! You have your time, but God has eternity. God lets you act, He interferes not with your liberty; your time is short. Eternity never ends!

### III. Injury Caused by Scandal

1. *Injury to others.* — Oh! what harm does not scandal do to the world!

"Woe to the world because of scandals." — Matt. xviii. 7.

Heresy, apostasy, infidelity, immorality, injustice, in fact all the evils in a religious point of view, have arisen from scandal; they have been strengthened and propagated by scandal. So also all the punishments and chastisements sent upon the world by God for its iniquities. "Woe to the world . . ."

But woe, especially, to the individual that is carried away by scandal. He is robbed of his greatest treasure. And he allows this, in order not to offend the scandal-giver. Scandal robs him not of his money, his property, not of honor and reputation, not of life, but of his soul and salvation, and that forever. And it is much more difficult for him to give up sin and do penance. The corruption caused by others is deeply rooted.

"Woe to you, because you shut the kingdom of heaven against men, for you yourselves do not enter in." — Matt. xxiii. 13. — "Put not a stumbling-block or a scandal in your brother's way," — Rom. xiv. 13, — over which he may fall and never rise again.

The persecutors of the Church made Saints of the Christians; the scandal-giver makes reprobates.

Who would ever have thought, when you were young, that after you had grown up, you would cause such evil! Oh! that you had died in your infancy!

Oh! that you had never been born!

"It were better for him if that man had not been born." — Matt. xxvi. 24.

2. *Injury to himself.* — Alas! this is great!

"Woe to the man by whom the scandal cometh." — Matt. xviii. 7.

*a.* By giving scandal he has by the one act made himself guilty of more than one sin. He is guilty of as many sins as he has scandalized persons.

*b.* He has exasperated God and has put the holy angels against himself, who accuse him before the throne of God.

"For I say to you, that their angels in heaven always see the face of my Father who is in heaven." — Matt. xviii. 10.

*c.* He has to answer for all the sins that those scandalized commit in consequence of his bad example, and all the sins that will be committed for all the future on account of his wicked word or deed.

"He that gives scandal ruins not only himself but drags also many others with him into perdition." — St. Cypr.

*d.* When he will appear before the tribunal of Christ, all those whom he has scandalized will appear against him. Those who are yet living will be represented by their angels.

*e.* The tortures inflicted upon him in hell will be in proportion to the evil that he has caused; and his torments must increase as the sins, caused by him, multiply on earth. As there is an accidental glory in heaven, so there are accidental torments in hell. Hence that woful sentence of our Lord:

"It were better for him that a mill-stone should be hanged about his neck, and that he should be drowned in the depth of the sea." — Matt. xviii. 6.

Better for himself, better for others, better for the place in which he lives, better for his friends, better for the Church, better for the world. For he is worse than a murderer, than the pestilence, than any public calamity, worse than the devil.

CONCLUSION. — Recapitulation.

Examine your ways, conduct, speech, visits, etc., whether there is nothing scandalous in them. But you have, no doubt, done so in the Mission. I must look to the future. Beautiful field is this parish, how beautiful now; but, alas! how soon may not the poisonous vapors of scandal arise from it! Therefore, but two words more:

One to you all, and that is: Shun the scandal-giver; and though he be as near and dear to you as your right eye, hand, foot, the Lord says, "cut them off and cast them away." Therefore, shun the scandal-giver!

The other word I direct to the angels of heaven, and it is: Accuse those who give scandal, take revenge on those who after this Mission dare scandalize again those who have made it, and for whom we have labored so much. Ask your heavenly Father to punish the scandal-givers, that they may not again ruin the souls under your charge, so that in union with you they may praise God and be happy with you for an endless eternity. Amen.

# X

## QUALITIES OF PRAYER

Text: "Lord, teach us to pray." — Luke xi. 1.

Exordium. — We spoke to you during the Mission on the necessity of prayer, telling you that without it perseverance is absolutely impossible. We showed you its efficacy, as well as its facility, and told you the particular times at which you should pray. Many of you complain that you cannot say a good prayer. The apostles, it seems, experienced the same difficulty; therefore they asked our Lord to instruct them how to pray well. May you do the same, and He will certainly answer your prayer by telling you through my humble words how you must pray.

I. The first quality of prayer is *attention*. When we pray, we ask God for some favor. We may do it in words expressed by our lips, or in thought. Prayer has no need of the voice. But we must *mean* what we say; our mind must attend to it.

"This people draw near me with their mouth, and with their lips glorify me, but their heart is far from me." — Is. xxix. 13.

In this manner those act who pray with a distracted mind. They recite excellent, divine words — Our Father, Hail Mary, Creed, Rosary, Litanies, . . . without thinking at all of what they are saying, or without *asking* for a particular favor.

"It is impossible for me to keep my thoughts from wandering. I have scarcely begun, and my mind is elsewhere. . . ."

This is a difficulty that has harassed even the greatest saints. What are we, then, to do?

1. Never become uneasy, but preserve perfect tranquillity of mind. 2. Collect your thoughts as soon as you notice the distraction, and continue your prayer quietly. 3. Do so as often as you find yourself distracted, although your entire prayer be nothing but a chain of distractions and subsequent recollections. 4. Humble yourself at the thought of your own weakness and utter incompetency to do any good. By so doing you will merit the blessing of God upon your prayer, as though every word of it had been said with the greatest recollection. For God it is enough to see your efforts in expressing your desires, wishes, supplications, . . . and He will take all as though it were most perfect.

II. The second quality of prayer is *humility* and *holy resignation*. We depend entirely on God for everything. Of this we must be convinced. Besides, we do not deserve to be heard by God, owing to our utter unworthiness, infidelities, sins. . . . Our petition is that of a wicked servant, to which, by right and justice, God should turn a deaf ear. Hence *humility*. God cannot listen to a prayer that is not humble.

"God resisteth the proud and giveth grace to the humble." — James iv. 6.

But as soon as this condition is fulfilled, God's compassion is moved toward us.

"The prayer of him that humbleth himself, shall pierce the clouds." — Eccli. xxxv. 21. — "A contrite and humbled heart, O God, thou wilt not despise." — Ps. l. 19.

In asking graces and heavenly favors of God, we must not presume to dictate to Him how and when He must hear us; hence *holy resignation*. We are blind to our own interests.  God knows best how to guide us through this valley of tears.  Such is especially the case in regard to *temptations*.  It may be much better for us to have them.

"There was given me a sting of my flesh, . . . for which thing thrice I besought the Lord that it might depart from me.  And he said to me: My grace is sufficient for thee: for power is made perfect in infirmity.  Gladly, therefore, will I glory in my infirmities, that the power of Christ may dwell in me." — II Cor. xii. 7–9.

The same is the case in our prayer under temporal embarrassments, sickness, . . . or when we rather imperatively demand the punishment of certain sinners, that they may be converted.  Our intention is good, so is our prayer; but God knows best when, where, and how, and to what extent He must grant our petition.

III.  The third quality of prayer is *firm confidence* in God.  It consists in a firm conviction of the mind that we shall certainly obtain what we pray for.

"Know ye that no one hath hoped in the Lord, and hath been confounded." — Eccli. ii. 11. — "Whatsoever you shall ask the Father in my name, that will I do." — John xiv. 13. — "Amen, amen, I say to you, if you ask the Father anything in my name, he will give it you." — John xvi. 23; — Matt. vii. ix.

Our Lord seemed to have nothing more at heart than to convince us of the efficacy of confident prayer.  But we must give credit to God for His goodness and power, unhesitatingly relying on His unfailing promises.

"Have the faith of God. . . . I say unto you, all things, whatsoever you ask when ye pray, believe that you shall receive; and they shall come unto you." — Mark xi. 22, 24.

It would even be wrong, it would be an insult to God, to think the contrary; and this is very often the reason why our prayer is not heard.

Examples of prayer offered with confidence: The Canaanite woman (Matt. xv. 22), the centurion (Matt. viii. 10), and others.

IV. The fourth quality of prayer is *perseverance*.

"It is necessary always to pray and never to faint." — Luke xviii. 1. — "Pray without ceasing." — I Thess. v. 17.

There are two reasons for this: 1. The constant need of the actual assistance of God for both body and soul. But God has made it a fixed law not to lend His assistance to any one before he asks for it, lest we forget our dependence upon Him for all things and at all times. Illustration: We are constantly in need of fresh air, which is near and around us in abundance; but we shall have no benefit of it unless we inhale it "without intermission." Application to grace and prayer. Prayer is the only good work that we are commanded to perform without interruption. It is not so with almsgiving, fasting, mortifications, Communion, etc.

How is this to be done? By keeping ourselves in constant union with God, by the recollection of His presence, and by every now and then communicating with Him in our thoughts. Can we not keep up a pleasant conversation with a dear friend at our side? Why not with God?

2. It is God's will that we should ask for the same favor repeatedly until we have obtained it: *a.* Because often our prayer is no prayer for want of attention, confidence, humility. Notwithstanding the imperfections of our prayer, God, however, will always grant us as much as we need at the time, and He will even bring our prayer to perfection, as Jesus Christ did with the Apostles (Luke ii. 1). *b.* Because God leaves us our weaknesses to keep us humble.

What benefit would it be for us to be heard at once, but to remain filled with pride? *c.* Because often God waits until we lay aside certain attachments, comforts, pleasures, vanities, etc. His generosity toward us is in proportion to our generosity toward Him.

"Blessed is the man . . . that watcheth daily at my gates, and waiteth at the posts of my door." — Prov. viii. 34.

CONCLUSION. — Recapitulation.

These, now, are the qualities of holy prayer — all most easy. No one can say that he cannot pray. Not because he has no time. It hardly requires any time. Good thoughts can be formed under any circumstances, even at work. Nor because he has no learning. No need of instruction to be able to pray to your heavenly Father in your heart. God is everywhere. He is in your soul; you can speak to Him there at all times. Nor because he is a sinner. As soon as you desire to give up sin God will hear you.

Oh! what a powerful and what an easy means of communicating with God and of drawing from Him all heavenly blessings for ourselves and for others!

Pray, then, pray, — pray always, — especially to the ever-blessed Virgin Mary, that she may pray with you and for you. Oh! what a sublime prayer is that which is united to the prayer of Mary, and through her addressed to Jesus Christ, and through Him, and in His name, to the Eternal Father!

# FOURTH PART

# INSTRUCTIONS FOR RENEWALS

# I

## SALUTARY EFFECTS OF A GOOD CONFESSION, AND THE EVIL CONSEQUENCES OF A SACRILEGIOUS CONFESSION

The most important duty of a Christian who professes the true faith, is to make his confessions well. On the part of faith his salvation is secure. It remains for him to procure for himself *purity of heart;* then he need not fear.

We gave full instructions on the Sacrament of Penance during the Mission. Some of you may have missed them. Others may have heard them without putting them in practice. It not unfrequently happens that bad, sacrilegious confessions are made even during the Mission.

For these reasons we give you this time one instruction on Confession, telling you, in general, what a *good confession* is, and what are its *salutary effects;* then, also, what a *sacrilegious confession* is, and what are its *evil consequences.*

A. *What is a good confession?*

1. A good confession is one which is made after a due *examination of conscience;* with a true, hearty, supernatural *sorrow;* with a firm *resolution* to sin grievously no more. It is a sincere, full and humble *accusation* of those mortal sins of which the sinner knows himself guilty, with an earnest will to do *penance* for them.

2. What are the salutary effects of such a confession? These are most consoling, and they are the following:

1. The sins are *surely* forgiven.  What a consolation!

"Whose sins you shall forgive, they are forgiven them." — John xx. 23. — "Be of good heart, son, thy sins are forgiven thee." — Matt. ix. 2.

2. *All the sins* are forgiven, including all those which the penitent has forgotten in this or in a former confession, and those which were not forgiven on account of some essential defect in former confessions, but not known to the penitent, provided he make an act of contrition for all his sins.

"Many sins are forgiven her, because she hath loved much." — Luke vii. 47.

3. God has *forgotten* them all.

"Thou hast delivered my soul that it should not perish, thou hast cast all my sins behind thy back." — Is. xxxviii. 17.

4. These sins will never be *brought to light against the soul* in judgment, nor will the sinner have to suffer for them, even though he should unfortunately sin again and be lost.

"I am, I am he that blot out thy iniquities for my own sake, and I will not remember thy sins." — Is. xliii. 25.

5. The fear of *death* and of *eternity* is changed into joy and consolation.  Thousands of examples prove this, of which every Mission is a witness.

"Thou hast turned for me my mourning into joy." — Ps. xxix. 12.

6. *Supernatural strength* is imparted to the soul to keep its good resolutions.  The good shepherd *carried* home the lost sheep on his shoulders after he had found it (Luke xv. 5).

7. The soul receives again its *former beauty* and merits.  The Prodigal Son, after his return, received a complete new outfit (Luke xv. 22).

B. *What is a sacrilegious confession?*

1. A sacrilegious confession is one in which any

of the above-named conditions required for a good confession is wanting.

2. What are the *evil consequences?* They are the following:

1. *No sin* is forgiven by such a confession.

"He that hideth his sins, shall not prosper." — Prov. xxviii. 13.

2. Another most grievous sin is added, *sacrilege*, which is greater than all the other sins that had to be told, put together, on account of the wanton profanation of the Sacrament.

"Son, for thy soul be not ashamed to say the truth. For there is a shame that bringeth sin." — Eccli. iv. 24, 25.

3. Generally one sacrilegious confession is followed by many more, and by many *unworthy Communions* and other sacrileges, committed with a cold heart.

"The wicked man when he is come into the depth of sins, contemneth." — Prov. xviii. 3.

4. The conscience of the sinner is in a *frightful state.* Terror and despair fill his soul.

"Because I was silent my bones grew old; whilst I cried out all the day long." — Ps. xxxi. 3. — "He that lives in mortal sin which he has often concealed in confession, carries a living prison, yea, hell itself in his conscience." — St. Chrys.

5. Such sinners are often *punished most terribly* on the spot. Example of Ananias and Saphira. (Acts v.)

6. The longer the sinner delays to confess his sins and his sacrileges, the harder he will find it. It requires an extraordinary grace. Many rather die in their sins than tell them to a priest.

7. On *Judgment-day* they must acknowledge all their sins before the whole world, and they will never cease confessing them for all eternity in hell.

Examine how you have made your confessions in the past. If badly, repair the evil at this Renewal by a good general confession.

## II

## BENEFITS DERIVED FROM A WORTHY COMMUNION, AND DISASTROUS CONSEQUENCES OF AN UNWORTHY COMMUNION

Holy Communion is the food of the soul, as nourishment is the food of the body. As the body must die without food, so must the soul die, that is, fall into grievous sin, without Holy Communion. For this reason we urged you at the Mission to receive it frequently.

But that this Sacrament may produce its wonderful effects, it must be received *worthily*. Immense harm is done to the soul by an unworthy Communion.

*A. What is a worthy Communion?*

1. A worthy Communion is one which is received in the *state of grace*, or by a Christian free from mortal sin. What those must do who are in the state of mortal sin, has been explained.

2. The *immense benefits* derived from a worthy Communion are the following:

1. Holy Communion produces the same effect in the soul that food produces in the body, because it *operates after the manner of food.*

"My flesh is meat indeed: and my blood is drink indeed." — John vi. 56.

This heavenly food nourishes the *mind* by imparting to it more light to understand divine truths; the *will* by giving it a certain vigor to resist and overcome temptations, no matter whence they come, great strength to bear with sufferings, and complete detachment from earthly goods. Example, the first Christians.

It sometimes extends its effects to the *body*, producing in it the same effects as corporal nourishment, as we see in the lives of some Saints who lived on Holy Communion. Examples are Blessed Nicholas of the Flue, Louise Lateau and others.

King Alphonsus VIII of Castile made his army go to Holy Communion before marching into battle, and he slew 200,000 of the enemy, while he lost only twenty men. A.D. 1212.

2. It effects the *remission of venial sins*, and even of mortal sins, if the soul should be in a bad state without knowing it, and of the temporal punishment due to sin. Trid. sess. 13. cap. 2.

3. It effects a most intimate *union between Jesus Christ and the soul*. They become together one flesh and blood (St. Cyril Jeros.); they are united like two pieces of wax melted together (St. Cyril. Alex.); as the nourishing substance of food is united to the body.

"He that eateth my flesh, and drinketh my blood, abideth in me and I in him." — John vi. 57.

4. The communicant is *transformed* into Jesus Christ, so that Christ lives in him (Gal. ii. 20), and the soul to a great extent imitates the actions and virtues of Christ.

"As I live by the Father, so he that eateth me, the same also shall live by me." — John vi. 58. — "Thou dost not change me into thee, as food into flesh, but thou art changed into me." — Christ speaking to St. Aug. conf. lib. 7.

5. Holy Communion is a pledge of *a glorious resurrection* and life everlasting.

"He that eateth . . . hath life everlasting; and I will raise him up in the last day." — John vi. 55.

All these salutary effects are produced to a greater or less extent according to the disposition and the devotion of the communicant, especially at thanksgiving. "A want of devotion," says St. Alph. (*Mor. Euch.* n. 270), "prevents in a great measure the good effects of Communion."

But what is to be said of those who receive Holy Communion unworthily?

*B. What is an unworthy Communion?*

1. An unworthy Communion is one which is received by a man in the state of mortal sin. Such a soul is supernaturally dead.

2. What benefit can it receive from this heavenly food?

1. *None at all.* It benefits the soul as little as food placed in the mouth of a corpse. The dead cannot eat. 2. It is, therefore, a *profanation* of the Holiest of Holies, hence a sacrilege than which there can be none greater.

"Whosoever shall . . . shall be guilty of the body and of the blood of the Lord." — I Cor. xi. 27.

3. This sin *stupefies* those who make themselves guilty of it; it takes away all light from the understanding, and makes the heart insensible to all religious influence. Examples of those who have made one or more unworthy Communions. An interior stupor has fallen upon them.

"Therefore, are there many weak among you, and many sleep." — I Cor. xi. 30.

4. God sometimes inflicts the most awful *punishment* upon the unworthy communicant.

About the year 862, King Lothaire of Lorrain was excommunicated because he lived in adultery. He went to Rome to be absolved by the Pope, without intending to give up sin. He and his followers, a few excepted, received Holy Communion on the promise that the king should return to his lawful wife. On their return they were attacked by a strange disease. All his followers, except those who had not communicated, died at Lucca; he himself died at Piacenza. (Smith's *Histor. Catech.*)

Mansius relates that a priest had refused absolution to a man, and had forbidden him to go to Communion. A little later the priest said Mass, and that man came to Communion. The priest could not refuse him on account of the seal of confession; but he said within himself: " May God judge between me and thee." The man received the Sacred Host and — dropped dead. (Wiser's *Lexicon.*)

5. He that receives Holy Communion unworthily, *eats judgment*, that is, damnation to himself.

"He that eateth and drinketh unworthily, eateth and drinketh judgment to himself." — I Cor. xi. 29. — "He that communicates unworthily receives life to his own condemnation." — St. Aug. — "Judas murmurs, Jesus bears with this; he is a thief, Jesus bears with this; he goes to betray his master, Jesus bears with this; he communicates unworthily — and the devil takes possession of him." — St. Chrys.

Go to Holy Communion *frequently*, as we told you in the Mission; but go *worthily* and receive it *devoutly*, and you will profit by it immensely.

# III

## HOLY MASS

Many could attend Mass on week-days but neglect
it. Others deem every little obstacle a sufficient
excuse to omit Mass even on days of obligation;
others again do not hear Mass with the proper devotion. The reason is, because they do not know
what the Mass is. The present instruction is to remedy
this defect.

No created mind can sound the depth of this great
mystery. Still we can learn so much concerning it as
to look upon it with the greatest awe and reverence.

### I. What is the Holy Mass

The Holy Mass is that solemn act by which, through
the ministry of the priest, Jesus Christ becomes present
on the altar under the species of bread and wine, and
then offers Himself to the Eternal Father in behalf
of His people. At the Mass Jesus Christ is present on
the altar as a victim of immolation. He there so
lowers Himself, that He appears as it were dead
(immolated), without the natural use of any of His
senses, prepared for men for their food and drink.

1. The Mass is the *most excellent sacrifice* that can
be made to God, on account of the victim, which is
nothing less than the God-man, Jesus Christ; and on
account of the offerer, who is again Jesus Christ.

"This is my beloved Son, in whom I am well pleased." — Matt.
iii. 17. — "Thou art a priest forever, according to the order of Mel-
chisedech." — Heb. v. 6.

2. The Mass is the same sacrifice as that on the *cross*. On the cross Jesus Christ was sacrificed in a bloody manner and only once; in the Mass He is sacrificed in an unbloody manner and all over the earth and through all times. In the Mass the sacrifice of the cross is reproduced and rendered present to all the people.

"By faith we must recognize in the offerings of the altar the Lamb of God lying on the holy table, that takes away the sins of the world and is sacrificed in an unbloody manner by the priests." — Council of Nice. — cf. Trid. sess. 22. cap. 2.

3. The Mass *includes* and absorbs *all other sacrifices*. All is contained in Jesus Christ. Therefore, as the stars disappear when the sun rises, so all other sacrifices ceased when the great sacrifice of the New Testament began.

"I will not receive a gift of your hand. For from the rising of the sun even to the going down . . . there is offered to my name a clean oblation." — Mal. i. 10, 11.

The Mass answers in a most sublime manner *all the ends* for which sacrifice may be offered. These are principally four: 1, To *adore* and worship the infinite Majesty of God; 2, To give *thanks* to God; 3, To *atone* for our sins; 4, To *ask* for new grace. How can these ends be accomplished better and more effectually than through Jesus Christ?

"The Mass comprises all the good contained in other sacrifices, it being as it were their consummation and perfection." — Trid. sess. 22. cap. 1.

4. The Holy Mass is the *most comprehensive sacrifice*, because it includes the universe in the offerer and in the victim offered.

a. *All creation is included in Christ.* Therefore, when Christ offers sacrifice *all creation sacrifices* to the Infinite God in Him. But He sacrifices principally as the head of the Church in union with all its members, and in particular in union with those who are present at the Mass. The entire act is performed through the ministry of the priest. Therefore the Mass is said in the plural number: *"Suscipiamur a te, Domine," "Offerimus tibi, Domine," "Rogamus ac petimus uti accepta habeas."* The Blessed in heaven are united with us, *"Communicantes."* But when the Mass arrives at the real act of the sacrifice, the consecration, Jesus Christ is alone, having absorbed all in Himself.

*b.* Again, in Jesus Christ *all creation is sacrificed.* All that exists is offered to God, the Infinite Being, when Jesus Christ is offered, because He represents all that exists.

"Through him, with him, and in him is given to Thee, God the Father, in union with the Holy Ghost, all honor and glory, throughout all ages without end." — Canon of the Mass.

Therefore, the people, especially those present, sacrifice to God with Christ, and are sacrificed to Him in Christ.

Of what infinite value, then, is a single Mass! What a privilege to be allowed to assist at it!

## II. Manner of Assisting at Mass

1. *We must hear the whole Mass,* that is, we must not come late, and not leave before the end.

"He that does not continue in prayer to the end of the mass is to be excluded from the communion of the faithful as a disturber of order and quiet." — Const. apost. can. 10. — "We command that the faithful attend the whole of the Mass on the Lord's day, and that no one presume to leave church before the blessing of the priest. He that acts thus is to be put to shame by the bishop." — Conc. Agathon. can. 47.

2. We should hear Mass *with devotion.* To do so it is, above all, necessary to attend to the three principal

parts of the Mass, the Offertory, the Consecration, the Communion. Those who pay no attention whatsoever to the Consecration have not heard Mass at all. For this reason the Church wants no singing then. The rest of the time may be filled up with other acts of devotion.

3. The following methods are the best to hear Mass with devotion: *a.* Read the *mass-prayers*, which in substance are the same as those which the priest says at the altar. *b.* Say the *Rosary*, as Leo XIII recently ordained. *c.* Offer the Mass with the priest for the *four principal ends*, in worship of God, in thanksgiving, in atonement, in prayer for graces. Always add one or more special intentions for yourself and others.

4. Remember that the Sacrifice of the Mass does not do away with the duty of making *personal sacrifices;* on the contrary, it enforces them. The faithful are to make offerings for the education and support of priests, for the building and the decorating of churches, and for many other needs. Those who neglect this duty are unworthy of receiving any benefit from this Holy Sacrifice.

Examine what esteem you have for the Mass, how you have attended it, how often you have perhaps neglected it, etc. Resolve to attend Mass whenever you can, even at a little sacrifice or at some inconvenience, to attend with true devotion, and to teach the same to your children.

# IV

## WORD OF GOD

Next to hearing Mass the most important duty of a Christian is to hear the Word of God.

### I. What is Comprised in the Word of God

1. By the Word of God we understand all that God has ever *made known to man*. He has spoken to the people of the Old Testament through the Patriarchs, Moses, and the Prophets; in the New Testament through Jesus Christ and the Holy Ghost.

"God, who, at sundry times and in divers manners, spoke in times past to the fathers by the prophets, last of all, in these days hath spoken to us by his Son." — Heb. i. 1, 2. — "I have yet many things to say to you; but you cannot bear them now. But when he, the Spirit of truth, is come, he will teach you all truth." — John xvi. 12, 13.

2. The Word of God *dates from all eternity;* it has been brought from heaven by Jesus Christ; it has been committed to the Apostles; and through them and their lawful successors it is to be made known to men to the end of time.

"I was set up from all eternity, and of old before the earth was made." — Prov. viii. 23. — "My doctrine is not mine, but his that sent me." — John vii. 16. — "I have not spoken of myself; but the Father who sent me, he gave me commandment what I should say, and what I should speak." — Ib. xii. 49. — "Go ye into the whole world, and preach the Gospel to every creature." — Mark xvi. 15.

3. It is through the Church and her lawfully established ministry that the Word of God is to be preached and not through others.

"He that heareth you, heareth me." — Luke x. 16. — "Faith cometh by hearing, and hearing by the word of Christ." — Rom. x. 17. — "You shall receive the power of the Holy Ghost and you shall be witnesses unto me to the uttermost parts of the earth." — Acts i. 8. — "They will heap to themselves teachers having itching ears." — II Tim. iv. 3.

The written Word of God, the Bible, is of value for us only in so far as it is explained to us by the Church.

## II. Necessity of Hearing Sermons

1. Sermons and instructions, given by the priests of the Church, are the *regular channels* through which the Word of God is to be made known. God has established this economy and He will not deviate from it.

This is proved by *examples:* When *St. Paul* was to be instructed, he was sent to the priest Ananias (Acts ix); *Cornelius* was told to send for St. Peter, then in Joppe (Acts x); St. Philip was even carried by an angel to instruct the *eunuch* on the road (Acts viii). God might have done all that by immediate illumination, or through the ministry of angels.

2. The Word of God is to be *preached*, and to be listened to, *again and again.*

*a.* Without seed nothing can grow, not on the very best soil. But "*semen est verbum Dei.*" Nor is it sufficient that the seed be *scattered but once* for several successive harvests, it must be scattered for each crop.

*b.* The *human passions* incline unto evil again and again, *the world* attracts unceasingly, *the devil* tempts without intermission; therefore *opportune remedies* must be given in the same proportion. These consist in sermons, preached time and again.

*c.* Travelers to unknown countries will not find

the road without repeated inquiries. So we are on the road to an unknown region. For a guide we have the Word of God.

"Thy word is a lamp to my feet." — Ps. cxviii. 105.

*d.* "Faith cometh by *hearing*" (Rom. x. 17).

"How shall they believe him, of whom they have not heard?" — Ib. x. 14.

Without preaching, *faith* cannot be acquired nor preserved. The same is true in regard to the principles of morality, which are the manifestation of the law of God.

A standing proof are those people who were once Catholics and who have lost the faith, because they had no priests to give instructions, or who, if they had priests, would not hear their sermons.

To these we may add a very large number of others in whom the faith has become weak, because although they go to Mass, they do not hear sermons.

3. For the same reason bishops and priests have the strict *commandment to preach* often. Are they perhaps to preach without an audience?

"I charge thee, before God and Jesus Christ . . . preach the word: be instant in season, out of season; reprove, entreat, rebuke in all patience and doctrine." — II Tim. iv. 1, 2.

The Council of Trent regards it as a grave obligation, resting upon all those who have the care of souls, to preach on all Sundays and feasts of obligation. (Sess. v. cap. 2.) Why so often, if it is not necessary for the people?

### III. Punishment for Neglecting to hear the Word of God

1. God looks upon such neglect as an act of contempt of Himself. And is it not an act of contempt

to refuse to listen to a friend who desires to speak to you concerning your highest interests?

"He that heareth you, heareth me; and he that despiseth you, despiseth me; and he that despiseth me, despiseth him that sent me." — Luke x. 16.

2. To neglect to hear the Word of God is a *sign of separation from God.*

"He that is of God, heareth the words of God. Therefore, you hear them not, because you are not of God." — John viii. 47. — "We are of God. He that knoweth God, heareth us. He that is not of God heareth us not. By this we know the spirit of truth, and the spirit of error." — I John iv. 6.

3. God will visit with the *severest judgments* those who refuse to hear the Word of God.

"He that despiseth me, and receiveth not my words, hath one that judgeth him; the word that I have spoken, the same shall judge him in the last day." — John xii. 48.

Worse things are said of those who refuse to listen to the preaching of the Apostles.

"And whosoever shall not receive you, *nor hear your words:* going forth out of that house or city, shake off the dust from your feet. Amen I say to you, it shall be more tolerable for the land of Sodom and Gomorrha in the day of judgment, than for that city." — Matt. x. 14, 15.

4. God threatens with *His curse* those who will not profit by the sermons that they hear; how much more those who neglect them. The Word of God is like the *rain that falls upon the earth.* If that earth bear no fruit, it is cursed.

"The earth that drinketh in the rain which cometh often upon it, . . . but which bringeth forth thorns and briers, is reprobate and very near to a curse, whose end is to be burnt." — Heb. vi. 7, 8.

What, then, about those who do not allow that rain to fall upon their souls?

IV. Conclusions to be Drawn

Whence the general spiritual desolation in our day? "He that hath ears to hear, let him hear." — Luke viii. 8.

A. Because many *do not hear* the Word of God at all: as, 1. *Infidels*, who believe in no religion; 2. *Careless Christians*, who avoid the Church; 3. Those who go to *another* Mass, or *go out* when the sermon begins, or pay *no attention*, acting just as though they were not present to listen.

B. Because many hear it *in the wrong way*. 1. They *despise* the preacher, criticize his language and manner, they are filled with prejudice against him; they take the sermon as the *word of man*, rather than the Word of God. 2. They do not allow it to *bear fruit*, — *a*, on account of *temptations* (Luke viii. 13). They say, "We must do as others do," "Can't be good," etc. They wish to serve two masters. — *b*. On account of *too much worldly care, business*. For such it "falls among briers." They believe in this world as their god, and the word of their god they keep more easily. "They have no time" to see to the affairs of their souls.

It is evident, therefore, why the sermons of five, ten, fifteen years have done no good.

Repent, change your mind, and say, "Speak, Lord for Thy servant heareth" (I Kings iii. 9), before it is too late, when God will speak to you no more.

# V

## LOVE OF OUR NEIGHBOR

Charity is the great law of God, which includes every other law.

"For all the law is fulfilled in one word: Thou shalt love thy neighbor as thyself." — Gal. v. 14.

For this reason the Gospels, and the Epistles of the Apostles are full of commands of charity, to be practised above everything else.

During the Mission we warned you against uncharitableness, enmity and hatred. This time we exhort you to love and charity in all its details.

### I. Why Must we Love our Neighbor

1. *Because the love of God and the love of our neighbor are one and the same love.* They are two rings but one chain, two actions but one virtue, two works but one motive, two streams from one source, two branches from one stem, two flames from one fire.

2. *Nature demands it.* We are all of the same nature, from the same parents, with the same inclinations, the same needs, faults, wants, affections, etc.

Charity is the basis and the strength of families, societies, communities, and states.

3. *It is the positive commandment of God.* Of the ten Commandments three only regard God, seven regard our neighbor. In six passages of the New Testament we are commanded to "love our neighbor as we love ourselves," *e.g.*, Matt. xix. 19. Rom. xiii.

9. Gal. v. 14. "It is the command of God (says St. John the Evangelist), and if this alone is done, it is enough." St. Jerome in ep. ad Gal.

4. *Our neighbor is entitled to our love.* We are all the property of God, all God's image and likeness, all God's children, all Christ's redeemed. We all wish to go to the same heaven, to enjoy the same glory, and desire to be one with God and in God forever. My neighbor owes me his love and I owe him my love; if I do not love him, I do him wrong, because I do not pay him what I owe.

5. *Charity is turned to our own great profit.*

"He that hath mercy on the poor, lendeth to the Lord; and he will repay him." — Prov. xix. 17. — "Give, and it shall be given to you: good measure and pressed down and shaken together and running over shall they give into your bosom. For with the same measure that you shall mete withal, it shall be measured to you again." — Luke vi. 38. — "But before all things have a constant mutual charity among yourselves; for charity covereth a multitude of sins." — I Pet. iv. 8. — "When thou shalt pour out thy soul to the hungry, and shalt satisfy the afflicted soul, then shall thy light rise up in darkness, and thy darkness shall be as noon-day . . . thou shalt be like a watered garden, and a fountain of water." — Is. lviii. 10.

6. It is impossible to love God without loving our neighbor.

"This commandment we have from God, that he, who loveth God, love also his brother." — I John iv. 21.

Who is our brother? Every human being, without distinction of nationality, color, or religion.

"Everybody is everybody's neighbor. Therefore, treat everybody as your neighbor; though he be no Christian, you know not what he is before God, or what God may intend to do with him. He may be converted and worship the true God more devoutly than you. — We must even love the wicked because they are the image and likeness of God. We do not love their evil work, because that is the work of man; but we love them, because they are the work of God." — St. Aug. — "He that loves me loves even my little dog." — St. Bernard.

## II. How Must we Love Our Neighbor

1. *As we love ourselves,* — as regards our actions, words, wishes and desires.

"All things, whatsoever you would that men should do to you, do you also to them." — Matt. vii. 12. — "See thou never do to another what thou wouldst hate to have done to thee by another." — Tob. iv. 16.

2. *With sincerity,* — not superficially, not with nice words, politeness, etc.

"Consider thy neighbor as part of thyself, and act toward him in every respect as thou dost toward thyself." — St. Aug.

3. *With disinterestedness.* — Seek not your own gain in the love of your neighbor.

"Charity seeketh not her own." — I Cor. xiii. 5.

Example of the first Christians, who gave away everything to let others have a part in it. Worldly charity is promoted by self-interest, hope of gain, ambition, political aims, even by evil lust.

4. *With activity,* — because charity is a fire which acts and is always active.

"My little children, let us not love in word, nor in tongue, but in deed, and in truth." — I John iii. 18.

Example of the Good Samaritan. "Go thou and do likewise," says Jesus Christ. Our active charity must extend to the body and the soul of our neighbor.

5. *With patience and perseverance.* — Hence, self-denial and overcoming our aversions, antipathies, little animosities and ill-feelings.

"Charity is patient, . . . is not provoked to anger, . . . beareth all things, endureth all things, charity never falleth away." — I Cor. xiii. 4, 5, 7, 13. — "Bear ye one another's burdens, and so shall you fulfil the law of Christ." — Gal. vi. 2.

Let everyone be mindful of his own weakness, his own failings, and of the difficulties which others have to bear with in him, and he will easily bear with others.

Hatred reigns supreme in hell, love reigns supreme in heaven. Earth would be heaven, if love and charity were allowed to reign here.

# VI

## TEMPTATIONS, CROSSES AND TRIALS

Life is given to man for a trial. During the brief period of his existence here below he will be given thousands of occasions to show his love and fidelity to God, by making the necessary efforts to overcome the obstacles in his way.

"The life of man upon earth is a warfare, and his days are like the days of a hireling." — Job vii. 1.

This warfare is caused by *Temptations*, and by *Crosses* and *Trials*.

### I. Temptations

A *Temptation* is an occasion on which man is *put to the test*, to show whether he prefer good to evil, God to the devil, heaven to hell, salvation to damnation.

1. *Origin* of temptation. Man, who either never fell into grievous sin, or who has been converted from *sin*, is tempted, often and fiercely.

*a.* By his own *nature*, which always inclines unto evil, or which is still accustomed to it after conversion.

"For the flesh lusteth against the spirit: and the spirit against the flesh; for these are contrary one to another." — Gal. v. 17. — "Every man is tempted by his own concupiscence, being drawn away and allured. Then when concupiscence hath conceived, it bringeth forth sin. But sin, when it is completed, begetteth death." — James i. 14, 15.

*b.* By the *devil*, man's adversary, "who, as a roaring lion, goeth about seeking whom he may devour" (I Pet. v. 8); and who, after a man's conversion, returns "with seven other spirits more wicked than himself" (Luke xi. 26), trying to gain back the soul that he has lost.

*c.* By *God*, Who subjects His servants to a trial. Some temptations are sent by God directly, as for instance in the case of Abraham.

"The Lord your God trieth you, that it may appear whether you love him with all your heart, and with all your soul, or not." — Deut. xiii. 3. — "Because thou wast acceptable to God, it was necessary that temptation should prove thee." — Tob. xii. 13.

Other temptations He simply permits, especially those which incline directly to sin.

"Let no man, when he is tempted, say that he is tempted by God. For God is not a tempter of evils, and he tempteth no man." — James i. 13.

2. Temptations, provided we overcome them, turn out to our *greatest profit.* They are for us occasions of *triumph* over our greatest enemies, the world, the devil, and our own flesh. We shall receive a greater glory in heaven for our victory over temptations than for many other good works that we may have performed.

"*Blessed* is the man that endureth temptation; for when he hath been proved, he shall receive the crown of life, which God hath promised to them that love him." — James i. 12. — "My brethren, count it all joy, when you shall fall into divers temptations." — Ib. i. 2.

Virtue is of no value except it has been tried by many temptations.

"What doth he know, that hath not been tried?" — Eccli. xxxiv. 9.

3. We possess *infallible means* for overcoming our temptations. Salvation depends at all times on ourselves; it is never impossible to keep from sin.

*a.* God *never allows* us to be tempted beyond our

strength. In *Holy Communion* we receive the strength of Jesus Christ Himself.

"Wisdom walketh with him in temptation." — Eccli. iv. 18. — "No evils shall happen to him that feareth the Lord: but in temptation God will keep him and deliver him from evil." — Ib. xxxiii. 1. — "God is faithful, who will not suffer you to be tempted above that which you are able; but will make also with temptation issue, that you may be able to bear it." — I Cor. x. 13.

*b.* We can greatly diminish our temptations by shunning the *occasions of sin.* Many have themselves to blame for their temptations, because they constantly seek them.

"If thou do well, shalt thou not receive? But if ill, shall not sin forthwith be present at the door? — But the lust thereof shall be under thee and thou shalt have dominion over it." — Gen. iv. 7.

*c.* We always have a most powerful help in *prayer.*

"No evils shall happen to him that feareth the Lord. . . ." — Eccli. xxxiii. 1. — "There was given me a sting of my flesh, an angel of Satan, to buffet me. For which thing thrice I besought the Lord, that it might depart from me. And he said to me: My grace is sufficient for thee; for virtue is made perfect in infirmity." — II Cor. xii. 7-9.

Strict *watchfulness* over ourselves and *prayer* are the two great means against temptation recommended by the Lord Jesus Himself.

"Watch ye, and pray that ye enter not into temptation." — Matt. xxvi. 41.

But, it may be asked, How is it that some people pray and yet fall into sin?

*a.* Because while praying they *love sin.* *b.* Keep gazing at or dallying with it, as Eve gazed at the apple. *c.* Because they do not pray *from the beginning,* but only after partly giving way to sin. *d.* Because in their pride, they still think that they can master the temptation at any time, which is not true.

4. It is a common *artifice of the devil* to induce those

who have many temptations, to believe that they cannot be in the state of grace, or, if the temptation has been very strong, that they have given consent to it. Be on your guard against this deception.

"The life of the just is not a triumph but a battle." (St. Aug. serm. 45 de temp.) "Rest is to be expected only in heaven, where we receive the palm of victory. In this life we must be between fear and hope, but the latter must prevail." (St. Francis de Sales.) "Everything may be in confusion in body and soul; but the delight that pleases the exterior of man, displeases the interior." (St. Francis de Sales, *Philothea.*)

NOTE. — This first part is given at greater length that it may serve as an instruction by itself where it may be deemed necessary to give it alone.

## II. CROSSES AND TRIALS

*Crosses* and *Trials* are either exterior or interior, as they affect either the body or the soul.

1. The life of a Christian ought to be a *life of suffering*. Such was the life of Christ, Who suffered all His life-time, because He chose for Himself a life of poverty and humility, and willingly received constant humiliations from others.

As the bridegroom is so must the bride be.

A soul that loves Jesus Christ will love suffering.

"If any man will come after me, let him deny himself and take his cross daily, and follow me." — Luke ix. 23. — "God forbid that I should glory, save in the cross of our Lord Jesus Christ, by whom the world is crucified to me, and I to the world." — Gal. vi. 14. — "Patience hath a perfect work: that you may be perfect and entire: failing in nothing." — James i. 4.

2. Crosses and Trials merit for us the *highest glory* in heaven.

"Through many tribulations we must enter into the kingdom of God." — Acts xiv. 21. — "The sufferings of this present time are not worthy to be compared with the glory to come." — Rom. viii. 18. — "For that which is at present momentary and light of our tribulation, worketh for us above measure exceedingly an eternal weight of glory." — II Cor. iv. 17.

3. Crosses and Trials, more than anything else, shorten *our sufferings in purgatory.* God, in His goodness, sends them to us, that we may the sooner atone for our sins.

"Murmur not, blaspheme not, do not say: why must I suffer so much? Rather say: the punishment that I suffer is not as great as my sins." — St. Isid.

4. The *way to act* under Crosses and Trials is simply to *bear them.* You cannot help feeling them very keenly, otherwise they would not be sufferings. Nor is it wrong to wish to be free from them; but let that wish be united to resignation. Slight complaints may also escape your lips, but let them not be expressions of impatience.

Above all, remember that sooner or later they will come to an end.

# VII

## RULE OF A CHRISTIAN LIFE

In a Christian life there must be *order*, else there is confusion and no success. This is the rule in regard to every sort of business. It must be so in particular in regard to the chief business of life — our salvation.

1. *Every day.* — Let there be a *fixed time* for *rising*, and for *retiring*.

When you awake give your first thoughts to God, bless yourself and rise without delay, thanking God that He has given you another day, and resolve to spend it according to His good pleasure.

After dressing kneel down and say three *Hail Marys* in honor of the purity of the Blessed Virgin Mary, that she may protect you against sin during the day. Then say an *"Our Father," "Hail Mary,"* the *Creed* and the *Confiteor*. Add the *Angelus*, and the *"Glory be to the Father,"* three times in honor of your Angel Guardian and your Patron-Saints.

When a *temptation* to sin befalls you during the day, ask Jesus and Mary to assist you, banish the bad thought and think of something else.

Let the *good intention* be repeated often during the day. Eat or drink as little as possible *between meals*, and thus practise some mortification; spend no time in *idleness*, vain talk; *rest a little* after meals; do nothing *in haste*, remembering that all your success depends on the *blessing of God*, not on your work. Preserve *patience* in little trials, or if things do not seem to succeed according to your expectation.

Fixed time *for meals*, with prayers before and after. Say the *Angelus* about midday.

Fixed time for *night prayer*, which should consist of the Holy Rosary, the Litany of the Blessed Virgin, the *Angelus*, three *Glorias* in honor of your Guardian Angel.

If you have time, read some pious book in the evening. Immediately before retiring, examine your conscience a little, and say the Christian Acts. If you do not know them, say at least an act of contrition. Lastly, say three *Hail Marys* in honor of the purity of the Blessed Virgin, that she may protect you against sin during the night. After retiring observe what you read in the Mission Remembrance.

In families there should be *divine service* in common once a day, in which all should join. Let them say night prayers together. This brings a special blessing upon the house.

If at all possible, at least one of the family should go to Mass every day. By this method the whole family partakes of the Mass, because the priest at the altar prays for those present and their relatives at home. "*Pro omnibus circumstantibus suisque omnibus.*"

2. *Every week.* — On Friday do not forget to keep the abstinence from flesh-meat. If you have sinned grievously during the week, go to *confession* on Saturday or Sunday, although it be out of your usual time. On *Sundays* and *Holy-days*, besides attending *Mass*, attend a *sermon* or *instruction;* if possible, try to hear a sermon or instruction every Sunday, or at least every other Sunday. Attend some *afternoon service*, so as to sanctify Sunday as a Christian should. Make *an offering* to God, that He may bless your work during the coming week; also, in thanksgiving for past bless-

ings, as. well as to fulfil one of your Christian
duties.

3. *Every month.* — Go to *confession* and *Holy Communion*, if you can, every month. Let all in the
family take *their turn* in doing so.

Become a member of some *confraternity* whose rule
is monthly Communion; and then assist at the exercises of the same. Examine whether you still keep
the resolutions taken at the *Mission*, and whether
every one under your charge (this includes servants)
fulfils his Christian duties.

4. *Every three months.* — Four times a year the
*Ember Days* are to be kept as days of fast and abstinence. Within the same period comes one or the other
day of fast and abstinence. Be careful to keep
them.

Also a Holy-day of obligation may come within
that period. Keep it as you keep Sunday.

Every quarter of a year you are reminded to pay
part of your regular dues to the church and to the
priest, by attending to your pew-rent, or by fulfilling
this duty in some other way.

5. *Every year.* — Once a year you are to keep Lent,
according to the diocesan regulations. You are also
to attend to your Easter duties, and see that every
one under your charge will do so.

Once a year set apart a day of special recollection.
Prepare for death by spending the day in more than
ordinary retirement. *Examine* your *conscience*, going
over the whole year. Make a *review* of your life during
the year to your confessor, repeating your principal
sins; give thanks to God for the many blessings
granted to you; visit the *Mission-Cross;* renew your
*resolutions* and baptismal *vows.*

*A good time for this* is the last day of the year, New

Year's day, your birthday, anniversary of the Mission, day of marriage, feast of your patron, etc.

If you spend your time in this manner, your life will be well spent. You will acquire immense treasures for heaven, and your reward will be exceedingly great in the land of the blessed.

# VIII

## INSTRUCTION FOR THE DYING

After having instructed you *how to live*, we shall also tell you *how to die.*

In the present instruction we have some very important advice to give to the dying themselves, and then to those who attend the dying.

### I. How Should the Dying Meet Death

1. There is something terrible about death for everybody; yet the man that has followed the rules of a Christian Life need not fear it. *"Sicut vita, finis ita"* is a general rule.

When you are very sick, ask your relatives, your physicians, not to conceal from you the danger, that you may at once prepare for your last moments. It is a notion to be condemned that we should conceal their danger from the dying, thus causing them to die without due preparation. The Church has issued her censures against physicians who do not insist on having their patients receive the Last Sacraments when they see that they are dangerously ill. However, these censures do not apply to this country. When you see the danger imminent, then

2. Put your *temporal affairs* in order; settle your *debts;* make *your will,* if necessary; and *forgive everybody* from your heart. After that *turn your mind and heart* altogether from this earth, which you know you must soon leave.

"Take order with thy house, for thou shalt die, and not live." —
Is. xxxviii. 1.

3. Then prepare for the reception of the *Last Sacraments*. Have the priest called while you still possess the full use of your mind.

Your last confession need not necessarily be a general confession if you have made one before, or if you have always made good confessions; yet a *general review* of your life is most useful, which you can make by telling in general terms the most grievous sins of your life without further details. But you should try to conceive a true and hearty sorrow for all the sins of your whole life.

Receive the *Viaticum* with true devotion. You need not be fasting for that. You may also receive it in that way more than once.

Then receive the Sacrament of *Extreme Unction*, the effect of which is threefold: restoration of health, if it be according to the will of God; purification of the soul from all sin and its last traces; strength of the soul at the last hour. This Sacrament may be received again in a new danger of death, independently of any former danger in which it had been administered.

Finally, you receive the last *Plenary Indulgence*, for which these are the conditions: invocation of the holy name of Jesus; contrition and detestation for all sin, including venial sin; acceptance of death with perfect resignation.

Those who possess any *pious articles* blessed for a happy death, or who are faithful members of some *confraternity*, have also a *Plenary Indulgence* for each, if they invoke with their lips, or at least in their heart, the holy names of Jesus and Mary, with true contrition for all their sins.

4. Fear not *at the approach of the hour of death.*

You may have severe temptations, especially to despair, but you will also have more than necessary strength to overcome them. When you see nothing more around you, when you have entered the *dark night of death*, do not lose confidence; keep on praying, make use of short aspirations, until you drop into the arms of Jesus.

## II. What is to be Observed by the Attendants

*As to the attendants* at the death-bed, they should,

1. *Know what is to be held in readiness* for the administration of the Last Sacraments, and have everything prepared: a *table* covered with a white cloth, a *crucifix*, one or two (blessed) *candles* to burn on the priest's arrival, a tumbler with fresh water, a clean tablespoon, a vessel with holy water, salt, or a few small slices of bread, cotton, a napkin to hold before the communicant. These things should be prepared before the priest arrives.

2. If the priest is expected to bring the Blessed Sacrament with him, meet him with a lighted taper at the door of the house or of the sick room. Remain kneeling until the priest bids you leave the room that he may hear the confession of the sick person. After returning remain kneeling until the priest has finished administering the Sacraments, and pray for the dying person.

3. After this *but few persons* should be allowed to be around the dying person, because their presence makes the room unhealthy; causes anguish to the dying, especially if they break forth into sobs and cries; and will keep him from recollection.

4. Let a *crucifix* be near the bed, and a *picture of the Blessed Virgin*, which the sick person can easily see;

also *holy water*, which should frequently be sprinkled upon the bed of the dying person, especially during the last agony. This is like a heavenly dew, and chases away evil spirits.

"Ad abigendos dæmones, non illic resideat spiritus pestilens, discedant omnes insidiæ latentis inimici, etc." — Rit. Ben.

A blessed *wax candle* should be kept burning near the bed during the agony. It represents the burning candle received at baptism, and the faith received then and kept until death. The blessed light has at the same time power to dispel the darkness of hell, as light and darkness cannot exist together.

"Talem benedictionem signaculo sanctæ crucis accipiant, ut quibuscunque locis accensæ sive positæ fuerint, discedant principes tenebrarum, et contremiscant et fugiant pavidi cum omnibus ministris suis ab habitationibus illis." — Rit. Ben.

5. When the dying person enters into his agony, read some of *the Passion of Christ* for him, that he may unite his death with that of Jesus; *then the prayers for the dying;* suggest some short and familiar *aspirations* to him, especially acts of faith, confidence, love, contrition, petition to Jesus, Mary and Joseph, the guardian angel, holy patrons. As he is unable to do this himself, do it for him, otherwise he will not even think of it. It is the best service that you can render him. Remember that he is on the point of entering eternity; all depends on these last moments. Do so for others, and you will not be left alone when you are about to die.

6. Immediately *after death* has closed the struggle, kneel down and say a prayer for the departed soul. Notify the priest to have a Mass said at once. Avoid having *wakes* around the body. Allow nobody to come to the house except those who are willing to pray for

the deceased; keep a candle burning near the body day and night. Be not in a hurry with the burial, except in cases of urgent necessity, and arrange the *funeral* according to approved customs and the prescriptions of the Church, without much display and expense.

# THE SACRAMENT OF CONFIRMATION

NOTE. — It often happens that at Missions or Renewals the
Sacrament of Confirmation is administered, and that it becomes
the task of the missionaries to give an instruction on this Sacrament. — The following sketch contains all that may be said on the
subject under those circumstances. It may be divided, especially
if the instruction is to be given before the Rosary, which, on most
occasions, is the best time for it.

The present instruction on the Sacrament of Confirmation is principally for those who are preparing
for the reception of this Sacrament, but it is also very
useful for all the rest, that they may be reminded of
what they received when they were confirmed.

## I. EFFECTS OF THE SACRAMENT OF CONFIRMATION

Confirmation is a Sacrament through which we
receive the Holy Ghost to make us strong and perfect
Christians and soldiers of Jesus Christ. This Sacrament, therefore, brings to perfection what Baptism
has begun.

1. The life of the soul is similar to that of the body.
First, man is born as an infant, then he grows up to
*perfect* manhood. So the soul is born as a Christian in
Baptism, in Confirmation it is brought to *perfection
as a Christian*. Hence, there is the same difference
between a Christian who is simply baptized and
another who is also confirmed, that exists between an
infant and a full-grown man.

2. The *Holy Ghost* is imparted in a special manner
to the baptized Christian who receives Confirmation,

giving him special strength and firmness against all attacks of the world and hell.

"God our Saviour saved us by the laver of regeneration, and renovation of the Holy Ghost." — Tit. iii. 5.

3. Confirmation *augments* sanctifying grace, by conferring upon the Christian a greater participation in the Divine Being. Life is stronger in a man than in an infant.

4. Confirmation makes out of weak Christians *soldiers of Christ*, and arms them against His enemies.

"By Baptism man is received into the army of Christ, by Confirmation he is provided with arms. In Baptism he comes to life, in Confirmation he receives strength for the battle of life. In Baptism man is regenerated unto salvation, in Confirmation he is prepared for the fight." — Pope St. Melch.— "Labor as a good soldier of Christ Jesus." — II Tim. ii. 3. — "The weapons of our warfare are not carnal, but mighty to God unto the pulling down of fortifications." — II Cor. x. 4.

5. Confirmation imparts to us the *seven gifts of the Holy Ghost*, mentioned by Isaias xi. 2, 3.

*a. Wisdom*, which induces man to despise the world, and to love and serve God;

*b. Understanding*, which comprehends the truths and teachings of faith;

*c. Counsel*, or prudence, by which man will always see and adopt the right means for working out his salvation;

*d. Fortitude*, by which man overcomes all obstacles in his way, and effects his perseverance;

*e. Knowledge*, which shows man at all times the right road to heaven and the dangers threatening him;

*f. Godliness*, which fills man's heart with unction and fervor;

*g. Fear of the Lord*, which gives man a holy awe for the majesty of God, and makes him dread sin as the greatest evil.

6. Confirmation puts a special *indelible seal* upon man's soul and marks him as a soldier of Christ. Soldiers are in a uniform by which they are distinguished from other people. Grown-up men are easily distinguished from children. Thus it is in Confirmation. This mark remains on the soul forever.

Confirmation is received *only once*, just as man grows up only once in his life.

"He that confirmeth us . . . and hath anointed us, is God: who also hath sealed us, and given the pledge of the Spirit in our hearts." — II Cor. i. 21, 22. — "In whom (Christ) believing you were signed with the Holy Spirit." — Eph. i. 13. — "Confirmation is a mark that can be not extinguished for all eternity." — St. Cyril of Jerusalem.

## II. OBLIGATION OF RECEIVING CONFIRMATION

1. Confirmation is not absolutely necessary for salvation. But it would be a sign of the greatest carelessness not to receive it when the opportunity is offered, because it confers so many graces and gives so much assistance in trials.

2. Therefore, it is generally to be regarded as a mortal sin wilfully to neglect this Sacrament. Hence, also those who have not received it in their younger days must receive it as adults.

3. It would be great recklessness and, therefore, a sign of intolerable pride, to neglect to procure great help in the dangerous warfare of life, and to risk the great battle without it.

"Although Confirmation is not absolutely necessary for salvation, yet no one must neglect it, because what God has ordained for the salvation of all, should be eagerly sought by all." — Rom. Catech. — "This Sacrament cannot be neglected without grievous sin, when the opportunity is given." — Ben. XIV.

The ancient discipline of the Church condemned to three years' penance parents who allowed their children to die without Confirmation.

### III. Preparation for Confirmation

For the reception of this Sacrament is required:

1. *Baptism.* Without this it would be invalid. No one can grow up who does not exist.

2. *Sufficient instruction* in all that a Christian is obliged to know and to believe, and a sufficient knowledge of this Sacrament.

3. *State of grace.* Therefore those who are in the state of mortal sin must go to confession. All who are to be confirmed generally go to confession a day or two before, unless they have received the Sacraments shortly before.

4. *Special devotion,* immediately before and after the administration of the Sacrament. The Pontifical gives the advice to receive it fasting; but there is no obligation to do so. The Apostles spent ten days in holy retirement before they received the Holy Ghost.

### IV. Ceremonies of Confirmation

1. The Bishop with outstretched hands *invokes the Holy Ghost* upon those to be confirmed, kneeling before him, that they may receive His sevenfold gifts.

2. Those to be confirmed are led before the Bishop by a *god-father*, who takes upon himself the obligation of directing his god-child in the duties of a good Christian, should it be necessary. Between this god-father and his god-child, henceforth, exists a spiritual relationship, as in Baptism. But this relationship is no longer (Canon 1079) an impediment of matrimony.

During the act of Confirmation the god-father places his right hand upon the right shoulder of his god-child.

3. It is customary that those to be confirmed take an *additional name,* so that they place themselves

under the protection of another Saint in heaven, as they are put in charge of another god-father on earth.

4. The Bishop anoints the forehead of the candidate with *Holy Chrism* in the form of the cross. Chrism is a mixture of balsam and olive oil, and denotes a great love for purity of life. The cross on the forehead warns the confirmed Christian never to be ashamed of his religion or its practices. The words which the Bishop pronounces express the effects of the Sacrament.

5. The Bishop gives a *slight blow* on the cheek to the candidate, signifying thereby that now he possesses strength enough to bear all sorts of insults for the sake of his religion. He says: "*Pax tecum*," expressing the peace of soul that the confirmed Christian enjoys under all trials and persecutions.

6. The Bishop, finally, gives a *blessing* to all who have been confirmed, praying that they may remain the living temples of the Holy Ghost, and enjoy the goods of the heavenly Jerusalem here on earth, and hereafter forever in heaven.

7. All those who are to be confirmed must be present from the *beginning to the end* of the ceremony. For this reason it is customary in some places to lock the doors of the church during the administration of Confirmation.

8. Before they leave the church all must say the *Creed* and the *Lord's Prayer*, showing that henceforth they will preserve a lively faith and practise prayer.

Let, then, all those who are confirmed live up to their faith and their religious obligations, taking good care not to drive the Holy Ghost from them by sin; being watchful lest they cause Him the least grievance, according to the warning of the Apostle: "Grieve not the Holy Spirit of God: whereby you are sealed unto the day of redemption." — Eph. iv. 30.

## FIFTH PART

SERMONS FOR MISSIONS AND
RENEWALS GIVEN ON CER-
TAIN OCCASIONS

# I

## TRUE CHURCH OF JESUS CHRIST

Faith in the true Church is fast disappearing even among Catholics, — hence the great number of apostates. Indifferentism, Liberalism, Latitudinarianism are gaining upon us to an astonishing degree.

*The object* of this sermon is not so much to convert Protestants, as to confirm Catholics in their faith and in fidelity to the Church. To gain this point, it must be shown that the Church is the organ of the Holy Ghost, Who by means of her teachers directs and guides men to heaven. Her authority is, therefore, the authority of God the Holy Ghost. For the same reason, the Church is infallible, she can never change, and she will never cease to exist.

Prudence suggests that the preacher make no direct attacks upon those outside of the Church, but confine himself to the truth to be established. Attacks can only exasperate non-Catholics; they will never convert them. This is to be neither a controversial nor a polemical discourse, but a solid instructive sermon.

It is well to publish the time when this sermon will be preached, and to invite Protestants, if there be a good number of them willing to attend.

In smaller Missions there will hardly be time enough for both sermons — on the true Church and the Precepts — while they are, perhaps, both very necessary to the people. In that case, both these sermons can very easily be united in one, under the head of *"Faith and Obedience due to the Church."* In this one sermon on both subjects, the principle is, first of all, demonstrated that no one who refuses to "hear the Church," can be a Christian. *"Non potest habere Deum patrem, qui non habet Ecclesiam matrem"* (St. Cypr.). Then, that this Church demands our implicit faith (give reasons), — and our perfect submission (give reasons). Lastly, the chief commandments of the Church are mentioned, and those most neglected are to be especially inculcated.

In an emergency, the sermon may be changed into a morning instruction, as was the custom in the past. However, among English-speaking Catholics, experience has proved the necessity of making an evening sermon out of it, if it be in any way possible.

In many places a sermon on *Faith* is preferable to the sermon on the Church. — There are no Protestants susceptible of the truth, attending the Mission; the Catholics all believe in the Church, but their faith may lack some of its essential qualities. Such is the state of things in many parishes. Hence a sermon on Faith will be in order.

The main point in this sermon is a good plain definition of faith. Then follow its necessary qualities, well described and supported by strong arguments. In this sermon the preacher may make it a point to speak on religious intolerance, and show that *faith* is, and must be, *exclusive*, while *Christian charity* is, and must be, *expansive*.

### SKETCH

TEXT: "In those days the God of heaven will set up a kingdom that shall never be destroyed . . . it shall stand for ever." — Dan. ii. 44.

EXORDIUM. — To be good Christians, we must be well grounded in faith.

"Without faith it is impossible to please God." — Heb. xi. 6.

Sad state of society at present.

"Men are tossed to and fro by every wind of doctrine." — Eph. iv. 14.

Or are given to a cold indifference. Even among Catholics many waver in their faith. It becomes our duty, then, to confirm our Catholic brethren in the faith, as well as to instruct those outside who show a good will toward the only saving faith. Let it be remarked, however, that it is by no means our intention to throw stones at others, although we cannot refrain from speaking out the plain truth. By this rule I will be guided in the present discourse.

### I. THERE CAN BE BUT ONE RELIGION

That *religion is necessary*, no reasonable man will call in doubt. There is a God, we must serve Him; we have immortal souls, we must save them; we have to live in harmony upon earth, we must observe certain laws to preserve our mutual relations. Hence, the necessity of religion, by which these ends will be attained.

Now, there can never be, there has never been, more than *one true* religion.

1. Religion *comes from God.* It tells us: 1, what we are to believe; and, 2, what we are to do or to avoid. Matters of faith can be made known by God alone, and through such means as leave no room for doubt. Under this condition only are we to give them our implicit and unwavering assent, divine faith. The commandments tell us what is good and what is evil. God alone can tell this, and to be binding in conscience this communication must be made known to man as coming from God. Without such assurance there can exist only religious opinions and general confusion.

2. Now, God cannot reveal a certain point of doctrine as divine truth, and then its very opposite as divine truth also. Neither can the same thing be true and false at the same time. Nor can God declare one and the same thing right and wrong at the same time. Therefore, that which is a sin, declared to be so by God, cannot at the same time be not a sin.

There exists either one religion or more in the world. If more, they either agree or disagree in matters of faith and morals. If they perfectly agree, then they make but one; if they do not agree perfectly, they must necessarily all be false except one.

"One Lord, one faith, one baptism, one God and Father of all, who is above all and through all, and in us all." — Eph. iv. 5, 6.

*Objection:* "We agree in essential points."

It matters not how insignificant in our eyes may be the point of doctrine or the commandment in regard to which we differ from one another, it proves what I have said. For in so much the authority of God is

in question, and let it be as little as the *tittle of an iota.*
— Forbidden fruit in Paradise.

But do we differ in non-essential points only? Church
authority or private judgment, necessity of certain
sacraments, real presence, forgiveness of sins by the
priest — are these non-essential points?

Therefore, the various religious denominations differ in essential points of doctrine and of morals. Hence
all are false save one — *i.e.,* the one established by God.
Which is it?

## II. The Roman Catholic Religion is the only Religion Established by God

1. In the Old Law, God manifested religion to men
in various ways (Heb. i. 2). In the New Law, through
Jesus Christ, Who has abundantly proved His divine
character and mission. Hence the religion of Jesus
Christ is the true one, and this we must profess and
practise in order to be saved. For this reason, sending the Apostles to preach His doctrine to the whole
world, He said:

"He that believeth and is baptized, shall be saved: but he that
believeth not shall be condemned." — Mark xvi. 16. — "Neither
is there salvation in any other. For there is no other name under
heaven given to men, whereby we must be saved." — Acts iv. 12.

The religion of Jesus Christ is, therefore, the religion
for all men, for all times, universal, *Catholic.* Jesus
Christ Himself foretold that this religion should never
disappear from the earth, never be changed in the
least.

"Amen, I say unto you, till heaven and earth pass, one jot or
one tittle shall not pass of the law." — Matt. v. 18. — "It is easier
for heaven and earth to pass, than one tittle of the law to fall." —
Luke xvi. 17. — Accordingly, St. Paul says: "Though we, or an
angel from heaven, preach a Gospel to you besides that which we
have preached to you, let him be anathema." — Gal. i. 8.

Therefore, the religion which Jesus Christ brought from heaven, established on earth, and commanded his Apostles to preach, is the only true religion.

What, then, about those men who attempt to spread a different Gospel?

2. *Where is that religion to be found?* That it still exists, and in its purity, is evident from the above. It must also be easy to discover it. For can anyone be pronounced guilty of hell-fire for not doing what he cannot do except under the greatest difficulties? Nor must it require much learning to discover it, else it would not be the religion for the poor and uneducated.

*Jesus Christ founded a Church.*

"Upon this rock I will build my Church." — Matt. xvi. 18.

He would remain with it always.

"And behold I am with you all days, even to the consummation of the world." — Matt. xxviii. 20.

This Church is a corporation, society, of such as believe in and practise His Gospel; His mystical body.

"We being many, are one body in Christ, and every one members one of another." — Rom. xii. 5.

Of this body He is the head.

"He [His Son] is the head of the body, the Church." — Col. i. 18.

His visible representative, the visible head of the Church, is Peter, and his successors, the Roman Pontiffs.

"Thou art Peter, and upon this rock I will build my Church." — Matt. xvi. 18. — "Feed my lambs, — feed my sheep." — John xxi. 15-17.

Hence, that must be the Church, the religion, of Jesus Christ, of which Peter and his successors are the visible head. Can you find this Church?

Nor can this Church cease to exist. Otherwise it

would be disconnected from its head, which is against the express declaration of Jesus Christ. Nor can it go astray, else the head would go astray with it; or the head would go one way, while the body goes another. This is an absurdity.

3. The mystical body of Christ, after its formation, was to be endowed *with a soul.*

"And the Lord God formed man of the slime of the earth: and breathed into his face the breath of life, and man became a living soul." — Gen. ii. 7.

The soul of the Church, which the Lord God breathed into it, is the Holy Ghost.

"The Spirit of truth . . . he shall abide with you, and shall be in you." — John xiv. 17.

The *Holy Ghost* gives it life, strength, and power; acts, directs, moves, speaks, by means of this mystical body, as the soul in the physical body. Hence the teaching and the commands of the Church are the actions of God the Holy Ghost.

The Holy Ghost teaches all truth.

"The Paraclete, the Holy Ghost, whom the Father will send in my name, he will teach you all things." — John xiv. 26.

He reveals in times of doubt the real meaning of Christ's doctrine.

"And bring all things to your mind, whatsoever I shall have said to you." — Ib.

He remains in the Church forever, as the soul in the body.

"The Father shall give you another Paraclete, that he may abide with you forever." — Ib. xiv. 16.

This makes it "the Church of the living God. the pillar and ground of truth." (I Tim. iii. 15.) *Infallible* and *indefectible* — *one* in doctrine and faith for all times and places. For how can the Holy Ghost teach false doctrine, introduce abominations, admit a variety or change of doctrine? . . . Impossible!

Ask now, How many of all our modern churches say that they are *infallible?* Only one. How many have always and everywhere held and taught the *same doctrine?* Only one. In how many is there *perfect unity?* Only in one. How many have *existed since the time of Christ*, always the same, in the midst of opposition? Only one; and that one is well known as a city built on the mountain, the *Roman Catholic Church*.

All the others exist only for one, two, three or four hundred years. They have changed again and again and there is still no end to their changing. Can such churches be the mystical body of Christ, with Himself as the head, whose soul is the Holy Ghost, the Church of the living God, the pillar and ground of truth, in which not a tittle is to be altered?

They go under the general name of *Protestant*, pretending, as they do, to protest against the horrid abuses introduced into the Catholic Church at some past time unknown, while they, as they say, are reproducing the Gospel in its original purity. And, because they have not yet fully succeeded in re-establishing the original purity of the doctrine of Christ, they find additional changes necessary. But the introduction of such abuses is impossible as regards the doctrine of the Church, as we have seen. Hence they protest against what does not exist. Abuses in the members of the Church are possible, however, and of this they are themselves a living proof.

St. Paul says that Christ established "the Church *glorious*, not having *spot* or *wrinkle*, or *any such thing*, but that it should be *holy*, and without *blemish*." — Eph. v. 27.

The Church, therefore, was pure from the beginning; so it had to be ever afterward, on account of its intimate union with God the Son and the Holy Ghost.

Hence no reformation ever was, or ever will be, needed for it; but it is needed for its members, whenever they deviate from its teaching.

4. Nor is the occasional *definition of an article of faith* an introduction of a new doctrine. The Church is the great teacher of all religious truth. Whenever disputes are rife in regard to certain points of doctrine, not yet clearly defined, the Church must speak and give us a clear definition concerning it. Children in school may vary in their opinion about the pronunciation of a certain letter. The teacher gives the right pronunciation, and all difference ceases. This, however, does not mean to change the letter, nor does it produce a new letter.

### III. Conclusion to be Drawn from this Doctrine

Recapitulation of first and second points.

Conclusion for non-Catholics: Either you have known this before, or not. If not, you cannot any longer excuse yourself on the plea of *ignorance*. At the present day, the doctrine of the Church is too well known all over the civilized world to make an allowance for such an excuse. And if the people's interest is awakened when some temporal loss or gain is in question, how much more should the doctrine about the only saving faith awaken it! At least this discourse puts you under the strictest obligation of examining into this matter. *Examine*, then, and *pray* for light. Your eternal salvation or damnation depends on it.

Let no human consideration prevent you from embracing and professing the religion that God gives you, and on the practice of which *all* depends. The great mistake has been made not by yourselves, but by your ancestors. No one can *blame* you for correcting it. You would do the same if some temporal loss or gain were at stake. This does not involve *a change* of religion, because there exists only the one.

CONCLUSION for Catholics: Be strong and steadfast in your faith! Away with religious indifference; especially with the false and absurd saying: "All religions are good." Be obedient to the laws and prescriptions of the Church, as coming from God.

"If any one will not hear the Church, let him be to thee as the heathen." — Matt. xviii. 17.

Be an ornament and not a disgrace to the Church by your conduct. See to the Catholic training of your children. As for those who have the misfortune to be separated from us, never hate any one. If they hate and persecute us, let them account for it. Pray for them, that they may receive the same light that has been given to you. Pray that soon the words of our Lord may be fulfilled: "And other sheep I have, that are not of this fold: them also I must bring, and they shall hear my voice, and there shall be *one fold and one shepherd*" (John x. 16).

## II

## FAITH

Text: "Without faith it is impossible to please God." — Heb. xi. 6.

Exordium. — Faith is diminishing more and more. Toward the end of time there will be left very little of it.

"The Son of man, when he cometh, shall he find, think you, faith on earth?" — Luke xviii. 8.

And the Faith of those who yet possess it, is not always what it ought to be in a true Christian. And what claim can a man have on the possession of God? All works of piety, all so-called religion, falls to the ground as useless without Faith. "Without faith. . . . " Text. Is your Faith what it ought to be? Let us examine it in the light of God. May Jesus and Mary assist us in this examination! May the Divine Spirit, Who "teaches every truth," enlighten us!

## I. Faith is Necessary to Salvation

1. God is the Creator and *Sovereign Lord* of heaven and earth. All creatures must bow to His will. Must we believe what God says? He is the *Infinite Truth*. Would it not be downright blasphemy to disbelieve or call in doubt what God has revealed? And when God reveals, makes known a certain truth, is it not His will, a *positive command* that man should believe it? What reason could He otherwise have for making known this or that truth? Therefore "it is impossible . . . " — Text.

2. In no point of doctrine is the *teaching of Jesus Christ* more explicit and more emphatic than in the necessity of Faith.

"He that believeth not, shall be condemned." — Mark xvi. 16. — "He that doth not believe, is already judged." — John iii. 18.

3. The same doctrine has constantly been held by the *Fathers* and the *Councils* of the Church.

"Whosoever wishes to be saved must before all hold to the Catholic faith; for any one who does not keep it entire and inviolate shall doubtless perish. — This is Catholic faith; any one who will not believe it faithfully and firmly cannot be saved." — Symb. Athan. — "Faith is the foundation of religion." — St. Chrys. — "Faith is the beginning of man's salvation, the foundation and the root of all justification." — Trid. sess. 6. cap. 8. — "Without faith no one has ever been justified." — Ib. cap. 7.

Therefore, Faith is absolutely necessary for salvation. Hence, it is most important to understand all about it.

## II. What do we Understand by Faith

Faith consists in a supernatural act of the human mind, by which a man gives his firm assent to those doctrines which the Church proposes as revealed, because God, the Infinite Truth, has revealed them. (Lehmkuhl.)

The Vatican Council defines Faith as a supernatural virtue by which, with the inspiration and the assistance of God, we believe to be true what has been revealed by Him, not because we understand by the light of reason the intrinsic truth of those things, but simply on the authority of God Himself, Who has revealed them, and Who can neither deceive nor be deceived. (Sess. 3. c. 3.)

That you may have a clearer idea about this, let me explain it.

1. We cannot believe as we ought, except *with the inspiration and the assistance of God*. Faith is a *gift* of God, bestowed upon us through the ministry of the Church in Baptism. "What dost thou ask of the Church of God? Faith." God must give it, God must preserve it.

"Not that we are sufficient to think anything (much less believe anything) of ourselves, as of ourselves; but our sufficiency is from God." — II Cor. iii. 5.

2. Faith is a *supernatural virtue*, because we believe with supernatural aid, supernatural things, unto supernatural life.

"Faith is the substance of things to be hoped for, the evidence of things that appear not." — Heb. xi. 1.

3. We believe on the *authority of God*, because He has made known what we believe. This excludes all mere human authority, and makes faith easy. For what is easier than to believe what He has said, with Whom deception is absolutely impossible?

"When you had received of us the word of God, you received it not as the word of men, but (as it is indeed) the word of God, who worketh in you that have believed." — I Thess. ii. 13. — "Though we, or an angel from heaven, preach a gospel to you besides that which we have preached to you, let him be anathema." — Gal. i. 8.

4. Not because we *understand* those things by the light of reason, or can *explain* them, nor because we have received some *private revelation*.

"Blessed are they that have not seen, and have believed." — John xx. 29. — The light of faith "shineth in a dark place, until the day dawn." — II Pet. i. 19. — "We see now through a glass in a dark manner." — I Cor. xiii. 12. — "Faith cometh by hearing; and hearing by the word of Christ." — Rom. x. 17.

Now you understand what is meant by Faith. But who assures me of what God has revealed? God Himself through His Church.

### III. Who Teaches the Faith of God in Truth

1. Through His only-begotten Son God has made known to the world the truths which He wants men to believe.

"God, in these days, hath spoken to us by his Son." — Heb. i. 2. — "This is my beloved Son, hear him." — Luke ix. 35.

2. To perpetuate His doctrine inviolate to the end of time Jesus Christ established a Church, which was to teach mankind the same truths that He brought from Heaven. With this Church He remains, although invisibly, truly united, so that she cannot fall into error.

"Go ye into the whole world, and preach the gospel to every creature." — Mark xvi. 15. — "Behold I am with you all days, even to the consummation of the world." — Matt. xxviii. 20. — "Christ is the head of the body, the Church." — Col. i. 18.

3. This same Church is inhabited by the Holy Ghost, Who in her teaches all truth, and Who speaks through her as the soul through the body.

"You shall receive the power of the Holy Ghost . . . and you shall be witnesses unto me in Jerusalem, and in all Judea, and Samaria, and even to the uttermost part of the earth." — Acts i. 8. — "The Church of the living God, the pillar and ground of truth." — I Tim. iii. 15.

He, therefore, who believes the Church, believes God.

4. Outside of this Church there is no ground or basis given to man on which he can rest his faith. For what will assure him that what he believes is divine truth? His preachers? Can they not deceive and be deceived? Other people? May they not labor under ignorance or error? The Bible? Is his copy correct? Does it contain all revealed truth? Does he understand

it aright?    Private judgment and revelation?    How unreliable!

Therefore, there is no true Faith except that which is, directly or indirectly, based on the authority of the Church.

"That we be no more children tossed to and fro, and carried about with every wind of doctrine by the wickedness of men." — Eph. iv. 14. — "He that will not hear the Church, let him be to thee as the heathen and publican." — Matt. xviii. 17.

## IV. Qualities of Faith

1. Divine Faith must be *firm*, without the least hesitation or doubt; hence it must not be a mere *opinion*, *persuasion*, but a *firm conviction*, resting on the authority of God Himself, Who assures me every moment, through the Church, of what is divine truth.

"Who raised Christ from the dead . . . that your faith might be in God." — I Pet. i. 21.

2. It must be *universal*, that is, we must believe all that the Church teaches, without making exceptions; because all is divine truth.    To deny one thing is to deny all, because if God cannot be believed in one thing, He cannot be believed in any.

"The Spirit of truth will teach you all truth." — John xvi. 13.

3. It must be *exclusive*.    It is impossible to believe that a certain truth has been revealed by God and believe also the opposite.

"One Lord, one faith." — Eph. iv. 5. — "I have confidence in you, that you will not be of another mind." — Gal. v. 10.

4. It must be *practical*.    What we believe we must put into practice.

"Faith, if it have not works, is dead in itself." — James ii. 17.

5. It must be *constant*.    We must profess our Faith at all times, even when persecuted for it, prefer to

suffer any loss, sacrifice even life itself, rather than give up the Faith. What is true to-day is true to-morrow. What was divine truth when you were young, is divine truth now, and will be always. Deplorable fact, that so many lose the faith. — Example of millions of martyrs.

"Heaven and earth shall pass away, but my words shall not pass away." — Luke xxi. 33. — "I count all things to be but loss for the excellent knowledge of Jesus Christ my Lord." — Phil. iii. 8.

CONCLUSION. — Recapitulation.

Therefore, preserve the Faith at all costs; learn it better and better, by hearing sermons and instructions, by good reading; have your children well instructed; profess it without fear; never be ashamed of it; shun the dangers through which you may lose it. The lighted candle given to the dying is the emblem of Faith, as is the one given at baptism. Happy will you be if you have carried that light through the storms of life without having it blown out. May Jesus and Mary grant that at the end of your lives you may be able to say with St. Paul:

"I have fought a good fight, I have finished my course, I have kept the faith. As to the rest, there is laid up for me a crown of justice (due to me) which the Lord the just judge will render to me in that day (of my death)." — II Tim. iv. 7, 8.

# III

## THE PRIESTHOOD

The *object* of this sermon is to inspire the people with due reverence and respect for the priest, wherever, for some cause or other, they may have failed in this duty. — Care must be taken against bringing out too glaringly the faults of certain priests in contrast with their sublime character. If scandals have taken place in certain localities it is sufficient simply to show that the wickedness of this or that priest does not in the slightest degree affect the priestly character, and that it should by no means diminish our respect for it.

For want of time during the Mission, this sermon may be left for the Renewal.

### Sketch

Text: "Let a man so account of us as of the ministers of Christ, and the dispensers of the mysteries of God." — I Cor. iv. 1.

Exordium. — Some people are very liable, by degrees, to lose their respect for the priest, and to consider him on an equality with themselves, or even below them. The priest is the channel of grace between God and the people. The salvation of the people depends on him. Those who lose their respect for the priest are punished with a sort of obstinacy that keeps them at a distance from him, and consequently cuts them off from all communication with God. To confirm your esteem and confidence in the priest, or to restore it to your souls, if lost, is the object of the present discourse.

### I. The Priest is Vested with the most Sublime Dignity and Power

What is the priest of the New Testament? A man ordained or consecrated to exercise the same power for the salvation of mankind as was exercised by Jesus Christ. All men descend directly from Adam by means of the propagation of human nature. So all true priests descend directly from Jesus Christ by means of Holy Orders. The priest is the vicegerent of Jesus Christ. God is in Christ, and Christ is in the priest, to effect the great work of the redemption to the end of time.

"I in them and thou in me." — John xvii. 23. — "All things are of God, . . . who hath given to us the ministry of reconciliation. For God was indeed in Christ, reconciling the world to himself, and he hath placed in us the word of reconciliation. For Christ therefore we are ambassadors, God as it were exhorting by us." — II Cor. v. 18–20.

1. *The priest, therefore, preaches the Gospel of Jesus Christ with the same authority as Christ Himself.*

Christ received His doctrine from the Eternal Father.

"My doctrine is not mine, but his that sent me." — John vii. 16

This same doctrine Jesus Christ delivered to the Apostles and their successors.

"The words which thou gavest to me, I have given to them." — John xvii. 8.

He commissioned them to preach the same to all nations.

"Going, therefore, teach ye all nations . . . teaching them to observe all things whatsoever I have commanded you." — Matt. xxviii. 19, 20.

Hence Christ wants the word of the priest to be listened to as His own.

"He that heareth you, heareth me." — Luke x. 16.

And any contempt shown to the priest reflects, on this account, upon Jesus Christ and the Eternal Father.

"He that despiseth you, despiseth me; and he that despiseth me, despiseth him that sent me." — Ib.

2. *The priest has full power and unlimited control over the powers of hell.*

"He gave them power over unclean spirits, to cast them out." — Matt. x. 1; also, Luke x. 19.

The Apostles exercised this power, as their successors, the priests, have done ever since.

"And the seventy-two returned with joy, saying: Lord, the devils also are subject to us in Thy name." — Luke x. 17; also, Mark vi. 13.

The priest, the anointed of the Lord, is an object of terror to hell.

3. *The priest possesses unlimited power to absolve from sin,* to deliver from the guilt of eternal damnation, and to restore the lost title to the possession of the kingdom of heaven.

This is indeed a divine power.

"Who can forgive sins, but God alone?" — Luke v. 21.

But God has given the power of forgiving sins to the priest by communicating to him a special power of the Holy Ghost.

"Receive ye the Holy Ghost: . . . whose sins you shall forgive, they are forgiven them." — John xx. 22, 23.

He has placed him by this on an equality with Himself.

This power is greater than that of raising the dead to life, because it restores spiritual, supernatural life to the soul, while the latter simply restores natural life. What power, to tear a soul from the grasp of Satan and restore it to heaven! Compare a man who goes to the graveyard and raises to life five or ten of the dead, with a priest who absolves fifty or a hundred every Saturday.

4. Greater than all this *is the power of consecrating*

*bread and wine into the true body and blood of Jesus Christ.*

To change one earthly substance into another, wood into silver, iron into gold, would be something most extraordinary. But what is it in comparison with the power of changing bread into the very being of the God-Man?

"The chalice of benediction, which we bless, is it not the communion of the blood of Christ? And the bread, which we break, is it not the partaking of the body of the Lord?" — I Cor. x. 16.

5. God has placed these powers in the hands of the priest for the benefit of mankind; yet it *depends entirely on the priest whether they shall be exercised or not.*

Thus no sin will be forgiven that the priest does not forgive.

"Whose sins you shall retain, they are retained." — John xx. 23.

The consecration does not take place unless the priest consecrates. The world depends on the priest for its salvation.

"O magna et inclyta Dei instrumenta, sacerdotes a quibus omnium populorum pendet beatitudo." — (Council of Milan.)

## II. Benefits that the People Receive from the Priest

1 *Immense sacrifice* that the priest makes of himself for the people.

He sacrifices, *a.* All his comforts, pleasures. . . . The ordinary comforts of life, although allowed to others, are not for the priest. *b.* His temporal property, in prosecuting his studies, giving up all that he can depend upon on earth, reducing himself to poverty, depriving himself of the right of carrying on business, etc. *c.* His time, which is not his own, but belongs to the people. The people have a claim on every hour of his time, by day or by night. *d.* His health and life, which he consumes in the ministry, every act of which tells severely on his constitution. He must enter the house of pestilence and death to administer the Sacraments to a dying Christian. *e.* He imperils his soul and salvation. The life of a priest is exposed to danger on every side. The world is more dangerous to him than to others, and yet he must dwell in it. Hell seeks with greater energy to strike down a priest than others.

"Simon, Simon, behold Satan has desired to have you, that he sift you as wheat." — Luke xxii. 31.

The administration of the Sacraments increases his responsibility a thousand-fold.

2. *Spiritual benefits* which the priest confers on the people. What Christ is to the world the priest is to the congregation, a saviour, *"alter Christus"* — Christ reproduced. He gives to the people, *a.* Good example. He is the light of the world and the salt of the earth. He reproduces Christ before his people by his own manner of living, thus giving to the people a living model according to which they are to be formed. *b.* He, as the minister of the infallible Church, reproduces the doctrine of Christ, the true road to heaven through the manifold trials and crosses of life. *c.* He applies to the souls of his people the infinite treasures of the merits of Christ. *d.* He reproduces the sacrifice of Christ offered on Mount Calvary. *e.* He patiently listens to the sad tales of their aberrations, consoles, directs and strengthens them in their troubles and tribulations, visits them on their death-bed, removes the fear of death, fortifies them against their last temptations, and leads them into the arms of Jesus Christ. *f.* He prays for his people daily, Divine Office, because they have not so much time for prayer. Often they are

enjoying a night's rest while the priest is still engaged in prayer for them. *g.* The priest suffers for his people. He, also, might lead a more comfortable life — one to which his science and learning entitle him. But he is a priest, and as such he must suffer. The ministry requires of him the sacrifice of his life.

### III. Conclusions to be Drawn

1. *The priest* is to be *honored* and *esteemed* as Christ Himself.

"He that despiseth you, despiseth me. . . ." — Luke x. 16. — "Honor God with all thy soul, and give honor to the priests." — Eccli. vii. 33. — Ananias and Saphira only told a lie to Peter, and they were punished with sudden death; "because they did not lie to man, but to God." — Acts v. 4.

2. Should the priest *fall from his state, he does not* by any means *lower the dignity of the priesthood.* Out of the first twelve priests of the New Testament one fell and was lost, yet Peter, John, James, etc., remained as great as before. It is a misfortune to be deeply deplored, but no cause for lessening the priestly dignity in our estimation. When one gold piece is lost, others do not lose their value thereby.

3. *The priest* must be *obeyed*, because on him depends our salvation. We must believe his teaching, receive his correction, and abide by his decision in receiving the Sacraments. If on Judgment-day Jesus Christ refuse us heaven, how glad would we be if we were allowed to return after a few weeks! We would not say: "I will no more bend a knee before a priest."

"Whosoever shall not receive you, nor hear your words; going forth out of that house or city, shake off the dust from your feet. Amen I say to you, it shall be more tolerable for the land of Sodom and Gomorrha in the day of judgment, than for that city." — Matt. x. 14, 15.

4. *The priest* must be *supported*.  We pay the work-man who renders us some valuable service; how much more the priest who secures for us the kingdom of heaven!  This is so much the more needed because the priest cannot carry on business, but is entirely dependent on the good-will of the people.

He who does not help to support the priest is not entitled to his services.  Ordinary punishment, the loss of faith.

"What can we give to this holy man?  I beseech thee to desire him, that he would vouchsafe to accept of one-half of all things that have been brought." — Tob. xii. 1, 4.

You need not give half your income; do you give the tenth part?

5. *Pray* that you may always have *good and zealous priests;* work with them hand-in-hand in the great work of salvation; like soldiers in an army, fight under the command of your officers, the priests, like one man, in this great warfare against the world and the powers of darkness.  Should God call one of your own sons to this holy dignity of the priesthood, place no obstacle in his way, but do all that you can to assist him in following his high vocation.

CONCLUSION. — Recapitulation.

What a great grace from heaven, to have a priest among you!  Poor people who clamor for priests and can have none! or who are deprived of their priests! Beware, lest such a calamity befall you!  Therefore, honor God in the priests whom He sends you, and do your duty toward them.  Be obedient to them, and willingly follow the guides whom God has given you through this earthly life, so that "when the Prince of pastors shall appear, you may all, people and priests, receive a never-fading crown of glory." — I Peter v. 4. Amen.

## IV

## ANOTHER SKETCH ON THE SAME SUBJECT

TEXT: "Jesus Christ yesterday, and to-day; and the same forever."
— Heb. xiii. 8.

EXORDIUM. — Our dear Lord is the same forever in heaven and the same on earth in the priesthood. In His priests He still lives on earth, and works for the redemption of mankind to the end of time. The priests of the New Testament are completely identified with Jesus Christ.

Very few people comprehend what they have in the priest, and therefore they do not understand their obligations toward him.

### I. THE PRIEST OCCUPIES A MOST SUBLIME POSITION; THEREFORE, ALL HONOR IS DUE TO HIM

1. As far as the *sublime powers* which the priest exercises are concerned, he is placed *on an equality with God* Himself. The priest exercises powers that God alone can exercise.

*a.* The priest announces God's word, makes children of God out of children of wrath, forgives sins, consecrates the body and blood of Jesus Christ, renews the sacrifice of Calvary, represents, in every respect, Jesus Christ.

*b.* God will not exercise these great powers except through the priest; and it *depends on the priest* whether the faithful will receive the benefit of them or not. Ordinarily, God will not save a soul except through the ministry of the priest.

Therefore, as far as the powers of the sacred ministry are concerned, the priest stands higher than the highest angels in heaven.

"Let a man so account of us as of the ministers of Christ, and the dispensers of the mysteries of God." — I Cor. iv. 1. — "God hath placed in us the word of reconciliation. For Christ therefore we are ambassadors, God as it were exhorting by us." — II Cor. v. 19–20.

2. If a man is to be honored according to his position, then the *highest honors* are to be bestowed upon the priest

"Render to all men their dues . . . honor to whom honor." — Rom. xiii. 7. — "Treat with honor such as he is (Epaphroditus the priest)." — Phil. ii. 29. — "We beseech you, brethren, to know them who labor among you, and are over you in the Lord. . . . That you esteem them more abundantly in charity, for their works' sake. Have peace with them." — I Thess. v. 12, 13. — "Honor God . . . and give honor to the priests." — Eccli. vii. 33.

## II. The Priest is a Pastor of Souls; therefore, Obedience is Due to Him

1. The entire flock of God on earth has been placed in charge of St. Peter and his successors. The bishops have charge of a certain portion of this flock, under the jurisdiction of the Supreme Pontiff; the priests have the care of a small portion of the diocese, under the jurisdiction of the bishop. To all has been said: "Feed my lambs" (John xxi. 16).

"For every high-priest taken from among men, is ordained for men in the things that appertain to God." — Heb. v. 1. — "Feed the flock of God which is among you, taking care of it." — I Pet. v. 2. — "Who is the faithful and wise steward, whom his lord setteth over his family, to give them their measure of wheat in due season?" — Luke xii. 42.

2. But who is to *rule*, the flock or the shepherd? And who is to *obey*, the shepherd or the flock? The

priest is, indeed, obliged to obey his bishop, but the people are to obey the priest.

There is obedience all over the earth, all over heaven, even in the three Divine Persons. There is only one independent being, and that is God the Eternal Father.

This is the order which God has instituted from all eternity. Jesus Christ submitted to it when on earth.

"Obey your prelates, and be subject to them. For they watch as being to render an account of your souls; that they may do this with joy, and not with grief. For this is not expedient for you." — Heb. xiii. 17.

III. THE PRIEST SACRIFICES EVERYTHING FOR THE PEOPLE; THEREFORE, THE PEOPLE OWE HIM HIS SUPPORT

1. Enumerate and explain the many *sacrifices* that the priest makes for the people from the day he begins his clerical studies. See preceding sermon on the Priesthood, P. II. n. 1.

2. Now, is the workman worthy of *his hire?* (Luke x. 7. I Tim. v. 18.) Is it not a sin crying to heaven for vengeance, to withhold from a laborer the wages due to him? (James v. 4.)

"Who serveth as a soldier at any time, at his own charges? Who planteth a vineyard, and eateth not of the fruit thereof? Who feedeth a flock, and eateth not of the milk of the flock? — Doth not the law also say these things?" — I Cor. ix. 7, 8. — "If we have sown unto you spiritual things, is it a great matter, if we reap your carnal things?" — Ib. 11.

Under the Old Law the tenth part of every man's income belonged to the priests for their own personal support. For a long time the same law existed in the New Testament. Give at least what the law of the Church commands you to contribute toward the support of priests at present, and give it cheerfully. — Explain this point.

## IV. What is Done for or against the Priest is Done for or against God

What is done for or against an ambassador or a representative is done for or against the dignitary represented. What is done for the priest is done to God, and what is done against him is regarded by God as though it were done against Himself. So God Himself has declared. (Examples of Moses and his sister Mary and Aaron, Num. xii; Core, Dathan and Abiron, Num. xvi; Saul and Samuel, I Kings xv; Ananias and Saphira, Acts v.)

"He that receiveth you, receiveth me; and he that receiveth me, receiveth him that sent me." — Matt. x. 40. — "He that despiseth you, despiseth me; and he that despiseth me, despiseth him that sent me." — Luke x. 16. — "He that toucheth you, toucheth the apple of my eye." — Zach. ii. 8.

This was said of the chosen people of God, the Jews. How much more true is it in regard to priests?

God Himself judges His priests most severely; He allows no one else to judge them, except their lawful superiors, who act in His stead.

"For a most severe judgment shall be for them that bear rule." — Wis. vi. 6.

Conclusion. — Recapitulation

Conduct yourselves toward your priests as you would toward Christ Himself, Who is represented by His priests. Through the priests Jesus Christ continues to communicate the blessings of the Redemption to men; through the priests the people must receive those blessings, try to please Jesus Christ and render to God the most acceptable service — the Holy Mass.

Be one with your pastor in Christ on earth, and you will be one with him in God in heaven.

# V

# JESUS IN THE BLESSED SACRAMENT.— REAL PRESENCE

This sermon is preached where a great part of the people have become weak in their faith in the Blessed Sacrament. — Among the arguments used should stand first and foremost the teaching of the Church. For Catholics there can be no stronger proof, and they should become accustomed to look to the Church and nowhere else, for instruction, because she is the teacher appointed by God to teach all nations, to teach all truth, and to teach with infallible authority. The teaching of the Church is gathered from her Councils and from her practices. *What* the Church teaches about the Blessed Sacrament should be explained in clear detail. — Then may follow other arguments taken from the Scriptures, the Fathers, the history of the Church, etc. — Finally, the most popular objections should be refuted.

The *object* of this sermon should be not merely the revival of the faith, but also the increase of love of Jesus in the Blessed Sacrament, of the Holy Mass, etc.

This sermon could be so arranged that, while the first part remains purely instructive or dogmatical, the second part might treat of the *necessity of the Blessed Sacrament*, as a sacrifice, and as nourishment for the human soul, by showing that the great work of the Redemption is finally accomplished in the Blessed Eucharist.

If it be thought advisable, an act of *public atonement* could be brought in connection with this sermon, for the unbelief of the world at large, for the lack of love and reverence on the part of Catholics, for the many sacrileges committed against our Lord in this Sacrament of Love. — If there is no time for it in the Mission, perhaps there may be in the Renewal.

## SKETCH

TEXT: "There hath stood one in the midst of you, whom you know not." — John i. 26.

EXORDIUM. — St. John the Baptist addressed these words to a large crowd of people who were ignorant of the presence of the Saviour of the world among them. There was an excuse for their ignorance, for no one had told them before. The same Lord and Saviour is personally among us. He has been among men for nineteen centuries; we are told of it constantly by an infallible teacher; and yet there are crowds of people who even make a boast of not recognizing His presence. Others know and believe that He is among us, but they act as though He were not present. Others, again, acknowledge and worship Him, but they will not allow Him to carry out the end for which He is principally hidden beneath the species of bread — Holy Communion. How will all these be able to justify themselves? Let, then, the faith in the Real Presence be revived in your souls, and let it awaken a lively desire of uniting yourselves frequently to Jesus Christ in Holy Communion.

## I. THE REAL PRESENCE

What is the Blessed Eucharist? A mystery of faith. Outwardly, in appearance, it is the species of bread as we behold it in the sacred host, and the species of wine as contained in the chalice. But in reality it is the true body and the true blood of Jesus Christ, together with His human and divine natures; or, *Jesus Christ as God and man.* That this is so, is proved beyond a doubt,

1. By the *authority of the Church,* which excludes from her communion all those who reject this article of faith.

"If any one deny that the Sacrament of the Eucharist contains really, substantially, and truly the body, the blood, the soul, and the divinity of our Lord Jesus Christ, and consequently Jesus Christ entirely . . . let such a one be anathema " — *i.e.,* cast out from the Church. — Trid. sess. xiii. can. 1.

A stronger proof cannot be brought; because here we have the living voice of the Holy Ghost, the Spirit of Truth, stating our doctrine in plain terms.

And this doctrine has been held by the Church throughout all ages. This proof is sufficient to convince any mind, not closed against conviction, of the truth of the doctrine on the Real Presence. For the Church is the infallible organ of the Holy Ghost, "the pillar and ground of truth." — I Tim. iii. 15.

In confirmation of it, let us add:

2. The *authority of Jesus Christ*, as given in the gospel. *a.* When first alluding to the Blessed Eucharist, He said:

"The bread that I will give, is *my flesh*, for the life of the world." — John vi. 52.

When His audience debated among themselves, saying: "How can this man give us his flesh to eat?" (Ib. 53) they proved that they understood Him in the genuine Catholic sense; and it is equally evident that He really meant to say this, or else He would most certainly have corrected their mistake, and He would not have allowed them to leave Him on that account, as they did (Ib. 67). On the contrary, He reasserted, even more emphatically and in the most unmistakable terms, what He had already said, saying:

"Amen, amen, I say unto you: except you eat the flesh of the Son of man, and drink his blood, you shall not have life in you." — Ib. 54.

Will any one, then, in the face of this, assert that it was *not His flesh* and *not His blood* which He on that occasion promised to give us to eat and to drink?

*b.* When instituting the Blessed Eucharist at the Last Supper, Jesus took *bread*, and blessed, and broke, and gave it to His disciples, and said:

"Take ye, and eat: *This* [what was bread before] *is my body.* And taking the chalice, he gave thanks: and gave to them saying: Drink ye all of this; for *this is my blood.*" — Matt. xxvi. 26–28.

Do you believe the word of Jesus Christ, the Eternal Truth? Will any one say the directly opposite, telling Him to his face: "No, this is *not* your body; it is *not* your blood"?

After this first consecration, Jesus Christ gave the power of doing the same to the Apostles and their successors, saying:

"Do this [in future] for a commemoration of me." — Luke xxii. 19.

And ever since that time the same power has been exercised by those who have been invested with it. Again, we have also in confirmation of this sacred doctrine:

3. The *authority of the Apostles.* That they consecrated and distributed Communion daily is shown by what is said of the first Christians.

"They were persevering in the doctrine of the Apostles, and in the communication of the breaking of the bread, and in prayers." — Acts ii. 42.

And what did they believe this bread to be?

"The chalice of benediction, which we bless, is it not the communion of the blood of Christ? And the bread, which we break, is it not the partaking of the body of the Lord?" — I Cor. x. 16.

The same Apostle that said this reprehended the Corinthians for their misbehavior in church and at Holy Communion, reminding them of what he had taught them about the Blessed Eucharist.

"I have received of the Lord that which also I delivered unto you, that the Lord Jesus . . . took bread . . . and said: Take ye, and eat: this is my body, which shall be delivered [crucified] for you," etc. — I Cor. xi. 23–24. — "Therefore whosoever shall eat this bread, or drink the chalice of the Lord unworthily, shall be guilty of *the body and of the blood* of the Lord." — Ib. 27.

This shows what the Apostles believed and taught about the Blessed Eucharist, although consecrated by other priests; for there was no Apostle at Corinth then.

To this we may add:

4. The *authority of the Fathers*, especially of the first centuries.

First Century. — St. Ignatius, martyr, exhorts to a worthy reception of Holy Communion.

"For it is the true flesh of our Lord Jesus Christ, and one chalice in union with his blood." — Ep. ad Phil.

Second Century. — St. Justin says, in his Apology of Faith sent to the Emperor Antoninus Pius:

"We believe that the bread and wine over which the sacramental words have been pronounced are the flesh and blood of Jesus Christ incarnate."

Third Century. — Tertullian says:

"He that communicates, nourishes himself with the body and blood of Jesus Christ" — quoting in confirmation of this doctrine the words of our Lord which He used at the Last Supper. — L. iv. c. Marc.

Fourth Century. — St. Ambrose expresses the doctrine of the Church in most distinct terms:

"This bread is *bread* before the words of the sacrament; as soon as the consecration takes place, the bread becomes the *flesh* of Christ. How can what is bread, be the body of Christ? Through the consecration. . . . It was not the body of Christ before the consecration, but after the consecration I say to thee, it is the body of Christ." — Lib. 4. c. 4. de Sacram.

In the same century. — St. Chrysostom:

"Behold you see him (Jesus), you touch him, you eat him." — Hom. 60 ad pop. Antioch.

Again in the same century. — St. Hilary:

"There can be no doubt in regard to the presence of the true flesh and blood of Christ in the consecrated bread and wine. When we receive them, they effect, that we are in Christ and Christ in us." — Lib. 8. de Trinit.

St. Cyril of Jerusalem, commenting on the words of St. Paul, says:

"The words of St. Paul seem to be amply sufficient to render your faith in the divine mysteries certain, by which you were made worthy to become one, in body and blood, with Christ. When Christ himself said of this bread, 'This is my body,' who should after that dare raise a doubt? And when he himself said, 'This is my blood,' who should throw in a doubt so as to say that it is not his blood? . . . Under the species of bread he gives his body and under the species of wine he gives us his blood. . . . We receive his body and blood into our members. . . . Judge not by the taste, but let faith assure you beyond any doubt." — Catech. 4.

Fifth Century. — St. Cyril of Alexandria, explaining the words of Christ, John vi. 57.

"As liquefied wax poured into other liquefied wax must become one mass, so he who receives the flesh and blood of the Lord, is so united with him, that Christ is in him and he in Christ." — Lib. 4. in Joan. c. 17.

What strong testimony to show that the faith in the Blessed Sacrament during the first ages was the same as at present!

For eleven centuries this doctrine remained unattacked. In 1045, Berengarius of Tours began to teach differently, but he was condemned by several Councils of the Church and by many Popes. Having retracted his false doctrine, he died penitent on an island near Tours. His strongest opponent, the learned Lanfranc, could boldly challenge him:

"Ask the Greeks, ask the Armenians, ask the Christians, of whatever nation they may be, all will answer that in this point they profess the same faith with us." — Dial. c. Ber.

Our argument, therefore, gains in strength even by

5. The *testimony of all the heresies* which arose prior to the fifteenth century. When, in 1570, the new reformers wished to unite themselves with the Greek

schismatics, the latter refused for many reasons, but especially because these modern heretics did not believe in the Real Presence. The Patriarch of Constantinople, Jeremias, wrote to them:

"It is a dogma of holy Church that in the consecration the bread is changed into the body of Jesus Christ, and the wine into his blood, through the power of the Holy Ghost."

*Obj.* — How is this possible?

Is it not sufficient to know that it is so? Why ask, how? We are ignorant of the *how* of many things in nature without denying their reality; how much more is this the case in things above nature!

The best answer is that of our Lord (John vi), *i.e.*, no explanation. There the audience was divided between believers and unbelievers. The former remained with Him, the latter kept away from Him, after that. So it is now. You are either a Christian or not, according as you believe in the Real Presence or do not.

Or, according to St. John Damascene, we give you the answer of the angel, if you ask the question with that modesty and deep reverence with which the Blessed Virgin asked of the celestial messenger. "How is this done?" We say, "Through the operation of the Holy Ghost."

## II. Conclusions Drawn from this Doctrine

Happiness of being a Catholic, who believes in the presence of Jesus Christ in the Blessed Sacrament, and draws innumerable blessings from it. How miserable those who have cast out of their temples the Lord Jesus, and who have thereby deprived themselves of the greatest consolation that a man can have on earth!

"He hath not done in like manner to every nation." — Ps. cxlvii. 20.

But learn from this to be grateful, and to show your gratitude in your actions. — In particular,

1. *Attend Mass* with great devotion, and as often as you can.

At the Mass Jesus Christ becomes present on the altar.

He then sacrifices Himself for you and in union with you.

At the Mass Jesus Christ performs, with you and for you, the most sublime acts of worship toward the Infinite God.

2. *Receive Holy Communion* devoutly and frequently, because

It is the greatest desire of Jesus Christ, to unite Himself with you.

"With desire I have desired to eat this pasch with you." — Luke xxii. 15.

By it the final object of the Incarnation is accomplished.

"As Thou, Father, in me, and I in Thee, that they also may be one in us." — John xvii. 21.

It is necessary for you, to preserve supernatural life.

"Except you eat the flesh of the son of man . . . you shall not have life in you." — John vi. 54.

3. *Visit Jesus Christ* in the Blessed Sacrament frequently and devoutly.

He is the source of all consolation; He will never let you go away with empty hearts.

"Behold I am with you all days, even to the consummation of the world." — Matt. xxviii. 20. — "My delights are to be with the children of men." — Prov. viii. 31. — "Come to me, all ye that labor and are burdened, and I will refresh you." — Matt. xi. 28.

4. *Reverence the Church*, which is truly the house of God, the dwelling-place of Jesus Christ. By contributing toward the erection and decoration of it, the payment of its debts, etc. By conducting yourselves with respect and awe when you enter it. When the great temple of Jerusalem was built, no noise was to be made in erecting it.

"And the house, when it was in building, was built of stones hewed and made ready: so that there was neither hammer nor axe nor any tool of iron heard in the house when it was in building." — III Kings vi. 7. — "The Lord is in his holy temple: let all the earth keep silence before him." — Habac. ii. 20.

By making a devout genuflection whenever you come before the tabernacle. What would you do, if you would see Jesus Christ there with the eyes of your body? And is He there less because you see Him only with the eyes of your soul?

Example of St. Anthony and the mule of an infidel at Rimini.

5. Have *great respect for the priest*, through whose mighty word Jesus Christ becomes present in the Blessed Sacrament.

"Let a man so account of us as of the ministers of Christ, and the dispensers of the mysteries of God." — I Cor. iv. 1.

Always speak to the priest and of him with great reverence; but, above all, show yourself as a true Catholic, who believes in the Real Presence, when the priest carries the Blessed Sacrament to some one in your house, or even in the neighborhood.

Look upon it as a great privilege if you or your children are deemed worthy to assist the priest in the celebration of the divine service.

CONCLUSION. — Brief recapitulation.

Thank God for your faith in the Blessed Sacrament.

Keep it, strengthen it by acting according to its teachings; revive it, if it has become dormant; never be ashamed to practise it, no matter in whose company you are.

Profoundly worship and adore the Most Blessed Sacrament of the altar, for it is Jesus Christ, as He is at the right hand of the Eternal Father. But realize, also, the object of its institution, namely, the nourishment of our souls for the preservation of the spiritual life.

May Jesus in the Blessed Sacrament be the object of your love, of all your affections! May He often enter your hearts and dwell there as in a living tabernacle!

May our Blessed Mother Mary obtain for us all a true love for Jesus in the Blessed Sacrament!

## ATONEMENT TO THE BLESSED
## SACRAMENT

Text: "The Son of man shall be betrayed into the hands of
sinners." — Matt. xxvi. 45.

Introduction. — When Jesus Christ said these
words He was so overcome by sadness that it was
enough to take His life. He looked for consolation
even at the hands of His own creatures, His Apostles.

"My soul is sorrowful even unto death: stay you here, and watch
with me." — Matt. xxvi. 38.

Jesus is sorrowful now, His Sacred Heart is grieved
above all measure, because again and again He is
ill-treated and delivered into the hands of sinners, in
the great Sacrament of love. He looks for consolation
from us. He expects us to make up for the indignities
to which He is subjected, by our acts of love, and
especially by acts of reparation and atonement.

Let us consider these indignities more in detail, and
then let us see how we can make reparation for them,
so as to console, as it were, the outraged Heart of
Jesus in this Sacrament of love.

### I. Various Outrages Committed against Jesus
### in the Blessed Sacrament

What is the Blessed Sacrament? Must I ask this
question in the presence of Jesus Christ Himself standing before us? It is Jesus Christ, true God and true
man, hidden under the species, *i.e.*, the mere outward

appearance of bread. Do we not believe this firmly? Is this not the doctrine of the infallible Church?

(For more proofs, if needed, see sermon on the Real Presence.)

And now, how is Jesus Christ treated in this Sacrament of love?

1. A considerable part of so-called Christians refuse to believe in His presence; and this in the face of the clearest proofs. I do not speak of heathens, of Jews, of Turks; but of those who call themselves believers in Christ.

And they glory in this ignorance. They would be ashamed to be found ignorant in some truth concerning ordinary natural sciences. But they are not ashamed of their ignorance of one of the most consoling truths of the Christian doctrine. How must this grieve the sweet Heart of Jesus!

2. But worse than this is the cold indifference shown toward this august Sacrament by those who believe all. They pass by the Catholic church, pass in and out of it, without reflecting who dwells in the sacred tabernacle.

Carelessness in acquiring a better knowledge of this divine mystery; hence, no love, no reverence, no devotion toward their hidden Saviour. Great neglect in instructing the children or in having them instructed in regard to this Sacrament, who grow up without knowing anything about Jesus in the Blessed Sacrament.

In fact, there are thousands of Catholics who would not care whether the Blessed Sacrament existed or not.

Hence, no care about building a church, or repairing it, or paying the debt of it. Great neglect in attending Mass, even on days on which it is commanded — no attention — no devotion at Mass — running in and out, coming late, talking, laughing, etc. There is more attention paid to a play in the theater than to the Mass. How can such Catholics believe that the Mass is the great Sacrifice of Calvary reproduced! Impossible!

3. Jesus Christ is constantly among us to be our consolation, to receive our visits. How do Christians correspond with this longing desire of Jesus?

"My delights are to be with the children of men." — Prov. viii. 31.

Is it our delight to be with Him, or are we disgusted with His presence? Are there not churches in which the Blessed Sacrament is never visited outside of the time of divine service? Is not this one of them? Jesus was better off when He was in the stable, "*inter duo animalia*," than He is "*in medio nostri*."

4. Jesus Christ is most desirous that we receive Him in Holy Communion. What a precious gift it is — and how necessary for us! In instituting this Sacrament it was His principal object to unite His flesh to our flesh, His soul to our soul, His divinity to our humanity, to make us one with Himself, and, through Himself, one with God. This is the ultimate end of the redemption.

"As the living Father hath sent me, and I live by the Father; so he that eateth me, the same also shall live by me." — John vi. 58.

And in order to remove all fear of approaching Him, He has hidden the glory of His being beneath the species of bread. The eye of the body does not perceive His presence, but only the eye of the soul, faith.

And nevertheless, how many are there who will go to Holy Communion but very seldom, and then only, as it were, by compulsion. It cost Jesus Christ so much, His very life, to become our food and strength.

How much must it not grieve Him to see His people so cold toward Him!

And when they do go to Holy Communion, what poor preparation do they make, what little thanksgiving, if any at all! What must Jesus Christ feel when He is so near a man's heart, but that heart is far away from Him.

When the Apostles had received Holy Communion from the hands of Jesus Christ, Judas left immediately; he was too busy. The others remained, conversed with Jesus, and Jesus with them.

And then, how long is the grace of Jesus Christ allowed to possess that heart, before it is driven from it again by sin and crime?

O Jesus! so full of love for men, how art Thou treated by men! Surely Thou art "betrayed into the hands of sinners."

But the worst of all the outrages against Jesus in the Blessed Sacrament is

## II. Sacrilegious Communion

1. The unworthy communicant subjects his beloved Saviour to *insults, pains, and sufferings* which He did not undergo even during His sacred Passion. To understand this fully it would be necessary to possess the mind of God, so as to comprehend the shocking sight which a soul in the state of mortal sin presents. The most disgusting object, a sink full of putrid matter, a carcass, etc., is a thousand times more agreeable to man than a sinful soul is to God. And down into that soul Jesus must descend, and there He must dwell until the sacred species are consumed.

Nero had dead bodies disinterred, and the Christians tied down upon them, mouth upon mouth, etc., thus leaving them to suffocate from the insupportable stench.

Thus is Jesus Christ tied down upon that putrefied soul, coming into the closest contact with what He abominates with supreme disgust.

2. By an unworthy Communion Jesus is thrown *under the feet of Satan.* Who governs in the sinner's heart? The devil. When Jesus arrives in Communion, He is thrown into the hands of His greatest enemy, and must crouch under the feet of Satan as long as He is kept there by the sacred species.

"By this sin the sinner throws Jesus under the feet of the devils, that they may trample upon him." — St. Ambrose.

Poor Jesus! is it thus that Thy excessive love is rewarded!

Judas delivered His Master into the hands of the Jews; the unworthy communicant delivers Him over to the devils. What a triumph and glory for hell!

"Thou hast given occasion to the enemies of the Lord to blaspheme." — II Kings xii. 14.

It is in this shocking manner that Jesus Christ is "betrayed into the hands of sinners," even of the devils.

3. *Fearful punishment* of the unworthy communicant, blindness of soul and obduracy of heart. Parable of the marriage-feast (Matt. xxii. 1–13). Preparation and invitation to the wedding-dinner — Communion. The banquet-hall was filled with guests — number of communicants. Man found without a wedding-garment, in his every-day clothes; a communicant not adorned with grace, in the state of sin. The man was silent — no excuse for the soul for coming in that state. "How did you come in hither?" What priest sent you? How did you dare, etc.?

Having his hands and feet bound, he is cast into exterior darkness — deprivation of the light of understanding and the pious emotions of the heart. Spiritual paralysis, utter inability to perform any spiritual functions.

"Therefore are there many weak among you, and many sleep." — I Cor. xi. 30.

Crimes follow without end. One sacrilegious confession follows another, one Communion another — Confirmation, Matrimony, Extreme Unction, recklessness in committing sin, until death, which will be followed by endless "weeping and gnashing of teeth." — Matt. xxii. 13.

When Judas had left the supper-room, the devil took possession of him, and drove him into greater sins, and into final despair.

"And after the morsel, Satan went into him." — John xiii. 27.

4. Unworthy Communion is *the seal of eternal damnation.* — A decree may be written and signed; so long as it is not yet sealed, it may be reversed. The sinner's sentence is written:

"The soul that sinneth, the same shall die." — Ez. xviii. 20.

He goes to confession in appearance; absolution is pronounced over his impenitent heart "in the name of the Father, and of the Son, and of the Holy Ghost"; this is the signature. He goes to Communion in that state. This puts the seal to it.

"He that eateth and drinketh unworthily, eateth and drinketh judgment to himself." — I Cor. xi. 29. — "He eats and drinks in — damnation." — St. Chrysostom, St. Ambrose, St. Anselm, and others.

It is the same as with one who swallows a cup of poison — he drinks in death.

A worthy Communion is the pledge of eternal salvation, as is expressed by "*Corpus D. N. J. C. custodiat. . . .* May the body of our Lord Jesus Christ preserve thy soul unto life everlasting." An unworthy Communion is the pledge of eternal damnation. The words of Baalam were turned in his mouth, a curse became a blessing. In our case the words of blessing are turned into a curse. They sound somewhat like this: "*Corpus D. N. J. C. condemnet animam tuam ad ignem æternum. Amen.* May the body of our Lord Jesus Christ condemn," etc. Hence the terrible state of soul in which the sinner returns from the railing.

Oza was killed instantly for having touched the ark of the covenant (II Kings vi. 7). Seventy men of rank and fifty thousand of the people of Bethsamy were slain for having gazed into the ark (I Kings vi. 19). The priest holds up the Sacred Host, saying, *Ecce Agnus Dei!* and the sinner looks up in his hypocrisy, strikes his breast, and is getting ready to approach Jesus Christ. What recklessness!

When Jesus asked the soldiers in the garden of Gethsemane, "Whom do ye seek?" they answered: "Jesus of Nazareth." He said: "I am he." At this they went backward and fell to the ground (John xviii. 4–6). I ask that sinner who is coming up to the railing, What do you want here? Whom do you seek? He says: I am going to Communion; I seek Jesus of Nazareth. Behold, here He is. *Ecce Agnus Dei!* Fear you not the consequences? Example.

You may ask now, like the Apostles at the Last Supper, "Father, is it I that you speak of?" On that occasion the guilty one knew who it was; so here. The guilty ones will be told by their own consciences. They are not ordinarily those who are afraid of an unworthy Communion, but rather those who are not afraid. Enumeration of unworthy communicants. And what excuse have they? None at all.

Alas! unfortunate sinners, what will you say now? You may perhaps say, "I am damned." This is what you have fully deserved; but your very presence on this occasion proves that God wishes to show you mercy. There is no sin that cannot be forgiven, and God evidently brought you here to-day that you might understand the grievousness of your sin, implore God's mercy, and be converted by a sincere confession and full atonement on your part. Your confession, I suppose, is made already, or will shortly be made. So I invite you now to make atonement in the presence of Jesus Christ Himself for the outrages committed against Him.

We shall all join you; for we are all more or less guilty of acts of irreverence toward Jesus Christ in the Blessed Sacrament. We shall make this atonement not only for ourselves, but also for all the outrages ever committed against Him.

NOTE. — If the sermon is preached without the exposition of the Blessed Sacrament, time will here be given, before the exposition, during which the *"Agnus Dei"* may be sung. Hence, the necessity of the interruption mentioned hereafter. — If the Blessed Sacrament is already exposed, the pause may or may not be made. In the latter case, all that is done here, is the removal of the veil, as directed by the preacher, — and the introduction to the act of atonement begins at once. See Prov. Stat. n. 45.

Before we perform this solemn act I shall give you some time for deep reflection, sorrow, and silent prayer for forgiveness. In the meantime let the mournful sounds of the organ introduce the hymn which is usually sung at High Mass before Communion: *"Agnus Dei, qui tollis peccata mundi, miserere nobis, dona nobis pacem."* Yes, O Lamb of God! Who takest away the sins of the world! have mercy on us;

take away from our souls those horrible crimes; . . . give to our troubled hearts that peace which is the only consolation of man — peace with God. Amen.

———————

## ACT OF ATONEMENT BEFORE THE BLESSED SACRAMENT EXPOSED

*Introduction of the Act.* — Raise your eyes! Look up toward the altar. There is that sweet Jesus, Who is so often offended by ungrateful men. Oh! how often is His loving Heart filled with grief at the awful outrages, irreverences, . . . committed against Him in this Most Holy Sacrament! Alas! we, too, have grieved Him! Let us now unite in making an act of atonement to Him. Atonement means reparation. Fully or adequately to repair such acts of ingratitude is impossible to poor, sinful mortals. But what we can do is this: we can at least express our great grief and sorrow for the sins committed against this Most Holy Sacrament by ourselves and others; we can declare ourselves willing to promote among men true love and reverence toward Jesus in the Blessed Eucharist; we can cheerfully undergo the sufferings and trials of our daily lives, uniting them to His sufferings on the cross, and thus offer them to God in atonement for those many acts of irreverence; we can make reparation by our frequent visits to the church, by worthy Communions, hearing Masses, and by the personal sacrifices which we shall make for His sake. With this disposition let us now proceed to the act of atonement. Follow me in silence and deep reverence while I recite the words aloud.

## THE ACT

O most adorable Jesus! worthy of the homage and love of all creatures, in the most profound sense of contrition for our sins, we prostrate ourselves before Thee, adoring Thee as our Lord and God. How great is Thy love for us miserable men; but, alas! how great is our ingratitude in return for it! Thou couldst do no more to show Thy love, and men could do no more to show their ingratitude. It pains us when we see that Thou art not known on this altar. It grieves us when we see Thee so much despised by those who have every reason to love Thee. But our hearts almost break at the sight of our own sins committed against Thee in this most holy mystery. We feel ourselves utterly unworthy of the privilege of kneeling here in Thy presence, much less of raising our eyes toward Thy holy tabernacle.

O most merciful Saviour! we trust that these sins are forgiven. Allow us now to express before Thee our most ardent desire of making atonement for our many and grievous sins, as well as for all the sins of unbelief, ingratitude, coldness, indifference, for the unworthy Communions, and every other outrage committed against Thee, since the institution of this Most Holy Sacrament down to this present hour, by Christians, heretics, infidels, and heathens. We declare ourselves willing to repair these offenses by frequent visits to Thy holy sanctuary; by offering up the Holy Sacrifice of the Mass; by worthy and frequent Communions. We offer ourselves as a living sacrifice in union with Thy sacred passion and death, ready to suffer everything, even death, in atonement for these manifold outrages. We offer to Thee all the love, praise, and thanksgiving that the angels and saints offer Thee in heaven. We ask Thee to pardon us and all those poor, wretched sinners, for our numberless acts of black ingratitude.

O merciful Jesus! enlighten our minds, that we may recognize, adore, and love Thee. May it please Thee this day to grant a lively faith and an ardent love for Thee to all mankind!

And now, O Jesus! as a token of forgiveness, grant us Thy most holy blessing; yes, O Jesus! bless us wretched but sorrowful sinners, as Thou didst bless the sorrowful Magdalen. Dismiss us from Thy feet with true peace in our hearts, which we hope to preserve undisturbed until we see Thee unveiled, face to face, in the blessed kingdom of heaven. Amen.

Tantum ergo, etc. — as usual at Benediction.

Immediately after Benediction the sinner's bell is tolled and the prayers for the conversion of sinners are recited.

# VII

## IMPENITENCE AND ITS CONSEQUENCES

Text: "Jesus seeing the city, he wept over it." — Luke xix. 41.

Exordium. — Description of the triumphant entry of Jesus into Jerusalem. When He saw the city He wept over it.

Grand solemnities are going on here, everybody is astir, the Mission. I see the Heart of Jesus weeping. Why? Because some souls of this congregation seem to be positively determined on their destruction.

A human soul is worth more than a city, more than all the cities of the world, more than heaven itself. To save it Jesus became man, established a Church . . . died on the cross. Jesus wept over the city of Jerusalem, not so much on account of its eventual destruction as over the eternal damnation of its inhabitants, for whose salvation He had done so much, but in vain.

What has He not done for the souls belonging to this congregation? The Mission, the Renewal. And yet, there are some who, after neglecting the Mission, will also let the Renewal pass without profiting by it. Over these Jesus Christ weeps; for the ruin that will come upon them will be terrible.

## I. The Abuse of the Grace of God is a Terrible Evil in Itself

1. Because it is the greatest outrage against the goodness of God. What an offense is sin! The sinner has forfeited life; yet God in His mercy bears with

him, calls him back repeatedly, makes his conversion easy. But the sinner refuses, remains stubborn, hardhearted, despises the offer, trampling under foot the most extraordinary of all graces.

"They would not hearken, and they turned away the shoulder to depart: and they stopped their ears, not to hear. And they made their heart as the adamant stone, lest they should hear the law, and the words which the Lord of hosts sent in his spirit by the hand of former prophets [missionaries]: so a great indignation came from the Lord of hosts. . . . He spoke, and they heard not. So shall they cry, and I will not hear, saith the Lord of hosts." — Zach. vii. 11–13.

2. Because the sinner despises grace, a treasure which Jesus Christ has purchased with His life. He deems as nothing His most precious blood, shed for his salvation.

"A man making void the law of Moses, dieth without any mercy. . . . How much more, do you think, he deserveth worse punishments, who has trodden under foot the Son of God . . . and hath offered an affront to the spirit of grace?" — Heb. x. 28, 29.

3. Because the impenitent abuse a means of which man stands in absolute need; conversion is absolutely impossible without the grace of God.

"If the Ethiopian can change his skin, or the leopard his spots: you also may do well, when you have learned evil." — Jer. xiii. 23.

And grace is granted in such abundance during the Mission, but despised and rejected by the hardhearted sinner. Comparison of a man dying of hunger, and casting away with contempt the food offered him.

4. And — what forms the climax of the malice of such sinners — grace is despised, abused, and cast away in consideration of a most miserable earthly good, for the meanest pleasure. Examples.

O sinner! after you have offended God's justice, you may have recourse to His mercy. What is left to you if you offend His mercy? No doubt, His justice.

## II. What will God do with Those who Abuse His Grace

1. He will abandon them.

"And now I will show you what I will do to my vineyard. I will take away the hedge thereof, and it shall be wasted: I will break down the wall thereof, and it shall be trodden down. And I will make it desolate: it shall not be pruned, and it shall not be digged; but briers and thorns shall come up: and I will command the clouds to rain no rain upon it." — Is. v. 5, 6.

Application of this text.

In the same sense Jêsus Christ pronounced that terrible woe over the obstinate city of Jerusalem:

"If thou also hadst known, and that in this thy day, the things that are to thy peace; but now they are hidden from thy eyes. For the days shall come upon thee: and thy enemies shall cast a trench about thee, . . . and beat thee flat to the ground: . . . and they shall not leave in thee a stone upon a stone: because thou hast not known the time of thy visitation." — Luke xix. 42, 44.

Obstinate sinner! apply this to yourself.

2. He will give those graces to others who will profit better by them. The number of the elect is certain, and it will be made full. The hard-heartedness of this or that sinner will not diminish it. They can do harm neither to God nor to heaven, but only to themselves.

The guests invited to the wedding-supper refused to come; others were invited, and the royal hall was filled (Matt. xxii). Saul was rejected and David put in his place (I Kings xv, xvi); Judas by his crime lost his apostleship, and Matthias was elected in his stead (Acts i. 26). The Jewish people rejected Christianity; they were rejected by God in turn, and their great privilege was conferred upon the heathens. Thus God casts away those who trample His grace under foot, and puts others in their place.

*Obj.:* "God is merciful." He is, but to those who fear Him; not to those who treat Him and His grace with contempt.

"And his mercy is from generation to generation *to them that fear him.*" — Luke i. 50.

### III. WHAT IS THE RESULT OF IMPENITENCE

A. *Blindness of Spirit.*

1. The blinded man sees no more what he saw before. So the blind in spirit believe not what they believed before. Countless examples of such as deny when old what they believed when young.

2. They cannot even believe, because the light of grace is taken away from them.

"They could not believe . . . for he hath blinded their eyes, and hardened their hearts, that they should not see with their eyes, nor understand with their hearts, and be converted, and I should heal them." — John xii. 39, 40.

You find many nowadays who say that they cannot believe. What to others is as clear as day these people find impossible to understand. The reason is obvious.

B. *Obduracy of Heart.*

1. Nothing will make an impression upon them, no sermon, no reflection, no misfortune, not even death. Their ease or quiet is never disturbed by what strikes the souls of others with fear and terror.

"Thou hast struck them, and they have not grieved; Thou hast bruised them, and they have refused to receive correction; they have made their faces harder than the rock, and they have refused to return." — Jer. v. 3.

This state of things remains even at death. They will not even then manifest any signs of despair, lest they be the cause of the conversion of others of similar dispositions.

2. They have a professed horror of all that is good,

the Church, the Sacraments, sermons, prayer, objects of devotion, religious people, priests, etc.

3. They ridicule faith, pure morality, and all religious practices.

"The sensual man perceiveth not these things that are of the spirit of God; for it is foolishness to him, and he cannot understand." — I Cor. ii. 14.

4. They are left to the ravages of their sinful desires, and by them are plunged into a bottomless abyss of crime.

"Their foolish heart was darkened: . . . wherefore God gave them up to the desires of their heart, unto uncleanness, to dishonor their own bodies among themselves. . . . God delivered them up to a reprobate sense, to do those things which are not convenient, being filled with all iniquity, malice, fornication, covetousness, wickedness, full of envy, murder, contention, deceit, malignity. . . ." — Rom. i. 21, 24, 28, 29.

5. They go so far as to deny the very existence of God.

"They have denied the Lord, and said, It is not he." — Jer. v. 12. — "The fool hath said in his heart, There is no God." — Ps. xiii. 1.

CONCLUSION. — Recapitulation.

Let me, therefore, warn every one of you against provoking the wrath of God to that extent that He must inflict so terrible a punishment upon him. Listen to the call of God, at least this time, and say with the Psalmist:

"I will keep Thy justifications. Oh! do not Thou utterly forsake me!" — Ps. cxviii. 8. "Cast me not away from Thy face, and take not Thy holy spirit from me!" — Ps. l. 13.

# VIII

## LEVITY OF MIND IN RELIGIOUS MATTERS

TEXT: "He that hath ears to hear, let him hear." — Luke viii. 8.

EXORDIUM. — These words were used by our Saviour whenever He wished to introduce something most important. They are used here for the same purpose. My object to-day is to draw your special attention to your most deadly enemy, who is stronger than hell itself, who finds his way into many families, deceiving men, women, and even children, so that "seeing they do not see, and hearing they do not understand." — Luke viii. 10. This enemy is a certain *Levity of Mind* in matters of religion. This unfortunate disposition makes people place at stake what is of the greatest importance to them; makes them forgetful of their greatest losses, and leaves them insensible to the consideration of the most important truths. It is fearful in *itself*, terrible in its *cause*, and most disastrous in its *consequences*.

### I. LEVITY OF MIND IN MATTERS OF RELIGION IS MOST FEARFUL IN ITSELF

In this state the soul is quite indifferent with regard to the most serious concerns of man.

Light-minded are those who act without consideration, attention; who simply do what inclination, instinct, or passion moves them to; who possess reason without consulting it; who have no taste for any serious occupation, least of all for religion; who go through life without ever stopping to ask themselves, *whence, where, whither;* who care not about conscience, Church, priest, parents. . . .

1. Such people *heap sin upon sin*, although the fearful consequences are before their eyes.

*a.* Sin brings on nothing but remorse, shame, and disgrace in time; an unhappy and often untimely death; a miserable eternity. Such are avarice, vanity, drunkenness, adultery, youthful indiscretions, sensual pleasures of every kind. And yet what do the light-minded care about it?

"Such is also the way of an adulterous woman, who eateth, and wipeth her mouth, and saith: I have done no evil." — Prov. xxx. 20. — "I have sinned, and what harm hath befallen me?" — Eccli. v. 4.

*b.* Light-minded people do not allow religion to take full possession of their hearts, nor do they permit the warning of their conscience to disturb them in the enjoyment of their pleasures.

["For the imagination and thought of man's heart are prone to evil from his youth." — Gen. viii. 21. — "For they that are according to the flesh, mind the things that are of the flesh." — Rom. viii. 5.

*c.* Such people know no law of God or the Church, no restraint, no limits; they become a mere mass of flesh, covered with sin and crime, as a putrid corpse is covered with worms, without feeling it.

2. The light-minded recklessly *squander away* their *most precious possessions:*

*a.* Temporal property, which belongs to their families; given to them by God for their support. Drunkards, gamblers, debauchees, worldlings.

*b.* Reputation, not caring what people think of them, not hesitating to mix in all sorts of company, entering houses of questionable character. . . .

*c.* Health. — The light-minded have but three steps more to make: the first, to utter dissoluteness; the second, to the sick-bed or hospital; the third, to the graveyard. And these are soon made.

*d.* Virtue and conscience, disregarding not only the warnings of others, but also the voice of God in their interior.

*e.* The light-minded squander away all that Baptism, Confirmation, and the other sacraments have conferred upon them. Indeed, they would not care if they were not Christians at all.

*f.* Respectful demeanor toward parents, priests, Church, holy things, equals, the world in general. The light-minded lose that Christian respect, so becoming a child of God and an heir of the kingdom of heaven.

They respect no one, and no one respects them.

Thus the light-minded cast off everything. But last of all, they are cast off themselves, the body into the grave, and the soul into the abyss of hell.

Therefore, take warning in good time, before it is too late.

## II. LEVITY OF MIND IS TERRIBLE IN ITS CAUSE

It rises from spiritual blindness, which includes deafness.

If we see people who believe in God, their own eternal existence, heaven, hell, Jesus Christ and the Church, act in the manner described, then we must conclude that, "seeing, they see not; hearing, they understand not," *i.e.*, that they are spiritually blind; whose state of soul becomes worse and worse from day to day.

*a.* If they were not blind, they would see the law of God in their hearts, their Saviour on the cross,

their Judge above them.   How can their recklessness
be accounted for otherwise?   State particular cases.

*b.* If they were not blind, they would recognize the
sweet voice that invites them to penance;   they would
see that they can do nothing better than to reconcile
themselves with God without delay.

*c.* If they were not blind;   were their eyes not
covered with a thick veil, which they have voluntarily
hung over them;   they, as fathers and mothers, would
give their children a better Christian education, because they would understand its importance;   as
children, they would be more strictly obedient to their
parents;   as Christians, they would practise more
submission to the Church.

*d.* If they were not blind, they would see and hear
Jesus Christ speaking to them, as He did to the blinded
inhabitants of Jerusalem:   "If thou hadst but known:
. . . but now they are hidden from thine eyes."—Luke
xix. 42.

But because they are blind, they walk on their
accustomed road further and further;   they approach
a fearful eternity without thinking of it, without
fearing it.   Like the blind man that drops into the
abyss before him, they fall into the abyss of hell, the
fire of which will make them see their misfortune when
it is too late.   Then they exclaim: *"Ergo erravimus!"*

"Therefore we have erred from the way of truth, and the light
of justice hath not shined unto us, and the sun of understanding
hath not risen upon us." — Wis. v. 6.

### III. Levity of Mind is Most Disastrous in its Consequences

The light-minded Christian hardly ever recovers
from the evil that has befallen him.   He lives and
dies in this state.

*a.* Some light-minded Christians live and die in a state of *false security*, or presumption. They try to persuade themselves that they are as good as others, or they falsely hope that God will not ask so strict an account of them. They may receive the Sacraments on their death-beds, but with the same careless disposition as in life: *"Sicut vita, finis ita."*

*b.* Others give themselves up to *despair.* Their sins rise before them in their gigantic magnitude, and make them forget the infinite mercy of God.

*c.* Others finally fall into rank *infidelity.* They despair of the mercy of God; they cannot bear the thought of His justice; so they give up the thought of God, eternity . . . altogether. They say: "Dead is dead, and there exists nothing on the other side of the grave." And in this state they fall into the hands of the living God.

Fearful end! No man would wish to die in this manner. Well, then, give up living in such a manner.

CONCLUSION. — Recapitulation.

"He that hath ears to hear, let him hear." Give ear to the voice of the most precious blood of Jesus Christ, which to-day calls upon you to consider well this terrible plague that is ravaging the entire Christian world. "With desolation is all the land made desolate; because there is none that considereth in the heart." — Jer. xii. 11. To effect a change for the better, let each one of you apply this sermon to himself.

"O ye sons of men, how long will you be dull of heart? Why do you love vanity, and seek after lying?" — Ps. iv. 3. — "Now is the hour for us to rise from sleep: for now our salvation is nearer than when we believed." — Rom. xiii. 11 — *i.e.*, nearer than at the ordinary season of grace.

# APPENDIX I

## THE ROSARY AT RENEWALS

The Rosary is recited every evening before the sermon, but no instruction is given. Instead, the mysteries are mentioned in a few words between the various decades, according to the method of St. Alphonsus,[1] prescribed by the Rule[2] for the Mission. Three, or at most, four short sentences are sufficient for each mystery. They are given out from the pulpit by the Father who says the beads with the people. In doing this he may rise or remain on his knees, but he should take care to be understood by the whole congregation.

At Renewals all that precedes the evening sermon should be finished in twenty minutes. On the closing night no reflections are made on the mysteries.

The Rosary on the opening day, although a Sunday, should always be said with the joyful mysteries, so that the simple people may not be led astray, by misunderstanding the order of the mysteries.

## REFLECTIONS ON THE MYSTERIES OF THE ROSARY

Every one may follow his own inspiration and devotion in making these reflections. Below, meditations are given for every day in the week of the Renewal, except for the Sunday of the close.

[1] *Exercises*, C. E., Vol. XV. p. 133.   [2] R., n. 137.

The meditations for Sunday, Tuesday and Wednesday are those given by St. Alphonsus in his *Exercises of the Missions.*

## I. SUNDAY. — JOYFUL MYSTERIES[1]

1. *The Incarnation of the Son of God.*

Consider the great love of God toward us! He did not send an angel to redeem us; but He came Himself to die for our salvation. How few are there who show their gratitude to God for this great love!

Let us ask the Blessed Virgin Mary to obtain for us a great love of God.

2. *The Visit of the Blessed Virgin Mary to her cousin, St. Elizabeth.*

Consider that when the Blessed Virgin Mary heard what blessings God had bestowed on Elizabeth, she made haste to visit her. This visit of Mary brought joy and gladness to the house of Elizabeth.

Blessed is he whom Mary visits.

Let us ask the Blessed Virgin Mary to visit our hearts often during this Mission, and to sanctify them.

3. *The Birth of the Infant Jesus at Bethlehem.*

Consider that the Blessed Virgin Mary was compelled to seek shelter in a cave near Bethlehem, which was used as a stable for animals, and that there she gave birth to the Son of God.

Jesus wished to appear upon earth as a helpless infant in a manger, to give great confidence to sinners to come to Him.

Let us ask the Blessed Virgin Mary to obtain for us great confidence in Jesus, her divine infant.

4. *The Presentation of the Infant Jesus in the Temple.*

Consider that Mary had no need of purification, because she was never defiled; but she wished to appear

[1] C. E., Vol. XV. p. 133.

like other mothers, to obey the law, and to practise humility.

Mary, most pure, wished to appear as unclean; and I, defiled by sin, am ashamed to confess my sins, because I wish to appear pure.

Ask the Blessed Virgin Mary to help you to overcome your false shame in confession.

5. *The Finding of Jesus in Jerusalem.*

Consider that the Blessed Virgin Mary and St. Joseph on their return from their visit to the temple of Jerusalem lost Jesus, Who had remained in the temple; and that they found Him in the temple after searching for Him in the deepest affliction for three days.

Mary had lost only the personal presence of Jesus, and yet she searched for Him with tears and sorrow. How much more should we search for Jesus Christ, who have lost grace by sin. If we wish it, we can surely find Him.

Let us ask the Blessed Virgin Mary for true sorrow or our sins.

## II. MONDAY. — JOYFUL MYSTERIES

1. *The Son of God becomes man.*

Reflect that the whole human race was doomed to eternal perdition through the fall of our first parents, and that Jesus Christ, moved by His infinite mercy, became man, to redeem us from sin and hell.

With what profound gratitude should we not adore the Word made flesh.

May the Blessed Virgin Mary obtain for us a great love for her divine Son, Jesus.

2. *Mary visits her cousin Elizabeth.*

Reflect that at this visit of Mary the mystery of the Incarnation was revealed to St. Elizabeth, and St. John the Baptist was purified from original sin.

The devotion to the Blessed Virgin causes in us great interior light and purity of heart.

May the Blessed Virgin Mary obtain for us a lively faith and a great love for virtue.

3. *Jesus is born in a stable.*

Reflect that Jesus Christ could not have chosen a more lowly place for His birth, and that poorer than He no one was ever born.

Our Lord wished thereby to teach us contempt of earthly goods, because the possession of them might prove a great hindrance to salvation.

May the Blessed Virgin Mary obtain for us complete detachment from earthly goods.

4. *Jesus is offered in the Temple.*

Reflect that Jesus Christ offered Himself when yet an infant, through the hands of His Blessed Mother, to his Eternal Father, for the promotion of His glory and the salvation of souls.

The entire life of a Christian should be spent in the service of God and in acts of charity.

Let us offer to God, through our dear Mother Mary, the remainder of our life, so that we may spend it in His holy service.

5. *Jesus is found at Jerusalem.*

Reflect that Jesus remained in Jerusalem, because this was the will of His heavenly Father, although He knew that thereby He would cause great affliction to His Mother and to St. Joseph.

When a commandment of God has to be observed, all human consideration must be laid aside.

May the Blessed Virgin Mary assist us in overcoming all human respect.

### III. Tuesday. — Sorrowful Mysteries [3]

1. *The Agony of Jesus in the garden.*

Consider that when Jesus arrived in the Garden of Olives, He was so overcome by interior sadness and affliction that it sufficed to cause His death.

Alas! it was the sight of our sins and the sufferings that He had to undergo for them, that caused Him this agony.

Let us ask the Blessed Virgin Mary to obtain for us a great sorrow for our sins.

2. *The Scourging of Jesus.*

Consider that this scourging was so cruel that the innocent body of Jesus was lacerated and covered with wounds from head to foot.

Jesus suffered these terrible tortures to atone for the sins of the flesh.

Let us ask the Blessed Virgin Mary to obtain for us the virtue of holy purity.

3. *The Crowning of Jesus with thorns.*

Consider that no sooner was the scourging at an end, than Jesus was most cruelly and most ignominiously treated in the crowning with thorns, and with all sorts of insults and derision.

This is also the way in which all those act who immediately after confession return to their sinful life again. They expose Jesus Christ to ridicule, and strike Him contemptuously in the face.

Let us ask the Blessed Virgin Mary to obtain for us a firm resolution rather to die than to sin again.

4. *The Carrying of the Cross to Calvary.*

Consider that in order to increase the shame and suffering of Jesus the cross was put on His shoulders, and that He carried it to atone for our sins.

[3] C. E., Vol. XV. p. 136.

We should also carry our crosses with resignation, in order to satisfy for our sins.

Let us ask the Blessed Virgin Mary to obtain for us patience in all our sufferings.

5. *The Crucifixion of Jesus.*

Consider how Jesus was stripped of His garments, was nailed to the cross, and died in presence of His sorrowful Mother.

We should frequently cast our looks on the crucifix and say: I love Thee, O my crucified Jesus!

Let us ask the Blessed Virgin Mary to obtain for us the grace often to think of the love of Jesus Christ toward us.


IV. Wednesday. — Glorious Mysteries [4]

1. *The Resurrection of Jesus from the dead.*

Consider the glory of Our Redeemer in His resurrection, having overthrown by His death the reign of Satan, and delivered man from his captivity.

What folly, therefore, to become again the slave of hell for the sake of earthly enjoyment!

Let us ask the Blessed Virgin Mary so to unite us to Jesus in holy love that we may never again be overcome by the devil.

2. *The Ascension of Jesus into Heaven.*

Consider that when Jesus ascended into heaven, He opened for those who love Him that celestial kingdom which was closed until then.

What misery! that so many forego heaven, which Jesus Christ opened for us again by so many sufferings, and condemn themselves to hell, for some vile pleasure.

Let us ask the Blessed Virgin Mary to obtain for us

[4] C. E., Vol. XV. p. 137.

light to see the vanity of this world, and to aspire to the joys prepared for us in heaven.

3. *The Descent of the Holy Ghost.*

Consider that the Apostles, so weak in faith before receiving the Holy Ghost as to abandon their divine Master, became so inflamed with the love of Jesus after the reception of the Holy Ghost that they sacrificed their lives for Jesus, their God.

The love of God surmounts pain in all sufferings, and turns them into sources of joy.

Let us ask the Blessed Virgin Mary to obtain for us the gift of the love of God.

4. *The Death and the Assumption of the Blessed Virgin Mary.*

Consider that Mary died a sweet death of love and was assumed into heaven, because she had led so holy a life.

Our death may not be so sweet, on account of our sins. But the servants of Mary are comforted by this good Mother when they come to die.

O Mary! we place all our confidence in thee. We are resolved to amend our lives; assist us in the hour of death.

5. *The Coronation of the Blessed Virgin Mary in Heaven.*

Consider that when Mary was crowned by her Divine Son in heaven, she was constituted our intercessor. She prays for us incessantly.

Mary prays for all, but she prays especially for those who invoke her. Let us pray: Holy Mary, Mother of God, pray for us sinners; O Mary! pray for us to Jesus!

## V. Thursday. — Joyful Mysteries

1. *The Second Person of the Most Blessed Trinity assumes human nature.*

Admire the extraordinary self-abasement of the Son of the Eternal Father in uniting to Himself the sinful nature of man. Admire also the dignity to which human nature was thereby raised.

And yet we commit so many sins!

May we, through the intercession of the Blessed Virgin Mary, obtain full knowledge of our dignity as members of the mystical body of Christ.

2. *Jesus, our Redeemer, when still in His Mother's womb, visits and sanctifies His precursor.*

What will Jesus Christ not do for us now, when He advocates our cause with God the Father, and especially when He descends from heaven, to enter our souls in Holy Communion!

Oh! may it please Mary to obtain for us greater confidence in Jesus Christ!

3. *Jesus is born as the lowest of men.*

When Jesus made His first appearance in this world He did everything to hide His divine and human perfections. He appeared as a helpless child.

And we are anxious to appear great and to be esteemed, though we are nothing.

Oh! may the Blessed Virgin Mary obtain for us true humility!

4. *Jesus is presented in the Temple.*

Although Jesus Christ is the maker and owner of heaven and earth, He desired to appear before the High-priest as the child of poor parents, who could not afford to make more than the offering of the poor for Him.

Never be ashamed of your poverty, nor of your poor offerings to God from the little that you possess.

Oh! may the Blessed Virgin Mary obtain for us a sincere contempt of hypocrisy under any guise, and of sham respectability!

5. *Jesus remains three days in the Temple.*

So much was Jesus occupied with the designs of His heavenly Father concerning the salvation of men that He neglected to notify His parents about His intention to remain longer in the temple.

We, on the contrary, neglect heavenly inspirations and divine callings rather than displease those near and dear to us.

May the Mother of Jesus obtain for us the grace to do in all things first the will of God!

## VI. FRIDAY. — SORROWFUL MYSTERIES

1. *Jesus sweats blood in the garden of Gethsemane.*

Reflect that our sins and cold ingratitude pressed so heavily on our dear Lord in the garden that they caused a bloody sweat.

Alas! how little are we concerned about our sins and ingratitude!

May the Blessed Virgin Mary obtain for us a true and hearty sorrow for them!

2. *Jesus is scourged at the pillar.*

Reflect that Jesus was stripped, tied to a pillar, and most unmercifully scourged for about an hour. His sacred body was thereby reduced to a bleeding mass of mangled flesh.

This is what the impure have done to Jesus Christ.

May the Blessed Virgin Mary obtain for us a true detestation of all sins of sensuality!

3. *Jesus is crowned with thorns.*

Reflect that Jesus was seated on a stone, with an old scarlet cloak thrown over His shoulders, and a reed in His hands. A bundle of thorns twisted into the shape of a crown was then pressed upon His sacred head. He was then ridiculed and abused as a mock-king.

Jesus suffered this torture and humiliation to atone for our sins of thought, especially those of pride and vanity.

May the Blessed Virgin Mary obtain for us true humility and simplicity of heart!

4. *Jesus carries the cross to Calvary.*

Reflect that it required superhuman strength to carry this heavy cross. Jesus took it willingly upon His shoulders, because men refuse to bow under the light burden of the commandments of God and His Church.

How often do we not complain against the commandments of God and the Church as though they were too heavy!

May the Blessed Virgin Mary obtain for us a greater regard for the holy laws of God and His Church, and more punctual submission to them!

5. *Jesus is crucified.*

Behold how Jesus Christ is nailed to the cross and dies on it, suffering the most excruciating pains for three long hours.

And after all this we refuse to suffer the least thing to save our souls, which Jesus ransomed at the cost of His divine life on the cross.

May the Blessed Virgin Mary assist us, that the unspeakable sufferings and the precious death of Jesus may not be lost to our souls!

## VII. Saturday. — Glorious Mysteries

1. *Jesus rises again from the dead.*

Reflect that on the third day after His death Jesus rose gloriously from the sepulcher, and began His life of triumph.

We are assured that we shall also one day rise glorious from the dead, if we go to the grave free from mortal sin.

May the Blessed Virgin Mary assist us to rise now from the grave of mortal sin and never to return to it again!

2. *Jesus ascends into heaven.*

Reflect that Jesus Christ has taken possession of the kingdom of heaven, in His name and ours. He has promised to share heaven with us forever, provided we have been His faithful followers on earth.

Should not our thoughts, therefore, be constantly occupied about our heavenly home?

May the Blessed Virgin Mary obtain for us a true and practical desire for heaven!

3. *The Holy Ghost is sent from heaven.*

Reflect that the Holy Ghost united Himself inseparably to the Church of Christ and to its members. He dwells in them as long as He is not banished by sin.

Alas! how often have we driven the Holy Ghost from our souls in the past!

May we, through the intercession of Mary, become again the living temples of the Holy Ghost forever.

4. *The Blessed Virgin Mary departs this life, and is assumed into heaven.*

The death of Mary was a death caused by the divine love in her heart. It is piously believed that she was assumed into heaven with body and soul.

By our numerous sins we have deserved to die a death of despair and of damnation.

May the glorious Virgin Mary obtain for us a death of deep sorrow and perfect contrition for all our sins, by which we abuse life and offend so good a God!

5. *Mary is crowned in heaven as Queen of angels and men.*

Reflect that this great Queen of heaven is truly our Mother and heavenly Queen. What a consolation for us poor pilgrims on earth!

Will we ever be admitted into the presence of our Mother in heaven?

Let us pray that we may always be the faithful children of the Blessed Virgin Mary on earth, so that we may also belong to the choir of her faithful servants in heaven.

# APPENDIX II

## SKETCHES FOR MISSION SERMONS FROM ST. ALPHONSUS

Excellent sketches for sermons to be preached on Missions and Renewals are found in each of the two works of St. Alphonsus, *Sermons for Sundays* (Vol. XVI, Centenary Edition), and *Preparation for Death* (Vol. I, Centenary Edition), as follows:

### I. For Missions

| Title | Vol. XVI Sermon | | Vol. I Meditation | |
|---|---|---|---|---|
| | number; | page | number; | page |
| 1. Invitation to Penance, | 32, | 322. | | |
| 2. Importance of Salvation, | 12, | 129; | 12, | 126. |
| 3. Mortal Sin, | 6, | 71; | 15, | 152. |
| 4. Sacrilegious Confession, | 17, | 172. | | |
| 5. Death in general, | 33, | 332; | 1, | 27. |
| | | | 4, | 51. |
| | | | 5, | 59. |
| Death of the Worldly-minded, | 44, | 448; | 7, | 78. |
| Death of the Sinner, | 38, | 390; | 6, | 68. |
| | 51, | 529. | | |
| 6. General Judgment, | 1, | 25; | 25, | 251. |
| 7. Hell, | 10, | 106; | 26, | 262. |
| Remorse of the Reprobate, | 8, | 91; | 28, | 283. |
| Loss of God, | 48, | 496. | | |
| 8. Mercy of God, | 18, | 181; | 16, | 162. |
| | 32, | 322. | | |
| 9. Delay of Conversion, | 52, | 540. | | |
| Measure of Grace and Number of Sins, | 15, | 155; | 18, | 182. |
| Sinful Habits, | 20, | 199; | 22, | 221. |
| Illusions of the Sinner, | 14, | 147; | 20, | 202. |

## II. For Renewals

# THE AMERICAN CATHOLIC TRADITION

*An Arno Press Collection*

Callahan, Nelson J., editor. **The Diary of Richard L. Burtsell, Priest of New York.** 1978

Curran, Robert Emmett. **Michael Augustine Corrigan and the Shaping of Conservative Catholicism in America, 1878-1902.** 1978

Ewens, Mary. **The Role of the Nun in Nineteenth-Century America** (Doctoral Thesis, The University of Minnesota, 1971). 1978

McNeal, Patricia F. **The American Catholic Peace Movement 1928-1972** (Doctoral Dissertation, Temple University, 1974). 1978

Meiring, Bernard Julius. **Educational Aspects of the Legislation of the Councils of Baltimore, 1829-1884** (Doctoral Dissertation, University of California, Berkeley, 1963). 1978

Murnion, Philip J., **The Catholic Priest and the Changing Structure of Pastoral Ministry, New York, 1920-1970** (Doctoral Dissertation, Columbia University, 1972). 1978

White, James A., **The Era of Good Intentions: A Survey of American Catholics' Writing Between the Years 1880-1915** (Doctoral Thesis, University of Notre Dame, 1957). 1978

Dyrud, Keith P., Michael Novak and Rudolph J. Vecoli, editors. **The Other Catholics.** 1978

Gleason, Philip, editor. **Documentary Reports on Early American Catholicism.** 1978

Bugg, Lelia Hardin, editor. **The People of Our Parish.** 1900

Cadden, John Paul. **The Historiography of the American Catholic Church: 1785-1943.** 1944

Caruso, Joseph. **The Priest.** 1956

Congress of Colored Catholics of the United States. **Three Catholic Afro-American Congresses.** [1893]

Day, Dorothy. **From Union Square to Rome.** 1940

Deshon, George. **Guide for Catholic Young Women.** 1897

Dorsey, Anna H[anson]. **The Flemmings.** [1869]

Egan, Maurice Francis. **The Disappearance of John Longworthy.** 1890

Ellard, Gerald. **Christian Life and Worship.** 1948

England, John. **The Works of the Right Rev. John England, First Bishop of Charleston.** 1849. 5 vols.

Fichter, Joseph H. **Dynamics of a City Church.** 1951

Furfey, Paul Hanly. **Fire on the Earth.** 1936

Garraghan, Gilbert J. **The Jesuits of the Middle United States.**
1938. 3 vols.

Gibbons, James. **The Faith of Our Fathers.** 1877

Hecker, I[saac] T[homas]. **Questions of the Soul.** 1855

Houtart, François. **Aspects Sociologiques Du Catholicisme Américain.**
1957

[Hughes, William H.] **Souvenir Volume. Three Great Events in the
History of the Catholic Church in the United States.** 1889

[Huntington, Jedediah Vincent]. **Alban: A Tale of the New World.** 1851

**Kelley, Francis C., editor. The First American Catholic Missionary
Congress.** 1909

Labbé, Dolores Egger. **Jim Crow Comes to Church.** 1971

LaFarge, John. **Interracial Justice.** 1937

Malone, Sylvester L. **Dr. Edward McGlynn.** 1918

**The Mission-Book of the Congregation of the Most Holy Redeemer.** 1862

O'Hara, Edwin V. **The Church and the Country Community.** 1927

Pise, Charles Constantine. **Father Rowland.** 1829

Ryan, Alvan S., editor. **The Brownson Reader.** 1955

Ryan, John A., **Distributive Justice.** 1916

Sadlier, [Mary Anne]. **Confessions of an Apostate.** 1903

**Sermons Preached at the Church of St. Paul the Apostle, New York,
During the Year 1863.** 1864

Shea, John Gilmary. **A History of the Catholic Church Within the
Limits of the United States.** 1886/1888/1890/1892. 4 Vols.

Shuster, George N. **The Catholic Spirit in America.** 1928

Spalding, J[ohn] L[ancaster]. **The Religious Mission of the Irish People
and Catholic Colonization.** 1880

Sullivan, Richard. **Summer After Summer.** 1942

[Sullivan, William L.] **The Priest.** 1911

Thorp, Willard. **Catholic Novelists in Defense of Their Faith, 1829-1865.**
1968

Tincker, Mary Agnes. **San Salvador.** 1892

Weninger, Franz Xaver. **Die Heilige Mission** *and* **Praktische Winke Für
Missionare.** 1885. 2 Vols. in 1

Wissel, Joseph. **The Redemptorist on the American Missions.**
1920. 3 Vols. in 2

**The World's Columbian Catholic Congresses and Educational Exhibit.**
1893

Zahm, J[ohn] A[ugustine]. **Evolution and Dogma.** 1896